Mastering Perl/Tk

Mastering Perl/Tk

Steve Lidie and Nancy Walsh

O'REILLY®

Beijing · Cambridge · Farnham · Köln · Paris · Sebastopol · Taipei · Tokyo

Mastering Perl/Tk
by Steve Lidie and Nancy Walsh

Published by O'Reilly & Associates, Inc., 1005 Gravenstein Highway North, Sebastopol, CA 95472.

O'Reilly & Associates books may be purchased for educational, business, or sales promotional use. Online editions are also available for most titles (*safari.oreilly.com*). For more information contact our corporate/institutional sales department: (800) 998-9938 or *corporate@oreilly.com*.

Editor:	Linda Mui
Production Editor:	Linley Dolby
Cover Designer:	Pam Spremulli
Interior Designer:	Melanie Wang

Printing History:

January 2002:   First Edition.

Library of Congress Cataloging-in-Publication Data

Lidie, Steve.
    Mastering Perl/Tk / Steve Lidie & Nancy Walsh.
      p. cm.
    ISBN 1-56592-716-8 (alk. paper)
    1. Perl (Computer program language) 2. Tk toolkit. 32. I. Title: Perl/Tk. II. Walsh, Nancy.
    III. Title.

QA76.73.P22 W363 2001
005.13'3--dc21

                                                                    2001045923

[M]

Table of Contents

Preface

Perl is arguably the most popular scripting language in use today. It is used for a wide variety of tasks, including file processing, system administration, web programming, and database connectivity. Early Perl users had to be content with command-line interfaces or full-screen interfaces using Curses or similar systems, but the splitting-off of the Tk widget library from the Tcl language opened a whole new world to Perl. Perl programmers could now easily create graphical interfaces for their programs using Tk's flexible and friendly widget set and, with little effort, those programs could be made to work across Windows and Unix platforms.

The relatively recent advent of the web browser would seem to have made the Tk interface obsolete. CGI programs are almost inherently cross-platform and provide many of the same widgets as Tk (this includes Menus, Buttons, text entry fields, and so on). However, the inherent statelessness of the Web makes it difficult to write some programs for it. Perl/Tk provides a richer widget set than that available to the CGI programmer. Server push and client pull try to get around some of these limitations, while JavaScript fills in other gaps, but the fact is, the user experience still falls short in many instances. It is for precisely this reason that Perl/Tk continues to flourish.

The Tk module gives the Perl programmer full access to the powerful Tk widget set. This rich and diverse library, like Perl itself, makes the easy things easy and the hard things possible. Easy things include designing graphical interfaces with Buttons, Checkbuttons, Menus, and text entry fields—all of which you will learn about in the first half of this book. The second half of the book contains more advanced topics, such as creating custom widgets, interprocess communication, images, animation, and key bindings. The goal of this book is to take you from Tk neophyte to Tk expert.

History of This Book

This book evolved from the book *Learning Perl/Tk* by Nancy Walsh (O'Reilly). While the response to that book made it clear that there were many avid and loyal

Perl/Tk users, readers also let us know that they wished the book showed advanced techniques, covered some nonstandard widgets, and included more extended examples of Perl/Tk programming.

So Nancy teamed up with Steve Lidie, already a seasoned Perl/Tk programmer and author, and together they doubled the size of the book and changed its title to befit its expansion. The baby emu on the cover of *Learning Perl/Tk* grew into the adult emu on the cover of this book. Programmers who are new to Perl/Tk can still learn from this book, but as the title says, this book will also turn you into a master.

What You Should Already Know

To get the most out of this book, you should already know the basics of programming in Perl, Version 5. You don't have to be a Perl guru to learn Perl/Tk, but it will help if you feel comfortable with the language.*

Perl/Tk utilizes the object-oriented features available in Perl 5, so even if you don't completely understand OO programming, you should be able to recognize it when you see it. The only other thing you'll need is prior knowledge of other graphical user interfaces (GUIs) and your opinions on them. This helps when deciding what features to include in your own applications. Take a look at the word processor you use on your PC, your web browser, or any program that has buttons and scrollbars and accepts both mouse and keyboard input.

In this book, we'll be covering each basic widget and all its associated options in detail. You'll learn how to make a window look the way you want it to look. You'll also learn how to make a window user-friendly and attractive. Other important topics include image creation and manipulation, interprocess communications, and mega-widget details. We also take a look inside the Tk event loop, encompassing events, bindings, and callbacks.

To complement the examples and code snippets, you will find complete programs scattered throughout the book and in Appendix C. These range from RPN calculators and LWP web clients to Robot Control programs written in Perl and Tcl.

If you want to know more about Perl in general, you should read *Learning Perl, Programming Perl, Advanced Perl Programming,* and *The Perl Cookbook,* which are all also published by O'Reilly & Associates, Inc. From other publishers, you might also try *Object Oriented Perl* (Manning), *Elements of Programming in Perl* (Manning), and *Effective Perl Programming* (Addison Wesley). There are also numerous FAQs and documents available on the Web.

---

* Here's the laundry list of things you should at least recognize: hashes, arrays, subroutines, and their anonymous versions, as well as $_ and @_.

What's in This Book

Here is the breakdown of what we cover in this book:

Chapter 1, *Hello, Perl/Tk*

The first chapter contains some interesting history about the Tk module, introductory comments, and the obligatory Hello World program.

Chapter 2, *Geometry Management*

Geometry management is probably the most important concept in using Perl/Tk. It determines how your widgets are drawn on the screen. Four geometry managers—pack, grid, place, and form—are covered here. Most of the examples in the book use pack.

Chapter 3, *Fonts*

You can easily make effective use of fonts in your Perl/Tk applications using Font objects. This chapter shows you how to utilize Fonts and what options are available for changing them. Several small applications are covered that demonstrate the use of Fonts.

Chapter 4, *Button, Checkbutton, and Radiobutton Widgets*

The Button widget is the first we cover, and we supply lots of details. There are tons of code snippets and screen shots showing different ways to manipulate the Button widget. Many of the options we discuss are common among the other standard widgets. In addition to the standard Button widget, we'll look at two derived variants: the Checkbutton and Radiobutton widgets.

Chapter 5, *Label and Entry Widgets*

The Label widget is the simplest of all. It is usually used with an Entry widget, which is why they are included in the same chapter. Typically, the Entry widget accepts user input, and the Label identifies the input. Perl/Tk has a special Tk::LabEntry widget that we'll examine in detail.

Chapter 6, *The Scrollbar Widget*

Certain widgets in Perl/Tk can be scrolled, which means they can contain more information than you can see on the screen. Scrollbars are used to navigate the data inside these widgets. This chapter tells you how Scrollbars communicate with each widget and how to create and use them. It also illustrates the Scrolled method, which automates Scrollbar creation.

Chapter 7, *The Listbox Widget*

A Listbox widget can contain any sort of data, but it usually contains a list of options from which the user can select. In this chapter, you'll learn how to create a Listbox, fill it with some items, and change the way the user selects items from the list.

Chapter 8, *The Text, TextUndo, and ROText Widgets*

The Text widget is a versatile widget you can use for many purposes besides just displaying text. This chapter covers the different things you can put inside a Text widget (such as text, images, or other widgets) and how to get the best use out of them. The derived TextUndo and ROText (Read-Only Text) widgets are also discussed.

Chapter 9, *The Canvas Widget*
A Canvas widget can display objects such as circles, rectangles, text, images, and even other widgets. This chapter covers all the options and methods available, and shows how to use them.

Chapter 10, *The Scale Widget*
The Scale widget is great for giving the user a range of numbers from which to select so that users can't type in numbers out of range or type in letters accidentally. This chapter includes examples of the Scale widget and covers all the methods available for setting it up and using it.

Chapter 11, *Frame, MainWindow, and Toplevel Widgets*
The Frame and Toplevel widgets are used to organize your other widgets on the screen to get the look you want. This chapter shows how you can use Frames and Toplevels in coordination with a geometry manager (covered in Chapter 2) to make your windows look the way you want them to. We also look closely at the MainWindow, which is a specialized Toplevel in disguise.

Chapter 12, *The Menu System*
Once an application gets complex enough, you will need to put a Menu in it. This chapter shows different ways to create menubars and pulldown, popup, tearoff, and option menus, and how they can best be used in an application. We also cover menu virtual events and briefly examine pie menus.

Chapter 13, *Miscellaneous Perl/Tk Methods*
There are many methods available for all widgets in Perl/Tk. We cover them in this chapter and show you how to use them. The two most important of these methods are configure and cget.

Chapter 14, *Creating Custom Widgets in Pure Perl/Tk*
Creating custom widgets is sometimes the only answer to a problem. This chapter covers all the details, including the Tk class hierarchy, and gives you several examples of composite and derived mega widgets to examine. You will find details here that appear nowhere else in the known universe. Featured widgets are Tk::Nil, Tk::CanvasPlot, Tk::LabOptionmenu, Tk::LCD, Tk::NavListbox, Tk::Thermometer, Tk::CollapsableFrame, and Tk::MacCopy.

Chapter 15, *Anatomy of the MainLoop*
This chapter explores the inner workings of Tk's event loop, including timers, I/O, mouse and keyboard events, bindings, and callbacks. Featured modules are Proc::Killfam, Tie::Watch, Tk::Trace, Tk::bindDump, and Tk::waitVariableX. Featured widgets are Tk::ExecuteCommand, Tk::MacProgressBar, and Tk::Splashscreen.

Chapter 16, *User Customization*
This chapter describes how to use the comand line and option database to customize your Perl/Tk application.

Chapter 17, *Images and Animations*

This chapter covers the various image types and how to use them. We examine Bitmaps, Pixmaps, Photos, and compound images, and touch on tile, transparency, and animation issues. Featured widgets are Tk::Animation, Tk::PhotoRotateSimple, Tk::Thumbnail, and Tk::WinPhoto.

Chapter 18, *A Tk Interface Extension Tour*

A detailed look at all the Tix widgets and ways to use them effectively in Perl/Tk applications, including display items and display styles.

Chapter 19, *Interprocess Communication with Pipes and Sockets*

With care, pipes and sockets can coexist with Tk's event loop. This chapter develops two illustrative client/server programs.

Chapter 20, *IPC with send*

Tk provides an unusual IPC mechanism that allows Tk programs to send messages amongst themselves. This chapter describes Perl-Perl, Tcl-Tcl, and Perl-Tcl intercommunications, and discusses security considerations. We compute π with multiple processes and develop a Perl plug-in for *tclrobots* so that Perl and Tcl Robot Control Programs can do battle. Featured modules include Tk::Receive and Tk::TclRobots.

Chapter 21, *C Widget Internals*

This chapter shows how to write, debug, and package a Tk widget written in C, using the Tk::Square widget as an example.

Chapter 22, *Perl/Tk and the Web*

LWP is a Perl library for accessing the World Wide Web. This chapter develops a web client, *tkcomics*, that displays our favorite comic strips. It details various nonblocking mechanisms for both Unix and Win32. Featured modules are LWP::Simple, LWP::UserAgent, and Tie::Win32MemMap. We then describe the PerlPlus Netscape plugin, which allows you to embed Perl in Netscape and run client-side programs.

Chapter 23, *Plethora of pTk Potpourri*

This chapter is a grab-bag of miscellaneous information and simple widgets such as Adjuster, Balloon, BrowseEntry, ColorEditor, Dialog, DialogBox, ErrorDialog, LabFrame, NoteBook, Pane, ProgressBar, chooseColor, getOpenFile, getSaveFile, and messageBox.

Appendix A, *Installing Perl/Tk*

The Tk module doesn't come with the standard Perl distribution. This appendix tells you where to download the latest release and updates, and how to install them.

Appendix B, *Options and Default Values for Each Widget*

This appendix lists all the options for every widget described in this book.

Appendix C, *Complete Program Listings*

This appendix includes complete code listings of sample programs that don't appear in the book proper.

Reading Order

This book was designed and written both for people new to Perl/Tk and those who are familiar with it. How you approach the book depends on which category best describes you.

Perl/Tk novices should probably start at the beginning. This book is designed to lead you into topics by building a foundation of knowledge. We'll start with a Hello World example in Chapter 1, and from there move into geometry management and the standard widgets. Using Perl/Tk is not really that hard once you understand the fundamentals of how it works.

Experienced programmers should feel free to skip around at will. We recommend reading through Chapter 2 so you have a complete understanding of how the geometry managers work. Then skip around to the different sections in which you are interested. This book has quite a few examples that will give you ideas on how to use Perl/Tk in different ways.

Typographical Conventions

The following typographical conventions are used in this book:

Italic

> Used for filenames, Unix command names, URLs, daemons, emphasis, and the first use of terms where defined

`Constant width`

> Used for function and method names and their arguments, and to show literal code in text

`Constant width italic`

> Used to identify replaceable values

`Constant width bold`

> Used to show default values in syntax lines and to indicate user input

We'd Like to Hear from You

Please address comments and questions concerning this book to the publisher:

> O'Reilly & Associates, Inc.
> 1005 Gravenstein Highway North
> Sebastopol, CA 95472
> (800) 998-9938 (in the United States or Canada)
> (707) 829-0515 (international or local)
> (707) 829-0104 (fax)

We have a web page for this book, where we list errata, examples, or any additional information. You can access this page at:

> *http://www.oreilly.com/catalog/mastperltk/*

To comment or ask technical questions about this book, send email to:

> *bookquestions@oreilly.com*

For more information about our books, conferences, Resource Centers, and the O'Reilly Network, see our web site at:

> *http://www.oreilly.com*

Acknowledgments

> What Descartes did was a good step. You have added much several ways, and especially in taking ye colours of thin plates into philosophical consideration. If I have seen further it is by standing on ye shoulders of Giants.
>
> —Newton to Hooke, 5 February 1676; Corres 1, 416.

Embodied in this statement is the simple truth that all work is derived, in one manner or another, from insights and knowledge gained from others. And so it is with this book. Its creation would have been impossible without a talented team of Giants, whose contributions we can only feebly recognize.

Steve

I'm especially grateful to my wife Carol, whom I neglected for all these months. It was her patience, love, and support that kept me going. And to my parents, Ken and Sally, thank you for providing the nurturing that made me what I am today.

Thanks to the creator of Tcl/Tk, John Ousterhout, who brought graphical programming from the dungeons of assembler to the bright light of high-level programming. And let's not forget the Tcl community, largely responsible for shaping the development of Tk. Thanks in particular to one Tcl illuminary, Cameron Laird, the maintainer of the Perl/Tk FAQ.

Many thanks to Linda Mui, our editor, and to the book's reviewers: Andy Duncan, Brand Hilton, Nick Ing-Simmons, Slaven Rezic, and Martin Stoufer. They all devoted lots of time and effort, and on short notice, to the task at hand. Unfortunately for me, but luckily for you, they spotted many typographical and technical errors, and provided many ideas that enhanced the quality of this work. I'm especially indebted to Andy, Brand, and Slaven who read the entire manuscript *multiple times*.

I would be remiss if I neglected to mention the many programmers from the Perl community who helped shape Perl/Tk, either by directly contributing code, or simply providing thoughtful and accurate answers to questions posted on the mailing list and on *comp.lang.perl.tk*. I've no doubt missed some names, and I apologize in advance. Here, then, is the partial list: Andrew Allen, William Asquith, Graham Barr, Booker C. Bense, Eric Bohlman, Achim Bohnet, H. Merijn Brand, John Cerney, Damian Conway, brian d foy, Marc Dashevsky, Chris Dean, Dominique Dumont, Jack Dunnigan, Toby Everett, Ron Hartikka, Hans Jørgen Helgesen, Grant Hopwood, Rajappa Iyer, Tim Jenness, Mark Lakata, Tripp Lilley, Greg London, Tad McClellan, Andrew Page, Phiroze Parakh, Ben Pavon, Bent B. Powers, Peter Prymmer, Ala Qumsieh, Andreas Reuter, Thomas Schmickl, Monty Scroggins, Rob Seegel, Jason A. Smith, Jonathan Stowe, Anthony Thyssen, Damion K. Wilson, and Ilya Zakharevich.

As an unsung hero, thanks to Malcolm Beattie, creator of *tkperl*, from which Perl/Tk sprang. And, lastly, copious thanks to Nick Ing-Simmons and Larry Wall. Together they have created my favorite language, Perl, and my favorite Perl module, Tk.

Nancy

My husband Michael has been an incredible source of support for me, encouraging me and allowing me to take the time out from our lives together to complete this. Thanks to our kitties, Thumper and Sasha, and the "puppies," Brandy and Theo. All our animals kept me company by walking across the keyboard at the perfect moment or barking just to keep me awake. As always, any typos are purely the cats' fault, but I love them anyway. Many thanks to my parents, Patricia and Delvin, who have been there for me my whole life helping me out when I needed it and sometimes when I didn't know I needed it.

Thanks to all the staff at O'Reilly, especially our editor Linda Mui. Thanks to all the technical reviewers; you did a great job: Andy Duncan, Brand Hilton, Nick Ing-Simmons, Slaven Rezic, and Martin Stoufer. I want to specifically thank Brand Hilton, who often encouraged me and sent me emails answering questions that I would toss to him out of the blue.

A huge thanks to everyone out there in the Perl community who has contributed to, or even just used, Perl/Tk. You all know who you are; keep up the great work.

## CHAPTER 1

Hello, Perl/Tk

Tk is a module that gives you the ability to create graphical interfaces with Perl. Most Perl programs are written with command-line interfaces, which can be cumbersome and intimidating to end users. Perl/Tk lets you communicate with buttons, menus, dialog boxes, scrolled text areas, and so on—all the features you need to develop simple or sophisticated GUI applications.

Why use a graphical interface? In the course of your programming experience, you've probably come across situations in which a text-based interface was insufficient for your needs, if not downright awkward. Certain applications can run with no input, but others, such as installation scripts, require the user to feed information to them constantly. They ask such questions as: Do you want to install this file? Can I overwrite this DLL? Do you want to create this directory? Do you want the help files?

A graphical user interface (GUI) adds a little flair and professionalism to an application. Here are some examples of good uses for a GUI:

- A mini web client that connects to a dictionary server
- An application that displays a map in a scrollable window
- A program that interfaces with a database and displays query results in several widgets, with labels to describe the data
- A mail reader that interfaces with your inbox and can also send out mail messages

A GUI can also be helpful when your boss just says "make it easy to use!," which usually means either adding a wrapper around a script or an interface that makes it easy for users to understand the decisions they have to make.

But don't take this to mean that you should start adding GUIs to all your Perl scripts. There are times when it would be overkill to add a GUI to a script. If all you are doing is reading one file, munging a bit with no user input, and generating another file, a GUI would be silly and unnecessary. GUIs work best when you require a lot of decisions and input from the user, such as in the installation scenario mentioned earlier.

Perl/Tk Concepts

Perl/Tk programs are written in an object-oriented (OO) style, but you don't need previous Perl object-oriented programming experience to code in Perl/Tk. You'll pick it up easily enough after seeing the first few examples. In a nutshell, Perl/Tk *widgets* (such as Buttons and Listboxes) are *objects* that have *methods* we invoke to control them. Besides widgets, Perl/Tk has *images*, which are also objects, and *fonts*, which can be objects or simple strings.

A Perl/Tk program is composed of a *hierarchy* of widgets. At the top of the hierarchy is the MainWindow, the parent widget for all other widgets in the application. The MainWindow widget acts as a container, within which we arrange child widgets using a *geometry manager*. The widget hierarchy is important for several reasons. Among other things, it's used by geometry managers to control the screen layout and the menu system to arrange menu items.

Each different widget belongs to a *class*. A widget's class defines its initial appearance and behavior, but individual widgets of the same class can be customized. As an example, you might create two Buttons that have different textual labels but are otherwise identical. Sometimes you'll read about *instantiating* a widget. This is simply OO-speak for creating a widget (a widget *instance)*. The class *constructor* is responsible for creating widget instances.

The class also defines a widget's initial behavior by creating *bindings*. A binding associates an *event* such as a button press with a *callback*, which is a subroutine that handles the event. You can add additional bindings (indeed, even change and remove them) to alter a widget's standard behavior. Callbacks have several formats, but we mostly use simple references to Perl subroutines.

You'll learn all about these topics as you continue reading.

Some Perl/Tk History

Perl/Tk has its roots in the X Window System and the Tcl language. So let's take a detour into the pages of history, to give you an idea of where Perl/Tk came from and how it got here.

The X Window System and Xlib

The X Window System (known to its friends as just "X" or "X11") was first released in 1987 as a graphical platform for Unix systems. Like most Unix software, X applications are almost universally written in the C language, using a library such as Xt, Motif, or (if you were really unlucky or just really brave) the underlying library for X-based applications, Xlib.

Xlib has the advantage that you can do anything, at the expense of dealing with everything. For instance, here's one way to make a simple pull-down menu using

Xlib (which is one statement in Tk). First, determine the dimensions of the longest menu item. For argument's sake, assume the menu label string is in the C variable menu_item. Subroutine XTextExtents determines several metrics about menu_item, such as its overall width in pixels in the current font and its pixel height, computed by summing the maximum ascent and descent (the number of pixels above and below the baseline, respectively). After accounting for the number of menu items, border widths, and including some slop for good luck, we arrive at the dimensions of the menu window itself, and its relative (x, y) position in the MainWindow.

```
XTextExtents( font_info, menu_item, strlen( menu_item ),
  &direction, &ascent, &descent, &overall );
menu_width = overall.width + 4;
menu_pane_height = overall.ascent + overall.descent + 4;
menu_height = menu_pane_height * menu_pane_count;
x = window_width - menu_width - ( 2 * menu_border_width );
y = 0;
```

XCreateSimpleWindow draws the menu with the proper border and background colors, although nothing appears on the display because the window hasn't yet been mapped.

```
theMenu = XCreateSimpleWindow( theDisplay, theWindow,
  x, y, menu_width, menu_height,
  menu_border_width, theBorderPixel,
  theBackgroundPixel );
```

But every menu item is itself a tiny window, so create them all, save the structure pointers for later use, and select the events they'll respond to. Notice that we haven't drawn the actual text of the menu items. To do that, we need to define font and graphic context items, then call XDrawImageString to paint the characters (that's all done in initialization and event handler code):

```
for( i = 0; i < menu_pane_count; i++ ) {
  menu[i].menu_pane = XCreateSimpleWindow(
    theDisplay, theMenu, 0, menu_height/menu_pane_count*i,
    menu_width, menu_pane_height, menu_border_width = 1,
    theForegroundPixel, theBackgroundPixel );
  XSelectInput( theDisplay, menu[i].menu_pane, EVENT_MASK3 );
}

XMapSubWindows( theDisplay, theMenu );
```

The symbol EVENT_MASK3 enumerates the events applicable to the menu item windows:

```
#define EVENT_MASK3 ButtonPresMask | ButtonReleaseMask |
  ExposureMask | EnterWindowMask | LeaveWindowMask
```

Now we must write the event handlers, including an Expose handler that actually draws the windows, our own event loop, and even our own event dispatching code, and on and on and on .... Whew!

Programming with higher-level libraries such as Motif or Xt is somewhat more civilized, but it's no walk in the park either. A significant stumbling block was that no matter what library you used, X remained in the clutches of C programmers. C is a fine language, but it kept X in the hands of the professionals—no hobbyists or hackers need apply. If you needed to develop an in-house tool (e.g., for tracking bugs), many companies would balk at spending the time and resources required for developing a C application, so you'd end up with a clunky script with a command-line interface.

Something had to be done, and something was.

The Coming of Tcl/Tk

The Tool Command Language (Tcl) was developed in 1987 by John K. Ousterhout of the University of California at Berkeley. Ousterhout envisioned an embeddable, extensible command language that many different applications could reuse. Each application would inherit identical basic features such as control structures, scalar variables and arrays, and built-in procedures. In turn, an application would add its unique commands, each of which had the same "feel" as any other Tcl command.*

But Ousterhout needed to prove his ideas, as much to himself as to others. Since he was interested in GUIs, he devised a toolkit of graphical components and tied them together using Tcl. He reasoned this approach would be more cost effective than writing C language code, even using a toolkit like Motif. His hunch was proven correct, bringing us to his next accomplishment: his graphical toolkit called Tk, from which Perl/Tk is derived.

In early 1991, Ousterhout released Tk Version 1.0, the graphical extension to the Tcl scripting language. Tk's high-level widget set (which ultimately uses Xlib as its drawing package) was an immediate hit. In the years following, thousands of Tcl/Tk applications were written and Tk was ported to languages such as Eiffel, Modula-3, Prolog, Python, Scheme, and more.

By November of 1993, Tcl/Tk was at Version 3.4 and, believe it or not, folks were busy pasting Tcl/Tk GUIs on top of their Perl programs. If only we Perlers had known that help was on its way, for that very same month Malcolm Beattie of Oxford University began his *TkPerl* project.†

---

* Years earlier, Control Data Corporation carried the concept of an embeddable, extensible command language to a logical conclusion with its operating system, NOS/VE. The command language was called System Command Language (SCL) and as the name implies it was used by the entire operating system, from utilities, compilers, and debuggers, to terminal servers and end-user scripts and applications. Any application could embed any other application—automatically, courtesy of the operating system—without *any* work from the user. The symmetry and consistency between applications was most amazing.

† While TkPerl is no longer available, Malcolm has two CPAN modules that allow you to use Tcl/Tk commands from a Perl script. Of course, they rely on Tcl/Tk libraries, so you need Tcl/Tk installed.

The Evolution of Perl/Tk

Malcolm's goal was a pure Perl 5, object-oriented interface to Tk without any dependence on Tcl, which meant converting Tcl code to Perl and writing XSUBs so Perl could call Tk C library routines. The marriage of Tk and Perl was complicated further because in those days Tcl/Tk C subroutines passed simple strings back and forth, which didn't fit well with Perl's model of native data types. Nonetheless, by the summer of 1994, TkPerl was available in alpha form for general use, sans the Text widget and a handful of lesser-used commands and bindings.

Here's an early TkPerl "Hello World" program:

```
use Tk;
$mw = tkinit;
$b = Button::new($mw, -text => 'Hello World');
$b->configure(-method => sub {exit});
tkpack($b);
tkmainloop;
```

If this looks odd to you, remember it was the state of affairs nearly eight years ago, when TkPerl was alpha, and Perl's object-oriented features were still beta. Notice that *pack* hadn't yet been turned into a widget method and was renamed *tkpack* so it didn't conflict with Perl's built-in function by the same name. Yet it worked, and it let us use Tk from Perl, which, after all, was the goal.

Around this time, another chap from the United Kingdom, Nick Ing-Simmons (then of Texas Instruments), began using TkPerl in earnest. He and Malcolm collaborated for a time, and they mutually agreed that Nick would continue development. From this came nTk, or "new Tk," or possibly "Nick's Tk," and thus began the evolution of Perl's Tk programming interface to what it is today. In May 1995, there was another name change, and Nick's package became known as pTk, for "pure Tk," or "portable Tk," or "Perl/Tk." Throughout the years, user-contributed widgets and Ioi Kim Lam's Tk Interface Extension (Tix) widgets found their way into the distribution. These Tks were all based on Tcl/Tk Version 4.x, a version for Unix only.

Remember the Xlib code we showed? Figure 1-1 shows a simple Perl/Tk window.

Figure 1-1. Hello, Perl/Tk

This window was created with the following Perl one-liner:

```
perl -MTk -e 'MainWindow->new->Label(-text => "Hello, Perl/Tk")->pack; MainLoop'
```

This example highlights just how far we've come.

Perl/Tk Meets Win32

In the meantime, the Tcl/Tk team members weren't resting on their well-deserved laurels. By the summer of 1995, Tcl/Tk 8.x* was running on Unix, MacOS classic, and Win32 operating systems, with a look and feel appropriate for each environment. It would take two more years for Perl/Tk to catch up.†

By the summer of 1997, Gurusamy Sarathy, a well-known and respected Perl porter, had produced a binary distribution of Perl 5.004 and Tk 40x.000 (and other useful modules) specifically for Window 95 and Windows NT. The growth of Perl/Tk took off exponentially. The only major complaint was that a Perl/Tk GUI looked too Motif-like, due to its Unix roots.

Nick, with his prodigious programming abilities, wasn't idling either, for in early 1998 he'd merged all of Perl/Tk, Tix, Jan Nijtmans' image package, and Tcl/Tk 8.0, thus creating the basis for the current Perl/Tk 800.000 series.

Simultaneously, Sarathy was heading the effort to combine the disparate Perl ports into a unified Unix and Win32 distribution, commonly called Oneperl. Finally, in the summer of 1998, we had one Perl, 5.005, for Unix and Win32. ActiveState Corporation distributes this unified Perl in binary form, used on most Win32 systems these days.

Around July 1998, Nick produced a unified Unix and Win32 Perl/Tk distribution, and placed a binary version of Perl/Tk 800.010 in ActiveState's PPM repository. The result is that Win32 users can simply download binary installation packages of Perl and Tk. For most Unix users, using a simple idiom, you compile Perl and Tk yourself. If you're really lucky, you can search the Web and find a binary distribution of Perl/Tk for your particular flavor of Unix.

Getting Started with Perl/Tk

Enough history. The remainder of this chapter is about the basics of using Perl/Tk, including how to create simple widgets and display them, a quick introduction to event-based programming, and an obligatory "Hello World" example. Before we continue, let's make sure you have everything installed properly.

Do You Need To Install Anything?

Since the Tk extension to Perl doesn't come with the standard Perl distribution, the first thing you should do is make sure you have a working Perl/Tk distribution.

---

* There were no Tk 5.x, 6.x, or 7.x versions. Tk jumped from a 4.x version number to 8.x to match the corresponding Tcl version. This made it easier to know which version of Tk matched which Tcl installation.

† On Windows, that is; Perl/Tk is still unavailable on Mac OS at the time of this writing.

Running Perl/Tk Programs on Win32

There are no differences between writing Perl/Tk applications on Unix or Windows machines. You can use any simple text editor on either system. However, there can be a small difference in the way you run them.

The lowest common denominator is to manually invoke Perl and specify the Perl/Tk program filename on the command line, like this:

```
perl myprog.pl
```

A Unix user commonly gives his program execute permission and ensures that the first line of the program is a valid "bang" line. This allows the user to invoke Perl/Tk programs by name. When invoking a program by name, the Unix command processor, called the shell program, inspects the file's first line and, if it begins with the characters #!, treats the remainder of the line as the command to execute, possibly with arguments. The ! character is the *bang*. A line of this form invokes Perl with the -w switch:

```
#!/usr/local/bin/perl -w
```

Conceptually, Win32 users do the same thing by associating the extension *.pl* with the Perl interpreter, so they can use Explorer and double-click the script to execute it. See Appendix A for more details.

Whether you're running Unix or Win32, the *perl* program should be in your path. Type the following at a command prompt to make the determination:

```
% perl -v
```

If you receive a "command not found" error message, see Appendix A and install Perl. If *perl* is found, you'll see output similar to this:

```
This is perl, v5.6.0 built for i686-linux

Copyright 1987-2000, Larry Wall

Perl may be copied only under the terms of either the Artistic License or the
GNU General Public License, which may be found in the Perl 5.0 source kit.

Complete documentation for Perl, including FAQ lists, should be found on
this system using `man perl' or `perldoc perl'. If you have access to the
Internet, point your browser at http://www.perl.com/, the Perl Home Page.
```

In particular, note the version number in the first line; anything earlier than 5.6.0 may not produce the results depicted in this book. Perl 5.005_03 *may* work, but nothing earlier will, guaranteed.

Now determine if the Tk module is available by using this command:

```
% perl -e "use Tk"
```

If you don't get the following error, you're ready to go:

```
Can't locate Tk.pm in @INC (@INC contains: C:\PERL\lib\site ...
```

Once again, to install Tk refer to Appendix A.

Assuming that Perl/Tk is up and running, you can determine its version with this command:

```
% perl -MTk -e 'print "$Tk::VERSION\n"'
800.022
```

Ideally, you want Version 800.022 or higher.

The best way to verify that all is well is to run the *widget* demonstration program. *widget* should already be in your path, so just invoke the command by typing **widget** at a command prompt. This program demonstrates most of the Perl/Tk widget set and lets you examine the Perl/Tk code, modify it, and rerun individual demonstrations. Clicking on About shows you the installed Perl and Tk versions.

Perl/Tk Versions

This book is based on the stable releases of Perl 5.6.0 and Tk 800.022. At the time of this writing, Perl 5.6.1 has been released, yet Tk continues to work as before, and all examples are known to work. Down the pipe is a major release of Tk, based on Tcl/Tk Version 8.3. Nick has seeded Tk 803.023 to a few Perl/Tk hackers, but the code is still far from prime-time ready.

When Perl/Tk 803.xxx becomes available, expect it to be thread-safe and Unicode (UTF-8) aware, but beware that if your application uses high-bit ISO-8859-1 characters, it will most likely break.

Creating Widgets

All widgets in Perl/Tk programs are created in the same basic fashion, with a few exceptions. Each widget must have a parent widget to watch over it as it is created and keep track of it while it exists in the application. When you create an application, you'll have a central window that will contain other widgets. Usually that window will be the parent of all the widgets inside it and of any other windows you create in your application. You are creating an order to the widgets so that the communication between child and parent widgets can happen automatically without any intervention from you once you set it all up.

Assuming that the $parent widget already exists, the generic usage when you create widget Widgettype is as follows:

```
$child = $parent->Widgettype( [ -option => value, . . . ] );
```

Note that the variables that store the widgets are scalars. (Actually, they are references to widget objects, but you don't need to know that right now.) If you aren't familiar with object-oriented syntax in Perl, using the -> between $parent and Widgettype invokes the method Widgettype from the $parent object. It makes the $parent related to the child $child. As you might guess, the $parent becomes the parent of the widget being created. A parent can have many children, but a child can have only one parent.

Specifying Options

When you invoke the Widgettype method, you usually specify configuration parameters to set up the widget and the interactions within the application. The configuration parameters will occur in pairs: an option (such as -text, -state, or -variable) and its associated value. Each option starts with a dash, but that's only by convention; the options are just strings used to indicate how to interpret their associated values.

Usually, it is not necessary to put quotation marks around option names because Perl is smart enough to recognize them as strings. However, if you are using the -w switch, Perl may complain about an option that it thinks is not text. You can stick quotes around all your options all the time to avoid this, but it shouldn't be necessary. The option names are all lowercase, except in a few rare cases that we'll note as we cover them.

Options are specified in list form:

```
(-option => value, -option => value, -option => value)
```

If you've never seen => in Perl before, don't be thrown by it. It's just a different way of saying "comma," except that the => operator auto-quotes the word to its left, eliminating possible ambiguities. For instance, the following code works properly because the auto-quoting resolves -text as a string:

```
sub text {}
$mw->Label(-text => 123);
```

With the comma syntax, however, -text resolves to -&text( ):

```
$mw->Label(-text, 123);
```

With this in mind, you can still use just the commas and not the => notation, such as:

```
(-option, value, -option, value, -option, value)
```

However, it's much harder to tell which are the option/value pairs. Consider the following syntactically equal statements (each of which create a Button widget that is 10 by 10 pixels, displays the word "Exit," and performs the action of quitting the application when pressed):

```
$bttn = $parent->Button(-text, "Exit", -command, sub { exit }, -width, 10, -height,
10);

$bttn = $parent->Button(-text => "Exit", -command => sub { exit }, -width => 10,
-height => 10);
```

In the second line, it is much more obvious which arguments are paired together. The option must be directly before the value associated with it: -text is paired with "Exit", -command has the value sub { exit }, and -width and -height both have values of 10.

Another favorite option/value specification syntax uses Perl's qw operator, which treats its arguments as a list of strings:

```
$bttn = $parent->Button(qw/-text Exit -width 10 -height 10 -command/ => sub { exit }/
);
```

This style is more reminiscent of Tcl's look, with whitespace-separated tokens. You tend to type fewer characters too. The string delimiter is often ( ) or {}, but // is most popular since it doesn't require a shift. Note that qw splits on simple words, so that option values can be only simple words, not multiword quoted strings, code references, and so on. That's why we moved the -command option to the end of the qw string.

Toplevel, MainWindow, and Frame Widgets

Time for another detour. In the next few chapters we'll be using widgets in our examples that we might not have covered yet. We trust that you'll figure out what most of them mean from the context in which they are presented, but a few require a short introduction.

MainWindow and Toplevel are the windows (or widgets—we often interchange the terms) that contain other widgets. MainWindow is a special version of a Toplevel widget, in that the MainWindow is the first window you create in your application.

The other type of widget you need to know about is a Frame widget. A Frame is a container that can also contain other widgets. It is usually invisible and is used just to arrange the widgets as desired.

Of course, there's more to it, but that's enough to know for now. For more information, see Chapter 11.

Displaying a Widget

Creating a widget isn't the same as displaying it in Perl/Tk. You need to use two separate commands to create a widget and display it, although sometimes they are combined into the same line and look like a single command. In the examples so far, we've used the Button method to create the Button, but nothing is displayed by using that method alone. Instead you have to use a geometry manager to cause the widget to be displayed in its parent widget or in another widget. The most commonly used geometry manager is pack. To use it, you simply call the pack method on the widget object, as follows:

```
$widget->pack();
```

For example:

```
$button->pack();
```

The arguments you can send to the pack method are covered in Chapter 2.

It is not necessary to invoke the pack method on a separate line. ->pack can be added to the creation of the widget:

```
$parent->Button(-text => "Bye!", -command => sub { exit })->pack( );
```

The other geometry managers available are grid, form, and place. All four behave differently; use what works best for your application. Again, look for information on the geometry managers in Chapter 2.

The Event Loop

When programming an application that uses a graphical interface rather than a textual interface, you need to rethink the way you approach the flow of the application. In a text-based application, you can read from standard input (STDIN), use command-line options, read files, or prompt the user for specific information. The keyboard is your main avenue of input from the user. In a GUI, input comes not only from those places but also from the mouse and the window manager.* Although this extra input allows more flexibility in our applications, it also makes our programming job more difficult. As long as we tell it what to do, Perl/Tk helps us handle all that extra input gracefully.

Input in a GUI is defined by events. Events are typically different combinations of using the keyboard and mouse at the same, or different, times. If the user pushes the left mouse button on Button "B," that is one type of event. Pushing the right mouse button on Button "C" is another event. Typing the letter "a" is another event. Holding down the Control key and clicking with the middle mouse button is yet another event. Events can also come from input and output operations or be generated virtually under program control. For an in-depth examination of the Tk event loop, see Chapter 15.

Events are processed during an *event loop*. The event loop, as its name implies, handles events during a loop. It determines what subroutines to call based on what type of event has happened. Here is a pseudocode event loop:

```
while (1) {
  get_event_info

  if event is left-mouse-click call process_left_mouse_click
  else if event is right-mouse-click call process_right_mouse_click
  else if event is keyboard-input call type_it
  else handle events for redrawing, resizing etc
}
```

This is obviously a simplistic approach to an event loop, yet it shows the basic idea. The event loop is a weeding-out process to determine what type of input has been given to the application. For example, the subroutine process_left_mouse_click

---

* For example, a "close" directive from a window manager such as *mwm* or MS Windows.

might determine where the pointer was when the mouseclick occurred and then call other subroutines based on that information.

In Perl/Tk, the event loop is initiated by calling a routine called MainLoop. Anything prior to this statement is just setting up the interface. Any code after this call will not execute until after the GUI has exited using $mw->destroy.[*]

If we forget to include the MainLoop statement, the program will think about things for a while and then go right back to the command prompt. None of the windows, Buttons, or widgets will be drawn at all. The first things that occur after calling MainLoop are the interface is drawn and the event loop is started.

Before we get too much further into the event loop and what it does (and what you need to do so it works properly), let's look at a working example program, Hello World. (You were expecting something else?)

Hello World Example

Every programming language goes through the Hello World example, which is a complete program that prints a string (typically "Hello World") and exits. "Hello World" may get its share of ridicule, but it's a remarkably effective tool that shows readers how to write and execute a working program while they're still in the first chapter of the book. In our Hello World example, we'll have the title of our window say "Hello World" and create a Button that will dismiss the application:

```
#!/usr/bin/perl
use Tk;
my $mw = MainWindow->new;
$mw->title("Hello World");
$mw->Button(-text => "Done", -command => sub { exit })->pack;
MainLoop;
```

Despite being only six lines long, there is quite a bit going on in our little program. The first line, as any Perl programmer knows, invokes Perl.[†] The second line tells Perl to use the Tk module.

The third line:

```
my $mw = MainWindow->new;
```

is how we create a window. The window will have the same basic window manager decorations as all your other windows.

The title of our window is changed using the title method. If we hadn't used this method, the text across the top of the window would be the same as the name of the

---

[*] Throughout the book, we use $mw to indicate the variable that refers to the MainWindow created at the beginning of the application.

[†] On Unix, that is. In Win32 you have to type **perl hello.pl** to invoke the program or twiddle with Explorer to call up the *perl* executable when *.pl* files are double-clicked.

file containing the code, excluding any extension. For instance, if the code were stored in a file named *hello_world*, the string "Hello_world" would appear across the title bar of the application (Tk automatically capitalizes the first character for you). Using the title method is not required, but it makes the application look more polished.

Any string we put as an argument becomes the title. If we wanted the title to be "Hey! Look at my great program!," this would be the place. This is akin to using the *-title* option when starting any standard X Windows application. We cover more methods for a MainWindow object later in Chapter 11.

The next line creates a Button widget, sets basic properties, and packs the widget. (See Chapter 4 for all available configuration options for Button.)

The Button is set to display the text "Done" and to perform the Perl command exit when pushed. Finally, the last item of concern is the MainLoop command. This starts the event loop in motion, and from then on the application will do only what we have told it to do: if the user clicks on the Button, the application will exit. Anything else the user does—minimizing, resizing, changing to other applications—will be processed by the window manager and ignored by our application. See Figure 1-2 for a picture of the Hello World window.

Figure 1-2. Hello World window

exit Versus destroy

In most of the examples in this book, you will see sub { exit; } (or its equivalent, \&exit) used to quit the Perl/Tk application. This works fine as long as you have done a use Tk; in the same file. Perl/Tk defines its own exit routine, which does some cleanup and various other things that are important to Tk. The program is then unconditionally terminated, and control returns to the operating system.

Another way to quit the Tk portion of the application is to call $mw->destroy, which destroys the MainWindow and returns to the code listed after MainLoop. This allows your program to do post-GUI processing before exiting.

Unsolicited Advice

Before we end this chapter, and you become engrossed in the details of Perl/Tk, we'd like to give you some suggestions on programming style and window design. Bear with us, this won't take long and might save you a lot of time in the future.

Programming Style

The code in a Perl/Tk script can get quite cumbersome and clunky because of all the option/value pairs used to define and configure each widget. There are several ways to format the code to deal with readability (and in some cases, "edit-ability"). Most just involve adding extra spaces or tabs to line up different portions of code. Once you get used to seeing the code, it won't seem quite so mysterious and unwieldy.

One coding style places each option/value pair on a separate line:

```
$bttn = $parent->Button(-text => "my text",
                        -command => sub { exit },
                        -width => 10,
                        -height => 10);
```

With this style, it is extremely obvious what the pairs are and what value is associated with which option. (You could also go to the extreme of aligning each => to make nice columns, depending on how much time you have to press the spacebar.) Some people like to start the option/value pairs on the next line and put the ending); on its own separate line, after the last option/value pair, which retains the comma for formatting ease:

```
$bttn = $parent->Button(
    -text => "Exit",
    -command => sub { exit },
    -width => 10,
    -height => 10,
);
```

This makes the code easier to edit; an option/value pair can be added or deleted on each line without having to mess with parentheses, semicolons, or commas. It also keeps the next lines closer to the left side of the page, so if you have several indentation levels, you don't end up with code quite so deeply nested to the right.

In either case, Emacs users may find the functionality of *cperl-mode.el* handy. This is an Emacs initialization file that adds color highlighting and special formatting that makes editing Perl code more efficient. You can find the file in the standard Perl distribution, in the *perl-5.6.0/emacs* directory.

Sometimes if there are only one or two option/value pairs, it makes sense to leave them all on the same line and conserve a little bit of space:

```
$bttn = $parent->Button(-text => "my text", -command => sub { exit });
```

You'll eventually come up with a style that works for the way you read and edit code. Whichever way you choose, try to be consistent throughout your scripts in case someone else takes over the maintenance of your code (it might even be you, a year or more down the road).

Naming Conventions for Widget Types

Sometimes your programs run away from you, getting so large and unwieldy that it becomes hard to remember what a particular variable was pointing to. If there are over 10 Buttons in a program, we would be hard-pressed to figure out which Button was $button3 without digging through a bunch of code.

So we've established a naming convention for our code. You don't need to use our convention, but it'll hopefully inspire you to come up with your own. Otherwise, we hope you have a really good memory.

For Buttons, you might use _b, _bttn, or Button as a type of qualifier to the variable name. For instance, you could name the Button in the Hello World example $done_b, $done_bttn, or $doneButton.

The topmost widget in an application's widget hierarchy is the MainWindow. Throughout this book, we use the variable $mw to represent this widget. You will see other programs use $main, $top, or $mainwindow as well.

Table 1-1 lists widget types and suggested naming conventions for them. Replace "blah" with a sensible description of the widget's purpose (e.g., exit). If you use this convention, you'll always know what type of widget you're working with.

Table 1-1. Naming conventions by widget type

Widget type	Suggested name	Examples
Button	$blah_b, $blah_bttn, or $blahButton	$exit_b, $apply_b, $newButton
Canvas	$blah_canvas or $blahCanvas	$main_canvas, $tinyCanvas
Checkbutton	$blah_cb or $blahCheckbutton	$uppercase_cb, $lowercaseCheckbutton
Entry	$blah_e or $blahEntry	$name_e, $addressEntry
Frame	$blah_f or $blahFrame	$main_f, $left_f, $canvasFrame
Label	$blah_l or $blahLabel	$name_l, $addressLabel
Listbox	$blah_lb or $blahListbox	$teams_lb, $teamsListbox
Menu	$blah_m or $blahMenu	$file_m, $edit_m, $helpMenu
Radiobutton	$blah_rb or $blahRadiobutton	$blue_rb, $grey_rb, $redRadiobutton
Scale	$blah_scale or $blahScale	$age_scale, $incomeScale
Scrollbar	$blah_scroll, $blah_sbar, or $blahScroll	$x_scroll, $yScroll
Text	$blah_t or $blahText	$file_text, $commentText
Toplevel	$blah_w or $blahWindow	$main_w, $fileopenWindow

Designing Your Windows

Before you decide what events to handle, it is worthwhile to spend some time sketching out a few windows on paper and deciding what should happen (from the user's perspective) when you click a button or invoke a menu item.

A GUI often makes the application look much more polished and purposeful than a command-line interface does, but it's easy to go overboard with a GUI and end up with something ugly, clunky, and impossible to navigate. So here are some things to consider when deciding how the GUI should look:

- Every widget should have a purpose that is intuitive and informative.
- Think about the way a user will use an application and design accordingly.
- Don't try to cram everything your application does into one window.
- Don't always try to separate everything into different windows. Sometimes the application is so simple that one window is all you need.
- Colors are great, but there are a lot of color-blind people out there. The same applies to fonts: many folks cannot read very small fonts. If you insist on using color and particular fonts, allow them to be customized via the resource database, through a file, or through the application itself.
- Some widgets do their jobs better than others. Use the proper widget for the job.

Debugging and Prototyping Perl/Tk Programs

Debugging a Perl/Tk program need not be different from debugging a nongraphical program; you can always sprinkle warn statements throughout the code to track progress and display intermediate results. We suggest using warn rather than print for three reasons: it adds the newline to the message automatically; the output includes the line number of the warn statement; and the output goes to STDERR, which is not normally buffered, thus the output appears immediately. Furthermore, you type fewer characters.

You normally run programs by typing the program name at the command prompt:

```
% hello_world
```

or:

```
C:\>perl hello_world
```

When you invoke the program this way, any printed output goes to that terminal window. If you don't put a \n on the end of the string to be printed, you won't see the information actually printed until you quit the program. You may have to unbuffer a file handle by setting the special Perl variable $|. If you use warn rather than print, these drawbacks are eliminated.

If that old-fashioned way isn't to your liking, perhaps the slightly newer old-fashioned way of using the standard Perl debugger is. The debugger has built-in Tk support, though you must use the O command and enable it by setting the variable tkRunning:

```
[bug@Pandy atk]$ perl -de 0
Default die handler restored.
```

```
Loading DB routines from perl5db.pl version 1.07
Editor support available.

Enter h or `h h' for help, or `man perldebug' for more help.

main::(-e:1):   0
  DB<1> 0 tkRunning
          tkRunning = '1'
  DB<2> use Tk
  DB<3> $mw = MainWindow->new
  DB<4> $b = $mw->Button(-text => 'Beep', -command => sub{$mw->bell})
  DB<5> $b->pack
  DB<6> x $b
0  Tk::Button=HASH(0x82ed434)
   '_TkValue_' => '.button'
  DB<7> q
```

As you see, we can not only print debug information, but also do simple prototyping.

An even better environment for this sort of activity is the program *ptksh*. It's part of a standard Perl/Tk installation and, as its name suggests, it's a Perl/Tk shell that allows us to interactively enter and test Perl and Tk commands. Figure 1-3 shows a sample *ptksh* session.

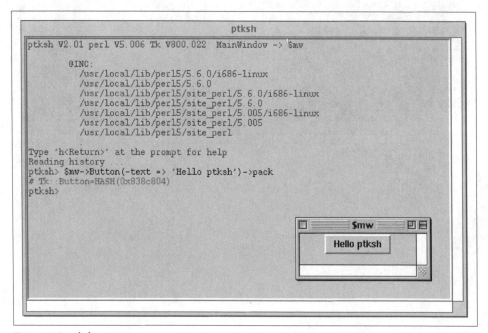

Figure 1-3. ptksh session

If you're really into graphical debugging, treat yourself to the CPAN module *Devel:: ptkdb*, an excellent, sophisticated Perl/Tk debugger. Simply invoke Perl with a -d argument such as this:

```
[bug@Pandy atk]$ perl -d:ptkdb group
```

Figure 1-4 shows a *ptkdb* session.

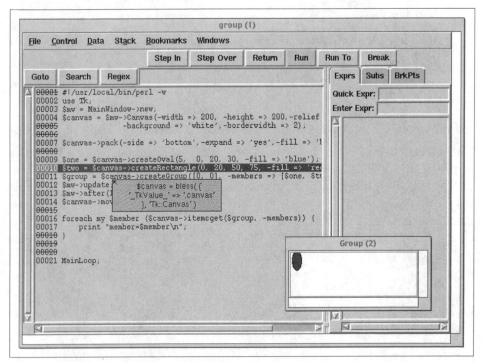

Figure 1-4. ptkdb session

## CHAPTER 2

Geometry Management

To display widgets on the screen, they must be passed to a *geometry manager*. The geometry manager controls the position and size of the widgets in the display window. Several geometry managers are available with Perl/Tk: pack, place, grid, and form.

All the geometry managers are invoked as methods on the widget, but they all have their own methodologies and arguments to change where and how the widgets are put on the screen:

```
$widget1->pack(); $widget2->place(); $widget3->grid(); $widget4->form();
```

When you organize the widgets in your window, it is often necessary to separate groups of widgets to get a certain look and feel. For instance, when you use pack, it is difficult to have widgets stacked both horizontally and vertically without grouping them in some fashion. We use a Frame widget or another window (a Toplevel widget) to group widgets inside a window.

We create our first window by calling MainWindow. The MainWindow is a special form of a Toplevel widget. For more detailed information on how to create/configure Frame and Toplevel widgets, see Chapter 11.

With the exception of place, differences between the geometry managers make it difficult (not entirely impossible, but definitely not recommended) to use more than one geometry manager within the same area.* In $mw, we can display many types of widgets, but if we start using pack, we should continue to use pack on all the widgets contained directly in $mw. Don't switch to grid in the middle, because the two geometry managers will get into a *race condition*: one will create its layout, which affects the geometry calculations of the other, which affects the layout of the first, causing it to recompute its geometries, ad infinitum. However, let's assume our MainWindow contains a Frame, which in turn contains other widgets. We could use pack to pack the Frame inside the MainWindow and then we could use grid to manage the widgets inside the Frame. See Figure 2-1.

---

* For an example that combines pack and place, see the NavListbox widget, described in Chapter 14.

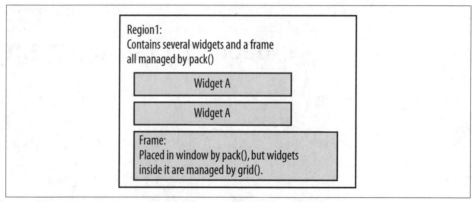

Figure 2-1. Frame within a window that uses a different geometry manager

Although the different geometry managers have their own strengths and weaknesses, pack is the most commonly used, so we'll discuss it first and in the most detail. The grid geometry manager has been improved greatly with the release of Tk 8.0 and subsequent porting to Perl. The place geometry manager is the most tedious to use, because you have to determine exact coordinates (relative or absolute) for every single widget. Finally, the form geometry manager is like a combination of pack and place.

The pack Geometry Manager

Remember when you were a child and you had those wooden puzzles to put together? Each piece in the puzzle had exactly one place where it could go and there weren't any overlaps allowed between pieces.

With the pack geometry manager, our windows are similar to the wooden puzzle, because widgets cannot overlap or cover each other, partially or completely (see Figure 2-2). If a Button is packed in a certain space on the window, the next Button (or any widget) will have to fit around the already packed Button. Luckily, our windows will be dealing only with rectangular shapes instead of funny-shaped puzzle pieces.

The order in which you pack your widgets is very important because it directly affects what you see on the screen. Each Frame or Toplevel maintains a list of items that are displayed within it. This list has an order to it: if widget A is packed before widget B, then widget A will get preference if space becomes scarce. This will become clear as we go through some examples. You will often get a different look to your window just by packing the widgets in a different order.

If you don't care what the window looks like and how the widgets are put in it, you can use pack with no arguments and skip the rest of this chapter. Here it is again:

```
$widget->pack();
```

To make your window look nicer and more manageable (and user friendly), there are arguments that can be sent to the pack method that will change the way the widgets

---

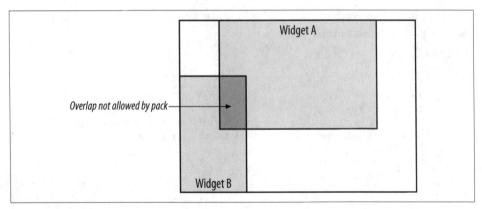

Figure 2-2. Overlap error

and the window look. As with anything in Perl/Tk, the arguments are arranged in key/value pairs. So the more sophisticated usage would be:

```
$widget->pack( [ option => value, ... ] );
```

Here is the code to create a window that doesn't use any pack options. We haven't covered all the widgets used in this example, but hang in there; it's pretty simple.

```
#!/usr/bin/perl -w
use Tk;

my $mw = MainWindow->new;
$mw->title("Bad Window");
$mw->Label(-text => "This is an example of a window that looks bad\nwhen you don't
send any options to pack")->pack;

$mw->Checkbutton(-text => "I like it!")->pack;
$mw->Checkbutton(-text => "I hate it!")->pack;
$mw->Checkbutton(-text => "I don't care")->pack;
$mw->Button(-text => "Exit",
            -command => sub { exit })->pack;
MainLoop;
```

Figure 2-3 shows the resulting window.

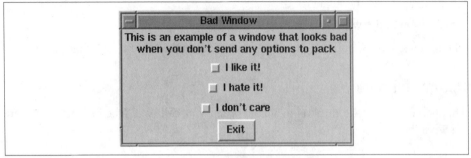

Figure 2-3. Window with widgets managed by pack

We can alter the preceding code and add some options to the pack calls that will make our window look much nicer:

```
#!/usr/bin/perl -w
use Tk;

my $mw = MainWindow->new;
$mw->title("Good Window");
$mw->Label(-text => "This window looks much more organized, and less haphazard\n" .
    "because we used some options to make it look nice")->pack;

$mw->Button(-text => "Exit",
            -command => sub { exit })->pack(-side => 'bottom',
                                           -expand => 1,
                                           -fill => 'x');
$mw->Checkbutton(-text => "I like it!")->pack(-side => 'left',
                                              -expand => 1);
$mw->Checkbutton(-text => "I hate it!")->pack(-side => 'left',
                                              -expand => 1);
$mw->Checkbutton(-text => "I don't care")->pack(-side => 'left',
                                                -expand => 1);
MainLoop;
```

Figure 2-4 shows the much more organized window.

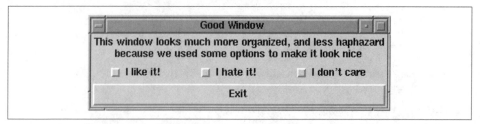

Figure 2-4. Window with widgets managed by pack using some options

Using pack allows you to control the:

- Position in the window relative to the window or Frame edges
- Size of widgets, relative to other widgets or absolute
- Spacing between widgets
- Position in the window's or Frame's widget list

The options, values, and defaults are listed and discussed in the following section.

Options for pack

This list shows all the options available when you call pack (the default values are shown in bold):

`-side => 'left' | 'right' | 'top' | 'bottom'`
> Puts the widget against the specified side of the window or Frame

`-fill => 'none' | 'x' | 'y' | 'both'`
> Causes the widget to fill the allocation rectangle in the specified direction

`-expand => 1 | 0`
> Causes the allocation rectangle to fill the remaining space available in the window or Frame

`-anchor => 'n' | 'ne' | 'e' | 'se' | 's' | 'sw' | 'w' | 'nw' | 'center'`
> Anchors the widget inside the allocation rectangle

`-after => $otherwidget`
> Puts $widget after $otherwidget in packing order

`-before => $otherwidget`
> Puts $widget before $otherwidget in packing order

`-in => $otherwindow`
> Packs $widget inside of $otherwindow rather than the parent of $widget, which is the default

`-ipadx => amount`
> Increases the size of the widget horizontally by *amount*

`-ipady => amount`
> Increases the size of the widget vertically by *amount*

`-padx => amount`
> Places padding on the left and right of the widget

`-pady => amount`
> Places padding on the top and bottom of the widget

Positioning Widgets

Each window (or Frame) has four sides to it: top, bottom, left, and right. The packer uses these sides as points of reference for widgets. By default, pack places the widgets against the top of the Toplevel or Frame.

You can control the side a widget is placed against with the -side option:

```
-side => 'left' | 'right' | 'top' | 'bottom'
```

For example, if we would like our Button against the left edge of the window, we can specify -side => 'left'.

Using our Hello World example as a base, let's look at what happens when we pack our Button against the different sides. In Figure 2-5, the only lines we change are the ->pack part of the Button creation line and the "Hello World" string in the $mw-> title command to easily show the new options to pack.

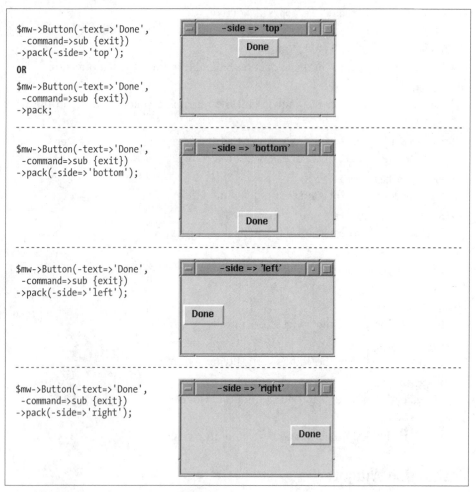

```
$mw->Button(-text=>'Done',
  -command=>sub {exit})
->pack(-side=>'top');

OR

$mw->Button(-text=>'Done',
  -command=>sub {exit})
->pack;
```

```
$mw->Button(-text=>'Done',
  -command=>sub {exit})
->pack(-side=>'bottom');
```

```
$mw->Button(-text=>'Done',
  -command=>sub {exit})
->pack(-side=>'left');
```

```
$mw->Button(-text=>'Done',
  -command=>sub {exit})
->pack(-side=>'right');
```

Figure 2-5. Packing a button against different sides

The windows in Figure 2-5 have been made a bit larger to emphasize the difference that using alternative values for -side makes. Normally, the window will be only as large as required to show the Button. When you are deciding how to place widgets in a window, it is always a good idea to see what happens when you make the window both larger and smaller. Make sure the behavior you get is what you want.

So far, pack seems pretty simple, but what if you want to put more than one Button in your application? What happens when we add more Buttons?

```
$mw->Button(-text => 'Done1', -command => sub { exit })->pack;
$mw->Button(-text => 'Done2', -command => sub { exit })->pack;
$mw->Button(-text => 'Done3', -command => sub { exit })->pack;
$mw->Button(-text => 'Done4', -command => sub { exit })->pack;
```

Since the default -side is top, we would expect all the Buttons to be mushed up against the top of the window, right? Sort of. The packer allocates space for each widget, then manipulates the widget inside that space and the space inside the window.

Figure 2-6 shows what the window with the four Done Buttons looks like; the next section explains why.

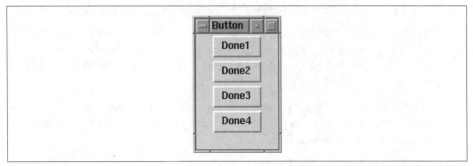

Figure 2-6. Four Buttons packed with default settings

Allocation Rectangles

When given an item to pack, the packer first looks to see which side (top, bottom, right, or left) to use. It then sets aside an invisible rectangular area across the length of that side for use only by that widget.

In Figure 2-7, the solid-line rectangle represents our empty window (or Frame), and the dotted-line rectangle is the area the packer sets aside for the first Button. It actually does go all the way across the width or height of the window, but to make it easier to see, it's shown indented slightly.

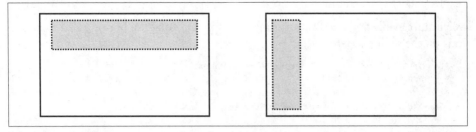

Figure 2-7. Rectangular areas set aside by the packer when using -side => 'top' and -side => 'left'

The dimensions for the dotted-line box, which we'll call the *allocation rectangle*, are calculated based on the size of the requesting widget. For both the top and bottom sides, the allocation rectangle is as wide as the window and only as tall as the widget to be placed in it. For the right and left sides, the allocation rectangle is as tall as the window but only as wide as required to fit the widget.

Our examples so far have used Buttons in which the text of the Button determines its width. If we create a Button with the text "Done" and one with the text "Done, Finished, That's it," the second Button is going to be much wider than the first. When these two Buttons are placed up against either the right or left side of the window, the second Button has a wider allocation rectangle than the first. If we place those same two Buttons against the top and the bottom, the allocation rectangles are the same height and width, because the window, not the widget, determines the width.

After the size of the allocation rectangle is determined, the widget is placed within the allocation rectangle according to other options passed and/or the default values of those options. We will go over those options and how they can affect the allocation rectangle later.

Once the first widget has been placed in the window, the amount of area available for subsequent allocation rectangles is smaller, because the first allocation rectangle has used some of the space (see Figure 2-8).

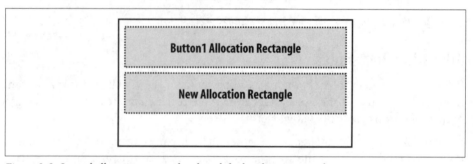

Figure 2-8. Second allocation rectangle when default side 'top' is used

When more Buttons are placed against different sides in the same window, the results will vary depending on the order.

We'll start by placing one Button along the top, one along the bottom, and then Buttons on the right and left:

```
$mw->Button(-text => "TOP", -command => sub { exit })
  ->pack(-side => 'top');

$mw->Button(-text => "BOTTOM", -command => sub { exit })
  ->pack(-side => 'bottom');

$mw->Button(-text => "RIGHT", -command => sub { exit })
  ->pack(-side => 'right');

$mw->Button(-text => "LEFT", -command => sub { exit })
  ->pack(-side => 'left');
```

Figure 2-9 shows the allocation rectangles for this window.

Figure 2-10 shows what the actual window looks like, both normal size and resized so it's a bit larger.

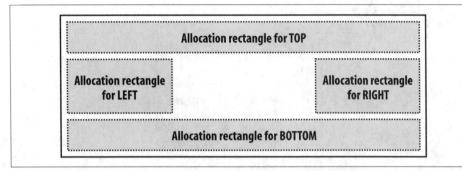

Figure 2-9. Allocation rectangles for four Buttons

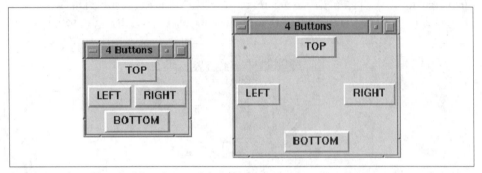

Figure 2-10. Four Buttons placed around the sides of the window

Filling the Allocation Rectangle

Normally, the widget is left at the default size, which is usually smaller than the allocation rectangle created for it. If the -fill option is used, the widget will resize itself to fill the allocation rectangle according to the value given. The possible values are:

```
-fill => 'none' | 'x' | 'y' | 'both'
```

Using the value 'x' will resize the widget in the x direction. Likewise, 'y' will cause the widget to resize in the y direction. Using -fill => 'both' is a good way to see exactly what size and placement was given to the allocation rectangle, because 'both' resizes the widget in both x and y directions. Using our four-Button example again, we'll specify -fill => 'both':

```
$mw->Button(-text => "TOP", -command => sub { exit })
  ->pack(-side => 'top', -fill => 'both');

$mw->Button(-text => "BOTTOM", -command => sub { exit })
  ->pack(-side => 'bottom', -fill => 'both');

$mw->Button(-text => "RIGHT", -command => sub { exit })
  ->pack(-side => 'right', -fill => 'both');

$mw->Button(-text => "LEFT", -command => sub { exit })
  ->pack(-side => 'left', -fill => 'both');
```

Figure 2-11 shows the resulting window.

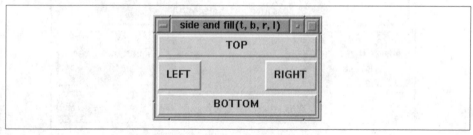

Figure 2-11. Four Buttons packed to each side using -fill => 'both'

If we switch the Button we create first, we get a different result. The window in Figure 2-12 was created by packing the widgets in this order: left, right, top, bottom.

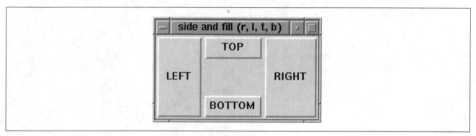

Figure 2-12. Four Buttons packed to each side in a different order using -fill => 'both'

Figure 2-13 demonstrates yet another order, which really shows that the allocation rectangles change size depending on which is packed first.

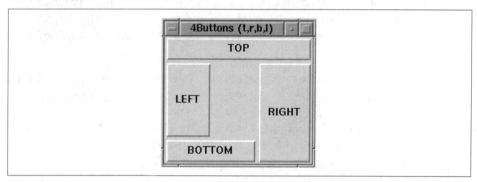

Figure 2-13. Four Buttons packed in order of top, right, bottom, and left

A common use of -fill is on widgets with Scrollbars: Listbox, Canvas, and Text. Usually the Scrollbars are along the edge of the window and you want the Listbox to fill the remaining area. See Chapters 6 and 7 for more information.

Expanding the Allocation Rectangle

The -expand option manipulates the allocation rectangle and not the widget inside it. The value associated with -expand is a Boolean value.

```
-expand => 1 | 0
```

Given a true value, the allocation rectangle will expand into any leftover space in the window, depending on which side the widget was packed.

Widgets packed with side 'right' or 'left' will expand in the horizontal direction. Widgets packed with side 'top' or 'bottom' will expand in the vertical direction. If more than one widget is packed with -expand turned on, the extra space in the window is divided evenly among all the allocation rectangles that want it.

In Figures 2-11 and 2-12, you saw that there was some space left in the center of the window that wasn't occupied by any widget. If we change the code and add -expand => 1 to the list of pack options for each Button, the result is the window in Figure 2-14.

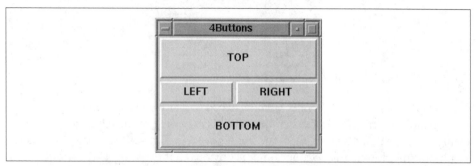

Figure 2-14. Four Buttons using the -expand => 1 and -fill => 'both' options

Note that in Figure 2-14, fill => 'both' is left in the code. If we omit the -fill option, the Buttons stay their original sizes, but the allocation rectangles (which are invisible) take over the extra space in the window (see Figure 2-15).

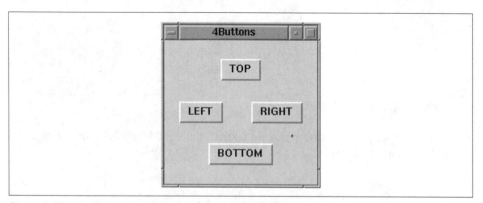

Figure 2-15. Four Buttons using -expand => 1 and -fill => 'none'

In Figure 2-15, the Buttons are centered in their allocation rectangles because of the default value of the -anchor option, which is 'center'.

Anchoring a Widget in Its Allocation Rectangle

The -anchor option manipulates the widget inside the allocation rectangle by anchoring it to the place indicated by the value passed in. It uses the points of a compass as references.

```
-anchor => 'e' | 'w' | 'n' | 's' | 'ne' | 'nw' | 'se' | 'sw' | 'center'
```

Figure 2-16 shows those locations in an example allocation rectangle.

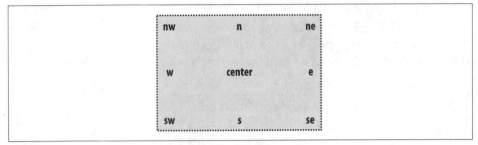

Figure 2-16. Allocation rectangle with -anchor points labeled

The default for -anchor is 'center', which keeps the widget in the center of its allocation rectangle. Unless the -expand option is set to a true value, this won't seem to change much of anything in the window. As seen in Figure 2-17, which shows the result of using the -expand => 1 option, it is obvious that the widget sticks to that center position when the window is resized.

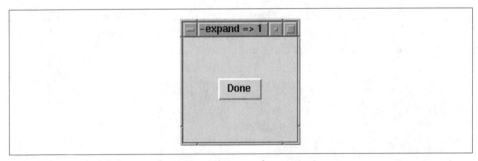

Figure 2-17. Default behavior of -anchor with -expand set to 1

If all other defaults are used to pack the widget, Figure 2-18 shows what -anchor => 'e' and -anchor => 'w' do.

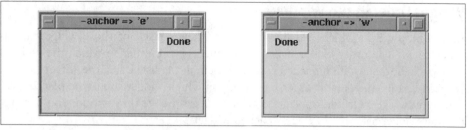

Figure 2-18. Examples of -anchor => 'e' and -anchor => 'w'

Remember that the allocation rectangle is created based on which side the widget is packed against, so certain combinations will appear not to have had any effect. For example:

```perl
$mw->Button(-text => "Done", -command => sub { exit })
    ->pack(-side => 'top', -anchor => 'n');
```

This code fragment will leave the widget exactly where it was if the -anchor option had not been specified, because the allocation rectangle does not change size at all. If the -expand option is also specified, when the window is resized, the widget sticks to the north side of the window. If -anchor => 's' is specified, when the window is resized, the widget sticks to the south side of the window.

The -anchor option is more often used to line up several widgets in a row. Figure 2-19 and Figure 2-20 show two common examples.

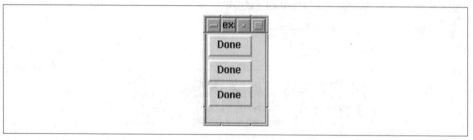

Figure 2-19. Window with three Buttons all packed with -side => 'top', -anchor => 'w'

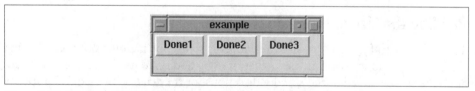

Figure 2-20. Window with three Buttons all packed with -side => 'left', -anchor => 'n'

Sometimes when -side and -anchor are used together, the results don't seem to be what you would expect at first glance. Always keep in mind that invisible allocation rectangle and how it affects what you see on the screen.

Widget Order in the Window

Each window into which widgets are packed keeps track of those widgets in an ordered list. The order of this list is determined by the order in which the widgets were packed; the last item packed is the last item in the list. Using the -after option, you can change the default order by specifying which widget should be placed after your new widget. On the opposite end, if you use the -before option, you can put the new widget before a previously packed widget:

```
-after => $otherwidget
-before => $otherwidget
```

As an example, let's create four Buttons ($widget1, $widget2, $widget3, and $widget4) and only pack three to begin with. The pack command for $widget4 might then be:

```
$widget4->pack(-after => $widget1);
```

Figure 2-21 shows two windows: one before $widget4 is packed and one after $widget4 is packed.

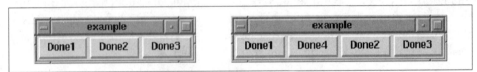

Figure 2-21. The window on the right has the Done4 Button packed using -after => $widget1

If we want to put $widget4 in front of $widget1, we use this command:

```
$widget4->pack(-before => $widget1);
```

Figure 2-22 shows the results.

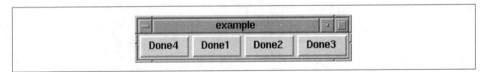

Figure 2-22. Button with Done4 label packed using -before => $done1

Padding the Size of the Widget

The final way to force pack to size the widget is to use the padding options. The first set of padding options affects the widget itself by adding to its default size. Different amounts can be added in the x and y directions, or they can be the same. To specify how much padding should occur in the x direction, use the -ipadx option:

```
-ipadx => amount
```

Specify padding for the y direction like this:

```
-ipady => amount
```

The *amount* is a number that is a valid screen distance. We'll discuss the definition of a valid screen distance in the next section.

Both the -ipadx and -ipady options change the size of the widget before the allocation rectangle is calculated. -ipadx adds the amount specified to both the right and left sides of the widget. The overall width of the widget is increased by $2 \times amount$. -ipady adds to the top and bottom of the widget, causing the overall height of the widget to increase by $2 \times amount$. Figure 2-23 shows how the -ipadx and -ipady options affect a Button.

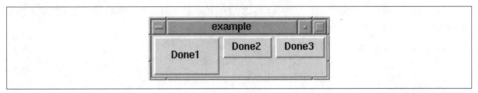

Figure 2-23. The Done1 Button was created with options -ipadx => 10, -ipady => 10

The other kind of padding is inserted between the edge of the widget and the edge of the allocation rectangle and is done with the -padx and -pady options:

```
-padx => amount
-pady => amount
```

Using -padx and -pady does not affect the size of the widget, but it does affect the size of the allocation rectangle. It acts as a buffer around the widget, protecting it from touching other widgets. Figure 2-24 shows the effects of using -padx and -pady.

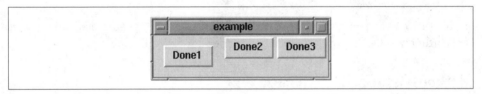

Figure 2-24. The Done1 Button was created with options -padx => 10, -pady => 10

A good way to remember the difference between -ipadx/y and -padx/y is that the "i" stands for "inside the widget" or "internal padding."

Valid screen distances

Many times you'll see options that require values specified in screen units (or what is called a valid screen distance). The options -ipadx and -ipady are examples of this type of option. Always check to see what value the option actually requires.

A screen unit is a number followed by a designation for the unit to use. If there is no designation, the units are in pixels. Table 2-1 shows all the possibilities.

Table 2-1. Valid screen units

Designator	Meaning	Examples
(None)	Pixels (default)	20, 30, "20", "40"
c	Centimeters	'3c', '4c', "3c"
i	Inches	'2i', "3i"
m	Millimeters	'4m', "4m"
p	Printer points (1/72 inch)	"72p", '40p'

To use these designators, it is necessary to use quotes (either single or double) around the value. Here are some examples:

```
$button->pack(-ipadx => 20);      # 20 pixels
$button->pack(-ipadx => '20');    # Also 20 pixels
$button->pack(-ipadx => "1i");    # 1 inch
$button->pack(-ipadx => '1m');    # 1 millimeter
$button->pack(-ipadx => 1);       # 1 pixel
$button->pack(-ipadx => "20p");   # 20 printer points
```

Remember that a p designator does not stand for pixels, but printer points.

Displaying in a Parent Other Than Your Own

By default, when a widget is packed, it is packed inside the region that created it. Sometimes it is necessary to display a widget inside a different region. Use the -in option to do so:

```
-in => $otherwindow
```

It puts the new widget at the end of the packing order for $otherwindow and displays it accordingly. All other options specified in the pack call still apply.

Methods Associated with pack

There are a few methods that are used in conjunction with the pack geometry manager. They allow the programmer to get information about either the widget that has been packed or the parent widget in which other widgets are packed.

Unpacking a widget

To unpack a widget from a window or Frame, use the packForget method:

```
$widget->packForget();
```

packForget makes it look like the widget disappears. The widget is not destroyed, but it is no longer managed by pack. The widget is removed from the packing order, so if it's repacked later, it appears at the end of the packing order.

Retrieving pack information

To return a list containing all the pack configuration information about a widget, use packInfo:

```
@list = $widget->packInfo( );
```

The format of the list is in option/value pairs. The first pair in the list is -in and the current window that contains $widget (usually also the parent). Here's an example of the information returned from packInfo:

```
-in MainWindow=HASH(0x818dcf4) -anchor n -expand 0 -fill none -ipadx 0 -ipady 0 -padx
10 -pady 10 -side left
```

From this we can tell that we packed our $widget into the MainWindow rather than into a Frame. Since the list has a "paired" quality to it, we could easily store the result from packInfo in a hash and reference the different option values by using a key to the hash:

```
%packinfo = $widget->packInfo;
print "Side used: ", $packinfo{-side}, "\n";
```

Disabling and enabling automatic resizing

Unless you've set a preferred window size via the geometry method explicitly, when you put a widget inside a window, the window (or Frame) will resize itself to accommodate the widget. If you are placing widgets inside your window dynamically while the program is running, the window will appear to bounce from size to size. You can turn this behavior off by using packPropagate on the Frame or Toplevel widget:

```
$widget->packPropagate(0);
```

If set to 0 or 'off', packPropagate changes the behavior of the widget so it doesn't resize to accommodate items packed inside of it. When a false value is sent to packPropagate before widgets are placed inside it, this automatic resizing doesn't happen, so you can't see any of the widgets placed inside the parent until it is manually resized. If you call packPropagate after the widgets have been placed inside it, the widget will ignore any size changes from its child widgets.

Listing widgets

You can determine the widgets your Frame or Toplevel holds with the packSlaves method:

```
@list = $parentwidget->packSlaves( );
```

packSlaves returns an ordered list of all the widgets that were packed into $parentwidget. An empty string (or empty list) is returned if no widgets were packed into $parentwidget.

The list returned from packSlaves looks like this:

```
Tk::Button=HASH(0x81b2970) Tk::Button=HASH(0x8116ccc) Tk::Button=HASH(0x81bcdd4)
```

Each item is a reference to a packed widget and can be used to configure it. For example, you can increase the size of each widget by 20 in both the x and y directions by looping through it and "packing" it with new information. Using our good window example in Figure 2-4, we can add a Button that will contain a subroutine that uses packSlaves:

```
$mw->Button(-text => "Enlarge",
            -command => \&repack_kids)->pack(-side => 'bottom',
                                             -anchor => 'center');
sub repack_kids {
  my @kids = $mw->packSlaves;
  foreach (@kids) {
    $_->pack(-ipadx => 20, -ipady => 20);
  }
}
```

Figure 2-25 shows the resulting window.

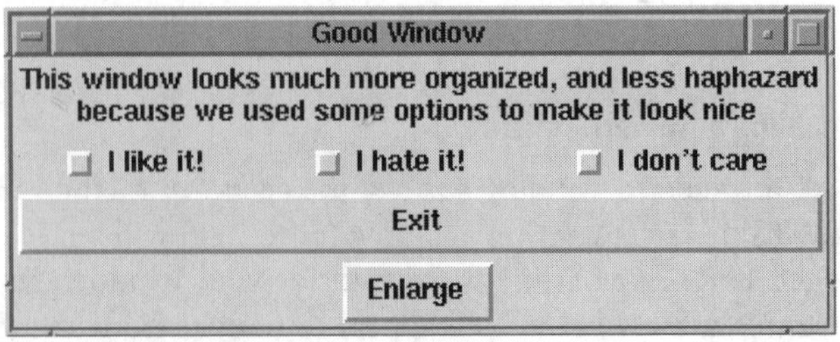

Figure 2-25. Window before pressing Enlarge Button

Let's look at what happens when we press the Enlarge Button. As shown in Figure 2-26, all the widgets are now repacked with additional parameters of -ipadx => 20, -ipady => 20. These new options are in addition to any other parameters with which the widgets were packed previously. If an option is repeated, the last one specified overrides the previous ones.

The window is suddenly huge! Subsequent presses of the Enlarge Button will do nothing more to the window, because each of the widgets already has an -ipadx and -ipady of 20. If we wanted to always add 20 to the values of -ipadx and -ipady, we would have to request the current values and add 20 to them:

```
sub repack_kids {
  my @kids = $mw->packSlaves;
  foreach (@kids) {
    %packinfo = $_->packInfo();
    $_->pack(-ipadx => 20 + $packinfo{"-ipadx"},
             -ipady => 20 + $packinfo{"-ipady"});
  }
}
```

We use packInfo to get the current configuration and add 20 to that value.

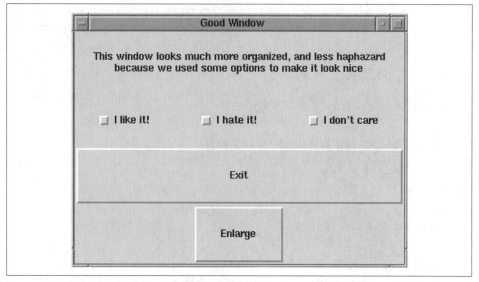

Figure 2-26. Window after pressing Enlarge Button

Demo Programs for pack

Here are three little programs that let you experiment with the packing options of an unspecified number of widgets.

As you can see in Figure 2-27, there is both a console window and an "output" window that show what is happening to widgets as you change their options. The complete code follows shortly.

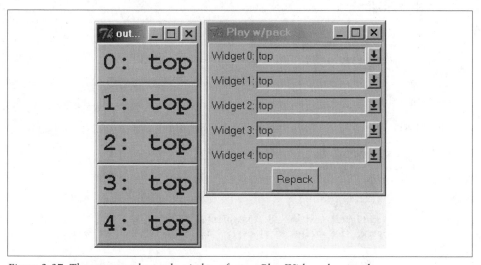

Figure 2-27. The output and console windows for our Play With pack example

There are a lot of widgets and methods in the code that we haven't covered yet. For now, it would be useful to download the code, run it, and play around with the options.

```
use Tk;
require Tk::BrowseEntry;

if ($#ARGV >= 0) { $numWidgets = $ARGV[0]; }
else { $numWidgets = 4; }

$mw = MainWindow->new(-title => "Play w/pack");
$f = $mw->Frame(-borderwidth => 2, -relief => 'groove')
    ->pack(-side => 'top', -fill => 'x');
my (@packdirs) = ();

$i = 0;
foreach (0..$numWidgets)
{
    $packdirs[$_] = 'top';
    my $be = $f->BrowseEntry(-label => "Widget $_:",
        -choices => ["right", "left", "top", "bottom"],
        -variable => \$packdirs[$_], -browsecmd => \&repack)
        ->pack(-ipady => 5);
}

$f->Button(-text => "Repack", -command => \&repack )
    ->pack(-anchor => 'center');

# use a separate window so we can see what the output
# looks like without clutter.
$top = $mw->Toplevel(-title => "output window");
my $c;
foreach (@packdirs)
{
    my $b = $top->Button(-text => $c++ . ": $_",
        -font => "Courier 20 bold")
        ->pack(-side => $_, -fill => 'both', -expand => 1);
}

MainLoop;

sub repack
{
    @w = $top->packSlaves;
    foreach (@w) { $_->packForget; }
    my $e = 0;
    foreach (@w)
    {
        $_->configure(-text => "$e: $packdirs[$e]");
        $_->pack(-side => $packdirs[$e++], -fill => 'both', -expand => 1);
    }
}
```

A more complicated version of our pack demo lets us alter not just the side the widget is packed against but the more commonly used pack options:

```
use Tk;
require Tk::BrowseEntry;

if ($#ARGV >= 0) { $numWidgets = $ARGV[0]; }
else { $numWidgets = 1; }

$mw = MainWindow->new(-title => "Play w/pack");

$f = $mw->Frame(-borderwidth => 2, -relief => 'groove')
    ->pack(-side => 'top', -fill => 'x');

# Initialize the variables
my (@packdirs) = ();
my (@anchordirs) = ();
my (@fill) = ();
my (@expand) = ();

$i = 0;
$top = $mw->Toplevel(-title => "output window");
my $addbutton = $f->Button(-text => "Add Widget",
    -command => \&addwidget )->pack(-anchor => 'center');

foreach (0..$numWidgets) {
    my $b = $top->Button(-text => $_ . ": $packdirs[$_]")->pack;
    my %pinfo = $b->packInfo;
    $b->packForget;
    &addwidget($_);
}
MainLoop;

sub repack {
    print "Repacking...";
    @w = $top->packSlaves;
    foreach (@w) { $_->packForget; }
    my $e = 0;
    foreach (@w) {
        $_->configure(-text => "$e: $packdirs[$e]");
        print "Expand is : " . $expand[$e]. "\n";
        $_->pack(-side => $packdirs[$e],
                         -fill => $fill[$e],
                         -expand => $expand[$e],
                         -anchor => $anchordirs[$e]);
        $e++;
    }
}

sub addwidget {
    my ($count) = @_;
    print "COUNT $count\n";
    if (! defined $count) {
```

```
                $numWidgets ++;
                $count = $numWidgets ;
        }

        $packdirs[$count] = 'top';
        $anchordirs[$count] = 'center';
        $fill[$count] = 'none';
        $expand[$count] = 0;

        my $f1 = $f->Frame->pack(-side => 'top', -expand => 1,
                -fill =>'y', -before => $addbutton);
        my $be = $f1->BrowseEntry(-label => "Widget $count:",
                -choices => ["right", "left", "top", "bottom"],
                -variable => \$packdirs[$count], -browsecmd => \&repack)
                ->pack(-ipady => 5, -side => 'left');

        $f1->BrowseEntry(-label => "-anchor",
                -choices => [qw/center n s e w ne se nw sw/],
                -variable => \$anchordirs[$count], -browsecmd => \&repack)
                ->pack(-ipady => 5, -side => 'left');

        $f1->BrowseEntry(-label => "-fill", -choices => [qw/none x y both/],
                -variable => \$fill[$count], -browsecmd => \&repack)
                ->pack(-ipady => 5, -side => 'left');

        $f1->Checkbutton(-text => "-expand", -onvalue => 1, -offvalue => 0,
                -variable => \$expand[$count], -command => \&repack)
                ->pack(-ipady => 5, -side => 'left');

        $top->Button(-text => $count . ": $packdirs[$count]",
                -font => "Courier 20 bold")->pack(-side => $packdirs[$count],
                -fill => $fill[$count], -expand => $expand[$count]);
}
```

Figure 2-28 shows what the new console looks like (the output window looks the same until you vary the options).

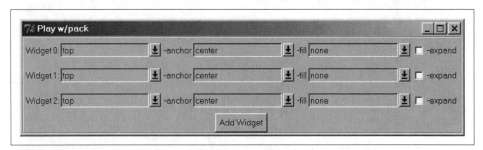

Figure 2-28. The console for the more complicated version of Play With pack

This sample switches packed widgets between a visible and invisible state. As the widgets are created, save their references as the array @w. The scalar $packed is associated with the Checkbutton. Whenever we click the Checkbutton, the value of $packed toggles between 1 and 0. The first click of the Checkbutton sets $packed to 0 and invokes the -command callback. For more information on callbacks, see Chapter 15.

The callback then removes the widgets from the display, using packInfo to fetch their pack attributes, which are stored in an instance variable. Refer to Chapter 14 for details on instance variables. When restoring widgets, the callback uses the saved pack information to exactly replicate the initial packing configuration.

```
my $f = $mw->Frame->pack;
my $packed = 1;

push  my @w, $f->Label(-text => "l1")->pack(-side => "bottom"),
    $f->Button(-text => "l2")->pack(-side => "right"),
    $f->Label(-text => "l3")->pack(-side => "top"),
    $f->Button(-text => "l4")->pack(-side => "left"),
;
$mw->Checkbutton(-text => "Pack/Unpack",
            -variable => \$packed,
            -command => sub {
                if ($packed) {
                foreach (@w) {
                    $_->pack(@{ $_->{PackInfo} });
                }
                } else {
                foreach (@w) {
                    $_->{PackInfo} = [ $_->packInfo ];
                    $_->packForget;
                }
                }
            })->pack;
```

The grid Geometry Manager

The grid geometry manager divides the window into a grid composed of columns and rows starting at (0, 0) in the upper-left corner. Figure 2-29 shows a sample grid.

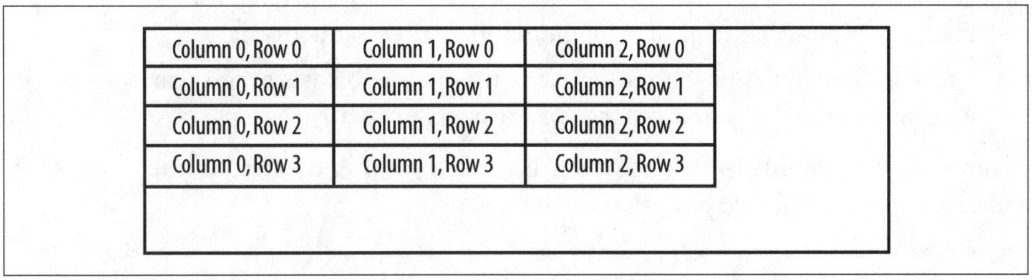

Column 0, Row 0	Column 1, Row 0	Column 2, Row 0
Column 0, Row 1	Column 1, Row 1	Column 2, Row 1
Column 0, Row 2	Column 1, Row 2	Column 2, Row 2
Column 0, Row 3	Column 1, Row 3	Column 2, Row 3

Figure 2-29. A window divided into grids

Rather than using the sides of a window as reference points, grid divides the screen into columns and rows. It looks a lot like a spreadsheet, doesn't it? Each widget is assigned a grid cell using the options available to grid.

The grid method takes a list of widgets instead of operating on only one widget at a time.* Here is the generic usage:

```
$widget1->grid( [ $widget2, ... , ] [ option => value, ... ] );
```

A specific example is:

```
$widget1->grid($widget2, $widget3);
```

Instead of using three separate calls, you can use one grid call to display all three widgets. You can also invoke grid on each widget independently, just as you can pack. Each call to grid will create another row in the window. So in our example, $widget1, $widget2, and $widget3 will be placed in the first row. Another call to grid creates a second row. This is what happens when you do not specify any additional options to the grid call.

The previous example can be rewritten like this:

```
Tk::grid($widget1, $widget2, $widget3);
```

But beware, this is not necessarily equivalent to the previous statement, due to *inheritance*, an object-oriented concept. For more information, please refer to Chapter 14. Essentially, using Tk::grid is the same as calling a subroutine directly, whereas the method call searches the widget's class hierarchy for a subroutine grid. It's certainly possible that $widget1 has its own special grid method, which we would rudely bypass. Is this a likely possibility? No. Just be aware when you make a procedural versus a method call.

For greater control, you can specify explicit -row and -column options for each widget in the window. We'll cover these options later.

When additional options are not specified, the following assumptions are made:

- The first widget in the row (e.g., $widget1 in the preceding example) invokes the grid command.
- All remaining widgets for that row will be specified as arguments to the grid command.
- Each additional call to grid will add another row to the display.
- Special characters can be used to change the -columnspan and -rowspan of the widget without using -columnspan or -rowspan explicitly.

A few examples will help demonstrate. Each call to grid creates another row, so in the following example we have two rows:

```
# Create two rows, each with four widgets
$widget1->grid($widget2, $widget3, $widget4);
$widget5->grid($widget6, $widget7, $widget8);
```

---

* Several people have mentioned that pack can also take a list of widgets. We don't cover this because it is not how pack is normally used.

In this example, we have created four rows and there is only one widget in each row:

```
# Create four rows, each with one widget
$widget1->grid( );
$widget2->grid( );
$widget3->grid( );
$widget4->grid( );
```

We can also create widgets as we go:

```
$mw->Button(-text => 'Button1', -command => \&call1)->grid(
        $mw->Button(-text => 'Button2', -command => \&call2),
        $mw->Button(-text => 'Button3', -command => \&call3),
        $mw->Button(-text => 'Button4', -command => \&call4));
```

Pay careful attention, because the second, third, and fourth calls to Button are inside the call to grid. All four of the Buttons will be placed in the first row. If we execute the same command again, the new widgets are placed in the next row.

Special Characters

There are several special characters that can be used to alter the way the widgets are gridded in the window. Each special character serves as a type of placeholder that indicates what to do with that position in the grid:

"-" *(a minus sign)*
> Tells grid that the widget specified just before this one in the list should span this column as well. To span more than one column, place a "-" in each widget position to span. A "-" cannot follow a "^" or an "x".

"x"
> Effectively leaves a blank space where a widget would otherwise be placed.

"^"

> A widget in row x will span row x and $x + 1$ when this character is placed in the grid command for row $x + 1$ in that row/column position. The number of "^" characters must match the number of columns the widget spans in row x. Similar to "-", but goes down, not across.

The following sections include some examples that illustrate what the special characters do.

Spanning columns

The following bit of code creates three rows of Buttons. The first two rows are normal and, in the third, the second Button spans three columns. Each "-" character adds one to the number of columns the Button uses, and the default is one. So the original column and two hyphens ("-","-") indicate that there are three columns to span. The -sticky option is necessary for the widgets to stick to the sides of the cells they span. If the -sticky option were left out, the Button would be centered across the three cells it spans.

```
$mw->Button(-text => "Button1", -command => sub { exit })->grid
  ($mw->Button(-text => "Button2", -command => sub { exit }),
   $mw->Button(-text => "Button3", -command => sub { exit }),
   $mw->Button(-text => "Button4", -command => sub { exit }));

$mw->Button(-text => "Button5", -command => sub { exit })->grid
  ($mw->Button(-text => "Button6", -command => sub { exit }),
   $mw->Button(-text => "Button7", -command => sub { exit }),
   $mw->Button(-text => "Button8", -command => sub { exit }));


$mw->Button(-text => "Button9", -command => sub { exit })->grid
  ($mw->Button(-text => "Button10", -command => sub { exit }),
   "-", "-",  -sticky => "nsew");
```

Figure 2-30 shows the resulting window.

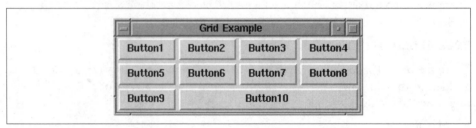

Figure 2-30. Example of column spanning using the "-" character

Empty cells

The "x" character translates to "skip this space" and leaves a hole in the grid. We removed the line that created Button6 and replaced it with an "x" in the following code. The cell is still there, it just doesn't contain a widget.

```
$mw->Button(-text => "Button1", -command => sub { exit })->grid
  ($mw->Button(-text => "Button2", -command => sub { exit }),
   $mw->Button(-text => "Button3", -command => sub { exit }),
   $mw->Button(-text => "Button4", -command => sub { exit }));

$mw->Button(-text => "Button5", -command => sub { exit })->grid
  ("x",
   $mw->Button(-text => "Button7", -command => sub { exit }),
   $mw->Button(-text => "Button8", -command => sub { exit }));
```

Figure 2-31 shows the resulting window.

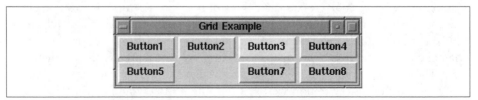

Figure 2-31. Leaving an empty cell between widgets

grid Options

The rest of the options are similar to those used with pack:

`"-"`
> A special character used in the grid widget list. Increases `columnspan` of the prior widget in the widget list.

`"x"`
> A special character used in the grid widget list. Leaves a blank space in the grid.

`"^"`
> A special character used in the grid widget list. Increases `rowspan` of the widget in the grid directly above it.

`-column => n`
> Sets the column to place the widget in ($n \geq 0$).

`-row => m`
> Sets the row to place the widget in ($m \geq 0$).

`-columnspan => n`
> Sets the number of columns for the widget to span beginning with `-column`.

`-rowspan => m`
> Sets the number of rows for the widget to span beginning with `-row`.

`-sticky => string`
> Sticks the widget to *string* sides. String contains characters n, s, e, or w.

`-in => $otherwindow`
> Indicates the widget is gridded inside $otherwindow instead the parent of $widget.

`-ipadx => amount`
> $widget becomes larger in x direction by *amount*.

`-ipady => amount`
> $widget becomes larger in y direction by *amount*.

`-padx => amount`
> Places buffer space equal to *amount* to the left and right of the widget.

`-pady => amount`
> Places buffer space equal to *amount* on the top and bottom of the widget.

Specifying Rows and Columns Explicitly

Rather than letting grid make assumptions, it is sometimes necessary to explicitly state the row and column in which the widget should be placed. This is done by using the `-row` and `-column` options. Each option takes a nonnegative integer as an argument:

```
-column => n, -row => m
```

When you use `-row` and `-column`, it is not necessary to build or grid the widgets in any sort of logical order (except for your own sanity when you are debugging). You could place your first widget in column 10 and row 5 if you like. All the other cells with lower row and column values will remain empty.

Spanning Rows and Columns Explicitly

It is also possible to indicate explicitly that a widget (or widgets) should span some columns or rows. The option to span columns is -columnspan. For spanning rows, the option is -rowspan. Both options take an integer that is 1 or greater. The value indicates how many rows or columns should be spanned, including the row or column in which the widget is placed.

For this example, we use the easy way to place widgets in columns and rows by not explicitly specifying the -row and -column options. Note that the second grid command applies to two Button widgets, so the single -columnspan option applies to *both* Buttons created there.

```
$mw->Button(-text => "Button1", -command => sub { exit })->grid
  ($mw->Button(-text => "Button2", -command => sub { exit }),
   $mw->Button(-text => "Button3", -command => sub { exit }),
   $mw->Button(-text => "Button4", -command => sub { exit }),
   -sticky => "nsew");

# Button5 will span Columns 0-1 and Button6 will span 2-3
$mw->Button(-text => "Button5", -command => sub { exit })->grid
  ($mw->Button(-text => "Button6", -command => sub { exit }),
   -sticky => "nsew", -columnspan => 2);
```

The resulting window is shown in Figure 2-32.

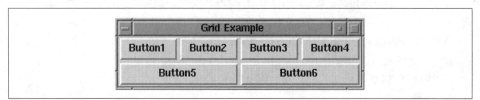

Figure 2-32. Nonexplicit -columnspan example

This window could also have been created using the "-" special character to indicate column spanning, like this:

```
$mw->Button(-text => "Button1", -command => sub { exit })->grid
  ($mw->Button(-text => "Button2", -command => sub { exit }),
   $mw->Button(-text => "Button3", -command => sub { exit }),
   $mw->Button(-text => "Button4", -command => sub { exit }),
   -sticky => "nsew");

# Button5 will span Columns 0-1 and Button6 will span 2-3
$mw->Button(-text => "Button5", -command => sub { exit })->grid
  ("-", $mw->Button(-text => "Button6", -command => sub { exit }), "-"
   -sticky => "nsew");
```

This example illustrates how to explicitly use the -row and -column options in addition to the -rowspan option:

```
$mw->Button(-text => "Button1", -command => sub { exit })->
    grid(-row => 0, -column => 0, -rowspan => 2, -sticky => 'nsew');
$mw->Button(-text => "Button2", -command => sub { exit })->
    grid(-row => 0, -column => 1);
$mw->Button(-text => "Button3", -command => sub { exit })->
    grid(-row => 0, -column => 2);
$mw->Button(-text => "Button4", -command => sub { exit })->
    grid(-row => 0, -column => 3);

$mw->Button(-text => "Button5", -command => sub { exit })->
    grid(-row => 1, -column => 1);
$mw->Button(-text => "Button6", -command => sub { exit })->
    grid(-row => 1, -column => 2);
$mw->Button(-text => "Button7", -command => sub { exit })->
    grid(-row => 1, -column => 3);
```

See Figure 2-33 for the resulting window.

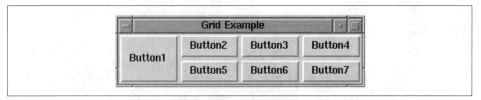

Figure 2-33. Explicit -rowspan example

Forcing a Widget to Fill a Cell

When you use the pack command, it is necessary to indicate both -fill and -expand options to get the widget to resize inside its allocation rectangle. The grid command doesn't have an allocation rectangle to fill, but it does have the cell within the grid. Using the -sticky option with grid is similar to using -fill and -expand with pack.

The value associated with -sticky is a string containing the compass points to which the widget should "stick." If the widget should always "stick" to the top of the cell, you would use -sticky => "n". To force the widget to fill the cell completely, use -sticky => "nsew". To make the widget as tall as the cell but only as wide as it needs to be, use -sticky => "ns". The string value can contain commas and whitespace, but they will be ignored. These two statements are equivalent:

```
-sticky => "nsew"
-sticky => "n, s, e, w"  # Same thing
```

If you use -sticky with your widgets and then resize the window, you'll notice that the widgets don't resize as you would expect. This is because resizing of the cells and the widgets in them is taken care of with the gridColumnconfigure and gridRowconfigure methods, which are discussed later in this chapter.

Padding the Widget

grid also accepts these four options: -ipadx, -ipady, -padx, and -pady. They work exactly the same as they do in pack, but instead of affecting the size of the allocation rectangle, they affect the size of the cell in which the widget is placed.

In this example, the -ipady and -ipadx options are applied to the top row of Buttons and not the bottom row:

```
$mw->Button(-text => "Button1", -command => sub { exit })->grid
  ($mw->Button(-text => "Button2", -command => sub { exit }),
   $mw->Button(-text => "Button3", -command => sub { exit }),
   $mw->Button(-text => "Button4", -command => sub { exit }),
   -sticky => "nsew", -ipadx => 10, -ipady => 10);

$mw->Button(-text => "Button5", -command => sub { exit })->grid
  ($mw->Button(-text => "Button6", -command => sub { exit }),
   $mw->Button(-text => "Button7", -command => sub { exit }),
   $mw->Button(-text => "Button8", -command => sub { exit }),
   -sticky => "nsew");
```

Notice in Figure 2-34 how Buttons 5 through 8 are also wider than they really need to be. This is because we used the -sticky => "nsew" option.

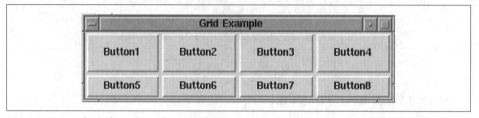

Figure 2-34. grid -ipadx and -ipady example

In the following example, the -pady and -padx options are applied to the top row of Buttons and not the bottom row. Figure 2-35 shows the results.

```
$mw->Button(-text => "Button1", -command => sub { exit })->grid
  ($mw->Button(-text => "Button2", -command => sub { exit }),
   $mw->Button(-text => "Button3", -command => sub { exit }),
   $mw->Button(-text => "Button4", -command => sub { exit }),
   -sticky => "nsew", -padx => 10, -pady => 10);

$mw->Button(-text => "Button5", -command => sub { exit })->grid
  ($mw->Button(-text => "Button6", -command => sub { exit }),
   $mw->Button(-text => "Button7", -command => sub { exit }),
   $mw->Button(-text => "Button8", -command => sub { exit }),
   -sticky => "nsew");
```

Specifying a Different Parent

The -in option works the same way in grid as it does in pack. $widget will be placed in $otherwindow and not in the default parent of $widget.

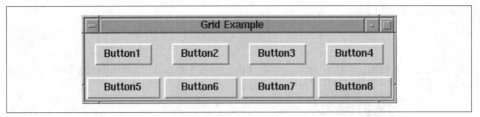

Figure 2-35. grid -padx and -pady example

Here is the usage:

```
-in => $otherwindow
```

Configuring Columns and Rows

As with any of the geometry managers, grid has a few methods associated with it. Each method is invoked via a widget that has been placed on the screen by using grid. Sometimes it is necessary to change the options of the group of cells that makes up your grid.

You can control resizing and the minimum size of a cell with the gridColumnconfigure and gridRowconfigure methods. Each takes a column or a row number as its first argument and then takes some optional arguments that will change the configuration of that column or row.

Both gridColumnconfigure and gridRowconfigure work similarly to the configure method used with widgets; however, the options you can specify with gridColumnconfigure and gridRowconfigure cannot be used with the grid command. The options you can use with gridColumnconfigure and gridRowconfigure are -weight, -minsize, and -pad.

If you send only a row or column number, a list of key/value pairs is returned with the current options and their values for that method:

```
@column_configs = $mw->gridColumnconfigure(0);
@row_configs = $mw->gridRowconfigure(0);
```

Depending on your sensibilities, you may want to store the results in a hash:

```
%column_configs = $mw->gridColumnconfigure(0);
%row_configs = $mw->gridRowconfigure(0);
```

In this example, we are getting the options and their values for the first column and the first row. The results of using the default values would look like this:

```
-minsize 0 -pad 0 -weight 0
-minsize 0 -pad 0 -weight 0
```

You can get the value of only one of the options by sending that option as the second argument:

```
print $mw->gridColumnconfigure(0, -weight), "\n";
print $mw->gridRowconfigure(0, -weight), "\n";
```

The results would be:

```
0
0
```

To change the value of the option, use the option followed immediately by the value you want associated with it. For example:

```
$mw->gridColumnconfigure(0, -weight => 1);
$mw->gridRowconfigure(0, -weight => 1);
```

You can also specify multiple options in one call:

```
$mw->gridColumnconfigure(0, -weight => 1, -pad => 10);
$mw->gridRowconfigure(0, -weight => 1, -pad => 10);
```

Now that we know how to call gridColumnconfigure and gridRowconfigure, we need to know what the three different options do.

Weight

The -weight option sets the amount of space allocated to the column or row when the window is divided into cells. Remember to use -sticky => "nsew" in your grid command if you want the widget to resize when the cell does. The default -weight is 0, which causes the column width or row height to be dictated by the largest widget in the column. Each -weight value has a relationship to the other -weights in the rows or columns.

If a column or row has a -weight of 2, it is twice as big as a column or row that has a -weight of 1. Columns or rows of -weight 0 don't get resized at all. If you want all your widgets to resize in proportion to the size of the window, add this to your code before you call MainLoop:

```
($columns, $rows) = $mw->gridSize( );
for ($i = 0; $i < $columns; $i++) {
  $mw->gridColumnconfigure($i, -weight => 1);
}
for ($i = 0; $i < $rows; $i++) {
  $mw->gridRowconfigure($i, -weight => 1);
}
```

This code will assign the -weight of 1 to every single row and column in the grid, no matter what size the grid is. Of course, this example works only if you want to assign the same size to each row and each column, but you get the idea.

Here is an example of how the -weight option works (Figure 2-36 shows the result):

```
$mw->Button(-text => "Button1", -command => sub { exit })->grid
  ($mw->Button(-text => "Button2", -command => sub { exit }),
   $mw->Button(-text => "Button3", -command => sub { exit }),
   $mw->Button(-text => "Button4", -command => sub { exit }),
   -sticky => "nsew");

$mw->Button(-text => "Button5", -command => sub { exit })->grid
  ("x",
```

```
    $mw->Button(-text => "Button7", -command => sub { exit }),
    $mw->Button(-text => "Button8", -command => sub { exit }),
    -sticky => "nsew");

  $mw->gridColumnconfigure(1, -weight => 1);
  $mw->gridRowconfigure(1, -weight => 1);
```

By giving row 1 and column 1 weights of 1 (whereas all other rows and columns have
0 weights), they take over any extra available space when the size of the window is
increased. Notice that columns 0, 2, and 3 are only as wide as is necessary to draw
the Buttons and their text, but column 1 has filled in the extra space. The same effect
happens for row 0 with a weight of 0 and row 1 with a new weight of 1. (The window has been resized larger to demonstrate the effects of -weight.)

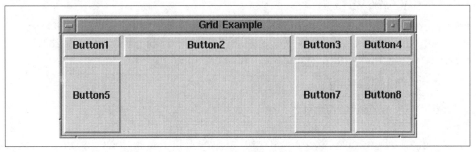

Figure 2-36. gridRowconfigure and gridColumnconfigure example

Minimum cell size

The option -minsize sets the smallest width for the column or the smallest height for
each row. The -minsize option takes a valid screen distance as a value. In this example, the minimum size of the cells in row 0 and column 0 is set to 10 pixels:

```
  $mw->gridColumnconfigure(0, -minsize => 10);
  $mw->gridRowconfigure(0, -minsize => 10);
```

If the column or row was normally less than 10 pixels wide, it would be forced to be
at least that large.

Padding

You can add padding around the widget and to the widget by using the -padx/y and
-ipadx/y options. You can also add a similar type of padding by using the -pad
option with the gridColumnconfigure and gridRowconfigure methods. This padding is
added around the widget, not to the widget itself. When you call
gridColumnconfigure, the -pad option will add padding to the left and right of the
widget. Calling gridRowconfigure with -pad will add padding to the top and bottom
of the widget. Here are two examples:

```
  $mw->gridColumnconfigure(0, -pad => 10);
  $mw->gridRowconfigure(0, -pad => 10);
```

Bounding box

To find out how large a cell is, you can use the gridBbox method:

```
($xoffset, $yoffset, $width, $height) = $master->gridBbox(0, 2);
```

This example gets the bounding box for column 0 and row 2. All the values returned are in pixels. The bounding box will change as you resize the window. The four values returned represent the x offset, the y offset, the cell width, and the cell height (offsets are relative to the window or Frame where the widget is gridded). The bounding box dimensions include any and all padding specified by the -padx, -pady, -ipadx, and -ipady options.

Removing a Widget

Like packForget, gridForget removes widgets from view on the screen. This may or may not cause the window to resize itself; it depends on the size of $widget and where it was on the window. Here are some examples:

```
$mw->gridForget();                  # Nothing happens
$widget->gridForget();              # $widget goes away
$widget->gridForget($widget1);      # $widget and $widget1 go away
$widget->gridForget($w1, $w3);      # $widget, $w1, $w3 go away
```

The widgets are undrawn from the screen, but the cells remain logically filled.

Getting Information

The gridInfo method returns information about the $widget in a list format. Just as with packInfo, the first two elements indicate where the widget was placed:

```
@list = $widget->gridInfo();   # Easier to print
%gridInfo = $widget->gridInfo();
```

Here are some sample results from gridInfo:

```
-in Tk::Frame=HASH(0x81abc44) -column 0 -row 0 -columnspan 1 -rowspan 2 -ipadx 0
-ipady 0 -padx 0 -pady 0  -sticky nesw
```

Widget Location

The gridLocation method returns the column and row of the widget nearest the given (x, y) coordinates, relative to the master:

```
($column, $row) = $master->gridLocation($x, $y);
```

Both $x and $y are in screen units relative to the master window (in our examples, $mw). For locations above or to the left of the grid, −1 is returned.

When given the arguments (0, 0), our application returns this:

```
0 0
```

This indicates that the cell is at column 0 and row 0.

Propagation

There is a gridPropagate method that is similar to packPropagate:

```
$master->gridPropagate( 0 );
```

When given a false value, gridPropagate turns off geometry propagation, meaning size information is not sent upward to the parent of $master. By default, propagation is turned on. If gridPropagate is not given an argument, the current value is returned.

How Many Columns and Rows?

To find out how large the grid has become after placing numerous widgets in it, you can use gridSize on the container widget to get back the number of columns and the number of rows:

```
($columns, $rows) = $master->gridSize( );
```

The list returned contains the number of columns followed by the number of rows. In many of the earlier examples, we had a grid size that was four columns by two rows.

```
($c, $r) = $f->gridSize( );     #$c = 4, $r = 2
```

It is not necessary for a widget to be placed in a column/row for it to be considered a valid column/row. If you place a widget in column 4 and row 5 by using -row=>5, -column=>4 and the only other widget is in row 0 and column 0, then gridSize will return 5 and 6.

gridSlaves

There are two ways to find out which widgets have been put in a window or Frame: use gridSlaves without any arguments to get the full list, or specify a row and column. Here are examples of both:

```
@slaves = $mw->gridSlaves( );
print "@slaves\n";
```

The preceding code might have printed this:

```
Tk::Button=HASH(0x81b6fb8) Tk::Button=HASH(0x81ba454) Tk::Button=HASH(0x81ba4cc) Tk::
Button=HASH(0x81ba538) Tk::Button=HASH(0x81b6fa0) Tk::Button=HASH(0x81ba5e0) Tk::
Button=HASH(0x81ba6dc) Tk::Button=HASH(0x81ba748)
```

We could have specified the widget in column 0, row 0:

```
$widget = $mw->gridSlaves( -row => 0, -column => 0 );
print "$widget\n";
# Might print this: Tk::Button=HASH(0x81b6fb8)
```

If you specify only the -row option, you'll get a list containing only the widgets in that row. The same goes for specifying only -column; your list will contain only the widgets in that column.

The place Geometry Manager

The place geometry manager is different than grid or pack. Rather than referencing against a cell location or a window's side, most of the time you'll be using a relative form of x and y coordinates. You can also use place to overlap portions of widgets, which isn't allowed in either grid or pack.

Invoking place is similar to calling the other geometry managers:

```
$widget->place( [ option => value, . . . ] );
```

The options specified when you call place affect how the widgets are put on the screen.

place Options

The following options can be used with place:

-anchor => 'n' | 'ne' | 'e' | 'se' | 's' | 'sw' | 'w' | **'nw'** | 'center'
> Sets the position in the widget that will be placed at the specified coordinates.

-bordermode => **'inside'** | 'outside' | 'ignore'
> Determines whether or not the border portion of the widget is included in the coordinate system.

-height => *amount*
> Sets the absolute height of the widget.

-in => $window
> Indicates that the child widget will be packed inside $window instead of in the parent that created it. Any relative coordinates or sizes will still refer to the parent.

-relheight => *ratio*
> Indicates that the height of the widget relates to the parent widget's height by *ratio*.

-relwidth => *ratio*
> Indicates that the width of the widget relates to the parent widget's width by *ratio*.

-relx => *xratio*
> Indicates that the widget will be placed relative to its parent by *xratio*.

-rely => *yratio*
> Indicates that the widget will be placed relative to its parent by *yratio*.

-width => *amount*
> Indicates that the width of the widget will be *amount*.

-x => *x*
> Indicates that the widget will be placed at *x*. *x* is any valid screen distance.

-y => *y*
> Indicates that the widget will be placed at *y*. *y* is any valid screen distance.

This code snippet produces the Button shown in Figure 2-41:

```
$b = $mw->Button(-text => "Exit", -command => sub { exit });
$b->place(-relx => 0.5, -rely => 0.5);
```

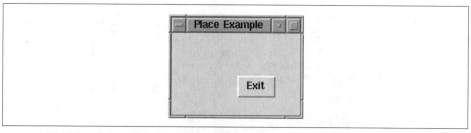

Figure 2-41. Using place with -relx => 0.5, -rely => 0.5

Although the Button in Figure 2-41 is placed in the middle of the screen, it looks off-center because the upper-left corner of the widget was placed in the middle of the window instead of the center. You can change this with the -anchor option, which we will discuss shortly. If we resize this window, the Button still stays in the middle of the window (see Figure 2-42).

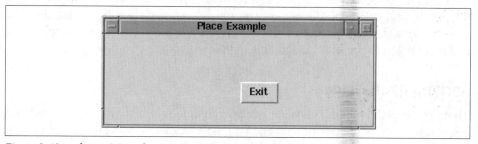

Figure 2-42. -relx => 0.5, -rely => 0.5 window resized to be larger

This next example creates two Buttons, both placed in the window with relative coordinates:

```
$mw->Button(-text => "Exit",
            -command => sub { exit })->place(-relx => 0.2,
                                             -rely => 0.2);
$mw->Button(-text => "Exit",
            -command => sub { exit })->place(-relx => 0.5,
                                             -rely => 0.5);
```

No matter what size the window is or where other widgets are in the screen, the two Buttons will stay in those relative locations (see Figure 2-43).

The left window in Figure 2-43 is the default size of the window when it was created. The right window is what it looks like after the window was resized to make it much smaller. Notice that the second Button placed in the window remains on top.

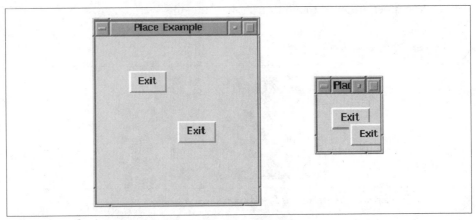

Figure 2-43. Two Buttons placed relative to the parent window

It does so because we are still maintaining the ordered list of widgets in the window; the second Exit Button, placed at (0.5, 0.5), is drawn last, so it's drawn on top of the other Button.

You can also combine the absolute and relative coordinate systems simply by using both in the argument list. The relative coordinate system is considered first, then the x or y value is added to that position. The options -relx => 0.5, -x => -10 place the widget 10 pixels to the left of the middle of the window.

Anchoring the Widget

Think of the child widget as a piece of paper that you want to put on your bulletin board (the board is the parent widget). You have a tack that you are going to use to keep the paper up on the board. You can put the tack right through the center of the paper, in the upper-left corner ("nw"), or in the lower-right corner ("se"). The point where the tack is going to stick the paper to the board is the -anchor point. The -anchor point on the widget is "tacked" to the coordinates given by -x, -y, and/ or -relx, -rely. The default -anchor is "nw". Figure 2-40 shows these -anchor points within the child widget.

It is important to know where the -anchor is, because it will affect how we see the widget within the parent.

In Figure 2-44, almost identical place commands were used to put the Exit Button in the window, but the -anchor value was changed. The left window's Button was created with this command:

```
$mw->Button(-text => "Exit",
            -command => sub { exit })->place(-relx => 0.5,
                                             -rely => 0.5);
```

The window on the right in Figure 2-44 used this command:

```
$mw->Button(-text => "Exit",
            -command => sub { exit })->place(-relx => 0.5,
                                             -anchor => "center",
                                             -rely => 0.5);
```

As with pack and grid, the possible values for -anchor are: 'n', 'e', 's', 'w', 'center', 'nw', 'sw', 'ne', and 'se'. However, the value now refers to the child widget instead of the position within the allocation rectangle.

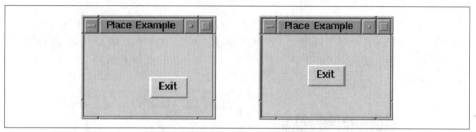

Figure 2-44. Different -anchor values affect where the widget is placed in the window

Width and Height

When you use place, you can specify the width and height of the widget in one of three ways:

- Allow the widget to determine its own size.
- Specify width and/or height in absolute measurements.
- Specify width and/or height in relative measurements (relative to the parent widget).

To let the widgets determine their own sizes, no options are specified. You can set the widgets' sizes with the following options: -width and -height, or -relwidth and -relheight, respectively.

The -width and -height options allow you to specify the exact width or height of the widget in a screen distance:

```
-width => amount, -height => amount
```

Each amount is a valid screen distance (discussed earlier in this chapter under pack). The widget will obey these options even if it has to cut off edges of the items displayed in it. Our Button looks quite silly on the screen when we use a -width of 40 pixels (see Figure 2-45).

```
$mw->Button(-text => "This Button Will Cause the Program to Exit",
            -command => sub { exit })->place(-x => 0, -y => 0,
                                             -width => 40);
```

The other two options, -relwidth and -relheight, determine the widget in relation to the parent widget.

```
-relwidth => ratio, -relheight => ratio
```

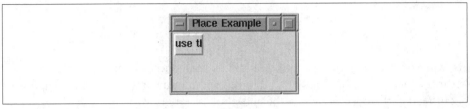

Figure 2-45. Using -width with place

The *ratio* is a floating-point number (similar to that specified by -relx or -rely). A value of 1.0 will make the widget as wide (or as tall) as the parent widget. A value of 0.5 will make the widget half as wide as the parent (see Figure 2-46).

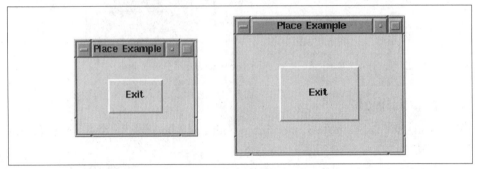

Figure 2-46. Example of the same window resized with -relwidth => 0.5, -relheight => 0.5

The options -width and -relwidth are additive when used together, and so are -height and -relheight.

Border Options

Normally the border of the widget is used as the edge of the possible space in the window, which means any widgets placed with either the absolute or relative coordinate system will be placed inside the border. This can be changed by using the -bordermode option:

```
-bordermode => 'inside' | 'outside' | 'ignore'
```

Using 'outside' will allow the coordinate system to use the space occupied by the border as well. A value of 'ignore' will have the coordinate system use the space designated as the official X area. Overall, this option is pretty useless, as you can see from the difference each makes in Figure 2-47.

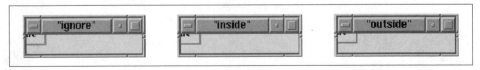

Figure 2-47. -bordermode examples

If you look very closely (get out your magnifying glass), you can see that the 'outside' version is two pixels higher and two pixels farther to the left than the 'inside' version. This is because with one window manager (*fvwm*), the border is defined as 2 pixels.

Methods Associated with place

The methods for place are simple and don't allow much manipulation of the widgets.

Removing the widget

As with pack and grid, there is a place version of the Forget method:

```
$widget->placeForget();
```

When you use this method, the widget is removed from view on the screen. It is also removed from the list maintained by the parent widget.

Place information

The placeInfo method returns a list of information related to the widget:

```
# For easier printing:
@info = $widget->placeInfo();
print "@info";
# Or for easier fetching of info
%info = $widget->placeInfo();

## Produced these results (there are blanks where there are no values)
-x 0 -relx 0 -y 0 -rely 0 -width  -relwidth -height -relheight -anchor nw
```

Place slaves

placeSlaves returns a list of the slave widgets that are within $parent:

```
@widgets = $parent->placeSlaves();
```

The list looks the same as it does when it is returned from packSlaves() or gridSlaves().

The form Geometry Manager

The final geometry manager we want to cover is form. Recently added into the Perl/Tk distribution, form is a very different geometry manager than those we've seen so far. To try and compare it with what we already know, it behaves like a combination of pack and place. Using form, it is legal to overlap widgets (as you would with place), but you can also display the widgets relative to each other and stretch them out to fill the entire available area and resize with the window (as you would with pack). The combination of all these abilities results in a powerful geometry manager.

When using form, each edge of a widget can be attached to something: the container's grid, another widget, or nothing at all. You can also use springs to push your widgets around in the window based on the strength (or weight) of the spring. As with the other geometry managers, you can add padding to your widget.

Let's look at the options briefly, then go into more detail on how to use them.

Options for form

The following are all the legal options for form. The following sections show you how to use these options to the best effect.

-bottom => *attachment*
> Uses the given attachment on the bottom side of the widget.

-bottomspring => *weight*
> Uses the given weight for a spring on the bottom side of the widget.

-fill => 'x' | 'y' | 'both' | 'none'
> Specifies the direction in which to fill when springs are used. There is no default value.

-in => $master
> Uses $master as the container to put the widget in. If used, the -in option must be the first one specified.

-left => *attachment*
> Uses the given attachment on the left side of the widget.

-leftspring => *weight*
> Uses the given weight for a spring on the left side of the widget.

-padbottom => *value*, -padleft => *value*, -padright => *value*, and -padtop => *value*
> Place padding on the given side of the widget.

-padx => *value*
> Places padding on the left and right sides of the widget.

-pady => *amount*
> Places padding on the top and bottom of the widget.

-right => *attachment*
> Uses the given attachment on the right side of the widget.

-rightspring => *weight*
> Uses the given weight for a spring on the right side of the widget.

-top => *attachment*
> Uses the given attachment on the top side of the widget.

-topspring => *weight*
> Uses the given weight for a spring on the top side of the widget.

Attachments

The edge (top, bottom, left, and right) of each widget can be attached to something else in the container. The left side can be attached to the grid (which we'll say more about in a minute), the right to another widget, and the top and bottom might be attached to nothing at all. In addition to an anchor point, you can specify a positive or negative offset from that point. An offset is a number given in screen units. A positive offset moves the widget to the right or down from the anchor point. A negative offset moves the widget to the left or up from the anchor point. An attachment is comprised of either an anchor point or an anonymous array of [anchor_point, offset]. The examples we go through to demonstrate each type will make this clear.

Attaching to the grid

There is an unseen grid in each container widget that uses form. Don't confuse this grid with the grid geometry manager. The default size of form's grid is 100 × 100, and does not change even if the container size changes. Within the container, the left and top are both at 0, the right and bottom are at 100. Using these numbers, we can specify a spot to attach a widget edge to. This is different from place because instead of using pixel points that change as the window changes size, the size of the grid remains static. To specify a grid attachment, use the form '%xx' replacing xx with the grid location. If you leave out the %, you are specifying an offset only, rather than a grid location. This example demonstrates using a grid attachment:

```
foreach (1..5) {
    # Create Buttons and attach them to grid at intervals of 5
    $mw->Button(-text => $_ * 5)->form(-left => '%' . $_ * 5,
                                       -top => '%' . $_ * 5);
}
```

This code creates five widgets, putting them on the grid at (5, 5), (10, 10), (15, 15), and so on. Take a look at Figure 2-48 and you'll see what happens when we resize this window. Notice that the widgets overlap each other and move as the window is resized. This demonstrates that the grid size stays the same as the window resizes, and the widgets move with the grid. If you make the window large enough, the widgets no longer overlap.

For the previous example, we used the -top and -left options to specify where to locate the widgets in the window. If you call form with no options at all, each widget is put at (0, 0), piled one on top of the other. The order in which the widgets are created is important in this case, because the last one created is placed on top of the pile.

You can change the size of the widget by attaching opposite sides to different points in the grid. The widget will resize with the window (see Figure 2-49):

```
# First Button is 'normal'
$b1 = $mw->Button(-text => "small")->form(-left => '%10');
# Second Button is attached to $b1 on left, and grid 70 on right
$mw->Button(-text => "BIG")->form(-left => $b1, -right => '%70',
                                  -top => '%0', -bottom => '%80');
```

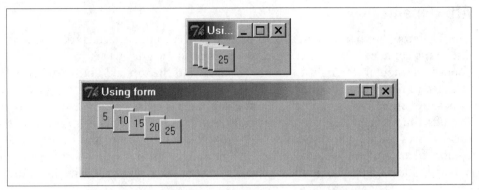

Figure 2-48. How the form grid works (both windows have grid sizes of 100x100)

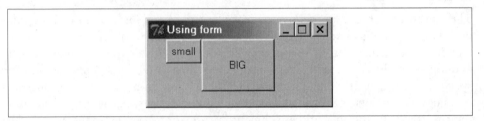

Figure 2-49. A widget attached to the grid on two sides stretches to stay attached

There are a few things to note about the code associated with Figure 2-49. We didn't specify a -top attachment point for the small Button. The default is always going to be 0 if there isn't a top/bottom or left/right attachment point explicitly used with form. Also, the -left attachment point for the BIG Button was another widget. That's a widget-to-widget attachment, which we'll cover next.

To shift your widget 10 pixels to the right of the grid coordinate (5, 5), you would use an anonymous array to specify the whole attachment:

```
$mw->Button(-text => "shifted right")->form(-left => ['%5', 10],
                                             -top => '%5');
```

If the offset is 0, you don't need to specify it at all.

Widget-to-widget attachments

There are two ways to attach one widget to another: by using the same side (both top, both bottom, and so on), or by using opposite sides. Any widgets attached to one another must be managed by form in the same parent container.

Here's an example of opposite side attachment:

```
$thisbutton->form(-left => $b1);
```

You would read that in English as "Attach the left side of $thisbutton to the opposite (right) side of $b1." Remember the option name you are using (-left, -right,

-top, or -bottom) applies to the widget on which you are currently calling form. If you want a bit of space between two widgets, add an offset to the -left attachment point:

```
$b1 = $mw->Button(-text => "small")->form(-left => '%10');
# Second Button is attached to $b1 on left, and grid 70 on right
$mw->Button(-text => "BIG")->form(-left => [$b1, 5], -right => '%70',
                                  -top => '%0', -bottom => '%80');
```

By changing the argument to -left (in bold), we add a bit of space between the two widgets, as shown in Figure 2-50.

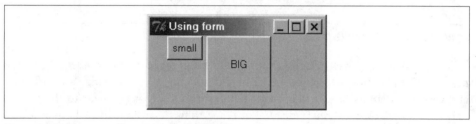

Figure 2-50. Using an offset with a widget attachment

What if we want to line up the left sides of a bunch of widgets? We use a same-side attachment. (In the docs this is called Parallel Side Attachment). To tell form you are using a same-side attachment, add the '&' character as the first item in an anonymous array.

```
$b1 = $mw->Button(-text => 'top widget')->form(-left => '%10');
$b2 = $mw->Button(-text => 'bottom widget')->form(-left => ['&', $b1],
     -top => $b1);
$mw->Button(-text => 'bottom widget(2)')->form(-left => ['&', $b1, ],
     -top => [$b2, 10]);
```

This code creates three Buttons, all left aligned, with the third Button 10 pixels from the bottom of the one above it. We are lining up both the second and third Button to $b1. See what this looks like in Figure 2-51.

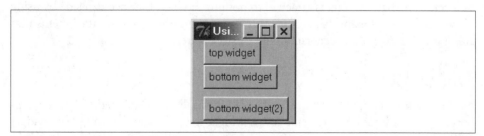

Figure 2-51. Using same-side and opposite-side attachments together

What if we want to stretch all three widgets to the same length? With pack we'd just use -fill => 'y' inside the container. With form, we add -right => '%100' to the options of each form call. This will stretch each widget all the way to the right edge of the container, as shown in Figure 2-52.

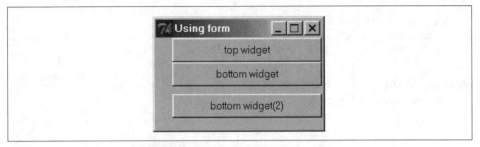

Figure 2-52. Stretching widgets to the same point in the container

Using form this way has one disadvantage: if you wanted to put something to the right of all those Buttons, you'd be better off sticking all three widgets in a Frame and treating them as one. A way around this is to use an attachment to the grid of -right => '%80' on all three widgets, but crazy things can happen if the window is sized smaller than you expect.

Here's an example of centering a widget directly in the container:

```
# Center a widget across the whole screen:
$w = -($a->reqwidth()/2);
$h = -($a->reqheight()/2);
print "W: $w, H: $h\n";
$a->form(-top => ['%50', $h], -left => ['%50', $w]);
```

We use reqwidth and reqheight to find out how large the widget should be, then use those values as offsets to the center grid position '%50' on both the top and left. In order to shift the widget correctly, we make the offsets negative. It isn't necessary to specify -right and -bottom edges.

Attaching to nothing

You can state that a widget is attached to nothing at all on the specified side by using 'none' as the attachment value. Since this is the default for any side attachments that aren't listed, it won't be necessary to use this very often.

Springs

As this book was being written, springs were not fully implemented.* They are supposed to act as forces on each side of the widget to adjust the position of the widget within its container. If the widget is attached to another widget, the result can be a widget that resizes properly, but doesn't overlap as things move around.

---

* It appears that top and bottom springs work, but left and right don't. Hopefully this will be fixed soon, as springs make form more powerful.

If you use a spring, it has a *weight*. The weight doesn't really matter except in relation to any other spring weights you are using in your parent container. If each spring has a weight of 1, they are all pushing with the same amount of force. The same can be said if every spring has a weight of 2. If one spring has a weight of 1, and another a weight of 2, then the second spring is twice as powerful as the first spring.

To discover what springs really do to your widgets, here's a "Play with form" widget displaying program:

```perl
use Tk;

$mw = MainWindow->new(-title => 'Play w/form');


# Create a Frame at the bottom of the window to use 'form' in
$f = $mw->Frame(-borderwidth => 2, -relief => 'groove')
    ->pack(-side => 'bottom', -expand => 1, -fill =>'both');

# Display the Button in the default position to start
$button = $f->Button(-text => "Go!", -command => \&reForm)->form;

# Use grid to create the Entry widgets to take our options:
$f1 = $mw->Frame->pack(-side => 'top', -fill => 'x');
$f1->Label(-text => '-top')->grid($f1->Entry(-textvariable => \$top),
    $f1->Label(-text => '-topspring'),
    $f1->Entry(-textvariable => \$topspring),
    -sticky => 'w', -padx => 2, -pady => 5);

$f1->Label(-text => '-bottom')->grid($f1->Entry(-textvariable => \$bottom),
    $f1->Label(-text => '-bottomspring'),
    $f1->Entry(-textvariable => \$bottomspring),
    -sticky => 'w', -padx => 2, -pady => 5);

$f1->Label(-text => '-left')->grid($f1->Entry(-textvariable => \$left),
    $f1->Label(-text => '-leftspring'),
    $f1->Entry(-textvariable => \$leftspring),
    -sticky => 'w', -padx => 2, -pady => 5);

$f1->Label(-text => '-right')->grid($f1->Entry(-textvariable => \$right),
    $f1->Label(-text => '-rightspring'),
    $f1->Entry(-textvariable => \$rightspring),
    -sticky => 'w', -padx => 2, -pady => 5);

# Add this Button in case the options we put in causes the 'formed' Button
# to go off screen somewhere.
$f1->Button(-text => "Go!", -command => \&reForm)
    ->grid('-', '-', '-', -pady => 5);

MainLoop;

sub reForm
{
    print "top => $top\t";
    print "topspring => $topspring\n";
```

```
print "bottom => $bottom\t";
print "bottomspring => $bottomspring\n";
print "left => $left\t";
print "leftspring => $leftspring\n";
print "right => $right\t";
print "rightspring => $rightspring\n";
print "----------------------------\n";

# Remove Button from container for now
$button->formForget;

my @args = ( );

if ($top ne '') { push (@args, ('-top', $top)); }
if ($bottom ne '') { push (@args, ('-bottom', $bottom)); }
if ($right ne '') { push (@args, ('-right', $right)); }
if ($left ne '') { push (@args, ('-left', $left)); }
if ($topspring ne '') { push (@args, ('-topspring', $topspring)); }
if ($bottomspring ne ''){push (@args, ('-bottomspring', $bottomspring));}
if ($rightspring ne '') { push (@args, ('-rightspring', $rightspring)); }
if ($rightspring ne '') { push (@args, ('-rightspring', $rightspring)); }
print "ARGS: @args\n";

# Put Button back in container using new args
$button->form(@args);

}
```

You can't enter anonymous arrays as values in this application, but you can play
with the basic way of attaching to a grid and with the springs. Take a look at
Figure 2-53 to see what the widget looks like after the options are changed.

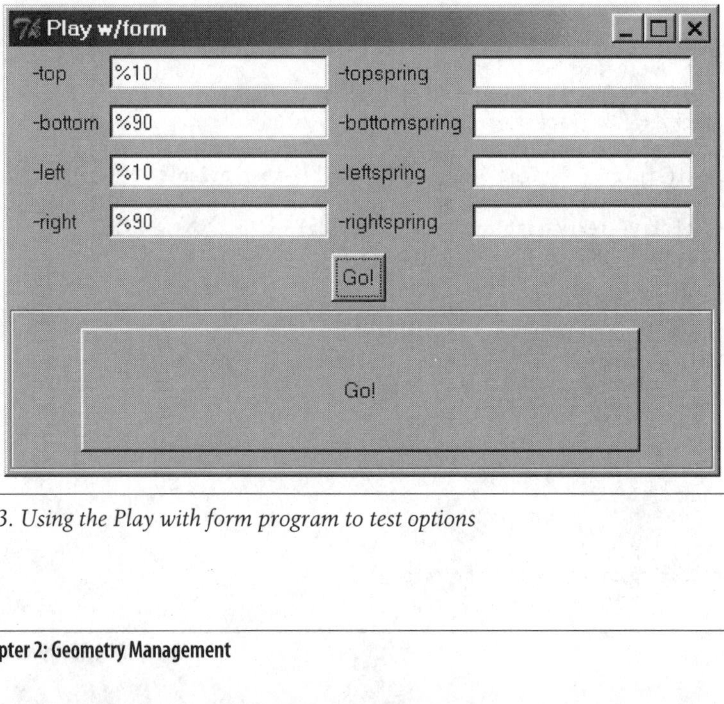

Figure 2-53. Using the Play with form program to test options

Using the top and bottom springs pushes the widget around a bit: if you enter 1 for both -topspring and -bottomspring, the height of the widget goes back to its default size and becomes centered in the screen.

form Methods

The following sections summarize form's methods.

Changing the grid size

You can change the grid at any time by calling formGrid with new x and y sizes. You can also determine the current size of the grid.

```
$parent->formGrid(200, 200);
($x, $y) = $parent->formGrid;
```

Removing a widget from a container

To take a widget out of its container, call $widget->formForget. Any attachments defined for this widget no longer apply.

Options info for form

Just like all the other geometry managers, form has an Info method to get detailed information about how a widget was put in its parent container:

```
%forminfo = $widget->formInfo;
$top_value = $widget->formInfo(-top);
```

What's managed by form?

To get a list of all the widgets managed by a parent container using form, call formSlaves on the parent. The order in the list is the same as how the widgets were added into the parent.

```
@widgets = $parent->formSlaves;
print "Widgets in $parent are @widgets\n";
```

Circular dependency check

You need to be careful that you don't end up with a circular reference when doing widget attachments. To check your setup, you can call $parent->formCheck. This will return true if it finds a circular dependency and false if it doesn't.

Geometry Management Summary

You now know more about the different geometry managers than you'll ever need to write a successful Perl/Tk application. Here are some helpful hints on deciding which geometry manager to use:

- pack is good for general purpose use and will be your choice about 95% of the time.
- grid is perfect for those situations in which you would like to create a columnar layout similar to a spreadsheet. Options allow you to change the sizes of rows and/or columns easily.
- place is most useful when you want your widget to stay in a position or size that is relative to the widget that created it. When used correctly, it can be very powerful.
- form is powerful, but difficult to get used to; not for the faint of heart. Check future releases of the Tk module for updates to this geometry manager.

No matter which manager you use, take the time to get the widgets on your window where they belong (or more likely, where you want them). There's nothing more unsettling than a Button that looks like it just doesn't belong in the window.

As you read through this book, you'll notice that some of the option names for the geometry managers are also option names when you are creating or configuring a widget type. For example, you can specify the -width of a Button without using place. Always keep in mind the context in which the option is used. Sometimes the functional difference is very subtle.

## CHAPTER 3

Fonts

Every computer system uses fonts. In Perl/Tk applications, you can change any of the fonts for items *inside* the application, but not the fonts used in the window decoration for titles (which are handled by the window manager). In this chapter, we'll show you how to use fonts in your Perl/Tk application.

What fonts do you have available? For MS Windows users, the available fonts can be found in the Font control panel. Users of the X Window System can get a font list by running *xlsfonts*. The font used in this chapter is Linotype Birka. While you can't do anything about the font used in this book, you can do something about the fonts in the applications you create or run in Perl/Tk.

The simplest way of altering an application's font is changing the base font for the entire application. You can do that with any Perl/Tk application by using a command-line option:

```
perl myTkApp.pl -font "Times 12"
```

Using the -font command-line option doesn't require any changes to your Perl script. The -font option works because of the way Tk::CmdLine works, described in Chapter 16. Note that you specify the –font option after the name of the program to run. As long as you haven't explicitly specified the font for any widgets in your application, all widgets will use the new font.

To change the font for only some widgets, you can use the option database, described in Chapter 16. For example, if you wanted to change only the font for Text widgets in your application, specify *text*font=Courier 16 in the option database.

Experimenting with Fonts

You don't generally want to hardcode font specifications in you programs. Simply put, it prevents your users from customizing your applications. There are extenuating circumstances, though; you might have an HP calculator that has a specific look that shouldn't be changed (see Chapter 15). Creating such a specific look might require one or more particular fonts.

One way to determine what font to use is to write a program using the `fontFamilies` method that displays various font specifications. So, before we get into the details of creating a font definition, let's look at a program that lets us play around with the fonts on our system. This program is useful no matter what operating system you're on.

```perl
use Tk;
use Tk::BrowseEntry;
use strict;

my $mw = MainWindow->new(-title => 'Font Viewer');
my $f = $mw->Frame->pack(-side => 'top');

my $family = 'Courier';
my $be = $f->BrowseEntry(-label => 'Family:', -variable => \$family,
  -browsecmd => \&apply_font)->pack(-fill => 'x', -side => 'left');
$be->insert('end', sort $mw->fontFamilies);

my $size = 24;
my $bentry = $f->BrowseEntry(-label => 'Size:', -variable => \$size,
  -browsecmd => \&apply_font)->pack(-side => 'left');
$bentry->insert('end', (3 .. 32));

my $weight = 'normal';
$f->Checkbutton(-onvalue => 'bold', -offvalue => 'normal',
  -text => 'Weight', -variable => \$weight,
  -command => \&apply_font)->pack(-side => 'left');

my $slant = 'roman';
$f->Checkbutton(-onvalue => 'italic', -offvalue => 'roman',
  -text => 'Slant', -variable => \$slant,
  -command => \&apply_font)->pack(-side => 'left');

my $underline = 0;
$f->Checkbutton(-text => 'Underline', -variable => \$underline,
  -command => \&apply_font)->pack(-side => 'left');

my $overstrike = 0;
$f->Checkbutton(-text => 'Overstrike', -variable => \$overstrike,
  -command => \&apply_font)->pack(-side => 'left');

my $stext = 'Sample Text';
my $sample = $mw->Entry(-textvariable => \$stext)->pack(-fill => 'x');

&apply_font;

MainLoop;

sub apply_font {
  # Specify all options for font in an anonymous array
  $sample->configure(-font =>
    [-family => $family,
     -size => $size,
     -weight => $weight,
```

```
        -slant => $slant,
        -underline => $underline,
        -overstrike => $overstrike]);
}
```

Figure 3-1 shows what the window looks like if we select Garamond, size 24, with slant and overstrike.

Figure 3-1. Font viewer

Those of you used to a Unix system will recognize this type of font viewer, since there is something similar that comes with X, called *xfontsel*.

In our font viewer, we can see the changes to the font are applied using the apply_font subroutine. We specify all aspects of the font so the user has the choice of changing any part of the font. Let's talk about those different parts.

Dissecting a Font

In the font viewer, we see that the Entry's font is changed with the -font option using an anonymous array. From this we know a font consists of the following things:

Family
> The actual name of the font, e.g., 'Courier', 'Times', and so on.

Size
> The size of the font in points. The larger the size, the larger the text displayed on the screen. A point is 1/72 of an inch. Negative values are interpreted as pixels.

Weight
> Determines if the font is shown bold or not. The value 'normal' means it is not shown bold, and 'bold' makes the font thicker.

Slant
> Shows straight up and down if 'roman' is used, and slanted if 'italic' is used.

Underline
> If the value used with -underline is true, the text will be underlined. If false, the text will not be underlined.

Overstrike
> If true, a line will be drawn through the center of the text.

If you are used to working with fonts on a Unix system, you are probably familiar with X Logical Font Descriptions (XFLD). This is the dash-delimited format used for fonts under X, for example:

```
*-helvetica-bold-r-*-*-*-240-*-*-*-*-*-*
```

This font description indicates a 24-point bold Helvetica font with Roman slant. The field order is as follows: *-foundry-family-weight-slant-sWdth-adstyl-pixelsize-pointsize-resx-resy-spacing-avgWidth-registry-encoding*.

When specifying a font in XLFD notation, an asterisk means you don't care what is used for that value, and the system will choose a default for you.

While a full description of X fonts is beyond the scope of this book, there are a few things you should know. First, it is entirely acceptable to specify a font in XLFD notation under either Unix or Windows. The code is:

```
font => '-*-helvetica-bold-r-*-*-*-240-*-*-*-*-*-*'
```

When you use this format under Unix, you get exactly what you ask for. Every field is honored. Under Windows, only family, weight, slant, pixelsize, and pointsize are honored. All the other fields are ignored.

If you would like to learn more about fonts under X, a good beginner's guide and bibliography may be found in "The X Window User HOWTO" by Ray Brigleb. This document may be found in many, many places on the Web, but the definitive location is *http://www.linuxdoc.org/HOWTO/XWindow-User-HOWTO.html*.

Using Fonts

Now that we know what comprises a font, let's look at a few ways we can specify them in code.

We simplify things in our Perl/Tk applications by being able to create a single name that refers to a combination of family, size, weight, slant, underline, and overstrike:

```
$code_font = $mw->fontCreate('code', -family => 'courier',
                             -size => 12);
```

Once we have created our new font, you can refer to the font by the variable $code_font or by the name, 'code':

```
$mw->Button(-text => "Show Code", -font => 'code');
$mw->Button(-text => "Show Code2", -font => $code_font);
```

It is much simpler to specify all the desired font options once and refer to them using the name or variable later in the program. If you don't want to use a name for the font, don't specify it; the system will generate a name for you automatically.

```
$code_font = $mw->fontCreate(-family => 'courier',
                             -size => 12);
```

Once the font is created, you can change any of its settings using the fontConfigure method, using the font name or reference as the first argument:

```
$mw->fontConfigure($code_font, -family => 'Verdana');
```

The changes will take effect immediately on any widgets using that font, making it very useful for on-the-fly changes.

The -font option will also accept an anonymous array containing the right parts, with or without the identifiers:

```
-font => ['courier', '14', 'bold']
# The same thing, but more verbose:
-font => [-family => 'courier',
          -size => '14',
          -weight => 'bold']
```

The second way is much more verbose, and easier to read, but those of us who prefer to keep our code small and compact might want to stick with the first method. You must specify at minimum the family name; all other specifications are optional.

If creating an anonymous array isn't to your liking, try just using a string containing the relevant parts:

```
-font => "courier 14 bold"
-font => "courier 12 bold italic"
-font => "{courier} 14"
-font => "{Calisto MT} 18 bold italic overstrike"
```

There are a few restrictions when using this specification. The family name must always come first, followed by the (optional) size, and any of weight, slant, and so on. If the family name has a space in it, you must put it between curly braces so the font parser can find the full family name. You can put any family name in curly braces, not just those that have spaces in them; if you like this way of specifying fonts, it might be best to always include the curly braces.

System Fonts

In addition to the fonts that are listed with *xlsfonts* or shown in the Font Control Panel, you can also specify fonts referred to as *system* fonts. Since these fonts are operating system specific, you will not get the same result from machine to machine, unless they happen to be running the same operating system. Table 3-1 lists system fonts on each of the popular operating system platforms.

Table 3-1. System fonts

Platform	System fonts
Unix	(Use *xlsfonts* for a complete listing)
Windows	system, systemfixed, ansi, ansifixed, device, oemfixed
Macintosh	system, application

Using Fonts Dynamically

Let's look at a program that creates fonts dynamically. This code will display each selected font in a window much the way Microsoft Windows does when you look at the Font control panel. To display the font in its different sizes, we simply use the ROText widget so the text is read-only (see Chapter 8 for further information on ROText widgets). The font changes are applied in the show_font sub using tags.

```perl
use Tk;
require Tk::TList;
require Tk::ROText;
use strict;

my $mw = MainWindow->new(-title => "Fonts");
$mw->minsize(700,400);
my $tl = $mw->Scrolled("TList", -font => ['Arial', '12'], -command => \&show_font)->
pack(-fill => 'both', -expand => 1);

# using a tlist, we have to insert each item individually
foreach (sort $mw->fontFamilies)
{
        $tl->insert('end', -itemtype => 'text', -text => $_);
}

MainLoop;

# called when user double clicks on a font name in the tlist.
sub show_font
{
        my ($index) = @_;
        my $name = $tl->entrycget($index, -text);
        my $top = $mw->Toplevel(-title => $name);
        my $text = $top->Scrolled("ROText", -wrap => 'none')
    ->pack(-expand => 1, -fill => 'both');

        $text->tagConfigure('number', -font => ['courier', '12']);

    # since we don't know what font they picked, we dynamically
    # create a tag w/that font formatting
        $text->tagConfigure('abc', -font => [$name, '18']);
        $text->insert('end', "abcdefghijklmnopqrstuvwxyz\
nABCDEFGHIJKLMNOPQRSTUVWXYZ\n1234567890.;,;(*!?')\n\n", 'abc');

        foreach (qw/12 18 24 36 48 60 72/)
        {
                $text->tagConfigure("$name$_", -font => [$name, $_]);
                $text->insert('end', "$_ ", 'number');
                $text->insert('end',
    "The quick brown fox jumps over the lazy dog. 1234567890\n", "$name$_");
        }
}
```

Figures 3-2 and 3-3 show the resulting windows.

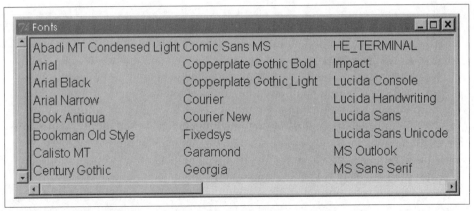

Figure 3-2. MainWindow in our control panel–like Font viewer

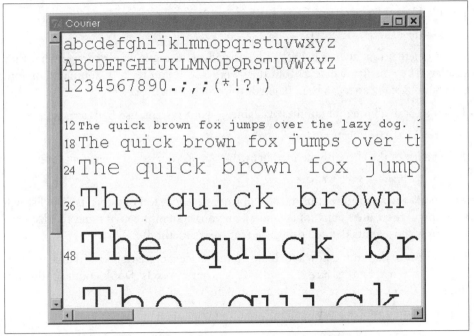

Figure 3-3. An individual font (Courier) viewed in a Toplevel widget

Font Manipulation Methods

Once you've created a font using fontCreate, you can use the following methods.

For a description of the font's attributes (some or all), use fontActual to query the font:

```
$mw->fontCreate('bigfont', -family => 'Arial', -size => 48);

%big = $mw->fontActual('bigfont');
print %big;
```

```
# prints:
-size 48 -overstrike 0 -underline 0
-weight normal -slant roman -family Arial

$size = $mw->fontActual('bigfont', -size);
print $size;
#prints:
48
```

To change (or query) a property of a font once it has been created, use fontConfigure:

```
if ($mw->fontConfigure('bigfont', -size) < 24) {
  $mw->fontConfigure('bigfont', -size => 48);
}

# same as $mw->fontActual('bigfont');
%bigfont = $mw->fontConfigure('bigfont');
```

If you'd like to delete a font definition, use fontDelete:

```
$mw->fontDelete('bigfont');
```

If you delete a font that is being used, the widgets using it won't change what they display. They display whatever font they were last. If you try to manipulate the font programmatically after it's been deleted, you will get an error.

To get a list of all the font families available on your system, use fontFamilies:

```
@families = $mw->fontFamilies;
```

To get a list of the currently defined named fonts on your system, use fontNames:

```
@definedfonts = $mw->fontNames;
```

The fontNames method returns a list of object references to Font objects. The list will be empty if there aren't any fonts defined on your system. Keep in mind this list contains only those fonts defined using the fontCreate method.

If you want to determine how much *horizontal* space a piece of text will take up with a given font, use fontMeasure. The answer is given in pixels. Don't count on this figure to be the exact size; it's more of an estimate.

```
print $mw->fontMeasure('bigfont', "SHORT"), "\n";
225
print $mw->fontMeasure('bigfont', "MUCH LONGER"), "\n";
480
```

For those of you who really understand the different ways you can measure a font, you'll be interested in the fontMetrics method. The vertical options it describes are -ascent (very top to baseline), -descent (very bottom to baseline), -linespace (separation between lines of text), and -fixed (whether or not the font is proportional).

```
$ascent = $mw->fontMetrics('bigfont', -ascent);
%metrics = $mw->fontMetrics('bigfont');
```

```
print %metrics;

-linespace 72 -descent 14 -ascent 58 -fixed 0
```

One Last Example

Just for fun we'll look at one last example. This program will display a banner in the selected font that continually rotates the text within it (see Figures 3-4 and 3-5).

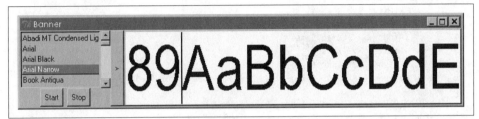

Figure 3-4. Banner program showing the font configuration widgets

Figure 3-5. Banner program without font configuration widgets

Here's the code for the banner program:

```
use Tk;
use strict;

# initial banner text. Entry is not read-only
my $str = "AaBbCcDdEeFfGgHhIiJjKkLlMmNnOoPpQqRrSsTtUuVvWwXxYyZz0123456789";

my $mw = MainWindow->new;
my $lframe = $mw->Frame->pack(-fill => 'both',
  -side => 'left', -expand => 1);
my $lb = $lframe->Scrolled("Listbox", -scrollbars => "e",
  -height => 3)->pack(-fill => 'both', -expand => 1, -side => 'top');

$lb->insert('end', sort $mw->fontFamilies);

# Button that will pop the config widgets in and out
my $hidebutton = $mw->Button(-text => ">")->pack(-side => 'left',
  -fill => 'y');
$hidebutton->configure(-command =>
  sub {
```

```perl
            if ($hidebutton->cget(-text) eq ">") {
              $lframe->packForget; $hidebutton->configure(-text => "<")
            } else {
              $lframe->pack(-before => $hidebutton, -fill => 'both',
          -side => 'left', -expand => 1);
              $hidebutton->configure(-text => ">");
            }
    }, -font => "courier 8");

  my $entry = $mw->Entry(
          -textvariable => \$str,
          -width => 12,
          -font => "{Comic Sans MS} 72",
          -relief => 'raised',
          -highlightthickness => 0,
          )->pack(-expand => 1, -fill => 'x', -side => 'left');

  $lb->bind("<Button>", sub { $entry->configure(
     -font => "{". $lb->get($lb->curselection) . "} 72"); });

  my $repeat_id = $mw->repeat(300, \&shift_banner);

  my $f = $lframe->Frame->pack(-side => 'bottom', -fill => 'y');
  my $start_button;
  $start_button = $f->Button(-text => "Start",
    -command => sub {
      $repeat_id = $mw->repeat(300,\&shift_banner);
      $start_button->configure(-state => 'disabled'); },
    -state => 'disabled')->pack(-side => 'left', -padx => 3);
  my $stop_button = $f->Button(-text => "Stop", -command => sub {
      $repeat_id->cancel();
      $start_button->configure(-state => 'normal'); }
    )->pack(-side => 'left', -padx => 3);

  MainLoop;

  # Causes text to be wrapped around in entry
  sub shift_banner {
          my $newstr = substr($str, 1) . substr($str, 0, 1);
          $str = $newstr;
  }
```

## CHAPTER 4

Button, Checkbutton, and Radiobutton Widgets

Almost all Perl/Tk applications use Buttons in one way or another. There are three different types of Button widgets available in the standard Perl/Tk set: Button, Checkbutton, and Radiobutton. This chapter covers all three types of Buttons and includes examples of where you might use one over the other.

Each of the Buttons we cover in this chapter look different, primarily in their use of *selection indicators*. The Button widget doesn't use indicators at all, but Checkbutton and Radiobutton widgets use them to indicate whether the Button has been selected or not. The Button widgets are:

Button
> A plain Button, shown in Figure 4-1. The user can press it and usually an immediate action results.

Figure 4-1. Button widget

Checkbutton
> A Checkbutton, shown checked in Figure 4-2. When checked or unchecked, only the visual representation is changed; the state is not validated until later in the program. Checkbuttons can be used singly or in groups.

Figure 4-2. Checkbutton widget

Radiobutton
> A Radiobutton, shown unchecked in Figure 4-3. When checked or unchecked, only the visual representation is changed; the state is not validated until later in the program. Radiobuttons are always used in groups of two or more.

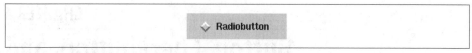

Figure 4-3. Radiobutton widget

A Button is one of the simplest Perl/Tk widgets: the user presses it and something immediately happens. The label of the Button should make the action clear; for example, text such as Quit, Save, or Print gives the user a good idea of what will happen when she clicks the Button. After the Button has been clicked, it will look exactly the same as before, unless programmed to change text or color.

Checkbuttons are for when you want to select none, some, or all items. For example, a shopping list might consist of Bread, Milk, Soda, and Eggs. Select none if you don't need any of them, or select all if you're out of everything. As the user clicks on each Checkbutton, the selection indicator will be filled in or left blank as appropriate (see Figure 4-4).

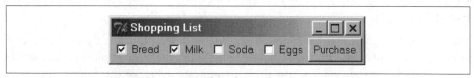

Figure 4-4. Checkbuttons used for a shopping list

After a user presses the Purchase Button, the code examines the value of each Checkbutton's variable to decide what tasks to perform next.

Radiobuttons, on the other hand, all assign the same variable and are necessarily related. Radiobuttons are used in situations when you must make a choice between items, such as on a multiple-choice exam, as shown in Figure 4-5.

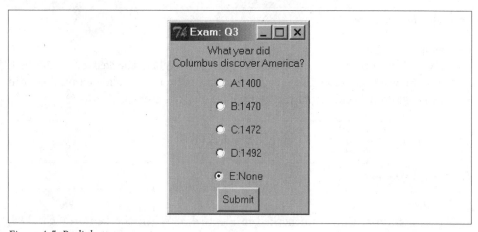

Figure 4-5. Radiobuttons

Because each Radiobutton in a group is associated with the same variable, you are forced to select one and only one choice in that group. If the default choice is always E and you click on D, E is unselected automatically.

Creating Button Widgets

As with any widgets you create, you call a method from the parent widget that matches the name of the widget:

```
$button = $mw->Button->pack;
$rb = $mw->Radiobutton->pack;
$cb = $mw->Checkbutton->pack;
```

These are unrealistic examples as you will most likely use some options when creating each different Button type:

```
# Create a Button widget
$mw->Button(-text => 'Go', -command => \&go_go_go)->pack;

# Create a Checkbutton
$cb = $mw->Checkbutton(-text => 'Red', -onvalue => 'Red',
    -offvalue => '')->pack;

# Create three Radiobuttons in Frame widget $f1
# Link them using $favcolor
foreach (qw/red blue green/) {
    $f1->Radiobutton(-text => $_, -variable => \$favcolor,
        -value => $_)->pack(-anchor => 'w');
}
```

We'll explain the options used in the previous examples in upcoming sections. In particular, -command expects a callback, which we'll mention briefly in the section "The -command Option," but we won't fully describe until Chapter 15.

The only time you might not want to save a reference is when you create a Button, set the text, and set a simple callback for it all at once:

```
$mw->Button(-text => 'Quit', -command => sub { print 'Bye!'; exit; })->pack;
```

Standard Options for Each Button Type

Before we get into all the options available for each of the Button widgets, let's take a look at the most common ones.

When creating a Button, use the -text and -command options. The -text option lets the user know what the Button is for, and the -command option makes something happen when the user clicks the Button.

```
$b = $mw->Button(-text => 'Exit', -command => sub { exit; } )->pack;

# Use the same sub for many Buttons
```

```
$b = $mw->Button(-text => 'Red', -command => [\&change_color, 'red'])->pack;
$b = $mw->Button(-text => 'Blue',
    -command => [\&change_color, 'blue'])->pack;
$b = $mw->Button(-text => 'Green',
    -command => [\&change_color, 'green'])->pack;
```

When creating Checkbuttons, you use -variable in addition to -text. Using -variable gives you an easy way to find out whether the Checkbutton is checked. (You will rarely use -command with a Checkbutton):

```
$mw->Checkbutton(-text => 'Print Header', -variable => \$print_header);

sub print_document {
    if ($print_header) {
        # Code to print header here...
    }
}
```

The value stored in $print_header is 1 or 0. A simple test will tell you if the Checkbutton was checked.

When creating Radiobuttons, we always create more than one and use the -text, -variable, and -value options:

```
$group1 = 100; # set default value
foreach (qw/1 10 100 10000 100000 1000000/) {
    $mw->Radiobutton(-text => '$' . $_, -variable => \$group1,
        -value => $_)->pack(-side => 'left');
}

print "User selected: $group1";
```

The variable $group1 relates all of the Radiobuttons, making it so the user can select only one at a time. Each Radiobutton must be given a -value to store in $group1 (there is no default).

Table of Options for Button-Type Widgets

The Button widgets share almost all of the same options. Table 4-1 shows a complete list of options and which widget they apply to. We'll cover these options in more detail as we explore what Buttons can do.

In the details following Table 4-1, all information applies equally to Buttons, Checkbuttons, and Radiobuttons unless explictly stated otherwise.

Table 4-1. Options for Button-type widgets

Option	Button	Checkbutton	Radiobutton
`-activebackground => color` Sets the color the background should be when the mouse cursor is over the Button. A color is a text string such as "red".	✓	✓	✓
`-activeforeground => color` Sets the color the text should be when the mouse cursor is over the Button.	✓	✓	✓
`-anchor => 'n' | 'ne' | 'e' | 'se' | 's' | 'sw' | 'w' | 'nw' | 'center'` Causes the text to stick to the specified position in the Button.	✓	✓	✓
`-background => color` Sets the background of the Button to `color`.	✓	✓	✓
`-bitmap => 'bitmapname'` Sets default bitmap or the location of a bitmap file (with @ in front of path). See Chapter 17 for more details.	✓	✓	✓
`-borderwidth => amount` Changes the width of the edge drawn around the Button and the thickness of the indicator. Emphasizes the `-relief` of the Button.	✓	✓	✓
`-command => callback` Indicates a pointer to a function that will be called when the Button is pressed.	✓	✓	✓
`-cursor => 'cursorname'` Indicates that the mouse cursor will change to `'cursorname'` when over the Button. See Chapter 23 for details.	✓	✓	✓
`-disabledforeground => color` Sets the color the text should be when the Button is disabled (`-state` will be `'disabled'`).	✓	✓	✓
`-font => 'fontname'` Changes the font of all text on the Button.	✓	✓	✓
`-foreground => color` Changes the text color to `color`.	✓	✓	✓
`-height => amount` Sets the height of the Button in characters if text is displayed and the screen distance if an image or bitmap is displayed.	✓	✓	✓
`-highlightbackground => color` Sets the color of the area behind the focus rectangle (shows when widget does not have focus).	✓	✓	✓
`-highlightcolor => color` Sets the color of the focus rectangle (shows when widget has focus).	✓	✓	✓
`-highlightthickness => amount` Sets the thickness of the highlight rectangle around the Button; indicates focus.	✓	✓	✓

Table 4-1. Options for Button-type widgets (continued)

Option	Button	Checkbutton	Radiobutton
`-image => $imgptr` $imgptr is a pointer to an Image object made with any supported image format. See Chapter 17 for details.	✓	✓	✓
`-indicatoron => 0	1` Determines whether to display the indicator.		✓	✓
`-justify => 'left'	'right'	'center'` Sets the direction against which multiline text will justify.	✓	✓	✓
`-offvalue =>` *newvalue* Sets the value used when the Button is off. Must be a scalar. Default is 0.		✓	
`-onvalue =>` *newvalue* Sets the value used when the Button is on. Must be a scalar. Default is 1.		✓	
`-padx =>` *amount* Adds extra space to the left and right side of the Button inside the Button edge.	✓	✓	✓
`-pady =>` *amount* Adds extra space to the top and bottom of the Button inside the Button edge.	✓	✓	✓
`-relief =>'flat'|'groove'|'raised'|'ridge'|'sunken'|'solid'` Changes the type of edges drawn around the Button. Default for Checkbutton and Radiobutton is `'flat'`.	✓	✓	✓
`-selectcolor =>` *color* Sets the color of the indicator when on.		✓	✓
`-selectimage =>` *imgptr* Indicates the image to display instead of text when Button is on. Ignored if `-image` is not used.		✓	✓
`-state => 'normal'	'disabled'	'active'` Indicates the Button's state of responsiveness. If set to `'disabled'`, the Button does not respond.	✓	✓	✓
`-takefocus => 0	1	undef` Indicates that the Button will never get focus (0), always get focus (1), or let the application decide (undef).	✓	✓	✓
`-text => 'text'` Sets the text string displayed on the Button.	✓	✓	✓
`-textvariable => \$variable` Points to a variable containing text to be displayed in Button. Button text will change as $variable does.	✓	✓	✓
`-underline =>` *n* Underlines the *n*th character in the text string. Allows keyboard input via that character when Button has the focus. It's important to note that the character is only underlined; any behavior must be supplied by the programmer via a `bind` command. See Chapter 15 for binding details.	✓	✓	✓
`-value =>` *newvalue* Sets the value assigned to $variable (with `-variable` option) when this Radiobutton is selected. Default is 1.			✓

Table 4-1. Options for Button-type widgets (continued)

Option	Button	Checkbutton	Radiobutton
`-variable => \$value` Associates the on/off values with `$variable`.		✓	✓
`-width => amount` Sets the width of the Button in characters if text is displayed and as a screen distance if an image or bitmap is displayed.	✓	✓	✓
`-wraplength => amount` Sets the screen distance for the maximum amount of text displayed on one line. The default is 0, which means that text is not wrapped at word boundaries, only at line breaks (newlines).	✓	✓	✓

Displaying Text on Buttons

To show what the Button will do when it is pressed, set its text string with the -text or -textvariable option. The descriptive text string should be short and simple.

The -text option is the more common way to assign a text string:

```
-text => 'Submit'
```

The string can be anything: alphanumeric, newline(s), or variables. The text string is just like any other string in Perl in that if it is put in single quotes, it is taken literally; if it is put in double quotes, it is interpolated. The interpolation only happens once (the first time the option is parsed). If a variable changes later in the program, it has no effect on the text in the Button. The only way the text in the Button can be changed after it has been created is by using the configure method to reset it (e.g., `$button->configure(-text => "newtext");`) or by using the -textvariable option.

There is no default for the -text option; if no text is specified, the Button will simply have no text.

The other way to display text on the Button is by using the -textvariable option. The -textvariable option allows a scalar variable to be associated with the Button; anything in the variable will be displayed on the Button. Specify the scalar variable as follows:

```
-textvariable => \$variable
```

This means the text of the Button will change as the contents of $variable change. When the text within the Button changes, the Button may become larger or smaller, and the entire window may change size.

This piece of code shows how the -textvariable option is used:

```
$count = 0;
$mw->Button(-text => "Add 1",
            -command => sub { $count++ })->pack(-side => 'left');
```

```
$mw->Button(-textvariable => \$count)->pack(-side => 'left');
$mw->Button(-text => "Exit",
            -command => sub { exit })->pack(-side => 'left');
```

Figure 4-6 shows two windows. The first shows how the window looks when it is first created, and the second shows what it looks like after clicking the "Add 1" Button fifteen times. Even though we don't show any specific examples using the -textvariable option for the Checkbutton and Radiobutton widgets, the option works exactly the same way.

Figure 4-6. Example of using -textvariable

Displaying an Image or Bitmap

The simplest way to replace the text on your Button with an image is to use a bit-map.* The image will take the place of the text; you can't display both at the same time. The -bitmap option takes a string that specifies which bitmap to use:

```
-bitmap => 'bitmapname'
```

There are several built-in bitmaps: error, gray12, gray25, gray50, gray75, hourglass, info, questhead, question, warning, Tk, and transparent. Figure 4-7 shows all the built-in bitmaps. To more easily show you the bitmaps, Figure 4-7 was grabbed from the *widget* demonstration program.

Using -bitmap for a Label is exactly the same as for a Button. You'll notice that the Tk bitmap is the same as that used in the upper-left corner of the application. Here are some examples using -bitmap when creating a Button:

```
$mw->Button(-bitmap => 'error', -command => \&handle_error)->pack;
```

To specify a bitmap from a file, you need to put an @ in front of the path:

```
$mw->Button(-bitmap => '@/usr/nwalsh/mybitmap',
            -command => sub { exit })->pack;
```

Note that if you use double quotes, you have to escape the @ with a backslash (e.g., "\@/usr/nwalsh/mybitmap").

If you don't want to use a bitmap, or have a different format of file (such as a GIF), you can use the -image option. First create an image pointer and then use the -image option to display the image. To create an image pointer, use the Photo method to

---

* In deference to our Win32 readers, a Tk bitmap file refers to an X11 XBM file, not a Win32 BMP formatted file. For complete details, please refer to Chapter 17.

Figure 4-7. Window showing all the default bitmaps

point to the image file, supplying the full pathname if the file is not in the current directory. Then pass the image pointer as a value to the -image option:

```
$image = $mw->Photo(-file => "bigredbutton.gif");
$mw->Button(-text => 'Exit', -command => sub { exit },
            -image => $image)->pack;
```

When using an image, only the image will be displayed, because Buttons can display either a text string or an image, not both. (In other words, -image will always override -text.) To display a bitmap using -image, use the Bitmap method to create an image pointer.

Images are covered in extensive detail in Chapter 17. Figure 4-8 shows an example of a Button with a GIF file on it.

Figure 4-8. Button with an image instead of text

Images with Checkbuttons and Radiobuttons

You can also use the -bitmap option with Checkbuttons and Radiobuttons. The bitmap will replace the text just as it does with a Button, and the indicator will remain showing. To display a different type of image (such as GIF), use the -image option. To display a different image when the Checkbutton or Radiobutton is selected, use the -image and -selectimage options. Both -image and -selectimage take an image pointer created with the Photo method.

```
# Create Photo objects with gif files
$folder = $mw->Photo(-file => "folder.gif");
$openfolder = $mw->Photo(-file => 'openfolder.gif');

$leftframe->Checkbutton(-image => $folder,
    -selectimage => $openfolder)->pack(-expand => 1);
$leftframe->Checkbutton(-image => $folder,
    -selectimage => $openfolder)->pack(-expand => 1);
```

```
# Create Bitmap objects with bitmap files
$bmpopen = $mw->Bitmap(-file => 'openfolder.xbm');
$bmpfolder = $mw->Bitmap(-file => 'folder.xbm');
$rightframe->Radiobutton(-image => $bmpfolder,
    -selectimage => $bmpopen, -variable => \$vvv,
    -value => 1)->pack(-expand => 1);
$rightframe->Radiobutton(-image => $bmpfolder,
    -selectimage => $bmpopen, -variable => \$vvv,
    -value => 2)->pack(-expand => 1);
```

Figure 4-9 shows the resulting window.

Figure 4-9. Using both -image and -selectimage

You'll notice in this example that in addition to the image changing when you click on the Checkbutton, there's also a selection indicator. If this seems redundant, that's because it is: the selection indicator is unnecessary when using -selectimage, and you're better off using -indicatoron => 0 to disable the indicator. Figure 4-10 shows the resulting images.

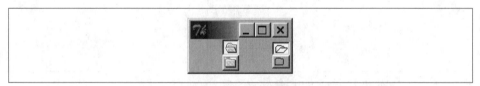

Figure 4-10. Using Checkbuttons and Radiobuttons with -indicatoron => 0

Both Checkbuttons and Radiobuttons look much like Button widgets with the indicators turned off, but their behavior is very different. In Figure 4-10, the very top two widgets are selected (just as in Figure 4-9). When selected, a Checkbutton will stay down (a relief of 'sunken') and when unselected it will be up (relief of 'raised'). The same is true of a Radiobutton with no indicator, but selecting a Radiobutton will cause all other Radiobuttons in that group to be deselected. Using -relief with -indicator => 0 is pointless; it won't change the relief of the Button.

Checkbutton and Radiobutton Indicator Status

With Checkbutton and Radiobutton widgets, you must include a -variable option to associate a variable with the status of the indicator.

```
-variable => \$value
```

How the variable is used, however, varies between Checkbuttons and Radiobuttons. When a Checkbutton is clicked, $value contains the status of the indicator; typically 0 if the indicator is off and 1 if the indicator is on. You can use the -onvalue and -offvalue options to change those defaults (more on that soon).

With Radiobuttons, there is no default value, and you need to explicitly assign $value with the -value option. We'll show some examples of this in the section, "Radiobutton Values."

By changing the contents of $value, you can change the status of the indicator. Changing the contents of $value will toggle the indicator on a Checkbutton; on a Radiobutton, the currently selected Radiobutton might change. It is important to note that the subroutine associated with -command (if there is one) is *not* invoked when the value of $value is changed. (See the next section for more information on using the -command option.)

Reading the value associated with -variable is usually the easiest way to check the status of the indicator on the Button. Here is an example with two Buttons that change the $cb_value variable:

```
$cb_value = 0;
$cb = $mw->Checkbutton(-text => "Checkbutton",
                       -variable => \$cb_value,
                       -command => sub { print "Clicked! $cb_value\n" }
                       )->pack(-side => 'top');

$mw->Button(-text => "CB on",
              -command => sub { $cb_value = 1 })->pack(-side => 'left');
$mw->Button(-text => "CB off",
              -command => sub { $cb_value = 0 })->pack(-side => 'left');
```

See Figure 4-11 for the resulting window.

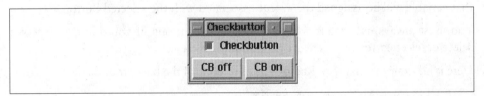

Figure 4-11. Buttons changing the value of a Checkbutton

The value stored in $cb_value can be changed in three ways: clicking the Checkbutton, clicking the "CB off" Button, or clicking the "CB on" Button. Only when you click on the Checkbutton will you see the word "Clicked!" written in the shell window from which it was run, followed by the value of $cb_value.

There are other ways to change the value associated with the Checkbutton. See invoke, select, deselect, and toggle, later in this chapter.

On and Off Values for a Checkbutton

Depending on how you want the Checkbutton to interact with the rest of your application, sometimes it makes sense to use different values instead of 0 and 1. If you don't like the default value of 1, you can use the -onvalue option to change it:

```
-onvalue => newvalue  ## Default is 1
```

Similarly, if you want to use something other than 0 for an off value, use -offvalue:

```
-offvalue => newvalue  ## Default is 0
```

The *newvalue* could be anything, as long as it is a scalar value. This means you can use references to arrays and hashes if you really want to.

It is good practice to keep the meaning of -onvalue the opposite of -offvalue. If -onvalue is now the string "ON", logically -offvalue should be "OFF". Of course, if the purpose of this Checkbutton is to use a more accurate value of pi, then -onvalue could be "3.14159265359" and -offvalue could be "3.14".

Be careful when you use unusual values for -onvalue and -offvalue. If you set the variable to something that doesn't equal either one of them, the Checkbutton will be considered off, even though the value of the $variable will not equal the -offvalue. For instance, if you set -onvalue => 1, -offvalue => 0, and you set $variable to 3, the Checkbutton will be considered off.

Radiobutton Values

Groups of Radiobuttons are designed to all use the same -variable option but with unique -value options for each individual Radiobutton. When you select a Radiobutton, any other Radiobuttons assigned the same -variable will be unselected, and that variable will be assigned the -value associated with the selected Button.

You must always use -value when creating Radiobuttons. If you don't, they won't select/deselect correctly. There are no defaults for -value.

Here is an example that uses Radiobuttons to control the background color:

```perl
# setup the default value we would like
$rb_value = "red";
$mw->configure(-background => $rb_value);

# create the Radiobuttons that will let us change it
foreach (qw(red yellow green blue grey)) {
  $mw->Radiobutton(-text => $_,
                   -value => $_,
                   -variable => \$rb_value,
                   -command => \&set_bg)->pack(-side => 'left');
}

# function to change the background color using $rb_value
```

```
sub set_bg {
   print "Background value is now: $rb_value\n";
   $mw->configure(-background => $rb_value);
}
```

We are storing the status of our Radiobutton group in $rb_value. We set it to an initial value of "red", which happens to match the first Radiobutton we are creating. When any of the Radiobuttons are clicked, including the one currently selected, the subroutine set_bg will be called. This subroutine will print the new value of $rb_value and then change the background of our MainWindow to that color.

If you look at the code closely, you see that we call the configure command and send it $rb_value. Even though the default value of our Radiobutton group is "red", that doesn't mean that the background of the window has been set to red as well. We could also have set the background color using an explicit call to the set_bg routine, or back when we created the MainWindow.

The window we have created looks like Figure 4-12.

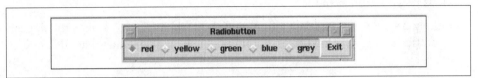

Figure 4-12. Radiobuttons that change the background color of the window

You might notice that for this example, rather than just setting a variable and waiting for the user to do something with it, we needed the Radiobutton to take action immediately when pressed. To do this, we used the -command option. Let's talk more about the -command option and callbacks in general.

The -command Option

You'll almost always create Button widgets with the -command option. This is because for the Button to do something when pressed, we have to associate a callback with the Button. A *callback* (see Chapter 15) is actually a Perl subroutine that's invoked when mouse button 1 is released over the Button.* (Note that we specified *released*; if you click down on the Button but move the cursor away from it before releasing, nothing happens, because the mouseclick was aborted.)

---

* Mouse button 1 is the leftmost mouse button, mouse button 2 is the middle mouse button, and mouse button 3 is the rightmost mouse button. On a 2-button mouse, mouse button 2 is often simulated by pressing buttons 1 and 3 simultaneously.

The simplest way to specify a -command callback is using a *code reference*. In many of our examples, we use an *anonymous* code reference to a subroutine that simply executes an exit statement:

```
$mw->Button(-text => "Done", -command => sub { exit })->pack;
```

We might also reference an *explicit* subroutine (that can then be called from multiple places):

```
$mw->Button(-text => "Done", -command => \&save_and_exit)->pack;
```

Note that in both examples, -command expects a reference to some Perl code. There are other callback formats, fully explained in Chapter 15.

Whereas Button widgets are nearly useless without callbacks, Checkbutton and Radiobutton widgets are designed to change the value of variables. Often, no immediate action is necessary: when a Checkbutton or Radiobutton is toggled, the value of a variable is changed, and then the widget simply waits until the user tells it to do something about it. However, sometimes we do want immediate results, as in the previous Radiobutton example.

One thing a Checkbutton might do immediately when clicked is alter the appearance of the window. The Checkbutton might look something like the one in Figure 4-13.

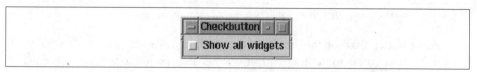

Figure 4-13. Checkbutton that will display other widgets on the screen when clicked

When the user clicks the Checkbutton to turn it on, the window changes to look like Figure 4-14.

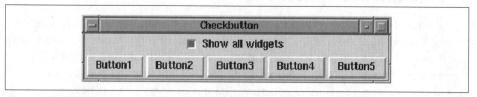

Figure 4-14. Window after clicking the Checkbutton

Here's the code that makes the magic happen:

```
#!/usr/bin/perl -w
use Tk;
$mw = MainWindow->new;
$mw->title("Checkbutton");

## Create other widgets, but don't pack them yet!
for ($i = 1; $i <= 5; $i++) {
```

```
        push (@buttons, $mw->Button(-text => "Button$i"));
      }

      $mw->Checkbutton(-text => "Show all widgets",
                       -variable => \$cb_value,
                       -command => sub {
                         if ($cb_value) {
                           foreach (@buttons) {
                             $_->pack(-side => 'left');
                           }
                         } else {
                           foreach (@buttons) {
                             $_->pack('forget');
                           }
                         }
                       })->pack(-side => 'top');
      MainLoop;
```

To display some widgets later in the program, we create them ahead of time and store references to them in the @buttons array. (Observant readers will notice that the Buttons in this example are rigged just for show and don't even have -command options associated with them. Normally, each would have a specific task to perform when pressed.)

Then we create our Checkbutton. When the Button is clicked (regardless of the status of its indicator), it will call the subroutine pointed to by -command. Our subroutine looks at the current value of $cb_value, shows the Buttons if it is on, and hides them if it is off. The value in $cb_value is changed before this subroutine is called. When our Checkbutton is clicked again, the extra Buttons will be removed from the window and the window will shrink back to its previous size.

This setup is great when you want to keep a basic window uncluttered while maintaining the ability to show more widgets (if the user can handle the advanced functions of the extra widgets). For example, you can create a Find window that has a place to enter text, a Button to start the find, and an Advanced Search Checkbutton. Clicking on Advanced Search would add more widgets to the bottom of the window, allowing you to match case, use regular expressions, and use other fancy search mechanisms.

Disabling a Button

Typically, Buttons are meant to be pressed. But sometimes you display a Button that you want to be disabled. For example, you may not want users to submit a form unless they've filled out some required fields.

To disable a Button, use the -state option.

```
-state => "normal" | "disabled" | "active"
```

The "normal" state is what we've been describing throughout this chapter so far: the Button changes colors when the mouse passes over it and performs the assigned callback (or changes indicator status) when clicked. The "active" state is when the mouse cursor is physically over the Button and is used internally by Perl/Tk. The "disabled" state is when the Button appears grayed out (or with whatever colors have been specified by -disabledforeground and -disabledbackground) and will not respond to the mouse at all.

For example, suppose we have a Button that disables another when it is pressed. The code would look like this:

```
my $exit_b = $mw->Button(-text => 'Exit',
                         -command => sub { exit })->pack;
$var = "Disable Exit";
$mw->Button(-textvariable => \$var,
            -command => sub { my $state = $exit_b->configure(-state);
                              if ($state eq "disabled") {
                                $exit_b->configure(-state => 'normal');
                                $var = "Disable Exit";
                              } else {
                                $exit_b->configure(-state => 'disabled');
                                $var = "Enable Exit";
                              }})->pack;
```

In this example, a reference to the Exit Button is saved because it needs to be used later to change the state of the Button. Also, note that $exit_b is used inside the scope of the anonymous subroutine. This will work only if $exit_b is left in the global scope of the entire program, so $exit_b will be defined when the anonymous subroutine is executed. Be careful not to set $exit_b to something else; if you do, the anonymous subroutine will refer to the new value in $exit_b when it is invoked, not the value you wanted.

Figure 4-15 shows the window after we have clicked the Disable Exit Button once.

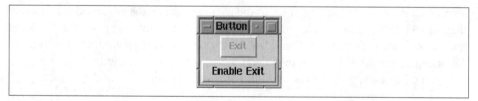

Figure 4-15. Window with disabled Button (Exit) and normal Button

A Button should not be available for selecting unless it makes sense in the application. By disabling widgets when they can't do anything, you give users visual hints about what they can and cannot do in the application.

Sometimes the terminology becomes confusing when talking about state and status. With Checkbuttons and Radiobuttons, there is the indicator's status (or value) and the state of the Button itself. The *status* of the button is either on or off, depending on whether it is checked. The *state* of the entire Checkbutton (including the indicator) can be normal, active, or disabled.

Text Manipulation

You can alter the appearance and location of the text within the Button. The simplest way is to use the -font option to change the font. Chapter 3 covers fonts in detail so we'll just look at a few simple ways to change the font:

```
-font => "{Times New Roman} 12 {normal}"
```

There can be only a single font for each Button, so the text string cannot change font in the middle of a word. However, each Button (or widget) in an application can have a different font. Here is an example of two Buttons in a window, one with the default font and the other with "lucidasans-14" (a Unix font) as its font:

```
$mw->Button(-text => "Exit",
            -command => sub { exit })->pack(-side => 'left',
                                            -fill => 'both', -expand => 1);
$mw->Button(-text => "Exit",
            -font => "lucidasans-14",
            -command => sub { exit })->pack(-side => 'left',
                                            -fill => 'both', -expand => 1);
```

Figure 4-16 shows the resulting window.

Figure 4-16. Buttons with various fonts

You can also move the text around within the Button. As in a word-processing document, you can change where the text will justify. The option that controls this is -justify:

```
-justify => 'left' | 'right' | 'center'
```

The default for -justify is 'center'. Normally the text displayed in a Button is a quick one- or two-word statement; for example, Exit, Done, Yes, No, or Cancel. The justification of the text isn't too obvious unless multiple lines of text are used. By default, the Button will display multiple lines only if a \n is included in the string. If you want the program to wrap the text automatically, use the -wraplength option:

```
-wraplength => amount
```

The *amount* indicates the maximum length of the line as a valid screen distance. If the length of the text string in the Button exceeds this amount, the text will wrap around to the next line. The default for -wraplength is 0.

Here is an example that uses both the -justify and -wraplength options:

```
foreach (qw(left center right)) {
    $b =  $mw->Button(-text =>"This button will be justified $_",
                      -command => sub { exit },
```

```
                    -wraplength => 53,
                    -justify => $_)->pack(-side => 'left',
                                          -fill => 'both',
                                          -expand => 1);
}
```

Figure 4-17 shows the results of the three Buttons. Although this example doesn't show it, it is possible for text to be wrapped in the middle of a word.

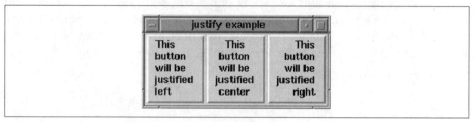

Figure 4-17. Effects of -justify and -wraplength in Buttons

The final possible adjustment to the text (or bitmap) is its position within the Button. This is controlled by the -anchor option, which is similar to the -anchor option used with the geometry managers:

```
-anchor => 'n' | 'ne' | 'e' | 'se' | 's' | 'sw' | 'w' | 'nw' | 'center'
```

Like the window, the Button has compass points that define locations within the Button. Figure 4-18 shows where these points are.

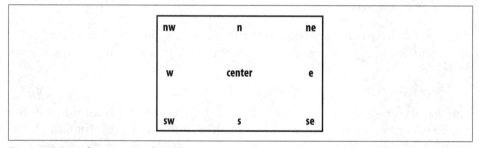

Figure 4-18. Anchor points within a Button

The default position for the text is 'center'. When the position is changed, it is not obvious that this option is in effect unless the Button is resized larger. In Figure 4-19, the Button is the same one created in the -justify example (Figure 4-17), except -anchor => 'nw' has been added to the option list.

As mentioned earlier, this option is similar to the pack command's -anchor option, except this option changes the position of the text in the Button, whereas the pack -anchor option changes the position of the widget in the window.

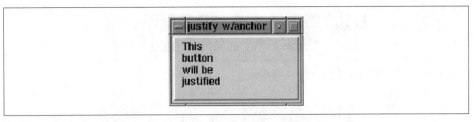

Figure 4-19. Anchor on Button set to 'nw'

Altering the Button's Style

By default, a Button looks like it's raised slightly off the surface of the window. By using the -relief option, you can change the style of the Button edges:

```
-relief => 'flat'|'groove'|'raised'|'ridge'|'sunken'|'solid'
```

The default for a Button widget is 'raised' and for Checkbuttons and Radiobuttons it is 'flat'.

Each value changes the look of the Button slightly, as you can see in Figure 4-20. Here is a list of the styles:

flat

> No edges are drawn around the Button at all. Makes it look like only text is present in the window.

groove

> Gives a slightly depressed look to the edge (as if there were a ditch around the text).

raised

> Gives a 3D look with a shadow on the lower and right sides of the Button, which causes it to look higher than the window surface. This is the default.

ridge

> Makes it look like a ridge is around the text. The opposite of 'groove'.

solid

> Draws a solid line around the widget.

sunken

> Gives the 3D effect of being below the surface of the window. The opposite of 'raised'.

No matter which value is specified for the -relief option, when the Button is pressed with the mouse, its relief will change to 'sunken'.

The Checkbutton and Radiobutton start with flat relief. Figures 4-21 and 4-22 show these.

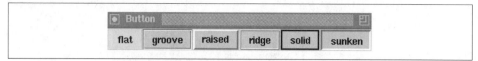

Figure 4-20. Different relief types for a Button

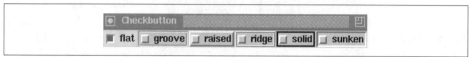

Figure 4-21. Different relief types for a Checkbutton

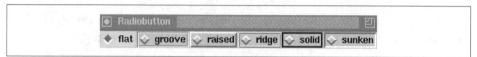

Figure 4-22. Different relief types for a Radiobutton

In addition to changing the type of edge drawn around a Button, you can change the thickness of the edge by using -borderwidth:

```
-borderwidth => amount
```

The default -borderwidth for a Button is 2 and for a Checkbutton and a Radiobutton is 0. The wider the -borderwidth, the more dramatic the effects of the -relief option become. Figure 4-23 shows what a -borderwidth of 10 does to each relief type for a Button. When changing the -borderwidth on a Checkbutton or Radiobutton, be careful you don't use too large a value, because the indicators do funny things at larger values. Take a look at Figures 4-24 through 4-27 for clarification. Hopefully seeing how silly these look here, you won't waste time wondering why your own indicators don't work.

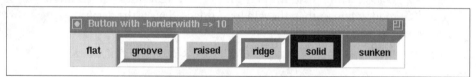

Figure 4-23. Different relief types for a Button with -borderwidth set to 10

Figure 4-24. Checkbuttons with -borderwidth => 4

Note that using -borderwidth with values greater than 4 makes widgets look extremely odd. In each of the widget chapters, you'll find a screenshot showing what happens to the widget with a larger -borderwidth value for each of the possible -relief values. The best use of -borderwidth is making one widget stand out more

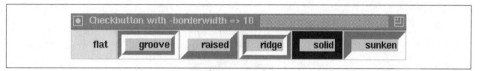

Figure 4-25. Checkbuttons with -borderwidth => 10

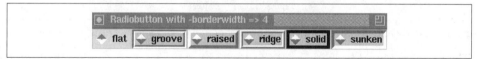

Figure 4-26. Radiobuttons with -borderwidth => 4

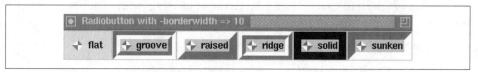

Figure 4-27. Radiobuttons with -borderwidth => 10

than the others temporarily during development. (You can also use this trick with Frames to figure out where the Frame is. Normally they are invisible. See Chapter 11 for more on this.)

Changing the Size of a Button

Normally the size of the Button is automatically determined by the application and is dependent on the text string or image displayed in the Button. The width and height can be specified explicitly by using the -width and -height options:

```
-width => x, -height => y
```

The values specified for x and y vary depending on whether a bitmap/image or text is displayed in the Button. When a bitmap or image is displayed, the values in x and y represent valid screen distances. If text is displayed on the Button, x and y are character sizes.

This example shows one Button that is the default size and another drawn with -width of 10 and -height of 10. (It is not necessary that the amounts for -width and -height be the same or that you use both options.)

```
$mw->Button(-text => "Exit",
            -command => sub { exit })->pack(-side => 'left');
$mw->Button(-text => "Exit",
            -width => 10, -height => 10,
            -command => sub { exit })->pack(-side => 'left');
```

In Figure 4-28, which illustrates this example, the second Button is much taller than it is wide, because text characters are taller than they are wide.

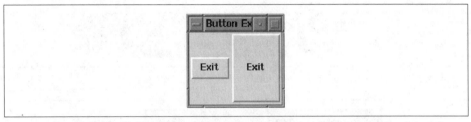

Figure 4-28. Default -width and -height (left) versus Button with -width and -height set (right)

The values specified for both -width and -height are characters, because the Button is displaying text. When -width and -height are used with a bitmap, the amount specified is in screen distance. Here is an example of using -width and -height with a bitmap:

```
$mw->Button(-bitmap => 'error',
            -width => 10, -height => 10,
            -command => sub { exit })->pack(-side => 'left');
$mw->Button(-bitmap => 'error',
            -command => sub { exit })->pack(-side => 'left');
$mw->Button(-bitmap => 'error',
            -width => 50, -height => 50,
            -command => sub { exit })->pack(-side => 'left');
```

The first Button is created with a restriction of 10 on the -width and -height. The middle Button looks like it would normally. The third Button is created with a -width and -height of 50. Figure 4-29 shows the resulting window.

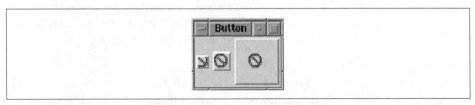

Figure 4-29. A bitmap displayed three times, with different values for -width and -height

The default value for both -width and -height is 0. Using 0 allows the program to decide the height and width of the Button dynamically.

The total width for Buttons with text is calculated by the width the text takes up plus 2 × -padx amount. The height is the text height plus 2 × -pady amount. The width and height of a Button with a bitmap is just the width and height of the bitmap itself. Any -padx or -pady options are ignored when a bitmap is displayed.

As an alternative to specifying an explicit width or height, it is possible to increase the size of the Button by using the options -padx and -pady to add padding between the text and edge of the Button:

```
-padx => amount, -pady => amount
```

The *amount* specified with -padx is added to both the left and right sides of the Button. The *amount* specified with -pady is added to both the top and bottom of the Button. Figure 4-30 shows an example.

By using these options you are telling the Button to be sized larger than it normally would, but you don't have to worry that it will be sized too small, as you would if you set -width and -height explicitly.

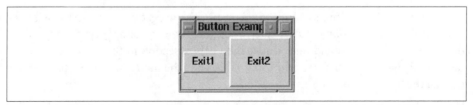

Figure 4-30. Default width and height (left) versus Button with -padx => 20, -pady => 20 (right)

Remember, -padx and -pady are ignored when a bitmap is displayed.

Adding a Keyboard Mapping

A Button is traditionally invoked by clicking mouse button 1 when the mouse cursor is over the Button. It can also be invoked by pressing the Tab key until the Button has the keyboard focus, then pressing the spacebar. The effects are the same: the callback associated with the Button is called, and the Button -relief changes momentarily. The keyboard focus is indicated visually by a thin black rectangle drawn around the widget (see Figure 4-37, later in this chapter).

To allow an additional keyboard character to invoke the Button, use the -underline option in a Button displaying text:

```
-underline => N
```

This will underline the *N*th character in the text string. The first character of the text string is the 0th character, so the text string "Exit", -underline => 1 will underline the second character in the string, the "x" (see Figure 4-31).

Don't forget to actually create the binding for the underlined character.

Figure 4-31. Example of -underline => 1

The default value for -underline is −1, which means no characters will be underlined in the text string.

Color Options

The options that can change the Button's colors are -background, -foreground, -activebackground, -activeforeground, and -disabledforeground. Each option takes a string that identifies a color. This string could be either a color description such as "blue" or a hex string such as "#d9d9d9", which also describes a color but is much more cryptic.

For either Win32 or Unix systems, you can run the *widget* demo included with the Tk module. If the *perl/bin* directory is in your path, you can simply type **"widget"** on the DOS or Unix command line. Under the Listbox section in the demo is an example that displays color names. You can double-click the names in the list to see them change the application's color.

Valid values for the color string are available on your Unix system in a file called *rgb.txt*. This file is typically located in the X11 *lib* directory, for example, */usr/X11R6/lib/rgb.txt*. You can also use the X application *xcolors* or *showrgb*. Check the manpages for each command to determine the best way to use it.

Another place to look for valid color names (and this applies to Win32 as well) is in your Perl distribution directory. Look for the file *xcolors.h*. It is a text file that contains the RGB values and names for quite a few colors. On a Win32 machine, it might be in *C:\Perl\lib\site\Tk\ptk*.

The color of the Button depends on the Button's state. When the Button has a state of 'normal', the colors assigned to -foreground and -background are in effect. The background of the Button is the area behind the text string but within the edges of the Button.

The background is specified like this:

```
-background => color
```

The default background color is light gray. Figure 4-32 shows the results of changing the second Exit Button's background to blue.[*]

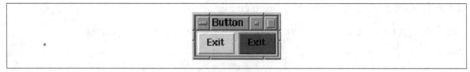

Figure 4-32. Example of -background => 'blue'

---

[*] Although we are talking about color, the figures are in black and white. Unfortunately, using color figures would have made the book too expensive to produce. We've tried to make color choices that contrast so the figures look as good as possible. The best way to determine what happens with each color option is to experiment and run the examples.

The foreground of the Button is the text (or bitmap). The foreground color is specified like this:

```
-foreground => color
```

By default, -foreground is 'black'. Make sure whatever color you pick contrasts enough with the background color to be readable. In the example in Figure 4-32, we left the text the default color, which doesn't contrast well with the background color of the Button. If we change -foreground to 'white', we will be able to see the text much more easily, as you'll see in Figure 4-33. (The shortcut for -foreground is -fg, which may or may not work on other types of widgets. For total compatibility, always stick with -foreground as the option name.)

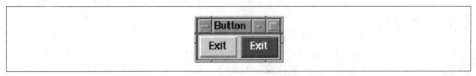

Figure 4-33. Example of -background => 'blue' and -foreground => 'white'

When you use the -foreground and -background options with a bitmap, the bitmap foreground and background will change to the specified colors. The effect of the colors depends on the bitmap. See Figure 4-34.

Figure 4-34. 'error' bitmap with -foreground => 'white' and -background => 'black'

The -foreground and -background options control what color the Button is in the 'normal' state. When the Button has the mouse cursor over it, the -activebackground and -activeforeground colors are used:

```
-activebackground => color, -activeforeground => color
```

These colors are different because we want users to have some visual clues that they can press the Button. By having the colors change slightly when the mouse cursor is over the Button, users know that the Button can be pressed to do something. The default for -activebackground is a slightly darker gray color ("#ececec").

The final color option, -disabledforeground, is the color of the text when the Button's state is 'disabled'.

```
-disabledforeground => color
```

When the Button is in a disabled state, it will not respond when the mouse cursor is over it or if it is pressed. The default text color (or bitmap color) is "#a3a3a3".

Figure 4-35 shows the difference between the text colors of one disabled Button and one normal Button. (We also saw this example in Figure 4-15. Look there for the code that created this window.)

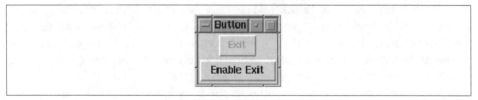

Figure 4-35. -disabledforeground example

Indicator Colors

You can use the -selectcolor option to alter the color that fills the indicator when the Checkbutton or Radiobutton is selected:

```
-selectcolor => color
```

The default value is "#b03060" (a dark pink). Changing the value for -selectcolor will also change the background of the Button when the Button is selected and -indicatoron => 0.

Hiding the Indicator

One way a Checkbutton or Radiobutton differs from a standard Button is the indicator. Use the -indicatoron option to tell Perl/Tk not to draw that funny little square Button at all:

```
-indicatoron => 0 | 1
```

As we have seen in previous examples, the default for -indicatoron is 1 (i.e., show the indicator). If we change this -indicatoron to 0, the Checkbutton will look almost like a normal Button (without quite as much space around the text, however). Though it looks a lot like a regular Button, its behavior when clicked (to turn the hidden indicator on) is completely different (see Figure 4-36). Note that the -relief option is ignored completely when -indicatoron is set to 0.

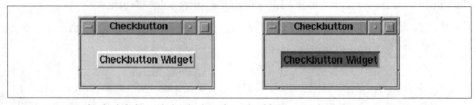

Figure 4-36. Unchecked (left) and checked (right) Checkbutton with -indicatoron => 0

In this example, the color for the background on the checked Button is the -selectcolor, not the -backgroundcolor. You might want to use the nonindicator configuration if you change the text of the Button to reflect the new state of the Checkbutton (for instance, changing Logging Enabled to Logging Disabled).

Focus Options

In an application, you can tab between widgets to make them available for input from the keyboard. The application indicates that a widget is available for keyboard input by drawing an outline around it in black (this is called the highlight rectangle; see Figure 4-37). If a widget has this outline around it, it is said to have the *focus* of the application. (You can force the focus of an application to start with a specific widget by using $widget->focus;.) Once a Button has the focus, you can use the spacebar on your keyboard to activate it instead of using the mouse.

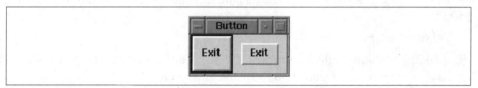

Figure 4-37. The first Button has the input focus

You can force the application not to allow your Button to receive the keyboard focus at all by using the -takefocus option:

```
-takefocus => 0 | 1 | undef
```

The -takefocus option is normally set to an empty string (undef), which allows the application to dynamically decide if the widget will accept focus. If a widget has its state set to 'disabled', it will be skipped over when users tab through all the widgets. To have the application always ignore the widget when tabbing through, use -takefocus => 0. To have the application always allow focus to the widget, use -takefocus => 1.

Altering the Highlight Rectangle

The highlight rectangle is normally displayed with a thickness of 2 pixels.[*] This can be changed using the -highlightthickness option:

```
-highlightthickness => amount
```

The amount specified is any valid screen distance. In Figure 4-38, the Exit Button on the right has a -highlightthickness of 10 and has the focus.

---

[*] On Win32 systems, the highlight rectangle is drawn as a dashed line within the widget.

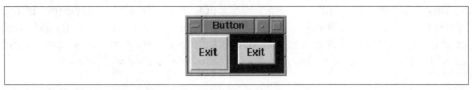

Figure 4-38. Example of -highlightthickness => 10

When the Button doesn't have the keyboard focus, a small space is left around it. If this extra space bothers you, you can set -highlightthickness to 0 and the space won't display, even if that widget has the focus. It is bad style to set the -highlightthickness to 0 without setting -takefocus to 0.

The color of the highlight rectangle can also be changed. There are two values for this: the color of the highlight rectangle when the Button does not have the focus and the color of the highlight rectangle when it does have the focus. The option -highlightcolor is the color of the highlight rectangle when the Button does have focus:

```
-highlightcolor => color
```

Figure 4-39 shows the right Button with the focus and with -highlightcolor set to 'yellow'. Compare it to Figure 4-38 to see the difference.

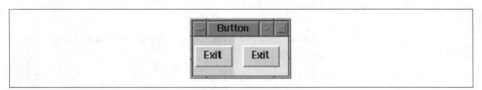

Figure 4-39. Example of Button with -highlightcolor => 'yellow'

To change the color of the space left around the Button when it doesn't have the focus, use the option -highlightbackground:

```
-highlightbackground => color
```

Normally, the highlight rectangle is the same color as the background of the window, which allows it to blend in with the background of the window or Frame that contains the Button.

Figure 4-40 shows an example where both Buttons have the following configuration:

```
-highlightcolor => 'blue', -highlightbackground => 'yellow'
```

The left Button has the focus.

Configuring a Button

Typically, you create a widget and then display it at some later time. What we haven't explicitly talked about yet is what you can do in between.

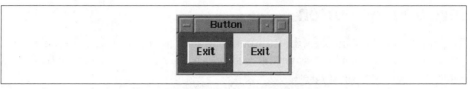

Figure 4-40. Button with -highlightcolor => 'blue' and -highlightbackground => 'yellow'

All options do not have to be specified when you create a widget. You can configure a widget further at a later time using the configure method, as long as you still have a reference to the widget. In addition, you can find out how a widget is already configured using the cget method. Here's an example:

```
$b = $mw->Button(-text => "Self referencing Button")->pack;
$b->configure(-command => [\&send_button, $b]);
```

In this example, we needed to use the actual widget reference in the callback for -command. We couldn't create the callback properly without the widget reference, so split that out using the configure method.* The configure and cget methods are generic to all widgets and are covered in Chapter 13.

To determine the current value of an option, call cget with only that option:

```
$state = $button->cget(-state);           # Get the current value for -state
```

To change the value associated with an option after the widget has been created, you call configure with the option and new value:

```
$button->configure(-text => "New Text"); # Change the text
$text = $button->cget(-text);            # Get the current text value
```

To get a list of lists describing every option and value for a widget, call configure without any arguments:

```
@all = $button->configure();              # Get info on all options for Button
foreach $list (@all) {                    # Print options, not very pretty
    print "@$list\n";
}
```

Flashing the Button

The flash method will cause the Button to appear to be "flashing" on the screen. It changes back and forth from the normal state colors to the active state colors:

```
$button->flash();
```

---

* Actually, we could create the callback as the widget is created if the widget reference was predeclared with a my $b statement.

Invoking the Button

The invoke method invokes the subroutine to which the -command option points. Once you use -command to assign the callback, whenever you need to perform that same task, you can use invoke:

```
$button->invoke( );
```

Turning a Checkbutton/Radiobutton On and Off

You can force the Checkbutton or Radiobutton from on to off or vice versa using the deselect and select methods.

The deselect method will always set the indicator to the off state and the variable assigned by -variable to the value in -offvalue. On a Radiobutton, using deselect causes the Radiobutton to be unselected. It sets the $variable to an empty string. If you use this method, make sure you account for it in any code that evaluates the value of $variable.

```
$cb->deselect( );
$rb->deselect( );
```

The opposite of deselect, select, sets the indicator to the on state and the variable assigned by -variable to the -onvalue or -value, if using a Radiobutton.

```
$cb->select( );
$rb->select( );
```

Both methods are ignored if -state is 'disabled'.

You can also toggle the indicator from on to off or vice versa using the toggle method:

```
$cb->toggle( );
$rb->toggle( );
```

Calling toggle does not cause the subroutine associated with the -command value to be called.

## CHAPTER 5

Label and Entry Widgets

There are times you'll want users to type in specific information, such as their names, addresses, or even serial numbers. The simplest way to do this is to use Entry widgets. You can use a Label widget with an Entry to clearly communicate to the user what should be typed in the Entry. Most often, you'll see the Label and Entry combination used multiple times in a database Entry–type window where there are many different pieces of information the user must enter.

The Label Widget

A Label is like a Button that doesn't do anything. It is a noninteractive widget and by default cannot have the keyboard focus (meaning you can't tab to it). It does nothing when you click on it (see Figure 5-1).

Figure 5-1. Label widget

Excluding Frame-like widgets, the Label is the simplest widget. It is similar to a Button in that it can show text (or a bitmap), have relief (default is flat), display multiple lines of text, have a different font, and so on. Figure 5-2 shows a simple window, with both a Button and Label, created with this code:

```
use Tk;
$mw = MainWindow->new();
$mw->Label(-text => "Label Widget")->pack();
$mw->Button(-text => "Exit", -command => sub { exit })->pack();
MainLoop;
```

Here are some typical uses for a Label:

- Put a Label to the left of an Entry widget so the user knows what type of data is expected.

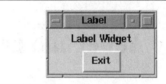

Figure 5-2. A simple window with Label and Button

- Put a Label above a group of Radiobuttons to clarify its purpose (e.g., "Background Color:"). You can do the same with Checkbuttons if they happen to be related or along the same theme.

- Use a Label to tell users what they did wrong: "The number entered must be between 10 and 100." (Typically, you would use a Dialog composite widget to give messages to the user like this, but not always.)

- Put an informational line across the bottom of your window. Each of the other widgets would have a mapping that displays a string containing information about that widget.

- Add an icon or decorative image to your application.

Creating a Label

The command to create a Label is, of course, Label. Here's the basic usage:

```
$label = $parent->Label( [ option => value . . . ] )->pack( );
```

Hopefully you are starting to see a trend in the creation command. As you might expect, when you create a Label, you can specify options that will change its appearance and how it behaves.

Label Options

The following is a comprehensive list of options for Labels:

-anchor => 'n' | 'ne' | 'e' | 'se' | 's' | 'sw' | 'w' | 'nw' | **'center'**
    Causes the text to stick to that position in the Label widget. This won't be obvious unless the Label is forced to be larger than standard size.

-background => *color*
    Sets the background color of the Label to *color*.

-bitmap => *bitmap*
    Displays the bitmap contained in *bitmap* instead of text.

-borderwidth => *amount*
    Changes the width of the edges of the Label.

-cursor => *cursorname*
    Changes the cursor to *cursorname* when the mouse is over this widget.

`-font => `*`fontname`*
> Indicates that the text in the widget will be displayed with *fontname*.

`-foreground => `*`color`*
> Changes the text of the Button (or the bitmap) to *color*.

`-height => `*`amount`*
> Sets the height of the Label to *amount*; *amount* is a valid screen distance.

`-highlightbackground => `*`color`*
> Sets the color of the focus rectangle when the widget is not in focus to *color*.

`-highlightcolor => `*`color`*
> Sets the color of the focus rectangle when the widget has focus to *color*.

`-highlightthickness => `*`amount`*
> Sets the width of the focus rectangle. Default is 0 for the Label.

`-image => `*`imgptr`*
> Displays the image to which *imgptr* points, instead of text.

`-justify => 'left' | 'right' | `**`'center'`**
> Sets the side of the Label against which multiline text will justify.

`-padx => `*`amount`*
> Adds extra space inside the edge to the left and right of the Label.

`-pady => `*`amount`*
> Adds extra space inside the edge to the top and bottom of the Label.

`-relief => `**`'flat'`**` | 'groove' | 'raised' | 'ridge' | 'sunken'`
> Changes the type of edges drawn around the Button.

`-takefocus => `**`0`**` | 1 | undef`
> Changes the ability of the Label to have the focus or not.

`-text => `*`text`*
> Displays a text string in the Label.

`-textvariable => \$variable`
> Points to the variable containing text to be displayed in the Label. Label will change automatically as $variable changes.

`-underline => `*`n`*
> Causes the *n*th character to be underlined. Allows that key to invoke the widget when it has the focus. Default value is –1 (no character underlined).

`-width => `*`amount`*
> Causes the Label width to be *amount*.

`-wraplength => `*`amount`*
> Indicates that the text in the Label will wrap when it gets longer than *amount*.

This list briefly describes each option and what it does. Some of the options have different defaults for the Label widget than we are used to seeing with Button-type widgets, causing the Label to behave a bit differently.

How a Label Differs from Other Widgets

When we created Button-type widgets, we could either click them with the mouse or tab to them and then use the keyboard to press the Button. A Label widget, on the other hand, does not interact with the user unless we add explicit bindings. It is there for informational purposes only, so there is no -command option.

The default value for the -takefocus option is 0, which means you cannot tab to it. When tabbing between widgets on the screen, the highlight rectangle shows us which widget currently has the keyboard focus. Since we don't allow the Label to have the focus (remember, -takefocus is set to 0), it doesn't make sense to have a visible highlight rectangle. The default value for the -highlightthickness option in a Label widget is 0. You can make a rectangle appear around a Label by setting -highlightthickness to something greater than 0, and setting -highlightbackground to a color, such as blue or red.

The Label widget also doesn't have a -state option. Since we shouldn't be able to click a Label, we should never have to disable it.

Relief

In Figure 5-3, you can see what happens when you change the Label's -relief option. Notice that the edges of the widget are very close to the text. Unlike a Button, you usually don't want much extra space around the Label (space is controlled by the -padx and -pady options). Normally you want the Label widget to sit right next to the widget (or widgets) it is describing.

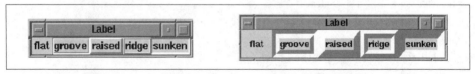

Figure 5-3. Labels with different relief values; window on right has a -borderwidth of 10

Seeing what a widget looks like with different relief values sometimes helps determine where the widget ends, especially with a widget that has a default value of 'flat'. Also, changing the relief of different widgets ensures that we know which widgets are where on the screen. After creating 10 Entries and Labels with less-than-creative variable names, it's easy to lose track. Changing the border width is bound to make that one widget stand out. Color is also a good way to make a diagnostic message.

Status Message Example

You can use the groove or ridge relief when making a help or status Label along the bottom of a window. Such a Label is packed with -side => 'bottom' and -fill => 'x'. There are two different ways you can use a status Label:

- Set the variable associated with it so it changes as your program progresses, announcing to the user that it is busy or that something is happening.
- Have the help Label give information on each of the different widgets in your application when it becomes active, using the bind command.

Both types are demonstrated in the following sample code.

This code shows the "What I'm doing now" type of help Label:

```
$mw->Label(-textvariable => \$message, -borderwidth => 2,
           -relief => 'groove')->pack(-fill => 'x',
                                       -side => 'bottom');
$mw->Text()->pack(-side => 'top',
                  -expand => 1,
                  -fill => 'both');

$message = "Loading file index.html...";
...
$message = "Done";
```

The Label is created across the bottom of the screen. We pack it first because we want it to stay on the screen if we resize the window (remember, the last widgets packed get lower priority if the window runs out of room). As the program executes (represented by the ...), it changes the Label accordingly.

This code shows an example of using a widget-helper help Label:

```
$mw->title("Help Label Example");

$mw->Label(-textvariable => \$message)
   ->pack(-side => 'bottom', -fill => 'x');

$b = $mw->Button(-text => "Exit", -command => \&exit, -relief => 'groove')
        ->pack(-side => 'left');
&bind_message($b, "Press to quit the application");

$b2 = $mw->Button(-text => "Do Nothing")->pack(-side => 'left');
&bind_message($b2, "This Button does absolutely nothing!");

$b3 = $mw->Button(-text => "Something",
   -command => sub { print "something\n"; })->pack(-side => 'left');
&bind_message($b3, "Prints the text 'something'");

sub bind_message {
   my ($widget, $msg) = @_;
   $widget->bind('<Enter>', [ sub { $message = $_[1]; }, $msg ]);
   $widget->bind('<Leave>', sub { $message = ""; });
}
```

This example is a bit longer, because we are using the bind method (the bind method is explained in more detail in Chapter 15). We want to associate a help message with each widget we create. We do this by adding bindings to each widget, which change the variable $message to a specified string when the mouse enters the widget and to an empty string if the mouse leaves the widget. We use a subroutine to avoid writing the same two bind lines over and over. Figure 5-4 shows what our window looks like with the mouse over the center Button.

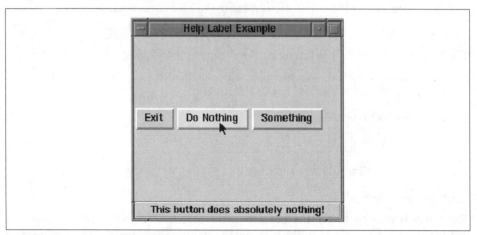

Figure 5-4. Window with Label across the bottom

Container Frames

In Figure 5-4, you can see the example text is centered within the Label widget. When using a single line Label and filling the widget across the screen, the text remains centered, even if you add the -justify => 'left' option. You can get around this by creating a container Frame, giving it the desired relief, filling the Frame across the screen (instead of the Label), and placing the Label widget within the Frame:

```
$f = $mw->Frame(-relief => 'groove',
                -bd => 2)->pack(-side => 'bottom',
                               -fill => 'x');
$f->Label(-textvariable => \$message,)->pack(-side => 'left');
```

This allows the Label to grow and shrink within the Frame as necessary, while the text sticks to the left side. Even better, perhaps, is to simply use -anchor => 'w' when configuring the Label.

If you've typed in this short example and played with the strings bound to each widget, you might have noticed that the window will resize itself if the text assigned to $message is too long to display in the Label. This can get annoying if your window is fairly small to begin with. There are two ways to deal with this: first, you can always use really short text strings; second, you can tell the window not to resize when the Label changes size.

The drawbacks with each approach aren't too bad, and which one you pick just depends on the application you are working on. If you can write really short sentences that make sense, great. Telling the window not to resize is almost as easy, though; it is accomplished by adding one line to your program:

```
$mw->packPropagate(0);
```

Using packPropagate will cause your window not to resize when a widget is placed inside the window (we first talked about packPropagate in Chapter 2). This means that your window might not show all your widgets right away. You can deal with this by keeping packPropagate on until you get all your widgets in, figuring out a good starting size for your window, and using $mw->geometry(*size*) to request that size initially. (See Chapter 11 for info on the geometry method.)

Label Configuration

Label is a pretty boring widget, so there are only two methods available to change or get information on it: cget and configure. Both methods work for Label the same way they work for the Button widget. Please refer to Appendix A for details on arguments and return values.

The Entry Widget

Until now, the only input we knew how to get from the user was a mouseclick on a Button widget (Button, Checkbutton, or Radiobutton), which is handled via the -command option. Getting input from a mouseclick is useful, but it's also limiting. The Entry widget (Figure 5-5) will let the user type in text that can then be used in any way by the application. Here are a few examples of where you might use an Entry widget:

- In a database form that requires one entry per field (e.g., Name, Last name, Address)
- In a software registration window that requires a serial number
- In a login window that requires a username and password
- In a configuration window to get the name of a printer
- In an Open File window that requires the path and name of a file

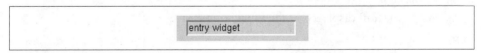

Figure 5-5. Entry widget

Normally, we don't care what users type in an Entry widget until they are done typing, and any processing will happen "after the fact" when a user clicks some sort of Go Button. You could get fancy and process each character as it's typed by setting up a complicated bind, but it's probably more trouble than it's worth.

The user can type anything into an Entry widget. It is up to you to decide whether the text entered is valid or not. When preparing to use the information from an Entry, we should do some error checking. If we want an integer but get some alphabetic characters, we should issue a warning or error message to the user.

An Entry widget is much more complex than it first appears to be. The Entry widget is really a simplified one-line text editor. Text can be typed in, selected with the mouse, deleted, and added. An Entry widget is a middle-of-the-line widget; it's more complicated than a Button, but much less complicated than the Text or Canvas widget.

Creating the Entry Widget

No surprises here:

```
$entry = $parent->Entry( [ option => value . . . ] )->pack;
```

When the Entry widget is created, it is initially empty of any text, and the insert cursor (if the Entry had the keyboard focus) is at the far-left side.

Entry Options

The following list contains a short description of each option available for configuring an Entry widget. Several of the options are discussed in more detail later in this chapter.

-background => *color*
> Sets the background color of the Entry widget. This is the area behind the text.

-borderwidth => *amount*
> Changes the width of the outside edge of the widget. Default value is 2.

-cursor => *cursorname*
> Changes the cursor to *cursorname* when it is over the widget.

-exportselection => 0 | **1**
> If the Boolean value specified is true, any text selected and copied will be exported to the windowing system's clipboard.

-font => *fontname*
> Changes the font displayed in the Entry to *fontname*.

-foreground => *color*
> Changes the color of the text.

-highlightbackground => *color*
> Sets the color the highlight rectangle should be when the widget does not have the keyboard focus.

-highlightcolor => *color*
> Sets the color the highlight rectangle should be when the widget does have the keyboard focus.

`-highlightthickness` => *amount*
> Sets the thickness of the highlight rectangle around the widget. Default is 2.

`-insertbackground` => *color*
> Sets the color of the insert cursor.

`-insertborderwidth` => *amount*
> Sets the width of the insert cursor's border. Normally used in conjunction with `-ipadx` and `-ipady` options for the geometry manager.

`-insertofftime` => *milliseconds*
> Sets the amount of time the insert cursor is off in the Entry widget.

`-insertontime` => *milliseconds*
> Sets the amount of time the insert cursor is on in the Entry widget.

`-insertwidth` => *amount*
> Sets the width of the insert cursor. Default is 2.

`-invalidcommand` => *callback*
> Specifies a callback to invoke when -validatecommand returns a false result—undef disables this feature (default). Typically, just call the bell method.

`-justify` => **'left'** | 'right' | 'center'
> Sets the justification of the text in the Entry widget.

`-relief` => 'flat'|'groove'|'raised'|'ridge'|**'sunken'**|'solid'
> Sets the relief of the outside edges of the Entry widget.

`-selectbackground` => *color*
> Sets the background color of any selected text in the Entry widget.

`-selectborderwidth` => *amount*
> Sets the width of the selection highlight's border.

`-selectforeground` => *color*
> Sets the text color of any selected text in the Entry widget.

`-show` => *char*
> Sets the character that should be displayed instead of the actual text typed.

`-state` => **'normal'** | 'disabled' | 'active'
> Indicates the state of the Entry.

`-takefocus` => 0 | 1 | **undef**
> Allows or disallows this widget to have the keyboard focus.

`-textvariable` => \$variable
> Sets the variable associated with the information typed in the Entry widget.

`-validate` => *validateMode*
> Specifies the events that invoke the -validatecommand callback: none (default), focus, focusin, focusout, key, or all.

`-validatecommand` => *callback*
> Specifies a callback that validates the input; `undef` disables this feature (default). The callback returns false to reject the new input and invoke the `-invalidcommand` callback or true to accept the input.

`-width` => *amount*
> Sets the width of the Entry in characters.

`-xscrollcommand` => *callback*
> Assigns a callback to use when scrolling back and forth.

The following options behave as expected; we won't discuss them further: `-background`, `-cursor`, `-font`, `-highlightbackground`, `-highlightcolor`, `-highlight-thickness`, `-foreground`, `-justify`, `-takefocus`, and `-state`. For more detailed information on these how these options affect a widget, see Chapter 3.

Assigning the Entry's Contents to a Variable

The `-textvariable` option lets you know what the user typed in the Entry widget:

    -textvariable => \$variable

By now you should be familiar with this option from several of our Button examples. Any text input to the Entry widget will get assigned into $variable. The reverse also applies. Any string that gets assigned to $variable will show up in the Entry widget.

It is important to remember that no matter what the user enters, it will be assigned to this variable. This means that even if you are expecting numeric input (e.g., **314**), you might get something like **3s14** if the user accidentally (or on purpose!) presses the wrong key(s). Before using any information from an Entry widget, it's a good idea to do some error checking to make sure it's the information you expect or, at the very least, in the correct format. Trying to use 3s14 in an equation would most likely produce undesired results.

The other way to find out what is in the Entry widget is to use the get method:

    $stuff = $entry->get();

You can use get whether or not you have used the `-textvariable` option.

Relief

As with all the widgets, you can change the way the edges are drawn by using the `-relief` and/or `-borderwidth` options:

    -relief => 'flat' | 'groove' | 'raised' | 'ridge' | **'sunken'**
    -borderwidth => *amount*

The default relief for an Entry is `'sunken'`, which is a change from what we've seen so far. Figure 5-6 shows the different relief types at different `-borderwidth` values, incrementing from the default (2) to 4 and to 10.

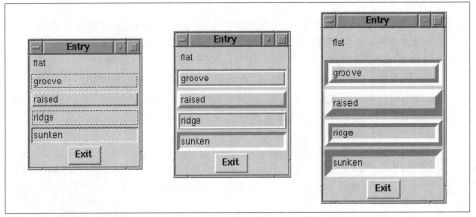

Figure 5-6. Different relief types for an Entry widget: -borderwidth of 2 (the default), 4, and 10

This is the code snippet that created the five Entry widgets and used the relief name as the Entry widget's text:

```
foreach (qw/flat groove raised ridge sunken/) {
    $e = $mw->Entry(-relief => $_)->pack(-expand => 1);
    $e->insert('end', $_);  # put some text in the Entry
}
```

Entry Indexes

To manipulate the text in the Entry widget, you need some way to identify specific portions or positions within the text. The last example actually used an index in it. The line $e->insert('end', $_) uses the index 'end'. Just like the insert method (covered later in the chapter), all of the methods that require information about a position will ask for an index (or two, if the method requires a range of characters). This index can be as simple as 0, meaning the very beginning of the text, or something more complicated, such as 'insert'.

Here are the different forms of index specification and what they mean:

n (any integer)

A numerical character position. 0 is the first character in the string. If the Entry contains the string "My mother hit your mother right on the nose" and we use an index of 12, the character pointed to is the t in the word hit.

'insert'

The character directly following the insertion cursor. The insertion cursor is that funny-looking little bar thing that shows up inside the Entry widget when text is typed. You can move it around with the arrow keys or by clicking on a different location in the Entry widget.

`'sel.first'`

The first character in the selection string. This will produce an error if there is no selection. The selection string is the string created by using the mouse or Shift-arrow. The selected text is slightly raised from the background of the Entry.

If our selected text was the word nose in this string (shown here in bold):

```
My mother hit your mother right on the nose
```

`'sel.first'` would indicate the n.

`'sel.last'`

The character just after the last character in the selection string. This will also produce an error if there is no selection in the Entry widget. In the preceding example, this would mean the space after the e in nose.

`'anchor'`

The `'anchor'` index changes depending on what has happened with the selection in the Entry widget. By default, it starts at the far left of the Entry: 0. It will change if you click anywhere in the Entry widget with the mouse. The new value will be at the index you clicked on. The `'anchor'` index will also change when a new selection is made—either with the mouse (which means the `'anchor'` will be wherever you clicked with the mouse) or by Shift-clicking—and `'anchor'` will be set to where the selection starts. Mostly, this index is used internally, and you'll rarely find a case where it would be useful in an application.

`'end'`

The character just after the last one in the text string. This value is the same as if you specified the length of the entire string as an integer index.

`'@x'`

This form uses an x coordinate in the Entry widget. The character that contains this x coordinate will be used. `"@0"` indicates the leftmost (or first) character in the Entry widget. This form of index specification is also one you'll rarely use.

Text Selection Options

You can select the text in an Entry widget and make several things happen. The indexes `'sel.first'` and `'sel.last'` point to the beginning and end of the selected text, respectively. You can also make the selected text available on the clipboard on a Unix system by using the -exportselection option:

```
-exportselection => 0 | 1
```

The -exportselection option indicates whether or not any selected text in the Entry will be put in the selection buffer in addition to being stored internal to the Entry as a selection. By leaving this option's default value, you can paste selected text into other applications.

The selected text also has some color options associated with it: -selectbackground, -selectforeground, and -selectborderwidth:

```
-selectbackground => color
-selectforeground => color
-selectborderwidth => amount
```

The -selectbackground and -selectforeground options change the color of the text and the area behind the text when that text is highlighted. In Figure 5-7, the word "text" is selected.

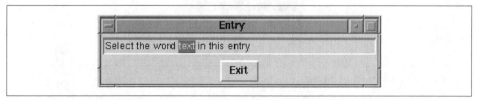

Figure 5-7. Entry with -selectbackground => 'red' and -selectforeground => 'yellow'

You can change the width of the edge of that selection box by using -selectborderwidth. If you left the size of the Entry widget unchanged, you wouldn't see the effects of it. The Entry widget cuts off the selection box. To actually see the results of increasing the -selectborderwidth value, use the -selectborderwidth option in the Entry command and -ipadx and -ipady in the geometry management command. Figure 5-8 illustrates -selectborderwidth.

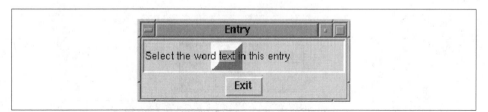

Figure 5-8. Entry widget with -selectborderwidth => 5

You might want to change the -selectborderwidth option if you like a little extra space around your text or if you really want to emphasize the selected text. Here's the code that generated the Entry widget in Figure 5-8:

```
$e = $mw->Entry(-selectborderwidth => 10)->pack(-expand => 1,
                                                -fill => 'x',
                                                -ipadx => 10,
                                                -ipady => 10);
$e->insert('end', "Select the word text in this Entry");
```

Notice the -ipadx and -ipady options in the pack command.

The Insert Cursor

The insert cursor is that funny-looking little bar that blinks on and off inside the Entry widget when it has the keyboard focus. It will only show up when the Entry widget actually has the keyboard focus. If another widget (or none) has the keyboard focus, the insertion cursor remains but is invisible. In Figure 5-9, the insertion cursor is immediately after the second "n" in the word "Insertion."

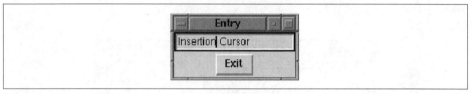

Figure 5-9. Default insertion cursor

You can change the thickness, border width, and width of the insertion cursor by using these options:

```
-insertbackground => color
-insertborderwidth => amount
-insertwidth => amount
```

The -insertwidth option changes the width of the cursor so it looks fatter. The -insertbackground option changes the overall color of the insertion cursor. Figure 5-10 shows an example.

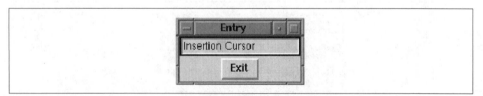

Figure 5-10. Insertion cursor with -insertbackground => 'green' and -insertwidth => 10

No matter how wide the cursor, it is always centered over the position between two characters. The insertion cursor in Figure 5-10 is in the same location it was in Figure 5-9. This can look distracting to users and might just confuse them unnecessarily, so you most likely won't change the -insertwidth option.

You can give the insertion cursor a 3D look by using -insertborderwidth (as in Figure 5-11). Like the -insertwidth option, the -insertborderwidth option doesn't have much practical use.

You can change the amount of time the cursor blinks on and off by using these options:

```
-insertofftime => time
-insertontime => time
```

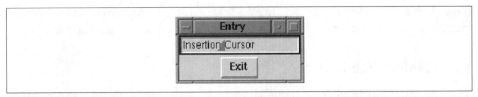

Figure 5-11. -insertborderwidth => 5, -insertbackground => 'green', and -insertwidth => 10

The default value for -insertofftime is 300 milliseconds. The default for -insertontime is 600 milliseconds. The default values make the cursor's blink stay on twice as long as it is off. Any value specified for these options must be nonnegative.

For a really frantic-looking cursor, change both values to something much smaller. For a relaxed and mellow cursor, double the default times. If you don't like a blinking cursor, change -insertofftime to 0.

Password Entries

There are times when you'll request information from the user that shouldn't be displayed on the screen. To display something other than the actual text typed in, use the -show option:

    -show => char

The *char* is a single character that will be displayed instead of the typed-in characters. For a password Entry, you might use asterisks (see Figure 5-12). If you specify a string, just the first character of that string will be used. By default, this value is undefined, and whatever the user actually typed will show.

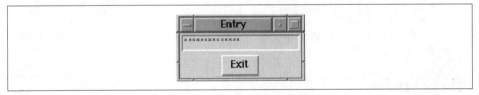

Figure 5-12. Entry displaying a password

When using the -show option, the information stored in the associated $variable will contain the real information, not the asterisks.

If you use this feature, the user can't cut and paste the password (regardless of the value of -exportselection). If it is cut and pasted to another screen, what the user saw on the screen (e.g., the asterisks) is actually pasted, not the information behind it. You might think that if you did a configure on the Entry widget, such as $entry-> configure(-show => "");, the words the user entered would suddenly appear. Luckily, this isn't true. A bunch of \x0s (essentially gibberish) show up instead. Any variable that uses the -textvariable option and is associated with the Entry will still contain the correct information. If you perform an $entry->get( )$, the correct (nongibberish) information will be returned. The get method is described later in this chapter.

Entry Widget Validation

You can perform input validation as characters are typed in an Entry widget, although, by default, validation is disabled. You enable validation using the -validate option, specifiying what events trigger your validation subroutine. The possible values for this option are focus and focusin (when the Entry gets the keyboard focus), focusout (when the Entry loses focus), key (on any key press), or all.

The -validatecommand callback should return true to accept the input or false to reject it. When false is returned, the -invalidcommand callback is executed.

The -validatecommand and -invalidcommand callbacks are called with these arguments:

- The proposed value of the Entry (the value of the text variable too)
- The characters to be added or deleted; undef if called due to focus, explicit call, or change in text variable
- The current value before the proposed change
- The index of the string to be added/deleted, if any; otherwise, −1
- The type of action: 1 for insert, 0 for delete, −1 if a forced validation or text variable validation

This Entry ensures that characters are restricted to those in the string "perl/Tk", without regard to case:

```
my $e = $mw->Entry(
    -validate       => 'key',
    -validatecommand => sub {$_[1] =~ /[perl\/Tk]/i},
    -invalidcommand  => sub {$mw->bell},
)->pack;
```

Using a Scrollbar

If the information requested from the user could get lengthy, the user can use the arrow keys to manually scroll through the text. To make it easier, we can create and assign a horizontal Scrollbar to the Entry widget by using the -xscrollcommand option:

```
-xscrollcommand => [ 'set' => $scrollbar ]
```

For now, we're going to show you the most basic way to assign a Scrollbar to the Entry widget. For more details on the Scrollbar, see Chapter 6.

The following code creates a Scrollbar and associates it with an Entry widget:

```
$scroll = $mw->Scrollbar(-orient => "horizontal"); # create Scrollbar
$e = $mw->Entry(-xscrollcommand => [ 'set' => $scroll ])->
  pack(-expand => 1, -fill => 'x'); # create Entry
```

```
$scroll->pack(-expand => 1, -fill => 'x');
$scroll->configure(-command => [ $e => 'xview' ]); # link them
$e->insert('end', "Really really really long text string");
```

Figure 5-13 shows the resulting window in two states: on the left, the window as it looked when it was created, and on the right, how it looks after scrolling all the way to the right.

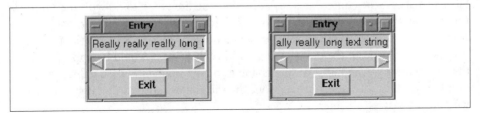

Figure 5-13. Scrollbar and an Entry widget

You'll rarely want to use a Scrollbar with an Entry widget. The Scrollbar doubles the amount of space taken, and you can get the same functionality without it by simply using the arrow keys when the Entry widget has the focus. If the user needs to enter multiple lines of text, you should use a Text widget instead. See Chapter 8 for more information on what a Text widget can do.

Configuring an Entry Widget

Both cget and configure are the same for the Entry widget as they are for any of the other widgets. The default options for the Entry widget are listed in Chapter 13.

Deleting Text

You can use the delete method when you want to remove some or all of the text from the Entry widget. You can specify a range of indexes to remove two or more characters or a single index to remove one character:

```
$entry->delete(firstindex, [ lastindex ])
```

To remove all the text, you can use $entry->delete(0, 'end'). If you use the -textvariable option, you can also delete the contents by reassigning the variable to an empty string: $variable = "".

Here are some other examples of how to use the delete method:

```
$entry->delete(0);       # Remove only the first character
$entry->delete(1);       # Remove the second character

$entry->delete('sel.first', 'sel.last')  # Remove selected text
    if $entry->selectionPresent();       # if present
```

Getting the Contents of an Entry Widget

There are two ways to determine the content of the Entry widget: the get method or the variable associated with the -textvariable option. Using the get method, $entry_text = $entry->get() will assign the entire content of the Entry widget into $entry_text.

How you access the content depends on what you are going to do with the information. If you only need to reference it once in order to write it to a file or insert it into a database, it doesn't make sense to waste memory by storing it in a variable. Simply use the get method in the print statement (or wherever it would be appropriate). If the information in the Entry widget is going to be a frequently used value, such as a number for a mathematical calculation, then it makes sense to initially store it in a variable for easy access later.

Moving the Insertion Cursor

The icursor method will place the cursor at the specified *index*:

```
$entry->icursor(index);
```

By default, the insertion cursor starts out wherever the last insert took place. To force the insertion cursor to show up elsewhere, you could do something like this:

```
$e_txt = "Entry Text";
$e = $mw->Entry(-textvariable => \$e_txt)->pack();
$e->focus;
$e->icursor(1); # put cursor at this index
```

We use the focus method (which is not specific to the Entry widget; it's generic to all widgets) to have the application start with the focus on our Entry widget. Then we place the insertion cursor between the first and second characters (indexes 0 and 1) in the Entry. See Chapter 13 for more information on focus.

You might want to move the starting position of your cursor if you are starting the text with a specific string. For instance, set $e_txt = "http://" and then $e->icursor('end').

Getting a Numeric Index Value

The index method will convert a named index into a numeric one:

```
$numindex = $entry->index(index) ;
```

One of the uses of index is to find out how many characters are in the Entry widget: $length = $entry->index('end'). Of course, if we used the -textvariable option, we could get the same result by using $length = length($variable).

As an example of using index to find where the current selection starts, use this code:

```
$startindex = $entry->selectionPresent() ?
                $entry->index('sel.first') : -1;
```

We discuss selectionPresent later in the chapter.

Inserting Text

The insert function will let you insert any text string at the specified index:

```
$entry->insert(index, string);
```

Here's a simple application that uses insert:

```perl
#!/usr/bin/perl
use Tk;
$mw = MainWindow->new;
$mw->title("Entry");

$e_txt = "Entry Text";    # Create Entry with initial text
$e = $mw->Entry(-textvariable => \$e_txt)->pack(-expand => 1,
                                                -fill => 'x');
$mw->Button(-text => "Exit",
            -command => sub { exit })->pack(-side => 'bottom');

# Create a Button that will insert a counter at the cursor
$i = 1;
$mw->Button(-text => "Insert #", -command =>
            sub {
               if ($e->selectionPresent()) {
                  $e->insert('sel.last', "$i"); $i++;
               }
            })->pack;
MainLoop;
```

We fill the Entry widget with "Entry Text" as a default. Then we create two Buttons. The first one is the obvious Exit Button that will allow us to quit the application. The second one is a bit more complicated. When pressed, it will check to see if any text is selected in the Entry $e. If text is selected, it will insert a number that keeps track of how many times we have pressed the Insert # Button.

In Figure 5-14, we first selected the word "Entry" and then pressed the Insert # Button four times. Each time it was pressed, it inserted a number at the index "sel. last". This index didn't change in between button presses, so it looks as if we are counting backward!

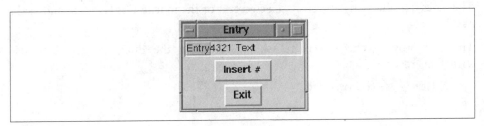

Figure 5-14. Using the insert method

Scanning Text

Both `scanMark` and `scanDragto` allow fast scrolling within the Entry widget. A call to `scanMark` simply records the x coordinate passed in for use later with `scanDragto`. It returns an empty string.

```
$entry->scanMark(x);
$entry->scanDragto(x);
```

The companion function to `scanMark` is `scanDragto`, which also takes an x coordinate. The new coordinate is compared to the `scanMark` x coordinate. The view within the Entry widget is adjusted by 10 times the difference between the coordinates.

And don't forget you can always drag the contents of the Entry widget left and right by holding down mouse button 2.

Working with the Selection

The `selection` method has several possible argument lists. If you look at the web page documentation, you'll see that you can use:

```
$entry->selectionAdjust(index).
```

You might also see the form `$entry->selection('adjust', index)`, where `'adjust'` is the first argument. Be aware that they mean the same thing as you read code written by other people.

You can adjust the selection to a specified index by using `selectionAdjust`:

```
$entry->selectionAdjust(index);
```

The selected text is extended toward the *index* (from whichever end is closest).

To clear out the selection:

```
$entry->selectionClear();
```

Any selection indicator is removed from the Entry widget, and the indexes `'sel.first'` and `'sel.last'` are now undefined. The selected text remains.

To reset the `'anchor'` index to the specified index, use `selectionFrom`:

```
$entry->selectionFrom(index);
```

This does not affect any currently selected text or the indexes `'sel.first'` and `'sel.last'`.

The only way to check if there is a selection in the Entry widget is to use `selectionPresent`:

```
if ($entry->selectionPresent()) {
}
```

It returns a 1 if there is a selection, which means you can safely use the 'sel.first' and 'sel.last' indexes (if there isn't a selection, an error will be printed when you refer to either index). selectionPresent will return a 0 if there is no current selection.

You can change the selection range by calling selectionRange:

```
$entry->selectionRange(startindex, endindex);
```

The two indexes indicate where you would like the selection to cover. If *startindex* is the same or greater than *endindex*, the selection is cleared, causing 'sel.first' and 'sel.last' to be undefined. Otherwise, 'sel.first' and 'sel.last' are defined the same as *startindex* and *endindex*, respectively.

The selectionTo method causes the new selection to be set from the current 'anchor' point to the specified index:

```
$entry->selectionTo(index);
```

Changing the View in the Entry Widget

xview is a method that will change its purpose based on what arguments are passed in. With no arguments, it will return a two-element list containing numbers from 0 to 1. These two numbers define what is currently visible in the Entry widget. The first number indicates how much of the text is off to the left and not visible. If it is .3, then 30% of the text is to the left of the Entry widget. The second number returned is how much of the text is not visible on the left side of the Entry widget plus the amount that is visible in the widget. In this case, 50% of the text is actually visible in the Entry widget (see Figure 5-15).

```
($left, $right) = $entry->xview( );
```

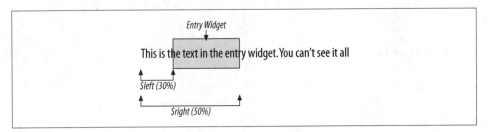

Figure 5-15. What $left and $right mean

When passing an index value to xview, the text in the Entry widget will shift position so that the text at the specified index is visible at the far-left edge:

```
$entry->xview(index);
```

The rest of the forms of xview have to do directly with scrolling (and are explained in detail in Chapter 6):

```
$entry->xviewMoveto(fraction);
$entry->xviewScroll(number, what);
```

The Perl/Tk LabEntry Mega-Widget

Perl/Tk provides special code that combines a Label with an arbitrary widget, so you can have LabArbitrary widgets. This is fully explained in Chapter 14. Perhaps the most common of these labeled widgets is LabEntry. It's configured using standard options, and ordinary options such as -font are directed to the Entry subwidget. To configure the Label subwidget, use options such as -labelFont, -labelBackground, and so on.

There's a special option, -labelPack, that accepts a reference to a list of packer options and controls the relative geometry of the Label and Entry subwidgets. By default, the Label is packed on top of the Entry. If you prefer left-side packing, use -labelPack as in the example below. This example shows how to use a fixed-width font to create a column of aligned LabEntry widgets:

```
foreach my $item (
  ['Copying', \$self->{file}],
  ['From', \$self->{from}],
  ['To', \$self->{to}],
  ['Bytes Copied', \$self->{bytes_msg}],
    ) {
  my $l = $item->[0] . ':';
  my $le = $cf_frame->LabEntry(
      -label        => ' ' x (13 - length $l) . $l,
      -labelPack    => [qw/-side left -anchor w/],
      -labelFont    => '9x15bold',
      -relief       => 'flat',
      -state        => 'disabled',
      -textvariable => $item->[1],
      -width        => 35,
  );
  $le->pack(qw/-fill x -expand 1/);
}
```

Please refer to Chapter 14 for a complete list of -label options.

## CHAPTER 6

The Scrollbar Widget

Scrollbars are used with widgets when there is more to see than can be shown at once. Scrollbars allow a user to scroll a widget's contents horizontally and/or vertically. This chapter shows how you can use Scrollbars with certain Perl/Tk widgets.

Defining Scrollbar Parts

Figure 6-1 shows all the different parts of a Scrollbar and their names.

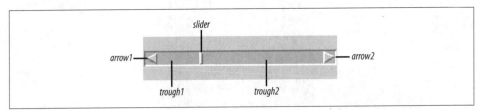

Figure 6-1. Different parts of a Scrollbar

The trough is the sunken part between the two arrows. It is divided into two parts, trough1 and trough2, by the slider. The slider is the rectangle that indicates how much of the window is available for scrolling. If you were in the middle of the list, you would see the slider rectangle in the center of the trough with space on either side of it. The arrows on either end are called arrow1 and arrow2. If the Scrollbar were vertical (rotated 90 degrees clockwise), arrow1 would be the top arrow.

Clicking on either arrow will move the information in the associated widget one unit at a time. What the unit is depends on the type of widget with which the Scrollbar is associated. With an Entry widget, the units are characters. With a Listbox widget and a vertical Scrollbar, the units are lines. Clicking in the trough on either side of the slider will page the information in the widget in that direction. You can also click directly on the slider and, holding the mouse button down, move it directly.

Scrollbars can be horizontal or vertical. They typically reside on the bottom and/or to the right of the widget they are scrolling, but not always.

Not just any widget can have scrollbars attached to it. Generally speaking, for a widget to be scrollable, it must have xview and/or yview methods. For the most part, if you think a widget should be scrollable, it probably is. Text, Listbox, Canvas, HList, Tiler, and Entry are all scrollable. One widget you might expect to be scrollable—but isn't—is the Frame widget. If you want a scrollable Frame widget, fetch Tk::Pane, described in Chapter 23, from CPAN. See Figure 6-2 through Figure 6-5 for examples of Scrollbars with various widgets.

Figure 6-2. Entry widget with a Scrollbar

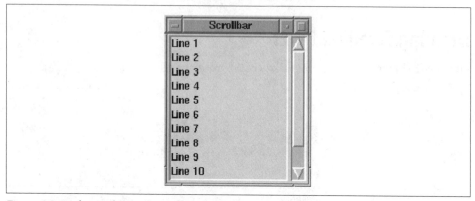

Figure 6-3. Listbox widget with Scrollbar

```
# Conversion from Tk4.0 scrollbar.tcl competed.
package Tk::Scrollbar;
require Tk;
use AutoLoader;

@ISA = qw(Tk::Widget);

Construct Tk::Widget 'Scrollbar';

bootstrap Tk::Scrollbar $Tk::VERSION;

sub Tk_cmd { \&Tk::scrollbar }

sub Needed
{
  my ($sb) = @_;
```

Figure 6-4. Text widget displaying Scrollbar.pm file with Scrollbar

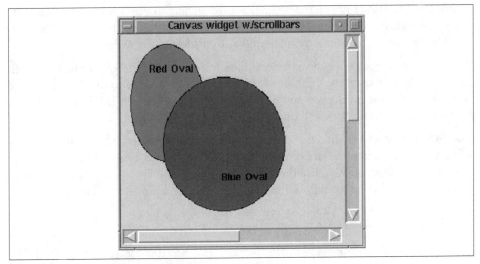

Figure 6-5. Canvas widget with Scrollbars

There are two ways to create and configure Scrollbars for use with widgets: you can use the Scrollbar widget creation command or you can use the Scrolled method to create the widget and associated Scrollbars. Both have their advantages and disadvantages. Using Scrolled is much less work and requires less coding, but it won't let you do anything fancy, such as associate the same Scrollbar with two different widgets. Creating the Scrollbar widgets yourself takes more code, but you can do much fancier things with them since you'll have direct control over where they go and which widget(s) they are associated with. This chapter will cover both methods of creating Scrollbars.

The Scrolled Method

To create a widget and Scrollbars at the same time, use the Scrolled method. Scrolled returns a pointer to the widget created. It is the easiest way to add Scrollbars to a scrollable widget. The Scrolled method creates a Frame that contains the widget and Scrollbar(s). You create them all in one command.

The usage for the Scrolled method is:

```
$widget = $parent->Scrolled('Widget',
                    -scrollbars => 'string' [, options ]);
```

The first argument is the widget to create, such as "Listbox" or "Canvas". The other argument you'll need to use is the -scrollbars option, which takes a string that tells it which Scrollbars to create and where to put them.

The possible values for -scrollbars are "n", "s", "e", "w"; or "on", "os", "oe", "ow"; or some combination of those that combines n or s with an e or w. The "n" means to put a horizontal Scrollbar above the widget. An "s" means to put a horizontal Scrollbar below the widget. The "e" means to put a vertical Scrollbar to the right of the widget. The "w" means to put a vertical Scrollbar to the left of the widget.

You can have a maximum of two Scrollbars for each widget. For instance, we can create one Scrollbar on the "n" side of the widget. It is possible to use "nw" to create two Scrollbars, one on the top and one on the left of the widget. It is not legal to use "ns", because "n" and "s" scroll in the same direction.

The "o" in front of the direction makes that Scrollbar optional. Optional Scrollbars will only display when the size of the widget makes it necessary to scroll the information in the widget. Always list the north or south value first (if you use either) to avoid complaints from the subroutine. Here are some examples to make this clearer:

```
# Create optional Scrollbar east (to the right) of widget
$lb = $mw->Scrolled("Listbox", -scrollbars => 'oe')->pack;

# Create Scrollbars to south (below) and east (to the right) of widget
$lb = $mw->Scrolled("Listbox", -scrollbars => 'se')->pack;

# Create optional Scrollbars south (below) and east (right) of widget
$lb = $mw->Scrolled("Listbox", -scrollbars => 'osoe')->pack;

# Create Scrollbars to the north (above) and west (to the left) of widget
$lb = $mw->Scrolled("Listbox", -scrollbars => 'nw')->pack;
```

Configuring the Scrollbar(s) Created with Scrolled

Any other options sent with the Scrolled method will configure only the widget created. If you need to configure the Scrollbars, use the Subwidget method from the widget reference. The Subwidget method can be used because a Scrolled widget is really a composite widget. Composite widgets are covered in Chapter 14.

To turn the background of your horizontal Scrollbar green, use this code:

```
$lb->Subwidget("xscrollbar")->configure(-background => "green");
```

To configure a vertical Scrollbar, use "yscrollbar" in place of "xscrollbar". If you try to configure a Scrollbar that you didn't create (e.g., you used -scrollbars => "e" and tried to configure the "xscrollbar"), an error occurs.

To configure just the widget, you can use $widget->configure after calling Scrolled, or you can use:

```
$widget->Subwidget("widget")->configure(...);
```

Using Subwidget this way is silly because you can just use $widget. The "widget" string is the same as the first argument sent to Scrolled except it's all lowercase. For instance, in the preceding example we called Scrolled with "Listbox", but we would use "listbox" with the Subwidget method.

Even better, Tk provides a subwidget named "scrolled", which is always the scrolled widget, whatever kind it might be.

The Scrollbar Widget

Instead of automatically creating one or more Scrollbars with the Scrolled method, you can use the Scrollbar widget method and perform the configuration yourself. It is better to create and configure your own Scrollbars when you need to do something nonstandard, such as have one Scrollbar scroll two Listboxes. Figure 6-6 shows a Scrollbar widget.

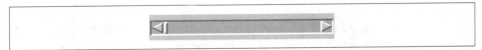

Figure 6-6. Scrollbar widget

Creating a Scrollbar Widget

To create the Scrollbar, invoke the Scrollbar method from the parent widget. It returns a reference to the newly created Scrollbar that you can use for configuration:

```
$scrollbar = $mw->Scrollbar([ options ...])
```

There are at least two other things you need to do to get a Scrollbar working with another widget. First, create the to-be-scrolled widget and use the Scrollbar with its -xscrollcommand or -yscrollcommand option. Then configure the Scrollbar so that it knows to talk to that widget. Here's an example that creates a Listbox widget (don't worry if you don't quite follow all of this now; we just want to show a complete example before we go on to talk about all the options):

```
# Create the vertical Scrollbar
$scrollbar = $mw->Scrollbar();
$lb = $mw->Listbox(-yscrollcommand => ['set' => $scrollbar]);
#Configure the Scrollbar to talk to the Listbox widget
$scrollbar->configure(-command => ['yview' => $lb]);

#Pack the Scrollbar first so that it doesn't disappear when we resize
$scrollbar->pack(-side => 'right', -fill => 'y');
$lb->pack(-side => 'left', -fill => 'both');
```

Creating the Scrollbar is pretty simple; we want all the default options for it. As we create the Listbox, we have to set up a callback so the Listbox can communicate with the Scrollbar when the contents of the Listbox move around. Our Scrollbar is vertical, so the -yscrollcommand option has the set command and our Scrollbar assigned to it (if it is horizontal, use -xscrollcommand). When the contents of the Listbox are scrolled by the user without using the Scrollbar, the Listbox will alert the Scrollbar by invoking $scrollbar->set(...).

The line $scrollbar->configure(-command => ['yview' => $lb]) does almost the opposite: it configures the Scrollbar to communicate with the Listbox. When the user clicks the Scrollbar, it will invoke $lb->yview(...) to tell the Listbox how to change the view of the contents. Use the y version of the view command, as it's a vertical Scrollbar.

There is more information on the details of yview in "How the Scrollbar Communicates with Other Widgets," later in this chapter. The last two lines in this example pack the Scrollbar and the Listbox in the window so the Scrollbar is the same height and lies to the right of the Listbox.

Always pack your Scrollbars first within the window or Frame. This allows the Scrollbars to remain visible when the user resizes the window smaller. It will then resize the Listbox (or other widget) but leave the Scrollbars visible on the edges of the screen.

Now that we've seen a complete example of how to create a Scrollbar and how to set up the widget it will scroll, we can go over the options with an idea of how they are used.

Scrollbar Options

This list contains the options available with a Scrollbar and their quick definitions. The important options are discussed in more detail later in this chapter.

-activebackground => *color*
> Sets the color the Scrollbar should be when the mouse pointer is over it.

-activerelief => 'flat' | 'groove' | **'raised'** | 'ridge' | 'sunken'
> Determines how active elements are drawn. The elements in question are arrow1, arrow2, and slider.

-background => *color*
> Sets the background color of the Scrollbar (not the trough color).

-borderwidth => *amount*
> Sets the width of the edges of the Scrollbar and the arrow1, arrow2, and slider elements.

-command => *callback*
> Sets the callback that is invoked when the Scrollbar is clicked.

-cursor => *cursorname*
> Sets the cursor that is displayed when the mouse pointer is over the Scrollbar.

-elementborderwidth => *amount*
> Sets the width of the borders of the arrow1, arrow2, and slider elements.

-highlightbackground => *color*
> Sets the color the highlight rectangle around the Scrollbar widget should be when it does not have the keyboard focus.

-highlightcolor => *color*
> Sets the color the highlight rectangle around the Scrollbar should be when it does have the keyboard focus.

-highlightthickness => *amount*
> Sets the thickness of the highlight rectangle. Default is 2.

`-jump =>` **0** `| 1`
Indicates whether or not the Scrollbar will jump scroll.

`-orient =>` `"horizontal"` `|` **`"vertical"`**
Sets the orientation of the Scrollbar.

`-relief =>` `'flat'|'groove'|'raised'|'ridge'|`**`'sunken'`**`|'solid'`
Sets the edges of the widget.

`-repeatdelay =>` *time*
Sets the number of milliseconds required to hold down an arrow before it will auto-repeat. Default is 300 ms.

`-repeatinterval =>` *time*
Sets the number of milliseconds in between auto-repeats. Default is 100 ms.

`-takefocus =>` `0 | 1 |` **`undef`**
Controls whether the Scrollbar can obtain the keyboard focus.

`-troughcolor =>` *color*
Changes the color of the trough (both `trough1` and `trough2`).

`-width =>` *amount*
Sets the width of the Scrollbar.

Scrollbar Colors

Within the Scrollbar, we have a new part of the widget called a trough. This trough gets its own coloring through the -troughcolor option. The trough is considered the part behind the arrows and slider. Figure 6-7 shows an example.

Figure 6-7. Scrollbar with -troughcolor set to 'green'

The background of the Scrollbar consists of the arrows, the slider, and a small portion around the outside of the trough. You change the color of the background by using the -background option. The -activebackground option controls the color displayed when the mouse cursor is over one of the arrows or the slider. Figure 6-8 shows two examples of -background; the second window uses both -background and -troughcolor.

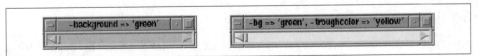

Figure 6-8. Examples of -background option

Scrollbar Style

The -relief and -borderwidth options affect both the outside edges of the Scrollbar and the arrow1, arrow2, and slider elements. This is similar to how the Checkbutton and Radiobutton widgets are affected by the -relief and -borderwidth options. See Figure 6-9 for a screenshot of different values for these two options, in the order 'flat', 'groove', 'raised', 'sunken', and 'solid'.

Figure 6-9. Different relief values; second row relief values have -borderwidth => 4

The -activerelief option affects the decoration of three elements—arrow1, arrow2, and slider—when the mouse cursor is over them. The -elementborderwidth affects the same three elements: arrow1, arrow2, and slider. The width of these elements' edges can be changed with this option. The -borderwidth option also changes the width of these elements but changes the width of the edges of the widget as well. Notice in Figure 6-10 how the edges of the Scrollbar remain at a width of 2.

Figure 6-10. Example of -elementborderwidth set to 4

The -width of the Scrollbar is the distance across the skinny part of the Scrollbar, not including the borders. Figure 6-11 demonstrates how the Scrollbar changes when you alter the -width.

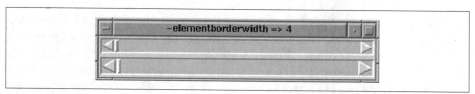

Figure 6-11. Top Scrollbar has width of 15 (default), bottom Scrollbar has width of 20

Scrollbar Orientation

As mentioned earlier, a Scrollbar can be vertical or horizontal. The default for a Scrollbar is 'vertical'. To change this, use the -orient option:

```
$scrollbar = $mw->Scrollbar(-orient => 'horizontal');
```

You could also use -orient => 'vertical', but it's the default, so it's not necessary.

Using the Arrows and the Slider

When you click on one of the arrows in a Scrollbar, you cause the slider to move in that direction by one unit. If you continue to hold down the mouse button, after a bit of a delay, the slider will auto-repeat that movement. The -repeatdelay option determines the amount of time you must wait before the auto-repeat kicks in. The default is 300 milliseconds.

Once you have held the mouse button down long enough to start auto-repeating, there is a short delay between each time it repeats the action. This delay is controlled by the -repeatinterval option. The default for -repeatinterval is 100 milliseconds.

Normally, when you click on the slider and move it around, the data within the widget will move accordingly. This is because the Scrollbar is updating the widget continuously as you move the slider. To change the Scrollbar so it will only update the widget when you let go of the slider, use the -jump option and set it to 1. The default for -jump is 0. You would most likely want to use -jump => 1 when your scrolled widget contains a large amount of data and waiting for the screen to update while you slide through it would make the application seem slow.

Assigning a Callback

When you create a Scrollbar, you tell it which widget to talk to and which method in that widget to call by using the -command option with an anonymous list. The list contains the name of the method to call and the widget from which that method should be invoked. In this code snippet, we can see that we want to use the yview command to scroll the widget $lb (a Listbox):

```
$scrollbar->configure(-command => ['yview' => $lb])
```

Now when the user clicks on the Scrollbar, it will invoke $lb->yview. We know that the Scrollbar associated with $lb is vertical because it uses the yview command. For a horizontal Scrollbar, use xview. Both yview and xview tell the widget to move the widget contents an amount that is determined by where the user clicked in the Scrollbar. The yview and xview methods are covered in the next section.

How the Scrollbar Communicates with Other Widgets

As described earlier, you use the -command option with the Scrollbar so it knows which widget and method to use when the Scrollbar is clicked. The command should be xview for horizontal Scrollbars and yview for vertical Scrollbars. You can call these methods yourself, but most of the time you won't want to.

Both xview and yview take the same type of arguments. Where the user clicks in the Scrollbar determines the value used, but the value will always be sent as one of the following forms:

```
$widget->xviewMoveto(fraction);
$widget->yviewMoveto(fraction);
```

This form is used when the user clicks on the slider, moves it around, and drops it again. The argument is a fraction, a real number from 0 to 1 that represents the first part of the data to be shown within the widget. If the user moves the slider all the way to the top or left of the Scrollbar, the very first part of the data in the widget should be seen on the screen. This means the argument should be 0:

```
$widget->xviewMoveto(0);
```

If the slider is moved to the center of the Scrollbar, the argument is 0.5:

```
$widget->xviewMoveto(0.5);
```

```
$widget->xviewScroll(number, "units");
$widget->yviewScroll(number, "units");
```

This form is used when the user clicks on one of the arrow elements in the Scrollbar. The widget should move its data up/down or left/right unit by unit.

The first argument is the *number* of units to scroll by. The value for *number* can be any number, but it's typically either 1 or –1. A value of 1 means the next unit of data on the bottom or right of the widget becomes visible (scrolling one unit of data off the left or top). A value of –1 means that a previous unit of data will become visible in the top or right of the widget (one unit will scroll off the bottom or right of the widget). For example, every time the user clicks on the down arrow in a vertical Scrollbar associated with a Listbox, a new line shows up at the bottom of the Listbox.

The second argument is the string "units". What a unit is depends on the widget. In a Listbox, a unit would be one line of text. In an Entry widget, it would be one character.

Here are some example calls:

```
# User clicked down arrow
$listbox->yviewScroll(1, "units");

# User clicked up arrow
$listbox->yviewScroll(-1, "units");

# User clicked right arrow
$entry->xviewScroll(1, "units");
```

```
$widget->xviewScroll(number, "page");
$widget->yviewScroll(number, "page");
```

This form is exactly like our previous one except the last argument is "page" instead of "units". When users click in the trough area of the Scrollbar (between the slider and arrows), they expect to see the data move by an entire page.

The type of page is defined by the widget being scrolled. For example, a Listbox would page up or down by the number of lines shown in the Listbox. It would page right or left by the width of the Listbox.

Scrollbar Configuration

You can get and set any of the options available with a Scrollbar by using cget and configure. See Chapter 13 for complete details on these methods.

Defining What We Can See

The set method, which we tell the scrolled widget about when we create it, defines what is visible. In our first example, we created a Listbox and told it to use our Scrollbar and the set method:

```
$scrollbar = $mw->Scrollbar();   # Vertical Scrollbar
$lb = $mw->Listbox(-yscrollcommand => ['set' => $scrollbar ]);
```

When the widget invokes the set command, it sends two fractions (*first* and *last*) as the arguments:

```
$scrollbar->set(first, last);
```

This will change the position in the data we are seeing. The arguments *first* and *last* are real numbers between 0 and 1. They represent the position of the first data item we can see and the position of the last data item we can see, respectively. If we can see all the data in our widget, they would be 0 and 1. The *first* value gets larger as more data is scrolled off the top, and the *last* value gets smaller as more data is scrolled off the bottom. You will probably never find a case in which to call set yourself, so just try to get an idea of what it does behind the scenes.

Figure 6-12 shows a hypothetical document that we are viewing with a vertically scrolled widget. The dashed rectangle represents the view of what we can currently see within the widget. When the widget calls set, it determines how far into the document the first viewable item is and sends this as the first argument. In Figure 6-12, this would be 10%, or 0.10. The second argument to set is how far into the document the last viewable item is. In our example, this would be 90%, or 0.90.

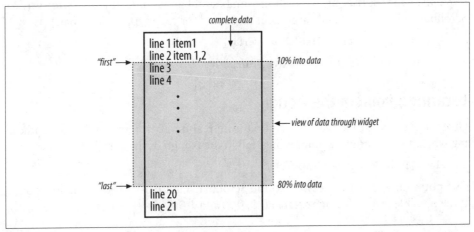

Figure 6-12. View of data through widget by set method (assumes vertical Scrollbar)

Getting the Current View

The get method returns in a list whatever the latest arguments to set were:

```
($first, $last) = $scrollbar->get();
```

This data can change if the widget requests a change in position of the data or if the Scrollbar requests a change.

Activating Elements in a Scrollbar

To determine which part of the Scrollbar is active, you can use the activate method:

```
$elem = $scrollbar->activate();
```

The value returned is an empty string (which means no element is currently active) or the name of the currently active element. The possible elements are "arrow1", "arrow2", or "slider".

If you send an element name as the argument to activate, that element will change to the color and relief specified by the -activebackground and -activerelief options. The element will continue to display that color and relief until an event (such as the mouse cursor passing over the element) causes it to change. Contrary to what you might believe, using activate does not invoke that element. Here are some examples:

```
$scrollbar->activate("arrow1");
$scrollbar->activate("arrow2");
$scrollbar->activate("slider");
```

There is no activate for "trough", because the trough doesn't change color when the mouse is over it.

Calculating Change from Pixels

The number returned by delta indicates how much the Scrollbar must change to move the slider *deltax* pixels for horizontal Scrollbars and *deltay* pixels for vertical Scrollbars. (The inapplicable argument is ignored for each type of Scrollbar.)

```
$amount = $scrollbar->delta(deltax, deltay)
```

The amount returned can be positive or negative.

Locating a Point in the Trough

Given a point at (x, y), fraction will return a real number between 0 and 1 indicating where that coordinate point would fall in the trough of the Scrollbar:

```
$loc = $scrollbar->fraction(x, y);
```

The point (x, y) must be relative to the Scrollbar. Figure 6-13 shows the location of three possible results from *fraction*: 0.0, 0.5, and 1.0.

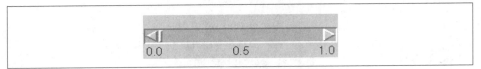

Figure 6-13. Example of values returned by the fraction method

Identifying Elements

The identify method returns a string containing the name of the element located at the (x, y) coordinate:

```
$elem = $scrollbar->identify(x,y);
```

If (x, y) is not in any element, the string will be empty. Both *x* and *y* must be pixel coordinates relative to the Scrollbar. The possible element names are "arrow1", "arrow2", "trough", and "slider".

Examples

These examples are included to hopefully clear up any confusion about using Scrollbars in the real world. Each example uses the Scrolled method if possible, then does the same thing manually. We haven't covered all the widget types we are using here, but we aren't doing anything fancy with them either. If you see an option or method you don't recognize, just see the appropriate chapter for that widget to learn more.

Entry Widget

The Entry widget can only be scrolled horizontally. The Entry can contain only one line of text at most, so a vertical Scrollbar would do nothing. Using Scrolled to create a scrolled Entry widget is easy:

```
$mw->Scrolled("Entry", -scrollbars => "s", -width => 30)->pack();
```

If you want to make the Scrollbar appear only when the data in the Entry widget requires it, use -scrollbars => "os". Using the Scrollbar method is a bit more work:

```
$scrollbar = $mw->Scrollbar(-orient => 'horizontal');
$entry = $mw->Entry(-width => 30,
                    -xscrollcommand => ['set' , $scrollbar]);
$scrollbar->configure(-command => ['xview', $entry]);
$scrollbar->pack(-side => 'bottom', -fill => 'x');
$entry->pack(-side => 'bottom', -fill => 'x');
```

Both will create an Entry that looks similar to the one in Figure 6-14.

Listbox, Text, and Canvas Widgets

A Listbox widget can be scrolled both horizontally and vertically, although you might not always want to use both options. If you know how wide your data is going

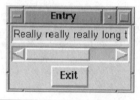

Figure 6-14. Entry widget with a Scrollbar

to be and the window can accommodate it, a horizontal Scrollbar is unnecessary. Our first example uses the Scrolled method and creates two Scrollbars:

```
$mw->Scrolled("Listbox", -scrollbars => "se",
              -width => 50, -height => 12)->pack();
```

To do the same thing manually, we need to use Scrollbar to create two Scrollbars and configure them to work with the widget:

```
$f = $mw->Frame()->pack(-side => 'top', expand => 1, -fill => 'both');
$xscroll = $f->Scrollbar(-orient => 'horizontal');
$yscroll = $f->Scrollbar();
$lb = $f->Listbox(-width => 50, -height => 12,
                  -yscrollcommand => ['set', $yscroll],
                  -xscrollcommand => ['set', $xscroll]);
$xscroll->configure(-command => ['xview', $lb]);
$yscroll->configure(-command => ['yview', $lb]);
$xscroll->pack(-side => 'bottom', -fill => 'x');
$yscroll->pack(-side => 'right', -fill => 'y');
$lb->pack(-side => 'bottom', -fill => 'both', -expand => 1);
```

As you can see, using Scrolled saves a lot of extra work. In Figure 6-15, we see a Listbox with two Scrollbars, one on the south and one on the east. This window was created using Scrolled. There is a subtle differencefrom one using Scrollbar: the small square of open space where the two Scrollbars meet in the southeast corner. When we create the Scrollbars ourselves, we don't get that small space (whichever Scrollbar gets packed first takes it).

Scrolled Text and Canvas widgets are created the same exact way as a scrolled Listbox widget, so we won't bother repeating the code again.

One Scrollbar, Multiple Widgets

There are times you want to use one Scrollbar with more than one widget. When the user clicks on the Scrollbar, it should scroll all the widgets in the same direction at the same time. In the following example, we create three Listboxes, each with eleven items. There is one Scrollbar that scrolls all three lists when the user clicks on it. When the user tabs to the Listboxes and scrolls up and down by using the arrow keys or the pageup/pagedown keys, the other Listboxes are also scrolled. Figure 6-16 shows what the window looks like.

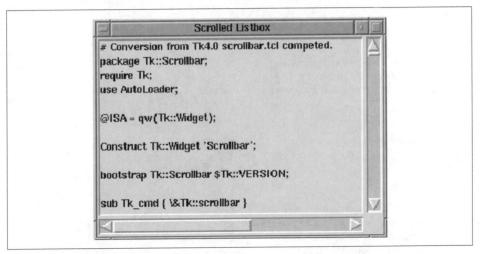

Figure 6-15. A Listbox with two Scrollbars

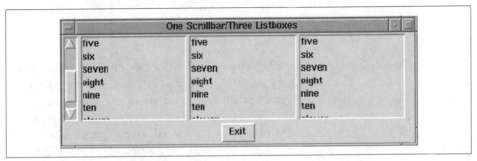

Figure 6-16. A window with three Listboxes all controlled by the same Scrollbar

The code is as follows:

```perl
use Tk;

$mw = MainWindow->new();
$mw->title("One Scrollbar/Three Listboxes");
$mw->Button(-text => "Exit",
            -command => sub { exit })->pack(-side => 'bottom');

$scroll = $mw->Scrollbar();
# Anonymous array of the three Listboxes
$listboxes = [ $mw->Listbox(), $mw->Listbox(), $mw->Listbox() ];

# This method is called when one Listbox is scrolled with the keyboard
# It makes the Scrollbar reflect the change, and scrolls the other lists
sub scroll_listboxes {
  my ($sb, $scrolled, $lbs, @args) = @_;
  $sb->set(@args); # tell the Scrollbar what to display
  my ($top, $bottom) = $scrolled->yview();
  foreach $list (@$lbs) {
```

```
        $list->yviewMoveto($top); # adjust each lb
    }
}

# Configure each Listbox to call &scroll_listboxes
foreach $list (@$listboxes) {
    $list->configure(-yscrollcommand => [ \&scroll_listboxes, $scroll,
                                          $list, $listboxes ]);
}

# Configure the Scrollbar to scroll each Listbox
$scroll->configure(-command => sub { foreach $list (@$listboxes) {
                                     $list->yview(@_);
                                 }});

# Pack the Scrollbar and Listboxes
$scroll->pack(-side => 'left', -fill => 'y');
foreach $list (@$listboxes) {
    $list->pack(-side => 'left');
    $list->insert('end', "one", "two", "three", "four", "five", "six",
                        "seven", "eight", "nine", "ten", "eleven");
}

MainLoop;
```

To connect multiple widgets to one Scrollbar, we first use the Scrollbar command to create the Scrollbar. Then we configure the Scrollbar so it calls yview for each of the Listboxes we are scrolling (the Listboxes are kept in an anonymous array so that all methods can reference them easily). The other part that makes the Listboxes truly connected is to configure each Listbox to call a special subroutine that scrolls all three Listboxes in addition to adjusting the Scrollbar. Normally, -yscrollcommand would have only ['set', $lb] assigned to it. Instead, we use a callback to \&scroll_listboxes and call set from within that subroutine.

## CHAPTER 7

The Listbox Widget

A Listbox widget is designed to list strings of text, one text string per line. You can then select a line or multiple lines from the Listbox on which to perform other operations. Some examples of things to place inside a Listbox include:

- An alphabetized list of cities.
- A list of servers to log in to. Select a server name and then enter a name and password into some Entry widgets. Click the OK Button to log in.
- A list of operating systems.
- A list of payment options: MasterCard, American Express, Visa, Check, Cash.

Figure 7-1 shows an example of a Listbox.

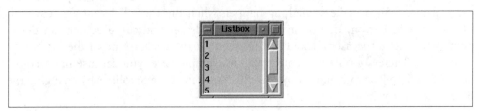

Figure 7-1. Listbox widget

A Listbox is ideal for replacing Radiobuttons or Checkbuttons that have become too numerous to display on the screen. Usually 3 or 4 Checkbuttons or Radiobuttons aren't a big deal, but if you try to display 10 at a time, the window could get a little crowded. A group of Radiobuttons can be replaced by a Listbox that limits the number of selections to one and has a default selection. A bunch of Checkbuttons can be replaced by a Listbox that allows multiple selections.

There are times when you'd like several Listboxes arranged side-by-side that scroll in parallel. While the standard Perl/Tk distribution doesn't have such a widget, Chapter 23 highlights some user-contributed "multi-Listbox" widgets.

An alternative to the plain Listbox are the HList and TextList widgets, which allow single lines to be configured individually.

Creating and Filling a Listbox

To create a Listbox widget, use the Listbox method on the parent of the Listbox:

```
$lb = $parent->Listbox( [ options ...] )->pack;
```

The Listbox method returns a reference to the Listbox that you've created. You can now use this reference to configure the Listbox, insert items into the Listbox, and so on. After creating a Listbox, use the insert method to insert items into it:

```
$lb->insert('end', @listbox_items);
# or...
$lb->insert('end', $item1, $item2, $item3);
```

The insert method takes an index value as the first argument; the rest of the arguments will be considered items to put into the Listbox. Listbox indexes are similar to the Entry widget indexes except they refer to lines instead of individual characters.

We could use a Listbox instead of Radiobuttons to select our window background color (see Chapter 4 for the Radiobutton example). The Listbox code looks like this:

```
$lb = $mw->Listbox(-selectmode => "single")->pack();
$lb->insert('end', qw/red yellow green blue grey/);
$lb->bind('<Button-1>',
          sub { $lb->configure(-background =>
                        $lb->get($lb->curselection()) );
              });
```

The -selectmode option limits the number of selections to one. We insert some colors from which to choose. There is no -command option for a Listbox, so we use bind (see Chapter 15) to make something happen when the user clicks on an item with the left mouse button. Using the Listbox methods get and curselection, we determine which item the user clicked on and then set the background of the Listbox to that color. There are only five colors in our example here; you can use more colors and add a Scrollbar to make it more useful. You can add a Scrollbar by changing the line with Listbox in it:

```
$lb = $mw->Scrolled("Listbox", -scrollbars => "e",
                    -selectmode => "single")->pack();
```

All the other lines in the program remain unchanged. For more information about adding and utilizing Scrollbars, see Chapter 6. Now that we've looked at an example, let's go over the options and methods that let us use the Listbox the way we want to.

Listbox Options

As with any of the widgets, you can configure the Listbox using options. The standard widget options are -cursor, -font, -height, -highlightbackground, -highlightcolor, -highlightthickness, -takefocus, -width, -xscrollcommand, and -yscrollcommand. The options specific to Listbox widgets will be further discussed later in this chapter.

`-background => color`
> Sets the color of the area behind the text.

`-borderwidth => amount`
> Sets the width of the edges of the widget. Default is 2.

`-cursor => cursorname`
> Sets the cursor to display when the mouse is over the Listbox.

`-exportselection => 0 | 1`
> Determines if the current Listbox selection is made available for the X selection as well. If set to 1, prevents two Listboxes from having selections at the same time.

`-font => fontname`
> Sets the font of any text displayed within the Listbox.

`-foreground => color`
> Sets the color of nonselected text displayed in the Listbox.

`-height => amount`
> Sets the height of the Listbox.

`-highlightbackground => color`
> Sets the color the highlight rectangle should be when the Listbox does not have the keyboard focus.

`-highlightcolor => color`
> Sets the color the highlight rectangle should be when the Listbox does have the keyboard focus.

`-highlightthickness => amount`
> Sets the thickness of the highlight rectangle. Default is 2.

`-relief => 'flat'|'groove'|'raised'|'ridge'|`**`'sunken'`**`|'solid'`
> Sets the relief of the edges of the Listbox.

`-selectbackground => color`
> Sets the color behind any selected text.

`-selectborderwidth => amount`
> Sets the width of the border around any selected text.

`-selectforeground => color`
> Sets the color of the text in any selected items.

`-selectmode => "single" | `**`"browse"`**` | "multiple" | "extended"`
> Affects how many items can be selected at once; also affects some key/mouse bindings for the Listbox (such as Shift-select).

`-setgrid => `**`0`**` | 1`
> Turns gridding off or on for the Listbox. Default is 0.

`-takefocus => 0 | 1 | undef`
> Determines whether the widget can have keyboard focus. 0 means never, 1 means always, undef means dynamic decision.

-width => *amount*
> Sets the width of the Listbox in characters. If amount is 0 or less, the Listbox is made as wide as the longest item.

-xscrollcommand => *callback*
> Assigns a horizontal Scrollbar to widget. See Chapter 6.

-yscrollcommand => *callback*
> Assigns a vertical Scrollbar to widget. See Chapter 6.

Selection Modes

As part of the Listbox widget, several choices exist for the way you can select items in the Listbox. You can have it so only one item at a time can be selected (emulating Radiobuttons) or you can have many different contiguous or noncontiguous items selected (emulating Checkbuttons). You control this behavior with the -selectmode option.

The possible select modes are "browse", "single", "multiple", or "extended". The default mode is "browse".

browse *and* single
> These modes are similar in that only one item can be selected at a time; clicking on any item will deselect any other selection in the Listbox. The browse mode has a slight difference: when the mouse is held down and moving around, the selection moves with the mouse. For bind purposes, a "<Button-1>" bind will be invoked when you first click down. If you want to catch the event when the mouse is released, define a ButtonRelease binding. (Binding events to widgets is discussed in Chapter 15.)

extended
> This mode lets you select more than one item at a time. Clicking on a single item with the left mouse button will deselect any other selection, but you can Shift-click or Control-click to add more items to your selection. Shift-clicking (holding down the Shift key while pressing a mouse button) will extend the selection from the already selected item to the newly selected item. Control-clicking (holding down the Control key while pressing a mouse button) will add the item being clicked to the selection, but it won't alter any of the other selections. You can also click an item with the mouse button, hold down the button, and then move the pointer over other items to select them. This is what's called a click-drag motion. Using "extended" allows for very fast selection of many different items in the Listbox.

multiple
> This mode also allows you to select more than one item. Instead of Shift-clicking or Control-clicking, you select items one at a time. Clicking on an unselected item will select it, and clicking on an already selected item will unselect it.

Operating System Differences

The -selectmode feature on Windows 95 does not allow the "multiple" selection mode, it behaves the same as "single" mode. On Unix and Windows NT, "multiple" mode works correctly.

When you select an item in a Listbox, by default it is made available as an X selection (meaning you can cut and paste it like any X selection in any window). Though this doesn't do anything with the clipboard on Win32 systems, it still affects the selection in multiple Listboxes. Items can be selected in only one Listbox at a time, even if you have more than one Listbox. The option -exportselection controls this. Use -exportselection => 0 to allow items to be selected in more than one Listbox at the same time.

Colors

In most widgets, there is a -background and a -foreground color. In addition to those, we also have the -selectbackground and -selectforeground color options in a Listbox. When a Listbox entry is selected, it appears in a different color.

Although you can change the color of the selected text, you can use only one color. You cannot make different lines in the Listbox different colors.

In Figure 7-2, the Listbox on the left has -foreground => 'red', -background => 'green'. The Listbox on the right has -selectforeground => 'red', -selectbackground => 'green'. Make sure the foreground and background values contrast with each other if you change these options.

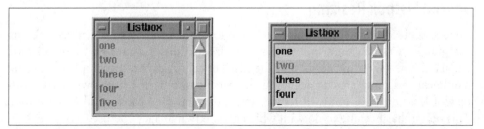

Figure 7-2. Examples of -foreground, -background, -selectforeground, and -selectbackground

Listbox Style

The default -relief of a Listbox is 'sunken'. The default -borderwidth is 2. Figure 7-3 shows the five different relief types (flat, raised, ridge, groove, and sunken). In the first window, the default -borderwidth is used; in the second window, a -borderwidth of 4 is used. To save space in the windows, we didn't draw any Scrollbars.

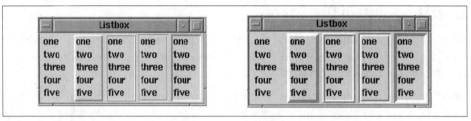

Figure 7-3. Examples of -relief and -borderwidth in Listboxes

Style of Selected Items

There is also a border width associated with any selected text. This is controlled by the -selectborderwidth option. Figure 7-4 shows what changing the selection border width to 4 does to the Listbox.

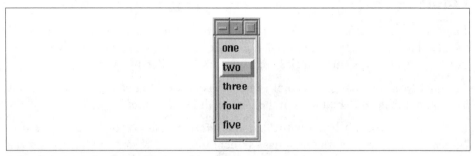

Figure 7-4. Example of -selectborderwidth => 4

Special Listbox Resizing

The -setgrid option changes how the window is drawn when it's resized. Using -setgrid => 1 causes the window to stay resized to the grid created by the Listbox widget. Essentially, this means that the Listbox will display only complete lines (no half lines) and complete characters. A side benefit is that the Listbox will always display at least one line and will remain in sight when the visible window is resized. This option has nothing to do with which geometry manager you use to put the Listbox in the window.

Configuring a Listbox

You can use the cget method to find out the current value of any of the Listbox options or the configure method to query or set any of the Listbox options. See Chapter 13 for more information on using the configure and cget methods.

Inserting Items

Use the `insert` method to add items to the Listbox:

```
$lb->insert(index, element, element ... );
```

Each *element* is another line in the Listbox. The *index* is a valid index (see the "Listbox Indexes" sidebar) before which the new elements will be inserted. For instance, to insert items at the end of the Listbox:

```
$lb->insert('end', @new_elements);
# Or
$lb->insert('end', "Item1", "Item2", "Item3");
```

To insert items at the beginning of the Listbox:

```
$lb->insert(0, @new_elements);
```

Deleting Items

You can use the `delete` method to delete items from the Listbox:

```
$lb->delete(firstindex [, lastindex ]);
```

The first argument is the index from which to start deleting. To delete more than just that one item, you can add a second index. The *firstindex* must be less than or equal to the *lastindex* specified. To delete all the elements in the Listbox:

```
$lb->delete(0, 'end');
```

To delete the last item in the Listbox:

```
$lb->delete('end');
```

Retrieving Elements

The get method returns a list of Listbox elements specified by the indexes *firstindex* to *lastindex*:

```
$lb->get(firstindex [,  lastindex ]);
```

If only the *firstindex* is specified, only one element is returned. The *firstindex* must be less than or equal to the *lastindex*. To get a list of all elements in the Listbox:

```
@elements = $lb->get(0, 'end');
```

To get the last item in the Listbox:

```
$lastitem = $lb->get('end');
```

To find out which items in the Listbox are selected, use the curselection method:

```
@list = $lb->curselection();
```

It returns a list containing the indexes of all currently selected items in the Listbox. If no items are selected, curselection returns an empty string. Here is an example of how the curselection method is used:

```
@selected = $lb->curselection;
foreach (@selected) {
   # do something with the index in $_
}
```

Remember that curselection returns a list of indexes, not elements.

Selection Methods

The curselection method, discussed in the preceding section, only tells you what the user has selected. You can also change the selection by using a form of the selection method.

Selecting Items

To select a range of items in a Listbox, you can use the "set" form of the selection method, selectionSet. selectionSet takes either a single index or a range. Any items not in the range are not affected. If you use a range, the *firstindex* must be less than or equal to the *lastindex*. Here are some examples:

```
# select everything
$lb->selectionSet(0, 'end' );
#select the first item
$lb->selectionSet(0);
```

Even if you have used -selectmode to limit the selection to only one item, you can force more than one item to be selected by using selectionSet(...).

Unselecting Items

To clear any selections in the Listbox, use the "clear" form of the selection method, selectionClear. Pass in an index or a range or indexes from which to clear the selection. For instance, to remove all the selections in the Listbox, you would do the following:

```
$lb->selectionClear(0, "end");
```

Any indexes outside the specified range will not be unselected; this allows you to unselect one item at a time. You can also clear the selection from just one item:

```
$lb->selectionClear("end");
```

Testing for Selection

To test if a specific index is already selected, use the "includes" form of selection, selectionIncludes. Calling selectionIncludes returns 1 if the item at the specified index is selected and 0 if it is not. For instance, to see if the last item in the list is selected:

```
if ($lb->selectionIncludes('end')) {
  ...
}
```

Anchoring the Selection

Using the "anchor" form of selection, selectionAnchor to set the index "anchor" to the specified index. The "anchor" is used when you are selecting several items within the Listbox with the mouse cursor. The first item you click (without letting up on the mouse button) becomes the "anchor" index. For example, use this to set the "anchor" as the first item in the list:

```
$lb->selectionAnchor(0);
```

Moving to a Specific Index

To cause the Listbox to show a specific item, use the see method:

```
$lb->see(index);
```

Given an index, see will cause the Listbox to page up or down to show the item at that index. For an example of using see, see "Listbox Example" later in this chapter.

Translating Indexes

The index method translates an index specification (such as "active") into the numerical equivalent. For instance, if the Listbox contains 12 items, $index = $lb-> index("end") sets the variable $index to 11. (Remember the first item in a Listbox is at index 0.)

Counting Items

The size method returns the total number of items in the Listbox:

```
$count = $lb->size( );
```

Active Versus Selected

The activate method sets the Listbox item at *index* to the active element. This allows you to access this item later using the "active" index. Figure 7-5 shows two windows with active elements underlined. Each Listbox also has the black highlight rectangle around it that indicates it has the keyboard focus (the active element isn't seen as marked unless the Listbox has focus).

```
# The first window activates the item "four"
$lb->activate(3);
$lb->focus();
# The second window activates the item "three"
$lb2->activate(2);
$lb2->focus();
```

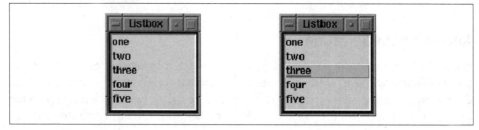

Figure 7-5. Windows showing a Listbox with an "active" element

Bounding Box

The method bbox returns a list of four elements that describes the bounding box around the text at *index*:

```
($x, $y, $w, $h) = $lb->bbox(index);
```

The four elements are (in order): x, y, w, and h. x and y are the (x, y) coordinates at the upper-lefthand corner of the bounding box. The w is the width of the text in pixels. The h is the height of the text in pixels. These measurements, relative to the Listbox, are shown in Figure 7-6.

Figure 7-6. Bounding box values around text

Finding an Index by y Coordinate

If you know a y coordinate in the Listbox, you can determine the index of the nearest Listbox item to it by using the nearest method:

```
$index = $lb->nearest(y)
```

The nearest method returns a number that corresponds to the index of the closest visible Listbox item.

Scrolling Methods

The Listbox can be scrolled both horizontally and vertically so it has both xview and yview methods and all their associated forms. These forms and how to use them are described in detail in Chapter 6.

The scan method allows you to use a really fast scrolling method. It is automatically bound to the second mouse button by the Listbox. Here is how you can do the same thing within your window:

```
$mw->bind("Listbox", "<2>",['scan','mark',Ev('x'),Ev('y')]);
$mw->bind("Listbox", "<B2-Motion>",['scan','dragto',Ev('x'),Ev('y')]);
```

When you click in the window with the second mouse button and then move your mouse around, you'll see the contents of the Listbox zip by at super-fast speed. You could change the second argument of each bind statement if you wanted to bind this to another combination of keys/mouse actions. The bind method is explained in Chapter 15.

Listbox Virtual Events

The Listbox widget has one virtual event, <<ListboxSelect>>, although it's not available in versions of Perl/Tk prior to 803.000. This event is generated any time the Listbox selection changes. So, when might we bind to this event?[*]

A common Listbox use is to bind <Button-1> to the widget, with the intent of executing a callback on the button click. Most people then assume that the active Listbox element is the one the button clicked on, but that's wrong, because Tk hasn't yet made that element active (unless it was already active). So if you *think* you want to do this:

```
$mpgs->bind('<1>' => sub {play $mpgs->get('active')}};
```

You probably *really* want this:

```
$mpgs->bind('<<ListboxSelect>>' => sub {play $mpgs->curselection}};
```

But until Tk 803.000 is here, do this instead:

```
$mpgs->bind('<ButtonRelease-1>' => sub {play $mpgs->get('active')}};
```

Or even this:

```
$mpgs->bind('<1>' => sub {
    play $mpgs->get( $mpgs->nearest($Tk::event->y) )
});
```

Listbox Example

Sometimes when you put a lot of items in a Listbox, it takes a long time to scroll through it. If you insert the items in the Listbox sorted, you can implement a search routine. Here's a quick script that shows you how to use an Entry widget to input the search text and search the Listbox every time you get a new character in the Entry:

```
use Tk;

$mw = MainWindow->new;
$mw->title("Listbox");
# For example purposes, we'll use one word for each letter
@choices = qw/alpha beta charlie delta echo foxtrot golf hotel india
              juliet kilo lima motel nancy oscar papa quebec radio sierra
              tango uniform victor whiskey xray yankee zulu/;

# Create the Entry widget, and bind the do_search sub to any keypress
$entry = $mw->Entry(-textvariable => \$search)->pack(-side => "top",
                                                     -fill => "x");
$entry->bind("<KeyPress>", [ \&do_search, Ev("K") ]);

# Create Listbox and insert the list of choices into it
my $lb = $mw->Scrolled("Listbox", -scrollbars => "osoe",
                       )->pack(-side => "left");
$lb->insert("end", sort @choices);

$mw->Button(-text => "Exit",
            -command => sub { exit; })->pack(-side => "bottom");
```

---

* Bindings and callbacks are described in Chapter 15.

```perl
MainLoop;

# This routine is called each time we push a keyboard key.
sub do_search {
  my ($entry, $key) = @_;

  # Ignore the backspace key and anything that doesn't change the word
  # i.e. The Control or Alt keys
  return if ($key =~ /backspace/i);
  return if ($oldsearch eq $search);

  # Use what's currently displayed in Listbox to search through
  # This is a non-complicated in order search
  my @list = $lb->get(0, "end");
  foreach (0 .. $#list) {
    if ($list[$_] =~ /^$search/) {
      $lb->see($_);
      $lb->selectionClear(0, "end");
      $lb->selectionSet($_);
      last;
    }
  }
  $oldsearch = $search;
}
```

## CHAPTER 8

The Text, TextUndo, and ROText Widgets

The Text widget is one of the most powerful standard widgets available in Perl/Tk. It is flexible, configurable, and easy to use for simple tasks. You can use Text widgets to:

- Display and edit a plain text file
- Display formatted text from an HTML document
- Create a scrollable color key, with Buttons that allow you change the colors
- Gather multiline, formatted text (including colors) from a user (act as a mini word processor)
- Display text with different colors based on the input
- Create hypertext windows that perform actions when clicked (either HTML or similar to the *widget* demo).*

You can put text as well as other widgets inside a Text widget. A Text widget can be used in conjunction with Scrollbars to allow many pages of information to be viewed in much less space.

Creating and Using a Text Widget

To create a Text widget, use the Text method from the desired parent widget:

```
$text = $parent->Text( [ options ... ] )->pack;
```

After the Text widget is created, there are several different ways to place text in it. The user can type directly into it, or you can use the insert method:

```
$text->insert('end', "To be or not to be...\nThat is the question");
```

The basic form of the insert method takes two arguments: an index value that indicates where to start placing the text, followed by the string to insert. For complete

---

* When you installed the Tk module with Perl, you also installed the *widget* demo. Type **widget** on the command line to see the capabilities of widgets in Perl/Tk.

details on the insert method and how to insert multiple strings at the same time, see the section "Inserting Text" later in this chapter.

A typical use of the Text widget is to read a file and place it in the Text widget as it's read:

```
$text = $mw->Scrolled("Text")->pack();
open (FH, "chapter1") || die "Could not open chapter1";
while (<FH>) {
  $text->insert('end', $_);
}
close(FH);
```

You can use the Text widget to display the file backward (line by line) by changing the insert line to $text->insert(0, $_). This will put the next line read at the top of the Text widget instead of at the end.

The Text widget can do a lot more than just display a file or two lines from a Shakespearean play. In addition to options, we also have tags, indexes, and marks to control how the contents of a Text widget are displayed.

Text Widget Options

Options used with the Text method change the way the text is displayed within the Text widget. The following options are standard for all the widgets (see Chapter 4, where the options were first covered, for further information):

-background => *color*
 Changes the color of the screen displayed behind the text.

-borderwidth => *amount*
 Sets the width of the edges of the widget.

-cursor => *cursorname*
 Sets the cursor displayed when the mouse cursor is in front of the Text widget.

-exportselection => 0 | **1**
 Determines if the text selected within the widget can also be used by the windowing system (such as X windows).

-font => *fontname*
 Sets the font in which the text is displayed.

-foreground => *color*
 Sets the color of the text.

-height => *amount*
 Sets the height of the widget. Default is 24.

-highlightbackground => *color*
 Sets the color the highlight rectangle around the widget should be when it does not have the keyboard focus.

`-highlightcolor => `*`color`*
> Sets the color the highlight rectangle around the widget should be when it has the keyboard focus.

`-highlightthickness => `*`amount`*
> Sets the thickness of the highlight rectangle around the widget. Default is 2.

`-insertbackground => `*`color`*
> Changes the color of the insert cursor.

`-insertborderwidth => `*`amount`*
> Changes the width of the insert cursor.

`-insertofftime => `*`time`*
> Sets the time the insert cursor blinks in the off position. Default is 300.

`-insertontime => `*`time`*
> Sets the time the insert cursor blinks in the on position. Default is 600.

`-insertwidth => `*`amount`*
> Sets the width of the insert cursor.

`-padx => `*`amount`*
> Adds extra space to the left and right of the text inside the Text widget's edge.

`-pady => `*`amount`*
> Adds extra space to the top and bottom of the text inside the Text widget's edge.

`-relief => 'flat'|'groove'|'raised'|'ridge'|`**`'sunken'`**`|'solid'`
> Sets the relief of the edges of the widget.

`-selectbackground => `*`color`*
> Sets the color of the area behind the selected text.

`-selectborderwidth => `*`amount`*
> Sets the width of the border of the selected area.

`-selectforeground => `*`color`*
> Sets the color of the selected text.

`-setgrid => `**`0`**` | 1`
> Enables gridding for the Text widget. Default is 0.

`-spacing1 => `*`amount`*
> Sets the amount of additional space left on top of a line of text that begins on its own line. Default is 0.

`-spacing2 => `*`amount`*
> Sets the amount of additional space left on top of a line of text after it has been wrapped around automatically by the Text widget. Default is 0.

`-spacing3 => `*`amount`*
> Sets the amount of additional space left after a line of text has been ended by a "\n". Default is 0.

`-state =>` **`'normal'`** `|` `'disabled'`
> Indicates the state of the Text widget. If set to `'disabled'`, no text can be inserted by either the user or the application (via the `insert` method).

`-tabs =>` *list*
> Specifies a list of tab stops to use in the Text widget. Default is every eight characters.

`-takefocus =>` `0` `|` `1` `|` **`undef`**
> Determines if widget can obtain keyboard focus.

`-width =>` *amount*
> Sets the width of the Text widget in characters. Default is 80.

`-wrap =>` `'none'` `|` **`'char'`** `|` `'word'`
> Sets the mode used to determine automatic line wrapping.

`-xscrollcommand =>` *callback*
> Determines the callback used when the Text widget is scrolled horizontally.

`-yscrollcommand =>` *callback*
> Determines the callback used when the Text widget is scrolled vertically.

Fonts

You can use the `-font` option to change the font, including how large or small the text is (see Figure 8-1). This defines the default font for the entire Text widget. Text that is inserted without a text tag (which allows you to specify formatting that applies only to certain portions of the text) will use this font.

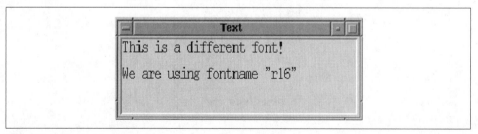

Figure 8-1. Text widget using -font => "r16"

The use of fonts was covered in Chapter 3, where we first discussed the `-font` option.

Widget Size

When you first create a Text widget, it will usually have a height of 24 lines and a width of 80 characters. Depending on how you put the Text widget in its parent window (whether you use `pack` with the `-expand` and `-fill` options or `grid` with `-sticky`

=> "nsew"), it can change size when the window changes size. To force the Text widget to a certain size, you can use the -width and -height options:

```
# Text widget 20 characters wide and 10 lines tall
$mw->Text(-width => 20, -height => 10)->pack;
```

While both options take numbers, they have different units associated with them. The value associated with -width is in characters* and the value associated with -height is lines of text. It's possible that the Text widget will not be that exact width and height if you force the main window to be larger via the minsize routine (i.e., $mw->minsize(400,400)), especially if you used -expand => 1 and -fill => 'both' with the pack command. So if you don't see what you expect on the screen the first time out, keep this in mind.

Widget Style

As with other widgets, you can change how the edges of the Text widget are drawn using the -relief and -borderwidth options. The examples shown in Figure 8-2 might not look much like Text widgets, but trust me, they are (they would look much more like Text widgets if there were scrollbars associated with each widget, but we were trying to save space in the screenshot)! Figure 8-2 also shows -width and -height options to force smaller size.

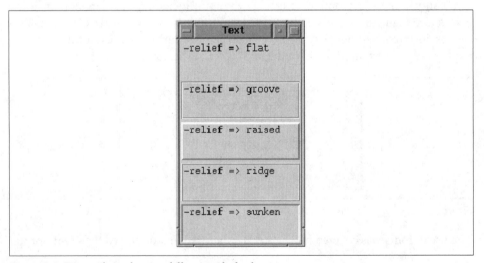

Figure 8-2. Text widgets showing different -relief values

---

* For a proportional font, the width is based on the width of the character "0".

Line Spacing

Long lines of text can wrap around automatically if the line becomes longer than the width the Text widget can display. The amount of room left between different types of lines is defined by using the -spacing*N* options. Figure 8-3 shows the different areas that -spacing1, -spacing2, and -spacing3 affect.

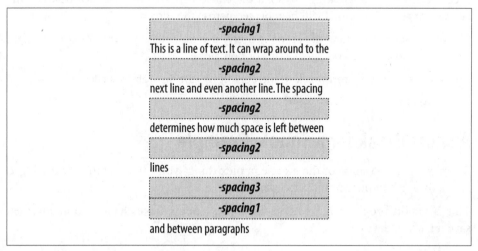

Figure 8-3. Example of -spacingN options

The -spacing1 option affects how much room is above a new line of text (the first line in a paragraph). The -spacing2 option affects the space between lines when text that is wrapped automatically is too long to fit on one line. The -spacing3 option determines how much room is left after a paragraph is finished (right after an explicit newline).

Tab Stops

The default setup for Text widget tab stops is every eight characters. Each tab equals eight spaces (but it doesn't actually use spaces). You can replace this default setting by using the -tabs option as follows:

```
-tabs => [qw/2 center/]   # Place tabs every 2 pixels
-tabs => [2, "center"]    # The same thing, different syntax
```

The argument that goes with -tabs is an anonymous list that specifies positions in which to place each of the tab stops. You can also specify an optional justification value for each tab stop (as in the preceding example) after each tab stop's numerical value. This all sounds much more confusing than it really is. Here are some examples to help clarify things:

```
-tabs => [qw/1i center/]   # every inch, text centered on tab-stop
-tabs => [qw/1i 1.5i/]     # ts at 1 inch, 1.5 inch and every .5 inch after
```

The default justification is "left". The possible justification values are "left", "right", "center", and "numeric".

When you specify the values (whether in centimeters, inches, or pixels), they are not cumulative. The list ["1i", "1.5i"] translates to one tab stop 1 inch from the left edge of the Text widget and the next tab stop 1.5 inches from the left edge. If the specified list isn't long enough to span the entire window, the distance between the last two tab stops specified will be repeated across the screen.

Of course, setting up new tab stops is pretty useless unless you're doing major text editing; in most cases, you'll leave this option alone.

You can reset the tab stops back to the default by setting -tabs to undef:

```
$text->configure(-tabs => undef);
```

A Short Break for a Simple Example

Before we get into some of the more complex things you can do with a Text widget, let's look at a complete application that uses it.

This is a short program that will display a file, let you make changes to it, and then save it back to disk:

```
use Tk;
$mw = MainWindow->new;
# Create necessary widgets
$f = $mw->Frame->pack(-side => 'top', -fill => 'x');
$f->Label(-text => "Filename:")->pack(-side => 'left', -anchor => 'w');
$f->Entry(-textvariable => \$filename)->pack(-side => 'left',
   -anchor => 'w', -fill => 'x', -expand => 1);
$f->Button(-text => "Exit", -command => sub { exit; } )->
  pack(-side => 'right');
$f->Button(-text => "Save", -command => \&save_file)->
  pack(-side => 'right', -anchor => 'e');
$f->Button(-text => "Load", -command => \&load_file)->
  pack(-side => 'right', -anchor => 'e');
$mw->Label(-textvariable => \$info, -relief => 'ridge')->
  pack(-side => 'bottom', -fill => 'x');
$t = $mw->Scrolled("Text")->pack(-side => 'bottom',
  -fill => 'both', -expand => 1);

MainLoop;

# load_file checks to see what the filename is and loads it if possible
sub load_file {
  $info = "Loading file '$filename'...";
  $t->delete("1.0", "end");
  if (!open(FH, "$filename")) {
    $t->insert("end", "ERROR: Could not open $filename\n");
    return;
  }
  while (<FH>) { $t->insert("end", $_); }
```

```
    close (FH);
    $info = "File '$filename' loaded";
}

# save_file saves the file using the filename in the Entry box.
sub save_file {
    $info = "Saving '$filename'";
    open (FH, ">$filename");
    print FH $t->get("1.0", "end");
    $info = "Saved.";
}
```

Text Indexes

When we talked about Listbox index values, each index referred to a line in the Listbox. The first line in the Listbox was at index 0, and so on. With a Text widget, the index can point to a specific line, but it can also point to a character within that line. An index for a Text widget is built using a base index and then optionally modifying that index. The entire index, base, and modifier should be put in double quotes.

Base Index Values

Here is a list of base index values:

'n.m'

> This format allows you to explicitly specify a line number and a character number within that line. Lines start at 1 (which is different than the Listbox widget), and characters start at 0.

'@x,y'

> The character in the widget that is closest to the (x, y) coordinate.

'end'

> The very end of the Text widget, after any "\n" characters as well.

'*mark*'

> This specifies the character after the location named *mark*. The two mark names provided by Tk are "current" and "insert". We'll discuss what they refer to later in this chapter.

'*tag*.first'

> A tag name is simply a placeholder for some special formatting instructions (discussed in the very next section). After creating tags, you can use this index form. *tag*.first is the first character in the Text widget that is of type *tag*. That is, you could create a "heading" tag and use a "heading.first" index.

'*tag*.last'

> This specifies the character directly after the text marked with *tag*.

$widget

> If you have an embedded widget, you can refer to its location within the Text widget by the variable referring to it.

$image

> You can have embedded images as of Tk 8.0. You can refer to their locations by using the variables referring to them.

Index Modifiers

The index modifiers can be used following a base index value.

[+ | -] count [chars | lines]

> You can use + and - to add or subtract lines and characters to a base index. The index "end - 1 chars" refers to text on the line before the "end". Be careful when you use this though, because any "\n" lines also count as complete lines.

linestart

> Modifies the index to refer to the first character on that line; that is, $t-> insert("end linestart", $string) will insert the string at the front of the last line in the Text widget. insert will place the new text before the index given.

lineend

> Refers to the last character in the line (usually the newline). It is useful when you don't know the exact number of characters in a line, but want to insert text at the end of it.

wordstart

> Adjusts the index to refer to the first character at the start of the word that contains the base index.

wordend

> Adjusts the index to refer to the character after the end of the word that contains the base index.

Text Index Examples

Here are some text index examples:

'end'

> The position right after the last line of text in the widget, no matter how much text is in the widget.

'1.0'

> The first character on the first line in the Text widget. The 1 represents the line, and 0 represents the character.

'2.0 - 1 chars'

> The last character on the end of the first line. We reference it by using the first character on the second line (2.0) and subtracting one character value from that.

If we use the `insert` method with this item, we insert the text right before the `"\n"` at the end of the first line.

`'1.end'`

Also the last character on the end of the first line. This is a simpler way of getting to it.

`'2.0 lineend'`

The end of the second line. It is necessary to specify 2.0, not just 2, because 2 is an invalid base index.

`'sel.first'`

The beginning of the current selection. This index might not exist if there isn't currently a selection.

The basic indexes are easy. When you start doing index arithmetic, it becomes a little more complicated. Just remember that you are referring to a position in the Text widget that may change if other text is inserted or deleted (either by the user or the application).

Although some of the combinations may seem silly (e.g., `'1.0 linestart'`), keep in mind that you will most likely be calling methods that return indeterminate information about an event. For example, a user clicks in the Text widget and presses a Button that will increase the font size of that entire line. The index arithmetic allows you to reference that entire line without even knowing for sure which line it is on.

Text Tags

Text tags give you another way to address portions of text in the Text widget. A tag has three purposes, and the same tag can serve all three or only one:

- Assigning formatting information to a portion (or portions) of text
- Associating a binding with text in the widget
- Managing selected text

Tags can change how the text appears on the screen; font, size, coloring, and spacing are a few of the text properties affected by tags. You change text properties by creating your own tags (with their own names) and using option/value pairs to assign formatting information. In addition to changing the formatting, you can use a tag to apply a specific binding (such as perform a task when the user double-clicks on that text). A special tag, `"sel"`, manages the selected text. Any time the user selects some text, the location of that text is marked with the `"sel"` tag.

Any of the text within the Text widget can have one or more tags associated with it. If you apply two tags to the same piece of text and they both alter the font, the last tag applied wins.

Tag Options

The options you can use to configure tagged text are mostly a subset of the configuration options of the Text widget itself. The configuration options for the Text widget are the defaults for all text in the Text widget. Using a tag allows you to change that formatting or binding on a case-by-case basis. There are some options that can be used only through tagged text.

-background => *color*
> Sets the color of the area behind the text.

-bgstipple => *pattern*
> Sets the pattern used to draw the area behind the text. Can create a shaded look.

-borderwidth => *amount*
> Sets the width of the relief drawn around the edges of the text, line by line.

-data => *scalar*
> Associates *scalar* with a tag, which allows you to store any amount of information for the tag. It can, of course, be a reference.

-elide => *boolean*
> If *boolean* is true, text covered by the tag is not displayed.

-fgstipple => *pattern*
> Sets the pattern used to draw the text.

-font => *fontname*
> Sets the font used for the text.

-foreground => *color*
> Sets the color of the text.

-justify => **'left'** | 'right' | 'center'
> Sets the position of the text within the Text widget.

-lmargin1=> *amount*
> Sets the amount of indentation from the left edge for the first line of a paragraph.

-lmargin2=> *amount*
> Sets the amount of indentation from the left edge for the second and greater lines of a paragraph. Sometimes called a hanging indent.

-offset => *amount*
> Sets the amount the text is raised or lowered from the baseline. Can be used to create superscripts and subscripts.

-overstrike => **0** | 1
> If a true value, causes the text to have a line drawn through it.

-relief => 'flat' | 'groove' | 'raised' | 'ridge' | 'sunken'
> Determines the way the edges of the text are drawn, line by line.

`-rmargin =>` *amount*

> Sets the amount of space left between the text and the right edge of the widget.

`-spacing1 =>` *amount*

> Sets the amount of additional space left on top of a line of text that begins on its own line. Default is 0.

`-spacing2 =>` *amount*

> Sets the amount of additional space left on top of a line of text after it has been wrapped around automatically by the Text widget. Default is 0.

`-spacing3 =>` *amount*

> Sets the amount of additional space left after a line of text has been ended by a "\n". Default is 0.

`-state =>` **'normal'** | 'hidden'

> Text is normally visible, but you may hide it if desired.

`-tabs =>` *list*

> Indicates the set of tab stops for this text. See "Tab Stops" earlier in this chapter for more detailed information.

`-underline =>` *boolean*

> Indicates that the text should be drawn with an underline.

`-wrap =>` 'none' | **'char'** | 'word'

> Determines the mode in which the text is wrapped. 'none' means lines that are longer than the Text widget is wide are not wrapped. 'char' will wrap at each character. 'word' will wrap between words.

A Simple Tag Example

Let's look at an example of how a simple tag is created and use it to insert some text into a Text widget (the resulting screen is shown in Figure 8-4):

```
$t = $mw->Text()->pack();
$t->tagConfigure('bold', -font => "Courier 24 bold");
$t->insert('end', "This is some normal text\n");
$t->insert('end', "This is some bold text\n", 'bold');
```

Line 1 creates the Text widget and places it on the screen.

Line 2 creates the 'bold' tag. Don't be fooled by the use of the word "configure" instead of "create." When you configure a tag, you are creating it. We created a tag named 'bold' and associated a different font with it (it happens to be the same as our Unix Text widget default font, just the bold version).

At this point, we haven't changed anything in the Text widget. We are just setting up to use the tag later in the code. You can use any name to indicate a tag as long as it is a valid text string. We could have named the tag "bold_font" or "big_bold_font" or "tag1". If you have good programming style (and want to be able to maintain your code), use a name that indicates what the tag does.

Line 3 inserts some text into the Text widget using the default formatting.

Line 4 inserts some more text into the Text widget but uses the 'bold' tag. The insert method allows us to specify a tag as the third argument. This causes that string of text to be inserted into the Text widget and assigned the tag 'bold'. The 'bold' tag was configured to change the font, so any text with the 'bold' tag will be shown with the different font.

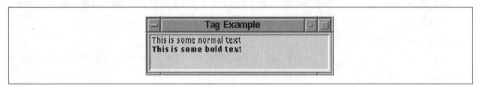

Figure 8-4. Text widget with normal and bold text

This is a pretty simplified example. What if we want to alter text that has been typed in by the user? We can't use the insert method then. We use the tagAdd method specifying a range of indexes to apply the tag to:

```
$t->tagAdd('bold', '1.0', 'end');
```

This applies the 'bold' tag to all the text within the Text widget.

Selections in a Text Widget Using the "sel" Tag

The "sel" tag is a special tag maintained by the Text widget. Any text the user selects will be assigned the "sel" tag. Unfortunately, there are no easy methods provided that help you determine if there is a selection or where it's located. Here are a few of the basic things you'll want to do with the selection.

To determine if the selection exists:

```
$if ($t->tagRanges('sel')) {
    ... do something with sel as an index ...
}
```

You may want to force the selection programmatically by using some of the tag methods (which we haven't covered yet) to put the "sel" tag on some text. For instance, to add the third line to the selected text:

```
$t->tagAdd('sel', '3.0', '3.0 lineend');
```

You can have multiple selections in the Text widget, and each time you call tagAdd, you're adding to the selection.

Here's an example that shows how to add another tag to the currently selected text:

```
$t->tagAdd('bold', 'sel.first', 'sel.last') if ($t->tagRanges('sel'));
```

When you use the "sel" tag as part of an index, you need to make sure the tag exists (using tagRanges) within the Text widget first or you'll get a really nasty error.

Here are two ways to get the currently selected text:

```
# Harder way:
$s1 = $t->get('sel.first', 'sel.last') if ($t->tagRanges('sel'));
# Easier way ($s2 is always set to something):
$s2 = $t->getSelected( );
```

The getSelected method is a convenience method for the Perl/Tk version of the Text widget. Look towards the end of this chapter in "The Perl/Tk Text Widget Extended Methods" for more selection convenience methods.

Configuring and Creating Tags

The first thing you'll do with a tag is create it by using tagConfigure (unless you're using the automatically defined "sel" tag). The first argument to tagConfigure is the name of the tag. The rest of the arguments (which are optional) are option/value pairs, as described earlier in the section "Tag Options." Here are some examples:

```
# creating a tag with no options
$text->tagConfigure("special");
# Creating a tag that will change the color
$text->tagConfigure("blue", -foreground => "blue");
# Creating a tag that will make underlined text
$text->tagConfigure("underline", -underline => 1);
# Creating a tag that changes the color and spacing
$text->tagConfigure("bigblue", -foreground => "blue", -spacing2 => 6);
```

You can change the settings for an already created tag by using tagConfigure a second time. Any changes you make to the tag immediately affect any text on the screen that has that tag:

```
# Add background color to "blue" tag
$text->tagConfigure("blue", -background => "red");
# Change the spacing for "bigblue"
$text->tagConfigure("bigblue", -spacing2 => 12);
```

As with widget configure methods, you can use tagConfigure to find the current settings for a specific tag. To get all the tag options and their values in a list of lists:

```
@listoflists = $text->tagConfigure("blue");
foreach $l (@list) { print "@$l\n"; }  # print it out
```

Each list within the list contains two elements: the option name and the value. You can limit the information you retrieve to a single option:

```
($option, $value) = $text->tagConfigure("blue", -font);
```

If you only want information on the value for a particular option, use tagCget:

```
$value = $text->tagCget("bigblue", -spacing2)
```

Adding a Tag to Existing Text

We've already seen an example of using the tagAdd method. It allows you to add a tag to portions of text in the Text widget. The usage of tagAdd is as follows:

```
$text->tagAdd('tagname', index1 [ , index2, index1, index2, ... ] )
```

You can add a tag to a single index or a range of indexes. This means you can add a tag to multiple places in the Text widget at the same time. Let's say you wanted to add the tag 'heading' to the 1st, 12th, and 30th lines because they are the location of some heading information that you want to look different than the rest of the text. The tagAdd line would look like this:

```
$text->tagAdd('heading', '1.0',  '1.0 lineend',
                         '12.0', '12.0 lineend',
                         '30.0', '30.0 lineend');
```

Now, assuming the formatting of 'heading' makes the font bigger, those lines show up differently than the defaults from the rest of the text in the widget.

You can add more than one tag to a section of text. For example, you can have both a 'heading' tag and a 'color' tag. If both tags try to alter the same option (such as -font), the last setting for that option wins.

Once you place a tag on a range of text, any text inserted between the beginning and ending indexes of that text will automatically get the tag of the characters surrounding it. This happens whether you are using insert without any specific tags or the user just types text into the Text widget. If you specify a tag with insert, it overrides the surrounding tags.

Using bind with Tags

One of the main reasons for tags is the ability to assign a binding to certain portions of the text. After creating a tag with tagConfigure, you can use bind so a callback will execute when a sequence of events happens (such as a mouseclick) on that tagged text. On our Button widgets, we have a default binding of <Button-1> that invokes the callback associated with the -command option. We can do the same thing with tagged text.

The best example is using text like a web hyperlink. When you click on the link, something happens: a new document is loaded, or another window is created and presented to the user. The basic form of a tagBind call is as follows:

```
$text->tagBind(tagname [, sequence, callback ] )
```

The callback is similar to that specified for the -command callback on a Button. The sequence is a description of the event that triggers the script. The only sequences you can specify are those that are keyboard or mouse related. (See Chapter 15 for more details on available events.)

The following code shows a psuedo-link example. All the link does when we click on it is show the end of the Text widget:

```
$t = $mw->Scrolled("Text", -width => 40)->pack(-expand => 1,
                                               -fill => 'both');
$t->tagConfigure('goto_end', -underline => 1, -foreground => 'red');
$t->tagBind('goto_end', "<Button-1>", sub { shift->see('end'); } );

# Setup Bindings to change cursor when over that line
$t->tagBind('goto_end', "<Any-Enter>",
            sub { shift->configure(-cursor => 'hand2') });
$t->tagBind('goto_end', "<Any-Leave>",
            sub { shift->configure(-cursor => 'xterm') });
$t->insert('end', "END\n", "goto_end");

# Insert a bunch of lines
for ($i = 1; $i <= 100; $i++) {
  $t->insert('end', "$i\n");
}
```

Inside the subs in the tagBind calls, we use the shift command to invoke a method. We can do this because the first argument sent to the bind callback is the Text widget. This is done implicitly for you. Whichever widget tagBind is invoked on is the widget that will be sent as the first argument to the callback. To use the Text widget more than once in the callback, assign it to a lexical variable; for example, my $widget = shift.

If we created our Text widget in the global scope of the program and placed a reference to the widget in the variable $t, we could also access the Text widget in the callback via the $t variable. This is only possible because $t is in the global scope and available during the callback. If you have two different Text widgets with which you want to use the same callback, use shift to get the correct Text widget:

```
$t1->tagBind('goto_end', "<Button-1>", \&goto_end );
$t2->tagBind('goto_end', "<Button-1>", \&goto_end );
sub goto_end {
  my $text = shift;
  $text->see('end');
}
```

Using the same callback for both Text widgets helps save space in your program.

To determine the bindings for a tagname, use tagBind with the tag name argument only:

```
@bindings = $text->tagBind("tagname");
```

The list will be empty if there are no bindings currently for that tag.

The Perl/Tk Text widget extended bindings

These bindings are particular to the Perl/Tk Text widget and do not exist in Tcl/Tk. The class methods are explained in the section "The Perl/Tk Text Widget Extended Methods."

<F1>Invokes the `clipboardColumnCopy` method.

<F2>Invokes the `clipboardColumnCut` method.

<F3>Invokes the `clipboardColumnPaste` method.

<Insert>Invokes the `ToggleInsertMode` method.

<3> Invokes the `PostPopupMenu` method.

Deleting All Instances of a Tag

Once a tag is created, you can use the `tagDelete` method to delete the tag:

```
$text->tagDelete(tagname [ , tagname ... ])
```

The tags are deleted completely when you use `tagDelete`. This means the text reverts back to the default configuration values, and any bindings or other information associated with those tags is also deleted.

The `tagDelete` method can be used if you are creating temporary tags dynamically within the program and need to delete the tags later when the information is no longer valid.

Removing a Tag from the Text

To remove the tag from a specific block of text, you can use the `tagRemove` method:

```
$text->tagRemove(tagname, index1 [, index2, index1, index2 ...])
```

Specify the name of the tag and an index or range of indexes from which to remove the tag. This leaves the tag intact; it merely removes it from the specific text indicated with the indexes.

Raising and Lowering Tags

When there are several tags applied to the same text, the last tag added to the text overrides the previous ones, and its configuration options are given priority. You can change the priority of the tags by using `tagLower` and `tagRaise`:

```
$text->tagLower(tagname [, belowtag ])
$text->tagRaise(tagname [ , abovetag ])
```

These methods take a tag name as the first argument. If there is no second tag argument, the first tag is given the highest or lowest priority. This affects the entire text in the Text widget, no matter where the tags are applied. If a second tag is specified, the first tag is placed specifically before or after the second tag.

Think of it as reordering a stack of tags (all applied to the same text). The tag on the top has the most say, and if it has a -foreground option of 'red', all the text with that tag will be red, regardless of what the other text tags set -foreground to. If we use tagRaise to move a tag with -foreground of 'blue' to the top, the tagged text will change to blue.

Getting Tag Names

You can find all the different tags that apply to a specific index, or to the whole Text widget, by using the tagNames method:

```
$text->tagNames([ index ])
```

If you specify an index, the list returned contains tags that apply only to that index. If a specific index isn't given, the list returned contains all the tags that apply to the entire Text widget whether or not that tag has been applied to text within the widget.

Determining Where a Tag Applies

If you know the name of the tag, you can find where it applies in the Text widget by using the range methods. The first method, tagRanges, returns a list that contains pairs of index values for the whole Text widget:

```
@list = $text->tagRanges("tagname")
# returns ( begin1, end1, begin2, end2 ... )
```

If no text in the Text widget has that tag, the returned list will be empty.

You can use the tagNextrange method to get the pairs of index values one at a time:

```
($start, $end) = $text->tagNextrange("tagname", index1 [ , index2 ])
```

The search for "tagname" will begin at index1 and go no farther than index2. If index2 is not specified, the search will continue until the end of the Text widget or until it finds the tagname, whichever comes first.

Inserting Text

Now that we've gone over text indexes and marks, we can talk in more detail about the methods for manipulating the widget's contents.

As we've seen from the many examples in this chapter, we use insert to put text into the Text widget. The first argument is an index and indicates where the text will be inserted. The second argument is the string to insert. The next argument (which is optional) is a single tag name or a reference to an array of tag names to assign to the inserted text. The usage is:

```
$text->insert(index, string, [ taglist, string, taglist ...] )
```

So far we've seen only single tags used with insert. If you want to specify more than one tag, put the tag names into square brackets, creating an anonymous array:

```
$t->insert('end', "This is a very tagged line",
           [ 'tag1', 'tag2', 'tag3' ]);
```

To use different sets of tags, supply additional text lines and additional tag lists:

```
$t->insert('end', "This is the heading", ['heading', 'underline'],
                  "Second line", ['bold', 'blue']);
```

When you use the insert command to insert more than one set of text with different tags, make sure they always come in pairs: text, tags, text, tags, and so on. If the tag used isn't defined (with tagConfigure), there will be no effect on the text, but the tag will still be assigned to that text. You can create the tag later if you wish.

You can also insert an entire newline-delimited file with a single insert call:

```
{
    local $/ = undef;
    $text->insert('1.0', <FILE_HANDLE>);
}
```

We set the input record separator to undef, so the entire file is slurped as a single string.

Inserting Lines Using print and printf

The Perl/Tk Text widget also has built-in TIEHANDLE methods for print and printf. This means that prints to file handles tied to a Text widget invoke these special subroutines. The subroutines then insert the print arguments into the Text widget.

The following example uses print and printf to insert lines into a Text widget (Figure 8-5 illustrates):

```
#!/usr/local/bin/perl -w
use POSIX 'acos';
use Tk;
use strict;

my $mw = MainWindow->new;
my $text = $mw->Text(qw/-width 40 -height 10/)->pack;

tie *STDOUT, ref $text, $text;

print "Hello Text World!\n";
printf "pi ~= %1.5f", acos(-1.0);

MainLoop;
```

Deleting Text

To remove text from the Text widget, you can use the delete method:

```
$text->delete(index1 [ , index2 ]);
```

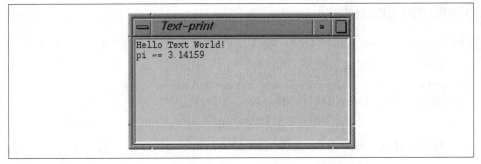

Figure 8-5. Lines inserted via print and printf

The first index argument is required, but the second is optional. If both are specified, the first index must be less than or equal to the second. All the characters from *index1* to (but not including) *index2* are removed from the Text widget. If you want to delete everything from the Text widget, you can use $text->delete("1.0", 'end').

Retrieving Text

The get function is one you'll use a lot. It returns the text located from *index1* to *index2*. If *index2* isn't specified, only the character located at *index1* is returned. The usage of get is as follows:

```
$t = $text->get(index1 [ , index2 ]);
```

As with any index ranges, *index1* must be less than or equal to *index2*, or an empty string will be returned.

Translating Index Values

When you work with indexes, it helps to convert a complicated index form into a simpler one. The index method returns an index with the form *line.char*:

```
$newvalue = $text->index(index1);
```

The *index1* value can be any valid index expression.

Comparing Index Values

You can compare two index values by using the compare method.

```
$text->compare(index1, op, index2);
```

You pass the first index, the test operation to perform, and the second index. The values for *op* are: "<", "<=", "==", ">=", and "!=". The function returns 1 if the test is true and 0 if it isn't. The following call returns 1 because the index "1.0" is less than "end":

```
$status = $text->compare("1.0", "<=", "end");
```

Showing an Index

The see method causes the Text widget to show the portion of it that contains *index*:

```
$text->see(index);
```

The text within the widget will be scrolled up or down as a result of this call. If the *index* is already visible, nothing happens.

Getting the Size of a Character

The bbox method returns a list containing four items that describe the box around the character at *index*:

```
($x, $y, $w, $h) = $text->bbox(index);
```

The first two items returned are the x and y coordinates of the upper-left corner. The last two are the width and height of the box. The bounding box describes only the visible portion of the character, so if it is half hidden or not visible at all, the values returned will reflect this.

Getting Line Information

The dlineinfo method returns a list of five items. These items describe the area of the line that contains *index*:

- X coordinate of the upper-left corner
- Y coordinate of the upper-left corner
- Width of the area
- Height of the area
- Baseline position of the line, measured from x

Here is an example call:

```
($x, $y, $w, $h, $base) = $text->lineinfo("index");
```

Unlike the bbox method, even areas not shown (due to nonwrapped characters) are used in the calculations, as long as some of the line is showing. However, if the line is not visible at all on the screen, the list will be empty. If the line happens to wrap to multiple lines, the entire area is used.

Searching the Contents of a Text Widget

You can use the search method to search the Text widget for a pattern or regular expression. The search method takes some optional switches, the pattern to search for, and an index at which to start searching:

```
$index = $text->search([switches], pattern, index, [ stopindex ])
```

Search Options

`-forwards`

Tells search to search forward through the Text widget starting at *index*. This is the default.

`-backwards`

Tells search to search backward through the Text widget starting at the character before *index*.

`-exact`

The *pattern* must match the text exactly. This is the default.

`-regexp`

The *pattern* will be considered as a regular expression.

`-nocase`

Ignores case between *pattern* and the text within the Text widget.

`-hidden`

Searches text even if it has a tag with `-state => hidden`.

`-count => varname`

varname is a pointer to a variable (i.e., `\$variable`). The number of characters matched will be stored within that variable.

`--`

This option does nothing except force the next argument to be taken as the *pattern* even if the next string starts with a `"-"`.

If a match is made, the index returned points to the first character in the match. If no match is made, an empty string is returned.

Here is a simple example of using search:

```
$result = $text->search(-backwards => "find me", 'end');

$location = $text->search(-nocase => "SWITCHES", "1.0");
```

See the "Search Options" sidebar for more information.

Scrolling

The Text widget can be scrolled both horizontally and vertically, so it implements both xview and yview methods. These two methods are described in Chapter 6.

Marks

There are several ways to refer to different positions throughout the Text widget. An index value refers to a character. A tag is a named reference to a specific character or group of characters. The term *mark* refers to the spaces between characters. Similar to tags, a mark has a name. For example, the "insert" mark refers to the position of the insert cursor. However, tags refer to the actual characters, and if those characters are deleted, the tag is no longer associated with those characters. The mark stays in place whether the characters surrounding it are deleted or other characters are added. Marks can refer only to one location within the Text widget at a time.

Once a mark is created, you can use it as an index. The gravity of the mark will determine if the mark moves or not when you insert text with it. Using a gravity of 'right' (the default) means that any text inserted using that mark will go to the left of the mark. A gravity of 'left' means that text inserted using that mark will go to the right of the mark. Another way to think about it is the gravity tells you which side the mark will stick to. For example, suppose we have the string "abcdef" and place the mark in between the c and the d. We'll represent the mark as a ^ character. Using 'right' gravity, "abc^def" becomes "abc1232^def" because the mark sticks to the character to its right. Using 'left' gravity, "abc^def" becomes "abc^123def" because the mark sticks to the character to its left.

There are two special marks that are set automatically by the Text widget: "insert" and "current". The "insert" mark is wherever the insert cursor is. The "current" mark is the position closest to the mouse and adjusts as the mouse moves (as long as a mouse button is pressed). Both marks are maintained internally and cannot be deleted.

You will also see a mark called "anchor" that shows up in the markNames method after you click in the Text widget. It always has the same index value as the "insert" mark, but "anchor" might not always exist.

Setting and Getting the Gravity

To set the gravity of the mark, you can use markGravity:

```
$text->markGravity(markname [ , direction ])
```

The possible values for *direction* are "right" and "left". The default gravity for new marks is "right". If you don't specify a gravity, the current gravity for that mark is returned.

Determining Mark Names

To get a list of all the marks in the Text widget, you can use markNames:

```
@names = $text->markNames()
```

There are no arguments to the markNames function, and it returns a list. Here is an example of how to report the marks within the Text widget:

```
$f->Button(-text => "Report",
           -command => sub { my @m = $t->markNames();
                 foreach (@m) {
                     print "MARK: $_ at ", $t->index($_), "\n";
           }})->pack(-side => 'left');
```

The results after clicking in the window to set the insertion cursor are as follows:

```
MARK: insert at 2.15
MARK: anchor at 2.15
MARK: current at 3.0
```

Creating and Deleting Marks

You can create a mark and set it at a specific index by using the markSet method.

```
$text->markSet(markname, index)
```

In addition to the *markname* you want to create, specify the *index* where the mark should be placed. For instance, if you always want to be able to insert at the end of line 3:

```
$text->markSet("end of line3", "3.0 lineend");
...
$text->insert("end of line3", "text to insert");
```

The markUnset method removes the mark from the Text widget and deletes the mark completely. It will no longer show up in the markNames list after it has been unset, and it can't be used as an index value either. You can specify more than one *markname* in markUnset:

```
$text->markUnset(markname [, markname, markname ... ])
```

Embedding Widgets

One of the best things you can do with a Text widget is put other widgets (such as Button or Entry widgets) inside it. One advantage of embedding widgets is you can create a scrolled set of widgets on a line-by-line basis.

Before we go over all the different functions available to work with embedded widgets, let's look at a quick example. We often want to do a lot of data entry in a program, which means we need a lot of Label and Entry widgets. Sometimes there are so many of them that it's hard to fit them all on the screen without making a mess of the window. By using a scrolled Text widget and putting the Label and Entry widgets inside it, we can create a lot more widgets in a smaller space. Here's the code:

```
use Tk;

$mw = MainWindow->new;
$mw->title("Data Entry");
$f = $mw->Frame->pack(-side => 'bottom');
$f->Button(-text => "Exit",
           -command => sub { exit; })->pack(-side => 'left');
$f->Button(-text => "Save",
           -command => sub {  # do something with %info;
                    })->pack(-side => 'bottom');
$t = $mw->Scrolled("Text", -width => 40,
                   -wrap => 'none')->pack(-expand => 1, -fill => 'both');
```

```
foreach (qw/Name Address City State Zip Phone Occupation
            Company Business_Address Business_Phone/) {
    $w = $t->Label(-text => "$_:", -relief => 'groove', -width => 20);
    $t->windowCreate('end', -window => $w);
    $w = $t->Entry(-width => 20, -textvariable => \$info{$_});
    $t->windowCreate('end', -window => $w);
    $t->insert('end', "\n");
}
$t->configure(-state => 'disabled'); # disallows user typing

MainLoop;
```

Figure 8-6 shows the Win32 version of this window.

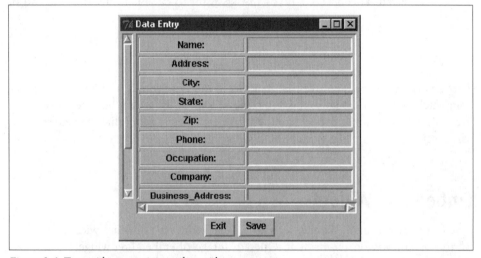

Figure 8-6. Text widget containing other widgets

We disable the Text widget before running MainLoop because we don't want the user to be able to type text directly into the Text widget. This only disables the ability to enter or delete text; the internal widgets still function normally. We also turn off the -wrap option so the Label and Entry widgets don't accidentally drop down to the next line when the window is resized.

You could put a Text widget inside another Text widget, but you probably wouldn't want to.

windowCreate, windowCget, and windowConfigure

As you can see from the preceding example, we use the windowCreate method to insert an embedded widget. The widget should have been created already, and it should be a child of the Text widget. The general syntax is:

```
$widget = $text->Widget( ... );
$text->windowCreate(index, -window => $widget,[option => value ] );
```

In the previous example, we used the 'end' index. You can use any valid Text widget index to insert the embedded widgets. The only option we used was a -window option with the reference to the new $widget.

Here are the available options for the windowCreate method:

-align => ['baseline' | 'bottom' | **'center'** | 'top']
Determines where the widget is placed within the line if it is not as tall as the line itself.

-padx => *amount*
-pady => *amount*
Adds space around the widget in the x and y directions, respectively (-padx => 10).

-stretch => 0 | 1
Takes a Boolean value (1 or 0). A true value will stretch the widgets to fill the line from top to bottom.

-window => $widget
Takes a reference to another widget.

There are several different forms of the window method. The first one, the "Create" form, creates the widget within the Text widget. The "Names" form lets you know what types of widgets are embedded in the Text widget:

```
@types = $text->windowNames();
```

The results use the format of the Tcl widget hierarchy (see Chapter 13):

```
.text.radiobutton .text.label .text.button .text.entry .text.checkbutton
```

Use the windowCget method to get information about the options used when the window was created in the Text widget:

```
$value = $text->windowCget(index, option);
```

To use windowCget, you need to know the index the widget is currently occupying (each widget occupies one character in the Text widget, even if it looks like it takes more space).

windowConfigure allows us to change the options associated with the widget at *index* or retrieve the value of the configuration option:

```
$text->windowConfigure(index [, option => value ] );
```

Remember that the only options you can use with this method are -align, -padx, -pady, -stretch, and -window. Other than this, windowConfigure(...) behaves just like a regular widget's configure method. To make changes on the $widget directly, use $widget->configure(...).

Internal Debug Flag

The debug function takes an optional Boolean argument:

```
$text->debug( [ boolean ] );
```

If the value passed in is true, internal consistency checks will be turned on in the B-tree code associated with Text widgets. If false, the checks will be left off. Without any argument, the debug method will return the value "on" if it has been turned on and "off" if not. All text widgets in the application share the same debug flag.

Scanning

The scanMark and scanDragto methods are used internally in the Text widget. A call to scanMark simply records the (x, y) passed in for use later with scanDragto. It returns an empty string:

```
$text->scanMark(x, y);
```

scanDragto also takes (x, y) coordinates, which are compared to the scanMark (x, y) coordinates. The view within the Text widget is adjusted by 10 times the difference between the coordinates:

```
$text->scanDragto(x, y);
```

The Perl/Tk Text Widget Extended Methods

These methods are available only with the Perl/Tk Text widget and are documented nowhere else but in this book. Another unique feature is the built-in Menu, activated by a <Button-3> click, which calls many of these methods for common text-related activities. The built-in Menu is shown in Figure 8-7.

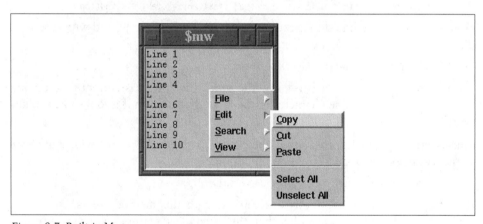

Figure 8-7. Built-in Menu

To disable the default Menu, use $text->menu(undef). To supply your own Menu, first create it and then use $text->menu(my_menu).

Here, then, is the complete list of extended Text widget methods. These methods should be considered experimental, so use them with caution and expect that you may have to change your code in the future.

$text->adjustSelect

Moves the end point of selection and anchor point to the mouse pointer location.

$text->clipboardColumnCopy

Performs a rectangular copy of the currently selected text, with basic compensation for tab characters.

$text->clipboardColumnCut

Performs a rectangular cut of the currently selected text, with basic compensation for tab characters.

$text->clipboardColumnPaste

Performs a rectangular paste of the text in the clipboard. The upper-left corner is specified by the current position of the insert mark, with basic compensation for tab characters.

$text->deleteSelected

Deletes the currently selected text.

$text->DeleteTextTaggedWith(*tag*)

Deletes the text tagged with the *tag* parameter.

$text->deleteToEndofLine

Deletes from the insert mark location to end of line.

$text->FindAll(*mode, case, pattern*)

First removes any current selections, then performs a global text search, tagging all matches with the sel tag. *mode* can be -exact or -regexp, and *case* can be -nocase or -case. *pattern* is an exact string to match if *mode* is -exact or a regular expression if the match *mode* is -regexp.

$text->FindAndReplaceAll(*mode, case, find, replace*)

Works just like FindAll, but additionally substitutes the matched text with the characters *replace*.

$text->FindAndReplacePopUp

Creates a find-and-replace popup if one doesn't already exist. If there is text currently selected, pre-fills the "find" field with it.

$text->FindNext(*direction, mode, case, pattern*)

First removes any current selections, then performs a forward or reverse text search, tagging a match with the sel tag. *direction* can be -forward or -reverse. *mode*, *case*, and *pattern* are as for FindAll.

$text->FindPopUp

Creates a find popup, if one doesn't already exist. If there is text currently selected, pre-fills the "find" field with it.

$text->FindSelectionNext

Gets the currently selected text and removes all selections. It then finds the next exact, case-sensitive string that matches in a forward direction, selects the new text, and makes it visible.

`$text->FindSelectionPrevious`
> Gets the currently selected text and removes all selections. It then finds the next exact, case-sensitive string that matches in a reverse direction, selects the new text, and makes it visible.

`$text->getSelected`
> Returns the currently selected text.

`$text->GetTextTaggedWith(`*tag*`)`
> Returns the text tagged with the *tag* parameter.

`$text->GotoLineNumber(`*line_number*`)`
> Sets the insert mark to *line_number* and displays the line.

`$text->GotoLineNumberPopUp`
> Displays a popup, pre-filling it with selected numeric text, if any, or the line number from `GotoLineNumber`, if any.

`$text->Insert(`*string*`)`
> Inserts *string* at the point of the insertion cursor. If there is a selection in the text, and it covers the point of the insertion cursor, delete the selection before inserting.

`$text->InsertKeypress(`*character*`)`
> Inserts *character* at the insert mark. If in overstrike mode, delete the character at the insert mark first.

`$text->InsertSelection`
> Inserts the current selection at the insert mark.

`$text->insertTab`
> Inserts a tab (\t) character at the insert mark.

`$text->markExists(`*markname*`)`
> Returns true if *markname* exists.

`$text->menu(?`*menu*`?)`
> Returns the Text widget's Menu reference if *menu* is omitted, disables the Menu if *menu* is undef, or changes the Menu if *menu* is another Menu reference.

`$text->openLine`
> Inserts a newline (\n) at the insert mark.

`$text->OverstrikeMode(?`*boolean*`?)`
> Returns the overstrike mode if *boolean* is omitted or sets the overstrike mode to *boolean*. True means overstrike mode is enabled.

`$text->PostPopupMenu(x, y)`
> Creates a popup Menu at the specified (x, y) pixel coordinates. The default Menu has File, Edit, Search, and View menu items that cascade to submenus for further commands. There is an implicit <Button-3> binding to this method that posts the Menu over the cursor.

`$text->ResetAnchor`
> Sets the selection anchor to whichever end is farthest from the index argument.

`$text->selectAll`
> Selects all the text in the widget.

`$text->selectLine`
> Selects the line with the `insert` mark.

`$text->selectWord`
> Selects the word with the `insert` mark.

`$text->SetCursor(`*`position`*`)`
> Moves the insert mark to *position*.

`$text->ToggleInsertMode`
> Toggles the current overstrike mode.

`$text->unselectAll`
> Unselects all the text in the widget.

`$text->WhatLineNumberPopUp`
> Creates a popup that displays the current line number of the `insert` mark.

For a demonstration of these extended Text widget features, run the widget demonstration "Gedi master advanced text editor"[*] from the "User Contributed Demonstrations" section of the program.

The TextUndo Widget

The TextUndo widget is derived from the Text widget, which simply means that it shares all the capabilities of its ancestor. In object-oriented terminology, we say that TextUndo is a subclass of Text (or, Text is a superclass of TextUndo). You'll learn more about this subject in Chapter 14.

Of course, we expect TextUndo to do *something* different from Text, and it does: it has unlimited undos and redos so that previous editing operations can be rescinded or redone.

Here are the TextUndo methods above and beyond those available for a Text widget:

`$textundo->ConfirmDiscard`
> Displays a messageBox that says "Save edits?". Returns 0 if yes or cancel, 1 if no.

`$textundo->ConfirmEmptyDocument`
> Displays a messageBox that says "Save edits?." The widget is cleared if the reply is no.

---

[*] Yes, that's "Gedi," not "Jedi" (with apologies to George Lucas).

`$textundo->ConfirmExit`
    Destroys the widget if you answer yes.

`$textundo->CreateFileSelect`
    Creates a popup file browser to select a filename.

`$textundo->deleteStringAtStartOfSelectedLines(`*`string`*`)`
    Deletes *string* from the start of every selected line.

`$textundo>->EmptyDocument`
    Deletes all text and undo/redo information; undefs the filename.

`$textundo->FileName(?`*`pathName`*`?)`
    Optionally updates the current filename to *pathName*. Returns the current file-name.

`$textundo->IncludeFile`
    Similar to Load, except it does not call EmptyDocument first.

`$textundo->insertStringAtStartOfSelectedLines(`*`string`*`)`
    Inserts *string* at the start of every selected line.

`$textundo->Load(`*`pathName`*`)`
    Loads the contents of *pathName* into the widget.

`$textundo->numberChanges`
    Returns the number of current undo operations.

`$textundo->redo`
    Redoes the previous operation.

`$textundo->ResetUndo`
    Deletes all undo and redo information.

`$textundo->Save(?`*`pathName`*`?)`
    Saves the contents of the widget to a file. If *pathName* is not specified, the file-name from the last Load call is used. If no file was previously loaded an error message pops up. The default filename of the last Load call is not overwriten by *pathName*.

`$textundo->SizeRedo`
    Returns the number of current redo operations.

`$textundo->undo`
    Undoes the previous operation.

TextUndo Virtual Events

The TextUndo widget supports two virtual events, <<Undo>> and <<Redo>>, which invoke the undo and redo methods, respectively. The key sequence Control-Z is bound to <<Undo>>, and Control-Y is bound to <<Redo>>.

The ROText Widget

The ROText widget is yet another widget derived from the basic Text widget. As you might suspect, RO stands for read-only. The ROText widget can only be manipulated programmatically via method calls; any bindings that might alter the contents of the widget have been removed. Other bindings that don't change the contents will remain the same; for instance, the user can still scroll up and down, as well as select, find, and copy text from within an ROText widget.

This widget is often used to present instructions, help information, or other data. One of the benefits of using a ROText widget over a Text widget is that you don't have to keep changing the state of the widget in order to insert data into it. If you set the -state of a Text widget to 'disabled', you need to set it back to 'enabled' even before you can do a programmatic insert. This is very tedious if you have a lot of updates and changes to the data in response to a user's action. Using ROText solves this problem for you nicely.

Other than the read-only aspect of ROText, you can simply pretend this a Text widget as you code. That's one of the beautiful aspects of object-oriented programming: this widget is used identically to a Text widget, at least from the programmer's point of view.

## CHAPTER 9

The Canvas Widget

The Canvas widget is used mainly for drawing items such as arcs, lines, rectangles, circles, and so on, but you can also place text and other widgets inside a Canvas widget. Here are some examples of how you can use a Canvas widget:

- Create a drawing program.
- Display a graph based on input from the user.
- Create a customized slider.

Figure 9-1 shows a Canvas widget.

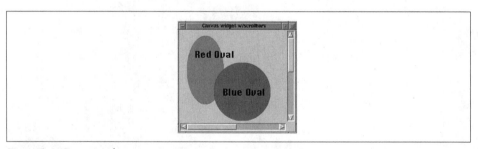

Figure 9-1. Canvas widget

Each item you create in a Canvas widget is assigned a unique *item ID*, which is a positive integer. Using an item's ID is a common way of addressing individual Canvas items, but you can devise tag names and use them as well. All Canvas items can have bindings attached to them for easy interaction with the user.

Creating a Canvas

It's easiest to always use the Scrolled method to create a Canvas, unless you know for sure your Canvas is going to be a fixed size that will fit in the window:

```
$canvas = $mw->Canvas( [ option => values, ... ] )->pack();
# or...
$canvas = $mw->Scrolled('Canvas', [ option => values, ... ])->pack();
```

The first line creates just a Canvas and the second creates a Canvas with Scrollbars. (See Chapter 6 for more information on the Scrolled method.) To create a Canvas widget, use the desired parent widget to invoke the Canvas method and pass any initial options in with their values. The Canvas method returns a reference to the newly created Canvas widget.

The Canvas Coordinate System

A Canvas widget uses a coordinate system to locate items within it, but the coordinate system isn't Cartesian, as you might expect. It's more like an upside-down coordinate system (much like the coordinate system described in Chapter 2).

Figure 9-2 shows a diagram that demonstrates the coordinate system a Canvas widget uses.

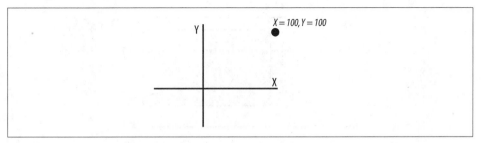

Figure 9-2. Canvas coordinate system

The x coordinates behave normally: the larger coordinates are to the right and the smaller ones are to the left. The y coordinates look like they have been drinking vodka: the larger y coordinates are on the bottom rather than on the top, because the (0, 0) point is in the upper-left corner. Although it is rare, you can use negative coordinates in a Canvas.

The coordinate system isn't too hard to deal with once you understand it, but if you try to draw a building with a standard coordinate system in mind, your building will be upside down.

There are several ways to deal with this. First, adjust your way of thinking so you always think y coordinates are larger at the bottom (never mind all those years we all struggled through geometry classes). Or, you can be stubborn and think in normal coordinates, and have your program multiply all y coordinates by –1 before sending them to the Canvas functions.

Whichever way you decide to deal with it, be consistent and make sure you comment your code.

The x and y coordinates can be specified in any valid screen unit. If you follow the coordinate number with a letter m, you are measuring distance in millimeters. The other letters you can use are p for printer points, i for inches, and c for centimeters. The default is pixels, which is what we'll use for all the examples in this chapter.

The Scrollable Region

The scrollable area is the portion of the Canvas widget you want the user to be able to see. If you don't create a scrollable area (by using the -scrollregion option), the user can scroll infinitely in any direction, and the Scrollbars don't reflect where items on the Canvas are.

Figure 9-3 shows an example of the scrollable area compared with the area that is visible in the Canvas. If these two areas are the same size, you don't need Scrollbars on the Canvas (if you use Scrollbars, their sliders will completely fill the trough area).

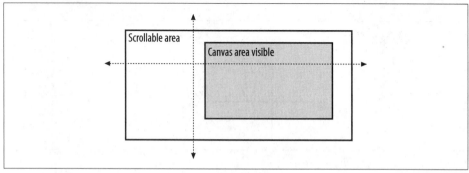

Figure 9-3. Scrollable area compared with visible area

The arrows on the axis markers in Figure 9-3 indicate that the Canvas can still be larger than the indicated scrolling area. For instance, if you decide to insert a circle beyond the scrolling area, you have to adjust the scrollable area so the user will be able to see the new circle.

The best way to do this is to use the bbox method, which returns a bounding box for all items that match the tags you send it. Here's what the code looks like:

```
$canvas->configure(-scrollregion => [ $canvas->bbox("all") ]);
```

Calling this after you add or remove items to the Canvas resets the scroll region to where it needs to be. Of course, if you are adding many different items all at once, you should wait until after you have added them all before updating the scroll region.

Using bind with a Canvas

When you try to use the bind method with a Canvas widget, you can easily run into unexpected problems. You may either get an error and your script won't run, or your script will run but your bind won't seem to have any effect. What's happening here is that Canvas objects have their own special bind method that works with tags and item IDs. To get around this, you'll need to use CanvasBind, a special method that binds events to the canvas as a whole:

```
$canvas = $mw->Canvas();
$canvas->CanvasBind("<Button-1>", sub { print "bind!\n"; });
```

If you used the Scrolled method to create your Canvas, you'll have an added difficulty; you'll have to use the Subwidget method to get to the Canvas widget:

```
$canvas = $mw->Scrolled("Canvas");
$real_canvas = $canvas->Subwidget("canvas");
$real_canvas->CanvasBind("<Button-1>", sub { print "bind!\n" });
```

Other than this one small annoyance, bind works just as you would expect. This example prints the Canvas coordinate you clicked on:

```
$c = $mw->Scrolled("Canvas")->pack();
$canvas = $c->Subwidget("canvas");
$canvas->CanvasBind("<Button-1>", [ \&print_xy, Ev('x'), Ev('y') ]);
sub print_xy {
  my ($canv, $x, $y) = @_;
  print "(x,y) = ", $canv->canvasx($x), ", ", $canv->canvasy($y), "\n";
}
```

To summarize, use bind to create event bindings to Canvas items, and use CanvasBind to create event bindings to the Canvas widget.

Canvas Options

The options listed in this section affect the entire Canvas widget and the items within it (such as circles, lines, rectangles, text, or other widgets). The following options act as you would expect (as explained in Chapter 4 for most options and in Chapter 6 for the Scrollbar options): -background, -borderwidth, -cursor, -height, -highlightbackground, -highlightcolor, -highlightthickness, -relief, -takefocus, -width, -xscrollcommand, and -yscrollcommand.

There are also several options that are unique to the Canvas widget. When selecting items in the Canvas with the mouse cursor, the Canvas widget does calculations to determine if the mouse cursor is inside or outside the item. The -closeenough option controls how close the mouse must be to the item before it is considered inside the item. The default value for -closeenough is "1.0", which is 1.0 pixels away. Any floating-point number is a valid value (and will always be in pixels) for -closeenough.

We discussed the -scrollregion option briefly in "The Scrollable Region" earlier in this chapter. It takes an array reference, which must contain four coordinates. The coordinates indicate a bounding region for the scrollable area in the Canvas. The coordinates are in this order: [*minx, miny, maxx, maxy*]. You can also think of the coordinates as if they were defining the [left, top, right, bottom] edges of the scrollable region.

Normally the Canvas widget limits the user to seeing only the area defined by the -scrollregion option. You can allow the user to scroll beyond this area by using -confine => 0. The default for -confine is 1.

Common Canvas Dash, Stipple, and Tile Options

Jan Nijtman's "dash and image" patches have been incorporated into Perl/Tk. In Chapter 17 we investigate the basic features of stipples and Jan's tiles. Here we introduce his Canvas "dash and tile" options. They are applicable to most Canvas items, although only -state and -updatecommand apply to embedded widgets.

The following describes a *dashSpec* and specifies how a dashed line is drawn.

-activedash => *dashSpec*
> Specifies the dash pattern of an active item.

-activefill => *color*
> Specifies the fill color of an active item.

-activeoutline => *color*
> Specifies the outline color of an active item.

-activeoutlinestipple => *bitmap*
> Specifies the outline stipple of an active item.

-activeoutlinetile => *image*
> Specifies the outline tile of an active item.

-activestipple => *bitmap*
> Specifies the stipple of an active item.

-activewidth => *outlineWidth*
> Specifies the outline width of an active item.

-dash => *dashSpec*
> Specifies a list of integers representing the number of pixels of a line segment (odd segments are the outline color; even segments are transparent) or a character list containing only the five characters .,-_ >. For example:
> ```
> -dash => '.'   = -dash => [2,4]
> -dash => '-'   = -dash => [6,4]
> -dash => '-.'  = -dash => [6,4,2,4]
> -dash => '-..' = -dash => [6,4,2,4,2,4]
> -dash => '. '  = -dash => [2,8]
> -dash => ','   = -dash => [4,4]
> ```

-dashoffset => *integer*
> Specifies the offset in the dash list where the drawing starts.

-disableddash => *dashSpec*
> Specifies the dash pattern for a disabled item.

-disabledfill => *color*
> Specifies the fill color of a disabled item.

`-disableoutline => color`
   Specifies the outline color of a disabled item.

`-disabledoutlinestipple => bitmap`
   Specifies the outline stipple of a disabled item.

`-disabledoutlinetile => image`
   Specifies the outline tile of a disabled item.

`-disabledstipple => bitmap`
   Specifies the stipple of a disabled item.

`-disabledwidth => outlineWidth`
   Specifies the outline width of a disabled item.

`-outline => color`
   Specifies the outline color of an item.

`-outlinestipple => bitmap`
   Specifies the outline stipple of an item.

`-outlinetile => image`
   Specifies the outline tile of an item.

`-state => normal | disabled | hidden`
   Specifies the state of the Canvas item. Overrides the Canvas' global `-state` option.

`-stipple => bitmap`
   Specifies the stipple of an item.

`-updatecommand => callback`
   Specifies the callback invoked when an item is updated on the display.

`-width => outlineWidth`
   Specifies the outline width of an item.

Additional Scrolling Options

The `-xscrollcommand` and `-yscrollcommand` options both work as described in Chapter 6, but there are two additional options that affect how the Canvas scrolls its contents: `-xscrollincrement` and `-yscrollincrement`. Each option takes a valid screen distance for a value. This distance is the unit the Canvas will use to scroll in the associated direction. For instance, if you specify `-xscrollincrement => 10`, each time you click an arrow on the horizontal Scrollbar, the contents of the Canvas will shift so the left edge of the contents is an even multiple of 10. Essentially, the Canvas will shift the contents 10 pixels in the arrow's direction.

If the value associated with `-xscrollincrement` or `-yscrollincrement` is 0 or less, scrolling is done in normal increments.

Canvas Widget Option List

These options all are used with the Canvas method:

`-background => color`
> Sets the background of the Canvas to *color*.

`-borderwidth => amount`
> Changes the width of the edges of the Canvas to *amount*.

`-closeenough => float_amount`
> Sets the amount of distance from the item when the cursor is considered inside the item.

`-confine => 1 | 0`
> Indicates that the Canvas will limit itself to the area defined by `-scrollregion` if set to 1.

`-cursor => cursorname`
> Indicates that the cursor will change to *cursorname* when it is over the Canvas.

`-height => amount`
> Sets the height of the Canvas to *amount*.

`-highlightbackground => color`
> Sets the color the highlight rectangle should be when the Canvas does not have the keyboard focus.

`-highlightcolor => color`
> Sets the color the highlight rectangle should be when the Canvas has the keyboard focus.

`-highlightthickness => amount`
> Sets the thickness of the highlight rectangle. Default is 2.

`-insertbackground => color`
> Sets the color of the area behind the text insert cursor.

`-insertborderwidth => amount`
> Sets the width of the borders on the insert cursor.

`-insertofftime => milliseconds`
> Sets the amount of time the cursor disappears from the screen when it is blinking off.

`-insertontime => milliseconds`
> Sets the amount of time the cursor appears on the screen when it is blinking on.

`-insertwidth => amount`
> Sets the width of the insert cursor.

`-relief => 'flat'|'groove'|'raised'|'ridge'|'sunken'|'solid'`
> Indicates the way the edges of the Canvas are drawn.

`-scrollregion => [ left, top, right, bottom ]`
> Defines the area the user is allowed to scroll.

`-selectbackground => `*`color`*
Sets the color of the area behind any selected text.

`-selectborderwidth => `*`amount`*
Sets the width of the border of the selected area.

`-selectforeground => `*`color`*
Sets the color of the selected text.

`-takefocus => 0 | 1 | `**`undef`**
Determines whether or not the Canvas can get keyboard focus. Default is for the application to decide.

`-width => `*`amount`*
Sets the width of the Canvas to *amount*.

`-xscrollcommand => `*`callback`*
Determines the callback used when the Canvas is scrolled horizontally (automatically set to the correct callback when the `Scrolled` method is used).

`-xscrollincrement => `*`amount`*
Sets the distance the Canvas contents move when the arrow on the horizontal Scrollbar is clicked.

`-yscrollcommand => `*`callback`*
Determines the callback used when the Canvas is scrolled vertically.

`-yscrollincrement => `*`amount`*
Sets the distance the Canvas contents move when the arrow on the vertical Scrollbar is clicked.

Creating Items in a Canvas

The whole point of having a Canvas is to put items in it. You can create arcs, bitmaps, images, lines, rectangles, ovals (circles), polygons, text, and widgets. Each has an associated create*XXX* method, where the type of item you want to create replaces the *XXX*. Each of the create methods returns a unique ID, which can be used to refer to the item later. When you see a method that takes a tag or an ID as an argument, the ID is the one returned from the create method.

The Arc Item

When you create an arc, you specify a bounding rectangle with two sets of x and y coordinates. The arc is drawn within the confines of the bounding box. The basic createArc statement is as follows:

```
$id = $canvas->createArc(x1, y1, x2, y2);
```

Any additional options used with createArc are specified after the coordinates:

```
$id = $canvas->createArc(x1, y1, x2, y2, option => value);
```

Each option for the arc item can be used later with the `itemcget` and `itemconfigure` Canvas methods. The options are:

-extent => *degrees*

> The length of the arc is specified in degrees by using the -extent option. The default -extent (or length) is 90 degrees. The arc is drawn from the starting point (see -start option) counterclockwise within the rectangle defined by (*x1, y1*) and (*x2, y2*). The *degrees* value should be between −360 and 360. If it is more or less, the value used is the specified number of degrees modulo 360.
>
> Here are some examples of the -extent option:
>
> ```
> # This draws half of an oval
> $canvas->createArc(0,0,100,150, -extent => 180);
> # This will draw 3/4 of an oval
> $canvas->createArc(0,0,100,150, -extent => 270);
> ```

-fill => *color*

> To fill the arc with the specified color. By default, there is no fill color for an arc.

-outline => *color*

> Normally the arc is drawn with a black outline. To change the default, use the -outline option. The outline color is separate from the fill color, so to make it a completely solid object, make the color for -outline and -fill the same.

-outlinestipple => *bitmap*

> To use -outlinestipple, you must also use the -outline option. Normally the outline of the arc is drawn solid. Use a bitmap with -outlinestipple to make the outline nonsolid; the specified bitmap pattern will be used to draw the outline of the arc.

-start => *degrees*

> The value associated with the -start option determines where Perl/Tk starts drawing the arc. The default start position is at three o'clock (0 degrees). The specified degrees are added to this position in a counterclockwise direction. Use -start => 90 to make the arc start at the twelve o'clock position, use -start => 180 to make the arc start at the nine o'clock position, and so on.

-stipple => *bitmap*

> The -stipple option fills the arc with a bitmap pattern, but the -fill option must be specified as well.

-style => **"pieslice"** | "chord" | "arc"

> The -style of the arc determines how the arc is drawn. The default, "pieslice", draws the arc and two lines from the center of the oval ends of the arc segment. The "chord" value draws the arc and a line connecting the two end points of the arc segment. The "arc" value draws just the arc portion with no other lines. The -fill and -stipple options are ignored if "arc" is used.

-tags => *taglist*

When you create an arc, you use the -tags option to assign tag names to it. The value associated with -tags is an anonymous array of tag names; for example:

```
$canvas->createArc(0,0,10,140,-tags => ["arc", "tall"]);
```

You don't need to use an anonymous array if you are only specifying one tag name:

```
$canvas->createArc(0,0,10,140,-tags => "arc");
```

-width => *amount*

This specifies the width of the outline. The default -width is 1.

The Bitmap Item

A Canvas widget can display a bitmap instead of text, just as a Button or Label can. You can use createBitmap to insert a bitmap into your Canvas widget:

```
$id = $canvas->createBitmap(x, y);
```

Of course, you must use the -bitmap option to specify which bitmap to display or you won't see anything. So we really create a bitmap like this:

```
$id = $canvas->createBitmap(x, y, -bitmap => bitmap);
```

The other options available for createBitmap are:

-anchor => **"center"** | "n" | "e" | "s" | "w" | "ne" | "nw" | "se" | "sw"

The -anchor option determines how the bitmap is placed on the Canvas relative to the (x, y) coordinates indicated. The default for -anchor is "center", which puts the center of the image at the (x, y) coordinates. Using a single cardinal direction (for example, "e") would place the center of that edge at the (x, y) coordinates.

-background => *color*

The -background option specifies the color to use for all the 0 (zero) bitmap pixels. If you don't specify a background color or use an empty string (""), the 0 pixels will be transparent.

-bitmap => *bitmapname*

You must use the -bitmap option to tell the Canvas which bitmap to display. You can use the built-in bitmaps (such as 'info' or 'warning') just as you can with the Button widget, or you can specify a filename. Remember, to specify a bitmap file, use an @ sign in front of the filename.

-foreground => *color*

The foreground color of a bitmap is the opposite of the background color. (By definition, bitmaps can have only two colors.) The -foreground option will color all the 1 pixels with this color. The default for -foreground is black.

```
-tags => taglist
```
Use the -tags option to assign tag names to a bitmap. The value associated with
-tags is an anonymous list of tag names; for example:

```
$canvas->createBitmap(0,0, -bitmap => 'info',
                       -tags => ["info", "bitmap"]);
```

You don't need to use the list if you are only specifying one tag name:

```
$canvas->createBitmap(0,0, -bitmap => 'info', -tags => "bitmap");
```

The Image Item

If we can create a bitmap on a Canvas, it makes sense that we can create an image as
well. We can do so with the createImage method:

```
$id = $canvas->createImage(x, y, -image => image);
```

Again, you have to specify an image to display or you won't see anything. The other
options available for createImage are:

```
-anchor => "center" | "n" | "e" | "s" | "w" | "ne" | "nw" | "se" | "sw"
```
The -anchor option for an image works the same as it does for a bitmap. The
-anchor option is how the image is positioned around the (x, y) coordinates.

```
-image => $image
```
The -image option indicates which image to display. The image value is actually
a reference to an image created with the Photo or Bitmap methods. (See Chapter 3
for more information on how to specify an image file.)

```
-tags => taglist
```
Use the -tags option to assign tag names to an image. The value associated with
-tags is an anonymous list of tag names; for example:

```
$canvas->createImage(0,0, -image => $imgptr,
                       -tags => ["image", "blue"]);
```

You don't need the list if you are specifying only one tag name:

```
$canvas->createImage(0,0, -image => $imgptr, -tags => "image");
```

The Line Item

The createLine method can actually create multiple connected lines, not just one.
The first two coordinate sets you supply create the first line, and any additional coordinates will continue the line to that point:

```
$id = $canvas->createLine(0,0, 400,400);           # creates one line
$id = $canvas->createLine(0,0, 400,400, -50, 240); # creates two lines
```

After the coordinates, you can specify any options and values you wish to configure
the line(s); the options and values are as follows:

`-arrow => "`**`none`**`" | "first" | "last" | "both"`

Use the `-arrow` option to place arrowheads at either end of the line (or both). If you have more than one line in your `createLine` method, only the first and/or last point can be made into an arrow. If you want each line to have an arrowhead, use multiple `createLine` statements.

`-arrowshape => [ `*`dist1, dist2, dist3`*` ]`

The `-arrowshape` option applies only if you use the `-arrow` option as well.

Specify the three distances by using an anonymous list such as this:

```
$canvas->createLine(10, 10, 200, -40, -arrow => "both",
                    -arrowshape => [ 20, 20, 20]);
```

Figure 9-4 shows what the distance values mean.

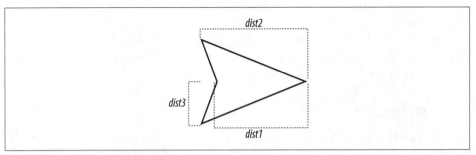

Figure 9-4. Definition of arrowhead

`-capstyle => "`**`butt`**`" | "projecting" | "round"`

Instead of arrowheads, you can make the ends of the line have one of these styles.

`-fill =>` *`color`*

The `-fill` option is misnamed, because it isn't actually filling anything. The line is simply drawn with this color instead of black.

`-joinstyle => "bevel" | "`**`miter`**`" | "round"`

The `-joinstyle` option affects how multiple lines are joined together. If there is only one line created, this option has no effect.

`-smooth => 1 | `**`0`**

If `-smooth` has a value of 1, then, using Bezier spline(s), the line(s) will be drawn as a curve. The first two lines make the first spline, the second and third line make up the second spline, and so on. To make a straight line, repeat the end points of the desired straight line (or use `createLine` again to make a separate line).

`-splinesteps =>` *`count`*

When you use the `-smooth` option, the more `-splinesteps` you use, the smoother the curve. To find out how many steps create the desired effect, you'll have to experiment with different values.

-stipple => *bitmap*

    To have the line drawn with a bitmap pattern (1 values in the bitmap have color; 0 values are transparent), use the -stipple option. The bitmap can be a default bitmap name or a filename. The wider the line (see -width), the more the stipple design will show up.

-tags => *taglist*

    When you create a line (or lines), assign tag names to them using the -tags option. The value associated with -tags is an anonymous list of tag names; for example:

```
$canvas->createLine(0,0, 100,100, -tags => ["line", "blue"]);
```

    You don't need to use a list if you are specifying only one tag name:

```
$canvas->createLine(0,0, 100, 100, -tags => "line");
```

-width => *amount*

    You can use the -width option to make the line(s) thicker. Normally the line is drawn only 1 pixel wide. The amount can be any valid screen distance (e.g., centimeters, inches).

The Oval Item

An oval can be a circle if you draw it just right. To create a circle or oval, use the createOval method and specify two sets of points that indicate a rectangle (or square) in which to draw the oval. Here is a simple example:

```
$id = $canvas->createOval(0,0, 50, 50);  # creates a circle
$id = $canvas->createOval(0,0, 50, 100); # creates an oval
```

The options for the oval will be familiar, so we'll just cover them briefly:

-fill => *color*

    Fills in the oval with the specified color. This color is different than the outline color. By default, the oval is not filled.

-outline => *color*

    The outline is the line drawn around the outside of the circle. Normally, the outline is black, but you can use the -outline option to change it. If you make the outline and the fill color the same, the oval appears solid.

-stipple => *bitmap*

    To fill the oval with a bitmap pattern (1 values in the bitmap are colored; 0 values are transparent), use the -stipple option. If the -fill option isn't used, -stipple has no effect. -stipple takes a default bitmap name or a file with a bitmap in it.

-tags => *taglist*

    When you create an oval, use the -tags option to assign tag names to it. The value associated with -tags is an anonymous list of tag names; for example:

```
$canvas->createOval(0,0, 100,100, -tags => ["oval", "blue"]);
```

You don't need to use a list if you are specifying only one tag name:

```
$canvas->createOval(0,0, 100, 100, -tags => "oval");
```

-width => *amount*

The -width option changes how wide the outline of the oval is drawn. The default for -width is 1 pixel.

The Polygon Item

A polygon is merely a bunch of lines where the first point is connected to the last point automatically to create an enclosed area. The createPolygon method requires at least three (x, y) coordinate pairs. For instance, the following piece of code will create a three-sided polygon:

```
$id = $canvas->createPolygon(1000,1000, 850,950, 30,40);
```

Additional (x, y) coordinate pairs can be specified as well; for example:

```
$id = $canvas->createPolygon(1000,1000, 850,950, 30,40, 500,500);
```

The options you can specify with createPolygon are the same as those you use with createLine: -fill, -outline, -smooth, -splinesteps, -stipple, -tags, and -width. Just remember that createPolygon connects the first point to the last point to enclose the area.

The Rectangle Item

As if being able to create a rectangle using createLine or createPolygon weren't enough, we also have the createRectangle method. It only takes two (x, y) coordinate sets, which are the opposite corners of the rectangular area:

```
$id = $canvas->createRectangle(10, 10, 50, 150);
```

Again, we have seen the options available for createRectangle with the other create methods: -fill, -outline, -stipple, -tags, and -width. Although we've covered these options already, here are a few examples:

```
# A blue rectangle with black outline:
$canvas->createRectangle(10,10, 50, 150, -fill => 'blue');
# A blue rectangle with a thicker outline:
$canvas->createRectangle(10,10, 50, 150, -fill => 'blue', -width => 10);
```

The Text Item

Finally, an item type that doesn't have lines in it! You can use the createText method to add text to a Canvas widget. It requires an (x, y) coordinate pair, which determines where you place the text in the Canvas and the text to be displayed:

```
$id = $canvas->createText(0,0, -text => "origin");
```

The -text option is actually optional, but then you wouldn't see any text on the screen. Because there is no point in that, we will assume that you will always specify -text with a text value to display. The other options available for text items are as follows:

-anchor => "**center**" | "n" | "e" | "s" | "w" | "ne" | "nw" | "se" | "sw"
> The -anchor option determines where the text is placed in relation to the (x, y) coordinate. The default is centered: the text will be centered over that point no matter how large the piece of text is.

-fill => *color*
> The text is normally drawn in black; you can use the -fill option to change this. The name of this option doesn't make much sense when you think about it in terms of text (normally our widgets use -foreground to change the color of the text). For example, -fill => 'blue' will draw blue text.

-font => *fontname*
> You can change the font for the displayed text by using the -font option.

-justify => "**left**" | "right" | "center"
> If the displayed text has more than one line, the -justify option will cause it to be justified as specified.

-stipple => *bitmap*
> This option is a bit strange, but here it is anyway. If you specify a bitmap name (or file) with the -stipple option, the text will be drawn by using the bitmap pattern. Most of the time, this will make the text unreadable, so don't use it unless you're using a large font.

-tags => *taglist*
> The *taglist* is a single tag name or an anonymous list of tag names to be assigned to the item.

-text => *string*
> This is not optional. The specified string is displayed in the Canvas widget at the (x, y) coordinate.

-width => *amount*
> This is another misnamed option, because it does not change the width of each text character. It determines the maximum length of each line of text. If the text is longer than this length, the line will automatically wrap to a second line. The default value for *amount* is 0, which will break lines only at newline characters. Lines are always broken at spaces so words won't be cut in half.

The following options, discussed earlier, work the same as they would for an Entry widget or a Text widget: -insertbackground, -insertborderwidth, -insertofftime, -insertontime, -insertwidth, -selectbackground, -selectborderwidth, and -selectforeground. See Chapter 5 and Chapter 8 for more details.

Text item indexes

Methods that affect text items will sometimes ask for an index value. Text indexes for the regular Text widget were covered in Chapter 8, and the index values for a Canvas text item are similar. The only difference is that each item is considered only one line (even if it has "\n" characters in it). Index values are as follows:

n

A number value. For example, 0 or 12. 0 is the first character, 1 is the second, and so on.

"end"

The character directly after the last one. Often used with the insert method to add to the end of the string.

"insert"

The character directly before the insertion cursor.

"sel.first"

The first character of the selected text. Only valid if there is a selection.

"sel.last"

The last character of the selected text. Only valid if there is a selection.

"@*x,y*"

The character closest to the point (*x, y*) of the Canvas (not screen coordinates).

Deleting characters

To delete characters from within a text item, use the dchars method: $canvas-> dchars(*tag/id, first* [, *last*]). Specify a tag or ID to match the text item(s) and the index at which to start deleting. If the end index isn't specified, all the characters to the end of the string will be deleted (including any "\n" characters).

Positioning the cursor

To specifically place the blinking text cursor, use the icursor method : $canvas-> icursor(*tag/id, index*). The cursor will only show up immediately if the specified item has the current keyboard focus. You can still set the position of the cursor if it doesn't, it just won't display until the item does get the keyboard focus.

Index information

To find an index based on another index, use the index method. Here's an example:

```
$index = $canvas->index("textitem", "sel.first");
```

This returns the numerical index associated with the first selected character in the text item. If more than one item matches the tag or ID indicated (in this case, it's a tag named "textitem"), then the first one found is used.

Adding text

To add more text to a text item, use the insert method: $canvas->insert(*tag/id*, *index*, *string*). The first argument is the tag or ID, which can match multiple items. The second argument is the index before which to insert the new string, and the last argument is the actual string to insert into the text item.

Selecting text

There are several methods you can use to programmatically select portions of the text. To clear the selection (any selection; there are no tags or IDs sent with this command), use $canvas->selectClear. To select a portion of text, use selectFrom and selectTo. The following two lines of code select the text from beginning to end for the first item that matches the tag "texttag":

```
$canvas->selectFrom("texttag", 0);
$canvas->selectTo("texttag", "end");
```

You can use the selectAdjust method to add to the selection: $canvas->selectAdjust("adjust", *tag/id*, *index*). To get the ID of the item that currently has the selection in it, use $id = $canvas->selectItem.

The Widget Item

You can put any type of widget inside a Canvas—Buttons, Checkbuttons, Text widgets, or even another Canvas widget (if you are a little crazy)—by using the createWindow method. Before calling createWindow, you must create the widget to put into the Canvas. Here's an example:

```
$bttn = $canvas->Button(-text => "Button",
                        -command => sub { print "Button in Canvas\n"; });
$id = $canvas->createWindow(0, 0, -window => $bttn);
```

There are a few things you should note about this example (which is fairly typical, except the subroutine associated with the Button doesn't do anything useful):

- The Button is a child of the Canvas widget. The Button could be a child of an ancestor of the Canvas (the Button could be a child of the MainWindow if the Canvas is also a child of the MainWindow). However, the Button should not be a child of a different Toplevel widget that has nothing to with the Canvas.

- The createWindow method doesn't actually create the widget; it just puts it in the Canvas. The Button is placed at the specified coordinates inside the Canvas and has not been placed on the screen with pack, grid, or place.

- The widget must be created before you call createWindow.

- You can click the Button and the callback associated with it will be invoked, just as with any other Button.

- When you create the widget, you can use any of that widget's options to configure it. To continue configuring the widget, use the reference to it (e.g., $bttn).

The following options, which you can use when you call createWindow, are more like options you use with pack than widget options:

-anchor => **"center"** | "n" | "e" | "s" | "w" | "ne" | "nw" | "se" | "sw"

The widget will be placed at the (x, y) coordinates according to the -anchor value. The default is "center", which means that the widget will have its center point placed on (x, y).

-height => *amount*

The widget will be given this height. If you don't use -height, the widget will have the height it was created with (usually the natural size of the widget).

-tags => *taglist*

The *taglist* associates a tag with the widget. You can specify either a single tag string or an anonymous list of tag names.

-width => *amount*

The widget will be given this width. If you don't use the -width option, the widget will have the width it was created with (the natural size of the widget).

-window => $widget

This is a nonoptional option. If you don't specify -window, there will be no widget put in the Canvas. The $widget is a reference to a widget item. You can create the widget beforehand or inline as follows:

```
$canvas->createWindow(0,0, -window => $canvas->Button(-text => "Button",
    -command => sub { print "Button!\"; }));
```

It makes sense to create the widget inline if you don't need to do anything fancy with it.

The Grid Item

Perl/Tk has an experimental *grid* item type that displays dotted, dashed, or solid lines, in both the x and y dimensions. The effect is reminiscent of old-fashioned graph paper.

Grid items cover the entire Canvas, but never enclose or overlap any area and are not near any point, so you cannot search for them using the closest, enclosed, or overlapping attributes. In most other regards, they behave like other Canvas item types. Currently, grids, like window items, do not appear in PostScript output.

Grid items are created like this:

```
$canvas->createGrid(x1, y1, x2, y2, ... );
```

x1 and *y1* specify the origin of the basal grid *cell*, and *x2* and *y2* specify its width and height, respectively; the cell is replicated over the entire surface of the Canvas widget. By default, dots are drawn at every grid intersection, unless the -lines option is set true. When drawing lines, dash specifications are honored.

This code generated Figure 9-5:

```
my $c = $mw->Canvas(qw/-width 300 -height 200/)->grid;
$c->configure("-scrollregion" => [0,0, 300, 200]);

$c->createGrid(0, 0, 10, 10);
$c->createGrid(0, 0, 50, 50, -lines => 1, -dash => '-.');
$c->createGrid(0, 0, 100, 100, -width => 3, -lines => 1);
```

One important note: *grid items remain invisible unless a scroll region is defined.* This may be construed as a bug, which is one reason why grids are deemed experimental.

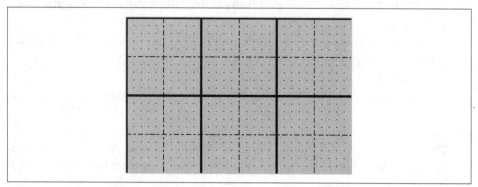

Figure 9-5. A canvas with three grid items

The Group Item

Perl/Tk sports a new Canvas item called a *group*. A group item is actually a collection of standard Canvas items that can be manipulated simultaneously. The following code creates an oval and a rectangle, then groups them together:

```
$one = $canvas->createOval(5,  0, 20, 30, -fill => 'blue');
$two = $canvas->createRectangle(0, 20, 50, 75, -fill => 'red');
$group = $canvas->createGroup([0, 0], -members => [$one, $two]);
$mw->update;
$mw->after(1000);
$canvas->move($group, 100, 100);
```

Figure 9-6 shows the outcome.

After a one-second delay, the group is moved to a new Canvas coordinate, shown in Figure 9-7.

Of course, sometimes you want to get to individual items within the group, perhaps to configure a special attribute. The current idiom is to iterate through the members of the group, like this:

```
foreach my $member ($canvas->itemcget($group, -members)) {
    print "member=$member\n";
}
```

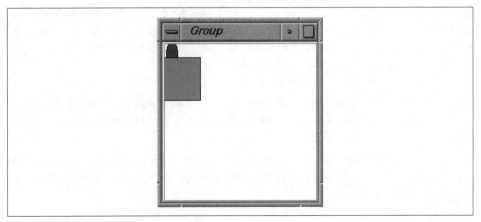

Figure 9-6. Before move

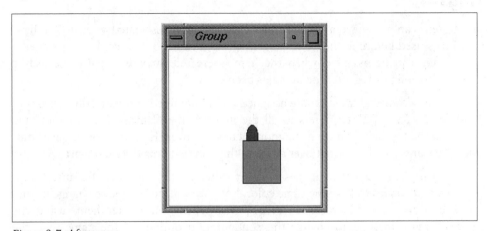

Figure 9-7. After move

This example prints out the item ID for each member of the group, but you can use the item IDs in an itemconfigure call.

Configuring the Canvas Widget

As usual, to configure or get information about the Canvas widget, you can use the configure and cget methods, explained in detail in Chapter 13. Remember, configure and cget operate on the entire Canvas widget (possibly affecting the items within it).

Configuring Items in the Canvas Widget

To change the configuration options of any of the items within the Canvas, you only need to know the tag name or the ID for that item. You can then use the itemcget and `itemconfigure` methods. They behave just like the `cget` and `configure` methods, except they take the tag or ID of the item(s) as a first argument. We say "item(s)" because a tag can refer to more than one item. Here are some examples:

```
$color = $canvas->itemcget("circle", -fill);
$canvas->itemconfigure($id_number, -fill => "yellow", -outline => 5);
```

Make sure the options you use with `itemconfigure` and `itemcget` are valid. Each item type has a list of valid options; they are listed earlier in this chapter with each create method.

When you set the `-tags` option, the `itemconfigure` method replaces any currently set tags for the item. The *taglist* associated with `-tags` can also be empty, which will essentially remove all tags.

Tags

Each item can also have a tag (or more than one tag) associated with it. We have seen tags used before in the Text widget, where sections of text could be assigned a tag. A tag can be assigned when the item is created, or you can use the `addtag` method to assign a tag after the item has been created.

There are two special tags that are assigned and maintained automatically: "current" and "all". The "all" tag refers to all the items in the Canvas. The "current" tag refers to the topmost item that the mouse cursor is over. If the mouse cursor is outside the Canvas widget or not over an item, the "current" tag does not exist.

You can use tags to make changes to many different items at once. For instance, if you want all circles to have the same color, but you want to be able to change it from time to time, give all circles a "circle" tag when you create them, using the `itemconfigure` method to change the configuration options of the items with the "circle" tag.

Tags can also be logical expressions by using the operators: &&, ||, ^, !, and parenthetical subexpressions. For example:

```
$c->find('withtag',   '(a&&!b)|(!a&&b)');
```

or equivalently:

```
$c->find('withtag', 'a^b');
```

will find only those items with either a or b tags, but not both.

The following are some sample syntax lines for creating tags:

`$canvas->addtag("newtag", "above", tag/id);`

> The "newtag" tag is added to the item that is above the *tag/id* item. If there is more than one match for *tag/id*, the last item found will be used so the "newtag" is directly above the *tag/id* item in the display list. The display list is created as you add items to the Canvas and can be manipulated with the `raise` and `lower` methods.

```
$canvas->addtag("newtag", "all");
```
The keyword "all" is a special tag that includes every item currently in the Canvas. Items added to the Canvas after the call to addtag will not contain "newtag" in their tag lists.

```
$canvas->addtag("newtag", "below", tag/id);
```
The "newtag" tag is added to the item that is directly below the *tag/id* item. If more than one item matches the below *tag/id* search, the lowest item in the list will be used.

```
$canvas->addtag("newtag", "closest", x, y);
```
Use the "closest" tag to select the item closest to the (x, y) coordinates (in Canvas coordinates). If more than one item matches, the last one found is used.

There are two more possible arguments for this form of addtag. You can specify a number that indicates how far out from the (x, y) coordinates items are to be considered. For instance, if you want an item that is within 10 pixels to be considered "closest", make the call as follows:

```
$canvas->addtag("newtag", "closest", 50, 100, 10);
```
You can also specify a starting tag or ID to start a search. The call would then look like this:

```
$canvas->addtag("newtag", "closest", x, y, 10, $tag_or_id);
```
Using this form, you can loop through all the closest items.

```
$canvas->addtag("newtag", "enclosed", x1, y1, x2, y2);
```
You can use the "enclosed" form of addtag to assign the same tag to several items within the area bounded by (*x1, y1*) to (*x2, y2*). Items will be given "newtag" only if they are completely within the area. The coordinates must make sense when you specify them: *x1 < x2* and *y1 < y2*.

```
$canvas->addtag("newtag", "overlapping", x1, y1, x2, y2);
```
To assign tags to any item that has any part inside a bounded region, use "overlapping" instead of "enclosed". Even if the item has only one pixel inside this area, it will still count. All other rules for the bounding area are the same as for "enclosed".

```
$canvas->addtag("newtag", "withtag", tag/id);
```
Assigns "newtag" to all the items with the tag or ID specified.

Binding Items Using Tags

Each item in a Canvas can have an event sequence bound to it so that a callback will be invoked when that event sequence happens. This is similar to adding an event sequence binding for widgets, except item tags or item IDs are used. (Remember, if you want to add a normal binding to the Canvas widget itself, you must use CanvasBind instead of just bind.)

The general form of bind is as follows:

```
$canvas->bind(tag/id [ , sequence, command ] );
```

The *sequence* would be similar to "<Button-1>" or "<Double-1>". A complete definition and explanation of event sequences is available in Chapter 15.

When you create item bindings, keep in mind that only mouse and keyboard bindings are valid for items. You can't do any of the weird, esoteric bindings that are
available for all widgets.

Here is an example that changes the color of any items tagged with "blue" when the
mouse is over them:

```
# When the mouse is over the item, color it blue
$c->bind("blue", "<Enter>",
         sub { $c->itemconfigure("blue", -fill => "blue"); });
# When the mouse is not over, color it black.
$c->bind("blue", "<Leave>",
         sub { $c->itemconfigure("blue", -fill => "black"); });
```

Finding Tags

You can use the find command to determine which items have a certain tag. The
possible ways to call find are the same as those of addtag (except for the newtag
argument). Here are the basic formats (see "Tags" earlier in this chapter for more
details on what they mean and how they work):

```
$canvas->find("above", tag/id);
$canvas->find("all");
$canvas->find("below", tag/id);
$canvas->find("closest", x, y [ , additional_area ] [ , tag/id ]);
$canvas->find("enclosed", x1, y1, x2, y2);
$canvas->find("overlapping", x1, y1, x2, y2);
$canvas->find("withtag", tag/id);
```

Getting Tags from a Specific Item

To get a list of all the tags associated with an item, use:

```
@list = $canvas->gettags(tag/id);
```

If the *tag/id* matches more than one item, the first item found is used. If the *tag/id*
doesn't match anything, an empty string is returned.

Retrieving Bounding Box Coordinates

When we talked about the scrolling region of a Canvas, we saw an example of the
bbox method. The bbox method returns a list with four elements that define the area
in which all the specified tags exist. The example used the special "all" tag, which

refs to every item in the Canvas. This was how we used it to define our scrolling region. You can specify more than one tag/ID to search for as follows:

```
($l, $r, $t, $b) = $canvas->bbox("blue", "red");
```

Assuming that you have been assigning the tags "blue" and "red" to color items appropriately, this code would return the region in the Canvas that encloses all blue and red items.

Translating Coordinates

When you set up a callback and use the Ev('x') and/or Ev('y') arguments to find out where the user clicked, you must translate that information into Canvas coordinates (Ev is explained in Chapter 15). To do this, use the canvasx and canvasy methods:

```
$x = $canvas->canvasx(screenx [, gridspacing ]);
$y = $canvas->canvasy(screeny [, gridspacing ]);
```

Each method takes an optional gridspacing argument; the Canvas coordinate value will be rounded to the nearest value to fit the grid.

Moving Items Around

Once an item has been created on the Canvas, use move or coords to move it around. The move method takes a tag or ID to indicate which items to move and the amounts to add to the x and y coordinates:

```
$canvas->move(tag/id, xdistance, ydistance);
```

For instance, the following code moves items with the "blue" tag 100 pixels in the x direction and 100 pixels in the y direction:

```
$canvas->move("blue", 100, 100);
```

To move an item in the negative direction, simply specify a negative value for the *xdistance* and/or *ydistance*. The other method, coords, allows you to specify a new x and y location for the first item found that is identified by the tag or ID:

```
$canvas->coords(tag/id, newx, newy);
```

If the item requires more than one set of (x, y) coordinates, you simply continue to specify them:

```
$canvas->coords(tag/id, newx1, newy1, newx2, newy2...);
```

To find where an item currently is in the Canvas, use coords without specifying the x or y coordinates:

```
@coords_list = $canvas->coords(tag/id);
```

Remember, the coords method only applies to the first item it finds that matches the given tag or ID.

Changing the Display List

Every time a method looks through all the items in the Canvas for a specific tag or ID, it looks through the display list. The display list is created as items are added to the Canvas. The first item added to the Canvas is the first item in the display list, and items are added in order as they are created. Also, items created later are drawn above the ones created earlier if they overlap at all. To change the display order, use the raise and lower methods:

```
$canvas->raise(tag/id, abovetag/id);
$canvas->lower(tag/id, belowtag/id);
```

The first argument for each method is the tag or ID of the item(s) you want to move in the display list. The second is the tag or ID next to which the first item should be placed (either above or below). If the first tag or ID matches more than one item, they are all moved.

Note that if you use the Scrolled method to create the Canvas, you can't use the item returned by that method to invoke either raise or lower; you'll get a nasty error about the wrong argument types, because Scrolled is not invoking this version of raise or lower, but another one. Use the subwidget to get the actual Canvas reference, and the call to raise and lower will work.

Deleting Items

To remove an item (or more than one item) from the Canvas completely, use the delete method. It takes a list of tags or IDs to remove from the Canvas. It will delete all matches it finds for the tag names, so be careful you aren't deleting something you don't want to delete. Here is an example that uses three separate tag/IDs:

```
$canvas->delete("blue", "circle", $id_num);
```

You can specify only one tag/ID or as many as you want.

Deleting Tags

To remove tags from items, use the dtag method. There are two forms:

```
$canvas->dtag(tag);
$canvas->dtag(tag/id, deltag);
```

The first one searches for items with the specified tag and then deletes the tag. The second searches for items that match the tag or ID and then deletes the deltag (if it exists) from that item. This allows you to delete a subset of the tags, rather than every single tag.

Determining Item Type

To determine an item's type, call the type method:

```
$canvas->type(tag/id);
```

If the tag or ID matches more than one item, only the type of the first item is returned. The returned value will be a string describing the item type: "oval", "text", "rectangle", and so on.

Setting Keyboard Focus

To assign the keyboard focus to an item, use the focus method:

```
$canvas->focus(tag/id);
```

If the item doesn't know what to do with the keyboard focus, nothing will happen. You'll use this to change the focus to a widget within the Canvas.

Rendering the Canvas as PostScript

To get a copy of the Canvas as PostScript, use the postscript method. It will either return the PostScript output or, if the -file option is specified, put it in a file:

```
$postscript = $canvas->postscript();
$canvas->postscript(-file => "ps.out");
```

The following options allow you to control the output of the PostScript:

-colormap => \@array
Specifies that each element in @array must be a valid PostScript command for setting color values (e.g., "1.0 1.0 0.0 setrgbcolor").

-colormode => "color" | "gray" | "mono"
Creates the PostScript in full color, grayscale ("gray"), or black and white ("mono").

-file => filename
Specifies the file in which to put the PostScript output.

-fontmap => \@array
Each element in @array is a two-element array that contains a font name and a point size. The font name should be a complete font name so Tk will parse it correctly (e.g., "-*-Helvetica-Bold-O-Normal--*-140-*").

-height => size
Sets the height of the area to print. The default height is the Canvas height.

-pageanchor => "n" | "e" | "s" | "w" | "center"
Indicates where the page should be placed over the positioning point specified by the -pagex and -pagey options.

-pageheight => *height*
> Sets the height of the printed page. The Canvas image will be scaled to fit. *height* is any valid screen distance.

-pagewidth => *width*
> Sets the width of the printed page. The Canvas image will be scaled to fit.

-pagex => *x*
> Sets the coordinate for the x positioning point. Can be any valid screen distance.

-pagey => *y*
> Sets the coordinate for the y positioning point. Can be any valid screen distance.

-rotate => **0** | 1
> If 1, the page is rotated into a landscape orientation. Default is 0, which is portrait orientation.

-width => *size*
> Sets the width of the Canvas area to be printed. Defaults to the width of the Canvas.

-x => *x*
> Sets the left edge of the area to be printed (in Canvas coordinates). Default is the left edge of the window.

-y => *y*
> Sets the top edge of the area to be printed (in Canvas coordinates). Default is the left edge of the window.

Scaling the Canvas

When you put a large number of items on the Canvas, it's sometimes hard to see them all without scrolling all over the place. It's possible to scale the Canvas; for example, so it will shrink everything in half or explode it to twice the original size. The usage for scale is as follows:

```
$canvas->scale(tag/id, xorigin, yorigin, xscale, yscale);
```

The scaling is centered around the *xorigin* and *yorigin*. It's best to use the real origin (0, 0) unless you can come up with a good reason not to. Both *xscale* and *yscale* are the scaling factors used on each coordinate in each item. Here are some examples:

```
$canvas->scale("all", 0, 0, 1, 1);    # no change!
$canvas->scale("all", 0, 0, .5, .5);  # make all 1/2 size
$canvas->scale("all", 0, 0, 2, 2);    # double everything
$canvas->scale("all", 0, 0, 3, 3);    # triple everything!
```

It's a great idea to add Zoom In and Zoom Out Buttons that take care of the scaling for you. Keep track of the scaling factor in a variable ($scale, for instance); set it to 1 to start with. Multiply it by .5 to zoom out and by 2 to zoom in. The last thing you'll need to do is make sure that if you insert any new items into the Canvas, you multiply those coordinates by the scale factor as well (otherwise they will look either too large or too small compared to the rest of the Canvas items).

Scanning

Use the scan method to implement scanning of the Canvas:

```
$canvas->scanMark(x, y);
$canvas->scanDragto(x, y);
```

The first call, $canvas->scanMark(x, y), records the x and y coordinates and the current Canvas view. The second call, $canvas->scanDragto(x, y), causes the view in the Canvas to be adjusted by 10 times the difference between these coordinates and the previous ones sent with scanMark. This makes the Canvas look as if it were moved at high speed.

Scrolling Methods

The Canvas widget can be scrolled both horizontally and vertically. The methods xview and yview are used to communicate with the Scrollbars. See Chapter 6 for more information on how these methods work.

A Drawing Program Example

The Canvas widget is very versatile and can be useful for displaying different types of items. One of the first things that comes to mind when people think of a Canvas is a drawing program. To save you the trouble, here is a rudimentary drawing program called Quick Draw you can use to draw rectangles, ovals, and lines. You can also change the thickness of the objects before you draw them. It requires only a tiny bit of error-checking to make it a slicker program. Here's the code:

```perl
use Tk;

$mw = MainWindow->new;
$mw->title("Quick Draw");

$f = $mw->Frame(-relief => 'groove',
                -bd => 2,
                -label => "Draw:")->pack(-side => 'left', -fill => 'y');
$draw_item = "rectangle";
$f->Radiobutton(-variable => \$draw_item,
                -text => "Rectangle",
                -value => "rectangle",
                -command => \&bind_start)->pack(-anchor => 'w');
$f->Radiobutton(-variable => \$draw_item,
                -text => "Oval",
                -value => "oval",
                -command => \&bind_start)->pack(-anchor => 'w');
```

```perl
$f->Radiobutton(-variable => \$draw_item,
                -text => "Line",
                -value => "line",
                -command => \&bind_start)->pack(-anchor => 'w');
$f->Label(-text => "Line Width:")->pack(-anchor => 'w');
$thickness = 1;
$f->Entry(-textvariable => \$thickness)->pack(-anchor => 'w');

$c = $mw->Scrolled("Canvas", -cursor => "crosshair")->pack(
                -side => "left", -fill => 'both', -expand => 1);
$canvas = $c->Subwidget("canvas");

&bind_start();

MainLoop;

sub bind_start {
  # If there is a "Motion" binding, we need to allow the user
  # to finish drawing the item before rebinding Button-1
  # this fcn gets called when the finish drawing the item again
  @bindings = $canvas->bind("<Motion>");
  return if ($#bindings >= 0);

  if ($draw_item eq "rectangle"||$draw_item eq "oval"||$draw_item eq "line") {
    $canvas->bind("<Button-1>", [\&start_drawing, Ev('x'), Ev('y')]);
  }
}

sub start_drawing {
  my ($canv, $x, $y) = @_;
  $x = $canv->canvasx($x);
  $y = $canv->canvasy($y);

  # Do a little error checking
  $thickness = 1 if ($thickness !~ /[0-9]+/);

  if ($draw_item eq "rectangle") {
    $canvas->createRectangle($x, $y, $x, $y,
      -width => $thickness, -tags => "drawmenow");
  } elsif ($draw_item eq "oval") {
    $canvas->createOval($x, $y, $x, $y,
      -width => $thickness, -tags => "drawmenow");
  } elsif ($draw_item eq "line") {
    $canvas->createLine($x, $y, $x, $y,
      -width => $thickness, -tags => "drawmenow");
  }

  $startx = $x; $starty = $y;
  # Map the Button-1 binding to &end_drawing instead of start drawing
  $canvas->bind("<Motion>", [\&size_item, Ev('x'), Ev('y')]);
  $canvas->bind("<Button-1>", [\&end_drawing, Ev('x'), Ev('y')]);
}

sub size_item {
  my ($canv, $x, $y) = @_;
```

```
        $x = $canv->canvasx($x);
        $y = $canv->canvasy($y);

        $canvas->coords("drawmenow", $startx, $starty, $x, $y);
    }

    sub end_drawing {
        my ($canv, $x, $y) = @_;
        $x = $canv->canvasx($x);
        $y = $canv->canvasy($y);

        # finalize the size of the item, and remove the tag from the item
        $canvas->coords("drawmenow", $startx, $starty, $x, $y);
        $canvas->dtag("drawmenow");

        # remove motion binding.
        $canvas->CanvasBind("<Motion>", "");
        &bind_start();
    }
```

Note that we didn't set the -scrollregion at all, so as to create a limitless drawing space for the user. (This was the easiest way to provide this functionality: do nothing!) It's a cute little program that demonstrates how to use bind and a few of the Canvas methods. Figure 9-8 shows a screenshot of the application after a few items have been drawn on it.

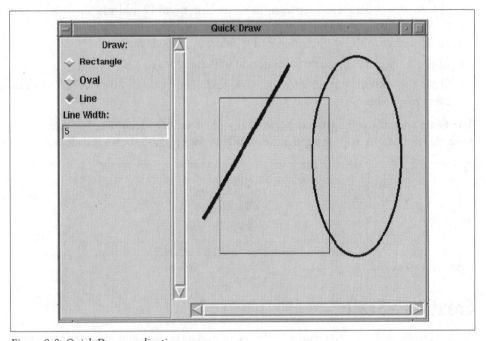

Figure 9-8. Quick Draw application screen

CHAPTER 10

The Scale Widget

A Scale widget looks similar to a Scrollbar but doesn't scroll anything other than itself. What it does is keep track of a number. When you change the position of the button in the Scale, the numeric value associated with the Scale changes. Some things you can do with a Scale widget are:

- Create a widget from which a user can select a number between 1 and 100.
- Create three Scales, each representing a value in an RGB (red, green, blue) number.
- Create four sliders, each representing a portion of an IP address. Each Scale can go from 0 to 255, and it would probably be smart to start them at 255. Use a Label widget to show the completed IP address, periods and all.
- Create a temperature Scale that starts at −50 and goes to 130 degrees.
- Show the amount of rainfall so far this year. The Scale can be marked to show every five inches.

The Scale widget can be placed horizontally or vertically, depending on where you have the most room in your application window. Figure 10-1 shows a scale widget.

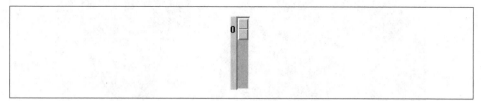

Figure 10-1. Scale widget

Creating a Scale

As with other widgets, to create a Scale, use a parent widget and pass options to the Scale to change its configuration:

```
$parent->Scale( [ option => value ] )->pack;
```

Use one of the geometry managers discussed in Chapter 2 to place it on the screen (such as pack, as shown in the preceding code).

Most of the options associated with the Scale widget are standard options used with all other widgets. All the possible options are in the following list. A discussion of special options that have slightly different meanings for the Scale and options that are specific to the Scale widget follows the list.

-activebackground => *color*
:   Sets the color the slider's background should be when the cursor is over the slider (-state is 'active').

-background => *color*
:   Sets the color the slider's background should be when the cursor is not over the slider (-state is 'normal').

-bigincrement => *amount*
:   Sets the amount by which the slider will change value when required to do so in large increments. Default is 0, causing the value to change by 1/10 the top value of the Scale. -bigincrement is used only when Control-Up/Down/Left/Right is pressed.

-borderwidth => *amount*
:   Sets the width of the edges of the widget. Default is 2.

-command => *callback*
:   Sets the callback invoked when the slider is moved.

-cursor => *cursorname*
:   Determines the cursor to display when the mouse is over the Scale.

-digits => *amount*
:   Indicates how many significant digits to retain when conversion from a number to a string takes place.

-font => *fontname*
:   Sets the font used to display any text in the Scale.

-foreground => *color*
:   Sets the color of the text displayed in the Scale.

-from => *value*
:   Indicates the low end of the Scale values. Default is 0.

-highlightbackground => *color*
:   Sets the color of the highlight rectangle displayed around the Scale when it does not have the keyboard focus.

-highlightcolor => *color*
:   Sets the color of the highlight rectangle displayed around the Scale when it has the keyboard focus.

-highlightthickness => *amount*
:   Sets the thickness of the highlight rectangle displayed around the Scale.

`-label => `*`labelstring`*
Describes a label for the Scale. Default is no label.

`-length => `*`amount`*
Sets the length of the slider (the long direction, regardless of the value of -orient) in a valid screen distance.

`-orient => `**`'vertical'`**` | 'horizontal'`
Sets the direction the Scale is drawn.

`-relief => 'raised'|'sunken'|`**`'flat'`**`|'ridge'|'groove'|'solid'`
Determines how the edges of the widget are drawn.

`-repeatdelay => `*`milliseconds`*
Sets the number of milliseconds the widget waits before repeating.

`-repeatinterval => `*`milliseconds`*
Sets the number of milliseconds the widget delays between repeats.

`-resolution => `*`value`*
Sets the increments by which the value in the Scale will change. Default is 1.

`-showvalue => 0 | `**`1`**
If set to 0, the value of the slider setting is not shown at all.

`-sliderlength => `*`value`*
Sets the size of the slider (inside the widget). Default is 25.

`-state => `**`'normal'`**` | 'active' | 'disabled'`
Determines the state of the widget and whether or not the user can interact with it.

`-takefocus => 1 | 0 | `**`undef`**
Determines whether or not the widget can receive keyboard focus. Default is to let the program decide.

`-tickinterval => `*`value`*
Describes the labels drawn by the right (or on the bottom) of the Scale. Labels are drawn for every value except 0 (which means no labels will be drawn at all). Default is 0.

`-to => `*`value`*
Sets the top value of the Scale. Default is 100.

`-troughcolor=> `*`color`*
Sets the color of the area behind the slider button (same as a Scrollbar).

`-variable => \$`*`variable`*
Sets the variable in which the slider value is stored.

`-width => `*`amount`*
Sets the width of the skinny part of the slider (regardless of the value associated with -orient).

Assigning a Callback

As usual, use the -command option to assign a callback for the widget. The callback is invoked every time the Scale value is changed. If you change the value from 50 to 100 and the Scale increment is 1, the callback will be invoked 50 times. The callback is also called when the widget is created. My recommendation is not to use -command unless you have a small number of possible values.

Orientation

To change the orientation of the Scale, use the -orient option. It takes a string value that should contain either "horizontal" or "vertical". The default for this option is "vertical". Figure 10-2 shows both a horizontal Scale and a vertical Scale.

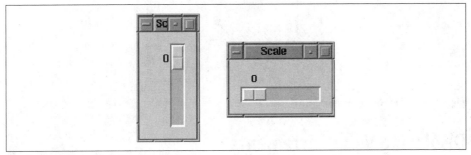

Figure 10-2. Vertical Scale (the default orientation) and horizontal Scale

Minimum and Maximum Values

Use the -from and -to options to change the possible range of values for the Scale. Usually the value associated with -from is smaller than the value associated with -to. If you happen to switch them, the Scale will still display the higher value on the right and the lower value on the left. Either or both values can be negative. Here are some examples:

```
$mw->Scale(-from => -10, -to => 10)->pack;
$mw->Scale(-from => 10, -to => -100)->pack;
$mw->Scale(-from => -100, -to => -50)->pack;
$mw->Scale(-from => -0.5, -to => 0.5, -resolution => 0.1)->pack;
```

As you can see, the values assigned to -from and -to don't need to be integers.

Displayed Versus Stored Value

Sometimes you are searching for a value that resides between two numbers that are very far apart, such as 0 and 1,000,000. Stepping through each of those values one by one would be tedious. You can change the step value of the displayed number using the -resolution option. The default for -resolution is 1, but it can be changed to any value that is less or greater than that.

Note that if the resolution is larger than 1, it is possible for the slider to have a value (set by the program, for example) that is smaller or larger than the displayed value.

Adding a Label

You can add a label to your Scale by using the -label option. The label is placed in a different location depending on the value associated with -orient (see Figure 10-3).

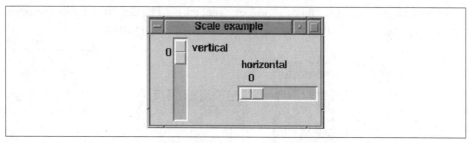

Figure 10-3. Two Scales with labels

Displaying Value Increments

The Scale displays its current value above or to the left of itself (depending on the value associated with -orient). Suppose you want to display labels (such as 0, 10, 20, ... 100) that show the user approximately where the button needs to be to select those values. If you want to display them underneath or to the left of the Scale, you can use the -tickinterval option. By default, it is set to 0 and no numbers are displayed. To show the values every 10 numbers, use -tickinterval => 10. The larger the range of values from which the Scale can select, the larger the value this should be, or you'll end up with a bunch of numbers so close together that you won't be able to tell what they are. See Figure 10-4.

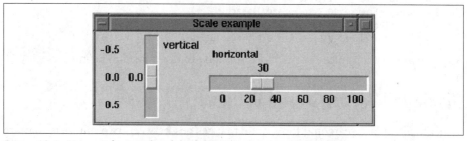

Figure 10-4. Using -tickinterval with both horizontal and vertical Scales

Changing the Size of the Scale

You can use the -length and -width options to change the size of the Scale. You can also change the size of the button displayed in the slider widget; to do so, use the -sliderlength option. It takes a value specified in screen units and will change the length of the slider button.

```
$mw->Scale(-sliderlength => 100); # make the button 100 pixels.
```

Figure 10-5 illustrates this.

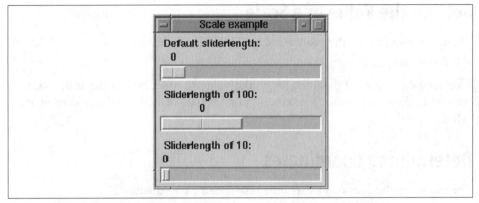

Figure 10-5. Different -sliderlength values

Options You'll Probably Never Need

The two final options for the Scale widget creation method are -bigincrement and -digits. The -bigincrement option specifies the size of jumps when using really large numbers. The default for -bigincrement is 0, which means it will jump in increments that are 1/10 the total range.

The -digits option represents how many digits will be used when converting from a number to a string. The default (0) forces the Scale to use a precision that allows for a different string for every possible value on the Scale.

Configuring a Scale

As usual, the Scale has both configure and cget methods, which let you query and set options for the Scale widget. See Chapter 13 for more details on how to use these methods.

Getting the Value of a Scale

The get method returns the current value of the Scale:

```
$value = $scale->get();
```

You can also specify x and y coordinates and retrieve the value of the Scale at that point:

```
$value = $scale->get(x, y);
```

Setting the Value of a Scale

The set method forces the value associated with the Scale:

```
$scale->set(value);
```

This method is great for setting an initial value if you aren't using the -variable option at all. If you're using -variable, just set that variable to the desired starting value.

Determining Coordinates

The coords method returns a list containing x and y coordinates:

```
($x, $y) = $scale->coords();
```

The coordinates indicate the position in which the current value is located in the Scale. You can also pass in a value to locate:

```
($x, $y) = $scale->coords(value);
```

Identifying Parts of a Scale

To find out what part of the Scale a coordinate resides in, use the identify method:

```
$value = $scale->identify(x, y);
```

The identify method returns a string containing one of the following values: "slider", "trough1", "trough2", or an empty string (if the coordinates don't refer to any of these parts).

## CHAPTER 11

Frame, MainWindow, and Toplevel Widgets

Frames and Toplevels are both designed specifically to be containers of other widgets. They differ in two ways: in their default settings and in their relationships to other widgets. A Frame, by default, has no visible border, relief, or anything to indicate that it's there, whereas all Toplevel widgets have decoration that is consistent with the system on which your application is run. Also, a Toplevel can be manipulated independently of other Toplevel widgets within the application, whereas a Frame always requires a parent (a Toplevel or another Frame) to reside in. It can't be independent.

We have already seen many examples using Toplevel widgets. The widget created by calling MainWindow->new is actually a Toplevel widget. If you print the variable, you see something like this:

```
print "$mw\n";    # prints: MainWindow=HASH(0x909a2d0)
```

This window is special because it displays itself automatically when you call MainLoop. In every other respect, that MainWindow widget is a Toplevel. By creating a Toplevel widget, you are creating another window as part of your application. Other Toplevel widgets in your program must be displayed explicitly somewhere in the code.

When to use an additional Toplevel is a design decision that you'll have to make. You should use another Toplevel widget instead of the MainWindow if there is too much information to fit in one window. Using Toplevels to group information is also sometimes a good idea. You don't want to have too many windows for the user to navigate, but a well-designed application might be able to make use of one or two.

Here are some examples of how you can use Toplevel widgets:

- Display informational text with a Close Button.[*]
- Provide data gathering output in different Toplevel windows that are triggered by something the user does (e.g., clicking a button).

---

[*] Look at Tk::Dialog. It is designed to do this and uses a Toplevel widget.

The entire purpose of a Frame widget is to provide a container for other widgets. This doesn't seem important, but it is. The geometry managers provided with Perl/Tk have some limitations (see Chapter 2), and we can use Frames to help them do their jobs better. We'll use pack as our example geometry manager throughout this chapter because it is the most popular, but remember that the basic rules for using a Frame apply to the other geometry managers as well.

When a Frame contains other widgets, it accommodates the size of the widgets inside it. If you don't have any widgets packed into the Frame, you won't see the Frame. If the widgets inside the Frame are resized for any reason, the Frame will try to resize as well.*

Creating a Frame

There is nothing special about creating a Frame widget, except you will usually save a reference to the widget so that you can put other things inside it.

```
# a Frame you'll never see
$frame1 = $mw->Frame;
$frame1->Button(-text => 'button1')->pack;
$frame1->Button(-text => 'button2')->pack;

# a more visible Frame
$frame2 = $mw->Frame(-borderwidth => 2, -relief => 'groove');
$frame2->Button(-text => 'button1, frame2')->pack;
$frame2->Button(-text => 'button2, frame2')->pack;

# a Frame in a Frame
$frame3 = $frame2->Frame(-borderwidth => 3, -relief => 'raised');
$frame3->Button(-text => 'button1, frame3')->pack;

$frame3->pack;  # not visible yet
$frame2->pack;  # still nothing visible...
$frame1->pack;  # now we can see all the Frames and Buttons
```

The Frame's parent can be a MainWindow, a Toplevel, or another Frame widget.† After the Frame is created, it can become a parent to other widgets. You must have created the Frame but not necessarily packed it on the screen for it to be the parent of other widgets. Keep in mind that even if you pack other widgets inside your Frame, if you don't pack the Frame as well, the other widgets won't show on the screen.

---

* To change this behavior, use packPropagate or gridPropagate.

† Technically, any widget can be a parent of another widget, but life is easier when widgets are children of a Frame, or else we have to use the -in option with pack, confusing everybody. Keep it simple, and you'll be much happier.

Creating a Toplevel Widget

To create a Toplevel, call `Toplevel` from the desired parent widget, usually the Main-Window widget (created with `MainWindow->new( )`). The returned item is a reference to the Toplevel widget; the reference allows you to configure the widget, call methods on it, and place items within it. Here is a simple example:

```
use Tk;
$mw = MainWindow->new;
$mw->title("MainWindow");
$mw->Button(-text => "Toplevel", -command => \&do_Toplevel)->pack( );

MainLoop;
sub do_Toplevel {
  if (! Exists($tl)) {
    $tl = $mw->Toplevel( );
    $tl->title("Toplevel");
    $tl->Button(-text => "Close",
                -command => sub { $tl->withdraw })->pack;
  } else {
    $tl->deiconify( );
    $tl->raise( );
  }
}
```

When you run this program, clicking on the Toplevel Button in the MainWindow creates the Toplevel widget (if it needs to) and displays it. Clicking Close hides the Toplevel from view. You need to test for the existence of the Toplevel before you show it, because you don't want to recreate it if it already exists, and you don't want to try to show something that doesn't exist.

When the Close Button is clicked, the Toplevel is withdrawn. It still exists, it is just not visible to the user. This saves time the next time around by redisplaying the same window. You can also use `withdraw` if you don't want to show the Toplevel while you are filling it with widgets. Simply use the `withdraw` method, place the interior widgets, then use `deiconify` and `raise` to redisplay the widget.

Options

Since Frame and Toplevel widgets share similar tasks in Perl/Tk, they share similar options, as listed here. The two following sections list the options that apply to both widgets. After that we'll cover the specific options that haven't yet been covered in a previous chapter.

`-background => color`
: Sets the color of the widget's background area (there is no foreground area).

`-borderwidth => amount`
: Sets the width of the widget's edges. Default is 0.

-class => *classname*

   Indicates the class associated with the widget instance in the option database. This option can actually be used on any widget, not just a Frame or Toplevel.

-colormap => "new" | $window

   Specifies whether to use a new colormap or share one with another widget in the application. If a colormap value is not specified, the window uses the display's colormap.

-container => **0** | 1

   If true, this Frame/Toplevel will be used to contain another embedded application, typically another Tk application.

-cursor => *cursorname*

   Changes the cursor to use when the mouse pointer is over the widget.

-height => *amount*

   Sets the starting height of the widget in a valid screen distance.

-highlightbackground => *color*

   Sets the color the highlight rectangle should be when the widget does not have keyboard focus.

-highlightcolor => *color*

   Sets the color the highlight rectangle should be when the widget does have the keyboard focus. Default color is black.

-highlightthickness => *amount*

   Sets the thickness of the highlight rectangle. Default is 0.

-relief => **'flat'**|'groove'|'raised'|'ridge'|'sunken'|'solid'

   Changes the appearance of the edges of the widget.

-takefocus => **0** | 1 | undef

   Specifies whether the widget should take the focus.

-visual => "*type #*"

   When used on an X Windows system, changes the depth of colors available to your application. Does nothing on Win32 systems.

-width => *amount*

   Sets the starting width of the Frame in a valid screen distance.

Frame-Specific Options

Here is a list of options specific to Frame widgets:

-label => *labelstring*

   Adds a label to the Frame with the text *labelstring*

-labelPack => [*pack options*]

   Specifies pack options for the label

```
-labelVariable => \$variable
```
Specifies a variable that contains the text for the label

Toplevel-Specific Options

Here is a list of options specific to Toplevel widgets:

```
-menu => $menu
```
Indicates that the Toplevel uses the Menu in $menu across the top of the window.

```
-use => $windowid
```
$windowid is the hexadecimal window ID of the containing widget within which this Toplevel is embedded. On Win32, use the window's handle, or HWND. The -container option should also be set to true.

```
-screen => screenname
```
Sets the screen on which to place the Toplevel. Cannot be changed by the configure method.

Viewing a Frame

The default for a Frame widget is not to be seen. In order to see it on the screen, you need use the -relief and -borderwidth options. The default -relief is 'flat', and the default -borderwidth is 0. If you want the Frame to have any edges at all, make sure you change -borderwidth to something higher than 0. Also, unless you put something in a Frame, you'll never see it. So, for the examples in Figure 11-1, we have inserted a Label widget and an Entry widget that state the relief of that Frame. Note that this is an actual Label widget, not the -label option described in the next section.

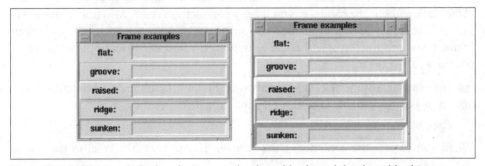

Figure 11-1. Different relief values for Frames; -borderwidth of 2 and -borderwidth of 5

Using -relief and -borderwidth is a great way to find where your Frame is in the window. If you have a complicated window, it's confusing to remember which Frame is where. A common trick is to add -borderwidth => 5, -relief => 'groove' when creating the Frame, which makes it stand out in the window.

Adding a Label to a Frame

With Perl/Tk, you can add a label to your Frame by using the -label option, which takes a text string as an argument:

```
$mw->Frame(-label => "My Frame:")->pack;
...
# configure label in Frame later :
$frame->configure(-label => "My Frame:")->pack;
```

By default, the label is placed at the top of the Frame, centered across the width (see Figure 11-2). Again, we put something in the Frame so you can see the Frame as well as the item in the Frame. In this case, we placed a Button with the default pack options in the Frame. We also created the Frame with -relief => 'groove', -borderwidth => 2 so you can see the edge.

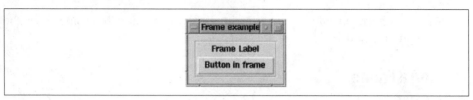

Figure 11-2. Frame with label in default position

To change the location of the label inside the Frame, use the -labelPack option. It takes an anonymous array as an argument, where the array contains any pack options for the label:

```
-labelPack => [ -side => 'left', -anchor => 'w']
```

Be careful to notice that this option has an uppercase letter in it. If you try to use -labelPack without the capital P, you'll get a compilation error. Also notice that there isn't a -labelGrid option available. You must use pack to put widgets inside your Frame if you are going to use the -label option. If you don't, your application might not run at all.

Instead of using a static text string with your Frame's label, use the -labelVariable option to assign a variable (again, notice the capital V):

```
-labelVariable => \$label_text
```

When you change the contents of the variable $label_text, the label in the Frame changes as well.

The instant you use the -label or -labelVariable option, a label is created and placed inside the Frame. You can use these options either in the initial Frame call or later with $frame->configure(...). If you use them later, the label is placed above all other widgets inside the Frame.

Frames Aren't Interactive

The Frame widget itself is not interactive. By default, it can't accept input from the user. The widgets inside it can, but the Frame cannot. As always, the focus ability is controlled by the -takefocus option:

```
-takefocus => 0
```

With a Frame widget, it is set to 0. If for some reason you need to get input from the user on your Frame, you will need to change it to -takefocus => 1.

Colormap Complications

When you are running several applications at once and you start a web browser, you'll sometimes notice that the colors become corrupted. When you switch from an application to the browser, the colors in your other applications suddenly change. If you switch back from your browser to an application, the browser colors change. This happens because the web browser is a color hog. It has requested more colors than the windowing system can allocate at once. The OS must alter the colormap between applications to allow the active application to use the colors it wants to use. The colormap simply gives the windowing system a way to keep track of who is using which colors.

Perl/Tk applications can have many colors too; you can get color-happy and make each Button a different color of the rainbow. This can cause problems if there are other applications running that want a lot of different colors too. If other applications are color hogs, Perl/Tk will switch to black-and-white mode. If you don't like this behavior, you can use the -colormap option to override it. -colormap takes either the word "new" or a reference to another window. If given "new", it will create its own colormap. When you use -colormap with another window, the two windows will share the colormap. But there is one catch, and that is the -visual option.

The -visual option takes as an argument a string that contains a keyword and a number. For example:

```
-visual => "staticgrey 2"
```

The keyword can be any one of the following: staticgrey, greyscale, staticcolor, pseudocolor, truecolor, or directcolor. The number indicates the depth of color used (2 = black/white).

When you use -colormap to share the colormap between two windows, the -visual option for both must be the same. This means that -visual must be undef for both (the default) or it must have the same value. Neither -colormap nor -visual can be altered by the configure method.

The Magical Class Option

To force your Frame or Toplevel to be in another class (besides Frame), use the -class option (see Chapter 16). Simply give it a string that is a unique class identifier:

```
-class => 'Myframe'
-class => 'MyToplevel'
```

Frame Methods

The only methods available with the Frame widget are cget and configure. These are described in detail in Chapter 13.

Toplevel Methods

The Toplevel widget methods are listed and explained in the following sections. It is important to note that all of these methods apply to a MainWindow as well; a Main-Window is just a specialized Toplevel widget. Also keep in mind that a lot of these methods were designed originally for use with a Unix windowing environment, and quite a few of them will state "No effect in Win32 system." Many of these functions serve no useful purpose to the typical ordinary Perl/Tk application, but we document them here for thoroughness.

Several of the methods here alter *window manager properties*, which often look like WM_PROPERTY_THING. These properties are also traditionally associated with the X Window system on Unix, but some still apply in Win32 systems. If a specific method doesn't say anything about which system it applies to, it will apply to both. If it applies only to one or the other (or only half-works in one system), this will be mentioned as well.

Sizing a Toplevel

You can use the geometry method to define or retrieve a geometry string. A *geometry string* determines the size and placement of a window on the screen. The geometry string is a concept that originated on Unix systems and is a bit cryptic at first glance. Here is a regular expression that describes a complete geometry string:

```
^=?(\d+x\d+)?([+-]\d+[+-]\d+)?$
```

The equals sign can be omitted completely (and usually is). The first portion (\d+x\d+) is the width and height (in that order), separated by an x. Both width and height are specified in pixels by default and in grid units if the window is gridded with the grid method (described later). The last portion of the geometry string represents the x and y coordinates of the location in which the Toplevel should be placed on the screen. Both x and y are always in pixels. Here are a few examples of what some geometry strings look like:

```
300x300       # width and height both = 300
300x450       # width = 300, height = 450
300x450+0+0   # width = 300, height = 450 placed in upper left corner
300x450-0-0   # width = 300, height = 450 placed in lower right corner
300x450+10+10 # width = 300, height = 450
              # placed 10 pixels out from upper left corner
+0+0          # window is 'natural' size, placed in upper left corner
```

When geometry is called with no arguments, the current geometry string is returned. You can also specify a new geometry by using geometry with the new geometry string as the argument. To set the size and position of the window immediately, you would do this:

```
$mw = MainWindow->new( );
$mw->geometry("300x450+0+0");
```

If you specify only the width and height, the placement of the window is determined by the window manager. If you specify only the positioning, then the size of the window will be determined by the widgets placed within the Toplevel, but the window will be placed at those x and y coordinates.

You can force the window back to its natural size by calling geometry with an empty geometry string:

```
$toplevel->geometry("");
```

Maximum Size

You can use maxsize to restrict the largest size of the window. It takes two integers as arguments, as follows:

```
$toplevel->maxsize(300,300);
```

If you call maxsize without any arguments, you get an empty string or a list with two items in it representing the current values. Calling maxsize with two empty strings cancels the limitation.

Minimum Size

You can also restrict the smallest size of the window by using minsize. The window will always be at least the size specified:

```
$toplevel->minsize(100,100);
```

Calling minsize without arguments returns an empty string or a list containing the width and height, respectively. Calling minsize with two empty strings eliminates the minimum size restriction.

Limiting Resizing

You can control whether a window can be resized in width and/or height by using resizable:

```
$toplevel->resizable(1, 0);
($canwidth, $canheight) = $toplevel->resizable();
```

Specifying 1 means it is resizable, and 0 means it is nonresizable in the specified direction. If you don't specify any arguments, resizable returns a list with two items. The first item is a 1 or 0 and indicates whether the width is resizable. The second item is a 1 or 0 and indicates whether the height is resizable. By default, a window is resizable in both directions.

Using a Size Aspect

You can use the aspect method to force the window to stay a certain width and height:

```
$toplevel->aspect( [ minN, minD, maxN, maxD ]);
```

In this example, the N in $minN$ and $maxN$ stands for "numerator" and the D in $minD$ and $maxD$ stands for "denominator."

The aspect method does some very subtle things, and you'll probably never use it. If you do, play around with different values (starting with the example that follows) to get the effect you want.

When you use the aspect method with no arguments, it returns either an empty string (if there are no constraints to the aspect of the window) or an array containing four elements:

```
($minN, $minD, $maxN, $maxD) = $toplevel->aspect;
```

Using these values, you can see how aspect controls the window:

```
($minN/$minD) < width/height < ($maxN/$maxD)
```

You can also send four empty strings to unset the aspect restrictions on the window. Try using $toplevel->aspect(1,2,3,1); the effect is subtle.

Setting the Title

To change the text across the top of the window, use the title method:

```
$toplevel->title("This will be the title");
```

Pass a string in with title and the new title will appear immediately in the window, assuming the window is currently visible. If you don't pass an argument with title, the current title string is returned. For the X Window System, the default title of a window is the name used to run the program, and the first character of the name is uppercase. For Microsoft Windows, the title always starts out as Toplevel.

Showing the Toplevel

The deiconify method causes the Toplevel to be displayed noniconified or deiconifies it immediately if the window has already been displayed once. If the window has been withdrawn, a $toplevel->raise( ) must also be done to display the window correctly.

If you call it with no arguments, the raise method brings the Toplevel to the front of all the other Toplevel windows in the application:

```
$toplevel->raise( );
```

You can also put the Toplevel in front of another Toplevel:

```
$toplevel->raise($other_toplevel);
```

It is sometimes necessary to use both deiconify and raise to get the window to show up on the screen.

Withdrawing the Toplevel

When you create a window, it is a good idea to make it invisible while you fill it with widgets. You can do so by using the withdraw method:

```
$toplevel->withdraw( );
```

If the window is already visible, withdraw will make the window manager forget about the window until it has been deiconified.

Iconifying the Toplevel

The iconify method forces the Toplevel into iconified form:

```
$toplevel->iconify( );
```

Iconifying is not the same as withdrawing the window. Withdrawing the window will not show an icon on the desktop. Also, note that window managers are free to decide what to do in the iconified state. Some window managers (such as Microsoft Windows or KDE) don't show icons but just mark the windows in the task bar differently.

Specifying the Icon Bitmap

When you iconify your application under the X Window System, it is represented on the screen with a bitmap. You use the iconbitmap method to specify this bitmap:

```
$toplevel->iconbitmap( );
$toplevel->iconbitmap("bitmap");
```

It takes a bitmap in the same form as the -bitmap option supported by the Button widget (see Chapter 4). Calling iconbitmap with no arguments returns the current bitmap or an empty string. Calling iconbitmap with an empty string removes the current bitmap.

On Win32 systems, the application is kept in the Start taskbar with an unchangeable Tk icon and the name of the application. Using the `iconbitmap` method on a Win32 system does nothing.

In recent versions of Perl/Tk, the `Icon` method should be used instead. The `Icon` method works with both Unix and Win32 and allows you to specify an image instead of a bitmap, if you prefer.

Specifying the Icon Mask

A mask for the icon bitmap can be specified by using the `iconmask` method (remember, this will only work with X Window Systems). It also takes a bitmap specified from a file or a default bitmap name (see the `-bitmap` documentation in Chapter 4). Where the bitmap mask has zeros, no part of the normal icon bitmap will be displayed. Where the mask has ones, normal icon bitmaps will be displayed.

Calling `iconmask` with no arguments returns the current bitmap mask or an empty string if no bitmap is being used. Calling `iconmask` with an empty string unsets the mask:

```
$currentmask = $toplevel->iconmask();  # get the mask
$toplevel->iconmask("bitmapname");     # set the mask
$toplevel->iconmask("");               # unset the mask
```

Setting the Name of the Icon

The `iconname` method sets or returns the current text associated with the icon that is displayed when the application is iconified. You can pass in a new string or an empty string:

```
$toplevel->iconname("newname");
$current_name = $toplevel->iconname();
```

If you don't specify an argument at all, `iconname` returns the current icon name or an empty string. You can query and set the icon name on a Win32 system, but it doesn't do anything. This method is used on the X Window System only.

Setting the Icon Position

The `iconposition` method suggests to the X Window System manager where the icon should be placed on the desktop when the application is iconified:

```
($x, $y) = $toplevel->iconposition();
$toplevel->iconposition($x, $y);
```

If x and y aren't specified, a list is returned containing only two items: the current x and y coordinates. If you call `iconposition` with two empty strings (one for each x and y), the suggestion to the window manager is canceled.

Using a Window Instead of an Icon

Some systems (not including Win32) support the idea of using a widget (or window) instead of a bitmap for an icon. Specify the widget by using the iconwindow method. To find out what the current widget is, call iconwindow with no arguments (an empty string is returned if there is no associated $widget). You can specify an empty string instead of $widget to cancel by using a widget for the icon:

```
$currentwindow = $toplevel->iconwindow(); # get
$toplevel->iconwindow($window);          # set
$toplevel->iconwindow("");               # unset
```

Determining the State

The state method returns one of three strings: "normal", "iconic", or "withdrawn".

```
$state = $toplevel->state();
```

The string indicates the state of the window when state is called.

Assigning a Client Name

Every graphical program has a WM_CLIENT_MACHINE window property, which should be the hostname of the machine the program is executing on. This property can be changed using the client method, as follows:

```
$mw->client (new_client_name);
```

If new_client_name is omitted, the current name is returned. Passing undef to the client method resets the WM_CLIENT_MACHINE property to its original value.

Window Properties

The protocol method controls the following window properties: WM_DELETE_ WINDOW, WM_SAVE_YOURSELF, and WM_TAKE_FOCUS. The callback (if any) associated with each property will be invoked when the window manager recognizes the event associated with the property:

```
$toplevel->protocol ( [ property_name] [, callback ] );
```

The WM_DELETE_WINDOW property callback is invoked when the window has been deleted by the window manager. By default, there is a callback assigned by Perl/ Tk that destroys the window. If you assign a new callback, your callback will be invoked instead of the default callback. If you need to save data associated with that window, do so in the callback, then invoke $toplevel->destroy() to mimic the correct behavior afterward.

The other two properties, WM_SAVE_YOURSELF and WM_TAKE_FOCUS, are used much less commonly. For instance, WM_TAKE_FOCUS is used in Unix systems but not in Win32. The presence of these properties is dependent on the window system you are running. If your application will be running on multiple systems, don't expect these properties to always be available. To find out if they are available, assign each one a callback that does a print, then run the application to see if the print is ever invoked.

If you leave out the callback when you use protocol, the current callback assigned to that property will be returned (or an empty string, if there isn't a current callback assigned). You can remove the callback by sending an empty string instead of the callback. If neither argument is specified, the method returns a list of all properties that have callbacks assigned to them.

The Colormap Property

The colormapwindows method affects the WM_COLORMAP_WINDOWS property. This property is used to talk to the window manager about windows that have private colormaps. Using colormapwindows with no arguments returns a list of windows. The list contains windows (in order of priority) that have different colormaps than their parents:

```
@list = $toplevel->colormapwindows();
```

You can pass a list of windows to colormapwindows as well:

```
$toplevel->colormapwindows(@list);
```

If you don't use this function at all, Perl/Tk will take care of everything for you, although the order of the windows might be different.

The Command Property

The command method (not to be confused with the -command option used with most of the widgets) controls the WM_COMMAND property. When used with no arguments, command returns a list reference:

```
$listref = $toplevel->command();
```

The list holds the words of the command used to start the application. Use this bit of code to determine what your application command was (which is sometimes nothing):

```
$listptr = $mw->command();
foreach (@$listptr) {
  print "$_\n";
}
```

You can unset the WM_COMMAND property by sending an empty string:

```
$toplevel->command("");
```

The Focus Model

The focusmodel method controls whether or not the Toplevel widget will give up the keyboard focus when another application or window should have it:

```
$toplevel->focusmodel( [ "active" | "passive" ] );
```

The default is "passive", meaning it will give up the keyboard focus. The changes present in your application depend completely on the type of window manager you use. Our testing revealed no changes under Win32 or the X Window System.

Getting a Widget's Window ID

If a widget has been reparented by the windowing system, the frame method returns the window ID of the window manager's decorative Frame. Otherwise, the returned window ID is that of the widget itself. See also the id method.

The Application Grid

The grid method restricts the size of a window. However, to avoid conflicts with the grid geometry manager (as described in Chapter 2), you must use the wm method to invoke grid indirectly, as follows:

```
$mw->wm('grid', ... );
```

When you tell the window to grid, you are restricting its size. The size must always snap to the grid as defined in grid. If you remember the Listbox widget and the -setgrid option to the Listbox widget back in Chapter 7, once you use -setgrid => 1 on a Listbox, you can use @list = $toplevel->wm('grid'); to determine the values used in the grid. Supposing the values you get are 10, 10, 7, and 17, this means the base width and height were each 10 pixels and each grid unit incremented by 7 pixels in width and 17 pixels in height. You can change the grid size and increments by calling wm('grid', ...) with new values if you desire; but if you don't, Tk manages everything quite nicely for any of the gridded widgets.

You should also know that you can unset the grid values by using empty strings for each instead of new values.

Being the Leader

This is another method you'll never use, but it's good to know about. The group method makes a widget the group leader of related windows. For each Toplevel that you want to be in $widget's group, call $toplevel->group($widget). If $widget isn't specified, it will return the current group leader of $toplevel; it will return an empty string if $toplevel isn't part of a group.

You can send an empty string to cancel Toplevel's association with that group. That is, to remove a Toplevel from the group, call $toplevel->group("").

Removing Decorations

To make a window with none of the normal window decorations (titlebars, borders, and so on), you can use the overrideredirect method with a true value:

```
$toplevel->overrideredirect(1);  # Remove all decorations
```

Be careful though; you won't be able to move the window on the screen once it is drawn. If you forgot to put an Exit Button on it, you won't be able to quit the application gracefully (although a Control-C in the window that started the script will kill it).

This is a way to make a splash screen (a screen that shows up as your application is loading). Remember that you must call MainLoop or update for it to show up at all. Chapter 15 discusses Tk::Splashscreen.

Calling overrideredirect with no argument returns the current value (1 or 0):

```
$current_value = $toplevel->overrideredirect();
```

Calling overrideredirect again with a 0 value will not turn decorations back on once the window has been displayed.

Who Placed the Window?

When the Toplevel widget is placed on the window, either the window manager tells the program where to be or the program tells the window manager where it wants to be. In some cases, the user positions the window manually when it comes up.

```
$who = $toplevel->positionfrom();
$toplevel->positionfrom("program");  # Try and force it
```

When called without argument, the positionfrom method returns information on which one happened. If it returns the string "program", an empty string, or a $widget, it means either the window manager or the program requested the position. If positionfrom returns the string "user", the user placed the window manually when it was created.

You can try to force which will happen by calling positionfrom with the "program" or "user" string, but it will only work if your window manager agrees with you.

Who Sized It?

The sizefrom method does the same thing positionfrom does except, it returns information regarding the size of the window.

```
$who = $toplevel->sizefrom(); # "program" or "user"?
$toplevel->sizefrom("user");  # Try and force it
```

Transient Windows

A transient window is one that isn't quite a real window (such as a pulldown menu). You can indicate to the window manager that the Toplevel (for example, the pulldown menu) is related to its master (the window in which it is displayed) by using the transient method:

```
$mymaster = $toplevel->transient();
$toplevel->transient($master);
```

If you don't use any arguments with transient, it returns either the current master or an empty string.

The appearance of transient windows is different among different window managers. On some window managers, there is no difference, whereas some allow for customization with their *.rc* files. Some only use a minimal title bar, and some show no title bar at all. Iconifying the master window may or may not iconify the transient window as well. Also, sometimes transient windows are always on top of the master window. All of this should be taken into consideration when writing portable code.

Creating Multiple MainWindows

Occasionally, you may need to create multiple MainWindows in the same application. Typically, having two MainWindows in one application isn't always a wise idea, since bitmaps and images aren't shared between MainWindows, and some Tk modules are unreliable when shared. But we're going to explore it anyway, because it's an interesting exercise. To show how it's done, we'll start with an advanced "Hello Worlds" program, so named because it uses two MainWindows.

You might be wondering what *useful* programs might exist that take advantage of more than one screen. Nonlinear digital video editing software is a great example. A fancy high-resolution screen displays the movie in progress, and secondary screens contain editing controls. Or, any application that requires lots of screen real estate can spread its windows across multiple screens. We won't be doing any of that fancy stuff, as you'll see.

Our little program begins typically enough, importing all the required Tk symbols, subroutines, variables, classes, widgets, and methods, then opening the first Main-Window, $mw1, in the normal fashion.*

```
#!/usr/local/bin/perl -w
#
# Advanced Hello World program using two MainWindows.

use Tk;
use subs qw/beep/;
use strict;

my $mw1 = MainWindow->new;
```

---

* It runs strict and with warnings enabled, as do most of the programs in this book; all yours should too, at least during development. If you fail to heed this warning, subtle (and sometimes overt) bugs will bite you, sooner rather than later.

By default, MainWindow opens its window on the display pointed to by $ENV{DISPLAY}, which in Unix is normally :0 (assuming you haven't pointed it elsewhere). Technically, a display specification consists of three fields: [*host*]:*server*[.*screen*], where *host* is the machine name and *server* and *screen* are usually zero.

The screen number is interpreted in at least two different ways. If there are multiple physical monitors that logically act as one, they are addressed via screen number. The screens are treated as a contiguous area, so if you want to move a window from one monitor to another, just grab it and drag. Alternatively, the screen number may specify special attributes of a single monitor. For instance, the MacX server treats screen zero as a monochrome monitor and screen one as color.

We open the second MainWindow just like the first but provide a command-line hook to send it elsewhere. (See Chapter 16 for details on command-line processing.)

```
my $mw2 = MainWindow->new(-screen => $ARGV[0] ||= $ENV{DISPLAY});
$mw1->Button(-text => 'MainWindow 1 Bell', -command => [\&beep, $mw1])->pack;
$mw1->Button(-text => 'MainWindow 2 Bell', -command => [\&beep, $mw2])->pack;
$mw1->Button(qw/-text Quit -command/ => \&exit)->pack;

MainLoop;

sub beep {shift->bell}
```

Note that the parameter for MainWindow's constructor is -screen, not -display as you might imagine. If nothing is supplied on the command line, then both MainWindows appear on the same display, as shown in Figure 11-3.

Now pack three Buttons in the first MainWindow and set up simple callbacks to ring the bell on either of the MainWindows. Notice that each callback passes its MainWindow reference to the beep subroutine, which shift grabs from @_. (See Chapter 15 for more about callbacks.) As you'd expect, pressing either of the Bell Buttons sounds the display's audible alert.

This program is more interesting when $mw2 is redirected to another display,[*] where pressing its Bell Button causes the *remote* machine to beep.

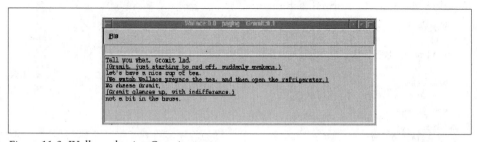

Figure 11-3. Wallace phoning Gromit

---

[*] Before you can use another display, its owner must give you permission. See the section on xauth authentication in Chapter 20 for details.

Putting Two MainWindows to Work

Here's a trickier dual-display program that has been slightly obfuscated by removing comments and disguising subroutine names. Before we discuss it, try to figure out what it does. To orient yourself, realize that variables beginning with "l" mean "local," and those beginning with "r" mean "remote." You have 60 seconds. Okay, GO!

```perl
my $lmw = MainWindow->new;
my $rmw = MainWindow->new(-screen => $ARGV[0] ||= $ENV{DISPLAY});
my($le, $lt) = &create_widgets($lmw);
my($re, $rt) = &create_widgets($rmw);
&config_widgets($le, $lt, $re, $rt);
&config_widgets($re, $rt, $le, $lt); $rmw->bell;
MainLoop;

sub create_widgets {
    my $screen = shift;
    my $e = $screen->Entry->pack(qw/-fill x -expand 1/);
    $e->focus;
    my $t = $screen->Text(qw/-height 10/)->pack;
    ($e, $t);
}

sub config_widgets {
    my($le, $lt, $re, $rt) = @_;
    $le->bind('<Return>' => [sub {
        my($le, $lt, $re, $rt) = @_;
        $rt->tagConfigure(qw/blue -underline 1/);
        my $input = $le->get . "\n";
        $le->delete(0, 'end');
        $lt->insert('end' => $input);
        $rt->insert('end' => $input, 'blue');
    }, $lt, $re, $rt]);
}
```

...5, 4, 3, 2, 1...time's up. Obviously, the key to understanding this program is the binding that config_widgets creates. (See Chapter 15 for more about bindings.)

Suppose Gromit is sitting in front of his Win32 computer and it happens to run an X server. In another part of the house, Wallace, an ever cheerful and willing-to-chat chap, runs our mystery program on his Linux box and specifies Gromit's display on the command line.

Figure 11-3 and Figure 11-4 show what might transpire and confirm that the mystery program is a Tk phone-clone.

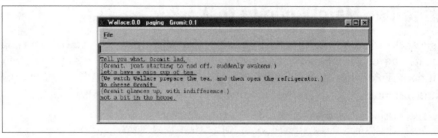

Figure 11-4. Gromit replying to a phone call from Wallace

There are several items worthy of note in the following code. First, here's the code:

```
1   #!/usr/local/bin/perl -w
2   #
3   # tkphone - Phone another X Display and have a line-mode conversation.
4   #
5   # Usage: see POD for details.
6
7   use Tk;
8   use subs qw/beep phone pconfig/;
9   use strict;
10
11  $ENV{DISPLAY} ||= ':0'; $ARGV[0] ||= $ENV{DISPLAY};
12
13  my $title = "$ENV{DISPLAY}   phoning   $ARGV[0]";
14  my $lmw = MainWindow->new(-title => $title);
15  my $rmw = MainWindow->new(-title => $title, -screen => $ARGV[0]);
16
17  my($le, $lt) = phone $lmw;
18  my($re, $rt) = phone $rmw;
19  pconfig $le, $lt, $re, $rt;
20  pconfig $re, $rt, $le, $lt; $rmw->bell;
21
22  MainLoop;
23
24  sub phone {
25
26      # Create the menubar and the phone Text Entry/display area.
27
28      my($screen) = @_;
29
30      my $menubar = $screen->Menu;
31      $screen->configure(-menu => $menubar);
32      my $file = $menubar->cascade(-label => '~File');
33      $file->command(-label => "Close", -command => [$screen => 'destroy']);
34      $file->command(-label => "Exit",  -command => \&exit);
35
36      my $e = $screen->Entry->pack(qw/-fill x -expand 1/);
37      $e->focus;
38      my $t = $screen->Text(qw/-height 10/)->pack;
39      ($e, $t);
```

```
40
41  }
42
43  sub pconfig {
44
45      # Configure local callbacks to talk to the remote party.
46
47      my($le, $lt, $re, $rt) = @_;
48
49      $le->bind('<Return>' => [sub {
50          my($le, $lt, $re, $rt) = @_;
51          $rt->tagConfigure(qw/blue -underline 1/);
52          my $input = $le->get . "\n";
53          $le->delete(0, 'end');
54          $lt->insert('end' => $input);
55          $rt->insert('end' => $input, 'blue');
56      }, $lt, $re, $rt]);
57
58  }
59  __END__
60
61  =head1 NAME
62
63  tkphone - Phone another X Display and have a line-mode conversation.
64
65  =head1 SYNOPSIS
66
67  B<tkphone> [I<display>]
68
69  =head1 DESCRIPTION
70
71  This program opens two MainWindows and arranges callbacks so they can
72  talk to each other.  It expects a single command line argument, the
73  remote
74  DISPLAY
75  specification
76  (defaults to :0 so you can phone yourself).
77
78  =head1 COPYRIGHT
79
80  Copyright (C) 1999 - 2000 ACME Rocket Supply, Inc. All rights reserved.
81
82  This program is free software; you can redistribute it and/or modify it under
83  the same terms as Perl itself.
84
85  =cut
```

On Win32, $ENV{DISPLAY} is undefined, so line 11 initializes it to quiet -w.

Lines 30 through 34 create a File menubutton with Close and Exit menu items. Examine them closely; destroying a MainWindow is not always sufficient to terminate the program, because Tk's MainLoop only ends when *all* MainWindows are destroyed (see Chapter 15). So, we provide Exit to really exit the application and Close, which destroys the local MainWindow, but only exits if the other MainWindow is already gone.

Lines 36 through 39 create and return an Entry widget for typing text and a Text widget that displays a transcript of the conversation between the phoner and phonee.

Lines 49 through 56 create the crucial <Return> binding that makes the application work.

Lines 51 through 55 get the data from the local Entry widget and insert it in the local and remote Text widgets, underlining the remote text. (The underline tag name is "blue", because it originally colored the remote text in blue, but colors won't show up well in this book. The Perl virtue of laziness took control, and the tag definition was changed rather than all occurrences of the tag name!) Which widgets are local and which are remote is relative to the particular MainWindow we are in front of. The fact that the binding works from either point of view is due to symmetry. Seek out symmetrical situations; they often simplify code.

Finally, lines 60 through 85 are the program's documentation, in the form of Plain Old Documentation (POD). We'll include POD examples throughout the book. Check out the *perlpod* and *perldoc* documentation for detailed information. On Unix, typing **perldoc tkphone** produces an output similar to Figure 11-5.

```
TKPHONE(1)      User Contributed Perl Documentation      TKPHONE(1)


NAME
        tkphone - Phone another X Display and have a line-mode
        conversation.

SYNOPSIS
        tkphone [display]

DESCRIPTION
        This program opens two MainWindows and arranges callbacks
        so they can talk to each other.  It expects a single
        command line argument, the remote DISPLAY specification
        (defaults to :0 so you can phone yourself).

COPYRIGHT
        Copyright (C) 1999 - 2000 ACME Rocket Supply, Inc. All
        rights reserved.

        This program is free software; you can redistribute it
        and/or modify it under the same terms as Perl itself.
```

Figure 11-5. How perldoc might render tkphone's POD

## CHAPTER 12

The Menu System

This chapter describes the menu system: its components, how to use them, and how they behave in a Unix and Win32 environment. Of primary interest are menubars and conventional linear menus (pulldown, option, and popup), although at chapter's end, we do visit a new kind of menu, the pie menu.

Typically, a menu contains commands that aren't used frequently, such as configuration options, File Open, File Close, Help, and so on. Commands that are used frequently may not be appropriate for menus and should be placed directly in the window to provide easier access for the user. Some examples of how menus might be used are for:

- Creating a File, Edit, and Help menubar across the top of your application
- Displaying a list of fonts from which the user can choose, with the selected font marked with a checkmark
- Displaying a list of editing commands that become available when the user right-clicks on another object in your window (such as a Listbox or Entry widget)
- Making a Menu pop up with a click of a button

You can build each of these different types of menus with the basic Menu widget.

Menu System Components

First, let's take a quick tour of the components of a menu.

Menus and Menu Items

The foundation of the menu system is the Menu widget, a rectangular window that, as a result of some event, appears out of the ether and displays one or more columns of *menu items*. The event that causes the menu to appear is often the press of a Menubutton or keyboard character, but could just as well be a mouseclick or even a callback. The action of making a menu appear is called *posting*; making a menu disappear is called *unposting*. There are six flavors of menu item, shown in Figure 12-1: *cascade, checkbutton, command, radiobutton, separator,* and *tearoff.*

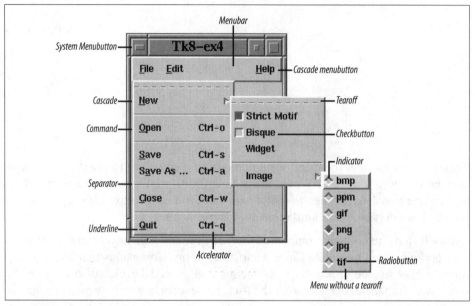

Figure 12-1. Important components of the menu system

With the exception of a separator, clicking a menu item initiates item-specific behavior, such as executing a callback, posting a menu, or perhaps setting a Perl variable. We'll examine the various menu items in detail shortly. Briefly:

- Clicking a cascade menu item posts another menu immediately to the right of the cascade. The new menu may have menu items of any number or type, including another cascade. A series of cascades are posted in quick succession from left to right, hence the menu item's name.

- A checkbutton menu item works just like the Checkbutton widget described in Chapter 4.

- Clicking a command menu item invokes a callback.

- A radiobutton menu item works just like the Radiobutton widget described in Chapter 4.

- A separator menu item is a passive line used to divide a Menu into logical sections.

- A tearoff menu item (when present) is always Menu index zero. After clicking a tearoff, you can drag the Menu somewhere so it's always available for fast access.

Menu Indexes

Many Menu methods expect a menu item *index* that specifies which menu item to operate upon. The following are valid menu indexes:

- Every menu item is identified by an integer ordinal, starting at zero for the top-most menu item and increasing linearly downward. By default, each menu has a tearoff menu item that is ordinal zero (tearoffs are the dashed lines at the tops of menus). Pressing the tearoff reparents the menu by cloning it in a new Toplevel, so you can move the menu about in its own window.

- The keyword active, which means the menu item that is currently selected (the mouse is over it and it is highlighted). If there are no menu items active, active means the same as none.

- The keywords end or last, which mean the last menu item in the Menu. If there are no items in the Menu, end means the same as none.

- The keyword none, which means no menu item is selected.

- A pixel y coordinate of the form @pixel_offset, where pixel_offset is an integer, relative to the Menu's top-left corner.

- A regular expression matched against the menu item's -label option. Typically, referring to a menu item by label rather than by ordinal is preferred, because the code should still work even if the number of menu items changes.

Manipulating Menus

Configure a Menu widget using the configure and cget methods, just like any other widget. If you're unfamiliar with these methods, see Chapter 13.

Here are some other Menu methods:

$menu->clone(*parent_menu, clone_type*)
: Clones a Menu, but you never call it yourself. Tk makes clones of menubar and tearoff Menus. Enter **perldoc Tk::Menu** for details.

$menu->post(*x, y*)
: Posts a Menu at root window coordinates (*x, y*). This method is most often superseded by the Post or Popup methods.

$menu->unpost
: Unmaps a Menu so it's no longer displayed.

Manipulating Menu Items

Configuring menu items is analogous to configuring widgets, except that we want to limit our activities to one menu item; that's what the entryconfigure and entrycget methods are for. The format is:

```
$menu->entryconfigure(index, -option => value);
```

The index, which can be in any of the previously described forms, specifies which menu item to configure. To fetch the value of a particular menu item option, use:

```
$menu->entrycget(index, -option);
```

Of course, there are other things you can do with menu items:

$menu->activate(*index*)

Makes the menu item at *index* the sole active menu item.

$menu->delete(*index* [, *index_end*])

Deletes menu item *index* or the range *index* through *index_end*

$menu->index(*index*)

Returns the integer ordinal of the menu item at *index*, where *index* can be any of the previously described forms

$menu->insert(*index*, *type* [, *options*])

Inserts a new menu item of *type* before *index*, where *type* may be cascade, checkbutton, command, radiobutton, or separator

$menu->invoke(*index*)

Executes the callback associated with menu item *index*

$menu->postcascade(*index*)

Posts the menu associated with the cascade menu item *index*

$menu->type(*index*)

Returns a string indicating the type of menu item at *index*

$menu->yposition(*index*)

Returns the y coordinate of the top-left pixel of the menu item at *index*

Menubars

Most nontrivial applications have *menubars* arrayed across the tops of their Main-Windows (or any Toplevels for that matter). Arranged within a menubar is a series of *menubuttons*, which, when pressed, post menus. Unfortunately, these days the term menubutton is somewhat of a misnomer, because in modern Tks, the menubutton is not an actual Menubutton widget but a cascade menu item. This came about because of menu system support for multiple operating systems.

Prior to Perl/Tk Version 8, menubars were Frames filled with Menubutton widgets, and programmers were responsible for managing the geometry and appearance of the entire apparatus. Perl/Tk Versions 8 and above support a native look and feel for Unix and Win32,[*] so to keep menubar management simple and consistent from the user

---

[*] Tcl/Tk also supports MacOS Classic. We'll mention menubar support code for this operating system even though it's not currently supported by Perl/Tk. But Apple's next generation operating system, Mac OS X, is BSD Unix-based, so it's possible to run Perl/Tk with a Unix look and feel on a Mac today. Work is in progress to convert the Tcl/Tk widgets to native Aqua, so we may see Perl/Tk with a Mac OS X look in the future.

and application developer points of view, a new menubar management scheme was devised. The basic idea is that the menubar is just a standard Menu widget associated with a MainWindow or Toplevel widget, and cascade menu items fill the role of Menubuttons. In fact, these statements created the menubar portion of Figure 12-1:

```
$mw->configure(-menu => my $menubar = $mw->Menu);

my $file = $menubar->cascade(-label => '~File');
my $edit = $menubar->cascade(-label => '~Edit');
my $help = $menubar->cascade(-label => '~Help');
```

To keep things simple, we'll call menubar buttons that post menus "menubuttons," whether they're real Menubuttons or just cascade menu items. Menubutton widgets are discussed in a later section.

The menu system is also aware of special operating system–dependent menubuttons, which is why the Help menubutton in Figure 12-1 is right justified (a custom in the Unix world). Under Mac OS, which always has a Help menubutton at the top of the display, Help menu items are *appended* to the existing Help items. Similarly, Apple menu items are *prepended* to the existing Apple menu items. Later on, we'll see how to augment the System menubutton on Win32 systems.

In summary, Tk 8 menubars have these benefits over the classical Frame/Menubutton approach:

- Identical programming interface regardless of the underlying operating system
- Native look and feel for enhanced user experience
- Automatic geometry management of the menubar and its buttons (cascades)
- Special processing for Apple, Help, and System menubuttons

Figure 12-2 shows how the code that produced Figure 12-1 is rendered on a Win32 machine. In particular, note how the Help menubutton is *not* treated specially and *not* right justified.

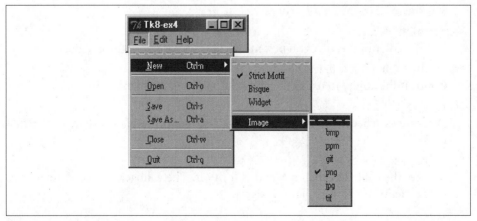

Figure 12-2. Compare this picture produced on Win32 with Figure 12-1, produced on Unix

Menu Options

As with any widget, there are options that affect how the Menu looks and behaves. The following is a list of the options available for the Menu widget:

-activebackground => *color*
> Sets the background color behind the active menu item.

-activeborderwidth => *amount*
> Sets the edge width of the active menu item's border.

-activeforeground => *color*
> Sets the text color of the active menu item.

-background => *color*
> Sets the background color of the entire menu.

-borderwidth => *amount*
> Sets the width of the menu's edge.

-cursor => *cursorname*
> Sets the cursor displayed when the mouse cursor is over the menu.

-disabledforeground => *color*
> Sets the text color of any disabled menu items.

-font => *font*
> Sets the font of the menu text.

-foreground => *color*
> Sets the color of the text in the menu.

-menuitems => *list*
> Defines a list of items to create in the menu.

-postcommand => *callback*
> Sets the callback that is invoked before the menu is posted to the screen.

-relief => 'flat' | 'groove' | **'raised'** | 'ridge' | 'sunken'
> Sets the relief of the menu's edges.

-selectcolor => *color*
> Sets the color of the selection box in checkbutton or radiobutton items.

-takefocus => **0** | 1| undef
> Controls the ability to use the keyboard to traverse the menu.

-tearoff => 0 | **1**
> Determines whether or not the menu will contain the tearoff item as the first item.

-tearoffcommand => callback | 1
> Invokes the callback when a Menu is torn off. The callback is passed references to the Menu and new Toplevel widgets.

-title => *string*
> Title of the torn-off Toplevel.

Menubars and Pulldown Menus

Perhaps the best way to learn about the menu system is to examine the program that produced Figures 12-1 and 12-2. We're going to show two ways to create those menus, first using a straightforward strategy and then a more elegant one.

Menubars the Clunky, Casual, Old-Fashioned Way

Here's one way to do it using Perl/Tk 8. We begin by creating a normal Menu and configuring it as the MainWindow's menubar:

```
use Tk 800.000;

my $mw = MainWindow->new;
$mw->configure(-menu => my $menubar = $mw->Menu);
```

Now create the cascade menubuttons. We save each menubutton's reference—an object of type Tk::Menu::Cascade—so we can add the requisite menu items later. (Note that unlike almost every other Perl/Tk object, a Tk::Menu::Cascade object is built from an array rather than a hash.) Each menubutton is assigned an identifying label that's displayed on the menubutton. The tilde character (~) represents the -underline character and is merely a convenience feature.

We already know the menu system handles a Toplevel menu specially. Since we didn't specify -tearoff => 0 when the menu was created, there's an implicit tearoff at index 0, meaning that the File, Edit, and Help cascades are menu item indexes 1, 2, and 3, respectively. Further, menubutton cascades are arranged from left to right rather than from top to bottom.

```
my $file = $menubar->cascade(-label => '~File');
my $edit = $menubar->cascade(-label => '~Edit');
my $help = $menubar->cascade(-label => '~Help');
```

Now create the menu items for the File menu. The New menu item, $new, is another cascade, whose menu we'll populate in short order. It's visually set apart from the other menu items by a separator: a thin horizontal rule. Command menu items accept callbacks and act like Buttons. Notice that for each label, we've explicitly used the -underline option rather than a ~, just to show that they both work. The -accelerator option displays a keyboard shortcut designed to activate a menu item. Note that we are responsible for adding the proper binding (See Chapter 15).

```
my $new = $file->cascade(
    -label       => 'New',
    -accelerator => 'Ctrl-n',
    -underline   => 0,
);
$file->separator;
$file->command(
    -label       => 'Open',
    -accelerator => 'Ctrl-o',
    -underline   => 0,
```

```
    );
    $file->separator;
    $file->command(
        -label        => 'Save',
        -accelerator  => 'Ctrl-s',
        -underline    => 0,
    );
    $file->command(
        -label        => 'Save As ...',
        -accelerator  => 'Ctrl-a',
        -underline    => 1,
    );
    $file->separator;
    $file->command(
        -label        => "Close",
        -accelerator  => 'Ctrl-w',
        -underline    => 0,
        -command      => \&exit,
    );
    $file->separator;
    $file->command(
        -label        => "Quit",
        -accelerator  => 'Ctrl-q',
        -underline    => 0,
        -command      => \&exit,
    );
```

Similarly, let's create the menu items for the Edit and Help menubuttons:

```
    $edit->command(-label => 'Preferences ...');

    $help->command(-label => 'Version', -command => sub {print "Version\n"});
    $help->separator;
    $help->command(-label => 'About',   -command => sub {print "About\n"});
```

Now it's time to populate the File/New cascade menu. The second and third menu items (the tearoff is the first) are checkbuttons created by iterating over a list of two-element anonymous arrays. Checkbuttons toggle between two values: an -onvalue and an -offvalue, which default to 1 and 0, respectively. We want each checkbutton in a known state, so we supply our own initialized variables. If -variable isn't specified, Perl/Tk uses a hidden, uninitialized instance variable.

```
    my($motif, $bisque) = (1, 0);

    foreach (['Strict Motif', \$motif], ['Bisque', \$bisque]) {
        $new->checkbutton(
            -label    => $_->[0],
            -variable => $_->[1],
        );
    }
```

To get to the actual checkbutton variable, we can do something like this:

```
    my $vr = $new->cget(-menu)->entrycget('Bisque', -variable);
    $$vr = 1;
```

This statement says, get the Menu reference for $new and, using that reference, get the -variable option value for the menu item whose label is Bisque. Now $vr is a reference to $bisque, which we de-reference and set "on."

The fourth menu item is another command, and the fifth a separator:

```
$new->command(-label => 'Widget');
$new->separator;
```

The sixth File/New menu item is yet another cascade, but this time we explicitly create its menu without a tearoff. It's important to note that the new menu must be a child of the current menu.

This highlights another special feature of the Perl/Tk menu system: we are not forced to explicitly create menus; Perl/Tk does that automatically when the first menu item is created. It's because of this behavior that we are forced to create a menu manually:

```
my $new_image = $new->cascade(
    -label => 'Image',
    -menu  => $new->cget(-menu)->Menu(-tearoff => 0),
);
```

The File/New/Image menu item is a cascade, so populate its menu with a radiobutton for each Photo image type (See Chapter 17). Like with checkbuttons, Perl/Tk uses an uninitialized instance variable if we don't supply one.

```
my $new_image_format = 'png';
foreach (qw/bmp ppm gif png jpg tif/) {
    $new_image->radiobutton(
        -label    => $_,
        -variable => \$new_image_format,
    );
}
```

Whew. That was a lot of work! If you're wondering why there isn't an easier way to manipulate such a common construct, then wonder no longer, because there is, and it's quite elegant. Once again, Perl/Tk has another unique option, -menuitems, which lets us specify all our menu items with a data structure.

Menubars the Slick, Sophisticated, New-Fashioned Way

In the following code, we create a menubar, add the menubutton cascades, and hide all the menu item details in subroutines. This is simple, modular, concise, and extremely cool.

```
use Tk 800.000;
use subs qw/edit_menuitems file_menuitems help_menuitems/;

my $mw = MainWindow->new;
$mw->configure(-menu => my $menubar = $mw->Menu);

my $file = $menubar->cascade(
    -label => '~File', -menuitems => file_menuitems);
```

```
my $edit = $menubar->cascade(
    -label => '~Edit', -menuitems => edit_menuitems);

my $help = $menubar->cascade(
    -label => '~Help', -menuitems => help_menuitems);
```

If you have lots of menubuttons, you might like this map approach, which produces an identical result. Here we feed map a code block and a list of anonymous arrays to work with. The code block prepends a tilde to the first element of each anonymous array and uses that as the menu item's -label option. The second element of each anonymous array is a subroutine call, which is invoked and returns a value for -menuitems.

```
map {$menubar->cascade( -label => '~' . $_->[0], -menuitems => $_->[1] )}
    ['File', file_menuitems],
    ['Edit', edit_menuitems],
    ['Help', help_menuitems];
```

Regardless of how we do it, the -menuitems option is key. Obviously, its value must be a Perl scalar; in fact, -menuitems expects an array reference and, within each element of the array, yet another array reference to a list of options that describe one menu item. We thus have a list of lists. For example, here's a definition for one command menu item, with the label "Preferences ...":

```
sub edit_menuitems {
    [
      ['command', 'Preferences ...'],
    ];
}
```

The first element of a menu item definition is the *type* of menu item (cascade, checkbutton, command, or radiobutton), and the second element is its -label value. These two values are required, but any other valid menu item option(s) can follow. In the case of a command menu item, we normally include a -command callback option and sometimes -underline (but that can be tilde-specified as part of the label), -accelerator, and so on.

Here are the Help command menu item definitions, including their callbacks. The null string between the Version and About menu items generates a separator. (-menuitems treats any array element that's not an array reference as a separator.)

```
sub help_menuitems {
    [
      ['command', 'Version', -command => sub {print "Version\n"}],
      '',
      ['command', 'About',   -command => sub {print "About\n"}],
    ];
}
```

Obviously, -menuitems must be powerful enough to generate the complex File menu shown in Figure 12-1. Let's examine the code:

```
1   sub file_menuitems {
2
3       # Create the menu items for the File menu.
4
5       my($motif, $bisque) = (1, 0);
6       my $new_image_format = 'png';
7
8       [
9         [qw/cascade ~New   -accelerator Ctrl-n -menuitems/ =>
10          [
11            ['checkbutton', 'Strict Motif', -variable => \$motif],
12            ['checkbutton', 'Bisque',      -variable => \$bisque],
13            [qw/command Widget/], '',
14            [qw/cascade Image -tearoff 0 -menuitems/ =>
15              [
16                map ['radiobutton', $_, -variable => \$new_image_format],
17                    qw/bmp ppm gif png jpg tif/,
18              ],
19            ],
20          ],
21        ],                                              '',
22        [qw/command ~Open  -accelerator Ctrl-o/],       '',
23        [qw/command ~Save  -accelerator Ctrl-s/],
24        [qw/command/, 'S~ave As ...', qw/-accelerator Ctrl-a/], '',
25        [qw/command ~Close -accelerator Ctrl-w/],        '',
26        [qw/command ~Quit  -accelerator Ctrl-q -command/ => \&exit],
27      ];
28
29   } # end file_menuitems
```

First, lines 8 through 27 encompass the array reference passed to -menuitems. Lines 22 through 26 define five command menu items (Open, Save, Save As, Close, and Quit) and three separators; we needn't go over this again. Lines 9 through 21 define the New menu item cascade and all its children. Let's look at the code more closely.

Line 5 declares and initializes the lexical variables used by the checkbuttons. The variables manage to survive past the end of the subroutine call because the checkbuttons keep references to them. Indeed, they'll never be destroyed until the checkbuttons go away and release the last reference.

Similarly, line 6 declares and initializes the default image format variables for the radiobuttons.

Line 9 declares the New cascade, the second File menu item (the tearoff is the first). Since cascades are menus that have their own menu items, we nest another -menuitems option, defined by lines 10 through 20.

Lines 11 though 19 define the menu items for the File/New menu. The first is the implicit tearoff, followed by the Strict Motif and Bisque checkbuttons (lines 11 and 12), the Widget command menu item, and a separator (line 13).

Line 14 generates the Image cascade, but its menu has no tearoff. Once again, we nest another -menuitems option, and lines 15 through 18 populate the menu.

Lines 16 and 17 define the radiobutton menu items for the File/New/Image menu, using the cool and concise map idiom.

If you've been paying close attention, you might be wondering if it's possible to specify a -menuitems option for the menubar itself; after all, the menubar is really just a menu filled with cascade menu items. As it happens, we can. First, delete the previous File/Edit/Help creation code and make these changes (shown here in bold) to our code:

```
use Tk 800.000;
use subs qw/edit_menuitems file_menuitems help_menuitems menubar_menuitems/;

my $mw = MainWindow->new;
$mw->configure(-menu => my $menubar = $mw->Menu(-menuitems => menubar_menuitems));
```

Then add subroutine menubar_menuitems, which returns a list of menubar cascades:

```
sub menubar_menuitems {

    [
      map ['cascade',  $_->[0], -menuitems => $_->[1]],
          ['~File', file_menuitems],
          ['~Edit', edit_menuitems],
          ['~Help', help_menuitems],
    ];

}
```

We can even go one more potentially ludicrous step and generate everything—menubar, menus, and menu items—from a single data structure. In this new version, all we've done is take the map construct and paste the File, Edit, and Help -menuitems definitions in place of a subroutine call. Gee, looks almost like assembly code.

```
use Tk 800.000;
use subs qw/menubar_etal/;
use strict;

my $mw = MainWindow->new;
$mw->configure(-menu => my $menubar = $mw->Menu(-menuitems => menubar_etal));

MainLoop;

sub menubar_etal {

    [
      map ['cascade',  $_->[0], -menuitems => $_->[1]],

          ['~File',
            [
              [qw/cascade ~New   -accelerator Ctrl-n -menuitems/ =>
                [
```

```
                ['checkbutton', 'Strict Motif'],
                ['checkbutton', 'Bisque'],
                [qw/command Widget/], '',
                [qw/cascade Image -tearoff 0 -menuitems/ =>
                  [
                     map ['radiobutton', $_],
                          qw/bmp ppm gif png jpg tif/,
                  ],
                ],
              ],
            ],                                                 '',
            [qw/command ~Open  -accelerator Ctrl-o/],          '',
            [qw/command ~Save  -accelerator Ctrl-s/],
            [qw/command/, 'S~ave As ...', qw/-accelerator Ctrl-a/], '',
            [qw/command ~Close -accelerator Ctrl-w/],          '',
            [qw/command ~Quit  -accelerator Ctrl-q -command/ => \&exit],,
          ],
        ],

        ['~Edit',
          [
            ['command', 'Preferences ...'],
          ],
        ],


        ['~Help',
          [
            ['command', 'Version', -command => sub {print "Version\n"}],
            '',
            ['command', 'About',   -command => sub {print "About\n"}],
          ],
        ],


    ];

} # end menubar_etal
```

The only things missing are the variables specifying the initial checkbutton and radiobutton values. We can make them file lexicals (globals) and include a -variable option, as we did previously. Or maybe limit their scope to some other block and pass references to them as formal parameters when calling menubar_etal. Or we can just use the default instance variables provided by Perl/Tk. All we need to know is how to access them.

It's easy because, once we have a reference to a Menu widget, we can entrycget and entryconfigure any menu item. Here we fetch the File Menu from the menubar cascade, the New Menu from the File cascade, and the Image Menu from the New cascade, and initialize the variables:

```
my $file_menu = $menubar->entrycget('File', -menu);
my $new_menu = $file_menu->entrycget('New', -menu);
my $image_menu = $new_menu->entrycget('Image', -menu);
```

```perl
my $motif = $new_menu->entrycget('Strict Motif', -variable);
$$motif = 1;
my $bisque = $new_menu->entrycget('Bisque', -variable);
$$bisque = 0;
my $new_image_format = $image_menu->entrycget('png', -variable);
$$new_image_format = 'png';
```

The Win32 System Menu Item

It's possible to add menu items to the Win32 System menubutton (the button at the top-left of a Perl/Tk window, labeled with the red *Tk* letters in script). Based on the operating system identifier, $^O, this code conditionally adds a command menu item that executes a DOS pipeline.

```perl
if ($^O eq 'MSWin32') {
    my $syst = $menubar->cascade(-label => '~System');
    my $dir = 'dir | sort | more';
    $syst->command(
        -label   => $dir,
        -command => sub {system $dir},
    );
}
```

Figure 12-3 illustrates.

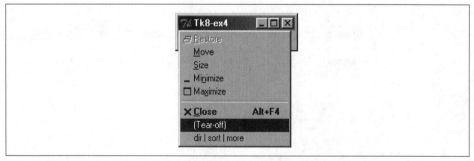

Figure 12-3. A System menu item that pages a sorted dir command

Figure 12-4 shows a DOS window and the contents of a particular directory. Then a Perl/Tk program is started and the "dir | sort | more" button is clicked; note the unsolicited, sorted directory listing.

The special menu item labeled "Tearoff" is really a tearoff menu item that, when clicked, tears off only the Tk portion of the System menu.

Classical Menubars

A classical menubar refers to the pre-Tk 8 idiom of arranging Menubutton widgets inside a Frame packed and stretched across the top of a MainWindow or Toplevel.

Figure 12-4. Output from pressing the "dir | sort | more" System menu button

Help Menubuttons are right justified on Unix machines. While you don't want to write new code in this style, it's important to know this idiom, because there's a lot of existing code written in this manner.

The following is typical classical menubar style, except for the use of -menuitems. Luckily for us, the three menu item subroutines are identical to our previous versions and generate a menubar that looks just like Figure 12-1. Most classical menubars create Menubuttons, Menus, and menu items as described in the section "Menubars the Clunky, Casual, Old-Fashioned Way."

```perl
use subs qw/edit_menuitems file_menuitems help_menuitems/;

my $mw = MainWindow->new;

my $menubar = $mw->Frame(qw/-relief raised -borderwidth 2/);
$menubar->pack(qw/-fill x/);

my $file = $menubar->Menubutton(qw/-text File -underline 0/,
    -menuitems => file_menuitems);
my $edit = $menubar->Menubutton(qw/-text Edit -underline 0/,
    -menuitems => edit_menuitems);
my $help = $menubar->Menubutton(qw/-text Help -underline 0/,
    -menuitems => help_menuitems);

$file->pack(qw/-side left/);
$edit->pack(qw/-side left/);
$help->pack(qw/-side right/);
```

Menubutton Options

The options specified with the Menubutton command (or via the configure method) can affect the Button part of the Menubutton, both the Button and the Menu, or just the Menu.* The options that affect the Menu are valid for the Menu widget as well as the Menubutton widget. Here is a brief synopsis of all the options and their effects. When the description says "Affects the Button only," the behavior is the same as it would be for a Button widget.

-activebackground => *color*
:   Affects the background color of the button and the currently highlighted menu item.

-activeforeground => *color*
:   Affects the text color of the button and the currently highlighted menu item.

-anchor => 'n' | 'ne' | 'e' | 'se' | 's' | 'sw' | 'w' | 'nw' | **'center'**
:   Affects the button only. Changes the position of the text within the button.

-background => *color*
:   Affects the button and the menu. All the background color changes to *color* when the state of the button and the menu items is 'normal'.

-bitmap => *bitmapname*
:   Affects the button only. Displays bitmap instead of text.

-borderwidth => *amount*
:   Affects the button only. Changes the width of the button edges.

-cursor => *cursorname*
:   Affects the button only. Changes the cursor when it's over the button part of the menubutton.

-disabledforeground => *color*
:   Affects the button and the menu item text when the -state for either is 'disabled'.

-direction => "above" | **"below"** | "left" | "right" | "flush"
:   Tk 8 option only. The value "above" puts the menu above the menubutton, "below" puts it below the button, and "left" and "right" put it on the appropriate side of the button. "flush" puts the menu directly over the button.

-font => *fontname*
:   Affects the button only. Changes the font of any text displayed in the button.

-foreground => *color*
:   Affects the button only. Changes the color of any text or bitmap to *color*.

---

* The Menubutton widget comprises other widgets (in this case, Button and Menu) to provide the overall functionality.

`-height` => *amount*

Affects the button only. Changes the height of the button.

`-highlightbackground` => *color*

Affects the button only. Changes the color of the highlight rectangle displayed around the button when the button does not have the keyboard focus.

`-highlightcolor` => *color*

Affects the button only. Changes the color of the highlight rectangle displayed around the button when the button has the keyboard focus.

`-highlightthickness` => *amount*

Affects the button only. Default is 0. Changes the width of the highlight rectangle around all edges of the button.

`-image` => *imgptr*

Affects the button only. Displays an image instead of text.

`-indicatoron` => **0** | 1

Affects the button; indirectly affects the display mechanism for the menu. When set to 1, a small bar appears on the right side of the button next to any text, bitmap, or image.

`-justify` => 'left' | 'right' | **'center'**

Affects the button only. Changes the justification of the text within the button.

`-menu` => $menu

Tells the menubutton to display the menu associated with $menu instead of anything specified via the -menuitems option.

`-menuitems` => *list*

Causes the menu to display a list of items to create.

`-padx` => *amount*

Affects the button only. Adds extra space to the left and right of the button inside the button edge.

`-pady` => *amount*

Affects the button only. Adds extra space to the top and bottom of the button inside the button edge.

`-relief` => **'flat'** | 'groove' | 'raised' | 'ridge' | 'sunken'

Affects the button only. The relief of the button changes to 'raised' when the button is pressed.

`-state` => **'normal'** | 'active' | 'disabled'

Affects the button; indirectly affects the menu (the menu cannot be displayed if state is 'disabled').

`-takefocus` => **0** | 1 | undef

Affects the button only. Determines whether or not the button can have the keyboard focus.

`-tearoff => 0 | 1`

Affects the menu only. If set to 0, does not display the tearoff dashed line in the menu.

`-text => text string`

Affects the button only. Displays the specified string on the button (ignored if the `-bitmap` or `-image` option is used).

`-textvariable => \$variable`

Affects the button only. The information displayed in `$variable` is displayed on the button.

`-underline => charpos`

Affects the button only. The character at the integer *charpos* is underlined. If the button has the keyboard focus, pressing the Alt key causes the button that corresponds to the underlined character to be pressed.

`-width => amount`

Affects the button only. Changes the width of the button to *amount*.

`-wraplength => pos`

Affects the button only. Default is 0. Determines the screen distance for the maximum amount of text displayed on one line.

Button-Only Options

The following options affect only the button portion of the menubutton, and behave exactly as described in Chapter 4: `-cursor`, `-anchor`, `-bitmap`, `-borderwidth`, `-font`, `-foreground`, `-height`, `-highlightbackground`, `-highlightcolor`, `-highlightthickness`, `-image`, `-justify`, `-padx`, `-pady`, `-relief`, `-state`, `-takefocus`, `-text`, `-textvariable`, `-underline`, `-width`, and `-wraplength`.

Popup Menus

Perl/Tk provides several ways to pop up menus. Thus far, all menus have been posted automatically by pressing a menubutton, but we can do it ourselves by binding keystrokes or button clicks to callbacks.

The post and Post Methods

The lowest-level mechanism is the Menu post method, which posts a menu at a specific screen coordinate. The Post method works like post, but additionally activates a specific menu item. In either case, we are responsible for determining *where* the menu is displayed.

Let's start with the code that produced Figure 12-5. It creates one menu, then displays it several ways. The toolbar across the top of the window contains a left-justified Menubutton and a right-justified labeled Optionmenu. The menu contains nine

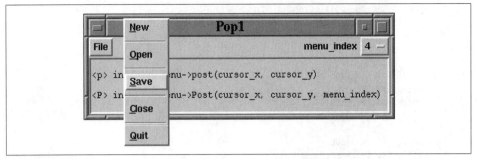

Figure 12-5. Post posts a menu and activates a menu item (here, index 4)

menu items, four separators, and five command menus at indexes 0, 2, 4, 6, and 8. Of course, the first way to post the menu is to press the File menubutton.

```
my $toolbar = $mw->Frame->pack(qw/-fill x -expand 1/);
my $file = $toolbar->Menubutton(
    -text   => 'File',
    -relief => 'raised',
);
$file->pack(qw/-side left/);;

my $menu = $file->Menu(-tearoff => 0, -menuitems => [
    [qw/command ~New/],
    '',
    [qw/command ~Open/],
    '',
    [qw/command ~Save/],
    '',
    [qw/command ~Close/],
    '',
    [qw/command ~Quit/, -command => \&exit],
]);
$file->configure(-menu => $menu);

my $menu_index = 0;
my $cursor = $toolbar->LabOptionmenu(
    -label     => 'menu_index',
    -labelPack => [qw/-side left/],
    -variable  => \$menu_index,
    -options   => [(0, 2, 4, 6, 8)],
);
$cursor->pack(qw/-side right/);
```

Here are two other ways to post the menu. Typing the character "p" invokes the post method and posts the menu so that its northwest corner is over the cursor. Typing the character "P" invokes the Post method and posts the menu so menu item $menu_index is centered over the cursor.

```
my $t = $mw->Text->pack;
$t->insert('end', <<"EOT");
```

```
<p> invokes \$menu->post(cursor_x, cursor_y)

<P> invokes \$menu->Post(cursor_x, cursor_y, menu_index)
EOT

$mw->bind('<p>' => [sub {
    my($w, $x, $y) = @_;
    $menu->post($x, $y);
}, Ev('X'), Ev('Y')]);

$mw->bind('<P>' => [sub {
    my($w, $x, $y) = @_;
    $menu->Post($x, $y, $menu_index);
}, Ev('X'), Ev('Y')]);
```

The Popup Method

You've probably had occasion to use a Dialog (or DialogBox) widget. These widgets are derived from a Toplevel and spend most of their time in a withdrawn state. It's also common to use Toplevels as containers for custom-built popup windows.* When it's time to display these dialogs, we call the special Perl/Tk window manager Popup method. Popup is essentially a wrapper around a call to Post, with three special purpose options that specify placement information in high-level terms rather than numerical coordinates. It's Popup's responsibility to take our human specifications and turn them into actual screen coordinates suitable for Post.

What has this got to do with Menus? As Figure 12-6 indicates, the *isa* program from Chapter 14 shows us that a Menu widget is a subclass of Tk::Wm, the window manager class. This means that Menus can invoke Popup too. Let's define some terms, then examine the three special options.

We can direct a popup menu (or, in general, any Toplevel) to appear in two general locations: either over another window—for example, the root window (screen) or a particular widget—or over the cursor. This is called the *popover location*. Once we've made this decision, we can further refine the exact placement of the popup relative to the popover location by specifying the intersection of two *anchor points*. The *popanchor point* is associated with the popup menu and the *overanchor point* is associated with the popover location (whether it be a window or the cursor). The point where the two anchor points coincide is the *popup locus*. Anchor points are string values and can be c (for center) or any of the eight cardinal compass points: n, ne, e, se, s, sw, w, or nw. See Figure 12-7.

---

* If you want a dialog window without window manager decorations, create the Toplevel and then call overrideredirect(1).

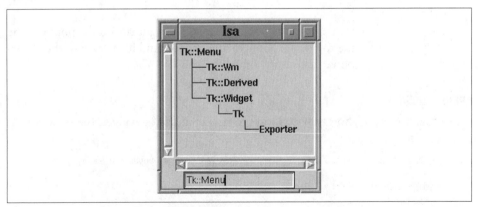

Figure 12-6. Popup is a method of Tk::Wm

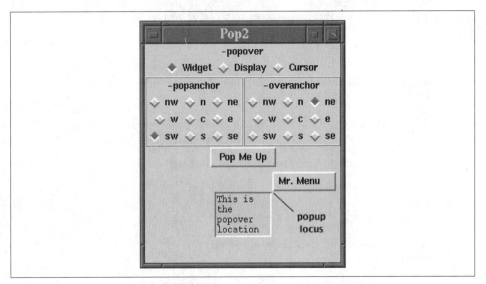

Figure 12-7. Two anchor positions define the popup locus

This spatial information is embodied in the following three options (which are applicable for any widget derived from Tk::Wm, including Menus, Toplevels, and dialog widgets like Dialog and DialogBox):

-popover

Specifies the popover location. It may be the string cursor, a widget reference, or undef to specify the root window (screen).

-overanchor

Specifies where the popup should anchor relative to the popover location. For instance, if east is specified, the popup appears over the right side of the popup location; if it's north, the popup is positioned above the popover location; and if it's northeast, the popup is positioned at the upper-right corner of the popover location.

-popanchor

Specifies the anchor point of the popup. If east, the right side of the popup is the anchor; if north, the top of the popup is the anchor; and if southwest, the lower-left corner of the popup is the anchor.

Popup examples

This program, *pop3*, shows various ways to pop up a Dialog widget; the same principles apply to menus:

```perl
my(@popup_opts) = (-popover => undef, qw/-overanchor sw -popanchor sw/);

my $d1 = $mw->Dialog(
    @popup_opts,
    -text => "Original options:\n" . join(' ', say(@popup_opts)) .
             "This Dialog should be in the screen's lower-left " .
             "corner.  When you dismiss this Dialog another will " .
             "popup in the southeast corner.",
);
$d1->Show;

@popup_opts = qw/-overanchor se -popanchor  se/;
$d1->configure(
    @popup_opts,
    -text => "Changed options:\n" . join(' ', say(@popup_opts)) .
             "1 second after you dismiss this Dialog another " .
             "will popup, without window manager decorations ".
             "(overrideredirect on), with its southeast corner " .
             "over the cursor.",
);
$d1->Show;
$mw->after(1000);

@popup_opts = qw/-popover cursor -popanchor se/;
$d1->configure(
    @popup_opts,
    -text => "Changed options:\n" . join(' ', say(@popup_opts)) .
             "1 second after you dismiss this Dialog another " .
             "will popup, with window manager decorations once ".
             "again (overrideredirect off), with its northwest " .
             "corner over the cursor.",
);
$d1->overrideredirect(1);
$d1->Show;

@popup_opts = qw/-popanchor  nw/;
$d1->configure(
    @popup_opts,
    -wraplength => '3i',
    -text => "Changed options:\n" . join(' ', say(@popup_opts)) .
             "End of demonstration.",
);
```

```
$d1->overrideredirect(0);
$mw->after(1000);
$d1->Show;

sub say {
    map {defined($_) ? $_ : 'undef'} (@_, "\n\n");
}
```

Option Menus

An option menu is a simple widget with a label and an indicator. Clicking the indicator posts a menu of selections from which we can choose any single value, which is then displayed in the label. An option menu has an associated Perl variable that keeps the current option value and may also have a -command callback that is invoked after the new option value is stored in the variable.

Perl/Tk has two option menu widgets: Tk::Optionmenu from the standard distribution and a native option menu that almost no one is aware of but that you will see shortly. Each has its pros and cons, so pick one based on the job at hand. Both option menus are based on a Menubutton widget, which posts its menu items when pressed.

Tk::Optionmenu

If we want to select a color from a *small* set of colors, we could use an Optionmenu like that shown in Figure 12-8. The operative word is small, because an Optionmenu's menu is limited to a single column. The -options option expects a reference to a list of options, which may be string values and/or array references of the form ['label' => 'value']. The 'label' is what's displayed in the menu, and the 'value' is stored in the variable. The -command option is a standard Perl/Tk callback. When the callback is invoked, the value of the option menu is appended to the callback argument list.

```
my $palette;
my @colors = qw/Black red4 DarkGreen NavyBlue gray75 Red Green Blue
    gray50 Yellow Cyan Magenta White Brown DarkSeaGreen DarkViolet/;

my $om = $mw->Optionmenu(
    -variable => \$palette,
    -options  => [@colors],
    -command  => [sub {print "args=@_.\n"}, 'First'],
);
$om->pack;
```

The Optionmenu widget has an addOptions method to add more items to the menu.

```
$om->addOptions(['chlorophyll' => '#8395ffff0000']);
```

And that's pretty much all you can do with a Tk::Optionmenu widget.

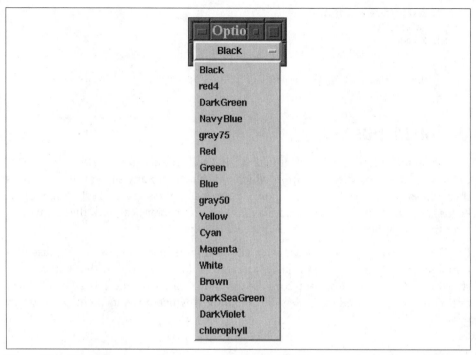

Figure 12-8. Tk::Optionmenu widgets are limited to a single column

A Native Option Menu

It's possible to build an option menu from standard Perl/Tk components that's more powerful than one created by Tk::Optionmenu. It is more complex and, because it's not part of the standard distribution, we have to carry extra baggage around. But we have direct access to its Menu, which provides us with a lot of flexibility.

Figure 12-9 illustrates how the new option menu displays our list of colors as an array of radiobutton menu items.* In this context, it's convenient to break the color list into several columns, plus the radiobutton's indicator serves to identify the widget's current value while the menu is posted.

The actual user code is very similar to the Tk::Optionmenu code. The main difference is we call a subroutine instead of invoking a Tk method. (As an exercise, turn this code into a Perl/Tk class.) The subroutine uses positional parameters rather than option/value pairs: the first argument is the widget's parent, the second argument is the variable, the third argument is the callback, and the remaining arguments are the menu options.

---

* In Chapter 17, we expand on this idea and use a color palette of Photo images rather than plain radiobutton menu items.

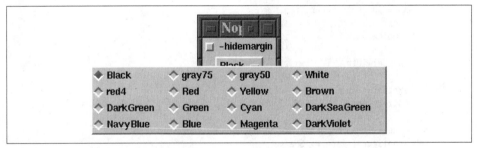

Figure 12-9. A multicolumn native option menu

```
use subs qw/native_optionmenu/;

my $palette;
my @colors = qw/Black red4 DarkGreen NavyBlue gray75 Red Green Blue
    gray50 Yellow Cyan Magenta White Brown DarkSeaGreen DarkViolet/;

my $nom = native_optionmenu(
    $mw,
    \$palette,
    [sub {print "args=@_.\n"}, 'First'],
    @colors);
$nom->pack;;
```

The following chunk of code breaks the menu into columns. The variable $nom is actually a reference to a Menubutton widget from which we fetch the menu reference. Then we loop, setting the -columnbreak option on every fourth menu item.

```
my $menu = $nom->cget(-menu);
for my $i (0 .. $#colors) {
    $menu->entryconfigure($i, -columnbreak => 1) unless $i % 4;
}
```

The native_optionmenu subroutine builds the actual option menu for us. First, we default the option menu variable to the first option value, which becomes the Menubutton's initial label. As the variable referenced by the -textvariable option changes, so does the text on the Menubutton. The -indicatoron option is what makes the Menubutton look and behave as an "OptionMenubutton." The -anchor and -direction options ensure that the tearoff-less menu pops up, centered directly on top of the Menubutton. Finally, we loop through the list of option values, populate the menu with radiobutton menu items, and return a reference to the Menubutton. The only trickiness is normalizing the -command callback and appending the correct "selected value" to the callback argument list.

```
sub native_optionmenu {

    my($parent, $varref, $callback, @optionvals) = @_;

    $$varref = $optionvals[0];
```

```
my $mb = $parent->Menubutton(
    -textvariable     => $varref,
    -indicatoron      => 1,
    -relief           => 'raised',
    -borderwidth      => 2,
    -highlightthickness => 2,
    -anchor           => 'c',
    -direction        => 'flush',
);
my $menu = $mb->Menu(-tearoff => 0);
$mb->configure(-menu => $menu);

my $callback = ref($command) =~ /CODE/ ? [$command] : $command;

foreach (@optionvals) {
    $menu->radiobutton(
        -label    => $_,
        -variable => $varref,
        -command  => [$callback, $_],
    );
}

$mb;

} # end native_optionmenu
```

Menu items have left and right margins, and it's in these margins that the radiobutton and checkbutton indicators are drawn. If you want to dispense with the margin, be aware that the indicators disappear too. This code sets each radiobutton's -hidemargin option based on the true/false setting of a Checkbutton widget:

```
sub hide {
    my $menu = $nom->cget(-menu);
    foreach (@colors) {
        $menu->entryconfigure($_, -hidemargin => ${$cb->cget(-variable)});
    }
}
```

Figure 12-10 shows a native option menu with a -hidemargin set to 1.

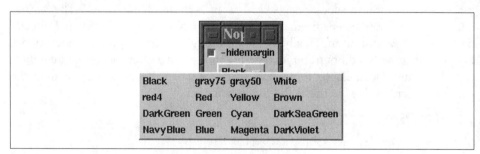

Figure 12-10. A native option menu with -hidemargin => 1

Menu Virtual Events

Currently, Perl/Tk generates a <<MenuSelect>> virtual event whenever a menu is posted and the active menu item changes.[*] This code binds a callback that prints on STDOUT the -label option of the active menu item. The special variable $Tk::event is a localized reference to the X11 event structure (the same thing returned by a call to *XEvent*, described in Chapter 15). Its W method returns the widget reference that the event occurred in, which is the Menu in this case. The use of Tk::catch isn't strictly necessary but does prevent the code from exiting if $menu isn't a Menu reference. Tk::Catch is essentially a block eval designed to trap and ignore exceptions.

```
$menu->bind('<<MenuSelect>>' => sub {
    my $label = undef;
    my $menu = $Tk::event->W;
    Tk::catch {$label = $menu->entrycget('active', -label)};
    print "palette=$palette, menu label=$label!\n" if defined $label;
});
```

Pie Menus

We are accustomed to using one-dimensional *linear* menus—not one-dimensional in appearance, but in usage. When a linear menu is posted, the cursor is positioned at the top of the menu and we are expected to move the cursor downward. If we overshoot the target menu item, we can move the cursor upward, but we're still moving in a single dimension. As the cursor moves over menu items, their reliefs change (unless disabled) to raised, meaning they are activated. To actually invoke a menu item we must release button 1 while the cursor is within the area defined by the menu item.

In contrast, pie menus are two dimensional: the cursor is initially positioned in the center of the pie, so all the wedge-shaped menu items are the same distance from the cursor but in different directions. Thus all menu items are equally accessible, spatially. Each pie piece has a virtual section that extends from the pie's perimeter to the edge of the display. To hit such a large target requires a gross, gestural motor movement, which your muscles easily learn and remember.

Pie menus were invented by Don Hopkins. For a history of Don's work, visit *http://catalog.com/hopkins/piemenus/index.html*. This experimental Perl/Tk pie menu implementation is based on a piece of Don's early work, written in 1992 for an early version of Tcl/Tk.

Figure 12-11 illustrates what a File pie menu might look like. The pie menu has six menu items, each occupying a 60 degree slice of the pie. To select an item, we just

---

[*] On Unix, multiple events are generated as the cursor moves over the menu. On Win32, a single event is generated whenever the active menu item changes.

click anywhere on the pie piece (or the virtual part that extends to the display's edge). There's no need to be particularly accurate; just make a fast, casual motion. Notice that this pie menu has its menu items floating in space.

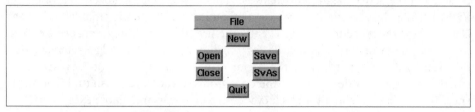

Figure 12-11. A pie menu with -shaped => 1

Figure 12-12 shows the same pie menu in a rectangular window with wedge dividers. Now, imagine those wedge dividers extending outwards to infinity (or as far as your arm is long or the display is big!). That huge pie slice defines the (virtual) pie menu item; you can click *anywhere* within that area!

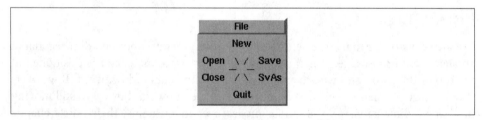

Figure 12-12. A pie menu with -shaped => 0

A pie menu is ideally suited for selecting two pieces of information simultaneously. Consider a word processor where we want to select a font and its size. Each font can be a pie piece, and its size is determined by how far from the center of the pie we click. Or think of a color wheel, where hue is a pie slice and its saturation varies from the pie's center to its circumference. Unfortunately, the current version of the Perl/Tk pie menu lacks this sophistication.

Fitts' Law

Pie menus are based on a model of human psychomotor behavior developed by P. M. Fitts. In his 1954 work, Fitts studied the time required to hit a target, based on target distance and size. Unsurprisingly, selecting a large menu item close at hand (a virtual pie menu item) with a mouse is faster than hunting for a small target far away (a tiny linear menu item).

We can write a Perl/Tk program to test this hypothesis. The basic idea is to start with the cursor at a known position, flash a target of random size and position, measure how long it takes to hit the target, and examine how this time depends on the target's distance and area. See Figure 12-13 for complete usage information.

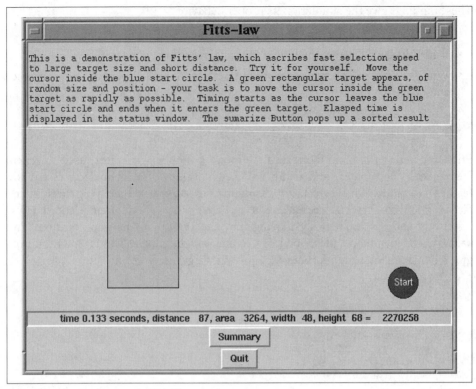

Figure 12-13. Demonstrating Fitts' law

The Fitts simulator uses a Canvas for the playing field, with a Canvas rectangle item as the target and an oval item as the starting point. The start circle is actually a canvas group[*] with a text item overlaid on top of the oval item. The group we'll tag with the string 'start' and the rectangle with the string 'rectangle', and we'll use those identifiers when addressing the canvas items.

```
my $c = $mw->Canvas(qw/-width 500 -height 500/)->grid;

$c->createGroup(0, 0,
    -tags    => 'start',
    -members => [
        $c->createOval(qw/ 0  0 40 40 -fill blue/),
        $c->createText(qw/20 20 -text Start -fill white/),
    ],
);
```

---

[*] Tk 800.018 added the canvasGroup Canvas method. As the name might imply, many individual canvas items can be logically grouped together and referenced as a single entity, in a manner not unlike a mega-widget.

These bindings give the simulation its proper behavior:

- When the cursor enters the blue start circle, create the green target.
- When the cursor leaves the blue start circle, record the current time.
- When the cursor enters the green target, compute and display the elapsed time, and delete the target.

```
$c->bind('start',     '<Enter>' => \&enter_start);
$c->bind('start',     '<Leave>' => \&leave_start);
$c->bind('rectangle', '<Enter>' => \&enter_rectangle);
```

Prior to entering the main loop, seed the random number generator, used to generate random coordinates, and width and height values. The main loop essentially fetches two random numbers and treats them as an (x, y) pair specifying the start circle's top-left corner. The coords method changes the 'start' item's coordinates, effectively and instantaneously moving the item (group) to its new location. The waitVariable command (described in Chapter 15) then logically suspends the program, but still allows event processing, until the target receives an <Enter> event.

```
srand( time ^ $$ );

while (1) {

    $rendezvous = 0;
    my($x, $y) = points 2;
    $c->coords('start', $x, $y);
    $mw->waitVariable(\$rendezvous);

}
```

Once the main loop has positioned the start circle, nothing happens until the cursor enters the circle. Once that happens, any rectangle is promptly deleted, which cures the pathological case of the user rapidly moving the cursor back and forth over the circle (hence generating multiple <Enter> events) and creating tons of rectangles. A random coordinate for the top-left corner of the rectangle is selected, as are random width/height values in the range 5 to 180, inclusive. Then the target is created and raised to ensure it's not obscured by the start circle.

```
sub enter_start {

    my($c) = @_;

    $c->delete('rectangle');
    my $w = int(rand 180) + 5;
    my $h = int(rand 180) + 5;
    my($x, $y) = points 2;
    $c->createRectangle($x, $y, $x+$w, $y+$h,
        -fill => 'green', -tags => 'rectangle',
    );
    $c->raise(qw/rectangle start/);
    $c->idletasks;

} # end enter_start
```

Now the start circle and target rectangle are visible on the Canvas, yet nothing further happens until we move the cursor out of the circle (and generate a <Leave> event); only then does timing commence. The Tk::timeofday function returns the number of microseconds since the Tk program started.*

```
sub leave_start {
    $t0 = Tk::timeofday;
}
```

At this point, we move the cursor to the target rectangle, which invokes the enter_rectangle callback. First, save the current time of day so we can compute the elapsed time. For the distance computation, we use the Pythagorean theorem that we all learned in high school. Since the start circle and target rectangle are both described by a bounding box, we can substitute the coordinates of the top-left corner in the distance equation. We mark this iteration of the simulation complete by modifying $rendezvous, which jogs the main loop into another iteration.

```
sub enter_rectangle {

    my($c) = @_;

    $t1 = Tk::timeofday();

    my(@rco) = $c->coords('rectangle');
    my(@sco) = $c->coords('start');
    my $dist = sqrt( ($sco[0] - $rco[0])**2 + ($sco[1] - $rco[1])**2 );

    my $w = $rco[2] - $rco[0];
    my $h = $rco[3] - $rco[1];

    $stat = sprintf "time %5.3f seconds, distance % 4.d, " .
        "area % 6.d, width %3.d, height %3.d = %10d",
        $t1 - $t0, $dist, $w * $h, $w, $h

    $rendezvous = 1;

} # end enter_rectangle
```

---

* That clock resolution may be a bit optimistic, but you can probably count on at least millisecond granularity.

CHAPTER 13

Miscellaneous Perl/Tk Methods

So far, most of the chapters in this book have concentrated on specific widgets. This chapter covers the methods and subroutines that can be invoked from any widget. You'll probably never need most of these methods, but there are a few that you'll use frequently, particularly configure and cget.

Most of the methods are based on the Tcl winfo command (window information). Generally, the commands are informational only, meaning you pass no arguments to them; you only get a value back.

This chapter also documents clipboard and selection methods for cut-and-paste operations between applications, focus and grab methods, and a few esoteric goodies.

Managing Widgets with configure and cget

Every widget included in the Perl/Tk distribution, as well as all user-contributed widgets available separately, can use the configure and cget methods, which set, change, and query widget attributes. No matter the widget, the format of the arguments to these functions is the same, and the results passed back have the same format.

The configure method allows you to assign or change the value of a widget option. It can also be used to retrieve the current value of the option. The cget method cannot assign values but simply retrieves them with simpler syntax than that of configure.

The configure Method

The basic format of the configure method is as follows:

```
$widget->configure( [ option => newvalue, ... ] );
```

Depending on the arguments passed to it, the configure method can do three things:

- Set or change the values of the options for $widget.
- Get the current value of any option for $widget.
- Get the current values of all of the options for $widget.

To set or change the value of an option, send the option pair exactly as it would have appeared in the widget creation command:

```
$widget->configure(-option => newvalue);
```

Whatever effect the option has will take place immediately. To see the current values for a single option, send it as the argument. The return value depends on whether configure is called in list context or scalar context. In the following line, configure is called in list context (since its return value is being assigned to an array):

```
@info = $widget->configure(-highlightthickness);
```

In list context, an array of scalars is returned:

```
-highlightthickness highlightThickness HighlightThickness 2 2
```

The following five values are in the returned array:

0   Option name

1   Option name from the option database (also as it would appear in the *.Xdefaults* file)

2   Class in the option database

3   Default value of the option

4   Current value of the option

Calling configure in scalar context returns a reference to the five configure items.

If you want to see the list of values for all the options the widget supports, use this format:

```
@config = $widget->configure;
```

@config is now an array of anonymous lists. The easiest way to print this information is to utilize Tk::Pretty, which will do all the hard work of traversing the arrays and then put the information into a readable form:

```
use Tk::Pretty;
@config = $widget->configure;
print Pretty @config;
```

The result is as follows:

```
['-activebackground',activeBackground,Foreground,'#ececec','#ececec'],
['-activeforeground',activeForeground,Background,Black,Black],['-activeimage',
activeImage,ActiveImage,undef,undef],['-anchor','anchor',Anchor,'center',
'center'],['-background','background',Background,'#d9d9d9','#d9d9d9'],['-bd',
borderWidth],['-bg','background'],['-bitmap','bitmap',Bitmap,undef,undef],
['-borderwidth',borderWidth,BorderWidth,2,2],['-command','command',Command,
undef,bless([CODE(0x8189888)],Tk::Callback)],['-cursor','cursor',Cursor,
undef,undef],['-disabledforeground',disabledForeground,DisabledForeground,
'#a3a3a3','#a3a3a3'],['-fg','foreground'],['-font','font',Font,'-Adobe
-Helvetica-Bold-R-Normal--*-120-*-*-*-*-*-*','-Adobe-Helvetica-Bold-R-Normal
--*-120-*-*-*-*-*-*'],['-foreground','foreground',Foreground,Black,Black],
['-height','height',Height,0,0],['-highlightbackground',highlightBackground,
HighlightBackground,'#d9d9d9','#d9d9d9'],['-highlightcolor',highlightColor,
```

```
HighlightColor,Black,Black],['-highlightthickness',highlightThickness,
HighlightThickness,2,2],['-image','image',Image,undef,undef],['-justify',
'justify',Justify,'center','center'],['-padx',padX,Pad,3m,9],['-pady',padY,
Pad,1m,3],['-relief','relief',Relief,'raised','raised'],['-state','state',
State,'normal','normal'],['-takefocus',takeFocus,TakeFocus,undef,undef],
['-text','text',Text,undef,Do_Something],['-textvariable',textVariable,
Variable,undef,undef],['-underline','underline',Underline,-1,-1],['-width',
'width',Width,0,0],['-wraplength',wrapLength,WrapLength,0,0]
```

Although this list may look nasty and ugly, it distinguishes between the different lists of lists for you by adding the [and] characters and the commas that separate them. Usually, you would look at this list only for debugging purposes.

You may find the output of Data::Dumper more pleasing:

```
use Data::Dumper;
@config = $widget->configure;
print Dumper @config;
```

Producing output similar to this:

```
$VAR22 = [
            '-highlightthickness',
            'highlightThickness',
            'HighlightThickness',
            '1',
            1
          ];
```

The configuration options for each widget described in this book are listed in Appendix B.

The cget Method

Instead of using configure to retrieve values, you can use the cget method:

```
$widget->cget(-option)
```

It returns only the current value (or address if the option stores a reference) of the option rather than the entire list that configure returns. Think of cget as standing for "configuration get." Here is an example of how to use cget:

```
print $b->cget(-highlightthickness), "\n";
## Prints this:
2
# return reference :
print $option_menu->cget(-textvariable), "\n";
# return actual value :
print ${$option_menu->cget(-textvariable)}, "\n";
# or...
$ref = $option_menu->cget(-textvariable);
print $$ref, "\n";
```

Building a Family Tree

The following methods deal with the ancestors or children of widgets and how they were created: children, name, PathName, parent, toplevel, manager, and class.

These methods tend to return either a widget reference or a string. A string is the Tcl-like name of a widget. Tcl uses string pathnames to reference widgets, with periods as pathname separators, and is how Tcl's widget hierarchy is defined. This is analogous to how Unix uses a forward slash as its pathname separator.

In Tcl, the MainWindow is always ".". From that point on, it's the programmer's job to name widgets that reflect the application's widget hierarchy. So, .frame might refer to the first Frame widget created as a child of the MainWindow, .frame1 might refer to the second, and so on. The programmer might call the first Button under the first Frame .frame.quit_button; this is the fully qualified pathname. The name its parent knows this Button by is simply quit_button. This name is the leaf part of the pathname, or, in Unix terminology, the basename.

As Perl/Tk programmers, we seldom explicitly assign a pathname to our widgets, but pTk does so on our behalf. Now you know what's happening when you see string pathnames. Ideally, we like to see real Perl object references, but sometimes Perl/Tk's Tcl underpinnings peek through.

Widget's Children

To determine the children of a widget (usually a Toplevel or a Frame), use the children method, which returns a list of widget references:

```
@kids = $widget->children;
# i.e. Tk::Button=HASH(0x85e3a0) Tk::Button=HASH(0x85e4a8)
```

The list returned contains scalars (widget references) that are the children of $widget. You can then use those references to perform actions such as setting a background color or font.

Name of a Widget

To determine what the parent calls the widget (the widget's leaf or basename portion of its pathname), use the name method:

```
$name = $widget->name;
```

You can combine the name and children methods like this:

```
@kids = $widget->children;
foreach (@kids) {
  print "Name: ", $_->name, "\n";
}
```

Here is example output from that code; notice you get strings:

```
button
button1
```

To see what string pathname Tk generated for a widget, use the `PathName` method. This method does not exist in Tcl/Tk, because you always know a widget's pathname. Do not confuse this method with `pathname`, described later.

```
print "\$button=", $button->PathName, "\n";
#i.e. .frame.button
```

Parent of a Widget

To get a widget reference to the parent of a widget, use the `parent` method:

```
$parent = $widget->parent;
```

The Widget's Toplevel

To get the Toplevel widget reference that contains a widget, use `toplevel`:

```
$path = $widget->toplevel;
```

Widget's Manager

You can find out which geometry manager `$widget` used by calling `manager`:

```
$manager = $widget->manager;
```

It returns a string that describes the geometry manager; for instance, if it is a Toplevel widget, it will return `"grid"`, `"pack"`, `"place"`, or `"wm"`. The `manager` method doesn't seem to work correctly on Windows 95, but it works on Unix and Windows NT.

The Widget's class

The `class` method returns a string that indicates the class to which it belongs. For example, `$listbox->class` returns `"Listbox"`, and `$menu->class` returns `"Menu"`.

Widget's ID

You use the `id` method to get X11 window ID or Win32 HWND for a widget:

```
$id = $widget->id;
print "$id\n";
# Prints 0x9c944c
```

This returns a hex value. A common use for this method is to embed a Tk window in another application. The PerlPlus Netscape plug-in does just this. It is described in Chapter 22.

Widget's PathName From Its X11 ID

You can get the PathName of the window by calling pathname and using the ID you retrieved with the id method:

```
$path = $widget->pathname($id);
```

Color-Related Methods

There are four methods that deal with color: colormapfull, rgb, cells, and depth. They are described in the following sections.

Is the Colormap Full?

To determine if the colormap for the widget is full, use colormapfull:

```
$isfull = $widget->colormapfull;
```

The colormapfull method returns a 1 if the colormap is full and 0 if it is not full.

Cell Count

The number of cells in the colormap can be obtained by using the cells method:

```
$count = $widget->cells;
```

The value returned is a number indicating the number of colors; for example, 64.

Color Depth

You can get the number of bits per pixel by using the depth method:

```
$depth = $widget->depth;
# $depth might contain "16"
```

Translate to RGB Value

You can translate a color name to the red, green, and blue values by using the rgb method. Send rgb a color name and it returns a list containing three items that represent the red, green, and blue numbers.

```
($red, $green, $blue) = $widget->rgb("color");
```

Now $red, $green, and $blue each contain an integer from 0 to 2^{n-1}, where n is the number of bit planes in your display. For 8-bit color, the maximum value is 255 (0xFF); for 16-bit color, it's 65,535 (0xFFFF).

When specifying a hexadecimal color, feel free to over-specify the value. For instance, if you want the color red, use 0xFFFF00000000. Tk will use it if possible, or will down-convert it to 0xFF0000 for an 8-bit display.

Setting Colors

You can have your entire application based on one color automatically by using the setPalette method:

```
$widget->setPalette(color);
```

The background color of $widget is set to the specified color, and the colors for all other widgets are calculated based on that color. So if a Button's edge is a lighter color than the background, it will show up a lighter shade of whatever color you pick. This method affects the entire application even if you only call it on a widget instead of a Toplevel.

You can set colors for explicit options by specifying the name and then the color to associate with it. For instance, the following code will set all foreground items in the application to red and all background items to blue:

```
$b->setPalette(background => "blue", foreground => "red");
```

Note that this is the only widget we know of where you cannot use a leading dash for an option.

Predefined Color Scheme

The bisque method sets the entire application to use a bisque scheme, the original Tcl color. Calling $widget->bisque is the same as calling $widget->setPalette("bisque"). This is the only predefined color scheme, mainly for Tcl old-timers who remember the days before the new steel scheme was voted in.

The Application's Name

The name of the application used in the option file is, by default, the name of the file from which the script is run. You can use the appname method to change the name of the application:

```
$mw->appname("newname");
```

You can find out the current name of the application by calling appname with no arguments:

```
$name = $mw->appname;
```

For more details about the significance of the application name, see Chapter 20.

Widget Existence

To determine if a widget has been created and not destroyed, use Exists($widget):

```
if (Exists($widget)) {
    ...
}
```

Note the uppercase E on this method. The `Exists` method is different from the built-in Perl exists function. Make sure you don't confuse the two.

Is the Widget Mapped?

To find out if the widget has been mapped to the screen, use the `ismapped` method:

```
if ($widget->ismapped)
  # Do something
} else {
  # map the widget
}
```

The `ismapped` method returns 1 if the widget is currently mapped to the screen and 0 if it is not.

Converting Screen Distances

If you prefer to use inches for screen distance but you want to print out pixels, you can use the `pixels` method to convert any valid screen distance string into a pixel value; for example:

```
$pixels = $widget->pixels("2i");    # What is 2 inches in pixels?
$pixels = $widget->pixels("2m");    # What is 2 millimeters in pixels?
```

The `pixels` method rounds to the nearest whole pixel. You can get a fractional pixel result by using `fpixels`:

```
$pixels = $widget->fpixels("2i");    # What is 2 inches in pixels?
$pixels = $widget->fpixels("2m");    # What is 2 millimeters in pixels?
```

Size of Widget

You can use the following methods to find out the size of a widget in several different ways.

Widget's Geometry

The `geometry` method returns the geometry string for the widget in the form of *width* × *height*+*x*+*y*.

```
$geom = $widget->geometry;
```

The geometry string was discussed in detail in Chapter 11. Geometry values are typically specified in pixels. An exception is a child widget that uses characters as its normal units, such as a Text or Listbox, with `-setgrid => 1` specified. In this case, the window manager forces a geometry in integral lines and characters.

Requested Height

The reqheight method returns the height of the widget:

```
$height = $widget->reqheight;
```

Requested Width

The reqwidth method returns the width of the widget:

```
$width = $widget->reqwidth;
```

Actual Width

To get the width of the widget as it currently is drawn, use the width method:

```
$cur_width = $widget->width;
```

When the widget is first created, width will return a 1 until the application has finished drawing everything. After that, it will return the actual width of the widget.

Actual Height

To get the current height, use the height method:

```
$h = $widget->height;
```

Just like the width method, height returns a 1 when the widget is first created. You can use the update or afterIdle method to force everything else to happen and then call height or width to get the finished values.

Widget Position

The methods in this section all deal with the position of a widget.

Position Relative to the Root Window

To determine which widget is at the point (x, y), use the containing method:

```
$which = $widget->containing($x, $y);
```

The $x and $y coordinates must be relative to the root window (or on a Microsoft Windows system, the desktop). An empty string is returned if there is no widget found at those coordinates. If there are several widgets located at those coordinates, the one closest to the front is returned.

Coordinates Relative to the Parent

You can get the coordinates of the upper-left corner of a widget by using the x and y methods. The coordinates they return are relative to the parent of the widget:

```
$x = $widget->x;
$y = $widget->y;
```

Coordinates Relative to the Root Window

To get the coordinates relative to the root window, use rootx and rooty on the widget:

```
$x = $widget->rootx;
$y = $widget->rooty;
```

The coordinates refer to the upper-left corner of the widget.

Virtual Desktop Coordinates

If you have a virtual desktop, there are special methods that give coordinates relative to the virtual desktop. Virtual desktops are very common on the X Window System (such as the *fvwm* and *tvtwm* window managers), but they exist on Microsoft Windows as well.

To determine the height and width of the virtual desktop, use the vrootheight and vrootwidth methods:

```
$height = $widget->vrootheight;
$width = $widget->vrootwidth;
```

To get the coordinates of the widget's upper-left corner relative to the virtual desktop, use vrootx and vrooty:

```
$x = $widget->vrootx;
$y = $widget->vrooty;
```

Each of these four methods returns an empty string if a virtual desktop is not found.

Cursor Coordinates Relative to the Desktop

You can use pointerx, pointery, and pointerxy to determine the cursor coordinates on the screen.

```
$x = $widget->pointerx;
$y = $widget->pointery;
($x, $y) = $widget->pointerxy;
```

All the coordinates returned are relative to the desktop (even if it is a virtual desktop).

Screen Information

The following methods all return information based on the screen (which can be a virtual desktop or a normal desktop) and the colors of the desktop.

Screen Name

Each screen you use has a name associated with it. To get the name, use the screen method:

```
$name = $widget->screen;
```

The name returned will be formatted as "*displayName.screenIndex*". For more details refer to Chapter 11.

Screen Height and Width

The screen height and width is really just the resolution of the screen. Sometimes you might need information to determine how large a window can fit on a user's display. To get the height and width of the screen in pixels, use the screenheight and screenwidth methods:

```
$height = $widget->screenheight;
$width = $widget->screenwidth;
```

If your display dimensions are 1024x768, then screenheight returns 768 and screenwidth returns 1024. If you prefer to get the size of the screen in millimeters, use screenmmheight and screenmmwidth:

```
$heightmm = $widget->screenmmheight;
$widthmm = $widget->screenmmwidth;
```

The same resolution, 1024x768, returns 203 millimeters as the height and 270 millimeters as the width.

Cell Count

The number of cells in the default colormap is retrieved by using screencells:

```
$count = $widget->screencells;
```

Screen Depth

To determine the number of bits per pixel your screen has, use the screendepth method:

```
$depth = $widget->screendepth;
```

Color Type

The type of color is defined by one of the following classes: "directcolor", "grayscale", "pseudocolor", "staticcolor", "staticgray", or "truecolor". To determine the class for the screen that contains the widget, use screenvisual:

```
$type = $widget->screenvisual;
```

To determine the class of color for the widget itself, use visual:

```
$type = $widget->visual;
```

To determine the X identifier for the visual for $widget, use visualid.

```
$xid = $widget->visualid;
```

To find out the entire list of classes available for the current setup, use the visualsavailable method:

```
@list = $widget->visualsavailable
```

Each element in @list describes the visual and the color depth for that visual. For instance, you might see:

```
pseudocolor 8
directcolor 8
grayscale 8
staticcolor 8
truecolor 8
staticgray 8
```

Server Type

The type of server is available through the server method:

```
$server_type = $widget->server;
```

An older Win32 machine has a server type of "Windows 4.0 67109975 Win32". Regardless, this information is generally inconsistent, if not incorrect, so treat it as suspect data.

Is the Widget Viewable?

A widget is determined viewable if the widget and all of its ancestors are mapped. You can ask the widget itself if it is viewable by using the viewable method:

```
$isviewable = $widget->viewable;
```

viewable returns 1 if the widget can be viewed and 0 if not.

Atom Methods

Atoms are an X11 concept. They map strings to an integer identifier allocated by the X server. In the context of Tk, each widget is assigned a pathname, which is stored as an *atom*. The atom has a string name (you can get it for each widget by using the PathName method) and a 32-bit ID. These methods are used internally to handle things such as the selection mechanism.

To get the 32-bit ID for a given widget, send the name of the widget to the atom method:

```
$id = $widget->atom($widget->PathName);
```

You can do the opposite and use the ID to get the name of the atom back. To do so, use the atomname method:

```
$name = $widget->atomname($id);
```

Ringing a Bell

To make the computer beep, call bell:

```
$widget->bell;
```

Clipboard and Selection Methods

Perl/Tk supports two kinds of selection. They are named after the atoms that identify them: CLIPBOARD and PRIMARY. Both selection buffers are capable of handling arbitrary data, but they default to simple ASCII text strings. Handling other data is beyond the scope of this book, thus we confine the discussion to strings.

When making a selection, standard Perl/Tk widgets—such as Text and Entry—select PRIMARY and highlight the selection. The widgets copy the selection to CLIPBOARD as well. This means that pasting text in Tk works in either of two ways:

- Using the middle button, which copies the PRIMARY selection
- Using the keyboard character Control-v, which copies the CLIPBOARD selection

Although we don't talk about virtual events until Chapter 15, participating widgets (effectively) bind <<Copy>>, <<Cut>>, and <<Paste>> virtual events to class methods that manipulate the CLIPBOARD selection. The MainWindow generates virtual <<Copy>>, <<Cut>>, and <<Paste>> events when it sees the characters Control-c, Control-x, and Control-v, respectively.

Applications differ as to which selection mechanism they use. The tendency these days is to use the CLIPBOARD and the characters c, x, and v. What differs is the lead-in character. It may be Control, Alt, or, on a Macintosh, the Apple key. Venerable Unix applications tend to use PRIMARY, where you copy with button 1 and paste with button 2. Your mileage may vary.

Clipboard Methods

The following methods manipulate the internal Tk clipboard, under Unix or Win32.

To clear out the clipboard, use `clipboardClear`:

```
$widget->clipboardClear;
```

Any data in the clipboard will be removed. `$widget` owns the clipboard.

To add data to the clipboard, use the `clipboardAppend` method:

```
$widget->clipboardAppend("data to add");
```

To find out what's in the clipboard, see the `SelectionGet` method in the following section.

Selection Methods

Some widgets allow the user to make a selection. For example, the user can make a selection by dragging the mouse over some characters in the Text, Entry, and Listbox widgets. You can manipulate the selection by using the following methods.

Clearing the selection

To clear the current selection from any widget, use `SelectionClear`:

```
$widget->SelectionClear;
```

You can specify a `-selection` option, which takes either `PRIMARY` or `CLIPBOARD`. The default is `PRIMARY`.

Getting the selection

To determine the current selection for the application, use `SelectionGet`:

```
$selection = $widget->SelectionGet;
```

You can specify the `-selection` option with the `SelectionGet` method:

```
$clipboard = $widget->SelectionGet(-selection => 'CLIPBOARD');
```

The `-selection` option takes, again, either `PRIMARY` or `CLIPBOARD`. The default is `PRIMARY`.

The `SelectionGet` command aborts if there is no selection, but you can catch errors using this idiom:

```
Tk::catch { $sel = $mw->SelectionGet };
if ( $@ ) {
    warn $@;
} else {
    print "selection = '$sel'\n";
}
```

Assigning a callback

You can call `SelectionHandle` to assign a callback that's automatically invoked when the selection associated with $widget changes:

```
$widget->SelectionHandle( \&callback );
```

When $widget owns the selection and there's a request for its selection, the callback is invoked. The callback should then return the selection. It's very possible that the caller may have insufficient space for the entire selection. Please read the Tk::Selection manpage for further details.

Determining the owner

You can find out which widget on the screen currently owns the selection by calling `SelectionOwner` (a widget owns the selection if something is selected in it):

```
$widget = $widget->SelectionOwner;
```

You can also specify the `-selection` option with either `PRIMARY` or `CLIPBOARD` as the value to determine who owns the selection or the current clipboard value, respectively.

Setting the owner

To force a widget to own the selection, call `SelectionOwn`:

```
$widget->SelectionOwn;
```

You can also specify which type of selection to force by using the `-selection` option with `PRIMARY` or `CLIPBOARD`. Finally, you can specify a `-command` option with an associated callback that will be invoked when that widget's selection is taken away.

Exporting the Selection to the Outside World

Here's a clever trick that inserts a string into both the `PRIMARY` and `CLIPBOARD` selections:

```
my $sel = 'frogs lacking lipophores are blue';

# Put a string in the CLIPBOARD buffer.

$mw->clipboardClear;
$mw->clipboardAppend('--', $sel);

# Put a string in the PRIMARY X buffer.

$mw->SelectionClear;
$mw->SelectionHandle( sub {$sel} );
$mw->SelectionOwn;
```

Destroying a Widget

You can destroy a widget by calling destroy on the widget (using if Tk::Exists is recommended):

```
$widget->destroy if Tk::Exists($widget);
```

If the widget is a parent of any other widgets, the other widgets are destroyed as well.

Focus Methods

When your application is running, you can force a widget to have the keyboard focus by calling focus on that widget:

```
$widget->focus;
```

You might want to do this if you have an Entry widget into which the user should start typing first. Calling focus right before MainLoop causes the widget to get the focus right away. If you press the Tab key, the focus automatically changes from one widget to the next. Shift-Tab can be used to change the focus to the previous widget. Control-Tab can be used in the Text widget. When in doubt, remember that you can tell when a widget has the focus by the highlight rectangle around it.

There are several methods that allow you to manipulate the focus.

To make the focus follow the mouse around, use focusFollowsMouse:

```
$widget->focusFollowsMouse;
```

To find out which widget has the focus, call focusCurrent:

```
$who = $widget->focusCurrent;
```

To force a widget to have the focus even if the application isn't currently active, call focusForce:

```
$widget->focusForce;
```

This is not a nice thing to do, so try to not use it.

To find out which widget had the focus last, call focusLast:

```
$which = $widget->focusLast;
```

If none of the widgets in the window has the focus, the Toplevel is returned.

You can use the focusNext and focusPrev methods to actually move the focus to the next or previous widget in focus order:

```
$nextwidget = $widget->focusNext;
$prevwidget = $widget->focusPrev;
```

So, what is *focus order*? First, focus order is constrained to $widget's Toplevel and the Toplevel's descendant widgets. focusNext follows the stacking order of $widget's children as it tries to determine which is the next widget to receive the focus. As it happens, the widget lowest (first) in the stacking order is the most eligible window to receive the focus. The search is then depth-first: the first widget in the stacking order and all its children are considered first, then the first widget's siblings.

Once a candidate widget to receive the focus is determined, the candidate widget's -takefocus option is evaluated. If -takefocus is 0, the widget never gets the focus. If 1, then the widget gets the focus. If undef, then Tk decides. Otherwise, the value of -takefocus is a standard callback, which should return 0, 1, or undef.

focusPrev sets the focus to the previous widget in the focus order.

Keyboard Traversal

What should you do when you don't want to use your mouse in your Perl/Tk application? There are ways you can move around in your application without having to touch the mouse.

Tabbing between widgets

Run any of the Perl/Tk applications you have and hit the Tab key. Assuming you haven't bound Tab to anything else, you'll see different widgets in your application get the focus, each in turn. You know a widget has the focus by a variety of ways. A Button will have a dotted or solid line drawn around it that wasn't there before it had the focus. An Entry will automatically select all the text in it when it has the focus. Only one widget in your application can have the focus at a time. When that widget has the focus, you are able to interact with it using the keyboard. With a widget such as Entry, this makes complete sense. You need to be able to type text into it using the keyboard. We'll talk about this in more detail in the next section.

Not all widgets will take the focus. A Label doesn't accept any keyboard or mouse input, so it won't ever get the focus. A Text widget is special because once it has the focus, a Tab is rebound to enter a Tab as part of the Text. Check with documentation on each widget to determine if you can Tab out of the widget or not.

The order in which the focus moves around matches the order that you packed the widgets into your application. If you are going to rely on using the Tab key to move between widgets in a logical fashion, you may need to redesign the packing order. Try using Shift-Tab; you'll now be moving between widgets in backwards order. Sometimes when Tab has been rebound to do something else, you can use Shift-Tab to get out of the widget and on to the next one (e.g., a Text widget).

Default widget bindings

So what happens when you start hitting other keys and a widget has the focus? A lot depends on what widget has the focus, because there are different built-in bindings for each widget. A Button will let you hit the spacebar to invoke it (this is true for a Button, Checkbutton, or Radiobutton). An Entry or Text widget will let you start typing text into the widget. A Listbox will let you use the arrow keys to move between different items in it. Each widget has its own set of default bindings that let you use the keyboard to interact with it. Check the documentation for each widget to determine what the default bindings are. You can also take a look at the bindDump module shown in Chapter 15 to get some interactive information about a widget.

Menu Traversal

One of the more common things you'll want to do with your application is allow shortcuts to commands that are in menus. Here is a typical file menu being created:

```
my $filem = $menubar->cascade(-label => "~File", -tearoff => 0);
$filem->command(-label => "~Open...", -command => \&open_file, -accelerator =>
    "Ctrl+O");
$filem->command(-label => "~Close", -command => \&close_file, -accelerator =>
    "Ctrl+W");
$filem->command(-label => "~Save", -command => \&save_file, -accelerator =>
    "Ctrl+S");
$filem->command(-label => "Save ~As...", -command => \&saveas_file);
```

You'll see we used the -accelerator option, which will show on the right side of the menu when it's dropped down. (See Figure 12-1 back in Chapter 12 for an example of accelerators.) This doesn't do anything but put text on the screen. In order to have something happen when the user clicks on "Control-W," you need to add a binding like this:

```
$mw->bind($mw, "<Control-s>" => \&save_file);
$text->bind("Tk::Text", "<Control-s>" => \&save_file);
```

By using bind on the MainWindow widget, we've effectively bound that key combination for all widgets in the application. No matter which widget has the focus, you'll be able to type Control-s and invoke the save_file method.

The second binding on the Text widget is necessary only in some cases where the Text widget will actually parse the entered command to try and insert text into the widget. Without that additional binding, you'll get a funny little rectangle if the Text widget has the focus and you'll type Control-s. This type of conflict reminds us to check out the default bindings for each widget we are using in our application. We might be replacing default widget functionality.

Take a look at Chapter 15 for more information on bindings and the different ways to create them.

Grab Methods

When a window does a *grab*, it holds all the keyboard and mouse input to itself. That window will not allow any other windows in the application to receive input. There is also a global grab, which means that no applications in the entire system can get input except the one window that has done the global grab. These methods are usually called from a Toplevel widget.

To do a local grab for the widget, use grab:

```
$widget->grab;
```

A local grab means that you can interact with other windows in the system, but not with other windows in the application. To do a global grab, use grabGlobal:

```
$widget->grabGlobal;
```

To ungrab, call grabRelease:

```
$widget->grabRelease;
```

To find out which widget has done a grab, call grabCurrent:

```
$who = $widget->grabCurrent;
```

To find out the current grab state of a $widget, call grabStatus:

```
$status = $widget->grabStatus;
```

The grabStatus method returns a string that is "none", "local", or "global".

To find out all the windows that are currently under the influence of grab, use grabs to get a list back:

```
@windows = $widget->grabs;
```

Marking a Widget Busy and Unbusy

When a widget (or application) is busy doing uninterruptable work and doesn't want to be bothered by mere mortals, the current idiom is to change the cursor shape (to a watch, a clock, or perhaps a spinning ball) as it passes over the busy widget(s). The Tk commands Busy and Unbusy automate this task for us.

```
$widget->Busy(?-recurse => 1,-option => value>?);
```

This method configures a -cursor option for $widget and, if -recurse => 1 is specified, all its descendants. If -cursor is not specified, it defaults to watch. Additional configure options are applied to $widget only. It also adds a special tag, Busy, to the bind tags of the widgets configured, such that KeyPress, KeyRelease, ButtonPress, and ButtonRelease events are ignored (with press events generating a call to bell). It then acquires a local grab for $widget.

The state of the widgets and the grab is restored by a call to:

```
$widget->Unbusy;
```

For cursor details, see Chapter 23.

Widget Mapping and Layering

Widgets exist in one of two basic states: unmapped or mapped. When a widget is first instantiated (created), it is unmapped, meaning that it exists but has not yet been displayed. Once it is managed by a geometry manager, a widget becomes mapped: its size and position on the display have been calculated, and it has been rendered on the display.

All geometry managers have a "forget" method that removes a widget from the display without destroying it. If the widget is remanaged it reappears on the display exactly where it used to be.

You can also unceremoniously map a widget without regard to its geometry manager:

```
$widget->MapWindow;
```

Doing this may confuse the geometry manager (pack, grid, place, form) that thinks it is managing the widget.

Similarly unceremoniously, you can yank a widget from the display:

```
$widget->UnmapWindow;
```

This unmaps the widget. It does for any widget what $widget->withdraw does for Toplevel widgets. It might confuse the geometry manager that thinks it is managing the widget.

Widgets have a stacking order (see Chapter 2 and Chapter 23 for details), which you can raise or lower using the raise and lower methods.

```
$widget->raise(?aboveThis?);
```

If the aboveThis argument is omitted, the command raises $widget so it is above all its siblings in the stacking order (it will not be obscured by any siblings and will obscure any siblings that overlap it). If aboveThis is specified, it must be a widget reference of a window that is either a sibling of $widget or the descendant of a sibling of $widget. In this case, the raise command will insert $widget into the stacking order just above aboveThis (or the ancestor of aboveThis that is a sibling of $widget); this could end up either raising or lowering $widget.

```
$widget->lower(?belowThis?);
```

If the belowThis argument is omitted, the command lowers $widget so it is below all its siblings in the stacking order (it will be obscured by any siblings that overlap it and will not obscure any siblings). If belowThis is specified, it must be the pathname of a window that is either a sibling of $widget or the descendant of a sibling of $widget. In this case, the lower command will insert $widget into the stacking order just below belowThis (or the ancestor of belowThis that is a sibling of $widget); this could end up either raising or lowering $widget.

Interapplication Communication

You can use the send command to have Perl/Tk (and even Tcl/Tk) applications communicate back and forth. The arguments include an application to talk to and the command to execute in that application.

```
$widget->send("application" => callback);
```

You can also specify the option -async, which will return control immediately instead of waiting for the callback to execute. For complete details, see Chapter 20.

By default, your application will return an error to another application trying to communicate with it. If you want to actually receive communications from other applications, define Tk::Receive($widget, "command") and be careful what you do with the command string. Allowing any application to send unknown commands to your application can be dangerous. Use the interps method to get a list of valid application names.

When engaging in interapplication communication, it is a good idea to run your Perl script with the -T switch, which forces taint checking. Again, see Chapter 20 for complete details and working programs.

Waiting for Events to Happen

At certain points in your application, it makes sense to wait until something happens. For instance, if you create a ColorEditor window and want it to assign the color the user selects to a variable, you can use waitVariable to wait until the variable is set. For complete details, see Chapter 15.

To have a program wait until a variable's value is changed, call waitVariable:

```
$widget->waitVariable(\$var);
```

Processing will continue as soon as the value contained within $var is changed to something different. To wait until a $widget is visible, use waitVisibility:

```
$widget->waitVisibility;
```

To wait until a widget is destroyed, call waitWindow:

```
$widget->waitWindow;
```

When you call these methods, nothing will happen in your program until the requested event has taken place.

An alternative to waitWindow is OnDestroy, where you specify a callback. The widget methods are still available when you use OnDestroy:

```
$widget->OnDestroy(sub { ... });
```

File Events

There is a special method in Perl/Tk called fileevent, which watches and notifies you when a file is readable or writable. For complete details see Chapter 15, Chapter 19, and Chapter 22.

Here is an example that shows how fileevent can be used (this code is meant to be executed on a Unix system because we use the Unix *tail* command):[*]

```
use Tk;
open (FH, "tail -f -n 25 text_file|") || die "Could not open file!\n";
my $mw = MainWindow->new;
my $text = $mw->Scrolled("Text",
                            -width => 80,
                            -height => 25)->pack(-expand => 1);
$mw->fileevent(FH, 'readable', [\&insert_text]);
MainLoop;

sub insert_text{
  my $curline;
  if ($curline = <FH>)   {
    $text->insert('end', $curline);
    $text->yview('moveto', 100);
  } else {
    $mw->fileevent(FH, 'readable', "");
  }
}
```

This short program sits around and waits until a file is readable and then inserts the newly read information into a Listbox. You can also use 'writable'.

```
$mw->fileevent(FH, 'writable', callback);
```

If you omit the callback portion, the callback will be returned. Replace the callback with an empty string ("") and the callback is removed.

Time Delays

There are times when you'll want to be able to delay the program a bit before going on, or maybe you'll want to execute the same command every minute. For complete details, see Chapter 15 and Chapter 17. To have the program sleep for *x* number of milliseconds, call after with the number of milliseconds:

```
$widget->after(milliseconds);
```

* Thanks to Phivu Nguyen for sharing this code.

You almost never want to do this, as the event loop is blocked.

To specify a callback that will be called after so many milliseconds instead of waiting, send a callback as the second argument to after:

```
$id = $widget->after(milliseconds, callback);
# i.e.
$id = $widget->after(1000, \&do_something);
```

If you want to execute a subroutine after the program has been idle for a while, call afterIdle:

```
$id = $widget->afterIdle(callback);
```

To cancel the call to after or afterIdle, use afterCancel with the $id returned by after:

```
$widget->afterCancel($id);
# You can also do this:
$id->cancel;
```

You can have the program repeatedly call the same callback by using the repeat method:

```
$widget->repeat(milliseconds, callback);
# i.e.
$widget->repeat(600, \&update_status);
```

If you destroy $widget, any calls to after and repeat are automatically canceled for you.

Parsing Command-Line Options

In the Unix world, it is standard practice to specify command-line options when you are invoking an application, especially a graphical program. Starting your program as myscript -geometry "80x40" would not be unusual. To have Perl/Tk parse and apply these command-line options for you automatically, just call CmdLine immediately after you create your MainWindow.

```
$mw->CmdLine;
```

For complete details, see Chapter 16.

Really Miscellaneous Methods

findINC returns the absolute pathname of a file:

```
$file = Tk->findINC("Xcamel.gif");
```

Tk->findINC searches for files in all Tk subdirectories of the current @INC path. This can also be a personal Tk directory, if it was added with use lib or push @INC,... earlier. If using the form Tk::findINC, then only @INC is searched, not the subdirectories.

FullScreen simply makes a Toplevel window as large as the display. On Win32, this does not include the taskbar area.

```
$mw->FullScreen;
```

Getimage looks for an image with the specified basename and returns the object reference. The subroutine appends extensions to the basename in the following order: xpm, gif, ppm, xbm until a valid image is found. If that fails, built-in images are searched.

```
$image = $widget->Getimage(name);
```

tainting returns a true value if the program is running with taint checks enabled.

```
$tainted = $widget->Tk::tainting;
```

scaling sets and queries the current scaling factor used by Tk to convert between physical units (for example, points, inches, or millimeters) and pixels. The number argument is a floating-point number that specifies the number of pixels per point on $widget's display. If the number argument is omitted, the current value of the scaling factor is returned.

A point is a unit of measurement equal to 1/72 inch. A scaling factor of 1.0 corresponds to 1 pixel per point, which is equivalent to a standard 72 dpi monitor. A scaling factor of 1.25 would mean 1.25 pixels per point, which is the setting for a 90 dpi monitor; setting the scaling factor to 1.25 on a 72 dpi monitor would cause everything in the application to be displayed 1.25 times larger than normal. The initial value for the scaling factor is set when the application starts, based on properties of the installed monitor (as reported via the window system), but it can be changed at any time. Measurements made after the scaling factor is changed will use the new scaling factor, but whether existing widgets will resize themselves dynamically to accommodate the new scaling factor is undefined.

```
$widget->scaling (number)
```

timeofday returns a floating-point number representing the universe's fractional time of the epoch. For most of us, the time is in the form ss.mmmmmm, where ss is seconds and mmmmmm is microseconds. If your operating system does not honor this, we apologize.

```
$self->{tm0} = Tk::timeofday;
```

## CHAPTER 14

Creating Custom Widgets in Pure Perl/Tk

In this chapter, we become implementers and learn how to build specialized *mega-widgets* using Perl, the existing Tk widget set, and object-oriented (OO) techniques. We use the term mega-widget because the net result is usually a bigger, better, faster widget. There are two basic types of mega-widgets we are going to cover: *composite* and *derived*. They are very similar with only subtle differences between them, and for this reason, we refer to them collectively as mega-widgets.

A composite widget is essentially one widget that is composed of several other widgets contained in a Frame or Toplevel, and maybe some methods, bindings, and configuration options that perform specific functions. The widgets comprising a composite are often called *subwidgets*. For instance, a Dialog consists of two Label and several Button subwidgets contained in a Toplevel, but it's neither Label-like nor Button-like. It's in a class by itself, as it were.

A derived widget is a *subclass* of an existing widget, and differs from the widget it's derived from by adding, changing, or subtracting functionality. It might also have different methods, bindings, and configuration options. For instance, ROText is a version of the Text widget with altered bindings that make the widget read-only (see Chapter 8).

But whether it is a composite or derived widget, our job as mega-widget writers is to make our new widget behave just like any other Tk widget, from how it's created, configured, and managed, to how it's destroyed.

A Mega-Widget Quick-Start

When first trying to decide if you need to write your own mega-widget, you need to know what you want it to do. What features should it have? Which features are absolutely necessary, and which are extras? After creating this list, prioritize the items according to necessity. At this point, you should have a general idea of what types of widgets your mega-widget requires. The next step is to take a look around at the various resources available (CPAN,* newsgroups, and this book) to see if there is already a widget out there. There is no sense in reinventing the wheel if a widget already exists. You might find one that is close enough to do what you want. If you find what you want, congratulations, you no longer need to keep reading this chapter. Still curious, or didn't find what you needed? Keep reading!

You won't learn object-oriented programming here; at least, we don't intend to try to teach it, as there are entire books devoted to the subject.† The actual techniques we use are pretty straightforward and are fully described in the standard Perl documentation. For instance, this code should make sense to you:

```
package Frog;

sub new {
    my($class, %args) = @_;
    bless \%args, $class;
}

sub get {
    my($self, $attr) = @_;
    $self->{$attr};
}

package main;

my $frog = Frog->new(qw/-color blue -poisonous 1/);
print "$frog: color = ", $frog->get(-color), "\n";

Frog=HASH(0x80ccf7c): color = blue
```

If this code is unclear, or if terms like base class, subclass, superclass, and @ISA are unfamiliar to you, then please read the Perl documents *perlsub*, *perlmod*, *perlmodlib*, *perlref*, *perltoot*, *perlobj*, and *perlbot* before continuing.

The class package Frog has a constructor (sometimes called a class method) named new that returns a reference to an anonymous hash, blessed into $class, which in this case is Frog. It also has an object method, get, which returns the value of any attribute of a Frog object. These object attributes are also known as *instance variables* and are stored in the object hash. All in all, this is pretty much standard OO Perl. Perl/Tk widgets are also modeled using an anonymous hash, exactly like the Frog object we just encountered.

You can create an entire mega-widget in fewer lines of code than class Frog's constructor. Of course, this is only because Perl/Tk does a lot of behind-the-scenes work.

```
package Tk::Nil;                # 1
use base qw/Tk::Toplevel/;     # 2
Construct Tk::Widget 'Nil';    # 3
```

---

* Visit *http://www.Lehigh.EDU/sol0/ptk/modlist* for a full list of Perl/Tk modules.

† *Object Oriented Perl* by Damian Conway (Manning) is an excellent read.

```
package main;
use Tk;
use strict;

my $mw = MainWindow->new(-title => 'Nil MW');
my $nil = $mw->Nil(-title => 'Nil object');
$nil->configure(-background  => '#d9d9d9');
print '-background = ', $nil->cget(-background), "\n";
MainLoop;
```

Running this program creates a Nil widget and produces this output:

```
-background = #d9d9d9
```

As Figure 14-1 shows, three lines of code define a Toplevel-based Nil widget class,*
including a constructor that can handle widget options and methods such as configure
and cget. In short, Perl/Tk does everything for you except give the widget an appearance and behavior. But it tries to, even in this minimalist case. You see, as a Nil widget
is created, Perl/Tk calls out to well-known methods (i.e., tries to invoke methods in
class Nil) that we widget writers can provide. These "gateways" allow us to create
bindings and arrange subwidgets within the Toplevel, thus breathing life into our
mega-widget. Any method we fail to provide, or override, in our new widget class, Perl
finds in one of our base classes by searching the @ISA array in the standard manner.

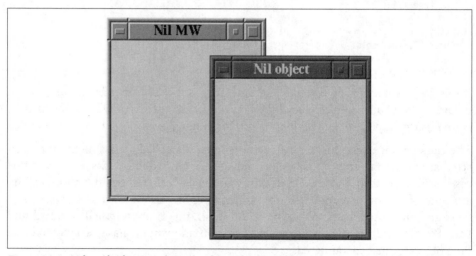

Figure 14-1. Nil, a (dis)functional, Toplevel-based mega-widget

There are two primary gateway methods of concern to us, ClassInit and Populate.
ClassInit is called once to initialize the class, where it typically creates class bindings.
Populate is called for every new widget instance, where, usually, it "populates" the
mega-widget with component subwidgets and defines configuration specifications.

---

* This new widget, unfortunately, doesn't do anything useful, hence its name.

The essence of making mega-widgets is learning how to effectively write these two subroutines. With that in mind, let's make a real mega-widget.

Risking oversimplification and technical inaccuracy, the remainder of this section gives a brief, to-the-point global view of mega-widget use and construction. (Don't worry. Further sections remedy any deficiencies.) The candidate mega-widget is a simple composite consisting of two subwidgets enclosed in a container Frame, so it's a Frame-based mega-widget. The Frame serves two functions. First, it bundles all the individual subwidgets that comprise the composite into a tidy package, which is then easily manipulated by a geometry manager. Second, through the object-oriented mechanism of inheritance, the Frame provides the widget's constructor and routines that handle option specification and configuration, method delegation, and other miscellaneous tasks.

From a user's perspective, using a mega-widget should be identical to using a coreTk widget. Given that, these statements create and configure the labeled Optionmenu widget shown in Figure 14-2. The Label is aligned across the top and the Option-menu is activated, displaying its list of choices.

```
my $mw = MainWindow->new;

use Tk::LabOptionmenu;
my $lo = $mw->LabOptionmenu(-label => 'Ranking', -options => [1..2]);
$lo->pack;
$lo->configure(-background => '#d9d9d9');
$lo->addOptions(3 .. 5);
```

This mega-widget has -label and -options arguments that apply to the Label and Optionmenu subwidgets, respectively. That's nice. We don't have to worry about Tk trying to apply -label to the Optionmenu or -options to the Label. On the other hand, applying a background color to *both* subwidgets is equally logical, and that's just what Tk does. These actions are described by a list of configuration specifications. Similarly, method calls such as addOptions are directed, or *delegated*, to one or more widgets. All of this heavy magic is initiated when Perl processes the use Tk:: LabOptionmenu statement, which reads the file *LabOptionmenu.pm* from somewhere in the *@INC* directory list.

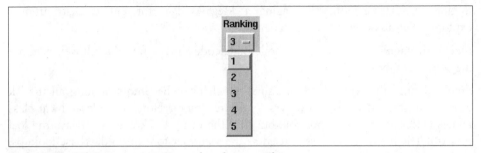

Figure 14-2. LabOptionmenu, a Frame-based mega-widget

This listing of *LabOptionmenu.pm* (including its POD documentation, which we'll examine shortly) serves as a good mega-widget template.

```perl
1   $Tk::LabOptionmenu::VERSION = '1.0';
2
3   package Tk::LabOptionmenu;
4
5   use Tk::widgets qw/Optionmenu/;
6   use base qw/Tk::Frame/;
7   use strict;
8
9   Construct Tk::Widget 'LabOptionmenu';
10
11  sub ClassInit {
12
13      my($class, $mw) = @_;
14      $class->SUPER::ClassInit($mw);
15
16  } # end ClassInit
17
18  sub Populate {
19
20      my($self, $args) = @_;
21
22      $self->SUPER::Populate($args);
23      my $o = $self->Optionmenu->pack;
24      $self->Advertise  ( 'optionmenu' =>  $o  );
25      $self->ConfigSpecs( 'DEFAULT'    => [$o] );
26      $self->Delegates  ( 'DEFAULT'    =>  $o  );
27
28  } # end Populate
29
30  1;
```

It's always good to maintain version information with a module, and it's required if it's distributed via the Comprehensive Perl Archive Network (CPAN) or ActiveState's Perl Package Manager (PPM) archive. In either case, this version information is used by MakeMaker, the utility that reads *Makefile.PL* files and installs Perl modules. There are several ways to define this version information; line 1 shows a possibility. Typically, some other program parses the module file and extracts this version information. A later section, "Packaging a Mega-Widget for Public Distribution," explores this and other distribution details.

Lines 3 through 7 are pretty much boilerplate code and are found in all well-behaved mega-widget modules.

Line 3 defines the widget's class name, which must be unique among all the Tk classes (unless you really know what you are doing). Note that hierarchical class names (Tk::A::B) are also possible but that the internal Tk class is always the leaf part (B). The internal Tk class is used as the identifier for option database lookups, as described in Chapter 16.

Line 5 imports widget definitions required by the new class, saving us from having to use or require them individually. (There is a reason we don't bother including Label, as we'll see soon.)

Line 6 initializes the class @ISA array by declaring the object-oriented base class or classes that the mega-widget is based upon. For composites, the choices are Tk::Frame or Tk::Toplevel. For derived widgets, the list includes Tk::Derived and the widget class being derived from. (Again, we'll clarify all this shortly.) You might see some modules declare their base classes by assigning directly to the @ISA array, but this form is deprecated: @ISA = qw/Tk::Frame/;.

Line 7: just do it.

Line 9 is the magic line. Briefly, it adds a &LabOptionmenu symbol table entry that calls a generic new constructor located in one of the base classes. When a LabOptionmenu widget is created, the generic new constructor creates the initial Frame widget, blesses it into the proper class, and then invokes the class' well-known subroutine, Populate, to create and arrange the Frame's subwidgets and to define configuration specifications and method delegation information. If this is the first LabOptionmenu instance for a MainWindow, ClassInit is called before Populate.

Lines 11 through 16 define subroutine Tk::LabOptionmenu::ClassInit. This subroutine is called once for each MainWindow and is commonly used to create class bindings. ClassInit must return a true result. This example depends on SUPER::ClassInit to do that for us.

Line 14 is obligatory. The statement invokes a ClassInit method in one of the mega-widget's base classes that may (or may not) perform a function on the behalf of our class. For a composite widget based on a Frame or Toplevel, this call currently does nothing, but that may change. However, a derived widget's superclass almost always has required initialization, so don't forget this statement.

Lines 18 through 28 define subroutine Tk::LabOptionmenu::Populate. This subroutine creates and arranges the composite's remaining widgets, advertises important subwidgets, defines configuration options, and specifies how these options (as well as widget methods) are applied to the various subwidgets. Generally, Populate should not configure any of these internal widgets, because Perl/Tk does that later. This is also the place to add subwidget bindings and/or modify the bindtags list. Populate is not expected to return a result.

Line 20 defines Populate's arguments. $self is not a simple Tk::Frame object, but a full-fledged Tk::LabOptionmenu object. $args is a reference to the keyword/value argument hash (in our sample code -label => 'Ranking', -options => [1..5]). If you need to make changes to the argument list, here's your chance.

Line 22 is obligatory. The statement invokes a Populate method in one of the mega-widget's base classes that may (or may not) perform a function on the behalf of our class. For a Frame-based composite such as LabOptionmenu this call invokes Tk::

`Frame::Populate`, which generates additional configuration specifications that transparently handle processing of the Label widget. Omitting this statement would break the mega-widget, because the built-in Label support provided by the Frame would be disabled. The LabEntry widget takes advantage of this feature too. For an exhaustive list of these Label options, see the later section "Mega-Widget Instance Variables."

Line 23 creates the Optionmenu subwidget and uses the packer to manage its geometry. The Label widget is created and packed automatically by the base class Tk:: Frame. (The implication here is that Tk uses pack to manage the Label's geometry, hence you must be wary if using grid in the same program, it's possible that the different geometry managers may enter a race condition as they compete with each other, causing the application to hang.)

Line 24 advertises the Optionmenu widget $o with the name optionmenu. In object-oriented programming, there's a de facto contract that forbids us from meddling with the internals of an object. By advertising a subwidget, it becomes part of the widget's public interface, and we can do with it as we please. Given an advertised name, the Subwidget method returns the corresponding widget reference.

Line 25 defines the mega-widget's configuration specifications. For this simple widget with a single primary subwidget, all configure and cget requests are directed to it. ConfigSpecs is fully described in the section "Subroutine ConfigSpecs."

Line 26 defines how methods targeted for the mega-widget are redirected to subwidgets. Again, the Optionmenu is the primary subwidget, so all mega-widget methods default to it. Delegates is fully described in the section "Subroutine Delegates."

Line 30 returns a true value and is the standard Perl way of indicating that a module "loaded" successfully.

Finally, this POD defines the mega-widget's public interface. It has many of the same headings as the POD for the phone program from Chapter 11. Additionally, it itemizes the mega-widget's new arguments and methods, lists advertised subwidgets, and provides an example.

```
__END__

=head1 NAME

Tk::LabOptionmenu - An Optionmenu with a descriptive label

=head1 SYNOPSIS

S<    >I<$lo> = I<$parent>-E<gt>B<LabOptionmenu>(I<-option> =E<gt> I<value>, ... );

=head1 DESCRIPTION

This widget is a standard Optionmenu with a descriptive label that can
appear on the top, left, right or bottom of the Optionmenu.
```

The following additional option/value pairs are supported:

=over 4

=item B<-label>

Label text to appear next to the Optionmenu. If I<-labelVariable> is
also specified, I<-label> takes precedence.

=item B<-labelPack>

Where to pack the label relative to the Optionmenu. This parameter
is a reference to a list of B<pack> options. WARNING: The implication
here is that Tk uses pack( ) to manage the Label's geometry, hence you
must be wary if using grid( ) in the same program - it's possible that
the different geometry managers may enter a race condition as they
compete with each other, causing the application to hang.

=item B<-labelVariable>

A reference to a Perl variable containing the label string.

=item B<-labelXYZZY>

The label attribute B<XYZZY>, where B<XYZZY> can be any valid Label
option except -text and -textvariable, which, obviously, are
superseded by -label and -labelVariable.

=back

=head1 METHODS

None.

=head1 ADVERTISED WIDGETS

Component subwidgets can be accessed via the B<Subwidget> method.
Valid subwidget names are listed below.

=over 4

=item Name: label, Class: Label

Widget reference of Label widget.

=item Name: optionmenu, Class: Optionmenu

  Widget reference of Optionmenu widget.

=back

=head1 EXAMPLE

I<$lo> = I<$mw>-E<gt>B<LabOptionmenu>(-label =E<gt> 'Ranking:',

```
-options =E<gt> [1 .. 5], -labelPack =E<gt> [-side => 'left']);

I<$lo>-E<gt>configure(-labelFont =E<gt> [qw/Times 18 italic/]);

=head1 AUTHOR

JPolooka@xy.zz.y

Copyright (C) 2001, Joe Polooka. All rights reserved.

This program is free software; you can redistribute it and/or
modify it under the same terms as Perl itself.

=head1 KEYWORDS

Optionmenu

=cut
```

The Perl/Tk Class Hierarchy

Mega-widgets are hierarchical in nature. Base classes are combined to create new classes of ever greater functionality and sophistication.

The following statement creates a Label widget as a child of the MainWindow, $mw, and stores a reference to it in the Perl variable $l:

```
my $l = $mw->Label;
```

In object-oriented lingo, it *instantiates* (makes an instance of) an object of class Tk::Label. If we don't know an object's class, we can determine it using the ref function:

```
print "l = $l, class = ", ref $l, "\n";

l = Tk::Label=HASH(0x822b3d0), class = Tk::Label
```

We see that in reality, $l is a reference to a hash that has been blessed into the package Tk::Label. What we don't know is where this class exists in the overall Tk class hierarchy. This useful bit of information not only tells us the path Perl follows when looking up object methods but also a widget's class relationship with other widgets.

We can write a program that uses an HList widget (fully described in Chapter 18) to graph a depth-first traversal of any widget's @ISA array. The program, *isa*, accepts a Tk class name as input via an Entry widget, then recursively calls isa_tree. This subroutine adds the class name to the HList tree, loads the module file so the symbol table is available, determines the module's base classes by evaluating the new module's @ISA array, and calls itself recursively as required.

```
use Tk;
use Tk::widgets qw/HList/;
use subs qw/isa_tree/;
use strict;
```

```
my $mw = MainWindow->new;
my $instance = 0;

my $hl = $mw->Scrolled(qw/HList
    -separator | -indent 35 -scrollbars sw/
)->pack(qw/-fill both -expand 1/);

my $m = 'Tk::Dialog';
my $e = $mw->Entry(-textvariable => \$m)->pack;
my $cb = sub {
    my $mod = shift->get;
    isa_tree $hl, $mod, $mod . $instance;
};
$e->bind('<Return>' => $cb);
$e->focus;

MainLoop;

sub isa_tree {
    my($h, $class, $path) = @_;

    $h->add($path, -text => $class);
    (my $file = $class) =~ s\::\/\g;
    require "$file.pm";

    foreach my $base_class (eval "\@${class}::ISA") {
        isa_tree $h, $base_class, "$path|$base_class";
    }
} # end isa_tree
```

Figure 14-3 shows the class tree for a Label widget, which is typical of most core
Perl/Tk widgets. Its immediate base class is Tk::Widget, a class module that provides over a hundred subroutines and methods common to all widgets, two of which
are ClassInit and Populate. Since Tk::Widget is the "lowest base class," Tk::Widget:
:ClassInit and Tk::Widget::Populate, both empty subroutines, are invoked if and
only if they are not overridden in a subclass. They act as safety valves, ensuring that
every Perl/Tk widget has Populate and ClassInit methods.

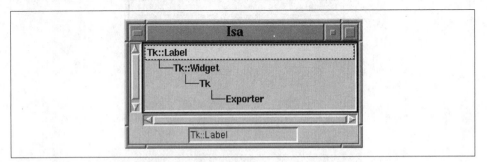

Figure 14-3. Class hierarchy for a Label widget

For historical reasons, *Tk.pm* acts as a base class for Tk::Widget and as an Exporter
module, where it provides over 60 subroutines and methods.

Figure 14-4 shows the class hierarchy for our Frame-based LabOptionmenu widget. When `Populate` and `ClassInit` are called on a LabOptionmenu widget, Perl first finds the methods in class Tk::LabOptionmenu. Each of these methods then passes the call to a superclass. For `Populate`, we know the call is satisfied by `Tk::Frame::Populate`, where the Label configuration specifications are generated. But Tk::Frame doesn't provide a `ClassInit` subroutine, so Perl keeps traversing the `@ISA` array until it finds the safety valve, `Tk::Widget::ClassInit`.

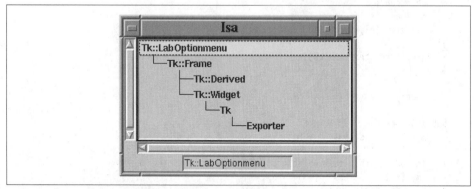

Figure 14-4. Class hierarchy for a LabOptionmenu widget

Note the special class Tk::Derived. It's an important base class for mega-widgets, because it provides more than 15 methods, including `configure` and `cget`, specially designed to make mega-widgets behave like core Tk widgets. Tk::Derived must be available, somewhere, in every mega-widget's `@ISA` tree.

Figure 14-5 shows that Dialog is a subclass of DialogBox, a Toplevel-based composite. We see several familiar classes it's based upon. We might even hazard to guess that a Toplevel is basically a Frame with some window manager attributes thrown in!

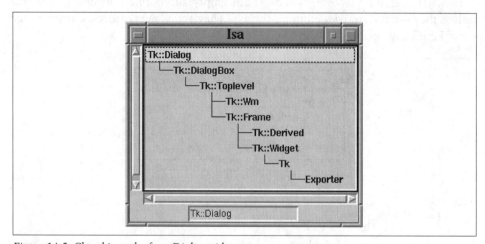

Figure 14-5. Class hierarchy for a Dialog widget

Mega-Widget Implementation Details

Once again, briefly, here's the basic structure of a Perl/Tk mega-widget, but this time using a derived NavListbox widget (described in the section "Derived Mega-Widgets") as the model:

```
1    package Tk::NavListbox;
2
3    use vars qw($VERSION);
4    $VERSION = '1.0';
5
6    use Tk::widgets qw(Listbox Dialog);
7    use base qw(Tk::Derived Tk::Listbox);
8    use strict;
9
10   Construct Tk::Widget 'NavListbox';
11
12   sub ClassInit {}
13   sub Populate {}
14
15   1;
```

Line 1 declares the widget's class name.

Lines 3 and 4 show another way of specifying the module's version number.

Line 6 concisely declares the widgets used by the module.

Line 7 is the signature line of a derived mega-widget, because the base class list starts with Tk::Derived and includes another Tk widget class. Tk::Derived provides all the option specification and configuration, and method delegation support methods. A composite mega-widget would list a single base class, either Tk::Toplevel or Tk::Frame. As Figure 14-4 shows, composite mega-widgets need not include Tk::Derived in their @ISA array, because Tk::Derived is a base class of Tk::Frame.

Line 10, also written as `Tk::Widget->Construct('NavListbox')`, creates a constructor named `NavListbox` in the class Tk::Widget. When the user types:

```
$nlb = $mw->NavListbox;
```

Perl eventually finds `Tk::Widget::NavListbox` via MainWindow's @ISA array. This constructor, like all Perl/Tk widget constructors, then calls `Tk::Widget::new` (described next) to actually create the widget.

Lines 12 and 13 are well-known methods invoked by `Tk::Widget::new`. As we are about to see, there are several other methods you may occasionally find useful.

Tk::Widget::new, the Real Perl/Tk Widget Constructor

In chronological order, `Tk::Widget::new` performs these six major steps when creating a Perl/Tk widget:

1. Calls `ClassInit` to perform class initialization, such as creating class bindings.

2. Calls `CreateArgs` to perform argument processing that is applicable only at widget creation time (as opposed to later configuration). Toplevel's -colormap option is an example.

3. Puts actual widget creation and blessing into the proper package. The only arguments specified at this time are the keyword/value pairs returned by `CreateArgs`.

4. Calls `SetBindtags` to initialize the widget's `bindtags` list. See Chapter 15 for details.

5. Calls `Populate` to perform widget initialization. `Populate` calls `ConfigSpecs` to generate configuration specifications and `Delegates` to describe how methods are dispatched to subwidgets. `Populate` is called only because Tk::Derived is in the widget's `@ISA` hierarchy.

6. Actually configures the widget using the configuration specification hash generated by the previous call to `Populate`.

As mega-widget writers, we have access to the widget in steps 1, 2, 4, and 5, detailed in the following sections.

Subroutine ClassInit

`ClassInit` is called once per MainWindow, allowing class customization on a MainWindow basis. Initialization typically consists of defining class bindings, but it might also initialize class variables, images, and/or data structures. It is passed two arguments:

- A class name, e.g., Tk::NavListbox
- A reference to the MainWindow

Where you place the call to `SUPER::ClassInit` can be important. If you want to override a superclass binding, place your `bind` command after the call. If, as in ROText, you do not want any superclass bindings, don't call `SUPER::ClassInit` at all!

`ClassInit` must return a true value.

```
sub ClassInit {
    my($class, $mw) = @_;
    $class->SUPER::ClassInit($mw);
    $mw->bind($class, '<Event>' => \&callback);
}
```

Subroutine CreateArgs

The rarely used CreateArgs method is called prior to actual mega-widget creation, allowing access to the widget argument hash for specialized processing. It is passed three arguments:

- A class name, e.g., Tk::NavListbox
- A reference to the MainWindow
- A reference to the argument hash

CreateArgs must return a list of keyword/value pairs that Perl/Tk supplies during the widget creation in step 3, described earlier. These keyword/value pairs are not available in step 6, when configure steps through the configuration specifications returned by Populate. The list of keyword/value pairs must also include any that the widget's superclasses might provide; this is very important.

```perl
sub CreateArgs {
    my($class, $mw, $args) = @_;
    my(%args) = (-special_arg => 'special_val');
    ($class->SUPER::CreateArgs($mw, $args), %args);
}
```

Subroutine SetBindtags

The SetBindtags method is called after mega-widget creation, providing a mechanism to alter the widget's bindtags list. It is passed one argument: a reference to the mega-widget.

The call to SUPER::SetBindtags initializes the bindtags list differently depending on the type of mega-widget. For Toplevels, the list is [class, instance, "all"], and for all others, it's [class, instance, Toplevel, "all"].

SetBindtags is not expected to return a result.

```perl
sub SetBindtags {
    my($self) = @_;
    $self->SUPER::SetBindtags;
}
```

Subroutine Populate

Finally, it's Populate time! This method is invoked only because Tk::Derived is somewhere in the @ISA method lookup hierarchy. Since composite widgets are based on Tk::Frame or Tk::Toplevel, they need not include Tk::Derived in their @ISA lists, because Tk::Derived is a base class of the Frame or Toplevel. Derived mega-widgets, on the other hand, must specifically declare Tk::Derived.

Populate is passed two arguments: a reference to the mega-widget and a reference to the argument hash. If the argument hash contains options that aren't destined for configure, they must be removed before calling SUPER::Populate. The idiom uses delete, like this:

```
my $frog = delete $args->{-frog};
```

$frog then contains the value of the -frog option.

As we learned earlier, SUPER::Populate often makes ConfigSpecs calls on behalf of the mega-widget, so remember to call SUPER::Populate.

Populate is also the appropriate place to create subwidget bindings. Note that if you want the subwidgets of a mega-widget to react to the class bindings created by ClassInit, you'll have to add the new class to the subwidget's bindtags list (see Chapter 15 for more details).

Populate is not expected to return a result.

```
sub Populate {
    my($self, $args) = @_;
    $self->SUPER::Populate($args);
    # Create and advertise subwidgets here.
    $self->ConfigSpecs();
    $self->Delegates();
}
```

In general, Populate should never perform any explicit mega-widget configuration, for these reasons:

- Doing so prevents the user from customizing the widget to her liking.
- Often it won't work anyway and only leads to frustration and confusion.

To see why, let's start with this tiny program, *el*, that uses a mythical EntList (Entry and Listbox) composite. Using the Subwidget method, the code fetches the widget references to the advertised Entry and Listbox widgets and inserts some text into each.

```
my $el = $mw->EntList->pack;
$el->Subwidget('entry')->insert('end', 'Entry!');
$el->Subwidget('listbox')->insert('end', 'Listbox!');
```

Suppose the user of this code has established some color and font preferences in his *.Xdefaults* file:

```
el*Foreground: purple
el*Font: -adobe-courier-bold-r-normal--34-240-100-100-m-200-iso8859-1
```

When the code is executed, the user expects large, purple text, shown in Figure 14-6.

Figure 14-6. Large, purple text

Now, it's okay to provide a default font and color scheme, but we can't mandate one. Let's examine *EntList.pm* to see the right and wrong way to do this. First, the incorrect way:

```
$Tk::EntList::VERSION = '1.0';

package Tk::EntList;

use Tk::widgets qw/Entry Listbox/;
use base qw/Tk::Frame/;
use strict;

Construct Tk::Widget 'EntList';

sub Populate {

    my($self, $args) = @_;

    $self->SUPER::Populate($args);

    my $e = $self->Entry->pack;
    my $l = $self->Listbox(-height => 2)->pack;
    $self->Advertise('entry'   => $e);
    $self->Advertise('listbox' => $l);

    # Wrong - hardcoding configurable options leads to
    # frustration and confusion.

    $e->configure(-font => '9x15', -foreground => 'red');
    $l->configure(-font => '9x15', -foreground => 'red');

} # end Populate

1;
```

When the poor user runs his code, instead of large, purple text, he sees small, purple text, as seen in Figure 14-7.

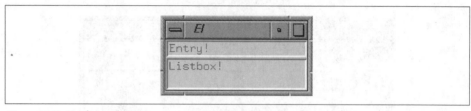

Figure 14-7. Smal, purple text

Now two people are confused: the user, because the font size is too small, and the programmer, because the foreground color is wrong! So replace the two configure lines with this call:

```
$self->ConfigSpecs(
    -font       => [[$e, $l], qw/font Font 9x15/],
    -foreground => [[$e, $l], qw/foreground Foreground red/],
);
```

Each ConfigSpecs entry (explained in the next section) is a reference to a list of values, the first of which specifies where to apply the option. In this case, it's another list of widgets. Now the user can customize the widget either via the option database or explicit configure calls, and if he doesn't, our default of 9x15, red lettering takes effect (see Figure 14-8).

Figure 14-8. 9x15 red lettering

The following sections describe other methods often called from Populate.

Subroutine ConfigSpecs

The ConfigSpecs method tells Perl/Tk what to do when a configure (or cget) request for an option is received. Any number of option/value pairs can be specified in the call, and ConfigSpecs can be called any number of times. (Indeed, we know that one or more of the mega-widget's superclasses may call ConfigSpecs.)

These are the three major ways of using ConfigSpecs:

```
$self->ConfigSpecs(
    'DEFAULT' => [where],
    -alias    => '-otherattribute',
    -option   => [where, DBname, DBclass, default_value]
);
```

If Perl/Tk can't find a ConfigSpecs entry for an option, the default where action is used (described later).

You can use the second flavor of ConfigSpecs to make aliases for options. Perl/Tk automatically aliases -bg and -fg for -background and -foreground, respectively.

The third form is the most common. DBname and DBclass are the name and class of the option in the X11 resource database, fully described in Chapter 16. If the option isn't specified when Tk::Widget::new autoconfigures the mega-widget, the option is assigned the default_value.

where specifies how Perl/Tk configures the mega-widget and/or its subwidgets. It's a scalar: either a single value from the following list or a reference to a list of the following values. All these values are strings except the last, which is a real widget reference:

'ADVERTISED'
:   The configure request is sent to all advertised subwidgets. A subwidget is advertised explicitly via an Advertise call or implicitly via a Component call.

'CALLBACK'
:   Treats the value of the option as a standard Perl/Tk callback: a code reference or a reference to an array with a code reference and subroutine arguments. The proper way to invoke the callback is to use the Callback method, e.g., $widget-> Callback(-option [=> @args]). Perl/Tk will look up the value of -option (the callback) and then call it, passing any optional arguments.

'CHILDREN'
:   The configure request is sent to the mega-widget's immediate children.

'DESCENDANTS'
:   The configure request is sent to the mega-widget's descendants (children, children of children, and so on).

'METHOD'
:   Perl/Tk invokes a subroutine having the same name as the option (excluding the leading dash). The method is called for configure and cget calls. For a configure request, it's called with two arguments: the mega-widget reference and the option value. For a cget request, it's called with only the mega-widget reference, and the subroutine should return the option's value.

'PASSIVE'
:   The option/value pair is simply stored in a hash instance variable. cget can retrieve the value at any time. See the section "Mega-Widget Instance Variables" for details you really shouldn't know!

'SELF'
:   The configure request is applied only to the mega-widget (the Frame, Toplevel, or derived widget).

$widget
:   The configure request is applied only to the specified widget.

ConfigSpecs Examples

This example defines a -validate option that expects a Perl/Tk callback as its value and supplies a default subroutine that always validates true:

```
$self->ConfigSpecs(
    -validate => ["CALLBACK", "validate", "Validate", sub { return 1 }],
);
```

This is an example from the section "Tk::Thermometer," described later in this chapter.

```
$self->ConfigSpecs(
    -background                =>
    [['DESCENDANTS', 'SELF'], 'background', 'Background', 'white'],
    -from                      => [$scale, qw/from From 500/],
    -highlightthickness =>
    [[@highlightthickness], qw/highlightThickness HighlightThickness 0/],
    -length                    => [$scale, qw/length Length 200/],
    -tscale                    => [qw/METHOD tscale Tscale/, $TSCALES[0]],
    -sliderlength              => [$scale, qw/sliderLength SliderLength 10/],
    -to                        => [$scale, qw/to To 0/],
    -width                     => [$scale, qw/width Width 10/],
    'DEFAULT'                  => [$scale],
);
```

The -background option is applied to the mega-widget ($self) and all it descendants, with a default value of white. The -from option is applied to the widget, $scale with a default of 500. The -highlightthickness option is applied to a list of widgets @highlightthickness, with a default of 0. The -length option is applied to $scale with a default of 200. The -tscale option is a method (when the option is configured, Tk invokes the subroutine tscale) with a default of $TSCALE[0]. The -sliderlength, -to, and -width options all apply to $scale, with the indicated default values. All other options default to $scale.

Finally, multiple options can be configured across multiple widgets simultaneously if where is a hash reference. Suppose we have this ConfigSpecs entry:

```
-option => [{-optionX => $w1, -optionY => [$w2, $w3]}, DBname, ... ]
```

Then:

```
$cw->configure(-option => value);
```

actually does:

```
$w1->configure(-optionX => value);
$w2->configure(-optionY => value);
$w3->configure(-optionY => value);
```

Subroutine Delegates

This method tells Perl/Tk how to dispatch mega-widget methods to the component subwidgets. Any number of option/value pairs can be specified in the call, and Delegates can be called any number of times.

```
$self->Delegates(
    'method1'   => $subwidget1,
    'method2'   => 'advertised_name',
    'Construct' => $subwidget2,
    'DEFAULT'   => $subwidget3,
);
```

The 'Construct' delegation has a special meaning. After 'Construct' is delegated, all widget constructors are redirected; e.g., after:

```
$self->Delegates('Construct' => $subframe);
```

$self->Button really does a $subframe->Button, so the Button is a child of $subframe and not $self. Delegates works only with methods that the mega-widget does not have itself.

Other Useful Methods

The following sections describe various methods that are useful when writing mega-widgets.

Subroutine Advertise

Advertise a subwidget reference so it's officially part of the mega-widget's public interface. Use the Subwidget method to map an advertised name to a widget reference.

```
$self->Advertise('advertised_name' => $subwidget);
```

Any other valid widget options can be appended as well.

Subroutine Callback

Execute an option's standard Perl/Tk callback. %args is an optional argument hash passed to the callback. The option -option (e.g., -command) is required and should be declared in a call to ConfigSpecs as type 'CALLBACK'. The Callback method looks up the actual callback associated with -option and invokes it with the optional arguments %args.

```
$self->Callback(-option  => ?%args?);
```

Subroutine Component

Create a widget of class WidgetClass as a child of $self and advertise it with the specified name. Use the Subwidget method to map an advertised name to a widget reference.

```
$self->Component('WidgetClass' => 'advertised_name');
```

Any other valid widget options can be appended as well.

Subroutine Descendants

Return a list of widgets derived from a parent widget and all its descendants of a particular class. If Class is not specified, it returns the entire widget hierarchy starting at $self.

```
$self->Descendants(? Class ?);
```

Subroutine Subwidget

Return the widget reference corresponding to an advertised name.

```
$subwidget_ref = $self->Subwidget('advertised_name');
```

Any Scrolled widget is actually a mega-widget. To get the actual widget reference, use the Subwidget command with the special advertised name scrolled.

Subroutine Walk

Traverse a widget hierarchy while executing a subroutine.

```
$self->Walk($code_ref => @args);
```

Mega-Widget Instance Variables

The mega-widget hash is Perl/Tk territory, but that hasn't stopped folks from using it as their private data structure. Typically, they just swipe a few hash keys to store their instance data, but there's always the risk of clobbering a key used by Perl/Tk. For the most part, Perl/Tk reserves keys beginning with an underscore. Unfortunately, over time, important keys not beginning with an underscore have crept into the mega-widget support code.

Now we're not supposed to peek at object internals, but for the record, these important mega-widget related keys are also reserved by Perl/Tk:

```
ConfigSpecs
Configure
Delegates
SubWidget
```

Since we're being bad, let's run this tiny program, named *xray*, and look inside an opaque LabOptionmenu widget. Each of the four hash keys is a reference to an anonymous hash, and *xray* just pretty-prints the keys and values from these hashes. Notice the tkinit convenience command that creates a MainWindow and returns its reference, which we use to create a widget of the class specified on the command line.

```
#!/usr/local/bin/perl -w

use Tk;
```

```
die "Usage:  xray widget" unless @ARGV >= 1;
my $class = shift;           # get class name from command line

require "Tk/$class.pm";
my $w = tkinit->$class(@ARGV)->pack;
print "X-ray data for widget $w\n";


foreach my $secret (
                    ["Advertised Subwidgets"    => 'SubWidget'],
                    ["Delegated Methods"         => 'Delegates'],
                    ["configure() Options"       => 'Configure'],
                    ["Configure Specifications" => 'ConfigSpecs'],
                   ) {
    printf "\n%-11s - %s\n", $secret->[1], $secret->[0];
    foreach (keys %{$w->{$secret->[1]}}) {
        printf "%20s: %31s\n", $_, $w->{$secret->[1]}->{$_};
    }
}

MainLoop;
```

We run the program by typing xray LabOptionmenu **–label X-ray** (which effectively does $mw->LabOptionmenu(-label => 'X-ray'), and we see this output:

```
X-ray data for widget Tk::LabOptionmenu=HASH(0x814d394)


SubWidget    - Advertised Subwidgets
            label:       Tk::Label=HASH(0x8251070)
       optionmenu:  Tk::Optionmenu=HASH(0x828884c)

Delegates    - Delegated Methods
          DEFAULT:  Tk::Optionmenu=HASH(0x828884c)

Configure    - configure() Options
        -background:                     #d9d9d9
        -foreground:                       Black
            -label:                       X-ray
      -labelVariable:            SCALAR(0x814d5c4)

ConfigSpecs - Configure Specifications
        -background:            ARRAY(0x814d3b4)
              -bg:                     -background
              -fg:                     -foreground
        -foreground:            ARRAY(0x814d420)
            -label:             ARRAY(0x82863b8)
       -labelAnchor:            ARRAY(0x81e0320)
   -labelBackground:            ARRAY(0x82a5158)
       -labelBitmap:            ARRAY(0x82a51dc)
  -labelBorderwidth:            ARRAY(0x82a5f34)
       -labelCursor:            ARRAY(0x82a5fb8)
         -labelFont:            ARRAY(0x82a603c)
   -labelForeground:            ARRAY(0x82a60c0)
```

```
         -labelHeight:            ARRAY(0x82a6144)
-labelHighlightbackground:        ARRAY(0x82a61c8)
     -labelHighlightcolor:        ARRAY(0x82a624c)
 -labelHighlightthickness:        ARRAY(0x82a6c04)
          -labelImage:            ARRAY(0x82a6c88)
         -labelJustify:           ARRAY(0x82a6d0c)
          -labelPack:             ARRAY(0x8286304)
          -labelPadx:             ARRAY(0x82a6d90)
          -labelPady:             ARRAY(0x82a6e14)
         -labelRelief:            ARRAY(0x82a6e98)
      -labelTakefocus:            ARRAY(0x82a6f1c)
          -labelText:             ARRAY(0x82a6fa0)
      -labelTextvariable:         ARRAY(0x82a7cd0)
       -labelUnderline:           ARRAY(0x82a7d54)
        -labelVariable:           ARRAY(0x8286340)
         -labelWidth:             ARRAY(0x82a7dd8)
     -labelWraplength:            ARRAY(0x82a7e5c)
              DEFAULT:            ARRAY(0x814cd3c)
```

The first thing to note is that the SubWidget key points to a hash of advertised widgets, with their names as keys and widget references as values. The Delegates key references a hash of Delegates options, and there we see our DEFAULT entry, the Optionmenu subwidget. Perl/Tk uses the anonymous hash referenced by Configure to store all PASSIVE option values and as instance variables for other options; notice -label and its value from the command line. Finally, the ConfigSpecs key points to all the ConfigSpecs entries, all but one (DEFAULT) of which Perl/Tk supplied automatically.

Composite Mega-Widgets

There are several composite mega-widgets in the Perl/Tk distribution; DialogBox and LabEntry are two simple ones. Before we delve into derived mega-widgets, here's a final, more complex composite.

Tk::Thermometer

This Thermometer widget is Frame-based and capable of displaying temperature in Kelvin, Celsius, or Fahrenheit. The default temperature scale is Kelvin, but is easily changed when the widget is instantiated.

```
my $therm = $mw->Thermometer(
    -label  => 'Reactants Temp',
    -tscale => 'Celsius',
)->pack;
$therm->set(-273);
```

Figure 14-9 shows the results of these statements. The mega-widget consists of a Scale widget packed on the left side of the Frame and three Radiobuttons packed vertically on the right. Instead of labeling the Radiobuttons with text, Pixmap images are used. Notice that the entire mega-widget is a uniform, white background color.

This is because the configuration specifications were cleverly devised so that the Frame, Scale, and Radiobuttons all receive -background configure requests. Other configuration specifications define the default look of the mega-widget, from its width and height to the size of the slider. The beauty of using configuration specifications is that none of this is hardcoded in the mega-widget. Users are free to make changes as they see fit, either during widget creation or in later calls to configure.

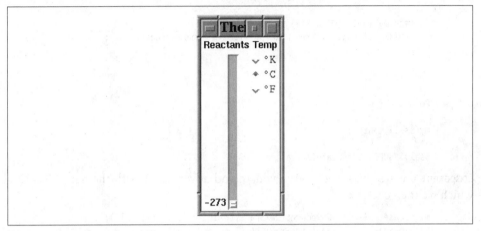

Figure 14-9. A Frame-based Thermometer widget

The module, *Thermometer.pm*, begins in the standard fashion by declaring the version, class name, required widgets, and base class, as well as building a constructor.

```
$Tk::Thermometer::VERSION = '1.0';

package Tk::Thermometer;

use Tk::widgets qw/Radiobutton Scale/;
use base qw/Tk::Frame/;
use strict;

Construct Tk::Widget 'Thermometer';
```

Here we declare two class variables[*] that manage data available to the entire class. %PIXMAPS stores the three Radiobutton Pixmap images. These images are created once during class initialization and shared by all Thermometer instances. @TSCALES is an array of supported temperature scales.

```
my %PIXMAPS;                          # images for the class
my @TSCALES = qw/Kelvin Celsius Fahrenheit/;
```

---

[*] This book is not about object-oriented techniques. Package-scoped lexicals are fine for this example, but you may find ideas in *perltoot* more to your liking.

We don't have any class bindings, but `ClassInit` is a perfect place to create all our images (see Chapter 17) and store their references in a hash indexed by temperature scale name.

```
sub ClassInit {

    my($class, $mw) = @_;
    $class->SUPER::ClassInit($mw);

    foreach my $unit (@TSCALES) {
        $PIXMAPS{$unit} = $mw->Pixmap(-file => "images/$unit.xpm");
    }

} # end ClassInit

sub Populate {

    my($self, $args) = @_;

    $self->SUPER::Populate($args);
```

`Component` creates the vertical Scale widget and advertises it with the name "scale", which we then pack left.

```
    my $scale = $self->Component(qw/Scale scale -orient vertical/);
    $scale->pack(qw/-side left -fill both -expand 1/);
```

Each Thermometer object holds two instance variables that store the old and new temperature scales. When a Radiobutton is pushed, changing the temperature scale, the current temperature is converted from the old to the new units. These two variables determine the name of the conversion subroutine.

```
    $self->{tscale} = $self->{old_tscale} = $TSCALES[0];
```

The `highlightthickness` borders surrounding the subwidgets create visual boundaries that detract from the overall appearance of the mega-widget. The `@highlightthickness` array stores a list of widgets whose -highlightthickness options we wish to configure, beginning with the Scale widget.

```
    my @highlightthickness = $scale;
```

Create a Radiobutton for each temperature scale and label it with a Pixmap. The current (or new) temperature scale is stored in the instance variable pointed to by -variable. When the Radiobutton is selected, the instance variable is updated with the new temperature scale and the -command callback is invoked. Also, add the Radiobutton to the `@highlightthickness` array.

```
    foreach my $unit (@TSCALES) {
        my $r = $self->Component('Radiobutton' => "radiobutton-$unit",
            -image    => $PIXMAPS{$unit},
            -variable => \$self->{tscale},
            -value    => $unit,
            -command  => [$self => 'tscale', $unit],
        )->pack(-side => 'top');
```

```
        push @highlightthickness, $r;
    }
```

The following ConfigSpecs call has several interesting features. To color the entire background, we need to specify SELF (the Frame) and DESCENDANTS (all widgets descended from the Frame: the Scale and Radiobuttons).

The -from, -length, -sliderlength, -to, and -width options all apply to only the Scale widget.

The -highlightthickness option applies to all subwidgets in the array @highlightthickness, which includes the Scale and Radiobuttons. But for this mega-widget, that's the same as saying DESCENDANTS, so we could have saved some code.

The -tscale option invokes the like-named method tscale. The method is supplied two arguments: the mega-widget reference and the new -tscale value (a temperature scale). We'll look at subroutine tscale shortly.

Any other mega-widget options default to the Scale.

In all cases, Perl/Tk uses the default ConfigSpecs value for options omitted by the user.

```
        $self->ConfigSpecs(
            -background    =>
              [['DESCENDANTS', 'SELF'], 'background', 'Background', 'white'],
            -from          => [$scale, qw/from From 500/],
            -highlightthickness =>
              [[@highlightthickness], qw/highlightThickness HighlightThickness 0/],
            -length        => [$scale, qw/length Length 200/],
            -tscale        => [qw/METHOD tscale Tscale/, $TSCALES[0]],
            -sliderlength  => [$scale, qw/sliderLength SliderLength 10/],
            -to            => [$scale, qw/to To 0/],
            -width         => [$scale, qw/width Width 10/],
            'DEFAULT'      => [$scale],
        );
        $self->Delegates('DEFAULT' => $scale);

    } # end Populate
```

When the Thermometer's temperature scale is changed, either programmatically by a configure(-tscale => $new_tscale) call or a Radiobutton click, we must convert the Scale's temperature value to the new units. The Thermometer class has various methods for converting from one temperature scale to another, having names of the form "old_scale2new_scale". All we need do is get the Scale's current temperature value, convert it to the new units, and update the Scale. Notice the use of Subwidget to fetch the advertised Scale widget reference.

tscale is called also on cget requests, so the subroutine both sets and gets the temperature scale.

```perl
sub tscale {

    # The temperature scale has changed - update the thermometer's
    # lower bound and reset the current temperature in the new scale.

    my($self, $new_tscale) = @_;

    if ($#_ > 0) {
        my $old_tscale = $self->{old_tscale};
        return if $new_tscale eq $old_tscale;

        my $subr = "${old_tscale}2${new_tscale}";
        $self->{tscale} = $self->{old_tscale} = $new_tscale;
        my $scale = $self->Subwidget('scale');
        $scale->set( $self->$subr( $scale->get ) );
    } else {
        $self->{tscale};    # cget() requests here
    }

} # end tscale

# Scale conversion data and subroutines.
#
#   Temperature      Kelvin   Celsius   Fahrenheit
#
#   Absolute Zero        0    -273.16     -459.69
#   Freezing        273.16          0          32
#   Boiling         373.16        100         212

use constant ABSZ_CELSIUS    => -273.16;
use constant ABSZ_FAHRENHEIT => -459.69;
use constant ABSZ_KELVIN     => 0;
use constant FREZ_FAHRENHEIT => 32;
use constant FIVE_NINTHS     => 5.0 / 9.0;
use constant NINE_FIFTHS     => 9.0 / 5.0;

# All conversion subroutines are called with two arguments, the
# mega-widget reference, and the temperature in the old scale.

sub Kelvin2Celsius {
    $_[0]->configure(-to => ABSZ_CELSIUS);
    $_[1] + ABSZ_CELSIUS;
}

sub Kelvin2Fahrenheit {
    $_[0]->configure(-to => ABSZ_FAHRENHEIT);
    NINE_FIFTHS * ( $_[1] + ABSZ_CELSIUS ) + FREZ_FAHRENHEIT;
}

sub Celsius2Kelvin {
    $_[0]->configure(-to => ABSZ_KELVIN);
    $_[1] - ABSZ_CELSIUS;
}
```

```
sub Celsius2Fahrenheit {
    $_[0]->configure(-to => ABSZ_FAHRENHEIT);
    NINE_FIFTHS * $_[1] + FREZ_FAHRENHEIT;
}

sub Fahrenheit2Kelvin {
    $_[0]->configure(-to => ABSZ_KELVIN);
    FIVE_NINTHS * ( $_[1] - FREZ_FAHRENHEIT ) - ABSZ_CELSIUS;
}

sub Fahrenheit2Celsius {
    $_[0]->configure(-to => ABSZ_CELSIUS);
    FIVE_NINTHS * ( $_[1] - FREZ_FAHRENHEIT );
}

1;
```

Derived Mega-Widgets

A derived widget is one directly descended from another widget rather than being comprised of two or more widgets. A classic example of OO subclassing is Dialog, a widget derived from DialogBox. Looking at Dialog's @ISA array:

```
use base qw(Tk::DialogBox);
```

you might wonder why Tk::Derived isn't included. The answer is Tk::DialogBox is itself a mega-widget and Tk::Derived is already part if its @ISA array (see Figure 14-5).

Tk::NavListbox

If you see limitations in the standard Listbox and want to make it more useful, perhaps the best thing to do is create your own derived widget. Let's start with a Listbox widget and add some features that allow a user to edit the items without need for additional controls.

We'll add these enhancements to our version of Listbox:

- Display one widget only, not a combination of widgets. We want to keep the widget simple for future programmers.

- Still be able to use scrollbars by using the built-in Scrollbars method, or let users attach scrollbars themselves.

- Provide a popup menu to give the user a mechanism to manipulate Listbox entries.

- Allow the programmer to define a validation routine for new/renamed entries; e.g., end user can enter only numbers.

Figure 14-10 shows what the NavListbox widget looks like while the user is editing an entry.

Figure 14-10. NavListbox, a derived mega-widget

The code to use the NavListbox might look like this:

```
$nlb = $mw->Scrolled("NavListbox", -width => 30, -height => 5,
  -font     => "Courier 12",
  -validate =>
    sub
    {
      my ($entry) = @_;
      print "Validate this: $entry";
      return 1 if ($entry =~ /^[0-9]*$/);
      return 0;
    })->pack(-fill => 'both', -expand => 1);
```

The -validate method does a simple check; it will allow only digits in the text. The rest of the code is just standard widget creation stuff.

The NavListbox class hierarchy, shown in Figure 14-11, is pretty much what we expect, although there is an additional class, Tk::Clipboard, that manages clipboard operations.

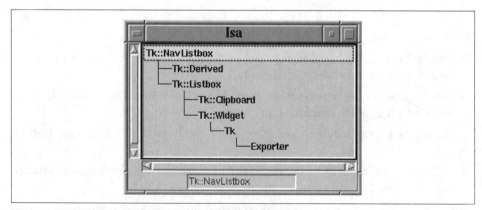

Figure 14-11. Class hierarchy for a NavListbox widget

Now that we have a good idea of what the enhanced Listbox should do, we need to decide how to code it. We're going to need to create a menu to display to the user. We'll have to make sure the menu displays only meaningful entries depending on what entry is right-clicked. The other bit of fancy coding we'll have to do is figure out how to edit an item in-place. We'll see how to accomplish this as we go through the code.

As always, the package statement declares the mega-widget class name. Now, specify the module version, required widgets, and base class list, then build the constructor. Notice Tk::Derived in the first base class entry, marking this as a derived widget.

```
package Tk::NavListbox;

use vars qw($VERSION);
$VERSION = '1.0';

use Tk qw(Ev);
use Tk::widgets qw(Listbox Dialog);
use base qw(Tk::Derived Tk::Listbox);
use strict;

Construct Tk::Widget 'NavListbox';
```

We define our class bindings inside ClassInit. For NavListbox, we don't want to remove any of the default bindings for the widget, so we call ClassInit in some superclass as well. Our binding is for the right mouse button. When the user right-clicks in a NavListbox, we invoke the method, show_menu, which actually does the work of posting the Menu so the user can select an action. The arguments to show_menu are some coordinates, so we can calculate which item in the Listbox they want to perform an action on.

The other bindings are key bindings. If the user holds the Alt button and the Up or Down arrow, we invoke move_item with the correct direction. This only works if the user has tabbed to the NavListbox so that it has keyboard focus.

```
sub ClassInit
{
    my ($class, $mw) = @_;

    $class->SUPER::ClassInit($mw);
    $mw->bind($class, '<Button-3>' => [\&show_menu, Ev('X'), Ev('Y'), Ev('y')]);
    $mw->bind($class, '<Alt-Up>'   => [\&move_item, -1]);
    $mw->bind($class, '<Alt-Down>' => [\&move_item,  1]);
}
```

In Populate, we first construct a Menu that's activated via button 3. We then call ConfigSpecs to set up the option to allow a validation callback, and supply a dummy subroutine that always validates true. Remember that Populate is actually called because we used Tk::Derived when setting up the inheritance chain for our widget.

```
sub Populate
{
    my ($self, $args) = @_;
```

```
$self->SUPER::Populate($args);

my $menu = $self->Menu(-tearoff => 0);
$menu->command(-label  => "New Item" ,
                -command => [$self => 'new_item']);
$menu->command(-label  => "Delete",
                -command => [$self => 'delete_item']);
$menu->command(-label  => "Duplicate",
                -command => [$self => 'dup_item']);
$menu->command(-label  => "Rename",
                -command => [$self => 'rename_item']);
$menu->separator;
$menu->command(-label  => "^ Move up",
                -command => [$self => 'move_item', -1]);
$menu->command(-label  => "v Move down",
                -command => [$self => 'move_item',  1]);
$self->{'lbmenu'} = $menu;

$self->ConfigSpecs(
    -validate => ["CALLBACK", "validate", "Validate", sub { return 1 }],
);
}
```

The first bit of fun is displaying the Menu to the user when she right-clicks somewhere in the NavListbox. This is handled by the show_menu routine. This routine is really quite boring; it's just housekeeping. We first want to select whatever entry the user right-clicked. The standard Listbox doesn't do anything when a user right-clicks, so we need to handle that ourselves.

Using the third of the coordinates passed in (x coordinate with respect to MainWindow, y coordinate with respect to the MainWindow, and y relative to the NavListbox), we can determine which item in the Listbox was selected.

Once we know which item the user clicked, we can determine which menu items to enable or disable. It doesn't make any sense for the user to be able to move the very first item in the Listbox up or the very last item in the Listbox down. If the user didn't actually right-click on an item (we'll find index -1), we want to disable all actions except "New Item."

The last statement in show_menu posts the Menu to the screen wherever the user clicked. If the user selects an item in the Menu, the appropriate callback is invoked. If she doesn't select anything, the menu is un-posted when she releases the mouse button.

```
sub show_menu
{
    my ($lb, $x, $y, $lby) = @_;

    # select the index we just clicked on.
    my $index = $lb->nearest($lby);
    $lb->selectionClear("0", "end");
    $lb->selectionSet($index);
```

```perl
    my $m = $lb->{'lbmenu'};
    if ($index == -1) {
        foreach (1..3,5,6) { $m->entryconfigure($_, -state => 'disabled'); }
    } else {
        foreach (1..3,5,6) { $m->entryconfigure($_, -state => 'normal'); }
        if ($index == 0) { $m->entryconfigure(5, -state => 'disabled'); }
        if ($index == $lb->size - 1) {
        $m->entryconfigure(6, -state => 'disabled'); }
    }

    # popup the menu; goes away when they select something
    $m->post($x, $y);
}
```

To create a new item in the list, we find out what item is selected (remember we selected whatever the user clicked on in show_menu) and insert the item at that index. We select the new item, then invoke the rename_item method to allow the user to edit the new item.

```perl
sub new_item
{
    my ($lb) = @_;
    my $index = $lb->curselection;

    $index = "end" if ! defined $index;
    $lb->insert($index, "<new item>");
    $lb->selectionClear("0", "end");
    $lb->selectionSet($index);
    $lb->rename_item;
}
```

To delete a list item, we find out what item is selected and simply delete it.

```perl
sub delete_item
{
    my ($lb) = @_;
    my $index = $lb->curselection;
    $lb->delete($index);
}
```

Copying a list item is similar to creating a new one, except we borrow the text from the currently selected item first. We also invoke rename_item so the user can edit the newly copied list item.

```perl
sub dup_item
{
    my ($lb) = @_;
    my $index = $lb->curselection;
    $lb->insert($index, $lb->get($index));
    $lb->selectionClear("0", "end");
    $lb->selectionSet($index);
    $lb->rename_item;
}
```

Inside rename_item is where the really neat stuff happens. Similar to all the other methods we have seen so far, we determine which item has been selected. Once we know that, we get some basic information about it so we can overlay it with an Entry widget that lets the user enter a new value while preserving the old value in the Listbox.

The bbox method will tell us how much space within the Listbox that item takes. In order to make our entry widget the correct size, we also have to find out how much space the NavListbox has allocated for the borderwidth. The borderwidth amount is doubled to account for both sides.

Creating the entry is standard, except we want our font size to match the size in our NavListbox. This will force the height of the entry to match the height of the item in the NavListbox, and also make it look like it belongs. The <Return> binding on the Entry is so that when the user finishes his editing by hitting the Return key, we check to see if he's entered valid information. We also bind to the Escape key, so he can abort editing at any time.

The rest of the code in the rename_item method handles the work of putting the widget inside the NavListbox using the place geometry manager, then keeping the user from doing anything else until editing is complete.

```perl
sub rename_item
{
    my ($lb) = @_;

    my $index = $lb->curselection;
    my ($x, $y, $w, $h) = $lb->bbox($index);
    my $bd = $lb->cget(-borderwidth) * 2;

    $y -= $bd;
    my $e = $lb->Entry(-font => $lb->cget(-font));
    $e->insert("end", $lb->get($index));
    $e->selectionRange("0", "end");

    $e->bind("<Return>",
        [sub {
            my ($e, $lb, $i) = @_;

            if ( $lb->Callback(-validate => $e->get) ) {
                $e->placeForget;
                # Must insert first, then delete item
                # so that scrolling doesn't get mussed up.
                $lb->insert($i, $e->get);
                $lb->delete($i + 1);
                $lb->activate($i);
                $e->destroy;
            } else { $e->bell; }
        }, $lb, $index]);

    # Allows us to abort the editing we began ( can leave a new item empty )
    $e->bind("<Escape>", sub {
        my ($e) = @_; $e->placeForget; $e->destroy; } );

    $e->place(-x => 0, -y => $y, -width => $lb->width - $bd);
    $e->focus;
```

```
        $e->grab;    # Don't let anything else happen until they finish w/entry.
        # Wait until the entry is destroyed before doing anything else
        $e->waitWindow;
    }
```

The move_item method simply moves an item up or down in one direction. We put in
some sanity checks, because this method can be called from either the Menu or from
the user hitting some keys.

```
sub move_item
{
    my ($lb, $direction) = @_;
    my $index = $lb->curselection;
    # Sanity checks
    return if ($index == 0 && $direction == -1);
    return if ($index == $lb->size()-1 && $direction == 1);

    my $newindex = $index + $direction;

    my $item = $lb->get($index);
    $lb->delete($index);
    $lb->insert($newindex, $item);
    $lb->selectionSet($newindex);
}
```

As always, the last thing in our module should be a 1, so that it loads correctly.

```
    1;
```

Tk::CanvasPlot

Tk::CanvasPlot is a widget derived from a Canvas that plots simple 2D line plots and
pie charts. Because a CanvasPlot widget is really a Canvas, you can do anything with
CanvasPlot that you can with a normal Canvas widget. Now don't get all excited and
assume this is a full-fledged plotting widget, because it's not. It's just an example of
how you can graft new methods onto an existing widget and extend its functionality. The many design and user-interface considerations required for a robust plotting
widget exceed the scope of this chapter.

The following code shows that CanvasPlot accepts a few more options than a regular Canvas, such as -font for labels and -colors for pie wedges. The new
createPiePlot method parallels the standard Canvas item-creation methods both in
name and calling sequence. To create a pie chart, we specify the pie's bounding box
(in other words, the upper-left and lower-right coordinates of a rectangular region
that just encloses the oval of the pie; the same as createOval) and pass an array reference pointing to the pie data.

```
my $cp = $mw->CanvasPlot(
    -background => 'white',
    -width      => 300,
    -height     => 200,
    -font       => $^O eq 'irix' ? '6x13' : 'fixed',
    -colors     => [qw/red green blue orange purple slategray cornflowerblue/],
```

```
)->grid;

my(@data) = qw/Mon 1 Tue 2 Wed 3 Thu 4 Fri 5 Sat 6 Sun 7/;
$cp->createPiePlot(25, 50, 125, 150, -data => \@data);
```

Figure 14-12 shows the resulting pie chart.

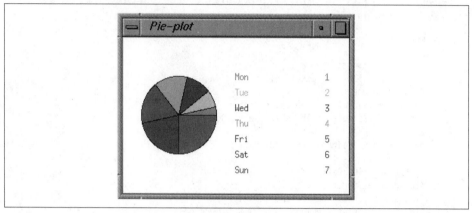

Figure 14-12. The derived mega-widget CanvasPlot can make pie charts

Here's an early version of the module and the standard mega-widget preamble: the module's version number, the module's class name, other Tk widgets required by the new module, the module's @ISA declaration (with Tk::Derived first), and the strict programming style.

```
$Tk::CanvasPlot::VERSION = '1.0';

package Tk::CanvasPlot;

use Tk::widgets qw/Canvas/;
use base qw/Tk::Derived Tk::Canvas/;
use strict;

Construct Tk::Widget 'CanvasPlot';
```

This particular widget doesn't do any class initialization, so we dispense with the ClassInit subroutine entirely. And all Populate does is initialize a few instance variables with PASSIVE configuration specifications, so we can cget them whenever required.

```
sub Populate {

    my($self, $args) = @_;

    $self->SUPER::Populate($args);

    my @def_colors = qw/red green blue/;
    $self->ConfigSpecs(
        -colors => ['PASSIVE', 'colors', 'Colors', \@def_colors],
        -font   => ['PASSIVE', 'font',   'Font',        'fixed'],
```

```
    );

} # end Populate
```

Actually creating the pie chart isn't too difficult, although we'll soon run into details that require some changes to this code. For now, just fetch the –data array reference, total the pie data to determine the number of degrees per unit, and create a series of arcs and labels of varying colors:

```
sub createPiePlot {

    my($self, $x1, $y1, $x2, $y2, %args) = @_;

    my $data = delete $args{-data};
    croak "createPiePlot:  No -data option." unless defined $data;

    my $total;
    for(my $i = 0; $i < $#{@$data}; $i += 2) {
        $total += $data->[$i+1];
    }

    my $colors = $self->cget(-colors);
    my $color;
    my $dp_unit = 360.0 / $total;

    my $degrees = 0;
    for(my $i = 0; $i < $#{@$data}; $i += 2) {
        my $d = $data->[$i+1];
        my $arc = $d * $dp_unit;
        $color = $$colors[ $i / 2 % @$colors ];
        $self->createArc(
            $x1, $y1, $x2, $y2,
            -start  => $degrees,
            -extent => $arc,
            -style  => 'pieslice',
            -fill   => $color,
        );
        $degrees += $d * $dp_unit;
        my $label = sprintf("%-15s %5d", $data->[$i], $data->[$i+1]);
        $self->createText(
            $x2 + 25, $y1 + ($i * 10),
            -text   => $label,
            -fill   => $color,
            -font   => $self->cget(-font),
            -anchor => 'w',
        );
    } # forend

} # end createPiePlot
```

Creating a line plot is even easier: it's just a call to createLine. You might say this is cheating, and you're probably correct. But the user doesn't have to know and besides, we might want to add various options that draw and label axes. Or we might just provide additional methods, such as createPlotAxis.

```perl
sub createLinePlot {

    my($self, %args) = @_;

    my $data = delete $args{-data};
    croak "createLinePlot:  No -data option." unless defined $data;

    $self->createLine(@$data, %args);

} # end createLinePlot
```

Figure 14-13 shows an interesting line plot of terminal server activity.

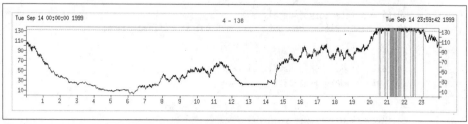

Figure 14-13. createLinePlot highlighting a terminal server failure

The –data option points to an array of x-y pairs, where y is the number of connected users and x is the second of the day (all 86,400 of them). If we scale all the x values by 0.01, they'll fit comfortably on most of today's monitors (the y values require no scaling). createLinePlot then draws the line in canvas coordinates. createPlotAxis draws the x axis, and left and right y-axes, and labels all three.

```perl
my $x_scale = 0.01;            # pixels per second
my $hour = 60 * 60;            # seconds per hour
my $day = 24 * $hour;         # seconds per day
my $x_margin = 30;            # left margin in pixels
my $x_max = 864 + $x_margin;
my $ports = 138;
my $y_max = $ports + 30;

my $cp = $mw->CanvasPlot(
    -height     => $y_max + 30,
    -width      => $x_max,
    -background => 'white',
    -font       => $font,
)->grid;
$cp->createLinePlot(-data => \@data);

$cp->createPlotAxis(
    $x_margin, $y_max, $x_margin + ($x_scale*$day), $y_max,
    -fill => 'red',
    -tick => ['blue', $font, 's', 0, 24, 1, $x_scale*$hour],
    -label => ['blue', $font, '', 1 .. 23, ''],
);
my @labels = ('', 10, '', 30, '', 50, '', 70, '', 90, '', 110, '', 130);
$cp->createPlotAxis(
```

```
            $x_margin, $y_max-$ports, $x_margin, $y_max,
            -fill => 'blue',
            -tick  => ['blue', $font, 'w',  0, 139, 10, 10],
            -label => ['blue', $font, @labels],
    );
    $cp->createPlotAxis(
            $x_margin + ($x_scale*$day), $y_max-$ports,
            $x_margin + ($x_scale*$day), $y_max,
            -fill => 'blue',
            -tick  => ['blue', $font, 'e', 0, 139, 10, 10],
            -label => ['blue', $font, @labels],
    );
```

There's an implementation detail we've neglected: how we should reference these plots and charts. That is, Tk assigns normal canvas items identifiers that we can use to manipulate them, but these plots are composed of multiple canvas items. What shall we do?[*]

One idea is to return a list of all the Canvas items used in the plot, so createPiePlot might do something like this:

```
push @ids, $self->createArc( ... );
push @ids, $self->createText( ... );
...
return @ids;
```

And user code would do this:

```
@pie_ids = $cp->createPiePlot( ... );
...
$cp->delete(@pie_ids);
```

So far so good, but most canvas methods accept only one item ID, not a list, so we've placed the extra burden of differentiating between normal canvas items and Canvas-Plot mega-items on the user. Not nice.

Let's try shifting the work into the class itself. A normal canvas returns positive integers for items it creates, so let's have CanvasPlot return negative integers for its plot mega-items. That means we need a class variable to count the mega-items and, for each mega-item, another variable to store its component items. Sounds like a scalar and an array or hash are what we need. We'll use a hash so we can delete the key when the mega-item is deleted.

```
# Class data to track mega-item items.

my $id = 0;
my %ids = ( );
```

---

[*] In the interest of full disclosure, we should tell you that the real solution is to use a *canvas group*. Nick introduced the concept of canvas groups in Tk 800.018, which act as containers for any number of other canvas items. A group item has its own unique canvas ID and is manipulated just like any other atomic canvas item. It's precisely the solution we should use here.

Now createPiePlot can do this:

```
push @ids, $self->createArc( ... );
push @ids, $self->createText( ... );
...
--$id;
$ids{$id} = [@ids];
return $id;
```

And user code can be written normally:

```
$pie_id = $cp->createPiePlot( ... );
...
$cp->delete($pie_id);
```

Except this won't work because the Canvas delete method has no idea what to do with a negative item ID. But we can override the superclass method by writing our own. This delete method can delete normal canvas items and our mega-items.

```
sub delete {
    my($self, @ids) = @_;
    foreach my $id (@ids) {
        if ($id >= 0) {
            $self->SUPER::delete($id);
        } else {
            $self->SUPER::delete(@{$ids{$id}});
            delete $ids{$id};
        }
    }
}
```

Now all we have to do is override every Canvas method that accepts an item ID. This is a satisfactory solutionand is the preferred solution if this is to be a drop-in replacement for the Canvas widget.

However, there's a middle ground that saves undue work for us, the mega-widget writers, and the user, if we're willing to stick to Canvas tags for identifying mega-items. User code can just do this:

```
$cp->createPiePlot(-tags => 'pie-tag', ... );
```

The only modification to CanvasPlot is to pass %args on all item creation commands:

```
$self->createArc(
    $x1, $y1, $x2, $y2,
    %args,
    -start  => $degrees,
    -extent => $arc,
    -style  => 'pieslice',
    -fill   => $color,
);
```

This allows users to supply any Canvas options they desire.

Tk::LCD

The Liquid Crystal Display (LCD) widget is derived from the Canvas widget and displays positive or negative integers. Each digit of the number is shown in an LCD *element*, consisting of seven *segments* that can be turned on or off. We'll label these segments a through g, as shown in Figure 14-14.

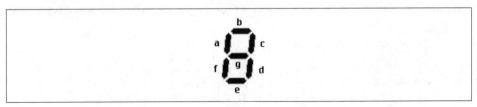

Figure 14-14. LCD widget

The segment shapes are defined using Canvas polygon items.* Figure 14-15 shows an LCD widget with 11 elements. You can easily see the segments, as well as which segments are on and which are off for each digit.

Figure 14-15. LCD widget with 11 elements

Here's how to use the widget:

```
use Tk::LCD;
my $lcd = $mw->LCD(-elements => 11)->pack;
```

Simple, eh? Since the segments are polygons, they have fill and outline colors too, so we can colorize the widget. There are two ways to specify the number to display: the set method or the -variable option. The -variable option requires Tie::Watch, which isn't discussed until Chapter 15, so we'll only touch on it briefly here. Let's look at the module in detail now.

Here is the standard mega-widget header, marking Tk::LCD as a derived Canvas widget. We also declare some class global variables.

```
$Tk::LCD::VERSION = '1.0';

package Tk::LCD;

use base qw/Tk::Derived Tk::Canvas/;
use vars qw/$ELW %SHAPE %LLCD %ULCD/;
use subs qw/ldifference/;
```

---

* Their coordinates came from Donal K. Fellows' game of Maze.

```
use strict;

Construct Tk::Widget 'LCD';

# LCD class data.

$ELW = 22;                          # element pixel width
```

Here are the relative Canvas coordinates for the shapes of each of the seven segments:

```
%SHAPE = (
    'a' => [qw/ 3.0  5  5.2  3  7.0  5  6.0 15  3.8 17  2.0 15/],
    'b' => [qw/ 6.3  2  8.5  0 18.5  0 20.3  2 18.1  4  8.1  4/],
    'c' => [qw/19.0  5 21.2  3 23.0  5 22.0 15 19.8 17 18.0 15/],
    'd' => [qw/17.4 21 19.6 19 21.4 21 20.4 31 18.2 33 16.4 31/],
    'e' => [qw/ 3.1 34  5.3 32 15.3 32 17.1 34 14.9 36  4.9 36/],
    'f' => [qw/ 1.4 21  3.6 19  5.4 21  4.4 31  2.2 33  0.4 31/],
    'g' => [qw/ 4.7 18  6.9 16 16.9 16 18.7 18 16.5 20  6.5 20/],
);
```

To display an LCD symbol we must turn certain segments on and off. %LLCD defines a list of segments to turn on for any particular symbol.

```
%LLCD = (
    '0' => [qw/a b c d e f/],
    '1' => [qw/c d/],
    '2' => [qw/b c e f g/],
    '3' => [qw/b c d e g/],
    '4' => [qw/a c d g/],
    '5' => [qw/a b d e g/],
    '6' => [qw/a b d e f g/],
    '7' => [qw/b c d/],
    '8' => [qw/a b c d e f g/],
    '9' => [qw/a b c d e g/],
    '-' => [qw/g/],
    ' ' => [''],
);
```

Similarly, %ULCD defines a list of LCD element segments to turn off for any particular symbol. Rather than manually generating the list of unlit segments, %ULCD is dynamically computed as the set difference of qw/a b c d e f g/ and the lit segments.

```
$ULCD{$_} = [ ldifference [keys %SHAPE], \@{$LLCD{$_}} ] foreach (keys %LLCD);
```

Subroutine Populate only defines additional configuration specifications for the new mega-widget. Construct has done all the hard work of making LCD like a Canvas, remember?

```
sub Populate {

    my($self, $args) = @_;
    $self->SUPER::Populate($args);

    $self->ConfigSpecs(
        -elements   => [qw/METHOD  elements   Elements   5/  ],
        -height     => [$self, qw/ height     Height     36/ ],
        -onoutline  => [qw/PASSIVE onoutline  Onoutline  cyan/ ],
```

```
                -onfill     => [qw/PASSIVE onfill     Onfill     black/],
                -offoutline => [qw/PASSIVE offoutline Offoutline white/],
                -offfill    => [qw/PASSIVE offfill    Offfill    gray/ ],
                -variable   => [qw/METHOD  variable   Variable/, undef ],
        );

} # end Populate
```

The only public method is set, which is responsible for creating all the lit and unlit segments and moving them to the proper spots on the Canvas. Each segment is tagged with the string lcd so it can be deleted on the next call.

```
# Public methods.

sub set {                           # show an LCD number

    my ($self, $number) = @_;

    my $offset  = 0;
    my $onoutl  = $self->cget(-onoutline);
    my $onfill  = $self->cget(-onfill);
    my $offoutl = $self->cget(-offoutline);
    my $offfill = $self->cget(-offfill);

    $self->delete('lcd');

    foreach my $c (split '', sprintf '%' . $self->{elements} . 'd', $number) {
        foreach my $symbol (@{$LLCD{$c}}) {

            $self->move(
                    $self->createPolygon(
                        $SHAPE{$symbol},
                        -tags    => 'lcd',
                        -outline => $onoutl,
                        -fill    => $onfill,
                    ),
            $offset, 0);

        }
        foreach my $symbol (@{$ULCD{$c}}) {

            $self->move(
                    $self->createPolygon(
                        $SHAPE{$symbol},
                        -tags    => 'lcd',
                        -outline => $offoutl,
                        -fill    => $offfill,
                    ),
            $offset, 0);

        }
        $offset += $ELW;
    } # forend all characters

} # end set
```

Now for Tk::LCD private methods. Subroutine elements is invoked when the user configures the LCD -elements option. The Canvas is resized to fit the new LCD dimensions exactly.

```perl
sub elements {

    my ($self, $elements) = @_;
    $self->{elements} = $elements;
    $self->configure(-width => $elements * $ELW);

} # end elements
```

Subroutine ldifference (list difference) computes the difference of two lists. It's basically right from the Camel (*Programming Perl*, O'Reilly) or The Perl FAQ.

```perl
sub ldifference {              # @d = ldifference \@l1, \@l2;

    my($l1, $l2) = @_;
    my %d;
    @d{@$l2} = (1) x @$l2;
    return grep(! $d{$_}, @$l1);

} # end ldifference
```

Subroutine variable handles the -variable option. Like other widgets with this option, it expects a reference to a scalar. When the scalar changes, the LCD display changes too. It uses Tie::Watch (described fully in Chapter 15) to watch the variable and magically invoke the set method. Notice the OnDestroy handler that removes the watchpoint when the LCD widget is destroyed.

```perl
sub variable {

    use Tie::Watch;

    my ($lcd, $vref) = @_;

    my $st = [sub {

        my ($watch, $new_val) = @_;
        my $argv= $watch->Args('-store');
        $argv->[0]->set($new_val);
        $watch->Store($new_val);

    }, $lcd];

    $lcd->{watch} = Tie::Watch->new(-variable => $vref, -store => $st);

    $lcd->OnDestroy( [sub {$_[0]->{watch}->Unwatch}, $lcd] );

} # end variable

1;
```

Packaging a Mega-Widget
for Public Distribution

Before you even begin writing a publicly consumable Perl/Tk widget, check the Perl/Tk mega-widget home page at *http://www.lehigh.edu/sol0/ptk/modlist*,* where you'll learn about your responsibilities as a module writer. The idea is to stop duplication of effort and coordinate the naming, development, and testing of modules. It's also important to keep the Perl/Tk mailing list *ptk@lists.stanford.edu* and the news group *comp.lang.perl.tk* advised of your module. You'll get invaluable feedback that will make your final result more polished.

Assuming you've followed the protocol and have a pure Perl/Tk widget module ready for distribution, you must register yourself as a CPAN developer and get a CPAN ID. Link to *http://www.perl.com/CPAN-local/modules/04pause.html* to get registration and upload instructions.

With all the paperwork complete, you need to package your new module so it installs in the standard Perl manner:

```
% perl Makefile.PL
% make
% make test
% make install
```

We'll use the NavListbox widget as our example in the next two sections. The first section details packaging the widget for CPAN and the second for ActiveState's Perl Package Manager (PPM).

To begin, create a new, empty distribution directory and copy to it the widget module file, *NavListbox.pm*. For completeness, we need to populate the distribution directory with at least three more files, as shown in the next section. The files are *MANIFEST*, *Makefile.PL*, and *test.pl*.

Packaging for CPAN

Every well-formed Perl module requires a file named *Makefile.PL*, which is an actual Perl program that describes the module. Perl executes this file, resulting in a generated *Makefile* that we use to build, test, and install the module.

Now create a file named *Makefile.PL*, containing these lines:

```
use ExtUtils::MakeMaker;

my $pm = 'NavListbox';

WriteMakefile(
```

---

* Originally developed by Graham Barr, the page is now maintained by Achim Bohnet.

```
    NAME         => "Tk::$pm",
    DISTNAME     => "Tk-$pm",
    VERSION_FROM => "$pm.pm",
    dist         => {COMPRESS => 'gzip', SUFFIX => 'gz'},
    ($] >= 5.005 ?
        (ABSTRACT => 'Navigatible Listbox',
         AUTHOR   => 'Flaz T. Bizzo (ftb@xy.zz.y)') : (),
    ),
);
```

This *Makefile.PL* program stores the module name in a Perl variable, so it's easy to reuse. The `WriteMakefile` subroutine can take many arguments, fully described in its POD:

```
% perldoc ExtUtils::MakeMaker
```

The minimum attributes we require are:

NAME
> The actual module name.

DISTNAME
> The distribution tar filename.

VERSION_FROM
> The name of the file containing the module's version information. We've always included it in the module itself.

dist
> The distribution is compressed with *gzip* and given the extension *.gz*.

ABSTRACT
> The description line from the module list entry.

AUTHOR
> Who wrote the module.

The last two attributes, particularly important for modules destined for a PPM archive, are conditional, because they weren't available prior to Perl 5.005.

To complete our distribution, we need two more files—*MANIFEST*, which lists all the filenames in the distribution, and *test.pl*, a Perl program for the make test phase—for a total of four files: *NavListbox.pm*, *Makefile.PL*, *MANIFEST*, and *test.pl*.

This configuration will likely work, but instead of using `ExtUtils::MakeMaker::WriteMakefile`, we should use its Tk counterpart, `Tk::MMutil::TkExtMakefile`.

As it happens, without even resorting to trickery, an improved *Makefile.PL* program using *TkExtMakefile* can do several more things:

- Create the *MANIFEST* file automatically.
- Create the *test.pl* file automatically.

Add an optional sample program to *widget*'s User Contributed Demonstrations section. *widget* is a Perl/Tk program that demonstrates most of the toolkit's capabilities

---

and is installed in your normal Unix or Win32 path. It's a multisection hypertext application that contains a special User Contributed Demonstrations section for highlighting nonstandard toolkit features. You can use the following special *Makefile.PL* to include a special demonstration of your new widget. For our purposes, this optional fifth file—the "widget contributed" (widtrib) demonstration file—is included.

Here's the widtrib file, *navtest.pl*:

```perl
# A NavListbox sample program.
use Tk;
use Tk::NavListbox;
use strict;

my $mw = MainWindow->new;
my $nlb = $mw->NavListbox->pack;
for (qw/one two three four five six seven eight none ten/) {
    $nlb->insert('end', $_);
}
MainLoop;
```

Our new *Makefile.PL* first writes the *MANIFEST* file containing the names of the four archive files plus the widtrib demonstration file, then writes *test.pl* after first substituting our module's name in the template.

```perl
# A generic Makefile.PL file for any pure Perl/Tk mega-widget. Set
# $pm to the name of the Perl module, and update %widinfo.  Leave
# $widtrib undefined unless you have an addition for widget's User
# Contributed Demonstrations section.
#
# This program creates the MANIFEST and test.pl files, then invokes
# MakeMaker to create the Makefile.  solo@Lehigh.EDU, 2001/01/01

use Tk::MMutil;
use vars qw/$pm $widinfo $widtrib %widtrib/;

$pm = 'NavListbox';              # widget Class name
%widinfo = (                     # PPM widget information
    ABSTRACT => 'Navigatible Listbox',
    AUTHOR   => 'Nancy Walsh (nw@xy.zz.y)',
);
$widtrib = 'navtest.pl';         # widtrib demo file name

print "Writing MANIFEST for Tk::$pm\n";
open MANIFEST, ">MANIFEST" or die "Cannot open MANIFEST: $!";
print MANIFEST <<"end-of-manifest";
MANIFEST
Makefile.PL
$pm.pm
test.pl
end-of-manifest
print MANIFEST "$widtrib\n" if $widtrib;
close MANIFEST or die $!;
```

```perl
print "Writing test.pl for Tk::$pm\n";
open TEST, ">test.pl" or die "Cannot open test.pl: $!";
while (<DATA>) {
    s/NavListbox/$pm/o;
    print TEST;
}
close TEST or die $!;

%widtrib =
  ($widtrib => "\$(INST_ARCHLIB)/Tk/demos/widtrib/$widtrib") if $widtrib;

Tk::MMutil::TkExtMakefile(
    NAME          => "Tk::$pm",
    DISTNAME      => "Tk-$pm",
    VERSION_FROM  => "$pm.pm",
    PM            => {"$pm.pm" => "\$(INST_LIBDIR)/$pm.pm", %widtrib},
    dist          => {COMPRESS => 'gzip', SUFFIX => 'gz'},
    ($] >= 5.005 ? %widinfo  : ()),
);
__DATA__
#!perl -w
use Test;
use strict;

BEGIN { plan tests => 12 };

eval { require Tk; };
ok($@, "", "loading Tk module");

my $mw;
eval {$mw = Tk::MainWindow->new();};
ok($@, "", "can't create MainWindow");
ok(Tk::Exists($mw), 1, "MainWindow creation failed");
eval { $mw->geometry('+10+10'); };

my $w;
my $class = 'NavListbox';

print "Testing $class\n";

eval "require Tk::$class;";
ok($@, "", "Error loading Tk::$class");

eval { $w = $mw->$class(); };
ok($@, "", "can't create $class widget");
skip($@, Tk::Exists($w), 1, "$class instance does not exist");

if (Tk::Exists($w)) {
    eval { $w->pack; };

    ok ($@, "", "Can't pack a $class widget");
    eval { $mw->update; };
    ok ($@, "", "Error during 'update' for $class widget");

    eval { my @dummy = $w->configure; };
```

```
        ok ($@, "", "Error: configure list for $class");
        eval { $mw->update; };
        ok ($@, "", "Error: 'update' after configure for $class widget");

        eval { $w->destroy; };
        ok($@, "", "can't destroy $class widget");
        ok(!Tk::Exists($w), 1, "$class: widget not really destroyed");
    } else {
        for (1..5) { skip (1,1,1, "skipped because widget couldn't be created"); }
    }

    1;
```

So now we have three files, *NavListbox.pm*, *navtest.pl*, and *Makefile.PL*, in an otherwise empty directory. Type this:

```
% perl Makefile.PL
% make
```

This automatically creates *MANIFEST* and *test.pl* for us. Now type this:

```
% make test
```

This creates the final distribution file, *Tk-NavListbox-1.0.tar.gz*, which you should then unpack and test as if you had just retrieved in from CPAN. If all is well, follow the CPAN upload instructions.

Packaging for PPM

If you're creating a PPM archive, we assume you're running in a Win32 environment, which usually lacks *make*, *tar*, and *gzip* programs. So first get *nmake* from *ftp://ftp.microsoft.com/Softlib/MSLFILES/nmake15.exe* and *gzip* from *http://www.itribe.net/virtunix*.

Create the four distribution files (*NavListbox.pm*, *Makefile.PL*, *MANIFEST*, and *test.pl*) as described in the previous section and build the distribution directory, *blib*:

```
% perl Makefile.PL
% nmake
```

Then pack the directory into an archive:

```
% tar -cvpf Tk-NavListbox-1.0.tar blib
% gzip --best Tk-NavListbox-1.0.tar
```

You now have an archive called (hopefully) *Tk-NavListbox-1.0.tar.gz*. Generate the PPD file:

```
% nmake ppd
```

You have to edit the resulting PPD file and add the location of the package archive into `<CODEBASE HREF=""/>`. The location is relative to the PPD file.

And that's it with regard to Perl/Tk mega-widgets. If you're interested in C-level widget information, check out Chapter 21.

CHAPTER 15

Anatomy of the MainLoop

As programmers, we all know what a "main loop" is. It's the heart of our programs, the repeating chunk of code that carries out the task at hand. But Perl/Tk programs are *event driven*, so even if we write what we believe is our program's main loop, it must coexist with a higher order main loop that's a fundamental part of Tk. The Tk main loop is typically referred to as the *event loop*, and its job is to invoke callbacks in response to events such as button presses or timer expirations.

Callbacks are Perl subroutines associated with Tk events. In Perl/Tk, we can define callbacks that, from our point of view, are automatically invoked when the appropriate event occurs. The Tk core defines hundreds of other callbacks on our behalf that we're not even aware of. It's the combination of our own callbacks and Tk-defined callbacks that gives behavior to our Perl/Tk applications.

The event loop is activated once the Perl/Tk program's MainLoop statement is reached. From that point on, MainLoop controls our program. As events happen, MainLoop dispatches them to a handler (a callback) for processing and puts the application to sleep for a short amount of time when the event queue is empty. This repeats until there are no more MainWindows, at which time MainLoop returns. Any code after the MainLoop statement is then executed.

Here is the salient portion of the actual MainLoop subroutine from the Perl/Tk source distribution:

```
use Tk ':eventtypes';

while (Tk::MainWindow->Count) {
    DoOneEvent(ALL_EVENTS);
}
```

As we see, the Tk main loop processes all events, one by one, until the count of MainWindows becomes zero. The use tag :eventtypes imports various symbols used by DoOneEvent, the subroutine that actually dispatches individual events. We'll learn more about DoOneEvent later. For now it's sufficient to know that the subroutine expects one argument, a bit pattern, specifying what types of events to process and whether to return immediately or to wait if there are no such events.

The symbol ALL_EVENTS is the inclusive OR of all the various event types, which we'll examine in detail later. The individual event types that DoOneEvent recognizes are as follows:

WINDOW_EVENTS

These include things such as keyboard entry, button clicks, and window size and visibility changes.

FILE_EVENTS

These deal with reading and writing files and network sockets.

TIMER_EVENTS

These are created by the after and repeat commands.

IDLE_EVENTS

These are low-priority callbacks executed only after all events of the previous types have been processed. The most common idle events are those that redraw widgets and refresh the display. You can queue idle callbacks using DoWhenIdle.

The :eventtypes tag defines one other symbol, DONT_WAIT, that can be inclusively ORed with a DoOneEvent bit pattern to make the subroutine call nonblocking. Notice that MainLoop does not include DONT_WAIT in its DoOneEvent bit pattern, meaning that DoOneEvent sleeps when there is nothing to do, instead of returning to MainLoop. This is actually a good thing, as it allows other programs running on our computer a slice of the CPU pie. Later we'll see when including DONT_WAIT works to our advantage.

MainLoop's job is to dispatch events to callbacks in a timely fashion. As you write callbacks, keep in mind you are in a mutually cooperative environment; all callbacks should be brief and nonblocking so the application remains responsive. A common novice mistake is to execute a long-running system command, then wonder why Buttons don't work and the display won't refresh. The novice fails to realize that MainLoop has been locked out, and the events responsible for Button actions and screen refreshes are being queued by the underlying operating system. We'll examine idioms to avoid blocking situations. The principle of mutual cooperation applies also when sharing events with other GUI packages, such as OpenGL.

And that, in a nutshell, describes the contents of this chapter. In summary, we'll learn:

- How to create callbacks
- About the different events, including virtual events
- How to associate events with callbacks
- About nonblocking programming techniques and how to cooperate with MainLoop
- How to share the event loop with OpenGL

Let us move on and examine the details.

Creating a Callback

Perl/Tk has an expressive and well-defined callback syntax. Anywhere an option expects a callback, you can use this syntax. The most common option name is -command, but you'll also see —validatecommand, -browsecmd, or something similar. For instance, when you create a Button widget, you use -command to specify the callback invoked when the button is pressed. Similarly, when you create an event binding, you specify the event of interest and a callback to invoke when the event occurs.

At its simplest, a callback is a subroutine reference:

```
-command => \&callback
```

or:

```
-command => sub { ... }
```

The first example is a code reference to a named subroutine. The second is a code reference to an anonymous subroutine. Notice that you cannot pass explicit arguments to the subroutines using this callback format. A common mistake is to assume a statement of this form will work:

```
-command => \&callback(arguments)
```

Well, it "works" in the sense that it compiles and produces a result, but the result is probably not what you expect. You aren't creating a code reference to a subroutine that will execute sometime in the future. Instead, the subroutine is executed immediately, and you get a reference to the subroutine's return value. A fast session in the Perl debugger shows us the scary details:

```
[bug@Pandy Anatomy]$ perl -de 0
Default die handler restored.

Loading DB routines from perl5db.pl version 1.07
Editor support available.

Enter h or `h h' for help, or `man perldebug' for more help.

main::(-e:1):   0
  DB<1> sub frog {print "frog args=@_!\n"; return 456}

  DB<2> &frog(1, 2, 3)
frog args=1 2 3!

  DB<3> $cref1 = \&frog

  DB<4> p $cref1
CODE(0x82c45f8)
  DB<5> $cref2 = \&frog(789)
frog args=789!

  DB<6> p $cref2
SCALAR(0x82c6818)
  DB<7> p $$cref2
```

```
456
    DB<8> q
```

Debug line 1 first creates the subroutine `frog` that prints its arguments and returns the integer 456. Line 2 then calls `frog` as a test. Line 3 takes a reference to `frog`, verified in line 4. Notice in line 5 that `frog` is called immediately and prints its argument 789. Line 6 shows us that we have failed to create a code reference but have a reference to a scalar instead. Line 7 dereferences `$cref2` and prints the result, which is 456, `frog`'s return value. You have been warned!

When you want to pass arguments to a callback, specify an array reference, with the callback code reference as first element and the callback arguments as subsequent array elements:

```
-command => [ \&callback, arg1, arg2 ...]
```

or:

```
-command => [ sub { ... }, arg1, arg2, ... ]
```

Finally, there's a third callback form in which you specify a method name as a string. This form is used more often in binding commands and when writing mega-widgets, because it's very easy for a subclass to override the subroutine by providing it's own method with the same name. We'll see examples later on in this chapter. Table 15-1 shows legal callback syntax.

Table 15-1. Legal callback syntax

Callback formats without arguments	Callback formats with arguments
`\&callback`	`[ \&callback, arg1, arg2, … ]`
`sub { … }`	`[ sub { … }, arg1, arg2, … ]`
`'methodname'`	`[ 'methodname', arg1, arg2, … ]`

Regardless of the syntax you use, Perl/Tk ends up creating a Tk::Callback object.

One final note: for callbacks with arguments, Perl/Tk evaluates the contents of the (anonymous) array when the callback is parsed. To defer evaluation of an argument until the callback is executed, use the `Ev` method, described in the section "Binding to a MouseWheel Event." The `Ev` method should only be used to construct parameters for event callbacks.

Callbacks and Closures

Creating a number of widgets using a Perl loop construct is a common programming task, which in itself is easy enough:

```
foreach $b (1 .. 5) {
    $mw->Button(
        -text    => $b,
    )->pack;
}
```

This code produces five Buttons aligned vertically, labeled 1 through 5. But the Buttons don't do anything, and trouble usually begins when you try to specify a callback. Since we're creating Buttons in a loop, the assumption is that they do similar things but vary slightly depending upon which one is pressed. So the problem reduces to how to tell the callback which button invoked it.

Here's a first attempt at creating a series of Buttons with unique identifiers (differences are shown in bold type). It's doomed to failure, because the scope of $b is local to the for loop only, and although the Button text is correct, by the time a Button callback is executed, $b has gone out of scope and no longer exists.

```
foreach $b (1 .. 5) {
    $mw->Button(
        -text    => $b,
        -command => sub {print "Button $b\n"},
    )->pack;
}
```

In the previous example, every time you click on any of the Buttons, you see this:

```
Use of uninitialized value in concatenation (.) at ./close1 line 12.
Button
```

Our second attempt at creating a series of Buttons with unique identifiers also fails, because the callback uses the value that $n had at the end of the for statement. This is simply a variation of our first attempt.

```
$n = 1;
foreach $b (1 .. 5) {
    $mw->Button(
        -text    => $b,
        -command => sub {print "Button $n\n"},
    )->pack;
    $n++;
}
```

When you click on any Button, you see this:

```
Button 6
```

For our third attempt, we declare $b a my, or *lexical*, variable, and voilà, it works! Every Button callback correctly prints its Button ID number.

```
foreach my $b (1 .. 5) {
    $mw->Button(
        -text    => $b,
        -command => sub {print "Button $b\n"},
    )->pack;
}
```

What's so magical about lexicals? In simple terms, when an anonymous subroutine is defined, the values of lexical variables it references outside its scope become "closed," or finalized, as the subroutine is defined. Closures are ideal for creating callbacks, because they can enclose current information in their definitions, which are available later in a different scope. For an authoritative essay on closures, please read the *perlref* manpage.

Here's another version, which also works as expected because Perl/Tk creates the closures for us. It's somewhat verbose, but it does the job.

```
foreach $b (1 .. 5) {
    $mw->Button(
        -text    => $b,
        -command => [\&do_button, $b],
    )->pack;
}

MainLoop;

sub do_button {
    $n = shift;
    print "Button $n\n";
}
```

Here's our final attempt at creating a series of Buttons with unique identifiers. This is a variation of our previous attempt that avoids the use of an explicit subroutine.

```
foreach $b (1 .. 5) {
    $mw->Button(
        -text    => $b,
        -command => [sub {print "Button $_[0]\n"}, $b],
    )->pack;
}
```

Generally, the preferred solution to this problem is either this most recent attempt or to use the lexical for loop variable (our third attempt).

Binding to Events

When creating a Button instance, the -command option specifies the callback to invoke when the user presses the Button. The button press must be button 1, because that's the Button's documented behavior. As a convenience, the Button constructor automatically creates the link between the button 1 press and our callback using the bind command. If it didn't, we'd have to do it manually for every Button we create, using syntax similar to this:

```
$button->bind('<ButtonRelease-1>' => callback);
```

If nothing else, -command => callback is fewer characters to type, but it also provides consistency, because the Button always reacts to the first button, not whatever button the programmer decided to use.

In the previous bind command, the string <ButtonRelease-1> is know as an *event descriptor*. It's composed of two fields enclosed in angle brackets, the *event type* and the *event detail*. In the case of a ButtonRelease event type, the detail portion specifies which button we are interested in. The event descriptor in this example is very specific: it invokes the callback only when button 1 is released over the Button widget (as opposed to when it's pressed). If you watch a Button closely, pressing button 1 only changes the widget's relief from raised to sunken. If you move the cursor away from the Button, the relief changes back, but the widget's callback is never invoked.

Event Descriptor Syntax

An event descriptor can be more complex than our first example; it can actually be one or more *event patterns*, and each pattern can have zero or more modifiers:

    <modifier-modifier-type-detail>

In the previous example, the event descriptor was comprised of one event pattern, which is typically all you'll ever use. Any of the fields may be omitted, as long as at least *type* or *detail* is present.

Tk also supports user defined *virtual events*. They are named entities surrounded by double angle brackets:

    <<virtual-event-name>>

Virtual events may not have modifiers. In previous chapters, we've discussed these virtual events: Tk::Text <<Undo>> and <<Redo>>, Tk::Menu <<MenuSelect>>, and Tk::Listbox <<ListboxSelect>>.

Use the eventGenerate command described later to trigger a virtual event.

Event descriptor modifiers

Table 15-2 lists the valid modifiers. Double and Triple modifiers repeat events. They are most often associated with buttons, so we often see event descriptors like <Double-Button-1>. Common keyboard modifiers include Alt, Control, Meta, Mod, and Shift; thus, <Control-Key-c> would trap a Control-c.

Table 15-2. Event modifiers

Alt	Control	Mod3, M3
Button1, B1	Double	Mod4, M4
Button2, B2	Lock	Mod5, M5
Button3, B3	Meta, M	Shift
Button4, B4	Mod1, M1	Triple
Button5, B5	Mod2, M2	

Event descriptor types

An event descriptor can include any of the types described in Table 15-3.

Table 15-3. Legal event types

Event type	Brief description
Activate	Currently unused.
ButtonPress (or Button)	A mouse button was pressed.
ButtonRelease	A mouse button was released.
Circulate	A widget's stacking order has changed.
ColorMap	A widget's colormap has changed.
Configure	A widget has changed size or position and may need to adjust its layout.
Deactivate	Currently unused.
Destroy	A widget was destroyed.
Enter	The cursor has moved into a widget.
Expose	All or part of a widget has been uncovered and may need to be redrawn.
FocusIn	A widget has gained the keyboard focus.
FocusOut	A widget has lost the keyboard focus.
Gravity	A widget has moved because its parent changed size.
KeyPress (or Key)	A key has been pressed.
KeyRelease	A key has been released.
Motion	The cursor is in motion over a widget.
MouseWheel	The mousewheel is scrolling.
Leave	The cursor has moved out of a widget.
Map	A widget has been mapped onto the display and is visible.
Property	A widget property has changed.
Reparent	A widget has been reparented.
Unmap	A widget has been unmapped from the display and is no longer visible.
Visibility	A widget's visibility has changed.

Of all these event types, most of the time you'll only deal with ButtonPress, ButtonRelease, Destroy, Enter, KeyPress, KeyRelease, Leave, and Motion.

We know that for Button events, the detail field of the event descriptor is a button number. Valid numbers are one through five. If the Button detail is omitted, *any* button triggers the callback. For Key events (KeyPress and KeyRelease), the detail field is a *keysym*, an identifier for the desired keyboard character. For alphabetic characters, the keysym is simply the character itself. For example:

```
$mw->bind('<KeyRelease-a>' => callback);
```

invokes the callback when the lowercase character "a" is typed in the MainWindow. If you want to bind to an uppercase character, use the uppercase keysym:

```
$mw->bind('<KeyRelease-A>' => callback);
```

Other keysyms are not so easy to figure out; for instance, what's the keysym for the page-down key? Well, let's find out....

The Event Structure

When Tk invokes a callback, it provides detailed information about the event that triggered the callback. In C, this data is stored in a structure and has been historically called the *event structure*. The internal Tk event structure is still a real C structure, but we don't fiddle with it directly. Instead, Perl/Tk gives us an *event object*, which we use to call methods that return the pieces of data of interest to us.

To see how this works, let's examine a program that prints the keysym for any keyboard character:

```
$mw->bind('<KeyPress>' => \&print_keysym);

sub print_keysym {
    my($widget) = @_;
    my $e = $widget->XEvent;     # get event object
    my($keysym_text, $keysym_decimal) = ($e->K, $e->N);
    print "keysym=$keysym_text, numeric=$keysym_decimal\n";
}
```

Notice the KeyPress binding is for the MainWindow, which lets us type anywhere in the window, even if it's filled with other widgets. The KeyPress event descriptor is missing its detail field, which means the callback is invoked when *any* key is pressed. Also notice that we've used a callback syntax that doesn't allow us to pass explicit arguments to print_keysym.

But print_keysym is expecting an argument; in fact, Tk implicitly passes the bound widget reference as the first argument to the callback, adding any of our explicit arguments afterwards. This is usually what we want, but sometimes the implicit argument gets in our way. To prevent bind from supplying the widget reference, specify your own object:

```
$a->bind(event_desciptor => [$b => callback]);
```

bind invokes the callback with widget $b rather than $a.

Using the widget reference, we call XEvent, which returns the event object for the KeyPress. The K method returns the key symbol, and the N method returns its decimal value.

In case you're wondering, the keysym for page down is Next.

The exporter tag :variables

The two most important pieces of information a callback needs are the event object and the widget the event object applies to. In newer Tks, Nick introduced two localized variables that represent this information: $Tk::event and $Tk::widget. These fully qualified variables are available to any callback. If you're particularly lazy, import them like so:

```
use Tk ':variables';
```

Then you can use the unqualified names $event and $widget in your callbacks. With this new information, we can write our keysym program more succinctly:

```
$mw->bind('<KeyPress>' => sub {
    print 'Keysym=', $Tk::event->K, ', numeric=', $Tk::event->N, "\n";
});
```

In the following example, we see the three different ways to get the event's widget reference:

```
my $b = $mw->Button(-text => 'Click B1 Then B2', -command => \&callback);
$b->bind('<ButtonRelease-2>' => \&callback);

sub callback {
    print "\n";
    print "callback args  = @_\n";
    print "\$Tk::event     = $Tk::event\n";
    print "\$Tk::widget    = $Tk::widget\n";
    print "\$Tk::event->W  = ", $Tk::event->W, "\n";
}
```

Clicking button 1 invokes callback with no arguments, and we see that $Tk::widget and the W event information method both return the same widget reference (that of the Button). Clicking button 2 invokes callback again, but this time, Tk supplies the bind widget reference as an argument: the Button reference.

```
callback args  =
$Tk::event     = XEvent=SCALAR(0x82920f0)
$Tk::widget    = Tk::Button=HASH(0x817fa00)
$Tk::event->W  = Tk::Button=HASH(0x817fa00)

callback args  = Tk::Button=HASH(0x817fa00)
$Tk::event     = XEvent=SCALAR(0x817ff70)
$Tk::widget    = Tk::Button=HASH(0x817fa00)
$Tk::event->W  = Tk::Button=HASH(0x817fa00)
```

Event information methods

Table 15-4 lists all the event information methods. Keep in mind that not all information is applicable to all events. For conciseness, we also list the corresponding eventGenerate options. The Tk::event documentation has more complete information.

Table 15-4. Event information methods

Method/option	Valid events	Comments
#[a] / -serial	All events	Integer
@	Events with x/y fields	"@x , y" used by Tk::Text

Table 15-4. Event information methods (continued)

Method/option	Valid events	Comments
A	KeyPress, KeyRelease	ASCII character
a / -above	Configure	Window object or ID
B / -borderwidth	Configure	Screen distance
b / -button	ButtonPress, ButtonRelease	Button number
c / -count	Expose, Map	Integer
D / -delta	MouseWheel	Integer
d / -detail	Enter, Leave, FocusIn, FocusOut	See Tk::event POD
E / -sendevent	All events	Boolean
f / -focus	Enter, Leave	All events
h / -height	Configure	Screen distance
K / -keysym	KeyPress, KeyRelease	Symbolic keysym
k / -keycode	KeyPress, KeyRelease	Integer
m / -mode	Enter, Leave, FocusIn, FocusOut	See Tk::events POD
N	KeyPress, KeyRelease	Decimal keysym
o / -override	Map, Reparent, Configure	Boolean (overrideredirect)
p / -place	Circulate	See Tk::event POD
R / -root	KeyPress, KeyRelease, ButtonPress, ButtonRelease, Enter, Leave, Motion	Window object or ID
S / -subwindow	KeyPress, KeyRelease, ButtonPress, ButtonRelease, Enter, Leave, Motion	Window object or ID
s / -state	All events	See Tk::event POD
T	All events	The event type
t / -time	KeyPress, KeyRelease, ButtonPress, ButtonRelease, Enter, Leave, Motion, Property	Integer
W	All events	Widget reference
/ -when	All events	now|tail|head|mark See Tk::event POD
w / -width	Configure	Screen distance
X / -rootx	KeyPress, KeyRelease, ButtonPress, ButtonRelease, Enter, Leave, Motion	Screen distance (the event's x coordinate relative to the root window)
x / -x	KeyPress, KeyRelease, ButtonPress, ButtonRelease, Motion, Enter, Leave, Expose, Configure, Gravity, Reparent	Screen distance (the event's x coordinate relative to the widget)
Y/ -rooty	KeyPress, KeyRelease, ButtonPress, ButtonRelease, Enter, Leave, Motion	Screen distance (the event's y coordinate relative to the root window)
y / -y	KeyPress, KeyRelease, ButtonPress, ButtonRelease, Motion, Enter, Leave, Expose, Configure, Gravity, Reparent	Screen distance (the event's y coordinate relative to the widget)

[a] Since # is an illegal method name, you must store it in a variable: $sn = '#'; $Tk::event->$sn().

Widget Class Bindings

Like most widgets, Buttons have a default behavior defined by bindings automatically created by Perl/Tk. That's why when we make a Button, we don't have to create its <ButtonRelease-1> binding. These default widget bindings are known as *class bindings*. We can see these bindings by using a second form of the bind command, where we pass it just a class name. bind then reports all the event descriptors for that class. We use the Perl built-in function ref to determine the widget's class:

```
my $b = $mw->Button(qw/-text Beep -command/ => sub {$mw->bell});
$b->pack;
my $class = ref $b;
print "Button \$b is an instance of class '$class'.\n" .
    "This class has bindings for these events:\n\n";
print join("\n", $b->bind($class) ), "\n";
```

This produces:

```
Button $b is an instance of class 'Tk::Button'.
This class has bindings for these events:

<Key-Return>
<Key-space>
<ButtonRelease-1>
<ButtonPress-1>
<Leave>
<Enter>
```

Without even referring to the Tk::Button documentation, we can guess what most of these bindings do. The <Enter> event is triggered when the cursor moves over the Button, and the Button's background color changes, indicating it's activated. The <Leave> event restores the Button's background color. The <ButtonPress-1> event changes the Button's relief to sunken, and the <ButtonRelease-1> event changes the relief back to raised and invokes the -command callback. The Key events also invoke the callback if the Button has the input focus.

You can add additional widget bindings to the class if you desire, so that all Buttons inherit this new behavior. Suppose you want button 2 to execute a Button callback twice. Here's how to do it:

```
my $b = $mw->Button(qw/-text Beep -command/ => sub {$mw->bell});
$b->pack;
my $class = ref $b;
$b->bind($class, '<ButtonRelease-2>' => \&twice);

print "Button \$b is an instance of class '$class'.\n" .
    "This class has bindings for these events:\n\n";
print join("\n", $b->bind($class) ), "\n";

sub twice {
    my $button = shift;
    $button->Callback(-command);
    $button->Callback(-command);
}
```

This produces:

```
Button $b is an instance of class 'Tk::Button'.
This class has bindings for these events:

<ButtonRelease-2>
<Key-Return>
<Key-space>
<ButtonRelease-1>
<Button-1>
<Leave>
<Enter>
```

Here we used a third variant of bind that ties an event to a class as a whole. There are three important facts to note:

- We've used a named subroutine rather than an anonymous subroutine for the callback. While not strictly required, it's still good style, because it lets others override the callback by providing their own subroutine of the same name. This is particularly relevant when writing mega-widgets.

- The new binding is retroactive. Widget instances of the class created prior to the new binding definition automatically inherit the new binding.

- The Callback method is the proper way to invoke a Perl/Tk callback. It works like this: Callback takes its object (here, the Button widget), looks up the value of the option passed as its argument (here, -command), then invokes the callback. Callback takes care of the argument handling on our behalf; all the information it needs is contained in the Tk::Callback object.

Widget Instance Bindings

Sometimes you want a binding placed on a particular widget instance instead of the entire class. If you want one particular Button to invoke its callback twice, use this familiar bind format:

```
$b->bind('<ButtonRelease-2>' => \&twice);
```

To query instance bindings, use this fourth flavor of the bind command:

```
print $b->bind, "\n";
```

Which yields:

```
<ButtonRelease-2>
```

This is as expected. Remember, all other Button bindings are *class* bindings.

Table 15-5 shows bind syntax. tag represents a Tk class name, a widget reference, or a symbolic bindtags tag. We examine bindtags in the next section.

Table 15-5. Legal bind syntax

bind format	Comments
`$w->bind;`	Query `$w` for its event descriptors (same as `$w->bind($w);`).
`$w->bind(tag);`	Query `tag` for its event descriptors.
`$w->bind(event_descriptor);`	Query `$w`'s *event_descriptor* for its callback.
`$w->bind(tag, event_descriptor);`	Query `tag`'s *event_descriptor* for its callback.
`$w->bind(event_descriptor => callback);`	Set callback for `$w`.
`$w->bind(tag, event_descriptor => callback);`	Set callback for `tag`.

There are two callback formats we haven't yet talked about. They both query for the actual callback associated with an event descriptor, and you might wonder how they can be useful in the Perl/Tk world, where callbacks are code references. Well, the callbacks may be method names as well, and if we query for a callback, we might get a method name (as a string) instead of a code reference. One thing we can do with this information is write a drop-in replacement for the named subroutine in a widget subclass. Tk will invoke our new subroutine in deference to the superclass method. We can simulate this in non–mega-widget code using the `__PACKAGE__` construct. Here's a way of rewriting the previous instance binding as a fake method name:

```
$b->bind('<ButtonRelease-2>' => __PACKAGE__ . '::twice');
```

Now Tk invokes the named subroutine in the named package (usually package `main`). You do not want to qualify the subroutine with an explicit package name in a mega-widget, though; Perl will find the method via its normal lookup mechanism.

Here is example code for a hypothetical calculator that binds the digits and arithmetic operators that drive the calculator, including those on the numeric keypad:

```
foreach my $key ( qw/0 1 2 3 4 5 6 7 8 9/ ) {
    $mw->bind( "<Key-$key>" => [\&key, $key] );
    $mw->bind( "<KP_$key>" => [\&key, $key] );
}

foreach my $key ( qw/period KP_Decimal/ ) {
    $mw->bind( "<$key>"      => [\&key, '.'] );
}

foreach my $key ( qw/Return KP_Enter/ ) {
    $mw->bind( "<$key>"      => \&enter );
}

foreach my $key ( qw/plus KP_Add/ ) {
    $mw->bind( "<$key>"      => [\&math3, $ad, $io,   undef] );
}
```

```perl
foreach my $key ( qw/minus KP_Subtract/ ) {
    $mw->bind( "<$key>"       => [\&math3, $sb, undef, undef] );
}

foreach my $key ( qw/asterisk KP_Multiply/ ) {
    $mw->bind( "<$key>"       => [\&math3, $ml, $an,     $dm] );
}

foreach my $key ( qw/slash KP_Divide/ ) {
    $mw->bind( "<$key>"       => [\&math3, $dv, $xr,     $dd] );
}

$mw->bind( '<Delete>'        => \&bspclrx );
```

Binding to a MouseWheel Event

Many machines of an Intel architecture include an IntelliMouse, a mouse with a wheel sandwiched between its two buttons. In a Unix environment, Linux in particular, the wheel acts as the middle button. Thus, one has full three-button capabilities. In a Win32 environment, however, the wheel serves as a scrolling device. As it happens, Tk can also use the wheel to scroll.

The following code is taken from Slaven Rezic's post on *comp.lang.perl.tk*. At last, we Unix Perl/Tk-ers can use the MouseWheel event. Slaven tested the code under NT, and we have tested it under Linux.

Until BindMouseWheel becomes part of core Perl/Tk, you can use code similar to this:

```perl
#!/usr/local/bin/perl -w
use Tk;
use strict;

my $mw = MainWindow->new;
my $t = $mw->Text->pack;
$t->insert('end', "line $_\n") for (1 .. 200);
$t->focus;

&BindMouseWheel($t);

MainLoop;

sub BindMouseWheel {

    my($w) = @_;

    if ($^O eq 'MSWin32') {
        $w->bind('<MouseWheel>' =>
            [ sub { $_[0]->yview('scroll', -($_[1] / 120) * 3, 'units') },
                Ev('D') ]
        );
    } else {

        # Support for mousewheels on Linux commonly comes through
        # mapping the wheel to buttons 4 and 5.  If you have a
```

```
        # mousewheel ensure that the mouse protocol is set to
        # "IMPS/2" in your /etc/X11/XF86Config (or XF86Config-4)
        # file:
        #
        # Section "InputDevice"
        #      Identifier  "Mouse0"
        #      Driver      "mouse"
        #      Option      "Device" "/dev/mouse"
        #      Option      "Protocol" "IMPS/2"
        #      Option      "Emulate3Buttons" "off"
        #      Option      "ZAxisMapping" "4 5"
        # EndSection

        $w->bind('<4>' => sub {
            $_[0]->yview('scroll', -3, 'units') unless $Tk::strictMotif;
        });

        $w->bind('<5>' => sub {
                $_[0]->yview('scroll', +3, 'units') unless $Tk::strictMotif;
        });
    }

} # end BindMouseWheel
```

There's an interesting item here. Notice the funny Ev('D') construct in the Win32 callback. This is the Perl/Tk way of postponing argument evaluation until the callback is executed. Here, it's the D field (MouseWheel delta) from the event structure. Equivalently, we could omit the Ev call and use the Tk::event object to manually fetch the mousewheel delta within the callback:

```
my $delta = $Tk::event->D;
```

where $delta corresponds to $_[1] in the callback.

Ev is even more sophisticated. You can pass it yet another Perl/Tk callback that doesn't get evaluated until the main event callback is executed. And Ev is recursive, so an Ev call can contain other Ev calls.

Canvas Bindings

Some final notes. A Canvas widget has its own bind method that binds callbacks to individual Canvas items rather than the Canvas as a whole. Unsurprisingly, the syntax parallels the normal bind:

```
$canvas->bind(tagorid, event_descriptor => callback);
```

where *tagorid* identifies the particular Canvas item. To create a binding for the Canvas instance, we use this special method:

```
$canvas->CanvasBind(event_descriptor => callback);
```

If CanvasBind isn't available with your version of Perl/Tk, you can always fall back to the old syntax:

```
$canvas->Tk::bind(event_descriptor => callback);
```

The bindtags Command

So, we know that a Button has a predefined binding for a `<ButtonRelease-1>` event. What do you suppose will happen if we make an instance binding to `<ButtonRelease-1>` as well? Which callback gets invoked, the class or the instance? Or are both invoked? If both callbacks are invoked, in what order do they occur?

Both callbacks are invoked: first the class, then the instance. To understand why, we need to study the `bindtags` command. Whenever a binding is created, it is always associated with an identifying tag. Thus far, each of our Button binding examples has used two tags, a class name and a widget instance, which represent the Button's class tag and the instance tag, respectively. Except for Toplevels, every widget has two additional binding tags: the widget's Toplevel window and the global string `all`. Toplevels are their own instances, so they have only three binding tags.

When an event occurs, it's compared against all the event descriptors for every tag that a widget owns, and if the event matches one of the tag's list of event descriptors, the associated callback is executed. The search continues through the `bindtags` list until all the tags have been examined and every possible callback executed.

A widget's `bindtags` list is ordered. It is always searched from left to right (starting at array index 0). The `bindtags` command queries, adds, deletes, or rearranges a widget's binding tags list.

Let's do a `bindtags` query command on our `$twice` button from the previous section:

```
my $twice = $mw->Button(qw/-text Beep -command/ =>  sub {$mw->bell});
$twice->pack;
$twice->bind('<ButtonRelease-1>' => \&twice);

my (@bindtags) = $twice->bindtags;
print "\$twice's bindtags:\n\n", join("\n", @bindtags), "\n";
Which yields:
$twice's bindtags:

Tk::Button
.button
.
all
```

Ignoring the fact that the $twice instance tag is represented by the string ".button", and the Toplevel tag by the string ".", a vestige of Perl/Tk's Tcl origins, the tag list order is class, instance, Toplevel, all.

As an aside, these string names are internal widget identifiers that you should never intentionally use; always use the real Perl/Tk reference. They are actually Tcl/Tk pathnames and are created by Perl/Tk when a widget is instantiated. "." Is the Tcl/Tk name for the MainWindow and `.frame2.text.radiobutton10` is the name of a Radiobutton deep inside the widget hierarchy. The `PathName` method shows a widget's internal pathname.

Now let's iterate through the binding tags and print the event descriptors for each tag:

```
print "\nHere are \$twice's binding tags, and each tag's bindings:\n\n";
foreach my $tag ($twice->bindtags) {
    print "  bindtag tag '$tag' has these bindings:\n";
    print "    ", $twice->bind($tag), "\n";
}
print "\n";
```

Here's the output:

```
Here are $twice's binding tags, and each tag's bindings:

  bindtag tag 'Tk::Button' has these bindings:
    <Key-Return><Key-space><ButtonRelease-1><Button-1><Leave><Enter>
  bindtag tag '.button' has these bindings:
    <ButtonRelease-1>
  bindtag tag '.' has these bindings:

  bindtag tag 'all' has these bindings:
    <Key-F10><Alt-Key><<LeftTab>><Key-Tab>
```

Now we can see exactly what happens when a button 1 release event occurs. First the class binding is executed, and we hear a beep. Perl/Tk then looks at the next tag in the binding tag list, finds a matching event descriptor, and executes its callback, which beeps the bell twice. The search continues through the Toplevel and all bindings, but no other matching event descriptor is found.

How Might We Use bindtags?

One way to use bindtags is to completely remove every binding tag belonging to a widget. If you want a "view only" Text widget that displays some fancy instructions but can't be modified by the user, remove all binding tags and render the widget inert.

```
my $mw = MainWindow->new;
my $b = $mw->Button(qw/-text Quit -command/ => \&exit)->grid;
my $t = $mw->Text->grid;
$t->insert(qw/end HelloWorld/);
$t->bindtags(undef);
```

A second use allows us to override a class binding for a widget instance. The idiom is to create the instance binding, reorder the widget's bindtags list, placing the instance tag before the class tag, then use break in the instance callback to short-circuit the bindtags search so the class callback can never be invoked.

In the following example, pretend we want to override the <Enter> binding for one Button instance only. When the cursor moves over that oddball Button, the bell sounds rather than the background color changing.

We also show how to override a binding for an entire class. The idiom is to derive a subclass that establishes the new bindings in ClassInit. Refer to Chapter 14 for mega-widget details.

This is how it's done:

```
package MyButton;
```

MyButton is a subclass of the standard Button widget. A MyButton behaves just like a normal Button except that it prints a message when the cursor moves over it instead of changing color. ClassInit first establishes normal Button bindings and then overrides the <Enter> event descriptor.

If there is no SUPER::ClassInit call, MyButton widgets would have no default behavior at all.

```
use base qw/Tk::Button/;
Construct Tk::Widget 'MyButton';

sub ClassInit {
    my ($class, $mw) = @_;
    $class->SUPER::ClassInit($mw);
    $mw->bind($class, '<Enter>', sub{print "Entered a MyButton\n"});
}
```

Make a Button and a MyButton:

```
package main;

my $mw = MainWindow->new;
$mw->Button(-text => 'NormalButton')->pack;
$mw->MyButton(-text => 'MyButton')->pack;
```

Although MyButton has overridden <Enter> on a class-wide basis, both Button and MyButton widgets have the same bindtags order: class, instance, Toplevel, all.

Now create a Button, $swap, and print its bindtags list to prove that, by default, the order remains class, instance, Toplevel, all.

```
my $swap = $mw->Button(-text => 'SwapButton')->pack;
my (@swap_bindtags) = $swap->bindtags;
print "\$swap's original bindtags list is : @swap_bindtags\n";
```

Reorder $swap's bindtags by swapping the class and instance order, yielding instance, class, Toplevel, all. bindtags expects a reference to an array of tags, which we provide after slicing the original array.

```
$swap->bindtags( [ @swap_bindtags[1, 0, 2, 3] ] );
@swap_bindtags = $swap->bindtags;
print "\$swap's new      bindtags list is : @swap_bindtags\n";
```

Override <Enter> for the instance $swap only. Now, when the cursor enters $swap, first the instance callback is executed, then break halts further searching of the bindtags list. $_[0] is $swap, the implicit callback argument provided by Perl/Tk.

```
$swap->bind('<Enter>' => sub {
    $_[0]->bell;
    $_[0]->break;
});

MainLoop;
```

In summary, to alter class bindings for many widgets, it's best to subclass them. For a single instance, break with a reordered bindtags list might be easiest.

This is why the bindtags order differs from Tcl/Tk's order of instance, class, Toplevel, all. Under object-oriented Perl/Tk, we are expected to use subclassing.

bindDump—Dump Lots of Binding Information

bindtags, in conjunction with bind, is a powerful debugging tool, since it can display tons of useful widget binding data. We've encapsulated it into a module that exports one symbol: the subroutine bindDump. Here's what it has to say about our $twice Button widget. For this example, we're using the "fake method" binding syntax:

```
my $twice = $mw->Button(qw/-text Beep -command/ =>  sub {$mw->bell});
$twice->bind('<ButtonRelease-2>' => __PACKAGE__ . '::twice');
&bindDump($twice);
```

The bindDump output follows. For each binding tag, it lists the event descriptor, the event descriptor's callback, plus all the callback arguments. Notice that without exception, the callback is a method name and not a code reference.

bindDump also lists the arguments passed to the callback, expanding Ev calls. Notice that the all tag's <Alt-Key> event uses Ev('K'), the event's keysym. The all binding tag affects menu and focus traversal.

```
## Binding information for '.button', Tk::Button=HASH(0x81803f0) ##

1. Binding tag 'Tk::Button' has these bindings:
             <Key-Return> : Tk::Callback=SCALAR(0x818024c)
                              'Invoke'
              <Key-space> : Tk::Callback=SCALAR(0x8180234)
                              'Invoke'
         <ButtonRelease-1> : Tk::Callback=SCALAR(0x818021c)
                              'butUp'
               <Button-1> : Tk::Callback=SCALAR(0x8180204)
                              'butDown'
                  <Leave> : Tk::Callback=SCALAR(0x81801d4)
                              'Leave'
                  <Enter> : Tk::Callback=SCALAR(0x81801e0)
                              'Enter'

2. Binding tag '.button' has these bindings:
         <ButtonRelease-2> : Tk::Callback=ARRAY(0x81808d0)
                              'main::twice'

3. Binding tag '.' has no bindings.

4. Binding tag 'all' has these bindings:
                <Key-F10> : Tk::Callback=SCALAR(0x82910a8)
                              'FirstMenu'
                <Alt-Key> : Tk::Callback=ARRAY(0x829103c)
                              'TraverseToMenu'
                    Tk::Ev=SCALAR(0x8164f3c)        : 'K'
```

```
        <<LeftTab>> : Tk::Callback=SCALAR(0x829100c)
                        'focusPrev'
         <Key-Tab> : Tk::Callback=SCALAR(0x8290f10)
                        'focusNext'
```

You should try `bindDump` on a Text widget; there's information there that will be quite surprising.

The actual *bindDump.pm* file isn't particularly pretty, but it illustrates an Exporter module with POD documentation. In any case, with reservations, here it is:

```perl
$Tk::bindDump::VERSION = '1.0';

package Tk::bindDump;

use Exporter;

use base qw/Exporter/;
@EXPORT = qw/bindDump/;
use strict;

sub bindDump {

    # Dump lots of good binding information.  This pretty-print subroutine
    # is, essentially, the following code in disguise:
    #
    # print "Binding information for $w\n";
    # foreach my $tag ($w->bindtags) {
    #     printf "\n Binding tag '$tag' has these bindings:\n";
    #     foreach my $binding ($w->bind($tag)) {
    #         printf "  $binding\n";
    #     }
    # }

    my ($w) = @_;

    my (@bindtags) = $w->bindtags;
    my $digits = length( scalar @bindtags );
    my ($spc1, $spc2) = ($digits + 33, $digits + 35);
    my $format1 = "%${digits}d.";
    my $format2 = ' ' x ($digits + 2);
    my $n = 0;

    print "\n## Binding information for '", $w->PathName, "', $w ##\n";

    foreach my $tag (@bindtags) {
        my (@bindings) = $w->bind($tag);
        $n++;                       # count this bindtag

        if ($#bindings == -1) {
            printf "\n$format1 Binding tag '$tag' has no bindings.\n", $n;
        } else {
            printf "\n$format1 Binding tag '$tag' has these bindings:\n", $n;
```

```perl
            foreach my $binding ( @bindings ) {
                my $callback = $w->bind($tag, $binding);
                printf "$format2%27s : %-40s\n", $binding, $callback;

                if ($callback =~ /SCALAR/) {
                    if (ref $$callback) {
                        printf "%s %s\n", ' ' x $spc1, $$callback;
                    } else {
                        printf "%s '%s'\n", ' ' x $spc1, $$callback;
                    }
                } elsif ($callback =~ /ARRAY/) {
                    if (ref $callback->[0]) {
                        printf "%s %s\n", ' ' x $spc1, $callback->[0], "\n";
                    } else {
                        printf "%s '%s'\n", ' ' x $spc1, $callback->[0], "\n";
                    }
                    foreach my $arg (@$callback[1 .. $#{@$callback}]) {
                        if (ref $arg) {
                            printf "%s %-40s", ' ' x $spc2, $arg;
                        } else {
                            printf "%s '%s'", ' ' x $spc2, $arg;
                        }

                        if (ref $arg eq 'Tk::Ev') {
                            if ($arg =~ /SCALAR/) {
                                print ": '$$arg'";
                            } else {
                                print ": '", join("' '", @$arg), "'";
                            }
                        }

                        print "\n";
                    } # forend callback arguments
                } # ifend callback

            } # forend all bindings for one tag

        } # ifend have bindings

    } # forend all tags
    print "\n";

} # end bindDump

1;
__END__

=head1 NAME

Tk::bindDump - dump detailed binding information for a widget.

=head1 SYNOPSIS
```

```
    use Tk::bindDump;

    $splash->bindDump;

=head1 DESCRIPTION

This subroutine prints a widget's bindtags.  For each binding tag it
prints all the bindings, comprised of the event descriptor and the
callback.  Callback arguments are printed, and Tk::Ev objects are
expanded.

=head1 COPYRIGHT

Copyright (C) 2000 - 2001 Stephen O. Lidie. All rights reserved.

This program is free software; you can redistribute it and/or modify it under
the same terms as Perl itself.
```

Executing Nonblocking System Commands

One of the most common requests seen on the *comp.lang.perl.tk* newsgroup is how
to execute a system command and display its output in a Text widget. The typical
response is some variation of *tktail*, which uses fileevent to signal that output data
is available without blocking the application.

Here's the program:

```
open(H, "tail -f -n 25 $ARGV[0]|") or die "Nope: $!";

my $t = $mw->Text(-width => 80, -height => 25, -wrap => 'none');
$t->pack(-expand => 1);
$mw->fileevent(\*H, 'readable', [\&fill_text_widget, $t]);
MainLoop;

sub fill_text_widget {

    my($widget) = @_;

    $_ = <H>;
    $widget->insert('end', $_);
    $widget->yview('end');

}
```

The standard way to keep Perl/Tk programs from blocking is to use *multiple processes*. Here we use Perl's open function to create a separate process that sends its
output to a pipe. fileevent then defines a callback that gets invoked whenever the
file handle H has data available to read. The callback appends one line to the Text
widget and uses yview to ensure that we always see the end of the file.

There's a problem here. The statement $_ = <H> expects to read an entire line, one that's newline terminated. If only a partial line were available, the read would block, and so would *tktail*. To be rigorous, we should use sysread for our I/O, which handles partial lines:

```perl
sub fill_text_widget {

    my($widget) = @_;

    my($stat, $data);
    $stat = sysread H, $data, 4096;
    die "sysread error:  $!" unless defined $stat;
    $widget->insert('end', $data);
    $widget->yview('end');

}
```

Later we take this simple example and turn it into a first-class mega-widget that's more powerful and flexible.

fileevent Syntax

The syntax for fileevent is as follows:

```perl
$mw->fileevent(handle, operation => callback);
```

handle is a Perl file handle, which may be a reference to a glob (*STDIN), the return value from IO::Handle, etc.

operation may be readable or writable.

callback is a standard callback or the empty string "". The callback is invoked when the file is readable/writable. If *callback* is the empty string, the callback is canceled.

Please refer to Chapter 19 for more information on fileevent.

Tk::ExecuteCommand

Tk::ExecuteCommand runs a command yet still allows Tk events to flow. All command output and errors are displayed in a window. This ExecuteCommand mega-widget is composed of a LabEntry widget for command entry, a "Do It" Button that initiates command execution, and a ROText widget that collects command execution output. While the command is executing, the "Do It" Button changes to a "Cancel" Button that can prematurely kill the executing command.

We start with a typical Frame-based mega-widget prologue, fully detailed in Chapter 14. As with the previous example, it depends on fileevent to keep the application from blocking.

```perl
$Tk::ExecuteCommand::VERSION = '1.1';

package Tk::ExecuteCommand;
```

```
use IO::Handle;
use Proc::Killfam;
use Tk::widgets qw/ROText/;
use base qw/Tk::Frame/;
use strict;

Construct Tk::Widget 'ExecuteCommand';
```

The Populate subroutine in the next example defines the widget pictured in Figure 15-1. Type the command (or commands) to execute in the Entry widget and start it running by clicking the "Do It" Button. Once pressed, "Do It" changes to "Cancel." The subroutine _reset_doit_button ensures that the Button is properly configured to begin command execution. The leading underscore in the method name indicates a *private* method, one that the widget's users should not call. The OnDestroy call ensures that any running command is terminated when the widget goes away.

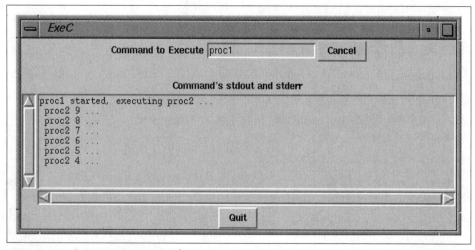

Figure 15-1. Tk::ExecuteCommand in action

The instance variable $self->{-finish} is true when it's time to kill the command. It can be set either by clicking the "Cancel" button or when the fileevent handler has sensed end-of-file. The widget's –command option is stored in another instance variable, $self->{-command}.

```
sub Populate {

    my($self, $args) = @_;

    $self->SUPER::Populate($args);

    my $f1 = $self->Frame->pack;
    $f1->LabEntry(
        -label => 'Command to Execute',
```

```
        -labelPack => [qw/-side left/],
        -textvariable => \$self->{-command},
    )->pack(qw/-side left/);

    my $doit = $f1->Button(-text => 'Do It!')->pack(qw/-side left/);
    $self->Advertise('doit' => $doit);
    $self->_reset_doit_button;

    $self->Frame->pack(qw/pady 10/);
    $self->Label(-text => 'Command\'s stdout and stderr')->pack;

    my $text = $self->Scrolled('ROText', -wrap => 'none');
    $text->pack(qw/-expand 1 -fill both/);
    $self->Advertise('text' => $text);
    $self->OnDestroy([$self => 'kill_command']);

    $self->{-finish} = 0;

    $self->ConfigSpecs(
        -command => [qw/METHOD command Command/, 'sleep 5; pwd'],
    );

} # end Populate

sub command {

    my($self, $command) = @_;
    $self->{-command} = $command;

} # end command
```

When the "Do It" Button is pressed, it begins flashing and continues to do so until the command has completed or is canceled. We use a Tcl/Tk idiom of rescheduling a timer callback that alternates the Button's background color. The first time through, the Button's background color is $val1, but the subsequent after callback reverses the colors so that $interval milliseconds later, the background changes to $val2. When the command finishes, no further timer callbacks are queued, and the flashing ceases.

```
sub _flash_doit {

    # Flash "Do It" by alternating its background color.

    my($self, $option, $val1, $val2, $interval) = @_;

    if ($self->{-finish} == 0) {
            $self->Subwidget('doit')->configure($option => $val1);
            $self->idletasks;
            $self->after($interval, [\&_flash_doit, $self, $option, $val2,
            $val1, $interval]);
    }

} # end _flash_doit
```

Here's a private method that reads command output and inserts it into the Text widget. It calls kill_command to perform cleanup operations when the command completes or the user clicks on the "Cancel" Button.

```
sub _read_stdout {

    # Called when input is available for the output window.  Also checks
    # to see if the user has clicked Cancel.

    my($self) = @_;

    if ($self->{-finish}) {
            $self->kill_command;
    } else {
            my $h = $self->{-handle};
            if ( sysread $h, $_, 4096 ) {
                my $t = $self->Subwidget('text');
                $t->insert('end', $_);
                $t->yview('end');
            } else {
                $self->{-finish} = 1;
            }
    }

} # end _read_stdout
```

The private method _reset_doit_button ensures that the "Do It" button is properly configured to start a new command. Besides setting the Button's text and appearance, it also configures the callback so that, once pressed, the Button is disabled (preventing a possible race condition), and command execution begins.

Notice it's not sufficient to use cget to fetch the background color, because the Button may have been flashing by alternating its background color. The only sure-fire way is to use configure and fetch the original default color from the configuration specifications. All Tk options are described by a five element array containing the option name, resource database name, class name, default value, and current value. The "Do It" Button's specifications might look like this:

```
-background background Background #d9d9d9 cyan

sub _reset_doit_button {

    # Establish normal "Do It" button parameters.

    my($self) = @_;

    my $doit = $self->Subwidget('doit');
    my $doit_bg = ($doit->configure(-background))[3];

    $doit->configure(
        -text       => 'Do It',
        -relief     => 'raised',
        -background => $doit_bg,
        -state      => 'normal',
```

```
    -command    => [sub {
        my($self) = @_;
        $self->{-finish} = 0;
        $self->Subwidget('doit')->configure(
            -text   => 'Working ...',
            -relief => 'sunken',
            -state  => 'disabled'
        );
        $self->execute_command;
    }, $self],
);

} # end _reset_doit_button
```

Here are all the public methods. execute_command creates a new file handle and stores it in an instance variable. Then it uses a pipe-open to execute the command, redirecting STDERR to STDOUT. If the open fails, the error is posted in the Text widget. The file handle is unbuffered, so data can be read as quickly as possible, and the readable fileevent is created. The "Do It" button is reconfigured into the "Cancel" button, and we start it flashing.

```
sub execute_command {

    # Execute the command and capture stdout/stderr.

    my($self) = @_;

    my $h = IO::Handle->new;
    die "IO::Handle->new failed." unless defined $h;
    $self->{-handle} = $h;

    $self->{-pid} = open $h, $self->{-command} . ' 2>&1 |';
    if (not defined $self->{-pid}) {
        $self->Subwidget('text')->insert('end',
            "'" . $self->{-command} . "' : $!\n");
        $self->kill_command;
        return;
    }
    $h->autoflush(1);
    $self->fileevent($h, 'readable' => [\&_read_stdout, $self]);

    my $doit = $self->Subwidget('doit');
    $doit->configure(
        -text    => 'Cancel',
        -relief  => 'raised',
        -state   => 'normal',
        -command => [\&kill_command, $self],
    );

    my $doit_bg = ($doit->configure(-background))[3];
    $self->_flash_doit(-background => $doit_bg, qw/cyan 500/);

} # end execute_command
```

kill_command sets the finish flag so that the flash and fileevent handlers know to quit. It releases resources by clearing the fileevent handler, killing the command and all its children, and closing the file handle. Then it resets "Do It."

The killfam command is an extension to the CPAN module Proc::ProcessTable. It accepts the same arguments as the Perl built-in kill command, but recursively kills subchildren. For the code, as well as the POD for this module, see Appendix C.

```
sub kill_command {

    # A click on the blinking Cancel button resumes normal operations.

    my($self) = @_;

    $self->{-finish} = 1;
    my $h = $self->{-handle};
    return unless defined $h;
    $self->fileevent($h, 'readable' => ''); # clear handler
    killfam 'TERM', $self->{-pid} if defined $self->{-pid};
    close $h;
    $self->_reset_doit_button;

} # end kill_command

1;
```

An MPG Player—tkmpg123

Using fileevent, the mpg123 library, and its Perl interface, Audio::Play::MPG123, we can write a Tk program to play our favorite tunes. Audio::Play::MPG123 sports an object-oriented syntax and methods that load, play, and pause a song.

Besides playing the music, our program needs a user interface. In this case, we've become extremely lazy and taken the skin from Apple's *iTunes* application and used it as a basis for our own. Briefly, we took a screenshot of the original application, shown in Figure 15-2, and placed that over the entire area of a Canvas. Then widgets and images were overlaid at key hot spots, which we bound to actions. For instance, the play and pause buttons are actually tiny images, which are selectively placed over the original play/pause button (see Figure 15-3).

The images, of course, we excised from *iTunes* while it was running.

As for the remainder of the interface, we've essentially ignored it, preferring to concentrate on listening to tunes instead. For instance, instead of an oval display and status window, we use a simple Frame. Instead of a multicolumn play list, we use a Scrolled Listbox. The complete program listing appears in Appendix C.

Figure 15-2. Apple's iTunes Player

Figure 15-3. Play and pause images

We start by creating an Audio::Play::MPG123 instance, $player, and retrieving the
player's input file handle, $phand, which we'll tie to a fileevent handler. The
mpg123 library has its own event loop, and when $phand is readable, we must empty
the mpg123 event queue in order to keep the music playing.

```
$player = Audio::Play::MPG123->new;
$phand = $player->IN;
```

Here we create the Canvas, overlay the *iTunes* skin, and configure the Canvas' width
and height to match the dimensions of the skin. See Chapter 17 for details on
images.

```
$c = $mw->Canvas(
    -width  => 1,
    -height => 1,
    -background => 'dark slate gray',
)->pack;
my $itunes = $c->Photo(-file => 'images/itunes.gif');
$c->createImage(0, 0,
```

```
        -image => $itunes,
        -tag   => 'itunes',
        -anchor => 'nw',
    );
    $c->configure(-width => $itunes->width, -height => $itunes->height);
```

Overlay the play button image on top of the static background button and tag it with
the string 'play-image'. Create a Canvas item button-1 binding that invokes the
pause subroutine. Subroutine pause toggles the player's pause state, as well as the
play/pause image.

```
    $paus = $c->Photo(-file => 'images/paus.gif');
    $play = $c->Photo(-file => 'images/play.gif');

    $c->createImage(80, 40, -image => $play, -tag => 'play-image');
    $c->bind('play-image', '<1>' => \&pause);
```

Every song has optional data associated with it, such as the title, artist, and album.
We can display this data in a simple Label widget, using a timer event to rotate
through the information list and update the Label's -textvariable, $infov.

Similarly, we use another Label to display the song's elapsed and total playing time,
in minutes and seconds.

```
    $infov = '';
    my $info = $f->Label(
        -textvariable => \$infov,
        -font         => $font,
        -background   => $green,
    );
    $info->pack(-side => 'top');

    $timev = 'Elapsed Time: 0:00';
    my $time = $f->Label(
        -textvariable => \$timev,
        -font         => $font,
        -background   => $green,
    );
    $time->pack(-side => 'top');
```

Create the Listbox and populate it with songs from the current directory. The button bindings says call subroutine play with the name of the song under the cursor as
its one argument.

```
    my $mpgs = $f2->Scrolled('Listbox')->pack(-fill => 'y', -expand => 1);
    foreach my $mpg (<*.mpg>, <*.mp3>) {
        $mpgs->insert('end', $mpg);
    }
    $mpgs->bind('<1>' => sub {play $mpgs->get( $mpgs->nearest($Tk::event->y) )});
```

When the play/pause button image is clicked, subroutine pause is called. It first toggles the player's state, pausing it if it was playing or resuming play if it was paused.
Then the play/pause image is updated appropriately.

```
    sub pause {
        $player->pause;
```

```
$c->itemconfigure('play-image',
    -image => ($player->state == 1) ? $paus : $play
);
}
```

We get here after a button click on a song name, where we load the song and start it playing. @info holds the title, artist, and album data (any of which may be undef).

```
sub play {
    my $song = shift;
    if (defined $song) {
        $player->load($song);
        @info = map {$player->$_} qw/title artist album/;
        start_play;
    }
}
```

Subroutine start_play does three things:

- Creates a timer event to display each song's title, artist, and album over and over again
- Creates another timer event that updates the song's elapsed playing time
- Creates a fileevent read handler to empty mpg123's event queue

The code for start_play is:

```
sub start_play {

    my $info_tid = $mw->repeat(5000 => sub {
    $infov = $info[0];
     unshift @info, pop @info;
    });

    my $time_tid = $mw->repeat(1000 => sub {
        my(@toks) = split ' ', $player->stat;
        $timev = sprintf( "Elapsed Time: %s of %s\n",
            &ctm($toks[3]), &ctm($toks[3] + $toks[4]) );
    });
```

At last, the heart of Tkmpg123, a single fileevent call pointing to an anonymous, readable subroutine. The subroutine calls poll in nonblocking mode (with 0 as its argument) to empty the mpg123 event queue, then update to empty Tk's event queue. This sequence repeats until the state method reports zero, meaning the song has ended. The stop method unloads the song, the fileevent is cleared, and the two timers are canceled.

```
    my $in_hand = sub {
    $player->poll(0);
    $mw->update;
    if ($player->state == 0) {
        $player->stop;
        $mw->fileevent(\$phand, 'readable' => '');
        $mw->afterCancel($info_tid);
        $mw->afterCancel($time_tid);
```

```
      }
   };
   $mw->fileevent(\$phand, 'readable' => $in_hand);

}
```

Figure 15-4 shows the *tkmpg123* program in action.

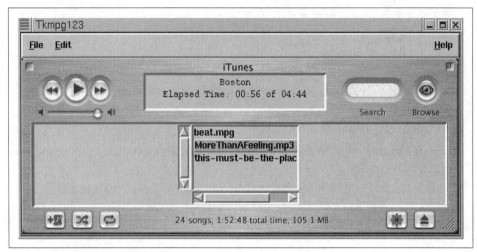

Figure 15-4. tkmpg123 playing a tune

Tracing Perl/Tk Variables

This is something of an oddball topic for this Anatomy lesson, but it introduces background information we'll use later. Plus, it lets us do some neat things.

The Perl way to trace (or set watchpoints upon) a variable is by using the built-in tie function or the CPAN module Tie::Watch. Tcl has three commands associated with variable tracing: trace variable, trace vdelete, and trace vinfo. We'll examine sample code that uses three similar Perl subroutines, then briefly illustrate how our new Trace module is implemented.

First we need to define three new commands, the analogs of the Tcl/Tk Trace commands. They are traceVariable (start tracing a variable), traceVinfo (show trace information), and traceVdelete (stop tracing a variable). Using these commands, we can write a program that animates an analog dial via a Scale widget (see Figure 15-5).

The dial is actually a fat Canvas line item with an arrow on one end. The Scale goes from 0 to 100, with the dial pointing straight up when it reads 50. The Scale's value is updated in the variable $v.

```
my $c = $mw->Canvas(qw/-width 200 -height 110 -bd 2 -relief sunken/)->grid;
$c->createLine(qw/ 100 100 10 100  -tag meter -arrow last -width 5/);
my $s = $mw->Scale(qw/-orient h -from 0 -to 100 -variable/ => \my $v)->grid;
$mw->Label(-text => 'Slide Me for > 5 Seconds')->grid;
```

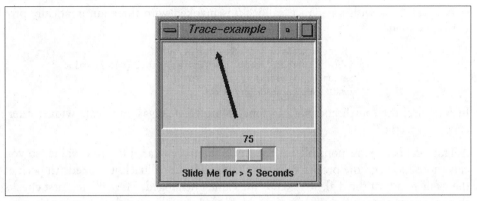

Figure 15-5. Animating a meter

The idea is to define a callback that's invoked whenever the Scale's variable $v changes value. The callback then redraws the dial appropriately. traceVariable expects three arguments: a reference to the traced variable; a letter from the set rwu that selects read, write, or undef (destroy) operations; and a standard Perl/Tk callback.

Here we call update_meter whenever $v is written.

```
$mw->traceVariable(\$v, 'w' => [\&update_meter, $c, $s]);
```

This code demonstrates the other Trace commands. After five seconds, we display trace information, then delete the trace. Once the trace is cleared, the dial stops moving. (This explains why the Scale's value does not correspond to the dial position in Figure 15-5.)

```
$mw->after(5000 => sub {
    print "Untrace time ...\n";
    my %vinfo = $s->traceVinfo(\$v);
    print "Watch info  :\n  ", join("\n  ", @{$vinfo{-legible}}), "\n";
    $c->traceVdelete(\$v);
});

MainLoop;
```

Here's the output from traceVinfo. It shows the variable being traced, two internal flags, the variable's value, and the three callbacks associated with the u (undef), r (read), and w (write) operations. Trace supplies default callbacks for any that we don't provide.

```
Untrace time ...
Watch info  :
  variable  : SCALAR(0x82a5178)
  debug     : '0'
  shadow    : '1'
  value     : '56'
  destroy   : ARRAY(0x82fd14c)
  fetch     : ARRAY(0x82fd224)
  store     : ARRAY(0x82fd110)
```

update_meter, as with any Trace callback, is invoked with three automatically provided arguments:

```
$_[0]        = undef for a scalar, index/key for array/hash
$_[1]        = variable's current (read), new (write), final (undef) value
$_[2]        = operation (r, w, or u)
$_[3 .. $#_] = optional user callback arguments
```

In our case, the fourth and fifth arguments are the Canvas and Scale widget references, respectively.

A Trace callback is responsible for returning the traced variable's new value, so you can choose to keep the proper value or change it. Our callback just needs to peek at the value to adjust the dial, so it keeps the value unchanged. The callback first checks the operation code and returns if the variable is being destroyed. Otherwise, it computes the dial's new position and redraws it.

```
sub update_meter {
    my($index, $value, $op, @args) = @_;
    return if $op eq 'u';
    my($c, $s) = @args[0,1];    # Canvas and Scale widgets
    my($min, $max) = ($s->cget(-from), $s->cget(-to));
    my $pos = $value / abs($max - $min);
    my $x = 100.0 - 90.0 * (cos( $pos * PI ));
    my $y = 100.0 - 90.0 * (sin( $pos * PI ));
    $c->coords(qw/meter 100 100/, $x, $y);
    return $value;
}
```

The Trace module is not a mega-widget. It's a plain old Exporter module, and a tad complicated at that. For the complete listing, see Appendix C. Trace is a wrapper around Tie::Watch, giving us a super-simple interface, at the expense of some loss of functionality. Let's see what Tie::Watch gives us, since we'll be using it in the future.

Tie::Watch

Tie::Watch is an object-oriented interface to Perl's built-in tie function, which lets us define a variable's implementation. The implementation is carried out using subroutines of our own devising that are invoked as the variable is operated upon. For a Perl scalar, there are only three operations: fetch, store, and destroy. Here's how to watch a scalar:

```
$watch = Tie::Watch->new(
    -variable => \$v,
    -fetch    => [\&fetch, 'arg1', 'arg2', ..., 'argn'],
    -store    => \&store,
    -destroy  => sub {print "Final value=$v.\n"},
}
```

The only required argument is -variable. We can provide behavior for any or all of the operations, or none at all. fetch and store callbacks look like this:

```
sub fetch{
    my($self) = @_;
    $self->Fetch;
};

sub store {
    my($self, $new_val) = @_;
    $self->Store($new_val);
};
```

These callbacks return the variable's new value by calling the underlying tie method. If you really want to confuse someone, make the traced variable read-only with this store callback:

```
sub store {
    my($self, $new_val) = @_;
    $self->Store($self->Fetch);
};
```

Tie::Watch can also watch arrays and hashes, but watching scalars is sufficient for our current needs.

Nonblocking Wait Activities

Perl/Tk provides three commands that wait for particular events to occur. Although the wait is nonblocking (Tk events continue to be processed), program flow is logically suspended at the wait point only until the appropriate event occurs. The commands are:

$widget->waitVariable(*varRef*)
> Waits until the variable referenced by *varRef* changes (i.e., it is written or undef).

$widget->waitVisibility
> Waits until $widget's visibility state changes. The most common use for this command is to wait for a window to appear on the display. (Event type = Visibility.)

$widget->waitWindow
> Waits until $widget is destroyed. (Event type = Destroy.)

waitVariable can be employed in a number of ingenious situations. In Chapter 23, we use it as a means of effecting interprocess communications. But perhaps the most common is waiting for a user response to, say, a Dialog widget. A Dialog posts a message and one or more Buttons, then waits for the user to make a selection by clicking a Button. The specified Button label text is then stored in the variable that waitVariable is watching, and logical program flow continues.

Tk::waitVariableX

Although waitVariable is nonblocking in the sense that Tk events continue to be processed, the program flow at the wait point is blocked until the variable changes. If the variable never changes, then that thread of execution can never continue. So, we can imagine a waitVariable with a timeout such that, after a certain amount of time, program flow resumes even if the variable never changes. We can go a step further and wait for a list of variables with a timeout. It's actually very easy to implement these features, using the existing waitVariable command and Tie::Watch.

We'll call this new command waitVariableX. The scheme is sublimely simple and clever. Our new command employs waitVariable to wait for a single scalar to change value. That scalar is set either by a timer callback or a Store callback invoked by watchpoints placed on the list of variables. Furthermore, waitVariableX tells us why it completed, by returning zero if the timer expired or a reference to the variable that changed.

Here is a typical calling sequence, where we wait for $splash_var to change value, or 3000 milliseconds, whichever occurs first. If the timeout is zero, no timer callback is queued.

```
$mw->waitVariableX(3 * 1000, \$splash_var);
```

In typical Perl/Tk style, we've decided that the first argument passed to waitVariableX can also be an array reference. In this case, the first element is the millisecond timeout value (or zero) and the second, a standard Perl/Tk callback that is invoked just before waitVariableX returns:

```
$self->waitVariableX( [$millis, $destroy_splashscreen] );
```

Here's the code for waitVariableX:

```
$Tk::waitVariableX::VERSION = '1.0';

package Tk::waitVariableX;

use Carp;
use Exporter;

use base qw/Exporter/;
@EXPORT = qw/waitVariableX/;
use strict;

sub waitVariableX {

    use Tie::Watch;

    my ($parent, $millis) = (shift, shift); # @_ has list of var refs

    croak "waitVariableX:  no milliseconds." unless defined $millis;
    my ($callback, $st, $tid, @watch, $why);
```

```perl
    if (ref $millis eq 'ARRAY') {
        $callback = Tk::Callback->new($millis->[1]);
        $millis = $millis->[0];
    }

    $st = sub {my $argv = $_[0]->Args('-store'); $why = $argv->[0]};
    foreach my $vref (@_) {
        push @watch,
            Tie::Watch->new(-variable => $vref, -store => [$st, $vref]);
    }
    $tid = $parent->after($millis => sub {$why = 0}) unless $millis == 0;

    $parent->waitVariable(\$why); # wait for timer or watchpoint(s)

    $_->Unwatch foreach @watch;
    $parent->afterCancel($tid);
    $callback->Call($why) if defined $callback;

    return $why;             # why we stopped waiting: 0 or $vref

} # end waitVariableX

1;
```

Once again, we have an Exporter module, not a mega-widget class module. We first save the parent widget reference and the milliseconds arguments, leaving the list of variables in @_. If the milliseconds argument is really an array reference, we create a Tk::Callback object and reset $millis.

Now we create the Store callback used by the list of variable watchpoints. If and when invoked, the callback calls the Tie::Watch method Args to fetch a reference to the list of Store arguments we supply to the Tie::Watch constructor, new. The first argument in the argument vector $argv is a reference to the watched variable, which is then stored in the lexical $why.

The foreach loop creates the actual watchpoint objects, using our callbacks $st and $vref, which, because we have a closure, uniquely point to each watched variable in turn. If and when the $st callback is invoked, it uses Args to fetch the closed $vref. Each variable's Store callback then stores $vref in the same lexical variable, $why.

If a millisecond timeout was specified, we use after to queue a timer event that sets $why to zero, assuming the timer ever expires. This is the same lexical variable set by the Store callbacks.

Finally, with everything in place, we wait for $why to change. When it does, we destroy all the watchpoint objects, cancel any outstanding timer event, execute the optional completion callback (passing it $why for completeness), and return $why; why waitVariableX is returned.

Note that:

- The list of variables is optional. If omitted and milliseconds is greater than 0, the command behaves much like `after`.

- If a variable list is specified but the millisecond timer is zero, the command behaves much like `waitVariable`.

- If the variable list is omitted and the millisecond timer is zero, the command waits forever. Hmm, perhaps we should disallow this possibility!

Splash Screens

Splash screens are those windows that pop up for the amusement of the user while a long-loading program gets underway. Some folks display their splash screens during program initialization sequentially, so that if a splash screen stays on the display for three seconds, the program takes three seconds longer to load. We, however, prefer that our splash screens run in parallel with program initialization. One approach might be:

1. Create a Toplevel splash screen.
2. Queue a timer event to set a variable after X seconds.
3. Initialize program.
4. Wait for splash timer to expire with `waitVariable`.
5. Destroy splash screen and enter `MainLoop`.

There's a problem with this scheme: if initialization takes too long and the splash timer expires, the `waitVariable` will hang. This can also happen if the splash delay is set too small. We *could* use `waitVariableX` with a timeout, resulting in code that might look like this:

```
my $mw = MainWindow->new;
$mw->withdraw;

my ($splash_scr, $splash_tid, $splash_var) = splash 3000;

# - program initialization.

my $why = $mw->&waitVariableX(3000, $splash_var);
$splash_scr->afterCancel($splash_tid);
$splash_scr->destroy;

$mw->deiconify;
```

But this just doesn't feel right. First, having the splash screen remain on the screen for X seconds one time, and X+3 seconds at others, is an unsatisfactory hack. Second, too much of the work is left to the application. We need to encapsulate things in a mega-widget. Besides, there are some subtle details, as we are about to see.

Tk::Splashscreen

We've just written *tkhp16c*, our version of the venerable RPN programming calculator, shown in Figure 15-6. As Tk programs go, this application loads slowly, because it's composed of so many widgets. So we'll incorporate a splash screen.

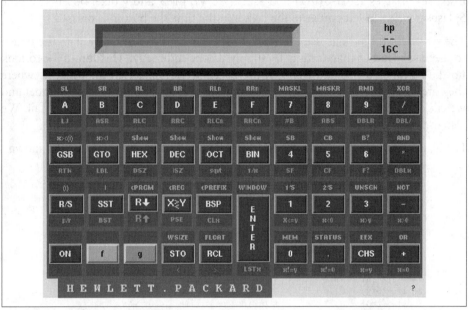

Figure 15-6. An HP-16C RPN calculator

Tk::Splashscreen is a Toplevel mega-widget providing all the display, destroy, and timing events. All we do is create the Splashscreen widget, populate it, then invoke Splash to display it and Destroy to tear it down. The plan for our splash screen is that it contain a progress bar; we'll be sure to sprinkle update calls throughout our initialization code so that any Splashscreen events are handled.

Here's the mega-widget preamble. If it's unfamiliar, please read Chapter 14 for complete details. Note that for this mega-widget, we import the DoOneEvent bit patterns.

```
$Tk::Splashscreen::VERSION = '1.0';

package Tk::Splashscreen;

use Tk qw/Ev/;
use Tk qw/:eventtypes/;
use Tk::waitVariableX;
use Tk::widgets qw/Toplevel/;
use base qw/Tk::Toplevel/;

Construct Tk::Widget 'Splashscreen';
```

Subroutine `Populate` immediately removes the empty Toplevel from the display so *tkhp16c* can fill it at its leisure. Then `overrideredirect` removes the window manager decorations. Of course, with the decorations gone, the Toplevel can't be moved around by normal means, so we'll have to create our own movement bindings. The widget uses mouse button 3 for this purpose and keeps state information in the instance variables `$self->{ofx}` and `$self->{ofy}`, the x and y pixel offsets from the Splashscreen's top-left corner to the cursor at the time the button is pressed.

The two button bindings use the special format where we explicitly state the object to use, `$self` rather than letting Tk supply us one indirectly. This forces Tk to look up the methods `b3prs` and `b3rls` in the package Tk::Splashscreen, which is where they are located. Otherwise, if for instance the Splashscreen contained a Label and we clicked on it, Tk would try to invoke `Tk::Label::b3prs`, and that would fail. We also use the `Ev` subroutine to pass event data to the callback.

Lastly, instance variable `$self->{tm0}` stores the time the Splashscreen is first shown.

```
sub Populate {
    my ($self, $args) = @_;

    $self->withdraw;
    $self->overrideredirect(1);

    $self->SUPER::Populate($args);

    $self->{ofx} = 0;          # X offset from top-left corner to cursor
    $self->{ofy} = 0;          # Y offset from top-left corner to cursor
    $self->{tm0} = 0;          # microseconds time widget was Shown

    $self->ConfigSpecs(
        -milliseconds => [qw/PASSIVE milliseconds Milliseconds 0/],
    );

    $self->bind('<ButtonPress-3>'   => [$self => 'b3prs', Ev('x'), Ev('y')]);
    $self->bind('<ButtonRelease-3>' => [$self => 'b3rls', Ev('X'), Ev('Y')]);

} # end Populate
```

At this point, we have an empty Splashscreen widget. Before we show it, let's put something inside. We'll keep it simple, with a MacProgressBar and a picture of an actual HP-16C calculator, as shown in Figure 15-7.

A MacProgressBar widget has a 3D look, exactly like the classic Macintosh progress bar. We won't examine the code here, but it's listed in Appendix C. It's a versatile widget. Here's a pseudo-volume meter:

```
$pb = $mw->MacProgressBar(-width => 150, -bg => 'cyan')->pack;

while (1) {
    my $w = rand(100);
    $pb->set($w);
```

```
    $mw->update;
    $mw->after(250);
}
```

Figure 15-7. tkhp16c initialization is 90% complete

Anyway, we keep the MacProgressBar widget reference in the global variable $MAC_PB, so we can access it throughout the various initialization subroutines. For our Splash-screen, we've use the -milliseconds option to specify that the Splashscreen remain posted for a minimum of three seconds.

```
$splash = $mw->Splashscreen(-milliseconds => 3000);
$splash->Label(-text => 'Building your HP 16C ...', -bg => $BLUE)->
    pack(qw/-fill both -expand 1/);
$MAC_PB = $splash->MacProgressBar(-width => 300);
$MAC_PB->pack(qw/-fill both -expand 1/);
$splash->Label(-image => $mw->Photo(-file => 'hp16c-splash.gif'))->pack;
```

Here's how we use the Splashscreen. First, withdraw the MainWindow and show the Splashscreen. Now perform program initialization. Note how we use the set method to update the MacProgressBar to 100% before destroying the Splashscreen. With the Splashscreen gone, redisplay the MainWindow containing the completed calculator.

```
my $mw = MainWindow->new;
$mw->withdraw;
$splash->Splash;           # show Splashscreen

build_help_window;
build_calculator;

$MAC_PB->set($MAC_PB_P = 100);
$splash->Destroy;          # tear down Splashscreen

$mw->deiconify;            # show calculator
```

The Splash method serves to record the second of the epoch that the Splashscreen is first displayed. This datum is used to ensure that the Splashscreen remains visible for the specified minimum amount of time. Then Splash maps the widget in the center of the screen.

```
sub Splash {
```

```
    my ($self, $millis) = @_;

    $millis = $self->cget(-milliseconds) unless defined $millis;
    $self->{tm0} = Tk::timeofday;
    $self->configure(-milliseconds => $millis);
    $self->Popup;

} # end_splash
```

Destroy's first duty is to ensure that the Splashcreen remains visible for its allotted minimum time. It does this with a simple computation, which, if positive, gives the time to delay. If the result is negative, we set it to zero so there is no wait.

We then create a generic completion callback that does one final update call (to ensure all pending events are completed) and destroys the Splashscreen.

Now, if the program initialization has taken longer than the minimum Splashscreen time, we call the completion callback and return. Otherwise, we process all timer events, wait the requisite amount of time, and destroy the Splashscreen.

```
sub Destroy {

    my ($self, $millis) = @_;

    $millis = $self->cget(-milliseconds) unless defined $millis;
    my $t = Tk::timeofday;
    $millis = $millis - ( ($t - $self->{tm0}) * 1000 );
    $millis = 0 if $millis < 0;

    my $destroy_splashscreen = sub {
            $self->update;
            $self->after(100);# ensure 100% of PB seen
            $self->destroy;
    };

    do { &$destroy_splashscreen; return } if $millis == 0;

    while ( $self->DoOneEvent (DONT_WAIT | TIMER_EVENTS)) {}

    $self->waitVariableX( [$millis, $destroy_splashscreen] );

} # end Destroy
```

These are the private methods responsible for moving a Splashscreen widget. On a button press, we record the cursor's x and y coordinates relative to the Splashscreen's top-left corner. When the button is released, we compute new x and y coordinates relative to the display's top-left corner and use geometry to move the Toplevel.

```
sub b3prs {
    my ($self, $x, $y) = @_;
    $self->{ofx} = $x;
    $self->{ofy} = $y;
} # end b3prs
```

```
sub b3rls {
    my($self, $X, $Y) = @_;
    $X -= $self->{ofx};
    $Y -= $self->{ofy};
    $self->geometry("+${X}+${Y}");
} # end b3rls
```

To complete our discussion on Tk::Splashscreen, here is a bindDump output:

```
## Binding information for '.splashscreen', Tk::Splashscreen=HASH(0x83a6874) ##

1. Binding tag 'Tk::Splashscreen' has no bindings.

2. Binding tag '.splashscreen' has these bindings:
            <ButtonRelease-3> : Tk::Callback=ARRAY(0x83aaaf8)
                                Tk::Splashscreen=HASH(0x83a6874)
                                'b3rls'
                                Tk::Ev=SCALAR(0x83aab1c)                    : 'X'
                                Tk::Ev=SCALAR(0x83aab58)                    : 'Y'
                   <Button-3> : Tk::Callback=ARRAY(0x83aaae0)
                                Tk::Splashscreen=HASH(0x83a6874)
                                'b3prs'
                                Tk::Ev=SCALAR(0x839a348)                    : 'x'
                                Tk::Ev=SCALAR(0x83aab04)                    : 'y'

3. Binding tag 'all' has these bindings:
                    <Key-F10> : Tk::Callback=SCALAR(0x839a3fc)
                                'FirstMenu'
                    <Alt-Key> : Tk::Callback=ARRAY(0x839a390)
                                'TraverseToMenu'
                                Tk::Ev=SCALAR(0x816e198)                    : 'K'
                <<LeftTab>> : Tk::Callback=SCALAR(0x839a360)
                                'focusPrev'
                    <Key-Tab> : Tk::Callback=SCALAR(0x839a264)
                                'focusNext'
```

Synthesizing Virtual Events

Tk supports a generic event command to define, generate, query, and delete virtual events. These are events that we make (or are made on our behalf) above and beyond those in Tk. We've mentioned the eventGenerate method previously, which generates events just as if they'd come from the window system. Using eventGenerate, we can simulate a person typing characters and clicking buttons, as well as invoking other real and virtual events.

The following code "types" the characters "Hello Perl/Tk" in the Entry widget $e. It's important to note that the Entry widget must have the keyboard focus, otherwise the data falls into the bit bucket. The update command is also important, as it ensures that all events have been processed. $evar is the Entry's -textvariable and, if all goes well, it will contain the "typed" characters.

```
my %keysyms = (' ' => 'space', '/' => 'slash');
my $evar;
```

```
my $e = $mw->Entry(-textvariable => \$evar)->pack;

$b = $mw->Button(
    -text    => 'Show $evar',
    -command => sub {print "$evar\n"},
)->pack;

$e->focus;
$mw->update; # prevents lost characters
```

Figure 15-8 shows the outcome.

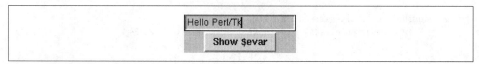

Figure 15-8. Data synthesized by eventGenerate

Here's the input loop. Most of the characters in the string "Hello Perl/Tk" are their own keysyms, but for those that aren't, we provide a mapping through the hash %keysysms.

```
foreach (split '', 'Hello Perl/Tk') {
    $_ = $keysyms{$_} if exists $keysyms{$_};
    $e->eventGenerate('<KeyPress>', -keysym => $_);
    $mw->idletasks;
    $mw->after(200);
}
```

After a short delay, we enter the Button's space, press it, and release it. The release event invokes the Button's callback, which prints "Hello Perl/Tk".

```
$mw->after(1000);

$b->eventGenerate('<Enter>');
$b->eventGenerate('<ButtonPress-1>');
$b->eventGenerate('<ButtonRelease-1>');
```

We create a virtual event using eventAdd. Once a virtual event is defined, we must create an actual binding to trigger the event. The following code creates the virtual event <<Gromit>>. Notice that virtual event names are surrounded by double angle brackets to distinguish them from real event names.

The <<Gromit>> virtual event is bound to the real event, <KeyPress>. Once defined, we bind <<Gromit>> to the subroutine look_for_gromit, which simply searches for the string "Gromit" (in this case, from an Entry widget).

We call bindDump and eventInfo to display interesting binding and event information.

```
my $e = $mw->Entry->pack;
$e->focus;
$e->eventAdd('<<Gromit>>' => '<KeyPress>');
$e->bind('<<Gromit>>' => \&look_for_gromit);
```

```
    &bindDump($e);
    print $e->eventInfo, "\n";

    sub look_for_gromit {
        my $text = $_[0]->get;
        print "Found Gromit in '$text'\n" if $text =~ /Gromit/i;
    }
```

Figure 15-9 shows the Entry and what we typed in it.

123gROMit

Figure 15-9. Searching for Gromit

As soon as we type the t and ! characters, look_for_gromit prints this:

```
Found Gromit in '123gROMit'
Found Gromit in '123gROMit!'
```

This is an excerpt from the bindDump output, showing the Entry widget's instance bindings.

```
2. Binding tag '.entry' has these bindings:
                <<Gromit>> : Tk::Callback=ARRAY(0x82d5160)
                             CODE(0x8270928)
```

The eventInfo method can return the event descriptor(s) associated with a virtual event. If no virtual event is specified, it returns a list of all virtual events.

```
<<LeftTab>><<Copy>><<Gromit>><<Undo>><<Cut>><<Redo>><<Paste>>
```

There's also an eventDelete method to remove an event descriptor from a virtual event or delete a virtual event entirely.

Coexisting with Other GUI Main Loops

It's perfectly possible to have more than one GUI main loop running concurrently. It's a simple matter of cooperation and balance. By balance, we mean how the events are portioned out. It's very easy for one main loop to "take control" and "starve" the other loop of processing time. In this section, we'll demonstrate how to use both OpenGL and Tk widgets in the same application. We've found that, generally, to keep Tk events flowing, it's sufficient to call update once in a while. If update starves OpenGL, we fall back to DoOneEvent.

DoOneEvent allows us to fine tune a Tk event loop by processing only selected events, which we specify by bit pattern. We can inclusively OR the following symbols together and define the desired bit pattern: WINDOW_EVENTS, FILE_EVENTS, TIMER_EVENTS, and IDLE_EVENTS. To specify all possible events, use ALL_EVENTS, and to make the DoOneEvent call nonblocking, add DONT_WAIT.

When passed ALL_EVENTS, DoOneEvent processes events as they arise and puts the application to sleep when no further events are outstanding. DoOneEvent first looks for a window or I/O event and, if found, calls the handler and returns. If there is no window or I/O event, it looks for a single timer event, invokes the callback, and returns. If no window, I/O, or timer event is ready, all pending idle callbacks are executed, if any. In all cases, DoOneEvent returns 1.

When passed DONT_WAIT, DoOneEvent works as described, except that, if there are no events to process, it returns immediately with a value of 0, indicating it didn't find any work to do.

It's actually rather difficult to find a use for DoOneEvent. One example is the bouncing ball widget demonstration, although it might have been better written using timer callbacks. But it *is* simulating a simulation, and simulations typically want to run as fast as possible, so we can't fault the implementation.

Even games don't usually require DoOneEvent. Here are two scenarios in which you might use it. Example one probably never reaches the MainLoop statement. It runs as fast as possible, consuming all available CPU time, and depends on update to process events.

```
&run;
MainLoop;

sub run {
    while (1) {
        &dogame;
        $mw->update;
    }
}
```

Example two establishes a repeating timer event, then enters MainLoop to process events. The game progresses at a more or less stately speed, with an update occurring every 50 milliseconds. Unlike example one, this example does not consume all available CPU time.

```
$mw->repeat(50 => \&run);
MainLoop;

sub run {
    &dogame;
    $mw->update;
}
```

Embedding OpenGL in a Perl/Tk Window

Before we delve into the difficult stuff, here's a really simple static OpenGL program that draws into a Tk window. OpenGL's glpOpenWindow command lets us specify a parent window. This example stuffs the OpenGL window in a Tk Toplevel widget. We use waitVisibility to ensure that the Toplevel is mapped, so it has a valid window identifier.

```
use OpenGL;
```

```
$mw = MainWindow->new;
$mw->Button(-text => 'OpenGL Demo', -command => \&opengl)->pack;
$mw->Button(-text => 'Quit', -command => \&exit)->pack;

sub opengl {
    $top = $mw->Toplevel(qw/-width 500 -height 500 -background pink/);
    $top->title('OpenGL Demo');
    $top->waitVisibility;
    glpOpenWindow(parent=> hex($top->id), width => 450, height => 450);
    glClearColor(0, 0, 1, 1);
    glClear(GL_COLOR_BUFFER_BIT);
    glOrtho(-1, 1, -1, 1, -1, 1);
    glColor3f(0, 1, 0);
    glBegin(GL_POLYGON);

    $pi  =  3.141592654;
    $d2r = $pi / 180.0;
    $nvert = 8;
    $dangle = 360 / $nvert;
    for ($angle = 0; $angle <= 359; $angle += $dangle) {
        $x = cos($angle * $d2r);
        $y = sin($angle * $d2r);
        glVertex2f($x, $y);
    }
    glEnd;
    glFlush;
}
```

The results are shown in Figure 15-10.

Flying the Enterprise

OpenGL is the de facto 3D graphics package, created by SGI. Ports and look-alikes are widely available. For Linux, install the MESA graphics library and install the Perl interface from CPAN. Bundled with the Perl interface is an OpenGL program that flies the Starship Enterprise in a 3D world.

As with the previous example, we've embedded the flying simulation in a Tk Toplevel widget. Then we enter the OpenGL main loop, which processes all Tk events followed by all OpenGL events.

```
use Tk qw/:eventtypes/;

$mw = MainWindow->new;
$b = $mw->Button(-text => 'Quit', -command => \&exit);
$b->pack;
$mw->waitVisibility;

$gl = $mw->Toplevel(-width => 400, -height => 400);
$gl->waitVisibility;
&gl_init( hex($gl->id) );

while( 1 ){ # gl_MainLoop
```

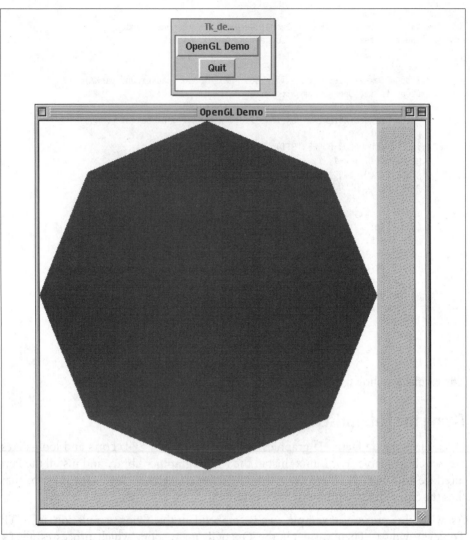

Figure 15-10. Embedding OpenGL in a Tk window

```
# ...

while (my $stat = $mw->DoOneEvent( DONT_WAIT | ALL_EVENTS )){}

while($p=XPending) {
        @e=&glpXNextEvent;
        &$s(@e) if($s=$cb{$e[0]});
}

# ...

} # end gl_mainLoop
```

Figure 15-11 shows the results.

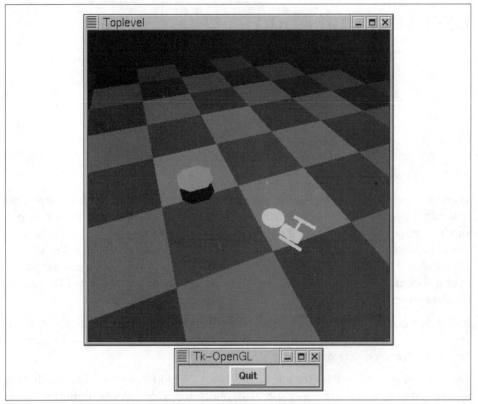

Figure 15-11. Perl/Tk and OpenGL main loops can coexist

The DoOneEvent statement was an experiment in which we tried various event masks, in an attempt to determine the optimal combination. You see what we arrived at, which, interestingly, is exactly equivalent to:

```
$mw->update;
```

CHAPTER 16

User Customization

When writing Perl/Tk applications, we can change the look of the application dramatically by using different options when creating widgets. We can give our users a similar type of control using the *resource database* or *command-line options*. The user has the ability to change the appearance of almost anything, from the width of widget edges and the fonts used to display text to the cursor shown as the mouse passes over a widget. A change can be global to every application that honors the option database or so specific that it changes a single option of a single widget.

In the first part of this chapter, we'll cover the ways users can change these visual aspects from the command line. Later in the chapter, we'll give you more ideas on how to utilize a resource database.

The term resource database originated in the X Window System. Essentially, the resource database provides user-specified values for widget configuration options. When creating a new widget, Tk queries the resource database for all options that the programmer did not explicitly specify on the widget creation command. If an option/value pair (sometimes called a *resource*) isn't found in the resource database, Tk uses the option's default value provided by the widget's class.

Actually, a resource is a bit more complicated. Although the resource identifies a single option/value pair, it may apply to more than a single widget. Using class names and the wildcard character (*), it's possible to pattern match multiple widgets. Each of those widgets subsequently has that particular option configured.

So, an option database resource is really a pattern/value pair. Resources have this general syntax:

```
pattern : value
```

where *pattern* identifies an option for one or more widgets and *value* is the value to assign to all matches. The colon acts as a separator (with or without whitespace). We'll see what all this means later.

Tk doesn't use the classical Unix resource database, but its own implementation, called the *option database*. Except for minor details, using the option database is identical to the resource database; thus, we'll use the two terms interchangeably.

Perl/Tk handles the option database slightly differently than Tcl/Tk. Prior to Main-Window creation, Perl/Tk calls the special command-line processing subroutine Tk::CmdLine::SetArguments. This subroutine extracts standard X11 options such as -background and adds them to the option database. Options that Tk::CmdLine::SetArguments doesn't recognize are left in @ARGV for the application to handle. We'll learn more about the Tk::CmdLine subroutines later.

When determining the value to assign to an option, Perl/Tk uses this order of precedence:

- If the programmer specified an option on a widget creation command, that value is used. It cannot be overridden by the option database.

- For an unspecified option, the option database is consulted. If a resource entry matches, the option database value is used for the widget option. As mentioned previously, this value may have come from the command line.

- Otherwise, Perl/Tk uses the default value supplied by the widget's class.

- All other command-line options remain in @ARGV.

Using the Command Line

You need to leave a way open for customization in your application. Mainly, this means you can take the easy way out and not hardcode many option values. If you hardcode too many configuration options, users cannot easily tailor your application using one of the methods listed in this chapter. For example, if you want to allow your users to change the font of all the widgets in the application, don't use the -font option when creating or configuring your widgets. If you want to do something such as change the size of a font, get the current font and then change the size.*

Often the easiest thing for a user to do is specify a command-line option when running the application. The options can be changed quickly and allow users to have immediate and direct control over their applications.

There are several command-line options that customize the way your application looks. When you run your application, the command line looks something like this:†

```
# On MS Windows systems:
> perl myScript.pl [ options... ]
```

---

* Sometimes your code might depend on the size of the font used (see NavListbox in Chapter 14). Rather than limiting your users or having your window look wrong, just determine the current font and calculate from there.

† In real life, MS Windows users might double-click on the *.pl* file or use a shortcut, but let's assume for now that you're typing this at a DOS prompt.

```
# On Unix systems:
% myScript [ options... ]
```

The supported options are standard X options that any user familiar with X Windows will recognize. None of these options are required, but they might be the simplest ways to do what you want (for example, changing the background color of everything in the application). When specifying a command-line list of options and values, do not use a comma separator. If any of the options have bad values, you'll get an immediate error, and the application won't run.

Customizing using only command-line options won't necessarily produce the most elegant-looking applications, but for something simple, such as changing colors or fonts, it's the quickest way to go. Also, remember that an option can't be changed by the user if you have set it inside the application. Table 16-1 lists the options that Tk::CmdLine::SetArguments recognizes.

Table 16-1. Command-line options recognized by Tk::CmdLine::SetArguments

Option	Description
-background, -foreground	Colors of nontext and text
-class	Class used for option DB lookups
-display, -screen	Display to use
-font	Default font of all text
-iconic, -geometry	Minimizes (or iconifies) size and position
-motif	Emulates look of Motif window manager
-name	Application name used for option DB lookups
-synchronous	Turn X buffering on or off
-title	Window title shown in decorative border
-xrm	Used to specify any other options

Colors, Fonts, and Titles

Changing all colors in an application is simplified by using the -background and -foreground command-line options. Each takes a color argument; it is wise to use contrasting colors since whatever you use for -foreground will be the text color.

Here's an example that changes your application to white on black:

```
% myScript.pl -foreground white -background black
```

If you are fond of a particular color for the text, use just the -foreground option:

```
% myScript.pl -foreground purple
```

To change the font of all widgets in the application, use the -font command-line option:

```
% myScript.pl -font "Arial 14"
```

For more information on fonts, take a look at Chapter 3.

Normally the title of a running Perl/Tk application is either its filename (excluding any extension), the value associated with the -title option when creating/configuring the MainWindow, or the title established with the title method. If the title isn't explicitly set, a user can use the -title command-line option:

```
% myScript.pl -title "This is my app!"
```

Initial MainWindow Placement

When you run a Perl/Tk application, the MainWindow immediately appears on the screen. If you would rather the window manager not display the MainWindow, specify the -iconic option on the command line:

```
% myScript.pl -iconic
```

In Windows, you'll see an entry on the Taskbar. For a Unix system, the icon is placed however your window manager normally does these things (perhaps in an icon bay, as an icon on the desktop, or not shown at all). This is a great way to start an application that has a lot of tasks to do (similar to a batch job), but you still want to be able to see the output in a nice format later. The program can even be written to deiconify itself if something urgent happens while it's running.

With the -geometry option, you can change the initial size and/or position of your application. To change the size of the MainWindow, use the -geometry option:

```
% myScript.pl -geometry "100x300"
```

The complete syntax for -geometry is:

```
widthxheight{+-}xoffset{+-}yoffset
```

where *width* and *height* are the window's x and y dimensions. If an offset value is positive, it is measured from the top or left edge of the display, and if negative, it is measured from the bottom or right edge of the screen. For example, a specification of -0-0 would place an application in the bottom-right corner of the display.

Choosing a Display

On Unix systems, you'll have to specify the full display name (take a look at the DISPLAY environment variable or look on the X manpage under Display Names for a bit more information). See Chapter 20 for complete details on DISPLAY and friends. It's normally set up automatically, although you can change it using the -display or -screen options.

Option Database Lookups

When using the option database, a resource pattern often contains class and application names. You can change these values for your application via the command-line options -class and -name. Using these options makes sense if you want to run the application several times simultaneously and easily distinguish between the different applications at a glance. You can make the one that points to a development server all blue and the production one red or green.

Further, you can pre-populate the option database by using the -xrm option with a value. The value is a standard *pattern:value* string. You can specify multiple -xrm pattern/value pairs as well, making this a very powerful command-line option. This option is particularly useful for adding options that do not have command-line equivalents.

```
% perl myScript.pl -xrm '*font: Arial 14' -xrm '*foreground: blue' -xrm '*pi: 3.14'
```

Synchronizing Window Messages

Normally your Perl/Tk application runs asynchronously, which means X messages are buffered. To turn off this buffering, use the -synchronous option. This is mainly a debugging technique, but we Perl/Tk programmers should never have to resort to it.

Using the Option Database

The option database is populated by several mechanisms. We already know Tk::CmdLine::SetArguments sets standard X11 options prior to MainWindow creation. Unix users should be familiar with the *.Xdefaults* file, a simple text file that can contain resource entries and is one of the files Tk::CmdLine::SetArguments reads during MainWindow initialization. Perl/Tk programs can load resources from other files as well by calling Tk::CmdLine::LoadResources or optionReadfile. Or, Tk::CmdLine::SetResources and optionAdd can add individual resources to the option database. For the location of other resources files, please read the manpage for Tk::CmdLine.

Here are some sample resource entries:

```
*font                      : 12x24
frog*Foreground            : blue
frog.button1.Background    : orange
frog.b3.foreground         : green
frog*Label*cursor          : gobbler
```

Note that the resource pattern is to the left of the colon, and its value to the right. The pattern can be general (such as the first entry, which changes the default font for every X and Tk application) or specific (such as the fourth entry, which changes only the foreground color of the widget named b3 of the application *frog*).

A resource pattern identifies an option and one or more widgets in the window hierarchy. Tk generates the hierarchy automatically, assigning string pathnames to each widget. In Chapter 13, we learned that Tcl/Tk programmers are required to do this manually. In Perl/Tk, we seldom need to refer to widget pathnames; rather, we use object references. If we need to see a widget's pathname, we use the `PathName` method. Pathnames are composed of words (components) separated by pathname separators (.), analogous to the forward slash in Unix pathnames or the backslash in Win32. For example, the pathname `.frame.text.button` might represent the Button created from these commands:

```
$mw->Frame;
$t = $mw->Text;
$b = $t->Button;
```

A resource pattern is also composed of words separated by . and * characters. These words may be program names, class names, option names, or widget names (a widget's name is the leaf portion of its pathname; if the pathname is `.a.b.c`, the leaf portion is c).

The characters . and * are used to provide tight and loose pattern match bindings. The . is the tight binding operator, separating adjacent pathname components. The * is the loose binding operator, separating any number of pathname components, including none. That's why the `*font` resource changes the font for any X or Tk program.

If you want a resource to apply to a particular program (or instance of a program), prepend the program name as the first component of the pattern. In the previous example, the second through fifth resources apply only to the program "frog". frog is in quotes because there are various ways to name a program frog. First, the program's filename can be *frog* or *frog.ext* (extensions are thrown away). Or, use the `-name` command-line option and name any old program *frog*.

A program's class name is its name with the first character capitalized or the value of the `-class` command-line option. Thus, if you have several frog-related programs, named, say, *tree-frog* and *sand-frog*, they could all be of class Frog and share resource entries, each of whose first component is Frog. Resource entries beginning with Frog are distinct from those beginning with frog.

Let's use the following program as an example. We create the MainWindow and disable its propagate feature, so it doesn't shrink-wrap itself around the widgets inside it. This lets us see its background color. Somewhere early on in this process, Tk::CmdLine::SetArguments is called to initialize the option database with command-line option/values. We print @ARGV so we can see what's left in the array after the call to MainWindow.

The Label's purpose is simply to show us the application's class and name, which affect how option database lookups work.

Now for the three Buttons, each designed for a special purpose. The first has a hardcoded background color, so it should remain yellow no matter what background-related resources are in the option database. The second button has no attributes set, so its background can be set from the option database. Finally, the third button has explicit set its name using the Name option. A widget's name can be changed only during widget creation; the name cannot be reconfigured afterwards. If the Name option is omitted, Tk automatically generates the name.

Lastly, we loop through all the widgets (ignoring Labels) and configure the Button's text to show its full pathname. It's the pathname we're interested in when creating resource entries.

```
my $mw = MainWindow->new;
$mw->packPropagate(0);

print "ARGV=@ARGV.\n";

my $l1 = $mw->Label(-text =>
    "Application class/name is\n'" . $mw->class . '/' . $mw->name . "'");
$l1->pack;
my $b1 = $mw->Button(-background => 'yellow')->pack;
my $b2 = $mw->Button->pack;
my $b3 = $mw->Button('Name' => 'B3')->pack;

foreach ($mw->children) {
    next if ref $_ eq 'Tk::Label';
    $_->configure(-text => "'" . $_->PathName . "'");
}
```

Let's assume the preceding code is saved in a file named *frog*. This means that the program's name is *frog* and its class is Frog.

For our test runs, we'll use the same resource entries that we saw before, which we've stored in our *.Xdefaults* file.

```
*font                     : 12x24
frog*Foreground           : blue
frog.button1.Background   : orange
frog.b3.foreground        : green
frog*Label*cursor         : gobbler
```

This file always resides in our home directory. Tk uses the value of the environment variable $HOME to locate the *.Xdefaults* file. Under Unix, the variable is always defined, but not so for you Win32 users, where the concept of a home directory doesn't exist. Nevertheless, you can define an MS-DOS HOME environment variable pointing to any directory you choose and store your *.Xdefaults* file there. If you want the *.Xdefaults* file on your desktop, use this command:

```
set HOME=c:\windows\desktop
```

Alternatively, you can create a batch (*.bat*) file, which might look like this:

```
set HOME=C:\Program Files\PerlApps
perl "C:\Program Files\PerlApps\fontviewer.pl"
```

This allows you to keep various resource files lying about.

Now run the program with the following command-line arguments and note the output. It shows us that `Tk::CmdLine::SetArguments` has indeed processed the `-geometry` option and left the unknown option in `@ARGV` for us to handle. Figure 16-1 displays the window.

```
[bug@Pandy atk]$ frog -geometry -0-0 -unknown-arg 123
ARGV=-unknown-arg 123.
```

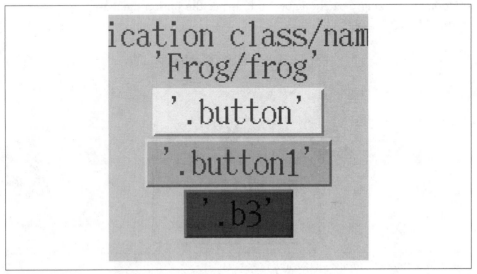

Figure 16-1. frog application with a huge font

It's immediately clear that the font is huge. That's due to a loose binding `*font :` `12x24` resource. This turns out to be a very unpleasant resource, as it trashes nearly every graphical application. Fortunately for us, we can still tell that the program's class and name are `Frog` and `frog`, respectively.

Although you can't tell from the grayscale image, the first Button (`.button`) has a yellow background with blue lettering. Indeed, the loose binding `frog*Foreground : blue` resource ensures that any widget attribute of class `Foreground` is set to blue, unless otherwise overridden.

The second Button (`.button1`) has an orange background and, again, a blue foreground.

The third Button (`.b3`) has the standard gray background with green lettering when inactive. In the figure, the Button is active, thus its background is blue and foreground is black. It's blue because a Button's `-activebackground` option is of class `Foreground`.

Let's remove the loose font resource binding by commenting it out. The option database comment character is the exclamation point.

```
!*font                      : 12x24
frog*Foreground             : blue
frog.button1.Background     : orange
frog.b3.foreground          : green
frog*Label*cursor           : gobbler
```

Figure 16-2 shows the result. First, the font is back to the Tk default. We've also left the pointer hanging over the Label and, as per the option database, the cursor has changed to a gobbler.

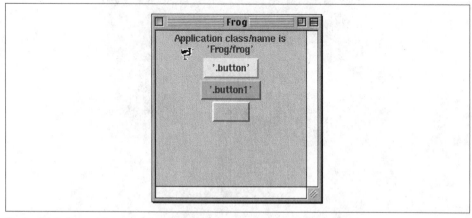

Figure 16-2. frog with normal fonts again

What do we do if we want to change the options on some Buttons but not others? From what we've covered, we know that all Button widgets nominally belong to the class Tk::Button, unless we do something to change it. If we want to group all Buttons with the text Ok on them, we can put them in the 'OkButton' class:

```
$mw->Button(-text => 'Ok', -class => 'OkButton');
```

Even if you create a Button with the text Cancel, as long as the -class option uses OkButton, it belongs to the proper class.

Manipulating Resources with option* Methods

optionClear, optionAdd, optionGet, and optionReadfile are the standard Tk resource handling methods. For complete details, read the Tk::option manpage. Briefly:

$widget->optionClear
    Clears the option database. The next time a resource is added to or removed from the database, *.Xdefaults* is reloaded automatically.

```
$widget->optionAdd(pattern => value ?, priority?)
```
Adds the specified resource to the option database, with a priority of *priority* (0–100). These are the recommended symbolic values:

widgetDefault *(20)*
: Used for default values hardcoded into widgets.

startupFile *(40)*
: Used for options specified in application-specific startup files.

userDefault *(60)*
: Used for options specified in the *.Xdefaults* file.

interactive *(80)*
: Used for options specified interactively after the application starts running. This is the default *priority*.

If an option database lookup results in multiple pattern matches, the one with the highest priority wins. If there are multiple matches at the same priority, the latest resource entered in the option database wins.

```
$widget->optionGet(name, class)
```
Returns a widget's option value given the specified *name* and *class*. *name* might be a configuration option like background, and class might be an application's class name or widget class, such as Tk::Button. This method is for looking up option database values only; it is not an analog of cget. In the context of the program *frog*, these commands both return green:

```
$b3->optionGet('foreground', ' Frog');
$b3->optionGet('foreground', ref $b3);
```

```
$widget->optionReadfile(pathName ?, priority?)
```
Loads the resources from file *pathName* at the given *priority*.

Be aware that Perl/Tk widgets can have hierarchical class names (Tk::A::B), but that the internal Tk class is always the leaf part (B). The internal Tk class is used as the identifier for option database lookups, as the following code demonstrates:

```
package Tk::Foo::Bar;
use base qw/Tk::Label/;
Construct Tk::Widget 'FooBar';

package main;
$mw = MainWindow->new;
$mw->optionAdd("*FooBar.background", "red"); # does not work
$mw->optionAdd("*Bar.foreground", "blue");    # works
$f = $mw->FooBar(-text => "foobar")->pack;
warn $f->Class;
```

Manipulating Resources with Tk::CmdLine Subroutines

In addition to the option* methods, Perl/Tk provides the following subroutines to manage the option database, fully described in the Tk::CmdLine manpage.

Tk::CmdLine::SetArguments([*args*])
> Parses the command-line–formatted option/value pairs in the array args and adds them to the option database. The array @ARGV is used by default. Perl/Tk implicitly calls this subroutine as it creates the first MainWindow.

Tk::CmdLine::cget([*option*])
> Returns the value of an option initialized by Tk::CmdLine::SetArguments. The only valid options are -class, -name, -screen, and -title. You might use this command to determine an application's class, which then might map to a particular resource file to load via Tk::CmdLine::LoadResources. The default option is -class.

Tk::CmdLine::SetResources(*resource* [, *priority*])
> Sets one or more resources. If *resource* is a scalar, it's interpreted as a resource pattern/value string. If *resource* is an array reference, its elements may be pattern/value strings or yet another reference to an array of two elements, the first being the pattern and the second the pattern's value. The *priority* defaults to userDefault.

Tk::CmdLine::LoadResources
> Loads resources from one or more files into the option database. This subroutine accepts four options, though none are required. Typically, you would use -file => pathName and perhaps -priority => priority. The -symbol option specifies the name of an environment variable that contains a colon-separated list of directory and/or file patterns. The -echo option expects a file handle reference (default is *STDOUT). For every resource file loaded, its filename is written to this file handle. Refer to the Tk::CmdLine manpage for details.

## CHAPTER 17

Images and Animations

In its early days, Tk pictures were limited to X11 bitmaps (XBMs), a two-color text-based format that let us enhance Labels and Buttons with simple drawings in place of plain text strings. XBM support still exists, but these days, we think in terms of *images*. Perl/Tk supports numerous image *types*, which may be further classified into distinct image *formats*. An image is an object in its own right, meaning it must be created before it can be used, has methods that manipulate it, and should be destroyed when we are through with it.

This chapter discusses the various image flavors and how we might use them, either as static pictures or dynamic animations.

An Overview of Perl/Tk Image Types

Perl/Tk supports the Bitmap, Pixmap, and Photo image types, illustrated in Figure 17-1.[*]

The Bitmap image type (column one) handles XBM files commonly found on Unix systems. XBM files are usually used for desktop icons and cursor shapes and are actually C language statements that define a two-dimensional array of source bits. In their simplest forms, an "on" source bit displays a foreground color and an "off" source bit displays a background color. There is an optional bitmap array of mask bits. If a mask is specified, pixels where the mask is zero display nothing, producing a transparent effect by allowing the background to show through. If the mask bit is one, the pixel displays the foreground color if the source bit is one and the background color if the source bit is zero.

The Pixmap image type (column two) handles X11 pixmap (XPM) files. XPM files are also text files of C language statements and are suitable for colored icons and cursor shapes. This format uses ASCII characters to define a color lookup table, then

---

[*] There's also a new Tix image type called the Compound type that we'll examine in a later section.

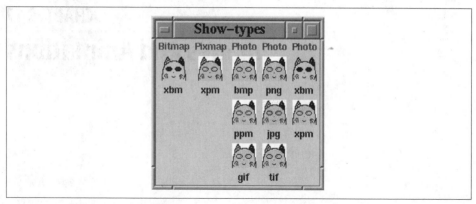

Figure 17-1. The three Perl/Tk image types

encodes the picture as a series of C strings containing characters from the color table. Each string represents a row of the picture and each character of the string a pixel from that row.

The most sophisticated image type, Photo, handles various image formats. The default Perl/Tk Photo formats are shown in Figure 17-1, column three. They include Win32 bitmaps (BMP), Unix portable pixmaps (PPM), and graphic interchange format (GIF) files. Available on CPAN are separately bundled modules (column four) for handling "ping" (PNG), joint photographic experts group (JPEG), and tagged image format (TIFF) files. You can find PNG, JPEG, and TIFF image format modules at *http://www.perl.com/CPAN-local/modules/by-category/08_User_Interfaces/Tk/*.

All these image formats consist of binary data. We'll see the significance of this in the section "The Photo Image Type."

Unlike Bitmap and Pixmap images, Photos have many methods that can manipulate the image, such as reading, writing, and copying ranges of pixels.

Column five shows that the Photo image type can even handle XBM and XPM files, although the Photo versions of these image formats are considerably larger than the native formats. Additionally, Photo supports many options that Bitmap and Pixmap do not, and vice versa, so you really don't want to do this.

Here's the program that generated Figure 17-1. Notice the Photo image formats JPEG, PNG, and TIFF—not part of the Perl/Tk distribution—must be specifically imported. It's easy to forget this, and if you do, Tk won't find the proper image handler and will display "couldn't recognize data in image file."

The foreach statement loops over a list of lists: a list of anonymous arrays, each of which is a list of strings. The first string element is an image type and the remaining elements are the image formats supported by that image type (they're actually common three-letter "file extensions").

All the widgets for each image type are contained in a Frame gridded at row zero of successive columns. Each column is labeled with its image type. The while block creates an image instance for each image format supported by the image type and displays it in a Label widget. Notice that Perl allows us to store the image constructor name in a variable, $image_type. The -file option specifies the name of the image file; in this case, a picture of a neko.*

```
#!/usr/local/bin/perl -w
use Tk;
use Tk::widgets qw/JPEG PNG TIFF/;
use strict;

my $mw = MainWindow->new;
my $column = 0;

foreach (
        [qw/Bitmap xbm/],
        [qw/Pixmap xpm/],
        [qw/Photo  bmp ppm gif/],
        [qw/Photo  png jpg tif/],
        [qw/Photo  xbm xpm/],
        ) {

    my $image_type = shift @$_;
    my $f = $mw->Frame->grid(-row => 0, -column => $column++, -sticky => 'n');
    my $l = $f->Label(-text => $image_type, -foreground => 'blue')->grid;

    while (my $image_format = shift @$_) {
        my $image = $mw->$image_type(-file => "Icon.${image_format}");
        $f->Label(-image => $image)->grid;
        $f->Label(-text  => $image_format)->grid;
    }

} # forend all image types

MainLoop;
```

Methods Common to All Image Types

Images are real objects; we need to create them and, when we're finished, destroy them; otherwise, their resources remain in use for the duration of program execution. For instance, if we create an image and assign it to a Label, then at some later time destroy the Label, like so:

```
my $l = $mw->Label(-image -> $image)
...
$l->destroy;
```

the image remains alive and ready for use again and again, even by multiple widgets simultaneously. If we want the image to go away, we must explicitly delete it:

```
$image->delete;
```

---

* Neko is Japanese for "cat." We'll see the neko throughout this chapter.

This applies to Bitmap, Pixmap, and Photo image types. Here are other methods available for any image type:

$image->cget(-*option*)
> Returns the value of the image option -option

$image->configure(-*option* => *value*)
> Configures the specified option

$image->delete
> Deletes the image

$image->height
> Returns the pixel height of the image

$image->type
> Returns the image type of the image

$image->width
> Returns the pixel width of the image

Bitmap Primitives

Prior to the advent of images, Tk supported simple bitmap operations. All the button-like widgets, plus Canvas, Dialog, and Label, have a -bitmap option whose value is either a string specifying a built-in bitmap name or an XBM filename with a leading @ character. This code displays the built-in bitmaps and an XBM file:

```
my $row = my $col = 0;
foreach my $b (qw/error gray75 gray50 gray25 gray12
        hourglass info questhead question Tk transparent warning/) {
    $mw->Label(-text => $b)->grid(-row => $row, -column => $col);
    $mw->Label(-bitmap => $b)->grid(-row => $row+1, -column => $col++);
    if ($col > 4) {$row +=2; $col = 0}
}

my $c = $mw->Canvas(qw/-width 35 -height 35/);
$c->grid(-row => $row, -column => 3);
$c->createBitmap(20, 20, -bitmap => '@images/Icon.xbm');
```

Figure 17-2 shows the bitmaps.

Bitmaps are also used as application icons and cursors. MainWindows and Toplevels have iconbitmap and iconmask methods that define an application icon:

```
$mw->iconbitmap('@images/Icon.xbm');
```

Tk provides scores of built-in cursors, depicted in Figure 23-2. To build your own cursor, you need an XBM file and a mask file. A cursor specification is a reference to an array of four elements:

```
[qw\@images/mouse.xbm images/mouse.mask blue yellow\]
```

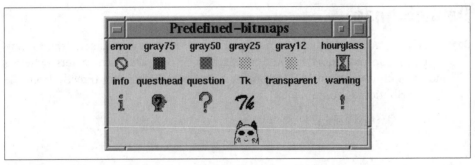

Figure 17-2. Bitmaps are built-in or read from a file

The array elements are the XBM filename, the mask filename, the foreground color, and the background color. The file *mouse.xbm* looks like this:

```
#define cursor_width 17
#define cursor_height 12
#define cursor_x_hot 8
#define cursor_y_hot 1
static char cursor_bits[] = {
    0x20, 0x00, 0x00, 0x90, 0x20, 0x00, 0x40, 0x40, 0x00, 0x0c, 0x40, 0x00,
    0x14, 0x8f, 0x00, 0x94, 0xb0, 0x00, 0x7c, 0x20, 0x01, 0x0c, 0x4c, 0x01,
    0x0a, 0x42, 0x01, 0x42, 0x82, 0x00, 0x3b, 0x87, 0x00, 0xff, 0x7f, 0x00};
```

Notice that a cursor bitmap requires two extra statements, which comprise an x and y "hot spot" that specifies what part of the bitmap is the actual "pointer." Here is the content of file *mouse.mask*, the corresponding mask:

```
#define cursor_mask_width 17
#define cursor_mask_height 12
static char cursor_mask_bits[] = {
    0x20, 0x00, 0x00, 0x90, 0x20, 0x00, 0x40, 0x40, 0x00, 0x0c, 0x40, 0x00,
    0x1c, 0x8f, 0x00, 0x9c, 0xbf, 0x00, 0xfc, 0x3f, 0x01, 0xfc, 0x7f, 0x01,
    0xfe, 0x7f, 0x01, 0xfe, 0xff, 0x00, 0xff, 0xff, 0x00, 0xff, 0x7f, 0x00};
```

Configuring a widget's -cursor option with these bitmap and mask files produces the mouse cursor shown in Figure 17-3, which the neko might find very interesting.

Figure 17-3. Neko mouse cursor

Note that the -bitmap and -cursor options can take only a built-in name or XBM filename (with the leading @). You'll have to use DefineBitmap or a Bitmap image to specify your bitmap as inline data. For more details on cursors, see Chapter 23.

DefineBitmap

DefineBitmap generates bitmaps at runtime. It expects four parameters: the bitmap name, the bitmap width and height, and a *static* area of packed characters, where a "1" indicates an on bit and a "." indicates an off bit. This idiom, directly from the Perl/Tk distribution, is common:

```
my $bits = pack("b8" x 5,
    "........",
    "...11...",
    "..1111..",
    ".111111.",
    "........");
$mw->DefineBitmap('increment' => 8, 5, $bits);
```

The 'increment' bitmap is an "up arrow" eight bits wide and five bits high and is usable anywhere a built-in bitmap name is valid. It's important to note the DefineBitmap keeps a reference to $bits, so you must not redefine it, or else the original bitmap pattern is lost.

Canvas and Text widgets have stipple options useful for producing mottled effects and dashed lines. The following program dynamically produces a series of stipples, numbered 1 through 8, which we can use to draw various dashed lines. Note that the eight stipple bit patterns are stored in an anonymous array. Each stipple is 1 bit wider than the previous, so we can select dashes of varying widths. We first draw a solid reference line, then eight stippled lines for comparison.

```
my $stipple_bits = [];              # important
foreach my $b (1 .. 8) {
    push @$stipple_bits, pack('b8', '1' x $b . '.' x (8 - $b));
    $mw->DefineBitmap("stipple$b" => 8, 1, $stipple_bits->[$b-1]);
};

my $c = $mw->Canvas(qw/-width 200/)->grid;
$c->createLine(qw/20 20 180 20/);
my $y = 40;

for my $b (1 .. 8) {
    $c->createText(10, $y, -text => $b);
    $c->createLine(20, $y, 180, $y, -stipple => "stipple$b");
    $y += 20;
}
```

Figure 17-4 shows the resulting window.

The Bitmap Image Type

The Bitmap command can read XBM data from a file or directly from data embedded in your Perl/Tk program. Suppose we have a bitmap of a circle. The following code

---

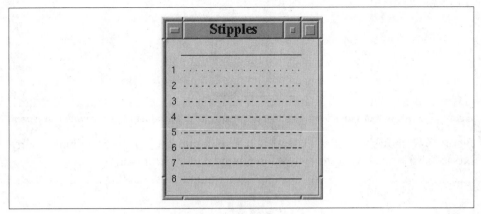

Figure 17-4. Stipples produce dashed Canvas lines

creates the bitmap image from the XBM file and gives it a black foreground (the circle) and a white background. The image is placed inside a Label with a gray background, and then it's packed:

```
my $b = $mw->Bitmap(-file       => 'circle.xbm',
                    -foreground => 'black',
                    -background => 'white',
);

my $l = $mw->Label(-image => $b, -background => 'gray')->pack;
```

Since the Label shrink-wraps around the image, all we see is the picture shown in Figure 17-5. Notice also that we've omitted any mask file.

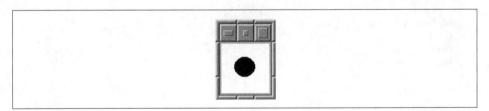

Figure 17-5. A bitmap of a circle without a mask

Suppose we copy the original bitmap and invert it (that is, toggle all the bits so ones become zeros and zeros become ones) and save the result as a mask file. This statement reconfigures the Bitmap image and adds a -maskfile option, producing a transparent area where the circle used to be (Figure 17-6), allowing the Label's gray color to show through:

```
$b->configure(-maskfile => 'images/circle.msk');
```

Notice the bitmap's background color appears wherever the mask has an on bit and the original source bit is off.

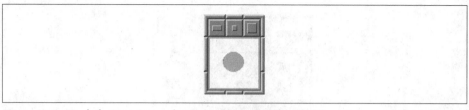

Figure 17-6. Mask that's an inverted version of bitmap makes the bitmap's foreground transparent

Figure 17-7 shows a similar mask that has some bits set where the original source bits are also set, allowing the source foreground to show through.

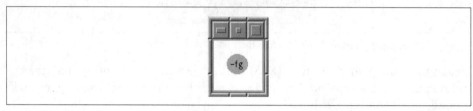

Figure 17-7. Mask bits set over on source bits show the foreground color

The Bitmap command can read data inline instead of from a file, using the -data and -maskdata options.

Cool Tricks with an Empty Bitmap

We can make the cursor totally invisible by assigning it an empty, or transparent, bitmap such as this:

```
#define trans_cur_width 1
#define trans_cur_height 1
#define trans_cur_x_hot 0
#define trans_cur_y_hot 0
static unsigned char trans_cur_bits[] = {
    0x00};
```

a mask such as this:

```
#define trans_cur_width 1
#define trans_cur_height 1
static unsigned char trans_cur_bits[] = {
    0x01};
```

and a -cursor specification similar to this:

```
my $c = $mw->Canvas->grid;
$c->configure(-cursor =>
  ['@trans_cur.xbm', 'trans_cur.msk', 'black', 'white']);
```

How can this possibly be useful? Just wait and see.

An invisible cursor

The tiny mote that represents the display's cursor is an X11 bitmap. For some applications (mostly games), the built-in cursors are not sufficient. Playing Doom with an X pointer just won't work! But if we use a transparent bitmap, the cursor is completely invisible when it's over the Canvas, although it's possible to track it programmatically with a simple <Motion> binding:

```
$c->CanvasBind('<Motion>' => sub {
    my($c) = @_;
    my($x, $y) = ($Tk::event->x, $Tk::event->y);
    print "cursor at canvas coordinate ($x,$y)\n";
});
```

Filling a transparent Canvas item

An interesting problem cropped up on the pTk mailing list. The task at hand was to create a series of transparent Canvas items that also responded to bound events. Creating a transparent item such as an oval, polygon, or rectangle is simple enough: just don't give it a -fill color. Then all we see is the item's outline, and the Canvas background color or image shows through. Unfortunately, events such as <Motion> aren't generated unless the cursor is precisely over the item's outline. Waggling the cursor in the item's interior has no effect. To verify, run this code and notice that the print statement is executed only if we carefully and deliberately position the cursor over the oval's red outline.

```
my $cb = sub {
    print "Over circle, args = @_!\n";
};

my $c = $mw->Canvas->grid;
my $o1 = $c->createOval(25, 25, 100, 100,
    -outline => 'red',
);
$c->bind($o1, '<Motion>' => $cb);
```

If we give the oval a -fill color, the binding is triggered anywhere over the item, as we'd like, but the transparent effect is lost, and the Canvas background is obscured. But we can surmount this problem with an empty stipple bitmap (even a cursor bitmap!) coupled with any -fill color.

```
my $o2 = $c->createOval(155, 25, 225, 100,
    -outline => 'red',
    -fill    => 'blue',
    -stipple => '@trans_cur.xbm',
);
$c->bind($o2, '<Motion>' => $cb);
```

This oval has a red outline just like the first but is transparently filled such that it generates events anywhere, yet allows us to see through it. This feature was deemed important enough that a new built-in bitmap named transparent was added to Tk 800.020, which means that we can say -stipple => 'transparent' in newer Tks.

The Pixmap Image Type

Applications often use pixmaps rather than bitmaps for their icon images, because pixmaps provide more than two colors. Here's how to do that:

```
my $pixmap = $mw->Pixmap(-file => 'Icon.xpm');
$mw->Icon(-image => $pixmap);
```

Pixmaps are plain text, so they easily embed in your Perl/Tk program. The Pixmap constructor has only one other option, -data, for just such a case. The following Pixmap has four RGB colors: white, black, tabby-orange, and green, represented by the characters " ", ., X, and o, respectively.

```
my $pixmap_data = <<'end-of-x11-pixmap-data';
/* XPM */
static char * Icon_xpm[] = {
"32 32 4 1",
"    c #FFFFFFFFFFFF",
".   c #000000000000",
"X   c #FFFFBDBD0000",
"o   c #0000FFFF0000",
"                                ",
"                                ",
"          ..            ..      ",
"          ...           ...     ",
"          .X..          .....   ",
"          ..XX..         ......  ",
"          .X..X.         ...X... ",
"          ..X.X.X. .......  ...X... ",
"          .X.XXX....XXXXX............ ",
"          ..X.X..XXXXXXXXXXX........ ",
"          .XX...XXXXXXXXXXXXX...... ",
"          .X..XXXXXXXXXXXXXXXX..... ",
"          ...XXXXXXXXXXXXXXXXXX.... ",
"          .XXXXXXXXXXXXXXXXXXXXX... ",
"          .XXXXXXXXXXXXXXXXXXXXXX. ",
"          ..XXX.....XXXXXX.....XXXXX. ",
"          .XXX.ooooo.XXXXX.ooooo.XXXX. ",
"          .XX.ooooo.o.XXX.o.ooooo.XXX. ",
"          ..XX.oooooooo.XXX.oooooooo.XXX. ",
"          .XXXX.ooooo.XXXXX.ooooo.XXXXX. ",
"          .XXXXX.....XXXXXXX.....XXXXXX. ",
"          .XXXXXXXXXXXXXXXXXXXXXXXXXXXX. ",
"          .XXXXXXXXXXXXX.XXXXXXXXXXXXXX. ",
"          .XXXXXXXXXXXXXXXXXXXXXXXXXXXX. ",
"          ..XXX..XXXXXXXXXXXXXXXXXXXXXXX.",
".XXX.XX.XXXXXXXXXXXXXXX...XXX..",
".XX.XX.XXXXXXXXXXXXXXX..XX.XX..",
".XX.X.X.XXXX.XXX.XXXXX.X.XXX...",
".XXXX.X.XXXXXX...XXXXXXX.X.XX.X.",
"..XXX.X.XXXXXXXXXXXXXXX.X.XX.X.",
".X.XXXXXXXXXXXXXXXXXXXX.XXX.XX.",
".XXXXXXXXXXXXXXXXXXXXXXXXXXXX.",
".XXXXXXXXXXXXXXXXXXXXXXXXXXXX."};
```

```
end-of-x11-pixmap-data
```

```
$mw->Icon(-image => $mw->Pixmap(-data => $pixmap_data));
```

The Photo Image Type

Like Bitmap and Pixmap image types, a Photo supports -data and -file options.
Unlike those simpler images, Photos additionally support several image formats and
manipulation methods. The Photo constructor attempts to auto-detect the format of
an image, but failing that, we can state it explicitly. The -format option is a case-
insensitive string that can be one of "bmp", "ppm", or "gif" (or "png", "jpeg", or
"tiff", if you have those image extensions installed).

All current Photo image formats are binary data, so to incorporate them into our
Perl/Tk code we need to encode the data into printable characters. All Photo image
formats that support the -data option require that the data be Base64 MIME
encoded. Given a filename, encode_photo_data does just that and returns the resulting string:

```
sub encode_photo_data {

    my($file) = @_;

    use MIME::Base64;
    my ($bin, $data, $stat);

    open PHOTO, $file or die "Cannot open $file: $!";
    while ( $stat = sysread PHOTO, $bin, 57 * 17 ) {
        $data .= encode_base64($bin);
    }
    close PHOTO or die $!;
    die "sysread error: $!" unless defined $stat;

    $data;

} # end encode_photo_data
```

The Photo data method can do the encoding for us as well. All we need to do is specify the format:

```
my $encoded_data = $photo->data(-format => 'png');
```

In either case, you can print the encoded results to a file and insert the data directly
into your Perl/Tk program.

Unfortunately, the Photo format handlers are not created equally where -data is concerned. Currently the PPM handler doesn't support -data at all, and the Photo constructor won't recognize a GIF format without a -format hint. Table 17-1 lists the
photo formats.

Table 17-1. Photo formats

Photo format	-data supported?	-format required to recognize -data?
BMP	Yes	No
PPM	No	n/a
GIF	Yes	Yes
PNG	Yes	No
JPEG	Yes	No
TIFF	Yes	No

Photos allow direct manipulation of the image pixels. We'll look at the copy method in detail shortly. It allows us to copy selected pixels from one Photo to another or to subsample, zoom, clip, rotate, or re-aspect a Photo. Here a list of the other Photo methods:

$photo->blank
> Blanks the Photo so it's transparent

$photo->get
> Fetches the RGB value of a pixel

$photo->put
> Stores an array of RGB pixel values

$photo->read
> Reads an array of pixels from a file into the Photo

$photo->redither
> Redithers the Photo

$photo->write
> Writes an array of Photo pixels to a file

Creating a Color Palette with the put Method

We can spiff up the native option menu example from Chapter 12. Rather than displaying textual menu items, create tiny Photo color swatches and show them instead. Figure 17-8 shows an example.

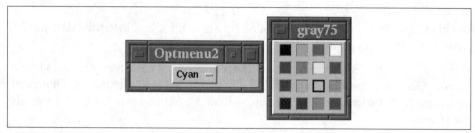

Figure 17-8. A multicolumn color palette menu; cyan is selected

As a reminder, the menu items are radiobuttons, each of which accepts an -image option used when the radiobutton is not selected and a -selectimage option used when the radiobutton is selected. Essentially, we'll create two Photo images per radiobutton, a color swatch for the -image option, and a color swatch with a black border for the -selectimage option.

Examine Figure 17-8 closely, and note that each of the images (excluding cyan, which is selected) has a sunken relief. This illusion is created by drawing a one pixel wide line of the color $topborder along the top and left edges of the color swatch and a similar line of the color $bottomborder along the bottom and right edges. The top and left edges are a darker shade of gray, fooling us into thinking that the light originates from the upper left.

```
my $topborder    = 'gray50';
my $bottomborder = 'gray75';

foreach my $i (0 .. $#colors) {
```

Each menu item has a -label option that is its actual color name, such as 'red4', 'NavyBlue', or 'Cyan', which we'll use to paint the color swatch. To begin, create an empty Photo 16 pixels on a side that is addressed using a scheme just like Canvas coordinates: (0, 0) is the upper-left coordinate and (15, 15) is the lower-right coordinate.

Now it gets a little tricky. The first put method draws the top border line, so we want to paint pixels 0 through 15 in row zero. The -to option specifies the rectangular region to color, but the last row and last column of the rectangle are not drawn! So the 2-row by 17-column rectangle defined by the coordinates (0, 0) and (16, 1) actually paints one row of 16 pixels. The next three put calls complete the relief border, and the last put colors the remaining interior pixels.

```
my $color = $menu->entrycget($i, -label);
my $p = $mw->Photo(qw/-width 16 -height 16/);
$p->put($topborder,    qw/-to 0  0 16  1/);
$p->put($topborder,    qw/-to 0  1  1 16/);
$p->put($bottomborder, qw/-to 1 15 16 16/);
$p->put($bottomborder, qw/-to 15 1 16 15/);
$p->put($color,        qw/-to 1  1 15 15/);
```

The second image (-selectimage) is similar to the first, except the border is solid black and two pixels wide.

```
my $r = $mw->Photo(qw/-width 16 -height 16/);
$r->put(qw/black      -to 0  0 16  2/);
$r->put(qw/black      -to 0  2  2 16/);
$r->put(qw/black      -to 2 14 16 16/);
$r->put(qw/black      -to 14 2 16 14/);
$r->put($color      , qw/-to 2  2 14 14/);
```

Now reconfigure the menu item and specify the two images.

```
$menu->entryconfigure($i, -columnbreak => 1) unless $i % 4;
$menu->entryconfigure($i,
```

```
      -image       => $p,
      -hidemargin  => 1,
      -selectimage => $r,
   );

}
```

And finally, add a tearoff so we can float the palette wherever we want.

```
$menu->configure(-tearoff => 1);
```

Using put to Create a Progress Bar with a 3D Look

We can use Photo's put method to generate dynamic images with minimal overhead. And, if we paint the pixels just right, we can add a lighting effect that simulates depth. The following progress bar image was borrowed from Mac OS 9 by initiating a copy and grabbing the Mac's progress bar in action, zooming in "fat bits" mode, and sampling individual pixels to determine their component RGB color values.

Like the previous color swatch example, the light originates from the left and behind us, slightly above the horizon, as shown in Figure 17-9. The actual Mac progress bar consists of three main segments: the concave base on the left, a repeating column of pixels that represent the progress bar proper, and a dark cap on the right. Taken together, the three segments emphasize the desired lighting and 3D effect. This example ignores the right-side cap, but see Chapter 15, where we turn this progress bar example into a real Perl/Tk mega-widget and treat the cap too. (We can imagine other uses for our progress bar; for instance, a volume meter that indicates the instantaneous level of an audio channel.)

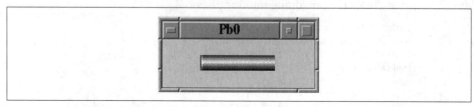

Figure 17-9. A 3D progress bar image

The Mac progress bar is 10 pixels high and dark blue on the top and bottom, graduating to almost pure white in the middle (which accentuates its protruding, rounded appearance). But for our purposes, we use a progress bar 20 pixels in height for clarity. We do this by doubling each row of a column so it occupies 2 pixels. Let's see how to accomplish this task.

First, we use a Canvas with a cyan background as the backdrop for the progress bar. Then we create an empty Photo wide enough for a 100 pixel image and place the empty image at Canvas coordinates (100, 30).

```
my $c = $mw->Canvas(qw/-width 200 -height 60 -background cyan/)->grid;

my $w = 100;
```

```
my $h = 20;

my $i = $c->Photo(-width => $w, -height => $h);
$c->createImage(100, 30, -image => $i);
```

Now paint the bar's left-side base segment. The base is normally 2 pixels wide, but it's expanded to 4 pixels in this example: each of the two columns is painted over two columns. The left two columns are a single shade of dark blue, while the right two columns are dark on the top and bottom and grow brighter toward the middle. The net effect is a concave, 3D look.

```
$i->put('#6363ce', -to => 0, 0, 2, $h);
$i->put([
    '#6363ce', '#6363ce',
    '#9c9cff', '#9c9cff',
    '#ceceff', '#ceceff',
    '#efefef', '#efefef',
    '#efefef', '#efefef',
    '#efefef', '#efefef',
    '#ceceff', '#ceceff',
    '#9c9cff', '#9c9cff',
    '#6363ce', '#6363ce',
    '#31319c', '#31319c',
], -to => 2, 0, 4, $h);
```

Now for the progress bar itself. It's a single column of pixels (again, doubled in height for clarity) that's repeatedly laid out from left to right, one column every 25 milliseconds.

```
for (my $col = 4; $col < $w; $col++) {
    $i->put([
        '#30319d', '#30319d',
        '#6563cd', '#6563cd',
        '#9c9cff', '#9c9cff',
        '#ceceff', '#ceceff',
        '#f0f0f0', '#f0f0f0',
        '#ceceff', '#ceceff',
        '#9c9cff', '#9c9cff',
        '#6563cd', '#6563cd',
        '#30319d', '#30319d',
        '#020152', '#020152',
    ], -to => $col, 0, $col + 1, $h);
    $mw->update;
    $mw->after(25);
}
```

To complete the effect, we should add a right-side end cap and some sort of border. Chapter 15 shows us how to do this.

Capturing a Window with Tk::WinPhoto

There's a special Photo format called WinPhoto (available only on Unix) that makes Photo images not from files or embedded data but from a window on your display (hence the format's name). The WinPhoto format is not available by default; you have to use it:

```
use Tk::WinPhoto;
```

To ensure that you capture the image you want, always update the display:

```
$mw->update;
```

Create the Photo image by specifying the X11 window ID of the desired window with the -data option. You can manipulate the Photo as you see fit, including writing an image file in any supported format.

```
my $img = $mw->Photo(-format => 'Window', -data => oct($mw->id));
$img->write('win.ppm', -format => 'ppm');
```

What you see is not always what you get

Here's a little program that "diffs" two XPM files: the original and one created by capturing a WinPhoto of an image of the original, then writing a new XPM file. We'll see that typically the two files will be different. "Pure colors" such as black, white, red, green, and blue might capture correctly, but "off-colors" such as tabby-orange might easily have varying pixel representations, depending on your display, pixel depth, and visual.

```
use Tk::WinPhoto;

# Create a Label with a picture of the neko.

my $mw = MainWindow->new;
my $neko = $mw->Label(-image => $mw->Photo(-file => 'Icon.xpm'),
                      -borderwidth => 0);
$neko->pack;

# Capture the window and write a new XPM file.

$mw->update;
my $win_img = $mw->Photo(-format => 'Window', -data => oct($mw->id));
$win_img->write('winphoto-neko.xpm', -format => 'xpm');

# Graphically compare the original and captured XPM files. First,
# read the original XPM file into a Text widget.
#
# Notice the $/ trick.  Setting the input record separator to undef
# means that the file is read as a single line with embedded newlines,
# which is then inserted into the Text widget as a single line without
# any tags. Otherwise, insert() would see a list of lines, insert the
# first, treat the second as a tag, insert the third, treat the fourth
# as a tag, etcetera.

my $f = $mw->Frame->pack;
my $t1 = $f->Text(qw/-width 35 -height 40 -font fixed/);
```

```
$t1->pack(-side => 'left');

open XPM, 'Icon.xpm' or die $!;
$/ = undef;
$t1->insert('end', <XPM>);
close XPM;

# Now create an empty Photo and read the new XPM image into it. We'll
# then loop through the image pixel by pixel, read the RGB values,
# and display them as a pseudo-XPM file.

my $neko_image = $mw->Photo;
$neko_image->read('winphoto-neko.xpm');

my $t2 = $f->Text(qw/-width 32 -height 40 -font fixed/);
$t2->pack(-side => 'left');

# Typically, the image captured by WinPhoto is not identical to the
# original.  This mapping approximates the original XPM file.

my %pixmap = ('000000' => '.',
              '00ff00' => 'o',
              'ffffff' => ' ',
              'ffd500' => 'X',
              'ffaa00' => 'X',
             );

$t2->insert('end', "The new pixmappings differ:\n\n");
foreach (keys %pixmap) {
    $t2->insert('end', " $pixmap{$_}       $_\n");
}

# Prior to Tk800.018, the get() method returned a string with
# 3 space-separated integers. Now get() returns a proper list.

my($w, $h) = ($neko_image->width, $neko_image->height);

foreach my $y (0 .. $h - 1) {
    foreach my $x (0 .. $w - 1) {
        #my($r, $g, $b) = split ' ', $neko_image->get($x, $y);
        my($r, $g, $b) = $neko_image->get($x, $y);
        my $code = sprintf "%02x%02x%02x", $r, $g, $b;
        $t2->insert('end', $pixmap{$code});
    }
    $t2->insert('end', "\n");
}
```

Figure 17-10 graphically shows the before and after images. In the original, the tabby-orange color is 0xFFBD00, but WinPhoto captured that color as two distinct (although very similar) colors, 0xFFD500 and 0xFFAA00.

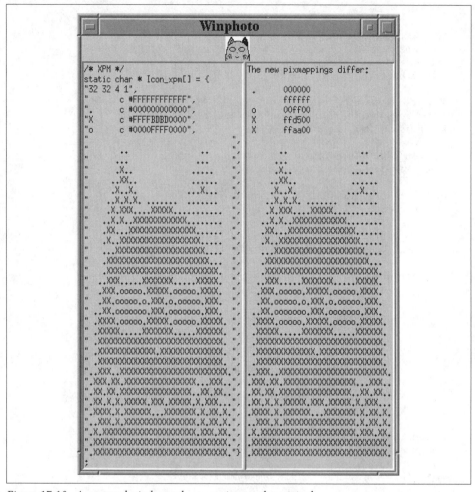

Figure 17-10. A captured window only approximates the original

Tk::Thumbnail

To appreciate the power of Photos, let's examine a Thumbnail widget. Thumbnails are shrunken images of larger (or zoomed images of smaller) pictures, typically arranged in a tabular format. Looking at Figure 17-11, Tk::Thumbnail's rendered POD documentation, we see the thumbnail width and height is selectable, the images can be labeled, and there's a -command option so we can supply a <Button-1> callback. The list of images (of any supported format) can be a mixture of filenames and/or existing Photo images. Tk::Thumbnail is responsible for disposing of any Photos it creates, thus it uses an OnDestroy callback to perform object cleanup.

```
NAME
        Tk::Thumbnail - Create a Tk::Table of shrunken images.

SYNOPSIS
            $thumb = $parent->Thumbnail(-option => value, ... );

DESCRIPTION
        Create a Table of thumbnail images, having a default size
        of 32x32 pixels.  Once we have a Photo of an image, shrink
        it by copying a subsample of the original to a blank
        Photo.

        -images
            A list of file names and/or Photo widgets.  Thumbnail
            creates temporarty Photo images from all the files,
            and destroys them when the Thumbnail is destroyed.
            Already existing Photos are left untouched.

        -labels
            A boolean, set to TRUE if you want file names
            displayed under the thumbnail image.

        -font
            The default font is fixed.

        -width
            Pixel width of the thumbnails.  Default is 32. The
            special value -1 means don't shrink images in the X
            direction.

        -height
            Pixel height of the thumbnails.  Default is 32. The
            special value -1 means don't shrink images in the Y
            direction.

        -command
            A callback that's executed on a <Button-1> event over
            a thumbnail image.  It's passed two arguments, the
            Label widget reference containing the thumbnail Photo
            image, and the file name of the Photo.

METHODS
        $thumb->free_photos;
            Deletes all the temporary Photo images.

EXAMPLE
        $thumb = $mw->Thumbnail(-images => [<images/*.ppm>],
        -labels => 1);

KEYWORDS
        thumbnail, image
```

Figure 17-11. POD documentation for Tk::Thumbnail

Given a desired thumbnail width and height, Tk::Thumbnail takes each image in turn and either shrinks it (via the copy -subsample method, described shortly) or enlarges it (via the copy -zoom method). This means that images of any size and format can be combined in the same Thumbnail widget.

This sample code, *tkthumb*, created Figure 17-12:

```
use Tk::Thumbnail;

my $mw = MainWindow->new;
my $skel = $mw->Photo(-file => 'tkskel.gif');
```

```
my $tn = $mw->Thumbnail(
    -images     => ['mouse.xbm', $skel, <*.ppm>],
    -command    => sub {
        my $i = $_[0]->cget(-image);
        print "args=@_, image=$i\n";
    },
    @ARGV);
$tn->pack;
```

The list of images consists of an XBM filename of the small mouse cursor, a large GIF Photo image, and a file glob of lots of medium-sized PPM images of the neko. In real life, the -command callback might actually do something when clicked over a thumbnail, but in *tkthumb*, it simply prints an informative message. Finally, note that @ARGV holds the command-line arguments, so we can run the program with different options and experiment with the Thumbnail widget.

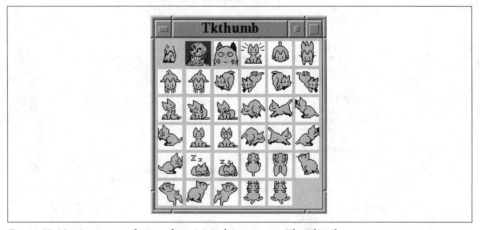

Figure 17-12. A mixture of image formats and sizes in one Thumbnail

From the discussions in Chapter 14, it should be clear that Tk::Thumbnail is a derived mega-widget based on Tk::Table. By the time Populate is called, Perl/Tk has already created the Table, $self, for us and blessed it into class Tk::Thumbnail.

```
$Tk::Thumbnail::VERSION = '1.0';

package Tk::Thumbnail;

use Carp;
use File::Basename;
use Tk::widgets qw/Table JPEG PNG TIFF/;
use base qw/Tk::Derived Tk::Table/;
use subs qw/free_photos/;
use strict;

Construct Tk::Widget 'Thumbnail';
```

Populate removes from the argument hash those options that are specific to the Thumbnail and needed only within itself. Scrollbars have proven to be distracting, so they're disabled unless the user specifically requests them. The thumbnail pixel dimensions also have default values unless overridden by options on the constructor call.

```perl
sub Populate {

    my($self, $args) = @_;

    my $img = delete $args->{-images}; # reference to array of images
    my $lbl = delete $args->{-labels}; # display file names IFF true
    my $pxx = delete $args->{-width};  # thumbnail pixel width
    my $pxy = delete $args->{-height}; # thumbnail pixel height
    $args->{-scrollbars} = '' unless defined $args->{-scrollbars};
    $pxx ||= 32;
    $pxy ||= 32;
    croak "Tk::Thumbnail: -images argument is required." unless defined $img;
    $self->SUPER::Populate($args);
```

This code computes the minimum dimensions required to fit all the thumbnail images in a square Table.

```perl
my $count = scalar @$img;
my $rows = int(sqrt $count);
$rows++ if $rows * $rows != $count;
```

For each element of the image array, we invoke UNIVERSAL::isa to test if it's already a Photo or if we need to create the Photo ourselves. (We could have used the ref function, but isa will detect derived Photo classes.) Once we have a Photo reference in $photo, we determine its width and height so we know whether to shrink or expand it to thumbnail size.

```perl
THUMB:
    foreach my $r (1 .. $rows) {
        foreach my $c (1 .. $rows) {
            last THUMB if --$count < 0;

            my $i = @$img[$#$img - $count];
            my ($photo, $w, $h);
            $photo = UNIVERSAL::isa($i, 'Tk::Photo') ? $i :
                $self->Photo(-file => $i);

            ($w, $h) = ($photo->width, $photo->height);
```

We start by making an empty Photo, $subsample, which will receive pixels from the main Photo, $photo. To shrink a picture, we subsample it, which means we extract every *n*th pixel from the source Photo before copying to the destination Photo. For example, if the source Photo is 64x64, we subsample every other pixel to reduce it to a 32x32 thumbnail. If the source Photo is 320x320, we subsample every tenth bit, and so on. We do this for both x and y. The special value −1 tells us not to subsample a particular dimension, keeping its size unchanged, and gives us one way to change the Thumbnail's aspect ratio.

```perl
my $subsample = $self->Photo;
my $sw = $pxx == -1 ? 1 : ($w / $pxx);
my $sh = $pxy == -1 ? 1 : ($h / $pxy);
```

So the variables $sw and $sh are typically integers greater than one, specifying how many pixels to subsample in width and height. If that's the case, invoke a subsample copy from $photo to $subsample, creating a shrunken thumbnail. But if the source Photo is smaller than the thumbnail size, the subsample width and height are fractional and we need to enlarge the Photo, so we zoom in for a closer look.

Finally, a little bookkeeping is required. We're responsible for deleting every thumbnail when the widget is destroyed, so we keep a list of Photos in an instance variable.

```
if ($sw >= 1 and $sh >= 1) {
    $subsample->copy($photo, -subsample => ($sw, $sh));
} else {
    $subsample->copy($photo, -zoom => (1 / $sw, 1 / $sh));
}
push @{$self->{photos}}, $subsample;
```

This uneventful code stuffs the thumbnail image in a Label and puts it in the Table widget, optionally adding a Label with the thumbnail's filename. The bind statement arranges for the user's -command callback (if any) to be invoked on a <Button-1> event over the thumbnail. Lastly, delete the source Photo, assuming we created it in the first place.

```
my $f = $self->Frame;
my $l = $f->Label(-image => $subsample)->grid;
my $file = $photo->cget(-file);
$l->bind('<Button-1>' => [$self => 'Callback', '-command',
                          $l, $file]);
$f->Label(-text => basename($file))->grid if $lbl;
$self->put($r, $c, $f);

$photo->delete unless UNIVERSAL::isa($i, 'Tk::Photo');

    } # forend columns
} #forend rows
```

Here's a rather typical ConfigSpecs call. See Chapter 14 for details.

```
$self->ConfigSpecs(
    -font       => ['DESCENDANTS',
                    'font',       'Font',        'fixed'],
    -background => [['DESCENDANTS', 'SELF'],
                    'background', 'Background', undef],
    -command    => ['CALLBACK',
                    'command',    'Command',     undef],
                );
```

When an OnDestroy callback is invoked, it's guaranteed to have an intact mega-widget hash, including all instance variables. The object method free_photos then has a chance to delete all the thumbnail Photos.

```
$self->OnDestroy([$self => 'free_photos']);

} # end Populate

sub free_photos {
```

```
    # Free all our subsampled Photo images.

    foreach my $photo (@{$_[0]->{photos}}) {
        $photo->delete;
    }

} # end free_photos

1;
```

Figure 17-13 and Figure 17-14 demonstrate the flexibility of the Photo copy method.

Figure 17-13. tkthumb -width 8 -height 8

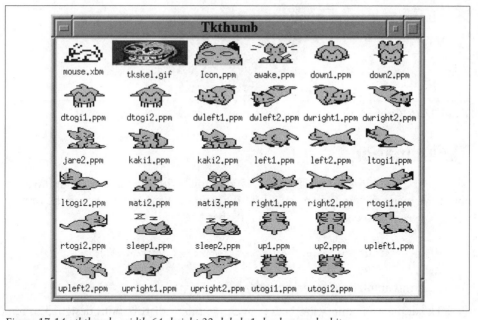

Figure 17-14. tkthumb -width 64 -height 32 -labels 1 -background white

The Compound Image Type

We can combine existing images, bitmap, and text characters to create a multiline mega-image called a Compound, which we then use just like any other image.

The first and third lines are vertical spacers, 10 pixels in height. The second line combines a bitmap, text, and an image separated by horizontal spacers. Although the components of a Compound have configurable foreground and background colors and can be justified and anchored in various ways, that's really all there is to Compounds.

```perl
my $c = $b->Compound;

$c->Space(-height => 10);  # line 1

$c->Line;                  # line 2
$c->Space(-width => 10);
$c->Bitmap(-bitmap => 'hourglass', -foreground => 'red');
$c->Space(-width => 10);
$c->Text(-text => "Searching for ", -font => 'times 19');
$c->Image(-image => $b->Pixmap(-file => 'Icon.xpm'));
$c->Space(-width => 10);

$c->Line;                  # line 3
$c->Space(-height => 10);
```

These statements created the three-line Compound in Figure 17-15.

Figure 17-15. Combining a bitmap, text, spaces, and an image

Tk::Animation

Recall our circle bitmap from Figure 17-5 and how, with the addition of an inverted mask, we made the circle transparent. Using a timer event, we can make the bitmap cycle between solid and transparent so it flashes like a pulsar.

```perl
$mw->repeat(100 => sub {
    $b->configure(-maskfile => $count++ % 2 ? undef : 'circle.msk');
});
```

Some call this animation, crude as it may be.

Perl/Tk supplies an Animation widget in the standard distribution, designed to render a series of Photos, like frames in a movie film. It's also smart enough to handle GIF89 images that contain multiple frames per image. Here's a program that accepts a list of image filenames from the command line and animates them.

```perl
my $animate;
if (@ARGV) {
    $animate = $mw->Animation;
    foreach (@ARGV) {
        $animate->add_frame($mw->Photo(-file => $_));
```

```
        }
    } else {
        my $gif89 = Tk->findINC('anim.gif');
        $animate = $mw->Animation(-format => 'gif', -file => $gif89);
    }
    $animate->set_image(0);

    my $lab = $mw->Label(-image => $animate);

    my $start = $mw->Button(
        -text => 'Start',
        -command => [$animate => 'start_animation', 500]);
    my $stop  = $mw->Button(
        -text => 'Stop',
        -command => [$animate => 'stop_animation']);
```

If no images are specified, the program defaults to the multiframe "Powered by Perl" GIF89 image, as Figure 17-16 shows.

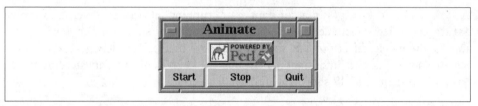

Figure 17-16. GIF89 images can be multiframe

tkneko—Animating the Neko on a Canvas

A more interesting task is emulating Masayuki Koba's *xneko* game, where a neko chases after the cursor, running up, down, left, right, and in circles, stopping only when the cursor stops. If the cursor stays motionless long enough, the neko falls into a deep sleep. When the cursor moves again, the neko awakens and resumes chasing the cursor. The neko is confined to the MainWindow, but if the cursor leads him to a window edge, he scratches to get free and eventually either falls asleep or resumes running.

To simulate motion, we display images of the neko at various positions on the Canvas at tenth of a second intervals (anything slower presents unacceptable flicker). The images we have to work with are shown in Figure 17-14. To make the neko run left, we repeatedly display the *left1.ppm* and *left2.ppm* images. (If the images display at the same Canvas coordinate, the neko runs in place. We might as well have used Tk::Animation if we wanted that effect.)

The neko's actions are state driven.[*] There are in fact five distinct states: the neko is either waking, moving, stopping, scratching, or sleeping. The *tkneko* states are

---

[*] The "togi" states are from the original Japanese code. We don't pretend to know what they mean, although they are the "scratching the wall" states.

encoded in a Perl hash with compiled (for efficiency) regular expressions as keys and code references (the state processors) as values:

```
%states = (
    qr/AWAKE/                                  => \&do_awake,
    qr/UP|UPRIGHT|RIGHT|DWRIGHT|DOWN|DWLEFT|LEFT|UPLEFT/ => \&do_move,
    qr/STOP/                                   => \&do_stop,
    qr/UTOGI|RTOGI|DTOGI|LTOGI/ => \&do_togi,
    qr/SLEEP/                                  => \&do_sleep,
);              # neko state table
```

The states that are dependent on the neko's direction (but otherwise equivalent) are further divided into substates, described by a regular expression with alternatives.

go_neko, the animation main loop, is activated by a repeating 100 millisecond timer event. The subroutine's job is simply to call a subroutine based on the animation's current state, $state. The subroutine in turn selects an appropriate PPM image and displays it on the canvas.

As long as the neko stays in a constant state, running left for example, the variable $state_count keeps incrementing, and the state processing subroutine do_move can use this to alternately select the *left1.ppm* or *left2.ppm* image. The debug -textvariable $where shows this state information as well as the neko's current Canvas coordinates, $nx and $ny. Figure 17-17 shows the neko in its sleep state.

```
$mw->repeat(100 => \&go_neko);

sub go_neko {

    $state_count++;                # current state's cycle count
    $where = sprintf("state=%-7s state_count=%05d, nx=%04d, ny=%04d",
                    $state, $state_count, $nx, $ny);

STATES:
    foreach my $regex (keys %states) {
        next STATES unless $state =~ /^($regex)$/;
        &{$states{$regex}}($1);
        return;
    }

} # end go_neko
```

We create all the PPM images during initialization, make Canvas image items of them, and store the item IDs in the %pixmaps hash, indexed by filename. But we don't want all these individual animation frames visible unless they're needed, so we position them off-Canvas at the invisible coordinates (−1000, −1000).

```
foreach my $pfn ( <$image_base/*.ppm> ) {
    my $bpfn = basename $pfn;
    $pixmaps{$bpfn} = $canvas->createImage(-1000, -1000,
        -image => $canvas->Photo(-file => $pfn));
}
```

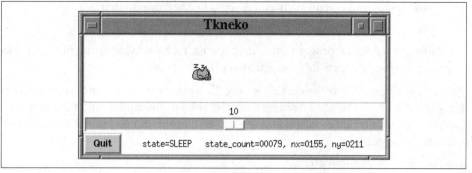

Figure 17-17. The neko has spent 79 cycles in the SLEEP state

---

Hidden Canvas Items

After this chapter was written, Tk 800.018 introduced the `-state` option for individual Canvas items, whose value can be `normal`, `disabled`, or `hidden`. We can take advantage of this and instead of moving an image offscreen, simply mark it as `hidden`:

```
$canvas->itemconfigure($pixmaps{$pxid}, -state => 'hidden');
```

This is the preferred solution, because to be sure that the image we move is offscreen, we need to factor in the current -scrollregion:

```
@scrollregion = @{$canvas->cget(-scrollregion) };
$canvas->coords($pixmaps{$pxid},
    $scrollregion[0] - 1000, $scrollregion[1] - 1000);
```

The `-scrollregion` option is a reference to an array of two canvas coordinates (four items): the top-left corner and bottom-right corner of a bounding box describing the maximum extents that one may scroll the canvas. For instance:

```
$canvas->configure(-scrollregion => [-1100, -1100, 400, 400]);
```

defines a square canvas 1500 pixels per side that in theory can be scrolled up-and-left so that our "hidden" Canvas items become visible. To be *really* sure the image is hidden, we should substitute the image's width and height for the constants 1000.

When a state processing subroutine selects an image (animation frame) for display, it calls the `frame` subroutine with the new pixmap name. After hiding the old image, `frame` moves the new image to the neko's current Canvas position.[*]

```
sub frame {
    $canvas->coords($pixmaps{$pix}, -1000, -1000);
    $pix = "$_[0].ppm";
    $canvas->coords($pixmaps{$pix}, $nx, $ny);
}
```

---

[*] Once again, for Tk Version 800.018 and newer it's preferable to set an image's state to `hidden` to make it disappear, and `normal` to make it visible.

So do_move might make a call such as this to make the neko run left:

```
frame 'left' . (($state_count % 2) + 1);
```

Of course, in the actual program, the direction isn't a hardcoded string but the back-reference $1 from the state table's regular expression match.

To make the neko follow the cursor, we use Tk's pointerxy command to get the cursor's coordinates, compute a heading from the neko to the cursor, and then map that value to a new state. $r2d is the radian-to-degree conversion factor, and $h is the new heading, in degrees.

```
($x, $y) = $canvas->pointerxy;

my $h = int( $r2d * atan2( ($y - $ny), ($x - $nx) ) ) % 360;
my($degrees, $dir);

foreach (
        [[ 22.5,  67.5], 'DWRIGHT'],
        [[ 67.5, 112.5], 'DOWN'],
        [[112.5, 157.5], 'DWLEFT'],
        [[157.5, 202.5], 'LEFT'],
        [[202.5, 247.5], 'UPLEFT'],
        [[247.5, 292.5], 'UP'],
        [[292.5, 337.5], 'UPRIGHT'],
        [[337.5,  22.5], 'RIGHT'],
        ) {
    ($degrees, $dir) = ($_->[0], $_->[1]);
    last if $h >= $degrees->[0] and $h < $degrees->[1];
} # forend

set_state $dir;
```

And that's really all there is to it. As you'd expect, there are many tiny details we've ignored, so the entire program is available at the O'Reilly web site.

Tile and Transparent Images

Like the -background color option, most widgets support a -tile option, as shown in Figure 17-18.

Figure 17-18. A 32x32 PNG file, tile.png

A tile is an image, typically small, patterned repeatedly across and down the widget. If a widget has both a -background and -tile option, the tile is applied over the background color, hence it takes precedence. Currently, the Button, Canvas, Checkbutton, Entry, Frame, Label, Listbox, MainWindow, Menu, Menubutton, Message,

Radiobutton, Scale, Scrollbar, Text, and Toplevel widgets support the -tile option. Here are the common tile-related widget options:

-activetile => *image*
> Specifies the tile image displayed when drawing an active widget.

-disabledtile => *image*
> Specifies the tile image displayed when drawing a disabled widget.

-offset => offsetSpec
> Specifies the offset of the tiles. It can have two different formats, -offset => [x, y] or -offset => *side*, where *side* can be n, ne, e, se, s, sw, w, nw, or center. In the first case, the origin is that of the Toplevel of the current window. For a Canvas and Canvas items, the origin is the Canvas origin, but putting a # character in front of the coordinate pair means use the Toplevel origin instead. For Canvas items, the -offset option is used for stippling as well. For line and polygon Canvas items, you can also specify an index as an argument, which connects the stipple or tile origin to one of the coordinate points of the line/polygon.

-tile => *image*
> Specifies the tile displayed as a widget's background.

-troughtile => *image*
> Specifies the tile displayed in the rectangular trough area of widgets such as Scrollbars and Scales.

We can think of the Canvas as having various layers. The lowest is the green background that is obscured by the tile layer. On top of these two layers is a single Canvas image item: a picture of the neko.

```
my $icon = $mw->Photo(-file=>'images/Icon.xpm');
my $tile = $mw->Photo(-file=>'images/tile.png');

my $c1 = $mw->Canvas(
    -tile       => $tile,
    -background => 'green',
    qw/-width 200 -height 200/,
);
$c1->pack(-side => 'left');
$c1->createImage(105, 105, -image => $icon);
```

This code produced Figure 17-19.

Figure 17-20 shows a GIMP[*] window where a transparent PNG picture is being edited. The picture starts out totally transparent, but we've deposited a lattice of blue dots with a feathered brush tool.

Figure 17-21 shows that if we create a second Canvas similar to the first and add an image item of this transparent PNG file (rather than a tile), we can expect the green

---

[*] GIMP stands for GNU Image Manipulation Program.

Figure 17-19. A Canvas with a tile

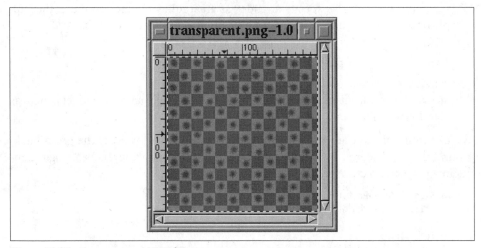

Figure 17-20. A transparent PNG lattice

Canvas background to show through. Notice that the neko image has been lowered in the Canvas' display list so it's behind the transparent PNG.

Here is the cod that produced Figure 17-21:

```
my $c2 = $mw->Canvas(
    -background => 'green',
    qw/-width 200 -height 200/,
);
$c2->pack(-side => 'left');
my $trans = $mw->Photo(-file => 'images/transparent.png');
$c2->createImage(105, 105, -image => $trans);
my $neko = $c2->createImage(105, 105, -image => $icon);
$c2->lower($neko);
```

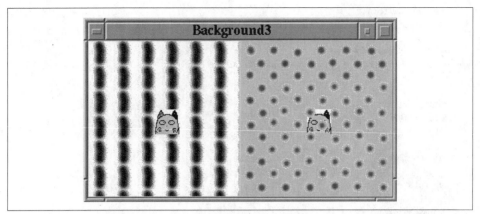

Figure 17-21. The background shows through a transparent PNG image

Miscellaneous Image Methods

Here is a list of miscellaneous image methods:

`$widget->Getimage(`*`image_name`*`)`
    Scans the images used by the MainWindow for an image, and `@INC` if the image is not already loaded, with the specified name and returns the Perl/Tk image reference. Search order is XPM, GIF, PPM, BMP, XBM. If an image is not located, the search continues with the built-in image names.

`$widget->imageNames`
    Returns a list of image names used by the MainWindow. Currently, these names are the actual image references. (Not available as an image method.)

`$widget->imageTypes`
    Returns a list of the image types currently used by the MainWindow, *not* the available image types. An image type appears in this list only if at least one instance has been created. (Not available as an image method.)

Simple Photo Rotations

Using standard Photo methods, it's possible to rotate an image 90 degrees clockwise, 90 degrees counter-clockwise, or flip it 180 degrees.[*] Once encapsulated in a module—call it Tk::PhotoRotateSimple—we can showcase its capabilities with this code, the result of which is shown in Figure 17-22.

```
use Tk;
use Tk::PhotoRotateSimple;
```

---

[*] This algorithm is courtesy of Ryan Casey's *img_rotate.tcl* script.

```
use subs qw/rotate/;
use strict;

my $mw = MainWindow->new;
my $p = $mw->Photo(-file => Tk->findINC('Xcamel.gif'));

rotate 'Original';
rotate 'flip';
rotate 'l90';
rotate 'r90';

MainLoop;

sub rotate {

    my $direction = shift;

    my $f = $mw->Frame(qw/-width 100 -height 100/)->pack(qw/-side left/);
    $f->packPropagate(0);
    $f->Label(-text => $direction)->pack;
    my $i = $f->Label(-image => $p)->pack(qw/-expand 1 -fill both -anchor c/);

    return if $direction eq 'Original';

    my $tmp = $mw->Photo;
    $tmp->copy($p);
    $tmp->rotate_simple($direction);
    $i->configure(-image => $tmp);

}
```

$p is our friendly camel Photo object. Using it as the original, we call rotate to rotate the image three times: 180 degrees, left 90 degrees, and right 90 degrees. The first call to rotate does no rotation, it just displays the original Photo and returns. The rotate_simple method rotates the actual Photo, so we make a temporary copy in order to preserve the original. Then call rotate_simple with flip, l90, or r90.

So much for the user's point of view; let's see the actual module.

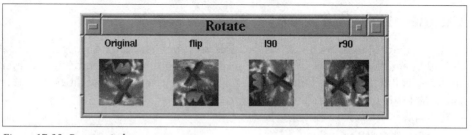

Figure 17-22. Rotate window

The first thing to note is that we are extending the class Tk::Photo by adding a new method, rotate_simple. The method's basic idea is to create a temporary Photo,

---

extract pixels from the original, stuff them into the temporary Photo appropriately rearranged, then copy the temporary image over the original.

```perl
$Tk::PhotoRotateSimple::VERSION = '1.0';

package Tk::Photo;
use Carp;
use strict;

sub rotate_simple {

    my ($photo, $rot) = @_;
    carp "Illegal rotation '$rot'." unless $rot =~ /l90|r90|flip/i;

    my $tmp = $photo->Tk::Widget::image('create', 'photo');
    bless $tmp, 'Tk::Photo';

    my $width = $photo->width;
    my $height = $photo->height;

    if ($rot =~ /l90/i) {
        for (my $x = 0; $x < $width; $x++) {
            my $curpix = $photo->data(-from => $x, 0, $x + 1, $height);
            $curpix = "{$curpix}";
            $tmp->put($curpix, -to => 0, $width - $x - 1);
        }
    } elsif ($rot =~ /r90/i) {
        for (my $y = 0; $y < $height; $y++) {
            my $curpix = $photo->data(-from => 0, $y, $width, $y + 1);
            $curpix =~ s/^{(.*)}$/$1/;
            $tmp->put($curpix, -to => $height - $y - 1, 0);
        }
    } else {
        $tmp->copy($photo, -subsample => -1, -1);
    }

    $photo->blank;
    $photo->copy($tmp);
    $photo->configure(-height => $width, -width => $height) if $rot !~ /flip/i;
    $photo->idletasks;

    $tmp->delete;

} # end rotate

1;
```

But there's one subtle gotcha: how to create the temporary Photo when all we've got to work with is a Photo object from the rotate_simple calling sequence. You see, the actual Photo method is a widget method, not a Photo method, so we can't simply say (and have it succeed):

```perl
my $tmp = $photo->Photo;
```

Instead, we do what we've been taught never to do: look inside an opaque object and take advantage of what we glean. In this case, we call image directly and bless the resulting object as a Tk::Photo.

```
my $tmp = $photo->Tk::Widget::image('create', 'photo');
bless $tmp, 'Tk::Photo';
```

The alternative is to have another parameter—say, -parent—that the user is required to supply so we have a widget reference. It's certainly safer to do this, if not as pleasing to the eye.

The rest of rotate_simple is straightforward. To rotate l90, grab to the left-most column and put it to the bottom row of the temporary Photo, repeating until all columns are rotated. To rotate r90, grab to the top-most row and put it to the right column of the temporary Photo, repeating until all rows are rotated. flip is the easiest of all, because copy's -subsample option flips automatically if its arguments are negative.

If you were actually looking at the earlier rotation code with the intent of understanding it, you should be wondering what those two regular expressions were all about. They're wrestling with vestigial Tcl semantics—remember most everything in Tcl is a string—so in one case we add curly braces, in the other we subtract curlies. If you're curious, the curlies are like hard quotes in Perl, ensuring that the data is not interpolated.

## CHAPTER 18

A Tk Interface Extension Tour

Tk Interface Extension (Tix) widgets are an additional set of widgets that come with the Tk module.

In this chapter, we cover the widgets from Ioi Lam's Tix 4.1.0 package. TList, HList, Tree, and DirTree are container-style widgets, designed to hold display items. This chapter covers:

TList
> A much more flexible Listbox that uses display items.

HList
> A hierarchical list widget, often used as a snazzy Listbox. It is the base class for Tree and DirTree.

Tree
> Based on HList, it displays items in tree format. Look at DirTree for an easy way to work with filesystems.

DirTree
> An extension of Tree, DirTree is designed to show directories and files in a hierarchical format.

You'd use the TList widget in place of a a ListBox when you want to display something other than text or want to display individual items in different fonts or colors. HList gives you the ability to structure a list hierarchically or with elegant column headings. The Tree widget provides a simpler interface for creating an HList with indicators, and DirTree is further simplified for displaying a filesystem hierarchy.

Before we talk about the widgets individually, we need to give you some background on how display items work and how to configure them. Once that's established, we can discuss the Tix widgets in detail.

Display Items

One of the things we gain when using Tix widgets is the ability to create a *display item* and then add it to a Tix widget for display. Display items are all rectangular, and the container widget manipulates those rectangles with little regard to anything other than the size of the rectangles and the order in which to display them.

There are four different types of items you can use in Tix widgets: text, imagetext, image, and window. A text item displays only text. An imagetext item can display both an image and text, or only an image, or only text. An image item displays only an image, and a window is another widget.

When creating each item in our TList, we specify the type using the -itemtype option:

```
$tl = $mw->TList->pack(-expand => 1, -fill => 'both');
foreach my $i (0..19) {
    $tl->insert('end', -itemtype => 'text', -text => "Display Item #$i");
}
```

In Figure 18-1, we see there are 20 different display items inserted. Each has an item type of 'text'.

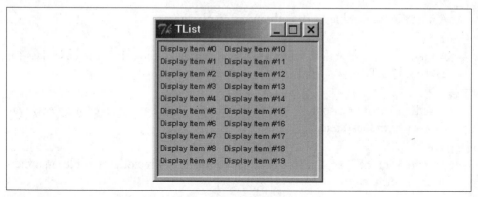

Figure 18-1. A TList widget showing display items

Now let's change our example to show different item types:

```
$tl = $mw->TList->pack(-expand => 1, -fill => 'both');
my $image = $mw->Getimage('folder');

foreach my $i (0..4) {
    $tl->insert('end', -itemtype => 'text', -text => "text Item #$i");
    $tl->insert('end', -itemtype => 'imagetext',
                -text => "imagetext item #$i", -image => $image);
    my $b = $tl->Button(-text => "Window item #$i",
                        -command => sub { print "Button pressed\n"; });
    $tl->insert('end', -itemtype => 'window', -widget => $b);
}
```

Figure 18-2 shows our screenshot, generated using the previous code, then manually resized to make it pretty with three items per column.

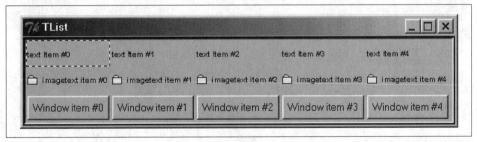

Figure 18-2. A TList widget showing different display item types

We didn't bother showing the 'image' type in this example, since it's just an image with no text on it. The fonts and colors used to display each item are the defaults for the TList widget, but we could change them on a per item basis using *item styles* (covered in the next section).

Table 18-1 lists the options you can use when creating each of the display item types. Different widgets use different methods to create item types. In our previous examples, we used TList, so the method to create a new item is insert. If we were using the HList widget, we would call itemCreate to create a new item.

Table 18-1. The options available for item types in Tix widgets

Option	Text	Imagetext	Image	Window
-bitmap => *bitmap* A bitmap to display in the item.		✓	✓	
-image => *image* An image to display in the item.		✓	✓	
-showimage => 0|1 Determines whether the image will be shown. Even if the image isn't being displayed, space will still be allocated for it.		✓		
-showtext => 0|1 Determines whether the text will be shown.		✓		
-style => *$style* A reference to a style created using the ItemStyle method. Will change how the item is displayed: font, colors, etc.	✓	✓	✓	✓
-text => *string* The text to be displayed. If using -showtext => 0 on an imagetext item, the text won't be seen.	✓	✓		
-underline => *index* The character index to underline in the text. First character in the text is at 0.	✓	✓		

Table 18-1. The options available for item types in Tix widgets (continued)

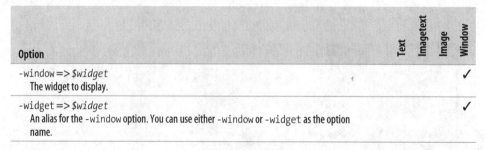

Option	Text	Imagetext	Image	Window
-window => *$widget* The widget to display.				✓
-widget => *$widget* An alias for the -window option. You can use either -window or -widget as the option name.				✓

Item Styles

Creating and using a style is very similar to creating and using a tag in the Text widget, except you get a bit more reusability with Tix item styles. If you predefine what you'd like the style to look like, you can use it throughout your program many times with different Tix widgets. If you need to change how those items are displayed, you can change the definition of the style instead of changing each individual item.

To create a new style, call the ItemStyle method:

```
$styleref = $parentwidget->ItemStyle('text',
        -stylename => 'stylename',
        [ option => value, ... ] );
```

The first parameter to ItemStyle must be an item type (image, text, imagetext, or window). What $parentwidget you use is important only because it determines the default values of all the style options. If you use a TList as the parent widget, with a default font of "Courier 14", then the style will use that font unless the -font option is explicitly changed. You can use any widget as the parent widget, including the MainWindow ($mw).

The rest of the arguments to ItemStyle are option/value pairs. You can use any of the following option/value pairs with ItemStyle:

-stylename => '*stylename*'
> Gives the style a name. Note that you don't really need this, because you use the reference to the style when creating items, not the name of the style. However, it's useful if you intend to let users create and manipulate styles, since it might help them remember which style is which.

-refwindow => $otherwidget
> Normally the default values for the style are taken from the parent widget. If you specify -refwindow, then the defaults are taken from $otherwidget.

-option => value
> Each item type has a different set of options you can change (font, color, etc.). See Table 18-2 for details on what is valid for the item type you're using.

To use the style you've created, specify it with the -style option as you create the item:

```
# Create the item style
$blue = $mw->ItemStyle('text', -foreground => 'blue',
    -selectforeground => 'white', -font => "Courier 8");
# Use item style with an item
$tl->insert('end', -itemtype => 'text', -style => $blue,
    -text => 'Blue text');
```

Now the item you've created will have blue text normally and white text when selected, and the text is displayed in 8 point Courier font. It is important that the style's item type and new item's type match, or you'll get an error (see Table 18-2).

Table 18-2. Style options by item type for Tix widgets

Option	Text	Imagetext	Image	Window
-activebackground => color The background color when the mouse is hovering over the item.	✓	✓	✓	
-activeforeground => color The text color when the mouse is hovering over the item.	✓	✓	✓	
-anchor => 'n' | 'ne' | 'e' | 'se' | 's' | 'sw' | 'w' | 'nw' | 'center' The anchoring direction for the item within its bounding box.	✓	✓	✓	✓
-background => color The color of the area behind the text.	✓	✓	✓	
-disabledbackground => color The color of the area behind the text when the item is disabled.	✓	✓	✓	
-disabledforeground => color The color of the text when the item is disabled.	✓	✓	✓	
-font => font The font to use for the text in the item.	✓	✓		
-foreground => color The color of the text.	✓	✓	✓	
-gap => amount The amount of space (in pixels) between the image and text.		✓		
-justify => 'left' | 'right' | 'center' The side of the bounding box against which the text will justify itself. Useless unless you also specify -wraplength.	✓	✓		
-padx => amount The amount of space to leave around the item on the right and left.	✓	✓	✓	✓
-pady => amount The amount of space to leave around the item on the top and bottom.	✓	✓	✓	✓
-selectbackground => color The color of the area behind the text or image when the item is selected.	✓	✓	✓	

Table 18-2. Style options by item type for Tix widgets (continued)

Option	Text	Imagetext	Image	Window
-selectforeground => *color* The color of the text when the item is selected.	✓	✓	✓	
-textanchor => 'n' | 'ne' | 'e' | 'se' | 's' | 'sw' | 'w' | 'nw' | 'c' The anchor position on the image where the text is attached. 'n' will cause the text to be centered above the image. Using ne, nw, se, or sw will look a bit strange, as the text will be hanging off a corner of the image.		✓		
-wraplength => *amount* The maximum amount of text (in a standard screen distance) displayed on one line.	✓	✓		

Let's look at a few examples of creating styles and using them with a Tix widget. The TList is the simplest to understand right now, so we'll use that as our display mechanism.

```
use Tk;
require Tk::TList;
require Tk::ItemStyle;

$mw = MainWindow->new(-title => 'TList');

# Create first style
$blue = $mw->ItemStyle('text', -foreground => 'blue',
  -selectforeground => 'white', -font => 'Courier 8');

# Create second style
$bluebig = $mw->ItemStyle('text', -foreground => 'blue',
  -selectforeground => 'white', -font => 'Courier 14');

$tl = $mw->TList->pack(-expand => 1, -fill => 'both');
$tl->insert('end', -itemtype => 'text', -text => 'small blue style',
            -style => $blue, -underline => 2);
$tl->insert('end', -itemtype => 'text', -text => 'big blue style',
            -style => $bluebig, -underline => 2);

MainLoop;
```

We've shown the whole program this time. When working with the Tix widgets, we require both Tk::TList and Tk::ItemStyle. We continue to create our MainWindow like we normally do, then start creating the styles we'd like to use. Notice that we are using $mw as the parent widget of our styles. Since we're doing this, the defaults for the style options we don't specify come from the MainWindow instead of from the TList we're going to use them in. If the user has configured any specific TList widget preferences, those preferences won't apply to these styles. (See Chapter 16 for information on allowing the user to specify options.)

Next in our example, we create our TList widget and insert some text. Figure 18-3 shows what the window looks like. You can see that the second item inserted is much larger than the first, and the font colors are blue when not selected and white when selected.

Figure 18-3. A TList that uses more than one style

If we had other Tix widgets that we wanted to use these styles with, we'd simply use the -style option (where applicable) when creating the new display items in those widgets as well. Unlike Text widget tags, which you can use only within the Text widget in which you created them (you can't even share tags between two different Text widgets in the same application), Tix styles are usable across multiple widgets and widget types.

Item Style Methods

We've already talked about the ItemStyle method itself, which creates a new style:

```
$style1 = $parent->ItemStyle('imagetext', .... );
```

Once you have a reference to that style, you can do only three things with it. You can call cget to get information about how the options are set, or you can call configure to change the values of options:

```
$color = $style1->cget(-foreground);
$style1->configure(-foreground => 'red');
```

The only thing you can't change when calling configure on a style is the type of item the style is designed to modify.

The last thing you can do with a style is delete it:

```
$style1->delete( );
```

The moment you delete a style, all items that use it will stop using the style and will be displayed using the Tix widget's default option values.

The TList Widget

The TList widget is very similar to a Listbox, because it displays a list of things. The Listbox is limited to displaying lists of text strings. The TList widget can display any item type, and each item can be a different color and/or font. One of the most common questions asked about a Listbox is whether it can display different color items. The answer to that is no, but a TList can. The TList can also handle displaying multiple columns of items.

When you create a TList, you specify options just as you would when creating any other widget. These options are completely standard and behave as expected: -background, -borderwidth, -class, -command, -cursor, -foreground, -font, -height, -highlightcolor, -highlightthickness, -padx, -pady, -relief, -selectbackground, -selectborderwidth, -selectforeground, -selectmode, -state, -xscrollcommand, -yscrollcommand, and -width.

The following options are specific to a TList widget:

-browsecmd => *callback*
> The callback is called when the user browses through the entries in the TList. Use -command if you want to invoke a callback when a user selects an item in the TList.

-itemtype => **'text'** | 'imagetext' | 'image' | 'window'
> The default item type to use for the TList. This allows you to call insert without specifying an item type, as it will use the one specified here.

-orient => **'vertical'** | 'horizontal'
> A TList will create columns if it can't fit everything in the first column. This option specifies if the items are displayed from top to bottom, go to the next column ('vertical'), or if items are displayed right to left, move down ('horizontal').

-sizecmd => *callback*
> This callback will be invoked whenever the TList size changes.

To see how the TList looks different from a Listbox, take a look at Figure 18-4.

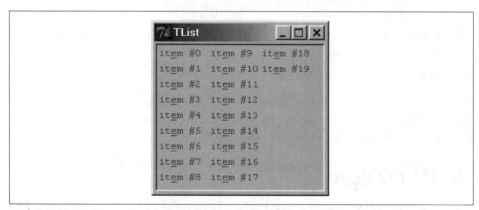

Figure 18-4. A TList showing the 'vertical' orientation

Scrollbars don't work quite as expected with a TList because of the automatic column feature. When using a vertical orientation on a TList, a horizontal scrollbar will work just fine, but a vertical one will never do anything because the TList wraps to the next column based on the current height of the window, regardless of whether there is a vertical scrollbar.

TList Indexes and Methods

Index specification works exactly the same way in a TList as it does in a Listbox. Please refer to Chapter 7 for information on index specification.

All of the methods listed as part of a Listbox work with the TList as well. The insert method for a TList is slightly different from a Listbox widget. It accepts the following additional option/value pairs related to item styles and creating display items:

-itemtype => 'text' | 'imagetext' | 'image' | 'window'
> Specifies the type of item to create. If not used, the default value for the TList will be used.

-data => $scalar
> You can store some data with the item by using this option. The information in $scalar is stored and can be retrieved using entrycget later.

-state => 'disabled' | 'normal'
> Each individual item in the TList can be disabled if you so choose.

-style => $style
> Causes the item to use the style's settings instead of the defaults for the TList.

The HList Family of Widgets

The HList widget is the basis for the two other Tix widgets we are examining: Tree and DirTree. The HList widget is a hierarchical list that uses the idea of paths to create the hierarchy it displays. You could also display a flat hierarchy and use HList as a type of Listbox that can have columns and column headings. Tree and DirTree are specialized versions of HList. DirTree is used to display a directory structure from a given starting point. All three of the widgets use display items.

The simplest way to use the HList widget is similar to a Listbox or TList. Create it and then add items to it:

```
use Tk;
use Tk::HList;
my $mw = MainWindow->new(-title => 'HList');

my $hlist = $mw->HList->pack;
foreach (qw/one two three four five/) {
  $hlist->add($_, -text => $_);
}
MainLoop;
```

Looking at this example, it isn't obvious at all that you can have display items or styles with an HList. The only non–self-explanatory item (given that you understand Listbox) is the first argument to the add method, which is a path. Since this example doesn't take advantage of any of the special hierarchical features of the HList, we're not going to bother showing a screenshot yet.

Just like a Listbox, the HList contains a list of entries. Each time you call the add method, you create another entry in the list. Each entry can contain one or more display items. If you want more than one display item with each entry, use the -columns option. Unlike TList, which automatically manages multiple columns based on its orientation, you need to manage columns manually for the HList. A later example will make this clear.

You need to give each entry in the HList a *path* (the first argument to the add method). The path for each entry must be unique; if it isn't, an immediate error will result.

A hierarchy results when you use the separator character in a path. Here is a simple hierarchy of colors using the separator character of .:

```
orange
orange.red
orange.yellow
green
green.blue
green.yellow
purple
purple.red
purple.blue
```

Changing our previous code to use these paths instead of one two three four five, we get the screen shown in Figure 18-5.

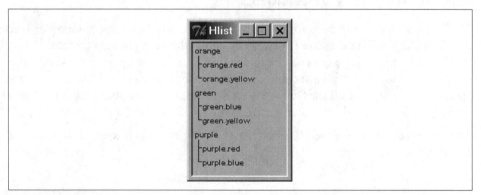

Figure 18-5. Simple hierarchy in an HList

The branches drawn on the left indicate which entries are below the others. orange is the parent of both orange.red and orange.yellow. If we tried to use a path of orange. green.blue, the call to add would fail, because we haven't set up the intermediate path of orange.green yet.

Another way to think of paths is like directory paths. If you don't have the parent directory of /home created, you can't create /home/nwalsh.

If you don't like the branch lines drawn between each parent and its children, you can always turn them off using the -drawbranch option with a value of 0. An empty space will be left in front of each child entry instead of the drawn branch. The amount of space or branch shown in front of each child entry is determined by the -indent option.

One advantage HList offers over Listbox is that it simplifies assigning a callback to be invoked when one of the entries in the list is double-clicked or when the Return key is pressed while one of the entries is active. To utilize this functionality, use the -command option to the HList constructor.

Using Indicators with HList

The information displayed in Figure 18-5 is static, meaning you can't manipulate the hierarchy (opening and closing various branches) without doing a lot of coding first. The most common feature people want in a hierarchical list is the ability to expand and collapse subtrees by clicking an indicator in the parent item. We don't see the indicators in Figure 18-5 because we haven't created any for the items in the list. The indicator can be any display item, and it is displayed to the left of the entry, on top of the branch line. Typical indicators are plus and minus signs, or open and closed folders.

The easiest way to create and use indicators with an HList is to use the Tree widget, because it's already coded internally in the widget. For example, if you don't mind thumbing ahead a few pages, you'll see that we used the Tree widget to create the screenshot shown in Figure 18-7. The indicators in the figure are the default Tree indicators of plus and minus images, displayed only on the entries that have children.

The work involved in setting up your own indicators with HList goes like this: create your HList with the -indicator option set to 1 and create an -indicatorcmd callback. For each entry in the list you want shown with an indicator, call indicatorCreate. Later, to change the appearance of the indicator inside the callback assigned to -indicatorcmd, you can use indicatorConfigure. Here's a version of our example that creates and uses indicators on every entry in the list:

```
use Tk;
use Tk::HList;

sub icmd {
  my ($path, $state) = @_;
  print "path is '$path', state is '$state'\n";
}

my $mw = MainWindow->new;
my $list = $mw->HList(-indicator => 1, -indicatorcmd => \&icmd)
            ->pack(qw/-fill both -expand yes/);
```

```
foreach (qw/orange orange.red orange.yellow
            green green.blue green.yellow
            purple purple.red purple.blue/) {
   $list->add($_, -text => $_);
   $list->indicator('create', $_,
                    -itemtype => 'image',
                    -image => $mw->Getimage('plus'));
}
MainLoop;
```

The best example of using indicators is in the source code for the Tree widget,
included with every distribution of the Tk module.

So what else might you want to use a HList widget for? You can create a list that has
columns and column headings. Let's change our initial code example to do just that:

```
my $hlist = $mw->HList(-columns => 4, -header => 1)
   ->pack(-expand => 1, -fill => 'both');

$hlist->headerCreate(0, -text => "Color Name");
$hlist->headerCreate(1, -text => "Red value");
$hlist->headerCreate(2, -text => "Green value");
$hlist->headerCreate(3, -text => "Blue value");

foreach (qw/orange red green blue purple/) {
   my ($r, $g, $b) = $mw->rgb($_);
   $hlist->add($_);
   $hlist->itemCreate($_, 0, -text => $_);
   $hlist->itemCreate($_, 1, -text => sprintf "%#x", $r);
   $hlist->itemCreate($_, 2, -text => sprintf "%#x", $g);
   $hlist->itemCreate($_, 3, -text => sprintf "%#x", $b);

}
```

We specified two options when creating the HList, -columns and -header. We want
to display four columns, and we'd like to be able to see the headings we give them as
well. After creating the HList, we create the headings, one for each column. The columns are numbered starting at zero. We don't create a hierarchy in this example, so
none of our path entries contain separator characters. (You can still create a hierarchy when using columns. The branch lines are drawn to the left of everything at that
point.) We want to display the color name in the first column and the RGB values in
the subsequent columns.

We still have to call add to create the entry with a path. After that, we can use the
itemXXX methods to put a text display item in each column. We call itemCreate with
the path to use, the column number, and then the text to display. As you can see in
Figure 18-6, a selection selects the whole entry, not just an individual column. There
is no way to select a single column entry in an HList.

Since we're using colors, we can change the background color of the HList when dou-
ble-clicking on an entry. We'll add the -command option and a subroutine to our code:

```
my $hlist = $mw->HList(-columns => 4, -header => 1,
   -command => \&change_background)
```

```
    ->pack(-expand => 1, -fill => 'both');
      .
      .
      .

  sub change_background {
    my ($path) = @_;
    print "color = $path\n";
    $hlist->configure(-background => $path);
  }
```

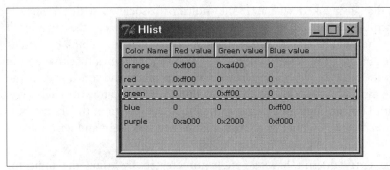

Figure 18-6. HList using columns and headings

Since we are using the color name as the path of the entry, we don't need to do any additional work, because we are given the pathname as the first argument to the callback. You could also get the text entered at one of the columns by calling itemCget:

```
$col0 = $hlist->itemCget($path, 0, -text);  # Text at column 0
```

If the text being displayed isn't what you want to retrieve, you can always store a piece of data using the -data option with the entry itself:

```
$hlist->add($_, -data => 'something else..');
  ...
$data = $hlist->infoData($path);
```

So now that we've seen some HList examples and how to use a few of the options and methods, here's a list of all the options and methods with short descriptions. HList uses these standard options (which behave as expected): -command, -foreground, -height, -selectbackground, -selectborderwidth, -selectforeground, -selectmode, and -width. The following options are specific to the HList widget:

-browsecmd => *callback*
    The callback is called when the user browses through the entries in the HList. Use -command if you want to invoke a callback when a user double-clicks (selects) an item in the HList.

-columns => *amount*
    The number of columns to use in the HList. Must be set when creating the HList.

-drawbranch => 1 | 0
    Determines whether HList shows the branch lines between parents and children.

`-header => 1 | 0`

If set to 1, headers will be shown when created. (See the `'header'` method.)

`-indent => amount`

The amount of screen space to indent a child entry from its parent. Default is 10.

`-indicator => 1 | 0`

If true, the indicator will be displayed for each item in the list.

`-indicatorcmd => callback`

A callback that is invoked whenever the indicator associated with an entry is pressed. Two additional arguments are passed to the callback: the entry path and a string that will be one of `<Arm>`, `<Disarm>`, or `<Activate>`. Think of Arm as similar to a Button Down event, except it is also sent to the callback when the user moves the mouse over the indicator with the mouse button down. If the user has the mouse button down and moves out of the indicator, the callback is invoked with Disarm. Activate happens when the user lets go of the mouse button while over the indicator. Typically, you'll see multiple Arm and Disarm calls before you get an Activate.

If the HList entry doesn't have an indicator created by using the indicator method, this callback will never be invoked for that entry.

`-itemtype => 'text' | 'imagetext' | 'image' | 'window'`

The default type of a display item. You can override the default item type when calling the `itemCreate`, `add`, or `addchild` methods.

`-sizecmd => callback`

This callback will be invoked whenever the HList size changes.

`-separator => character`

The character used to separate pathnames of entries. Default value is `'.'`.

HList Methods

The following methods can be called on an HList:

`$hlist->add($path, options ...);`

Adds a list item using one of the following options:

`-at => position`

Position is an index starting at zero.

`-after => entrypath`

Places the new entry after the given entry path.

`-before => entrypath`

Places the new entry before the given entry path.

`-data => $scalar`

Associates this scalar as data for this entry.

`-itemtype => type`

Uses this type of display item.

-state => 'normal' | 'disabled'
>   'disabled' makes the entry unselectable.

You can also specify any options that are valid for the item type this entry uses.

$hlist->addchild($parentpath, *options* ...)
>   Instead of using separators in the path of each entry and calling add, you can build your hierarchy using addchild once the parent is created (the path of '' is the top-level path). All the option/value pairs listed for add are valid with addchild as well.

$hlist->columnWidth($col, *options* ...)
>   Specifies the width of a column or, with no arguments, return the column's current width. The following options are also recognized:

>   '' *(empty string)*
>>   Resets the column width so it is just wide enough for all text in that column.

>   *width*
>>   Specifies the screen distance for this column.

>   -char => *numchars*
>>   Makes the column *numchars* wide.

$hlist->delete(*what, $path*)
>   Deletes some of the HList entries. *what* must contain one of the following: 'all', 'entry', 'offsprings', or 'siblings'. If using 'all', $path is optional. The entry at $path is not deleted if specifying 'offsprings' (all children of the entry at $path) or 'siblings' (all entries that have the same parent as $path).

$hlist->headerCreate($column, ...);
>   Creates the header for the $column. In addition to the following option/value pairs, you can specify valid option/values for the item type being created.

>   -itemtype => *type*
>>   Specifies what type of item to create.

>   -borderwidth => *amount*
>>   Specifies the width of the border all around the header item.

>   -headerbackground => *color*
>>   Specifies the color behind the text of the header item.

>   -relief => *type*
>>   Specifies the type of relief to use for the edges of the header item.

$hlist->headerConfigure($column, ...)
$hlist->headerCget($column, ...)
>   You can use headerConfigure to change or query any option that is valid with the headerCreate method and query current settings using headerCget. These methods work just like configure and cget, except they take a $column number as the first argument.

`$hlist->headerDelete($column)`

Deletes the header associated with $column.

`$hlist->headerExists($column)`

Returns 1 if there is a header item for the $column and 0 if there isn't.

`$hlist->headerSize($column)`

Returns a list containing the width and height (in pixels) for that header item.

`$hlist->hide('entry' $path)`

Makes the entry at $path invisible to the user. The $path still exists and can be made visible with the show method.

`$hlist->indicatorCreate($path, ... )`

Creates an indicator and associates it with the entry at $path. The indicator is also a display item, so indicatorCreate accepts the -itemtype option and all valid options for the item type used.

`$hlist->indicatorConfigure($path, ... )`
`$hlist->indicatorCget($path, ...)`

These methods allow you to configure the indicator at $path. Both of these methods work the same as configure and cget and, just like headerCget and headerConfigure, they require a $path as the first argument.

`$hlist->indicatorDelete($path)`

Deletes the indicator associated with the entry at $path.

`$hlist->indicatorExists($path)`

Returns a 1 if an indicator exists at $path and 0 if it doesn't.

`$hlist->indicatorSize($path)`

Returns a list with the width and height of the indicator at $path.

`$hlist->infoAnchor`

Returns the path of the current anchor or an empty string if there is no anchor set. The anchor is indicated visually by a dotted line. If selectmode is set to 'single', the anchor is always the same as the selection, but in 'multiple' selectmode, the first item selected is the anchor.

`$hlist->infoBbox($path)`

Returns a list that gives the entry's bounding box coordinates. The list is: $upperleft_x, $upperleft_y, $lowerright_x, $lowerright_y, all in pixels. Only the visible portion of the entry is given; if nothing is visible, an empty string is returned.

`$hlist->infoChildren($path)`

Returns a path list for all children of the given $path. To get a list of all the children, don't specify a $path at all.

`$hlist->infoData($path)`

Returns the data associated with the entry at $path.

`$hlist->infoDragsite`

`$hlist->infoDropsite`

Returns the path of the entry at the dragsite or dropsite, or an empty string if those don't exist.

`$hlist->infoExists($path)`

Returns 1 if the entry at $path exists and 0 if it doesn't.

`$hlist->infoHidden($path)`

Returns 1 if the entry at $path is hidden and 0 if it isn't.

`$hlist->infoNext($path)`

Returns the path of the entry immediately below the one at $path. If $path is the last entry in the list, infoNext returns an empty string.

`$hlist->infoParent($path)`

Returns the parent's path, or an empty string if $path is at the top level.

`$hlist->infoPrev($path)`

Returns the path of the entry immediately before the one at $path, or an empty string if $path is at the top of the list.

`$hlist->infoSelection($path)`

Returns a path list of selected entries, or an empty string if nothing is selected.

`$hlist->itemCreate($path, $column, ... )`

Creates an entry at $path and $column. The path must have already been created by a call to add or addchild. You can use the -itemtype option and any option/value pairs that are valid for that option type.

`$hlist->itemConfigure($path, $column, ...)`

`$hlist->itemCget($path, $column, ...)`

These methods allow you to configure the entry at $path and $column. Both of these methods work the same as configure and cget, except they require $path and $column as their first arguments.

`$hlist->itemDelete($path, $column)`

Deletes the entry at $path and $column.

`$hlist->itemExists($path, $column)`

Returns 1 if the entry at $path and $column exists and 0 if it doesn't.

`$hlist->nearest($y)`

Returns the path of a visible entry that is nearest the y coordinate specified in $y (a valid screen distance).

`$hlist->see($path)`

Changes the view of the HList so the entry at $path is visible.

`$hlist->selectionClear([from [$to]])`

Given no arguments, selectionClear removes the selection from the HList. Given a $from argument, only the item at the path in $from is taken out. If given $from and $to arguments, it removes the selection from those two paths and anything in between.

`$hlist->selectionGet`
> Same as `$hlist->infoSelection`; returns a list of entries that are currently selected, or an empty string if nothing is selected.

`$hlist->selectionIncludes($path)`
> Returns 1 if the entry at `$path` is included in the selection and 0 if it isn't.

`$hlist->selectionSet([$from [, $to ]])`
> Sets the selection to either only the path in `$from`, or the paths between `$from` and `$to`, inclusively.

`$hlist->show('entry', $path)`
> Unhides the entry at `$path`.

The Tree Widget

The Tree widget is based on HList, but it has a lot more built-in functionality. We mentioned earlier that if you want to be able to open and close parts of the heirarchy, you might as well use the Tree widget rather than recoding everything yourself. Here's our color hierarchy example again, but using Tree:

```perl
use Tk;
use Tk::Tree;
my $mw = MainWindow->new(-title => 'Tree');

my $tree = $mw->Tree->pack(-fill => 'both', -expand => 1);

foreach (qw/orange orange.red orange.yellow green green.blue
    green.yellow purple purple.red purple.blue/) {
  $tree->add($_, -text => $_);
}

$tree->autosetmode();
MainLoop;
```

Figure 18-7 illustrates this.

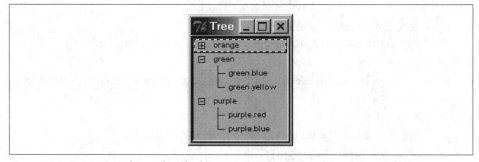

Figure 18-7. Tree using a hierarchy of colors

The only changes in our code are that we replaced HList with Tree and we made an additional call to autosetmode. This call is necessary for the widget to set up all its internal variables so it knows which branches are open. If you forget to make this call, the plus and minus indicators won't appear. Other than those small changes, everything else about a Tree is the same as an HList. All the HList methods and options apply to Trees as well. Here are a few additional options and methods:

-closecmd => *callback*

Called when a branch is closed. Assigning this callback overrides the default callback, so your branch won't actually close unless you add code to facilitate that. If you need to retain the functionality currently provided, save the reference to the callback first, then invoke it in yours:

```perl
my $closecmd = [
    sub {
        print "args=@_!\n";
        my $tree = shift;
        my $closecmd_orig = $tree->{'closecmd_orig'};
        $tree->$closecmd_orig(@_);
    },
    $tree,
];

$tree->configure(-closecmd => $closecmd);
```

-ignoreinvoke => 0 | 1

If set to false, the branch is opened or closed when the user selects the entry (not just the indicator).

-opencmd => *callback*

Called when a branch is opened. If you assign this callback, you are overriding the default callback, so your branch won't actually open unless you add code to facilitate that.

Tree Methods

The following methods are available for the Tree widget:

$tree->autosetmode

For the indicators to be created, you must call this after setting up all your entries in the Tree .

$tree->open($path)

Invokes the callback associated with the -opencmd option.

$tree->close($path)

Invokes the callback associated with the -closecmd option.

$tree->setmode($path, *mode*)

Sets the mode on an individual path. The first argument is the $path to use, and the second argument should be 'open', 'close', or 'none'. A mode of 'none' means the user cannot open or close that branch; a mode of 'open' means the path is ready to be opened by the user (all its children should currently be hidden), and a mode of 'close' means the path is ready to be closed by the user (all its children are currently visible). The meaning of each of these states is counter-intuitive at first glance. In brief, the mode you are using is what the path's going to be doing the next time the user interacts with it.

```
$tree->getmode($path)
```
> Returns the current mode of the given $path. The string returned will be one of 'open', 'close', or 'none'.

The DirTree Widget

The DirTree widget extends the Tree widget (which extends the HList widget) and inherits all the methods and options from both Tree and HList. A DirTree is designed to show directories from a given starting point (similar to the lefthand side of an MS Windows Explorer window). Here's a simple example showing DirTree reading the directories off a CD-ROM drive:

```
use Tk;
use Tk::DirTree;
my $mw = MainWindow->new(-title => 'Tree');
$mw->DirTree(-directory => "D:/")->pack(-fill => 'both', -expand => 1);
MainLoop;
```

Figure 18-8 shows the outcome.

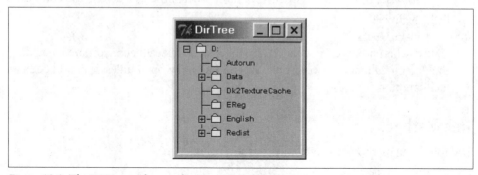

Figure 18-8. The DirTree widget reading my CD-ROM drive

The following options can be used with DirTree:

```
-dircmd => callback
```
> The callback to use when DirTree attempts to read a directory. By default, the DirTree assumes a Unix directory, which works most of the time.

```
-showhidden => 0 | 1
```
> If true, hidden directories are shown (following the Unix convention, any directory starting with a . is considered hidden).

```
-directory => directoryname
```
> The starting directory. For example, *C:/apps/perl* or *D:/*.

Adding a Directory

There is only one method specific to a DirTree widget. You can call chdir at any time to add to the directory listing:

```
$dirtree->chdir($directoryname);
```

If you take a peek at the actual code in *DirTree.pm*, you'll see that setting the -directory option calls chdir as well. When you call chdir, the widget doesn't remove any of the previous directory entries. If you want to remove other directories, you must use the delete method first to avoid confusion.

Tix Images

There are some additional images that are part of the Tix package: act_fold, file folder, info, minus, minusarm, no_entry, openfold, plus, plusarm, srcfile, textfile, and warning. You can use them just like any other images (See Chapter 17 for more details). They are shown in Figure 18-9.

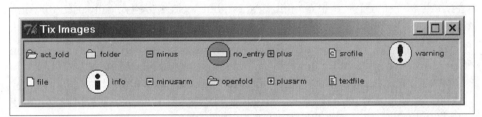

Figure 18-9. Tix images shown as imagetext items in a TList

Here's the code that created Figure 18-9:

```
use Tk;
require Tk::TList;

my $mw = Tk::MainWindow->new(-title => 'Tix Images');
my $tlist = $mw->TList->pack(-expand => 1, -fill => 'both');

foreach (qw/act_fold file folder info minus
            minusarm no_entry openfold plus
            plusarm srcfile textfile warning/) {
  $tlist->insert('end', -itemtype => 'imagetext', -text => $_,
            -image => $mw->Getimage($_));
}

MainLoop;
```

## CHAPTER 19

Interprocess Communication with Pipes and Sockets

The term *interprocess communication* describes a scenario in which two or more processes talk to one another. The processes may reside on the same computer or they may be on separate computers connected via a network. In Unix, there are several IPC mechanisms: pipes, semaphores, signals, shared memory, and sockets, to name a few. All are useful for local communication, but sockets are typically used for communication over a network.

The problem with reading and writing a network socket is that an I/O operation often takes a considerable amount of time to complete, which, as described in Chapter 15, might block the flow of Tk events. Your program then stalls, and the user becomes unhappy. But with care, it's possible to mix network programming with Perl/Tk and still maintain lively event processing.

In this chapter, we'll write some Perl/Tk network programs using pipes and sockets. In Chapter 20, we'll cover more examples using an IPC mechanism unique to Tk, the *send* command.

The first example in this chapter is a simple TCP/IP media change client/server, just to become familiar with the basic mechanisms. These programs help automate daily tape backups on a Linux computer. The client sends an operator message to a central machine, requesting a tape change, and the server posts the message in a Perl/Tk window and returns the operator's response.

Later, we'll develop a Tk user interface that updates flat files on a remote machine, but won't freeze in the face of I/O delays and timeouts due to network latency or disabled servers. The model is extremely simple; it depends on fileevent,[*] in conjunction with a helper process that uses Unix pipes to communicate with the Perl/Tk

---

[*] Although there have been success stories, fileevent on Win32 operating systems is at best problematic. We present two possible workarounds: polling and shared memory. The former solution appears in another section of this chapter, while the latter is written-up in Chapter 22. A newer Perl, combined with the upcoming Tk 8.3, should resolve these deficiencies.

client, and TCP/IP sockets to communicate with the remote daemon. Information is exchanged between the client and daemon using a command/response protocol mediated by the helper. The client pipes a command to the helper, which forwards it to the daemon. The daemon obliges by sending output (and errors) to the helper for piping to the Tk client.

Handling Unsolicited Media Changes

A good system administrator always implements backup procedures, which protect her machines from damaged disks, malevolent miscreants, or rash <Return>s. The venerable tape is still the backup medium of choice for most shops due to its low cost and high reliability. Typically, a full system backup is performed, say, once a week, followed by periodic incremental change dumps. It's not uncommon for a full dump to require several tape volumes, and some sort of operator intervention is required to swap tapes.

But our administrator, in accordance with Perl's First Virtue, Laziness, is also likely to initiate these backups via *cron* or some similar automated means, which means there is no terminal for the backup program to communicate with her. Fortunately, the backup program has an option to run a user-specified program when a media change is required. This alert program is typically a script to send a mail message or display a window that attracts the operator's attention. Sending mail seems to lack style. But opening a window is cool unless there are many machines, each with its own window, so let's write a TCP/IP server that displays media change messages in Tk windows on a single machine, as they arrive from any number of backup client machines.

The Media Change Client, mediachangec

When the system backup reaches end of volume, it executes this incredibly simple client code, specifying the IP address of the media change server plus a message string to display. The code first opens a socket to the server and unbuffers it.[*] The PeerAddr and PeerPort options specify the host to contact and the TCP/IP port the server listens on. The client code then outputs the message on the socket, reads the operator's response from the socket, and prints it on STDOUT.

```
use IO::Socket;

do {print "Usage:  mediachangec host message\n"; exit} unless @ARGV == 2;

$sock = IO::Socket::INET->new(
    PeerAddr => $ARGV[0],
    Proto    => 'tcp',
    PeerPort => 8979,
```

---

[*] The autoflush call is not required in recent versions of IO::Socket but is included for completeness.

```
);
die "Cannot connect: $!" unless defined $sock;
$sock->autoflush(1);

print $sock $ARGV[1], "\n";      # send operator message
print STDOUT <$sock>;            # display operator response
```

As shown in Figure 19-1, the response comes directly from a messageBox widget posted on the server's display and can be either "Ok" or "Cancel."

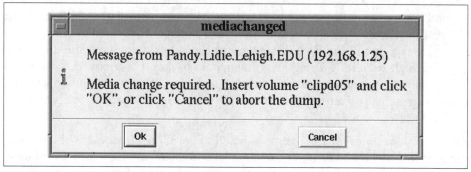

Figure 19-1. A media change operator message

The Media Change Server, mediachanged

We're about to see a forking TCP/IP server, sometimes called a network daemon. In typical Unix fashion, we'll call it *mediachanged*, with the trailing *d* identifying it as a daemon program. This bare-bones example serves as the basis for the much more complicated IPADM server discussed in the remaining sections of this chapter.

The following code is initiated on the media change server at boot time and runs forever. It opens a listen socket on the little-known port 8979 and, as requests arrive, it forks a new child that creates a Tk MainWindow with a lone messageBox widget. Here are the preamble statements:

```
#!/usr/local/bin/perl -w
#
# mediachanged - media change daemon.
#
# Wait for connect on our well known port, display the received message
# in a Tk messageBox, and return the operator's reply.

use 5.005;
use IO::Handle;
use IO::Socket;
use Net::hostent;
use POSIX qw/setsid/;
use Tk;
use subs qw/client_connect/;
use strict;
```

This statement ensures that the daemon's children are properly disposed of after they terminate:

```perl
$SIG{CHLD} = sub {wait};
```

The program backgrounds itself by forking and terminating the parent:

```perl
my $pid = fork;
die "fork failed: $!" unless defined $pid;
exit if $pid;                      # parent exits, daemon continues
setsid or die "setsid failed: $!";
```

Here we create a *listen socket*, distinct from the client's *connect socket*, differentiated by the Listen option that specifies how many simultaneous incoming connections on port 8979 are possible:

```perl
my $server = IO::Socket::INET->new(
    Proto     => 'tcp',
    LocalPort => 8979,
    Listen    => SOMAXCONN,
    Reuse     => 1,
);

die "Socket::INET::new failed: $!" unless defined $server;
```

At last, here is the daemon's main loop, where it blocks on the accept statement until a media change request arrives. It then makes a (very) feeble attempt at authentication by verifying that the peer's IP address is from a legal subnet (192.168.x.x). Unfortunately, an IP address is easily spoofed, so this authentication scheme is unreliable. Nevertheless, within the context of an isolated machine room, the data is useful enough, so we initialize the variable $from with the peer's human-readable IP name.

The daemon then quickly spawns a child to handle the request and resumes waiting on the accept. The child unbuffers the network socket, $ns, and calls client_connect to continue processing.

```perl
while (my $ns = $server->accept) {

    my $peeraddr = $ns->peeraddr;
    my $hostinfo = gethostbyaddr($peeraddr);
    my $remote_host = $hostinfo->name || $ns->peerhost;
    my(@inetaddr) = unpack('C4', $peeraddr);
    my $from = "Message from $remote_host (" . join('.', @inetaddr) . ')';
    unless ($inetaddr[0] == 192 and $inetaddr[1] == 168) {
        close $ns;
        next;
    }

    if (my $pid = fork) {
        close $ns or die "Client socket close failed: $!";
    } elsif (defined $pid) {
        $ns->autoflush(1);
        client_connect $ns, $from;
```

```
        } else {
            die "fork error: $!";
        }

    } # whilend forever network daemon
```

Subroutine `client_connect` first reads the media change message from the network socket. Then it creates the MainWindow, withdraws it, creates a 15-second repeating timer event to ring the bell and alert the operator, and posts an `OKCancel` messageBox dialog widget. Eventually the operator interacts with the messageBox, which returns either the string `OK` or the string `Cancel`. This reply string is sent to the peer via the network socket, and we're done.

```
    sub client_connect {

        # Process a client connect - send our client either an "Ok" or
        # "Cancel" string, depending upon how the media change went.

        my($ns, $from) = @_;

        chomp( $_ = <$ns> );

        my $mw = MainWindow->new;
        $mw->withdraw;
        $mw->bell;
        $mw->repeat(15 * 1000 => sub {$mw->bell});
        my $reply = $mw->messageBox(
            -icon       => 'info',
            -type       => 'OKCancel',
            -message    => "$from\n\n$_",
            -wraplength => '6i',
            -title      => 'mediachanged',
            -background => '#ECFFFF',
        );
        print $ns "$reply\n";
        close $ns;
        exit;

    } # end client_connect
```

Armed with the know-how to build a TCP/IP client/server, let's examine a more complicated scenario involving a Perl/Tk client.

IPADM Design Considerations

The programs detailed in the remainder of this chapter work in unison to help manage Dynamic Host Configuration Protocol (DHCP) and Domain Name System (DNS) configuration files. Now, you don't have to know anything about DHCP or DNS, or managing IP networks for that matter; we're more concerned with how to manipulate these files remotely, rather than with their actual content.

Suppose we have a company, ACME Rocket Supply, Incorporated, which has a class B IP network, 192.168.0.0.* The site administrator has subnetted this address space by department; for instance, IP numbers 192.168.1.0 through 192.168.1.255 are assigned to the accounting department, while 192.168.2.0 through 192.168.2.255 are for purchasing. The administrator also decided to make each department responsible for managing its own computers and printers, and has delegated and trained several responsible persons. But he doesn't want his helpers to have direct access to the server machine. So he has written a Perl/Tk TCP/IP client, *ipadm*, for remote IP administration.

There are various DHCP and DNS programs, and *ACME.com*'s network administrator chose not to limit his choices by writing *ipadm* for any particular flavors. Instead, he invented a metafile that describes an individual subnet, which can be sent to a filter to produce DHCP and DNS configuration files in whatever format is required. It's these metafiles (subnet definitions) that are remotely manipulated. Each subnet definition file consists of two sections, separated by a __NODES__ line. The following is a sample subnet description file:

```
Title = Subnet 128B, ACME Rubber Band Development
Domain = RubberBand.ACME.Com
Base_IP = 192.168.128.16
Subnet_Mask = 255.255.255.240
Gateway = 192.168.128.30
__NODES__
JetDirect3:192.168.128.17:00abcd00abcd:print::Network Print Server
Coyote:192.168.128.18:00abce00abce:Badguy:Mail.ACME.COM:SGI  1
Roadrunner:192.168.128.19:00abcf00abcf:Goodguy:Mail.ACME.COM:SGI  2
```

The first section lists characteristics of the subnet as a whole, while the second section defines every subnet node. (We'll learn more about each colon-separated field in a node definition in the section "The Subnet Widget Edits a Subnet Description.") Using flat file databases is a common technique in the Unix world, so we'll call these files SDBs, for subnet databases.

All the SDB files are centrally located in a single directory on the DHCP/DNS server machine, and a forking TCP/IP daemon serves them to Perl/Tk clients. The daemon, *ipadmd*, and client, *ipadm,* communicate using four IPADM messages, all originated by the client:

get_subnet_list
> Tells the daemon to return a list of all subnets. *ipadmd* does this by reading the Title line of each SDB file (Figure 19-2).

get_subnet_file
> Tells the daemon to lock an SDB file for exclusive access and return its contents.

---

* This is actually a private address space that anyone can use, as long as the addresses remain on the internal network. We'll freely use any of the 65,536 IP numbers in the range 192.168.0.0 through 192.168.255.255 without fear of interfering with a valid address.

`put_subnet_file`

Tells the daemon to expect an updated version of an SDB file, which it uses to rewrite the master copy. *ipadmd* then releases its exclusive lock on the SDB file.

`unl_subnet_file`

Tells the daemon to simply release its exclusive lock on an SDB, as the client has canceled all changes.

These four messages and their responses make up the IPADM protocol. Once the protocol is defined, we know *exactly* what each component of the system can and cannot do. But a formal protocol definition needs to be much more comprehensive and define in detail the format of each command and response. We won't do that here. Instead, we'll look at the actual code. Suffice it to say, each message consists of a command line, zero or more lines of data, and a terminator. The command line, which may have arguments, ends with a newline, as do the data and terminator lines. The terminator, which we'll refer to simply as $EOF, is a funny string guaranteed to be unique; that is, it will never occur anywhere in a message. The message response includes a one-line command completion status, zero or more lines of data, and the terminator, $EOF.

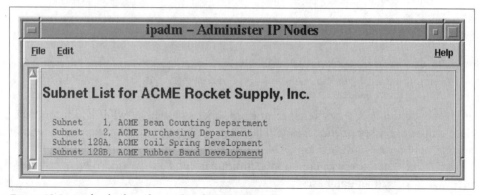

Figure 19-2. ipadm displays the results of a get_subnet_list command

The daemon also maintains an SDBM file containing the last modification times of all the SDB files. Periodically, it uses this information to see which SDBs have recently changed and invokes the filter procedure to create updated versions of the DHCP/DNS configuration files. Of course, the filter must exclusively lock SDB files before it can do its work.

The Perl/Tk IPADM Client, ipadm

The client's primary duties are to build the human interface and establish a communications link to the server, *ipadmd*. In order to talk to the server, *ipadm* starts the helper, *ipadmh*, as a separate process. Then *ipadm* sends a message to the daemon

requesting a list of subnet descriptions, which it uses to construct the hypertext interface shown in Figure 19-2. Each subnet description has tags and bindings that react
to mouseclicks and subsequently display the subnet's nodes, as shown in Figure 19-3.

The following sections explain all this in detail.

Creating the Hypertext User Interface

As Figure 19-2 shows, *ipadm*'s MainWindow is essentially a single, scrolled ROText
widget listing all of ACME Rocket Supply's subnets.

```
my $t = $MW->Scrolled('ROText',
    qw/-width 80 -height 10 -relief ridge -scrollbars w/);
```

As the cursor passes over a subnet line, it becomes "hot," is highlighted in green, and
is able to respond to a button click. Clicking on a hot item opens a Toplevel "subnet
editing" window, which we'll see shortly. All these actions are controlled by text tags
and bindings. First, we create and configure several tags:

```
$t->tagConfigure(qw/title -font/ => 'Helvetica 18 bold');
$t->tagConfigure(qw/subnet -lmargin1 .5c -lmargin2 1c -foreground blue/);
$t->tagConfigure(qw/hot -relief raised -borderwidth 1 -background green/);
```

The title tag is applied to the title line, giving it a nice, large font. The subnet tag is
applied to each subnet line, and the hot tag is applied to a subnet line as the cursor
moves over it and is removed as the cursor leaves.

This dynamic manipulation of the hot tag is handled by tag bindings for <Enter> and
<Leave> events.

```
my $last_hot = '';
$t->tagBind(qw/subnet <Enter>/ => sub {
    my $text = shift;
    my($x, $y) = ($Tk::event->x, $Tk::event->y);
    $last_hot = $text->index("\@$x,$y linestart");
    $text->tagAdd('hot', $last_hot, "$last_hot lineend");
});
```

As usual, the first argument to a bind callback is the bound object reference, here the
ROText widget. We can determine the text line on which the event occurred by
fetching the event's cursor coordinates and using *index* to convert them to a string in
"*line.character*" notation. The linestart modifier ensures that the character portion is always 0. Now we can add the hot tag to the entire line, changing its background color to green.

The <Leave> callback is even simpler, because we can unconditionally clear the hot
tag from the entire text area. Note the shift trick that returns the implicit ROText
widget reference.

```
$t->tagBind(qw/subnet <Leave>/ => sub {
    shift->tagRemove(qw/hot 1.0 end/);
});
```

Our tag bindings tell us when the cursor enters or leaves any text tagged with the subnet tag; they don't tell us when the cursor crosses line boundaries. If you place the cursor at the top of the *ipadm* window and drag it downward, a single <Enter> event is generated as the cursor hits the first subnet line, and a corresponding <Leave> event is generated as the cursor moves out the bottom of the window. Essentially, no events whatsoever are generated as the cursor moves over subnet lines between the first and last. We handle this with a <Motion> binding that checks to see when the cursor moves to a different line and updates the hot tags appropriately.

```
$t->tagBind(qw/subnet <Motion>/ => sub {
    my $text = shift;
    my($x, $y) = ($Tk::event->x, $Tk::event->y);
    my $new_hot = $text->index("\@$x,$y linestart");
    if ($new_hot ne $last_hot) {
        $text->tagRemove(qw/hot 1.0 end/);
        $text->tagAdd('hot', $new_hot, "$new_hot lineend");
        $last_hot = $new_hot;
    }
});
```

As we learned in the previous section, the actual data inserted into the ROText widget comes from a get_subnet_list IPADM command. The do_command subroutine, described later, handles all the busy work concerning the pipe I/O and protocol details, but note that it issues a single, human-legible command and returns the command status and data. Each line of data consists of two tokens: the SDB filename and the Title line from the SDB file. In the following code, each line is tagged with two strings: "subnet" and the SDB filename (the filename has the extension *.sdb*).

```
my($status, @subnet_list) = do_command "get_subnet_list\n";
die "Cannot get SDB list" unless  $status =~ /OK/;

foreach (sort numerically @subnet_list) {
    my($sdb, $title) = /^(\S+)\s+(.*)/;
    $t->insert('end', "$title\n", ['subnet', $sdb]);
}
```

To complete the user interface, we need to invoke the subnet editor when a subnet line is clicked:

```
$t->tagBind(qw/subnet <ButtonRelease-1>/ => \&open_subnet);
```

The open_subnet subroutine creates an instance of a Subnet widget for editing an SDB file. It fetches the list of tags associated with the current line and searches the list[*] for a tag ending in *.sdb*, the SDB filename. The SDB filename, plus a unique identifier used by the daemon for file-locking purposes (described in the later section "Locking an SDB File"), are supplied as parameters to the get_subnet_file IPADM command. The command status line and SDB contents are returned to the @sdb

---

[*] lsearch is a local subroutine that searches a list using the supplied regular expression and returns a match ordinal, or −1 if not found.

array. We are looking for either of two status responses indicating whether *ipadmd* acquired an exclusive or nonexclusive lock. Anything else is an error. Ideally, we'd like an exclusive lock so the subnet editor can modify the subnet, but failing that, the subnet editor lets us look at, but not modify, the subnet.

The subnet editor is really a composite widget that produces a window like that shown in Figure 19-3. After interacting with the subnet editor, we can either update the subnet or cancel all changes, so we supply callbacks that handle those actions (by issuing the appropriate IPADM command).

```
sub open_subnet {

    my($text) = @_;

    my @tags = $text->tagNames('current');
    my $i = lsearch('.*\.sdb', @tags);
    return if $i < 0;
    $text->Busy(-recurse => 1);
    my $id = "$ME\@$HN:$$";
    my(@sdb) = do_command "get_subnet_file $tags[$i] $id\n";
    if ($sdb[0] =~ /Have Lock|Lock Failed/) {
     $text->Subnet(
      -sdb_path  => $tags[$i],
      -sdb       => \@sdb,
      -id        => $id,
      -updatecmd => sub {do_command "put_subnet_file $tags[$i] $id\n", @sdb},
      -cancelcmd => sub {do_command "unl_subnet_file $tags[$i] $id\n"},
     );
    } else {
     $text->messageBox(-message => "SDB Open Error: $sdb[0]",
      -type => 'ok', -bitmap => 'error');
    }
    $text->Unbusy;

} # end open_subnet
```

The Subnet Widget Edits a Subnet Description

A Subnet widget has two sections, paralleling the two sections of an SDB file. The top section is a series of LabEntry widgets that display data from the SDB header, while the bottom section displays the characteristics of a single network node. In Figure 19-3, we see details of the node known as JetDirect3, a three-port print server used by the Rubber Band Development department.

The A (address) field is the unqualified IP name of the node. People on the Rubber Band subnet can refer to the print server using this name or the IP number 192.168. 128.17. People on other ACME subnets must use either the IP number or include the domain and use the fully qualified IP name, JetDirect3.RubberBand.ACME.Com. The CNAME (canonical name) field is an alias for the node's IP name. The MX (mail exchange) field typically points to a mail server that handles mail on behalf of the node; it's not relevant in this case. The Comments field is just that.

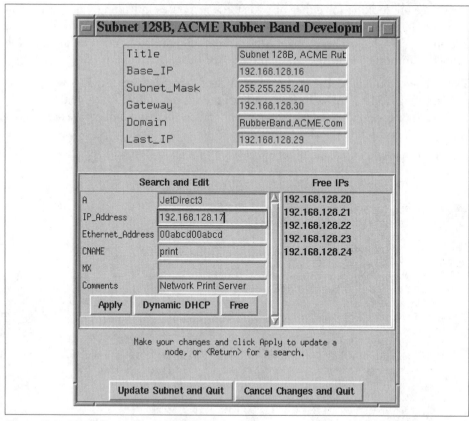

Figure 19-3. The Subnet widget edits an SDB description

As the balloon help suggests, the subnet administrator can type a search string in any node field to perform a search. Once a node entry is loaded, he makes his changes and clicks Apply. Or, to make a new node entry, he clicks on an available IP number in the Listbox on the right, moving it from the free list to the edit area, configures the node, and applies the changes. When complete, he can either update the subnet with his changes (put_subnet_file) or cancel them all (unl_subnet_file).

Although we won't spend much more time discussing the Subnet widget, it does have one trick up its sleeve, and that's how it uses watchpoints to track changes to any of the subnet header LabEntry widgets. The widget's Populate method reserves an instance variable in the composite hash, $cw->{Subnet_Changes}, so all we need do is register a STORE callback on an entry's -textvariable to set that flag. Since the composite widget reference, $cw, is in scope, we simply create a closure and feed that to the CPAN module Tie::Watch:

```
my $callback = sub {
    shift->Store(shift);
    $cw->{Subnet_Changes}++;
```

```
};

    Tie::Watch->new(-variable => \$title, -store => $callback);
```

Whenever the variable $title is written, the callback is invoked with two arguments: a reference to the Tie::Watch object and the watched variable's new value.

Starting the IPADM Helper Task

The IPADM client, *ipadm*, starts its IPADM helper, *ipadmh*, in the standard Unix manner[*] and talks to it via two unidirectional pipes. From our point of view (the parent), we use the file handles PR and PW to read and write data from/to the helper (our child). From the child's point of view, it simply reads from STDIN and writes to STDOUT/STDERR, which we connect to the opposite ends of the two pipes, CR and CW, respectively. Note that we unbuffer all the output file handles.

As its first task, *ipadmh* attempts to connect to the daemon, *ipadmd*, and pipes us an unsolicited message indicating whether or not the connect was successful. Calling do_command without a command reads this message for us.

Finally, note the dubious use of a signal handler to catch a SIGPIPE error. Generally, mixing signals with Perl/Tk causes unexpected application crashes, but in this case, losing contact with the helper is, for all intents and purposes, fatal, and this lets us exit gracefully.

```
    sub start_ipc_helper {

        $SIG{PIPE} = sub {print STDERR "ipadmh pipe failure.\n"; exit};

        pipe CR, PW or die "cr/pw pipe $!";
        pipe PR, CW or die "pr/cw pipe $!";

        if ($PID = fork) { # parent, ipadm/Tk
            close CR;
            close CW;
            PW->autoflush(1);
        } elsif (defined $PID) { # child, exec ipadmh
            close PR;
            close PW;
            open STDIN,  "<&CR" or die "STDIN  open $!";
            open STDOUT, ">&CW" or die "STDOUT open $!";
            open STDERR, ">&CW" or die "STDERR open $!";
            STDOUT->autoflush(1);
```

---

[*] Here we exec a non-Tk program after the fork (we don't require Tk functionality or desire its added baggage), but that's not strictly necessary; it's perfectly okay to have a Perl/Tk child, with two caveats. First, the child must not touch, reference, or manipulate Tk objects belonging to the parent in any way. Second, if the child terminates before the parent, it must override the standard Tk exit command and use CORE::exit, or better, POSIX::exit. Invoking plain exit(Tk::exit) unceremoniously destroys all widgets and data structures and terminates the application.

```
        STDERR->autoflush(1);
        exec("./ipadmh", $DAEMON_HOST, $DAEMON_PORT) or die "exec $!";
        die "exec warp $!";
    } else {
        die "fork $!";
    } # ifend fork

    my(@stat) = do_command undef;# did helper make a connection?
    return if $stat[0] =~ /Connect OK/;

    $MW->messageBox(-message => "Cannot connect to remote IPADM daemon " .
        "$DAEMON_HOST:$DAEMON_PORT.  Please try again later.",
        -title => 'Daemon is Dead', -icon  => 'warning',
        -type => 'OK');
    fini;

} # end start_ipc_helper

sub fini {
    kill 'SIGTERM', $PID;
    exit;
}
```

fileevent Keeps ipadm Happy

And now, here is do_command, the guts of *ipadm*'s message handling:

```
sub do_command {

    # Issue a single IPADM command and wait for a reply.  Using
    # pipes and fileevent() allows X11 events to continue flowing.

    pipe_out @_;
    return pipe_in;

} # end do_command
```

Recall that *ipadm* uses this code to get a list of subnets:

```
my($status, @subnet_list) = do_command "get_subnet_list\n";
die "Cannot get SDB list" unless  $status =~ /OK/;
```

do_command's helper pipe_out appends the terminating string, $EOF, to the outgoing data, then registers a callback that's invoked when the output pipe is writable. Because we're coding with use strict in effect, we cannot give fileevent a bare file handle but must use a reference to a glob instead. The callback outputs its data, including the $EOF, using syswrite, at which time it increments $wait. Meanwhile, waitVariable has logically suspended us, pending a change in $wait, at which time the writable callback is canceled.

```
sub pipe_out {

    # Issue an IPADM command by syswrite-ing all the data plus
    # the terminating $EOF.
```

```
        return unless defined $_[0];

        my($bytes, $offset, $sysdata, $sysstat, $wait);

        $sysdata = join '', @_, "$EOF\n";
        $bytes = length $sysdata;
        $offset = 0;

        $MW->fileevent(\*PW, 'writable' => sub {

            while ($bytes > 0) {
                $sysstat = syswrite PW, $sysdata, $bytes, $offset;
                die "ipadm: syswrite error $!" unless defined $sysstat;
                $bytes  -= $sysstat;
                $offset += $sysstat;
            }
            $wait++;

        });

        $MW->waitVariable(\$wait);
        $MW->fileevent(\*PW, 'writable' => '');

    } # end pipe_out
```

Unsurprisingly, pipe_in reads the reply data[*] in a similar manner.

```
    sub pipe_in {

        # Now that the IPADM command has been issued, keep sysread-ing
        # until the $EOF string is read, and return all the accumulated
        # data, excluding $EOF.

        my(@data, $sysbuf, $sysdata, $sysstat, $wait);

        $MW->fileevent(\*PR, 'readable' => sub {

            if ( $Tk::VERSION  le '800.015' ) {
                $sysbuf = <PR>;
            } else {
                $sysstat = sysread PR, $sysbuf, 4096;
                die "ipadm: sysread error $!" unless defined $sysstat;
            }
            $sysdata .= $sysbuf;
            if ($sysdata =~ /$EOF$/s) {
                @data = split /\n/, $sysdata;
                $#data--;          # throw $EOF away
                $wait++;           # unblock waitVariable()
            }
```

---

[*] Notice that Tk 800.015 and earlier do not use sysread due to differences in fileevent handling. This leaves us open to a potential deadlock, but our line-oriented protocol is simple enough that in practice, this never happens.

```
    });

    $MW->waitVariable(\$wait);
    $MW->fileevent(\*PR, 'readable' => '');

    @data;

} # end pipe_in
```

The IPADM Helper, ipadmh

The helper completes the communications link between *ipadm* and *ipadmd* by open-ing a socket. By far the easiest way of doing this is to use the IO::Socket module. *ipadm* provides the @ARGV values for the PeerAddr and PeerPort parameters, which specify the remote machine and port to contact. The connect status is piped to the Perl/Tk client by writing a message to STDOUT.

The helper then enters its main loop, transferring client IPADM commands over the socket to the daemon and piping responses back.

Notice that the helper is free to use signals, in particular SIGALRM, so it can time-out network reads and inform the client.

```
sub timeout {print "1 Socket Timeout\n$EOFn"; $SIG{ALRM} = \&timeout}
$SIG{PIPE} = sub {print "2 Pipe Error.\n$EOF\n"};

my $sock = IO::Socket::INET->new( PeerAddr => $ARGV[0],
                Proto => 'tcp', PeerPort => $ARGV[1]);
print +((defined $sock) ? "0 Connect OK" : "3 Connect Failed"), "\n$EOF\n";

while (1) {

    while(<STDIN>) {
        print $sock $_;          # send parent's command/data to daemon
        last if /^$EOF$/;
    }

    my(@data) = ();
    $SIG{ALRM} = \&timeout;       # reset handler
    alarm 60;

    while (<$sock>) {
        push @data, $_;          # accumulate command's reply
        last if /^$EOF$/;
    }

    alarm 0;
    print (/^$EOF$/ ? @data : "4 Daemon Failure\n$EOF\n");

} # whilend
```

The IPADM Daemon, ipadmd

The daemon's duties consist of:

- Creating the well-known server socket, then looping forever, accepting client connect requests and forking a copy of itself to handle them
- Processing IPADM messages for the duration of the session
- Employing advisory file locking so only one client has write access to an SDB at any point in time, thus ensuring the integrity of the SDB files
- Keeping the DHCP and DNS configuration files current by periodically checking for modified SDB files, and running the filter as required

We'll look briefly at how these functions are handled, but only briefly; we're beginning to stray far from the topic of choice.

The Forking Server

We want a forking server, because each connect typically takes many minutes to service; after all, there's a human on the other end of the socket, slowly clicking and typing away at the Tk client. With Perl and IO::Socket, writing such a server is a piece of cake. First, *ipadmd* creates its socket endpoint. The Listen parameter specifies the maximum number of simultaneous open sockets and indicates that this socket listens for connect attempts rather than attempting a connect itself.

The daemon main loop simply accepts connects as they arrive, storing the network socket handle in $ns, which the child inherits after the fork. While the child handles the current request, the parent closes its copy of $ns and resumes listening for network activity.

```
my $server = IO::Socket::INET->new
    Proto    => 'tcp',
    LocalHost => $DAEMON_HOST,
    LocalPort => $DAEMON_PORT,
    Listen   => SOMAXCONN,
    Reuse => 1,
);
die "Socket::INET::new failed: $!" unless defined $server;

while (my $ns = $server->accept) {

    my $pid = undef;
    if ($pid = fork) {
        close $ns or die "Client socket close failed: $!";
    } elsif (defined $pid) {
        $ns->autoflush(1);
        client_connect $ns;
    } else {
```

```
        die "fork error: $!";
    }

} # whilend forever network daemon
```

IPADM Message Handling

The child forked by *ipadmd* has yet another main loop, which lasts as long as the Perl/Tk client keeps the socket alive. The child reads the socket line by line until the $EOF terminator arrives and dispatches the IPADM message to the proper processing subroutine. This code also appends the $EOF terminator to whatever data the command processor might have returned, as required by the IPADM protocol.

```
CONNECTED:
  while (1) {
      my(@data) = ();

    COMMAND:
      while (1) {
          $_ = <$ns>;
          last CONNECTED unless defined $_;
          last COMMAND if /^$EOF$/;
          push @data, $_;
      } # whilend COMMAND

      $_ = $data[0];

    CASE:
      {
          /get_subnet_list/ and do { gsl $ns, @data; last CASE };
          /get_subnet_file/ and do { gsf $ns, @data; last CASE };
          /put_subnet_file/ and do { psf $ns, @data; last CASE };
          /unl_subnet_file/ and do { usf $ns, @data; last CASE };
          print $ns "1 Unknown command '$_'";
      } # casend

      print $ns "$EOF\n";
  } # whilend CONNECTED
```

Perhaps the simplest example of an IPADM command processor is the subroutine gsl, the get_subnet_list handler. Assuming it can open the SDB directory, it creates an array of filenames ending in *.sdb*, then reads the first line of each file, and outputs the filename and title line on the network socket. Notice gsl also provides status and/or error messages.

```
sub gsl {

    my($ns, @data) = @_;

    unless (opendir S, $SDB_PATH) {
        print $ns "1 Cannot Read SDB Directory $SDB_PATH: $!.\n";
        return;
    }
```

```
    my(@dirent) = grep /^.+\.sdb$/, sort(readdir S);
    closedir S;
    print $ns "0 OK\n";

    while ($_ = shift @dirent) {
        open S, "$SDB_PATH/$_" or die "Cannot open $_: $!";
        my $title = <S>;
        ($title) = $title =~ /^\s*Title\s*=\s*(.*)$/;
        print $ns "$_ $title\n";
        close S;
    }

} # end get_subnet_list
```

Locking an SDB File

Potentially, several network clients and this daemon could be vying for a single SDB file, so it's imperative that we provide a reliable locking mechanism. For example, the Perl/Tk client *ipadm* wants exclusive access so it can modify the SDB, while this daemon wants exclusive access so it can read the SDB without fear of it changing under its nose.

We have at our disposal a cool module that implements advisory file locking using LockFile objects. As the word advisory suggests, this module only advises us if we have an exclusive lock on a file; it can't actually enforce or guarantee exclusiveness. The underlying locking mechanism is implemented via the Perl built-in flock function, with all its caveats and limitations, although in this mutually cooperative environment where everyone uses LockFile, it works just fine.

But LockFile doesn't lock the SDB files; it's more clever than that. Instead, it locks access to an entire lock directory, where it creates special symbolic links that encode which SDBs are locked, who owns the locks, and when the locks were created.

An SDB is locked with a call like this:

```
my $lock = LockFile->new($sdb, $id);
```

where $sdb is the SDB pathname and $id is a unique user identifier composed of username, hostname, and process ID. LockFile interlocks the lock directory by *flock*-ing a special file named *single_thread.lock*, then proceeds to create the specially coded symbolic link. Here's an example of what the lock directory might look like:

```
lrwxr-xr-x Aug 11 23:33 Subnet_128B.sdb-lock -> bug@Pandy:193041
-rw-r--r-- Jul 10 21:54 single_thread.lock
```

The symbolic link tells us what subnet is locked (subnet 128B, the Rubber Band Development department), when it was locked, and what username, computer, and process ID has the lock.

Because we know the time a subnet was locked, it's possible to implement *lock time-outs*. Once granted exclusive access to an SDB, an administrator has a guaranteed minimum amount of time to complete his work. Other lock requests arriving in this time period are granted only concurrent read access. After the lock timeout interval expires, someone else can grab the SDB, but if no one does, the original person keeps the lock indefinitely. LockFile objects have these methods at their disposal:

check_my_lock

> Returns a true value if we still have an exclusive lock

extend_lock

> Attempts to reacquire an exclusive lock on the current SDB

free

> Returns the second of the epoch when the current lock expires

owner

> Returns the owner of an exclusive SDB lock

The entire module is too long to show, but here's a small section that interlocks the lock directory and recreates the symbolic link:

```perl
my $file = $self->{-file};
my $lockname = lockname $file;
my $lockstring = $self->{-user};

sysopen(LOCK, "$LOCK_PATH/single_thread.lock", O_RDWR|O_CREAT) or
    do {carp "Can't open single_thread.lock: $!"; return 0};
flock(LOCK, LOCK_EX) or
    do {carp "Can't flock single_thread.lock: $!"; return 0};

my (@ls) = lstat $lockname;
unless (@ls) {               # file not locked, grab it
    symlink $lockstring, $lockname or die $!;
    close LOCK;
    return 1;
} else {                     # file lock held
    my $expires = ($ls[10] ||= 0) + ($self->lock_time * 60); # seconds
    if ((time > $expires) or $self->check_my_lock) {
        unlink $lockname or die $!;# lock's expired, or is mine,
        symlink $lockstring, $lockname or die $!;# so recreate it
        close LOCK;
        return 1;
    } else {                 # lock belongs to someone else
        close LOCK;
        my $free = localtime $expires;
        my $owner = readlink $lockname or die $!;
        $self->{free} = $free;
        $self->{owner} = $owner;
        return 0;
    }
}
```

Updating the DHCP and DNS Configuration Files

ipadmd maintains a DBM file whose keys are SDB filenames and whose values indicate when the SDB file was last filtered, i.e., when it was incorporated in the DHCP and DNS configuration files. The following statements bind the DBM file $MOD_DB_PATH (creating it if needed) to the global hash %MODTIMES and initialize an alarm handler that calls update_network_dbs every minute.

```
tie %MODTIMES, 'SDBM_File', $MOD_DB_PATH, O_RDWR|O_CREAT, 0644;
$SIG{ALRM} = \&update_network_dbs;
alarm 60;
```

This crude version of update_network_dbs compares the DBM's last filter time with the SDB's last modification time (second of the Unix epoch), gets an exclusive lock on the SDB file, and updates the network configuration files and DBM last filter time.

However, a better approach might be to make a list of modified SDBs and have the filter operate on all of them, so the configuration files are updated only once. This minimizes DHCP and DNS query delays, since the process of reinitializing these daemons can be lengthy.

```
sub update_network_dbs {

    # Compare subnet database files and SDBM last modification
    # dates. Lock recently changed files and update dhcpd.conf
    # and the named zone files.

    opendir S, $SDB_PATH or warn "Cannot open $SDB_PATH: $!";
    my(@dirent) = grep /^.+\.sdb$/, readdir S;
    closedir S;

    while (my $subnet = shift @dirent) {
        $MODTIMES{$subnet} ||= 0;
        my $last_mod = (stat "$SDB_PATH/$subnet")[9];
        if ($last_mod > $MODTIMES{$subnet}) {
            # Lock the subnet file, update DHCP/DNS config files.
            $MODTIMES{$subnet} = $last_mod;
        }
    }

    $SIG{ALRM} = \&update_network_dbs;
    alarm 60;

} # end update_network_dbs
```

What About Security?

That's beyond the scope of this book. Really. See Recipe 17.7 in the *Perl Cookbook* (O'Reilly).

Polling Win32 Sockets

If fileevent fails us in a Win32 environment, a simple and effective remedy, suggested by Brand Hilton, is to poll the socket ourselves. Here we have a simple *poll* daemon that works on Unix and Win32. It waits for a connect on port 10254 and outputs 5 bytes on the socket every five seconds. (Please excuse the lack of error processing.)

```
use IO::Socket;
use Tk;
use strict;

my $socket = IO::Socket::INET->new(
    Listen    => 5,
    Reuse     => 1,
    LocalPort => 10254,
    Proto     => 'tcp',
) or die "Couldn't open socket: $!";

my $new_sock = $socket->accept();
while (1) {
    syswrite $new_sock, "polld";
    sleep 5;
}
```

Given that, we'd expect the following Tk *poll* client to work in both operating environments. The client packs a Text widget, connects to the *poll* daemon, and creates a fileevent handler to read the incoming socket data and append it to the Text widget. It works perfectly under Unix, but alas, on Win32, the I/O handler is never called.

```
use IO::Socket;
use Tk;
use strict;

my $mw = MainWindow->new;
my $text = $mw->Text->pack;
my $sock = IO::Socket::INET->new(PeerAddr => 'localhost:10254');
die "Cannot connect" unless defined $sock;
$mw->fileevent($sock, 'readable' => \&read_sock);
MainLoop;

sub read_sock {
    my $numbytes = 5;
    my $line;
    while ($numbytes) {
        my $buf;
        my $num = sysread $sock, $buf, $numbytes;
        $numbytes -= $num;
        $line .= $buf;
    }
    $text->insert('end',"$line\n");
}
```

Here's a revised *poll* client that still uses fileevent for Unix. But if it's running under Win32, it creates a timer event that uses select to poll the socket. You can use select directly, but the IO::Select OO interface is easier to use. So, $sel becomes our IO::Select object, to which we add one handle to monitor, the read socket. Subroutine read_sock uses the can_read method to determine if the socket has available data and, if so, sets $hand for sysread.

```perl
use IO::Socket;
use Tk;
use subs qw/read_sock/;
use vars qw/$mw $sel $sock $text/;
use strict;

$mw = MainWindow->new;
$text = $mw->Text->pack;
$sock = IO::Socket::INET->new(PeerAddr => 'localhost:10254');
die "Cannot connect" unless defined $sock;

if ($^O eq 'MSWin32') {
    use IO::Select;
    $sel = IO::Select->new;
    $sel->add($sock);
    $mw->repeat(50 => \&read_sock);
} else {
    $mw->fileevent($sock, 'readable' => \&read_sock);
}

MainLoop;

sub read_sock {
    my $hand = $sock;
    if ($^O eq 'MSWin32') {
        my (@ready) = $sel->can_read(0);
        return if $#ready == -1;
        $hand = $ready[0];
    }
    my $numbytes = length 'polld';
    my $line;
    while ($numbytes) {
        my $buf;
        my $num = sysread $hand, $buf, $numbytes;
        $numbytes -= $num;
        $line .= $buf;
    }
    $text->insert('end',"$line\n");
} # end read_sock
```

Be sure to check out Chapter 22 and see how we can employ a shared memory segment to bypass fileevent on Win32.

CHAPTER 20

IPC with send

There's an interprocess communication mechanism unique to Tk: the send* command. As originally implemented in Tcl/Tk, send transmits commands (which, in Tcl, are simply strings) to another Tcl application running on the same display. The receiving application then executes the commands and replies with the results. Think of it as an eval in the context of the receiver, performed automatically by Tcl/Tk.

Perl/Tk provides a send command too, but the default receiver is a simple stub that rejects all incoming send requests. Fortunately, we can override that behavior by writing our own receiver. And we're not constrained to merely evaling the incoming data, but can do whatever we please.

Using send, we can write remote controllers, client/server applications, parallel programs, and intriguing games. In this chapter, we'll see examples of some of these written in Perl and, in a mind-stretching twist, Tcl.

Security and Inter-Language Considerations

Tcl and Perl take slightly different approaches with regard to send security, and it's instructive to talk about each. Both require *xauth* server authentication, which essentially limits connections to the X server from trusted individuals on trusted hosts. Although *xauth* details vary, the basic idea is that a random key is generated for every X session, and an application must present this key to the X server before it's granted permission to run. The key, referred to as a magic cookie, is often stored in the file . *Xauthority* in your home directory. Only you can read the file, and your local X clients grab the key from there. Before other users or machines can access the display, you must explicitly give them the key, perhaps by providing them with a copy of your authorization file. But remember, if the key you loan to a friend falls into enemy

---

* Currently, send is not available on Win32 operating systems. This may change in the future.

hands, your machine can be hacked with deadly efficiency. If you suspect *xauth* authentication has been compromised, start a new X session, so the cookie changes.

Many modern X environments automatically initialize and use *xauth* authentication, and *ssh* (the secure shell) propagates this information automatically, so life is easy. But there are still lots of people using *xhost* authentication, and send will just not work. Rightly so, because, as its name implies, this mechanism only limits authentication to a list of hosts, and any process on those computers can connect to your display. If you must use send with *xhost*, you'll have to build Tk with TK_NO_SECURITY set to true.

This Unix patch, applied with a command similar to patch -p0 < file.pat, is relative to Tk 800.021 and is another way to disable security:

```
--- pTk/mTk/unix/tkUnixSend.c~      Sun Dec 12 08:58:37 1999
+++ pTk/mTk/unix/tkUnixSend.c       Fri Apr 21 13:13:30 2000
@@ -696,6 +696,8 @@
     int numHosts, secure;
     Bool enabled;

+    return 1;                    /* no security */
+
    secure = 0;
    addrPtr = XListHosts(dispPtr->display, &numHosts, &enabled);
    if (enabled && (numHosts == 0)) {
```

Application Names

To verify that send works, run the *rmt* program (also available from the Perl/Tk distribution). This is a Tk remote controller that can send Perl commands to itself, although before *rmt* can send anything, it needs to know the address, or application name, of the target application.

Every Tk program is automatically assigned a default application name, usually the filename of the program, although the appname method can set the name programmatically. To avoid ambiguities, Tk insists that application names be unique and appends a number if needed, as shown in Figure 20-1.

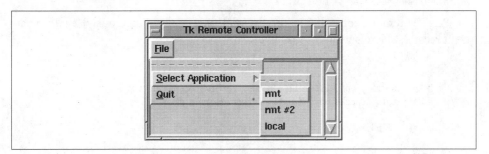

Figure 20-1. A remote controller showing application names

To find your own application name, use the name method, and to see a list of active Tk programs, use interps:

```
my $name     = $mw->name;

my(@interps) = $mw->interps;
```

For the test, select the *rmt* application and type this statement in the window:

```
print STDOUT $MW, "\n";
```

Something like "MainWindow=HASH(0x822b090)" should print on your terminal, indicating that send is functioning normally. If the widget reference of the text widget you just typed into was $t, and you didn't like its background color, the following code changes it for you:

```
$t->configure(-background => 'azure');
```

Let's look under the hood and see how all this works.

Tk::Receive

As mentioned earlier, it's impossible to send to a Perl/Tk program unless its author has explicitly overridden the default receiver, Tk::Receive, and supplied her own. In this regard, Perl/Tk is a bit more secure than Tcl/Tk, since Tcl/Tk receives by default and requires programmers to disable that behavior manually. Perl/Tk goes even further and assumes that incoming data is tainted, so the program must run with taint checks on (–T command-line parameter). Tainted data is untrusted information coming from outside the program, so all received data, user input, command-line arguments in @ARGV, and most environment variables should be treated with suspicion. In fact, the HOME environment variable needs initialization just to create the MainWindow:

```
$ENV{HOME} = '/home/frog';
```

This prevents the program from aborting with this taint error:

```
tainted at /usr/local/lib/perl5/site_perl/5.005/i686-linux/Tk/MainWindow.pm line 55.
MainWindow->new( ) at ./rmt line 19
```

The Perl/Tk remote controller naturally (and potentially dangerously) evals whatever it receives. Here's what it looks like:

```
sub Tk::Receive {

    # For security you must roll you own `receive' command, run
    # with taint checks on and untaint the received data.

    my($mw, $cmd) = @_;

    $cmd =~ /(.*)/;
    $cmd = $1;
    eval $cmd; get_eval_status;

} # end Tk::Receive
```

The subroutine is called with two arguments: the application's MainWindow reference and a string containing whatever was sent, anywhere from a single line of text to an entire file. The string is then untainted and blindly evaled.

For completeness, this is how send is invoked:

```
$t->send($appname, $cmd);
```

The Perl/Tk remote controller is designed to talk to other Perl/Tk applications, although there's no reason it can't connect to a Tcl/Tk application, as long as we remember to send Tcl/Tk commands (and vice versa, depending on which end is sending). Then again, a Tcl/Tk application returns Tcl results to the Perl sender, so it becomes unclear exactly how send should behave between languages. Indeed, this is another reason Perl/Tk left the receiving side of the interoperability equation undefined.

In this section, we used send in a pure Perl environment. The following sections investigate send in other applications. The first is pure Tcl, while the second is a hybrid Tcl-Perl mix.

Computing π with Parallel Message Passing

Scientists demand the most powerful computing machinery available, whether they model global atmospheric conditions, decipher the human genome, study viscous fluid dynamics, visualize plasmas in 3 dimensions, or vibrate strings in 14. Besides tons of disk space (perhaps a terabyte for */tmp* alone) and tremendous I/O and memory bandwidth, they want raw CPU power. Since no single CPU will ever suffice, scientists work with vector and massively parallel computers.

In parallel programming, we try to divide the work of a sequential program into portions so that many processors can work on the problem simultaneously. For example, this code[*] computes π by integrating the function $4 / (1 + x^2)$ in the range $-.5 \leq x < .5$:

```
my $intervals = 1_000;
my $h = 1.0 / $intervals;
my $sum = 0.0;

for(my $i = 1; $i <= $intervals; $i++) {
    my $x = $h * ($i - 0.5);
    $sum += 4.0 / (1.0 + $x*$x);
}

my $pi = $h * $sum;
```

The variable $intervals defines the granularity of the summation and, hence, the accuracy of the computation. To get a good result, the interval must be very finely

---

[*] This is a Perl version of the C example from the public domain MPICH distribution, available at *http://www-unix.mcs.anl.gov/mpi/mpich/download.html*. Notice two optimizations: the factor $h is turned into multiplication because it's faster than division; likewise, multiplying $x by itself is faster than exponentiation.

divided, which, of course, increases the program's running time. But suppose we parcel out the work to two processors, with each one integrating only half of the curve? If we then add the two partial sums, the value of π is the same, but the computational wall-clock time is halved. In fact, putting 10 processors to work completes the job an order of magnitude faster, because this problem scales well.

The Message Passing Protocol

Writing parallel code requires some mechanism through which the processors can communicate with each other. Generally, there's a master processor that sets initial conditions and, later, collects results. In our case, assume the master is responsible for telling the slave processors which portion of the curve they are to integrate, collecting the slaves' partial sums, adding them together, and reporting the value of π.

To implement this communication, we use a message passing scheme very similar to that found on parallel supercomputers. The big iron might use shared memory or high-speed interconnects to transfer megabytes of data, but this example just sends a few scalars back and forth.

It's unlikely you have access to a parallel computer, so we'll make do using multiple processes on a single CPU. The first process, the master, creates a MainWindow, menubar, and two Entry widgets that select the number of intervals and slave processes, as shown in Figure 20-2. It's also responsible for starting the helpers, sending them their starting values, and collecting their results.

Each slave opens a MainWindow and populates it with a Label widget displaying intermediate results. When a slave finishes, it sends its result to the master.

With true message passing, there's a blocking receive command that reads the message queue and synchronizes the processors. There's nothing like that in Tk, but we can simulate it using tkwait variable, the Tcl way of saying waitVariable, which logically suspends a processor until a variable's value changes. As long as each processor understands the protocol—when and what to send, and when and what variable to wait for—we're okay. Protocol details follow in the next two sections, during the examination of the Tcl/Tk code.

Tcl/Tk Slave Processor Code

At less than 25 lines, the slave code *pihelp.tcl* makes a good starting point. It's simple, concise, and maps well to Perl/Tk, so you should follow it easily. I think you'll find learning a little Tcl/Tk to be worthwhile, and you can add another bullet to your resumé. Plus, there's a lot of Tcl/Tk code out there, and this small diversion might assist you when doing a Perl/Tk port.

```
wm title . "Pi helper [tk appname]"
wm iconname . "pihelp"
```

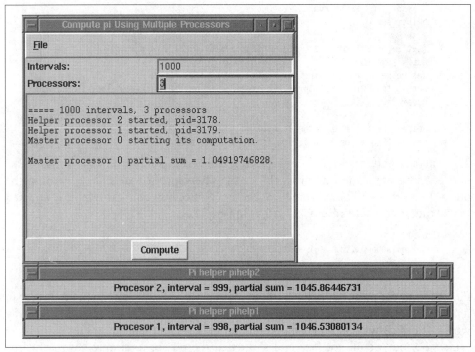

Figure 20-2. Computing pi with a master and two slave processors

In Tcl/Tk, strings identify widgets, not object references, and the MainWindow is always . (dot). These two window manager commands initialize the MainWindow's title and icon name. Tcl has double-quote interpolation just like Perl, as well as command substitution, indicated by square brackets. Here, Tcl fetches the program's application name before interpolating the title string and assigning it to the MainWindow.

```
set status ""
label .l -textvariable status -width 80
pack .l
```

Tcl has scalars just like Perl, and set assigns values to those variables. Notice that, as in shell programming, there's no leading $. The $ is used only when it's time to evaluate a variable. We then pack an 80-character Label widget, .l, a child of the Main-Window, with an associated text variable.

```
#set numprocs 0
#set proc 0
#set intervals 0
tkwait variable intervals
```

These three set commands are commented out, because it's up to the master processor to initialize these variables (we need to read them but dare not write them). So we idle, waiting for our master to send the three real set commands. When the set intervals command arrives, it changes the value of intervals, the tkwait completes, and we continue.

```
set h [expr 1.0 / $intervals]
set helper_sum 0

for {set i [expr $proc + 1]} {$i <= $intervals} {incr i $numprocs} {
    set x [expr $h * ($i - 0.5)]
    set helper_sum [expr $helper_sum +  4.0 / (1.0 + $x*$x)]
    set status "Processor $proc, interval = $i, partial sum = $helper_sum"
    update idletasks
}
set helper_sum [expr $h * $helper_sum]
set status "Processor $proc, final sum = $helper_sum"
```

This is a straightforward Tcl translation of the Perl-π-computing code we saw earlier. It only sums "one numprocs-th" of the interval, but that's okay, because the other "numprocs - 1" processors sum the rest. Notice how the status label is updated in real time, via update idletasks, just as in Perl/Tk.

```
while {1} {
    catch {send pi.tcl "set sums($proc) $helper_sum"}
    after 1000
}
```

Finally, send the partial sum back to the master, who is expecting to see it appear in its sums associative array, indexed by processor number. A Tcl associative array works the same way as a Perl hash; in fact, Perl used to call its hashes associative arrays too, but we all got lazy and shortened the phrase to simply hash (which is more descriptive anyway).

The catch construct ignores errors (perhaps the sendee has ended?) and works just like Tk::catch. The infinite loop, better written with repeat in Perl/Tk, broadcasts our result until the master receives it and kills us. The send is repeated to keep the master from deadlocking, because it's more likely harvesting another processor's result. The next section clarifies matters, as we bring together all the loose ends.

Tcl/Tk Master Processor Code

For brevity, we'll focus only on the three subroutines from *pi.tcl* that create the user interface (Figure 20-2) and handle the send/receive transactions.

create_interface places the MainWindow on the display and initializes its title and icon name. It then creates the MainWindow's menubar and adds the File menubutton cascade with a Quit menu item. With the exception of having to explicitly define the cascade menu, we do exactly this in Perl/Tk. Underneath the menubar are, essentially, two labeled Entry widgets, which are created from scratch by packing Label and Entry widgets side-by-side in container frames. (We'd use LabEntry widgets in Perl/Tk.) Finally, it packs a Text widget that displays results and a Compute button that initiates a computation.

```
proc create_interface {} {

    wm geometry . "+100+100"
    wm title . "Compute pi Using Multiple Processors"
    wm iconname . "pi"

    # Create menubar, menubuttons, menus and callbacks.

    menu .mb
    . configure -menu .mb

    .mb add cascade -label File -underline 0 -menu .mb.file
    menu .mb.file
    .mb.file add command -label Quit -command {destroy .}

    # Frame to hold itervals label and entry widgets.

    frame .f
    pack .f -fill x
    label .f.s -text "Intervals: "
    entry .f.e -width 25 -textvariable intervals
    pack .f.s -side left
    pack .f.e -side right

    # Frame to hold number of processors label and entry widgets.

    frame .f2
    pack .f2 -fill x
    label .f2.s -text "Processors: "
    entry .f2.e -width 25 -textvariable numprocs
    pack .f2.s -side left
    pack .f2.e -side right

    # Text widget to hold results.

    text .t -width 50 -height 14
    pack .t -fill both -expand 1

    button .c -text Compute -command {compute_pi}
    pack .c

}; # end create_interface
```

start_helpers_calculating first executes all the Tk helper programs, which then wait for a start message, as described in the previous section. It records all the process IDs and ensures that all instances of the helper (*pihelp.tcl*) have different application names (-name) and appear as nicely spaced columns on the display (-geometry). After a 2-second delay, which gives the helpers time to synchronize on their tkwait variable command, it sends each helper three Tcl set commands. After the set intervals command is evaluated in the context of the helpers, they begin computing their partial sums.

In contrast to the Perl way, note that each Tcl variable is local to a subroutine, and global variables must be explicitly declared with a global command (or, you can poke around the call stack using uplevel and upvar).

```
proc start_helpers_calculating {} {

    global helper intervals numprocs pids proc sums
    global wishexe

    set proc [expr $numprocs - 1]
    set y 420
    while {$proc > 0} {
        set pids($proc) [exec $wishexe -name pihelp${proc} \
            -geometry +100+${y} < $helper &]
        status "Helper processor $proc started, pid=$pids($proc)."
        incr y 50
        incr proc [expr -1]
    }
    after 2000

    set proc [expr $numprocs - 1]
    while {$proc > 0} {
            send pihelp${proc} "set numprocs $numprocs; \
                set proc $proc; set intervals $intervals"
            incr proc [expr -1]
    }

}; # end start_helpers_calculating
```

sum_reduce simulates a sum reduction, which is a message-passing operation that reads data from all helper processors and reduces the results to a single value by summing. It waits for each helper, in turn, to store its partial sum in the sums associative array and kills the helper afterward. Finally, it adds its own partial sum and returns the reduced result, π.

```
proc sum_reduce {} {

    # Do a sum reduction.  Fetch all the partial sums computed
    # by the helper processors, and then add them to our partial
    # sum.  The result is an approximation of pi.

    global helper intervals numprocs pids proc sums

    set pi 0
    for {set proc 1} {$proc < $numprocs} {incr proc} {
        tkwait variable sums($proc)
        status "Partial sum from processor $proc = $sums($proc)."
        set pi [expr $pi + $sums($proc)]
        exec kill $pids($proc)
    }
    return [expr $pi + $sums(0)]

}; # end sum_reduce
```

Figure 20-3 shows the outcome.

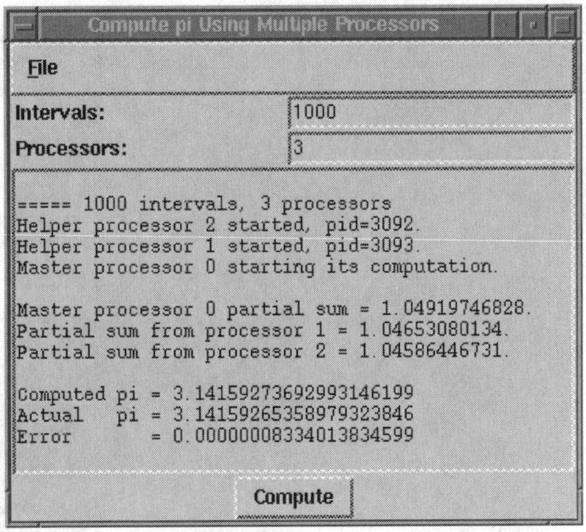

```
┌─────────────────────────────────────────────────┐
│ ─ │    Compute pi Using Multiple Processors    │ ▫ ▫ ▪│
│ ┌─────────────────────────────────────────────────┐ │
│ │ File                                              │ │
│ │ Intervals:        │1000                          │ │
│ │ Processors:       │3                             │ │
│ ├───────────────────────────────────────────────┤ │
│ │ ===== 1000 intervals, 3 processors             │ │
│ │ Helper processor 2 started, pid=3092.          │ │
│ │ Helper processor 1 started, pid=3093.          │ │
│ │ Master processor 0 starting its computation.   │ │
│ │                                                 │ │
│ │ Master processor 0 partial sum = 1.04919746828.│ │
│ │ Partial sum from processor 1 = 1.04653080134.  │ │
│ │ Partial sum from processor 2 = 1.04586446731.  │ │
│ │                                                 │ │
│ │ Computed pi = 3.14159273692993146199           │ │
│ │ Actual   pi = 3.14159265358979323846           │ │
│ │ Error       = 0.00000008334013834599           │ │
│ │                                                 │ │
│ │              ┌──────────┐                       │ │
│ │              │ Compute  │                       │ │
│ │              └──────────┘                       │ │
│ └─────────────────────────────────────────────────┘ │
└─────────────────────────────────────────────────┘
```

Figure 20-3. An estimated value of pi, with error

TclRobots

TclRobots, written by Tom Poindexter, is a test of programming prowess. The goal is to program a robot that battles other robots and hopefully, survives to become the victor. How well a robot performs depends mostly on the Robot Control Program (RCP) you write. As in real life, there is randomness built into the contest, so even the best RCP is occasionally defeated.

The TclRobots arena is a square, 1,000 meters on each side. Robots, identical other than their controlling RCPs, have drive mechanisms that move them each in a given direction at a given velocity within the arena, scanners for seeking out enemy robots, and cannons for firing at the enemy. A contest involves two, three, or four robots, each trying to outlast the others. In Figure 20-4, two robot scanners have targeted enemies, *complex.tr* has taken a severe hit, and a cannon shot is in mid-flight.

tclrobots starts a robot instance by execing a new *wish* interpreter,[*] then uses send to customize it. First, it transmits specially crafted subroutines that implement the RCP command set (commands such as drive, scan, and cannon). These commands define the RCP application programming interface (API), and they use send to invoke subroutines in *tclrobots*. Next, *tclrobots* sends the Tcl RCP source code to the robot and starts it running. (There's actually a *lot* more detail behind the scenes. Feel free to visit the *tclrobots* source code.)

---

[*] Just like in the message passing example, although this is Tom's idea, not mine.

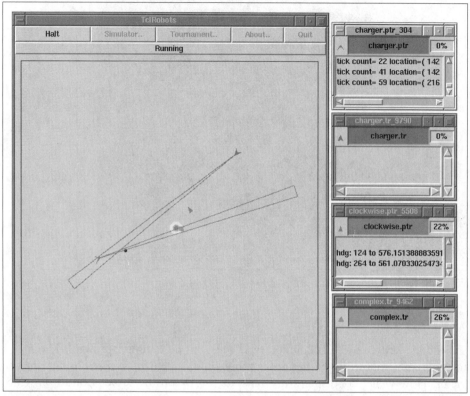

Figure 20-4. A TclRobots contest

Until now, the only RCP programming language available was Tcl, but my desire to write RCPs in Perl changed that, as we are about to see. Several things are required before a Perl RCP is possible. First, *tclrobots* needs to distinguish between a Tcl and Perl RCP. Since the convention of using the extension *.tr*, for TclRobot, was already in place, I selected *.ptr*, for PerlTclRobot. Thus, *tclrobots* checks for those extensions and differentially loads *perl* or *wish*. Second, incoming Tcl messages must be translated into proper Perl actions, and results returned in Tcl format. Lastly, the RCP API needs to be re-implemented in Perl so it sends Tcl commands and returns Perl results.

TclRobots.pm, the Perl Interface to TclRobots

This module implements a thin API so you can write RCPs in your favorite language—Perl—and do battle with all the existing Tcl RCPs. It's one of the strangest modules around, mixing Exporter subroutines; Perl, Tk, and Tcl code; and inter-language, bidirectional communications. You never knowingly *use* this module; rather, it's included when *tclrobots* runs an instance of `perl -MTclRobots`, at which time this module is loaded and begins execution on behalf of your RCP. It creates the main window of the required dimensions and at the proper location on the display, and adds all the widgets, text, and images. When instructed by *tclrobots*, the module then loads your Perl RCP via require, so be sure the code returns a true value. From that point on, incoming TclRobots messages are dispatched to Perl emulation handlers, and Perl RCP commands are converted to Tcl syntax and sent to *tclrobots*. The communication is handled transparently via send and Tk::Receive.

Tk::Receive handles tclrobots to Perl communications

To figure out the TclRobots protocol, the first version of Tk::Receive simply dumped messages to a file for study. A little experimentation determined what *tclrobots* sent and what it expected to receive. Some messages were easy to dechiper, like expr 1+1, which obviously must return 2. Other messages create and modify the Tk interface or start and stop the RCP. The final version of Tk::Receive follows; note that all global symbols are prefixed with an underscore, indicating they are private to *TclRobots. pm*. The CASE statement simply uses several regular expressions to pattern match the incoming Tcl commands and call a Perl handler.

```perl
sub Tk::Receive {

    # Accept Tcl strings from tclrobots and invoke
    # Perl/Tk emulation code.

    my($mw) = shift;        # main window
    $_ = shift;             # Tcl command

    return 2 if /expr 1\+1/;
    return if /(Knuth|^rename)/m;

CASE:
  {
        /setup window/m     and do {_setup_window_;        last CASE};
        /create|configure/  and do {_customize_window_ $_; last CASE};
        /set _start_ 0/     and do {_load_rcp_;            last CASE};
        /set _start_ 1/     and do {_start_rcp_;           last CASE};
        /^proc after/       and do {_disable_rcp_;         last CASE};
        /\.d\.l insert/     and do {_insult_rcp_ $_;       last CASE};
        /^_a_\d+ 0 _e_\d+/  and do {_destroy_rcp_;         last CASE};
        /^set/              and do {_set_variables_ $_;    last CASE};
        print STDERR "UNHANDLED cmd=$_!\n";
  } # casend

} # end Tk::Receive
```

As an example, _setup_window_ creates the small RCP MainWindow shown in Figure 20-4, containing a tiny Canvas and two Labels. These display the RCP's icon, filename, and damage percentage, respectively. Below these widgets is a scrolled Listbox for debug and status information. (The following section describes when and how the MainWindow, $_mw_, is created.)

```perl
sub _setup_window_ {

    # Setup the RCP's debug and damage window.
```

```
    my $f = $_mw_->Frame;
    $f->pack(qw/-side top -fill x -ipady 5/);
    $_fc_ = $f->Canvas(qw/-width 20 -height 16/);
    $_fl_ = $f->Label(qw/-relief sunken -width 30  -text/ =>
            "(loading robot code..)");
    $_fs_ = $f->Label(qw/-relief sunken -width 5   -text/ => "0%");
    $_fc_->pack(qw/-side left/);
    $_fs_->pack(qw/-side right/);
    $_fl_->pack(qw/-side left -expand 1 -fill both/);

    $_dl_ = $_mw_->Scrolled('Listbox', qw/-relief sunken -scrollbars se/);
    $_dl_->pack(qw/-side left  -expand 1 -fill both/);
    $_mw_->minsize(100, 70);
    $_mw_->update;

}
```

The RCP API handles Perl to tclrobots communications

TclRobots.pm is a plain old module that exports subroutines. Specifically, it exports
the RCP commands that control the robot. Unlike other Perl modules, however,
once loaded, this one begins executing, creates a MainWindow, enters the Tk event
loop, and never returns. I've distilled the salient portions:

```
$TclRobots::VERSION = '2.1';

package TclRobots;

# This module implements a thin API that interfaces ...

use Exporter;
@ISA = qw/Exporter/;
@EXPORT = qw/after alert cannon damage dputs drive dsp
    heat loc_x loc_y scanner speed team_declare team_get
    team_send tick update/;

use Tk;
use Tk::widgets qw/Dialog/;

use vars qw/$_mw_/;
use strict;

$ENV{'HOME'} = '/tmp';
$_mw_ = MainWindow->new;
MainLoop;

# Robot Control Program commands ...

sub drive {
}
sub scan {
}
sub cannon {
}
```

In Tcl, the RCP command to move a robot is drive:

```
drive $heading $velocity
```

The heading is given in degrees, 0 to 359, with 0 degrees due east, rotating counter-clockwise. The velocity is a percentage, from 0 to 100. Here's the Perl drive implementation; all RCP subroutines follow this format:

```
sub drive {
    my($deg, $speed) = @_;
    $_mw_->after(100);
    $_mw_->update;
    my $val = Tk::catch {$_mw_->send($_tclrobots_,
                "do_drive $_robot_ $deg $speed")};
    $_mw_->waitVariable(\$_resume_) if $_debug and $_step_;
    &_ping_check_;
    $_mw_->update;
    return $val;
}
```

The subroutine first delays for 100 milliseconds (reflecting the fact that hardware commands take a finite amount of time), invokes *tclrobots'* do_drive subroutine, and returns the result. For debugging purposes, the RCP can be single-stepped, which is what the waitVariable statement is for. An RCP can also define a callback alerting it when an enemy robot scans it; _ping_check_ invokes any such callback.

Robot Control Programs

"Do I flee when scanned, or do I turn and attack? How do I know where I am? I've kept a list of enemy robots and their locations, which do I shoot at first? How do I keep from running into an arena wall? How do I steer? How do I get from point A to point B? How do I compensate for my motion when computing a firing solution?" We certainly won't answer these questions, but just in case you think writing an RCP is easy, think again!

A good way to start writing your own RCP is to examine the samples, and the tournament entries at *http://www.neosoft.com/tcl/ftparchive/sorted/misc/TclRobots/*. Or search the Web; I've found Computer Science courses that teach RCP programming! And, of course, read the manpage.

Let's take a quick look at the Perl version of a sample RCP, *charger.ptr*. It's one of the shortest RCPs I've seen, yet it's surprisingly effective. Its strategy is simple: scan with a wide resolution until an enemy robot is found, charge the opponent, pinpoint the target with a narrow scan, and fire the cannon. Notice the code is strictly Perl, no Tcl or Tk required. The $status callback, executed every 10 seconds, demonstrates how to emulate repeat if it's not part of the language. It posts the robot's current position and the hardware tick count in the debug window. The scanner command expects the direction and resolution of the scan and returns the distance to the first target found. The cannon command fires a shell in the specified direction for the specified distance.

```
use vars qw/$dir $closest $limit $nothing $rng $start $status/;
use strict;

$dir = 90;
$nothing = 0;
$closest = 0;

$status = sub {
    dputs "tick count=", tick, "location=(", loc_x, ",", loc_y, ")";
    after 10_000 => \&$status;
};
after 0 => \&$status;              # Tcl idiom for repeat()

while (1) {
    $rng = scanner $dir, 10;      # look for an opponent
    if ($rng > 0 and $rng < 700) { # if found and in range
        $start = ($dir+20)%360;   # begin narrow scan
        for ($limit = 1; $limit <= 40; $limit++) {
            $dir = ($start - $limit + 360) % 360;
            $rng = scanner $dir, 1;
            if ($rng > 0 and $rng < 700) {
                $nothing = 0;              # charge!  fire a shell, and backup
                cannon $dir, $rng;         # scan so not to miss a moving target
                drive $dir, 70;
                $limit -= 4;
            }
        }
    } else {
        $nothing++;
        $closest = $dir if $rng > 700;
    }

    drive 0, 0;

    if ($nothing >= 30) {  # check for nothing found in reasonable time
        $nothing = 0;
        drive $closest, 100;
        after 10000 => sub {drive 0, 0};
    }
    $dir = ($dir - 20 + 360) % 360;
}

1;
```

Unsurprisingly, trigonometry plays an important part in any nontrivial RCP. Here are two formulas I've found useful. The first computes the distance between two points:

```
[expr hypot( ($x-$x0),($y-$y0) )]
```

You might use this to check if the robot has reached a particular coordinate or to calculate the range to a target. The second equation computes a heading between two points:

```
[expr (round($R2D * atan2(($y-$y0),($x-$x0))) + 360) % 360]
```

This is useful for steering the robot. The variable $R2D converts radians to degrees and is given by:

```
set R2D [expr 180.0 / π]
```

Of course, by now, you are fully capable of computing π and translating these simple Tcl statements to Perl.

Turn to Appendix C for a listing of *complex.ptr*, a sophisticated RCP written in Perl. This RCP is completely state driven and uses clock ticks to schedule internal events. It moves in a path described by an *n*-sided polygon that approximates a circle. The direction of movement is randomly chosen during preset, eliminating "wall" code (although the RCP may perform a "crazy Ivan" if it cannot find an enemy). The RCP also attempts to move as fast as possible, thus tracks its cooling rate to coordinate turns, eliminating "flee" code. There is also some watchdog code that periodically checks the RCP's health. Finally, the robot recognizes team members and targets only real enemies.

## CHAPTER 21

C Widget Internals

Chances are you'll never have to deal with Tk widgets at the C level, because the existing toolkit is so rich, and because you can quickly and efficiently build new mega-widgets using the powerful techniques described in Chapter 14. But there may come a time when you have to leave the cozy world of Perl and delve into C, perhaps because of efficiency considerations, or a missing system call, or maybe because you have an existing Tcl/Tk C widget you'd like to port to Perl/Tk.

In this chapter, we'll closely examine a simple (but real) C widget and see how to package, build, test, and install it. This is a Unix-centric chapter, because we have no Win32 development environment. But the porting essentials are still relevant.

The Tk::Square Widget

The Tcl/Tk distribution contains a Square widget that demonstrates the basic structure of a C widget. It's a simple square of variable size and color that can be moved around a window by dragging it with a mouse. It has a keyboard binding to an "a" that starts and stops an animation that varies the widget's size over time, so that it appears to throb.

Tcl/Tk Example

Although Perl/Tk code produced Figure 21-1, this Tcl/Tk example creates an identical window. The square widget, .s, is packed, assigned three bindings, and given the keyboard focus. The mouse button bindings move the square to the cursor's current position, and the "a" binding toggles the animation's state. In the Perl/Tk version, we'll see how to move the bindings into the Tk::Square class proper (seems reasonable, since it's unclear exactly what a square widget should do anyway).

```
square .s
pack .s -expand yes -fill both

bind .s <1> {move %x %y}
bind .s <B1-Motion> {move %x %y}
```

```
bind .s a animate
focus .s
```

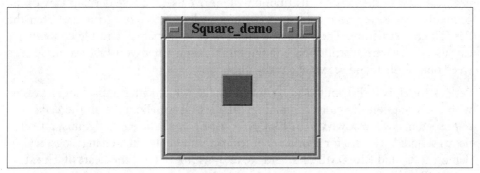

Figure 21-1. A Tk::Square with a raised relief

This procedure moves the square to a given position. The (x, y) coordinate comes from the %x and %y binding codes, analogous to the $Tk::event->x and $Tk::event->y calls. The size method returns the pixel length of the square's side, and the position method actually repositions the square.

```
proc move {x y} {
    set a [.s size]
    .s position [expr $x-($a/2)] [expr $y-($a/2)]
}
```

These procedures start and stop a 30-millisecond timer event that makes the square throb, cyclically changing its size from small to large. Trying to translate this Tcl/Tk code directly to Perl/Tk leads to deep recursion in the timer procedure, but we'll see the Perlish way around this problem in a later section. Note that size is a dual-purpose get/get command.

```
set inc 0
proc animate {} {
    global inc
    if {$inc == 0} {
        set inc 3
        timer
    } else {
        set inc 0
    }
}

proc timer {} {
    global inc
    set s [.s size]
    if {$inc == 0} return
    if {$s >= 40} {set inc -3}
    if {$s <= 10} {set inc 3}
    .s size [expr {$s+$inc}]
    after 30 timer
}
```

Overview of the Perl/Tk Distribution

A global view of the Perl/Tk distribution will prove useful as we develop C widgets, primarily because we need to pattern our new widgets' directory structures after the Perl/Tk core structure. There are also similarities in filenames and file contents we can use. The entire distribution is quite intimidating when you first see it, so let's weed out the chaff and see what's really important.

Perl/Tk for Unix is distributed as a gzipped tar file, which, after unpacking, leaves us with a distribution directory containing 201 files.[*] If we eliminate all the *demo* and *test* programs, we're down to 161 files. Now get rid of all the *bug* programs, miscellaneous scripts Nick uses for routine maintenance and debugging, change logs, widget demos, tests, and README files, and we're down to 43 files, the heart of Tk extension for Perl:

```
drwxr-xr-x  2 bug  users     65 Jan 18 14:45 Bitmap
drwxr-xr-x  2 bug  users     98 Jan 18 14:45 Canvas
drwxr-xr-x  2 bug  users     91 Jan 18 14:45 Compound
drwxr-xr-x  3 bug  users    101 Jan 18 14:45 Contrib
drwxr-xr-x  4 bug  users   4096 Jan 18 14:45 DragDrop
drwxr-xr-x  2 bug  users     63 Jan 18 14:45 Entry
drwxr-xr-x  3 bug  users   4096 Jan 18 14:45 Event
drwxr-xr-x  3 bug  users     27 Jan 18 13:11 Extensions
drwxr-xr-x  2 bug  users     80 Jan 18 14:45 HList
drwxr-xr-x  2 bug  users     57 Jan 18 14:45 IO
drwxr-xr-x  2 bug  users     84 Jan 18 14:45 InputO
drwxr-xr-x  2 bug  users     67 Jan 18 14:45 Listbox
-r--r--r--  1 bug  users  32646 Jan  8 07:21 MANIFEST
-r--r--r--  1 bug  users   3964 Dec 12 08:58 Makefile.PL
drwxr-xr-x  2 bug  users     73 Jan 18 14:45 Menubutton
drwxr-xr-x  2 bug  users     78 Jan 18 14:45 Mwm
drwxr-xr-x  2 bug  users     67 Jan 18 14:45 NBFrame
drwxr-xr-x  2 bug  users     63 Jan 18 14:45 Photo
drwxr-xr-x  2 bug  users     63 Jan 18 14:45 Scale
drwxr-xr-x  2 bug  users     71 Jan 18 14:45 Scrollbar
drwxr-xr-x  2 bug  users     63 Jan 18 14:45 TList
drwxr-xr-x  3 bug  users     89 Jan 18 14:45 Text
drwxr-xr-x  2 bug  users   4096 Jan 18 14:45 TixGrid
drwxr-xr-x  2 bug  users     65 Jan 18 14:45 TixPixmap
drwxr-xr-x  4 bug  users   4096 Jan 18 14:45 Tixish
drwxr-xr-x  3 bug  users   4096 Jan 18 14:45 Tk
-r--r--r--  1 bug  users  14457 Dec 23 17:22 Tk.pm
drwxr-xr-x  2 bug  users    100 Jan 18 14:45 WinPhoto
drwxr-xr-x  3 bug  users   4096 Jan 18 14:45 Xlib
-r--r--r--  1 bug  users   2029 Jul 27 14:20 chnGlue.c
-r--r--r--  1 bug  users   2944 Jul 27 14:20 evtGlue.c
-r--r--r--  1 bug  users  18202 Dec 12 08:58 objGlue.c
drwxr-xr-x  6 bug  users   4096 Jan 18 14:45 pTk
drwxr-xr-x  5 bug  users   4096 Jan 18 14:45 pod
```

---

[*] Tk 800.017 was used for this test.

```
-r--r--r--  1 bug  users     910 Jul 27 14:21 tixGlue.c
-r--r--r--  1 bug  users  104480 Jan  5 15:14 tkGlue.c
-r--r--r--  1 bug  users    2061 Nov 19 07:30 tkGlue.def
-r--r--r--  1 bug  users      55 Nov 20 16:19 tkGlue.exc
-r--r--r--  1 bug  users    3744 Dec 19 10:49 tkGlue.h
-r--r--r--  1 bug  users    1418 Dec 19 10:49 tkGlue.m
-r--r--r--  1 bug  users    1780 Dec 19 10:49 tkGlue.t
-r--r--r--  1 bug  users     562 Jul 27 14:21 tkGlue_f.c
-r--r--r--  1 bug  users     327 Jul 27 14:21 tkGlue_f.h
```

There are lots of familiar terms and widget names in that list, mostly directories containing *.xs*, *.pm*, and *make* files. Then there are the *glue* files that act as intermediaries between the Tcl C code and Perl. *Tk.pm* is important because it acts as the lowest Tk base class, even more basic than *Widget.pm*. And of course, where would we be without the *pod* directory of documentation? Important as these files and directories are, for our current task, this is all we are interested in:

```
-r--r--r--  1 bug  users   32646 Jan  8 07:21 MANIFEST
-r--r--r--  1 bug  users    3964 Dec 12 08:58 Makefile.PL
drwxr-xr-x  6 bug  users    4096 Jan 18 14:45 pTk
```

The *MANIFEST* is a MakeMaker utility file that lists the files and directories that must be in the distribution for Perl/Tk to build and function properly. *Makefile.PL* is an actual Perl program that uses MakeMaker commands to produce a customized *Makefile* suitable for maintaining, building, and installing a Perl extension. The *pTk* directory contains most of the Perl-ized C source code, and its subdirectory *pTk/mTk* ("m" for munge, modify, or mainline) contains the original Tcl/Tk (and Tix) C source code, with minimal hand edits.

We are going to build a parallel directory structure outside the Perl/Tk distribution (named *Tk-Square-1.0*), assemble required components, and port Tk::Square there (see Figure 21-2). And although, in practice, you shouldn't actually merge the code with the Perl/Tk core, we'll still review the requisite steps.

Layout of a Typical C Widget

Let's see how real C widgets are written. Typical Tcl/Tk widgets begin life in the directory *pTk/mTk/generic*, so we want to store *tkSquare.c*, the Tk::Square Tcl C source code, in a similar location. In its raw form, this C code has no hope of interfacing with Perl, but there's a tiny translator that handles the grunt work. The program, *pTk/Tcl-pTk*, works best on Tcl/Tk 8 source files, but can be of use even for Tix and Tcl/Tk 3/4 source files.[*] We don't usually run this program by hand, because the build process does it for us automatically. The translated source file is stored in the *pTk* directory.[†]

---

[*] Unfortunately it only makes simple syntax changes. The Tcl/Tk API changed so radically for Tk 8 that you'll be forced to make many more changes by hand. Common items include font structure and method changes, and API calls whose names changed from Tk_ to Tcl_ when the Tk event loop was moved into Tcl. Your best source of information will be the Perl/Tk discussion group and mailing list.

[†] Essentially, *make* runs *Tcl-pTk/mTk/generic/tkSquare.c tkSquare.c*.

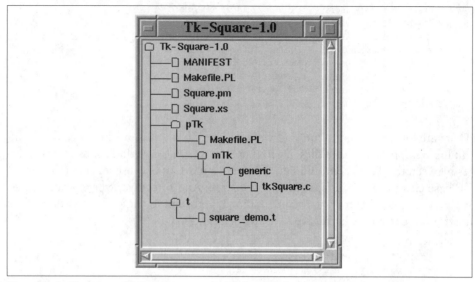

Figure 21-2. Tk::Square directory structure parallels core Tk

But the translator most likely won't do a perfect job, so any hand edits we make must be done to *pTk/mTk/generic/tkSquare.c*, and the *make* repeated. For instance, the Tcl name for the widget creation subroutine is SquareCmd, but the Perl/Tk convention requires it be Tk_SquareCmd. And the original include directives:

```
/*#include "tkPort.h"*/
/*#include "tk.h"*/
```

will not work and must be replaced with the following (it's critical to have all these includes in the proper order):

```
#include "tkPort.h"
#include "default.h"
#include "tkInt.h"
#include "tkVMacro.h"
```

To fully understand the following code, you should be familiar with Xlib programming and the Tk toolkit library. All the Tk documents have been podified and are located in the directory *pod/pTk*. Note that this code is the fully functioning Perl/Tk version, not the original Tcl/Tk source.

Tk::Square instance structure

Every Tk::Square instance is in reality modeled by a C Square structure. The widget creation subroutine, Tk_SquareCmd, mallocs memory for the structure, then initializes its members. Although programming at the C level is not object oriented, we can think of the Square structure as an object that maintains the widget's entire state. During widget destruction, we must release the structure's allocated memory.

```
typedef struct {
    Tk_Window tkwin;          /* Window that embodies the square.  NULL
```

```
                                * means window has been deleted but
                                * widget record hasn't been cleaned up yet. */
     Display *display;          /* X's token for the window's display. */
     Tcl_Interp *interp;        /* Interpreter associated with widget. */
     Tcl_Command widgetCmd;     /* Token for square's widget command. */
     int x, y;                  /* Position of square's upper-left corner
                                * within widget. */
     int size;                  /* Width and height of square. */

     int borderWidth;           /* Width of 3-D border around whole widget. */
     Tk_3DBorder bgBorder;      /* Used for drawing background. */
     Tk_3DBorder fgBorder;      /* For drawing square. */
     int relief;                /* Indicates whether window as a whole is
                                * raised, sunken, or flat. */
     GC gc;                     /* Graphics context for copying from
                                * off-screen pixmap onto screen. */
     int doubleBuffer;          /* Non-zero means double-buffer redisplay
                                * with pixmap;  zero means draw straight
                                * onto the display. */
     int updatePending;         /* Non-zero means a call to SquareDisplay
                                * has already been scheduled. */
 } Square;
```

Tk::Square configuration specifications

The following table of configuration specifications should look strikingly familiar. Yes, here we define the legal widget options, which can appear on the widget creation command, or cget and configure methods. The first element of each option describes what it is, followed by the option name, resource DB name, resource DB class, and default value (the same as a ConfigSpecs entry for a Perl mega-widget).

One interesting option is -dbl, which specifies how the widget is displayed. For efficiency, and to reduce flicker, widgets are often double buffered; that is, drawn in an off-screen pixmap and then displayed. If -dbl is disabled (false), the widget is drawn directly to the screen.

```
    static Tk_ConfigSpec configSpecs[] = {
        {TK_CONFIG_BORDER, "-background", "background", "Background",
                "#d9d9d9", Tk_Offset(Square, bgBorder), TK_CONFIG_COLOR_ONLY},
        {TK_CONFIG_BORDER, "-background", "background", "Background",
                "white", Tk_Offset(Square, bgBorder), TK_CONFIG_MONO_ONLY},
        {TK_CONFIG_SYNONYM, "-bd", "borderWidth", NULL,
                NULL, 0, 0},
        {TK_CONFIG_SYNONYM, "-bg", "background", NULL,
                NULL, 0, 0},
        {TK_CONFIG_PIXELS, "-borderwidth", "borderWidth", "BorderWidth",
                "2", Tk_Offset(Square, borderWidth), 0},
        {TK_CONFIG_INT, "-dbl", "doubleBuffer", "DoubleBuffer",
                "1", Tk_Offset(Square, doubleBuffer), 0},
        {TK_CONFIG_SYNONYM, "-fg", "foreground", NULL,
                NULL, 0, 0},
        {TK_CONFIG_BORDER, "-foreground", "foreground", "Foreground",
                "#b03060", Tk_Offset(Square, fgBorder), TK_CONFIG_COLOR_ONLY},
        {TK_CONFIG_BORDER, "-foreground", "foreground", "Foreground",
```

```
                  "black", Tk_Offset(Square, fgBorder), TK_CONFIG_MONO_ONLY},
        {TK_CONFIG_RELIEF, "-relief", "relief", "Relief",
                  "raised", Tk_Offset(Square, relief), 0},
        {TK_CONFIG_END, NULL, NULL, NULL,
                  NULL, 0, 0}
};
```

Tk::Square instance constructor

All C widgets have a creation command of the form 'Tk_' . $widget_class . 'Cmd', in
this case, Tk_SquareCmd. When an object of class Square is instantiated, the subroutine is called and it allocates, initializes, and configures a Square struct, and returns a
standard Tcl integer result. The next section describes how the function is advertised so the rest of Tk can see it, and we can create widgets.

In Tcl, the ClientData parameter is a single word that can hold an integer or pointer
value. Its interpretation is application specific, and Tk uses it to hold various data,
such as the Tk_Window or Square struct pointers. If this were Tcl/Tk code, Tcl_Interp
would point to an instance of the *wish* interpreter, but in Perl/Tk, it's a private Perl
object[*] that should be left alone. Arguments are passed just like shell command-line
arguments, with an argument count and a pointer to a list of strings.

```
int
Tk_SquareCmd(clientData, interp, argc, args)
    ClientData clientData;     /* Main window associated with
                               * interpreter. */
    Tcl_Interp *interp;        /* Current interpreter. */
    int argc;                  /* Number of arguments. */
    Arg *args;                 /* Argument strings. */
{
    Tk_Window mainw = (Tk_Window) clientData;
    Square *squarePtr;
    Tk_Window tkwin;
    char *name;

    if (argc < 2) {
        Tcl_AppendResult(interp, "wrong # args: should be \"",
                LangString(args[0]), " pathName ?options?\"",  NULL);
        return TCL_ERROR;
    }
```

Create the Square's window and initialize its class, used for resource database lookups. The window isn't visible on the display, because it hasn't been mapped by a
geometry manager. Note how users can change the widget's class by using -class.

```
    tkwin = Tk_CreateWindowFromPath(interp, mainw, LangString(args[1]),
            NULL);
    if (tkwin == NULL) {
        return TCL_ERROR;
```

---

[*] As of Tk 800.018, it maps Tk_Window pathnames to Perl objects and is subject to change without notice.

```
    }
    name = "Square";
    if ((argc>3) && !strcmp(LangString(args[2]),"-class")) {
        argc -= 2;
        args += 2;
        name = LangString(args[1]);
    }
    Tk_SetClass(tkwin, name);
```

Allocate the Square structure and initialize it:

```
    squarePtr = (Square *) ckalloc(sizeof(Square));
    squarePtr->tkwin = tkwin;
    squarePtr->display = Tk_Display(tkwin);
    squarePtr->interp = interp;
    squarePtr->widgetCmd = Lang_CreateWidget(interp,squarePtr->tkwin,
            SquareWidgetCmd, (ClientData) squarePtr,
            SquareCmdDeletedProc);

    squarePtr->x = 0;
    squarePtr->y = 0;
    squarePtr->size = 20;
    squarePtr->borderWidth = 0;
    squarePtr->bgBorder = NULL;
    squarePtr->fgBorder = NULL;
    squarePtr->relief = TK_RELIEF_FLAT;
    squarePtr->gc = None;
    squarePtr->doubleBuffer = 1;
    squarePtr->updatePending = 0;
```

Register the event processing subroutine SquareEventProc and the events that interest it. The ExposureMask bit selects Expose events, and the StructureNotifyMask bit selects both ConfigureNotify and DestroyNotify events. When SquareEventProc is called, its ClientData argument is the widget's structure pointer, squarePtr.

```
    Tk_CreateEventHandler(squarePtr->tkwin,
        ExposureMask|StructureNotifyMask,
        SquareEventProc, (ClientData) squarePtr);
```

Perform the initial widget configuration, using values from argc and resource database lookups.

```
    if (SquareConfigure(interp, squarePtr, argc-2, args+2, 0) != TCL_OK) {
        Tk_DestroyWindow(squarePtr->tkwin);
        return TCL_ERROR;
    }

    Tcl_ArgResult(interp,LangWidgetArg(interp,squarePtr->tkwin));
    return TCL_OK;
}
```

Tk::Square method processors

Now that we can create a Tk::Square widget, we need to write C code to handle method calls against it. Every C widget has a subroutine name of the form $widget_class.'WidgetCmd'; in this case, SquareWidgetCmd.

```
static int
SquareWidgetCmd(clientData, interp, argc, args)
    ClientData clientData;          /* Information about square widget. */
    Tcl_Interp *interp;             /* Current interpreter. */
    int argc;                       /* Number of arguments. */
    Arg *args;                      /* Argument strings. */
{
    Square *squarePtr = (Square *) clientData;
    int result = TCL_OK;
    size_t length;
    char c;

    if (argc < 2) {
        Tcl_AppendResult(interp, "wrong # args: should be \"",
                LangString(args[0]), " option ?arg arg ...?\"", NULL);
        return TCL_ERROR;
    }
    Tcl_Preserve((ClientData) squarePtr);
    c = LangString(args[1])[0];
    length = strlen(LangString(args[1]));
```

Here is the method processing code for the cget, configure, position, and size methods. Hopefully the code is obvious.

```
    if ((c == 'c') &&
            (strncmp(LangString(args[1]), "cget", length) == 0) &&
            (length >= 2)) {
        if (argc != 3) {
            Tcl_AppendResult(interp, "wrong # args: should be \"",
                    LangString(args[0]), " cget option\"", NULL);
            goto error;
        }
        result = Tk_ConfigureValue(interp, squarePtr->tkwin, configSpecs,
                (char *) squarePtr, LangString(args[2]), 0);
    } else if ((c == 'c') &&
            (strncmp(LangString(args[1]), "configure", length) == 0) &&
            (length >= 2)) {
        if (argc == 2) {
            result = Tk_ConfigureInfo(interp, squarePtr->tkwin,
                    configSpecs, (char *) squarePtr, NULL, 0);
        } else if (argc == 3) {
            result = Tk_ConfigureInfo(interp, squarePtr->tkwin,
                    configSpecs, (char *) squarePtr,
                    LangString(args[2]), 0);
        } else {
            result = SquareConfigure(interp, squarePtr, argc-2, args+2,
                    TK_CONFIG_ARGV_ONLY);
        }
    } else if ((c == 'p') &&
```

```
            (strncmp(LangString(args[1]), "position", length) == 0)) {
        if ((argc != 2) && (argc != 4)) {
            Tcl_AppendResult(interp, "wrong # args: should be \"",
                    LangString(args[0]), " position ?x y?\"", NULL);
            goto error;
        }
        if (argc == 4) {
            if ((Tk_GetPixels(interp, squarePtr->tkwin, LangString(args[2]),
                    &squarePtr->x) != TCL_OK) || (Tk_GetPixels(interp,
                    squarePtr->tkwin, LangString(args[3]), &squarePtr->y)
                    != TCL_OK)) {
                goto error;
            }
            KeepInWindow(squarePtr);
        }
        Tcl_IntResults(interp,2,0, squarePtr->x, squarePtr->y);
    } else if ((c == 's') &&
            (strncmp(LangString(args[1]), "size", length) == 0)) {
        if ((argc != 2) && (argc != 3)) {
            Tcl_AppendResult(interp, "wrong # args: should be \"",
                    LangString(args[0]), " size ?amount?\"", NULL);
            goto error;
        }
        if (argc == 3) {
            int i;

            if (Tk_GetPixels(interp, squarePtr->tkwin, LangString(args[2]),
                    &i) != TCL_OK) {
                goto error;
            }
            if ((i <= 0) || (i > 100)) {
                Tcl_AppendResult(interp, "bad size \"", LangString(args[2]),
                        "\"", NULL);
                goto error;
            }
            squarePtr->size = i;
            KeepInWindow(squarePtr);
        }
        Tcl_IntResults(interp,1,0, squarePtr->size);
    } else {
        Tcl_AppendResult(interp, "bad option \"", LangString(args[1]),
                "\": must be cget, configure, position, or size", NULL);
        goto error;
    }
```

Queue a DoWhenIdle callback to display the Square unless an update is already pending.

```
    if (!squarePtr->updatePending) {
        Tcl_DoWhenIdle(SquareDisplay, (ClientData) squarePtr);
        squarePtr->updatePending = 1;
    }
    Tcl_Release((ClientData) squarePtr);
    return result;

error:
    Tcl_Release((ClientData) squarePtr);
```

```
    return TCL_ERROR;
}
```

Tk::Square option configurator

Subroutine `SquareConfigure` handles all configuration requests for a Tk::Square
widget:

```
static int
SquareConfigure(interp, squarePtr, argc, args, flags)
    Tcl_Interp *interp;     /* Used for error reporting. */
    Square *squarePtr;      /* Information about widget. */
    int argc;               /* Number of valid entries in args. */
    Arg *args;              /* Arguments. */
    int flags;              /* Flags to pass to
                             * Tk_ConfigureWidget. */
{
    if (Tk_ConfigureWidget(interp, squarePtr->tkwin, configSpecs,
            argc, args, (char *) squarePtr, flags) != TCL_OK) {
        return TCL_ERROR;
    }
```

Set the window's background color. If double buffering, create a graphics context:

```
    Tk_SetWindowBackground(squarePtr->tkwin,
            Tk_3DBorderColor(squarePtr->bgBorder)->pixel);
    if ((squarePtr->gc == None) && (squarePtr->doubleBuffer)) {
        XGCValues gcValues;
        gcValues.function = GXcopy;
        gcValues.graphics_exposures = False;
        squarePtr->gc = Tk_GetGC(squarePtr->tkwin,
                GCFunction|GCGraphicsExposures, &gcValues);
    }
```

Set the window's geometry and queue a DoWhenIdle event to display it:

```
    Tk_GeometryRequest(squarePtr->tkwin, 200, 150);
    Tk_SetInternalBorder(squarePtr->tkwin, squarePtr->borderWidth);
    if (!squarePtr->updatePending) {
        Tcl_DoWhenIdle(SquareDisplay, (ClientData) squarePtr);
        squarePtr->updatePending = 1;
    }
    return TCL_OK;
}
```

Tk::Square event handler

Subroutine SquareEventProc is invoked by Tk's event dispatcher, based on the events
selected when `Tk_SquareCmd` queued this handler. If you've run the square
demonstration program and tried to drag the square outside its window, then you've
noticed that you can't. That's because the ConfigureNotify event makes calls to
KeepInWindow, the subroutine that enforces that rule.

```
static void
SquareEventProc(clientData, eventPtr)
    ClientData clientData;   /* Information about window. */
```

```
    XEvent *eventPtr;        /* Information about event. */
{
    Square *squarePtr = (Square *) clientData;

    if (eventPtr->type == Expose) {
        if (!squarePtr->updatePending) {
            Tcl_DoWhenIdle(SquareDisplay, (ClientData) squarePtr);
            squarePtr->updatePending = 1;
        }
    } else if (eventPtr->type == ConfigureNotify) {
        KeepInWindow(squarePtr);
        if (!squarePtr->updatePending) {
            Tcl_DoWhenIdle(SquareDisplay, (ClientData) squarePtr);
            squarePtr->updatePending = 1;
        }
    } else if (eventPtr->type == DestroyNotify) {
        if (squarePtr->tkwin != NULL) {
            squarePtr->tkwin = NULL;
            Lang_DeleteWidget(squarePtr->interp, squarePtr->widgetCmd);
        }
        if (squarePtr->updatePending) {
            Tcl_CancelIdleCall(SquareDisplay, (ClientData) squarePtr);
        }
        Tcl_EventuallyFree((ClientData) squarePtr, SquareDestroy);
    }
}

static void
KeepInWindow(squarePtr)
    register Square *squarePtr;        /* Pointer to widget record. */
{
    int i, bd;
    bd = 0;
    if (squarePtr->relief != TK_RELIEF_FLAT) {
        bd = squarePtr->borderWidth;
    }
    i = (Tk_Width(squarePtr->tkwin) - bd) - (squarePtr->x + squarePtr->size);
    if (i < 0) {
        squarePtr->x += i;
    }
    i = (Tk_Height(squarePtr->tkwin) - bd) - (squarePtr->y + squarePtr->size);
    if (i < 0) {
        squarePtr->y += i;
    }
    if (squarePtr->x < bd) {
        squarePtr->x = bd;
    }
    if (squarePtr->y < bd) {
        squarePtr->y = bd;
    }
}
```

Tk::Square drawing handler

Subroutine `SquareDisplay` runs as a DoWhenIdle handler. This is the code responsible for displaying the widget. Note that a Drawable is either the actual display or an off-screen pixmap.

```
static void
SquareDisplay(clientData)
    ClientData clientData;       /* Information about window. */
{
    Square *squarePtr = (Square *) clientData;
    Tk_Window tkwin = squarePtr->tkwin;
    Pixmap pm = None;
    Drawable d;

    squarePtr->updatePending = 0;
    if (!Tk_IsMapped(tkwin)) {
        return;
    }
```

If required, create the off-screen pixmap for double-buffering:

```
if (squarePtr->doubleBuffer) {
    pm = Tk_GetPixmap(Tk_Display(tkwin), Tk_WindowId(tkwin),
            Tk_Width(tkwin), Tk_Height(tkwin),
            DefaultDepthOfScreen(Tk_Screen(tkwin)));
    d = pm;
} else {
    d = Tk_WindowId(tkwin);
}
```

Redraw the widget's background and border, and display the square:

```
Tk_Fill3DRectangle(tkwin, d, squarePtr->bgBorder, 0, 0, Tk_Width(tkwin),
        Tk_Height(tkwin), squarePtr->borderWidth, squarePtr->relief);

Tk_Fill3DRectangle(tkwin, d, squarePtr->fgBorder, squarePtr->x,
        squarePtr->y, squarePtr->size, squarePtr->size,
        squarePtr->borderWidth, TK_RELIEF_RAISED);
```

Copy the pixmap to the display if double buffering:

```
if (squarePtr->doubleBuffer) {
    XCopyArea(Tk_Display(tkwin), pm, Tk_WindowId(tkwin), squarePtr->gc,
            0, 0, (unsigned) Tk_Width(tkwin), (unsigned) Tk_Height(tkwin),
            0, 0);
    Tk_FreePixmap(Tk_Display(tkwin), pm);
}
}
```

Tk::Square destructor

Subroutine `SquareCmdDeletedProc` is called by core Tk to destroy a Tk::Square widget:

```
static void
SquareCmdDeletedProc(clientData)
    ClientData clientData;      /* Pointer to widget record for widget. */
```

```
{
    Square *squarePtr = (Square *) clientData;
    Tk_Window tkwin = squarePtr->tkwin;

    if (tkwin != NULL) {
        squarePtr->tkwin = NULL;
        Tk_DestroyWindow(tkwin);
    }
}
```

Subroutine SquareDestroy is called in response to a DestroyNotify event and frees the
Square structure and any graphics context.

```
static void
SquareDestroy(memPtr)
    char *memPtr;           /* Info about square widget. */
{
    Square *squarePtr = (Square *) memPtr;

    Tk_FreeOptions(configSpecs, (char *) squarePtr, squarePtr->display, 0);
    if (squarePtr->gc != None) {
        Tk_FreeGC(squarePtr->display, squarePtr->gc);
    }
    ckfree((char *) squarePtr);
}
```

Interfacing tkSquare.c with Perl/Tk

After creating the *Tk-Square-1.0* directory structure depicted in Figure 21-2, copy the
hand-edited *tkSquare.c* to *pTk/mTk/generic*. Create the *MANIFEST* file containing
these lines:

```
MANIFEST
Makefile.PL
Square.pm
Square.xs
pTk/Makefile.PL
pTk/mTk/generic/tkSquare.c
t/square_demo.t
```

Makefile.PL

The topmost *Makefile.PL* is a Perl program written in a specialized MakeMaker language enhanced for generating Perl/Tk Makefiles. The OBJECT attribute includes *pTk/
tkSquare.o* to satisfy the external Tk_SquareCmd. For more information, read the
ExtUtils::MakeMaker documentation.

```
use Tk::MMutil;

Tk::MMutil::TkExtMakefile(
    'NAME'          => 'Tk::Square',
```

```
           'VERSION_FROM' => 'Square.pm',
           'OBJECT'       => '$(O_FILES) pTk/tkSquare.o',
    );
```

Square.xs

This extension subroutine, or XSUB, lets Perl call Tk_SquareCmd. Of special note are
Tk's VTABLES (vector tables), which are structs with pointers to functions as their
members. The vector tables provide a modular, operating system–independent
means for dynamically loadable Tk modules (*.so* for Unix, *.dll* for Win32) to call
externals in other loadables. The *.m* files define macros that transform apparent
function calls into vector table lookups.

```
    #include <EXTERN.h>          /* standard ... */
    #include <perl.h>            /* ... XSUB ... */
    #include <XSUB.h>            /* ... headers  */

    #include "tkGlue.def"        /* map Tcl structs to Perl SV * etc. */

    #include "pTk/tkPort.h"      /* OS dependant definitions */
    #include "pTk/tkInt.h"       /* Tk widget internals */
    #include "pTk/tkVMacro.h"    /* includes the *.m files etc. for you */
    #include "tkGlue.h"          /* _The_ Perl <-> Tk glue header */
    #include "tkGlue.m"          /* header functions as macros via table */

    extern int Tk_SquareCmd _ANSI_ARGS_((ClientData, Tcl_Interp *, int, Arg *));

    DECLARE_VTABLES;             /* declare the pointers to tables */

    MODULE = Tk::Square PACKAGE = Tk

    PROTOTYPES: DISABLE

    void
    square(...)
    CODE:
    {
        XSRETURN(XSTkCommand(cv, Tk_SquareCmd, items, &ST(0)));
    }

    BOOT:
    {
        IMPORT_VTABLES;
    }
```

Square.pm

This Perl module bootstraps the Tk::Square loadable and defines class and instance
methods and definitions. The *Makefile.PL* VERSION_FROM attribute directs *Make-*

Maker to get the module's version number from this file. As with pure Perl mega-widgets, `Construct` plugs a "Square" symbol in Tk::Widget's symbol table, which is a code reference that invokes Tk::Widget::new.

```perl
$Tk::Square::VERSION = '1.0';

package Tk::Square;

use AutoLoader;
use Tk qw/Ev/;
use strict;

use base qw/Tk::Widget/;
Construct Tk::Widget 'Square';

bootstrap Tk::Square $Tk::VERSION;
sub Tk_cmd {\&Tk::square}

Tk::Methods(qw/cget configure position size/);

1;
```

For better performance, *make* autosplits subroutines after the `__END__` statement, writing each to a separate *.al* file. Hopefully, the comments in each make the code self-explanatory.

```perl
__END__

sub ClassInit {

    # Establish bindings for class Square.

    my ($class, $mw) = @_;

    $class->SUPER::ClassInit($mw);

    my $move = ['move' =>, Ev('x'), Ev('y')];
    $mw->bind($class, '<1>'         => $move);
    $mw->bind($class, '<B1-Motion>' => $move);
    $mw->bind($class, '<a>'         => ['animate']);

} # end ClassInit

sub InitObject {

    # C widgets don't have a Populate() method (Tk::Derived
    # is not in their @ISA array). InitObject() performs per
    # instance Square initialization.

    my($self, $args) = @_;

    $self->SUPER::InitObject($args);
    $self->{-count} = 0;      # animation cycle count

} # end InitObject
```

```
sub animate  {

    # A <KeyPress-a> event invokes this callback to start or stop
    # a Square's animation.  Vary the size between 10 and 40 pixels.

    my $self = shift;

    if ($self->{-count} == 0) {
        $self->{-count} = 3;
        $self->{-tid} = $self->repeat(30 => [sub {
            my $self = shift;
            return if $self->{-count} == 0;
            my $s = $self->size;
            if ($s >= 40) {$self->{-count} = -3}
            if ($s <= 10) {$self->{-count} = +3}
            $self->size($s + $self->{-count});
        }, $self]);
    } else {
        $self->{-count} = 0;
        $self->afterCancel($self->{-tid});
    }

} # end animate

sub move {

    # Move a Square to the specified coordinate.

    my($self, $x, $y) = @_;

    my $s = $self->size;
    $self->position($x - ($s / 2), $y - ($s / 2));

} # end move
```

Finally, we complete the module with POD documentation.

```
=head1 NAME

Tk::Square - Create a Tk::Square widget.

=for pm Tk/Square.pm

=for category Tk Widget Classes

=head1 SYNOPSIS

S<    >I<$square> = I<$parent>-E<gt>B<Square>(I<-option> =E<gt> I<value>, ... );

=head1 DESCRIPTION

Create a B<Square> widget.

=over 4

=item B<-dbl>
```

Double buffer iff true.

=back

=head1 METHODS

=over 4

=item C<$square-E<gt>B<size>;>

Change the size of the Square.

=item C<$square-E<gt>B<position>(I<x>, I<y>);>

Move the Square to coordinate (I<x>,I<y>).

=back

=head1 DEFAULT BINDINGS

Perl/Tk automatically creates class bindings for Square widgets
that give them the following behaviour.

=over 4

=item B<<B1>>

Move Square's top-left corner to cursor position.

=item B<<B1-Motion>>

Continuously move Square's top-left corner to cursor position.

=item B<<a>>

Starts/stop the Square's animation mode.

=back

=head1 AUTHORS

The Tcl/Tk group, Nick Ing-Simmons and Steve Lidie.

=head1 EXAMPLE

I<$square> = I<$mw>-E<gt>B<Square>(-dbl =E<gt> 0);

=head1 KEYWORDS

square, widget

=cut

pTk/Makefile.PL

This special *Makefile.PL* program serves two main purposes: it determines the location of installation include and executable files, and it munges all the hand-edited C files in *pTk/mTk/generic*.

```perl
use File::Basename;
use Tk::MMutil;
use strict;

my $inst_tk = Tk::MMutil::installed_tk();
my $inst_inc  = "$inst_tk/pTk";

Tk::MMutil::TkExtMakefile(
    'OBJECT' => '$(O_FILES)',
    'INC'    => " -I${inst_inc}",
    'clean'  => {'FILES' => 'tkSquare.c'},
);

sub MY::post_initialize {

    my $self = shift;

    my $perl = $self->{'PERL'};
    foreach my $tcl (<mTk/generic/*.c>) {
        my $ptk = basename $tcl;
        print "Munging $tcl -> $ptk\n";
        system ($perl, "$inst_tk/pTk/Tcl-pTk", $tcl, $ptk );
    }

    push @{$self->{O_FILES}}, "\tttkSquare.o";

    '';
}
```

Building and Testing Tk::Square

Once all the files are in place, we simply run:

```
% perl Makefile.PL
```

which generates the topmost *Makefile* as well as *pTk/Makefile*. Then a simple *make* munges *pTk/mTk/generic/tkSquare.c*, compiles the munged *pTk/tkSquare.c*, runs *xsubpp* on *Square.xs*, and then compiles the generated *Square.c* file and links the *.o* files into a single *.so* loadable (for Unix). The autosplit subroutines, the *Square.pm* file, and the loadable are all copied into *blib*, the build library, for testing.

t/square_demo.t

Here's the test program. It's a rather normal Perl/Tk program with a few special-pur-
pose print statements. When we type **make test**, files in the *t* directory are executed,
each of which prints out the number of tests and strings of the form "ok 1" or "not ok
2", specifying the status of each test. For related information, check out the Test::
Harness module.

```
#!/usr/local/bin/perl -w

# This program creates Square widget.  The Square class
# has these default bindings:
#
# <1> press/drag : moves the Square to the pointer
# "a"            : toggles size() animation on/off

BEGIN {
    $| = 1;
    print "1..3\n";
}

use Tk;
use Tk::Square;
use strict;

my $mw = MainWindow->new;
print "ok 1\n";

my $sq = $mw->Square;
print "ok 2\n";
$sq->pack(qw/-expand yes -fill both/);
$sq->focus;

MainLoop;
print "ok 3\n";
```

How Not to Port Tk::Square

As we learned earlier, it's best to keep private C widgets distinct from the Perl/Tk
distribution. But if we were to do a merge, here are some considerations.

First, copy *tkSquare.c* (with the same hand edits described previously) to *pTk/mTk/
generic*, copy *square_demo.t* to *t*, and then fire up your favorite editor and add these
lines to the main Perl/Tk *MANIFEST*:

```
Square/Makefile.PL
Square/Square.xs
Square/Square.pm
```

```
pTk/mTk/generic/tkSquare.c
t/square_demo.t
```

Now make the *Square* directory and populate it with the preceding files. The files *Square.xs* and *Square.pm* are the exact same files we just used, but *Makefile.PL* looks like this:

```
use Tk::MMutil;
Tk::MMutil::TkExtMakefile(
    'dynamic_ptk' => 1
);
```

Secondly, we must add a single statement to three files so the Perl/Tk core is "aware of" Tk_SquareCmd.

To *pTk/mTk/generic/tk.h*, add the following around line 1880:

```
EXTERN int Tk_SquareCmd _ANSI_ARGS_((ClientData clientData,
        Tcl_Interp *interp, int argc, char **argv));
```

To *pTk/mTk/generic/tkWindow.c*, add the following around line 152:

```
{"square",        Tk_SquareCmd,        NULL,        1},
```

To *pTk/tk.exc*, add the following around line 96:

```
Tk_SquareCmd
```

It may be advisable to start fresh and begin with:

```
make distclean
perl Makefile.PL
```

Making and testing the widget code is similar to what we just did, although development is slower because it's a *make* from the top of the entire Perl/Tk hierarchy, with scores of dependencies and nested *makes*. You'll quickly find that the *make*; *make test* cycle is ridiculously slow.

Testing is sped up if we use a command of the form:

```
perl -Mblib Square/t/square_demo.t
```

This uses all the newly made code (both Perl and the loadable object) from *blib*, the build library.

We can even fake a *make install* with a script that might look like this (although the exact pathnames vary):

```
#!/bin/sh
make
cp blib/arch/auto/Tk/Square/Square.so /usr/local/lib/perl5/site_perl/5.005/i686-
linux/auto/Tk/Square/Square.so
```

Of course, this only "installs" the C loadable, not the *.pm* file or autosplit subroutines.

There are various techniques for debugging the C code, but perhaps the easiest is the tried-and-true fprintf statement (don't forget the #include <stdio.h>):

```
fprintf(stderr, "square size=%d\n", squarePtr->size);
```

## CHAPTER 22

Perl/Tk and the Web

In this chapter, we'll examine how Tk can access the wealth of information available on the World Wide Web. Using the Library for WWW Access in Perl (LWP), we'll develop *tkcomics*, a web client to fetch images of our favorite comics and display them in a Perl/Tk window.

One of the Web's most popular Clients is *Netscape*. It's an extensible application that allows developers to write *plug-ins*—loadable chunks of code often written in C—which add functionality to the basic browser. We'll learn how to execute client-side Perl/Tk programs via the PerlPlus plug-in.

Library for WWW Access in Perl

LWP is a Perl library providing access to the Web, used primarily for writing client applications. It "speaks" Hypertext Transfer Protocol (HTTP),* and one of its most basic duties is fetching the content of URLs. The beauty of LWP is that it hides all the operational details while allowing us to do our work with simple objects and methods.

In essence, a *user agent* object working on our behalf takes a *request* object and does whatever low-level communication and error handling is required to send a request for web content on its way. The user agent then waits for the reply (or error) and hands it back to our program in the form of a *response* object. Our job is to create the user agent, then use various LWP methods to manipulate requests and responses. But if all we want to do is simply fetch web content, we can use LWP in "simple" mode and just say "fetch this URL," and LWP creates the user agent and request/response objects internally, eventually returning content data to our program.

---

* Using HTTP as the underlying transport medium, LWP also supports gopher, FTP, news, file, mailto, and secure HTTP services.

At first glance, the simple LWP mechanism would appear to suffice for a client such as *tkcomics*, but it has some drawbacks. As you might suspect, they have to do with blocking, because there might be a considerable time delay between a request and when the network finally delivers the response. Even handling LWP's user agent manually can't surmount all of these problems. Thus, eventually, we'll have to resort to a multiprocess scheme. So let's begin and see how *tkcomics* might have evolved.

An excellent place for private viewing of your favorite comics is *http://www.comics. com*, although all the glamour, glitz, and advertisements may be too much for the stomach. But there's nothing to stop us from fetching just the comics and using Tk to display them.* We'll start by learning how to fetch and interpret the *http://www. comics.com* home page, and then build our Tk client around that framework.

LWP::Simple, the Easiest Way to the Web

The LWP::Simple module is so simple, it's not even object oriented; rather, it exports a handful of subroutines for fetching and mirroring web content. All we're interested in is fetching web content, accomplished with the get subroutine:

```
use LWP::Simple qw/get/;
```

To retrieve a web page, we call get with the desired URL:

```
my $comics_home = 'http://www.comics.com';
my $comics = get $comics_home or die "Can't get $comics_home.";
```

So now $comics contains a ton of raw Hypertext Markup Language (HTML), stuff we normally let our browser interpret and display for us. If we actually did browse that URL, one of the things we'd see is the actual comic selector widget, which appears to be an Optionmenu (see Figure 22-1).

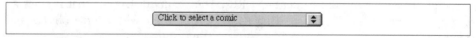

Figure 22-1. Comic selector widget

It's not a Tk Optionmenu, of course, but it's what the browser renders when it encounters a <SELECT> tag. Looking at the HTML, either by printing $comics or viewing the page source in the browser, we see this:

```
<SELECT NAME= ... >
    <OPTION>Click to select a comic
    <OPTION VALUE="/universal/adam/ab.html">Adam
    <OPTION VALUE="/comics/alleyoop/ab.html">Alley Oop
    <OPTION VALUE="/comics/andycapp/ab.html">Andy Capp
    <OPTION VALUE="/comics/arlonjanis/ab.html">Arlo & Janis
    <OPTION VALUE="/comics/askshagg/ab.html">Ask Shagg
```

---

* We can only use this material for private consumption. Any other use is illegal. Please read the letter of the law at *http://www.comics.com/info/site/copyright.html*.

```
    <OPTION VALUE="/comics/bc/ab.html">B.C.

...

    <OPTION VALUE="/comics/wizardofid/ab.html">Wizard of Id
    <OPTION VALUE="/universal/ziggy/ab.html">Ziggy
</SELECT>
```

That looks promising. We seem to have a list of URLs, one per comic. If we're lucky, we should be able to key on the string `"OPTION VALUE"`, then use the following code to pick out the comic names and their associated URLs:

```
my $n = 0;
foreach (split /\n/, $comics) {
    next unless /OPTION\s+VALUE/i;
    if (my($comic_url, $comic) = m\"([^"]+)">(.*)\) {
        $comic =~ s/\t//g;
        $comic =~ s/\r//g;
        printf "%-30s : %s\n", $comic, $comic_url;
        $n++;
    }
}
print "\nfound $n comics\n";
```

Indeed, luck is with us, for if we run the code, we see this output:

```
Adam                          : /universal/adam/ab.html
Alley Oop                     : /comics/alleyoop/ab.html
Andy Capp                     : /comics/andycapp/ab.html
Arlo & Janis                  : /comics/arlonjanis/ab.html
Ask Shagg                     : /comics/askshagg/ab.html
B.C.                          : /comics/bc/ab.html

...

Wizard of Id                  : /comics/wizardofid/ab.html
Ziggy                         : /universal/ziggy/ab.html

found 91 comics
```

As it happens, these URLs are not the comic images, but another page, relative to the site's home address, within which the actual URL of the comic is embedded. For instance, if we concatenate Ask Shagg's relative URL with $comics_home and view the HTML at *http://www.comics.com/comics/askshagg/ab.html*, we see an `<IMG>` tag with the relative URL of the actual GIF image:

```
<IMG SRC="/comics/askshagg/archive/images/askshagg21461240000515.gif" ALT="today's
comics strip" ALIGN=TOP BORDER="0">
```

tkcomics can easily extract this URL, fetch the image file, convert it to a Photo, and display it. So, we have proof-of-concept code. On the upside, it's extremely simple, but on the downside, it's blocking, and there's no timeout mechanism. Let's try to address these concerns.

Fetching Web Content with LWP::UserAgent

Although a tad more complicated than LWP::Simple, most people use LWP::User-Agent for their web clients, because it gives them complete control over their applications. Unlike LWP::Simple, we create the user agent manually and exert control by sending messages to it. All this means is that we create a user agent object and invoke methods on it. For instance, this is how we set a timeout so network requests won't take longer than 20 seconds:

```
use LWP::UserAgent;

my $ua = LWP::UserAgent->new;
$ua->timeout(20);
```

Nevertheless, at this (the Perl) level, a timeout still doesn't buy us anything, because no matter how short the timeout is, Tk is blocked until the LWP request is complete.

Even this trick of configuring a callback to read small chunks of network data is unlikely to be sufficient; blocking for 1 byte of data still prevents Tk from processing events. The following code defines a callback that appends data to a string. As network data arrives, the user agent invokes the callback on every byte. When the request completes (or times out), we use the response object to check the status of the request and die if there's an error. In addition to not solving our problem, processing data a byte at a time is incredibly inefficient.

```
my $comics_home = 'http://www.comics.com';
my $comics;

sub req_callback {
    my($content, $response, $protocol) = @_;
    $comics .= $content;
}

my $req_object = HTTP::Request->new('GET' => $comics_home);
my $res_object = $ua->request($req_object, \&req_callback, 1);
die "request failed" if $res_object->is_error;
```

Assuming the get request succeeds, $comics contains the same HTML page content as the LWP::Simple example, which can be processed as before.

While the LWP::UserAgent solution is slightly cooler than the LWP::Simple one, it can still block and ruin our comic-viewing experience. What we need is a nonblocking LWP request, and one sure-fire way to implement that is to use the *fork/pipe/exec* idiom we developed in Chapter 19. In that chapter, we saw that piping information between two asynchronous processes—one of which was a Tk program—and using fileevent prevented Tk from blocking. We can use the same technique here, and let the child fetch web content and pipe it back to *tkcomics* whenever the data becomes available.

lwp-request and fileevent Rule

To keep Tk events flowing, we need to use a separate process (or thread) and ensure that the two processes can talk in a nonblocking way. The first process, the Tk parent, handles the GUI and event processing, while the child fetches comic images and forwards them to the parent.

The IPC solution developed in Chapter 19 was unusually specialized, because it used bidirectional pipes for a two-way conversation between the Tk parent and the child. In contrast, if the *tkcomics* child can get its URL from the command line and send comics to standard output, we can use the pipe form of the open command and let Perl do the hard work.

Included in the LWP package is *lwp-request*, a standalone program perfectly matched for our needs. It accepts a URL on the command line and prints the resulting web content on its STDOUT. So that's our plan, and with Perl 5.6.0, it might work on Win32 too.

We start with needed declarations. All the comic images are binary data, but to use them in Tk we must first Base64 encode them; that's why we need MIME::Base64. Additionally, although most of the comics are GIFs, a few are in JPEG or PNG format. Note that Tk::JPEG and Tk::PNG are not bundled with Perl/Tk, so you'll have to install them yourself:

```
#!/usr/local/bin/perl -w
#
# tkcomics - display comics courtesy of http://www.comics.com
#
# Because LWP::Simple and LWP::UserAgent can block, do the
# network I/O in another thread, er, child, with fileevent().
# Add a Stop/Cancel button that kills the pipe.

use MIME::Base64;
use Tk;
use Tk::JPEG;
use Tk::PNG;
use subs qw/get_url show_comic status stop_get/;
use strict;
```

Here we open the MainWindow in the standard fashion, then initialize a few global variables. $photo holds the comic image object reference. $status displays periodic status messages that keep the user informed of the state of data transfers. $eof is set either when the *lwp-request* child completes, signaling the web fetch is complete, or by a user button click that prematurely interrupts a transfer. $pid is the process ID of the child, used to kill it if we tire of waiting for the network. The %ext hash maps a comic filename extension to a Tk Photo image processor.

```
my $mw = MainWindow->new;
my $photo = '';
my $status = '';
```

```
my($eof, $pid);
my %ext = qw/
    gif gif
    jpg jpeg
    png png
    tif tiff
    xbm xbm
    ppm ppm
/;                              # file extension => Photo format map
my $help = '<Button-1> fetch comic, <Button-2> interrupt transfer';
```

As Figure 22-2 shows, the entire application consists of just three Tk widgets: a List-box that holds the names of the comics, one Label that displays the comic images (except initially, when it displays the string "tkcomics" in large italic letters), and a second Label that displays relevant status information:

```
my $s = $mw->Label(-textvariable => \$status, -width => 100);
my $lb = $mw->Scrolled(qw/Listbox -selectforeground blue/);
my $l = $mw->Label(
    -text       => 'tkcomics',
    -foreground => 'blue',
    -font       => [qw/-size 100 -slant italic/],
);
$s->pack(qw/-side bottom -fill x -expand 1/);
$lb->pack(qw/side left -fill y -expand 1 -anchor w/);
$l->pack(-side => 'right');
```

The following code is essentially our old proof-of-concept example, except instead of printing comic names and URLs, we build a hash of comic URLs indexed by comic name. It's important to note that we've eliminated LWP::Simple, using our own get_url subroutine in place of LWP::Simple::get.

```
my $comics_home = 'http://www.comics.com';
my $comics = get_url $comics_home or die "Can't get $comics_home.";

my(%comics, $comic_url, $comic);
foreach (split /\n/, $comics) {
    next unless /OPTION\s+VALUE/i;
    if (($comic_url, $comic) = m\"([^"]+)">(.*)\) {
        $comic =~ s/\t//g;
        $comic =~ s/\r//g;
        $comics{$comic} = $comic_url;
    }
}
```

At this point, we display our first status message, telling us how many comics were found and how to use *tkcomics*. We'll stuff the names of all available comics in a List widget and use a <Button-1> event to select one for viewing. <Button-2>, obviously, is used to interrupt a long (or hung) transfer. Subroutine status simply sets the status Label's -textvariable, then invokes idletasks to flush Tk's low-priority idle events queue. This updates the entire Tk display so the status message appears immediately.

```
my $help = scalar(keys %comics) .
    ' comics, <Button-1> fetch comic, <Button-2> interrupt transfer';
```

```
status $help;

sub status {
    $status = $_[0];
    $mw->idletasks;
}
```

Finally, populate the Listbox with the comic names, sorted alphabetically; establish two button bindings that give life to *tkcomics*; and enter the main Tk event loop:

```
foreach (sort keys %comics) {
    $lb->insert('end', $_);
}

$lb->bind('<ButtonRelease-1>' => \&show_comic);
$mw->bind('<ButtonRelease-2>' => \&stop_get);

MainLoop;
```

Figure 22-2. Initial tkcomics display

The heart of *tkcomics* is the subroutine get_url, shown in the following code. Look it over before we explain it. Note that there's an implicit tradeoff between efficiency and simplicity. For an "important" program, it would be better to fork a persistent child once and establish a dialog between it and the Tk parent. In this case, however, it's considerably easier just to use a pipe open and run *lwp-request* for every URL:

```
sub get_url {

    my($url) = @_;

    status "Fetching $url";
    $pid = open PIPE, "lwp-request -m GET -t 20 -e $url 2>&1 |" or
        die "Open error: $!";
    binmode PIPE if $^O eq 'MSWin32';

    my $content;
    $mw->fileevent(\*PIPE, 'readable' => sub {
        my($stat, $data);
        while ($stat = sysread PIPE, $data, 4096) {
            $content .= $data;
```

```
        }
        die "sysread error:  $!" unless defined $stat;
        $eof = 1 if $stat == 0;
    });
    $mw->waitVariable(\$eof);
    $mw->fileevent(\*PIPE, 'readable' => '');
    close PIPE;

    $pid = undef;

    (my $response, $content) = $content =~ /(.*?)\n\n(.*)/is if $content;

    return wantarray ? ($response, $content) : $content;

} # end get_url
```

Subroutine get_url is passed a single argument, the URL to fetch, which is immediately posted in the status Label. The open statement does the requisite pipe, fork, and exec-ing of *lwp-request* for us, so all we (the TK parent) need do is establish a fileevent handler to read web content. The *lwp-request* option –t effects a 20-second timeout, and the –e option says to return the response headers along with the web content. The response headers are returned first, separated from the content by an empty line.

If you're running a Win32 operating system, the binmode statement is very important, because the comic images are binary data. On Unix, binmode isn't required, but it does no harm, either.

Now we set up the fileevent readable callback on the *lwp-request* output pipe. The callback simply appends up to 4K of web data to the $content variable and nominally ends at end-of-file. Meanwhile, Tk event processing continues because the Tk parent is spinning on the waitVariable statement, waiting for the $eof variable to change. $eof changes in one of two ways, either when the fileevent callback detects end-of-file, or, as we shall see, when the user clicks <Button-2>.

Once the waitVariable is satisfied, we cancel the fileevent readable callback, close the pipe handle, and undef $pid. Notice that get_url uses wantarray to determine if it was called in scalar or list context. In list context, we assume the caller wants two strings, the response headers and the actual URL content, or else just the content. We'll see how the response headers are used shortly.

To stop a web GET, we click <Button-2>, which invokes the stop_get subroutine. We then set $eof so the fileevent readable callback terminates, and, if $pid is defined (i.e., the *lwp-request* child is still running) we kill it.

```
sub stop_get {
    status "Stopping transfer ...";
    $mw->after(5000, sub {status $help});
    $eof = -1;
    kill 'TERM', $pid if defined $pid;
}
```

The Recipe for Displaying Web Images

Let's take a peek at what the *tkcomics* application looks like rendering a comic. Figure 22-3 depicts the program displaying a GIF file. To see how to render it, read on. Basically, using the active Listbox element, find the comic URL and fetch its contents. Within the page is an `<IMG>` tag with another URL pointing to the actual image, which we then fetch, convert to a Photo, and display. Periodically, we examine `$eof` to see if any transfer was aborted.

Figure 22-3. Ask Shagg Camel Facts

As with any binding callback of the form:

```
$lb->bind('<ButtonRelease-1>' => \&show_comic);
```

Perl/Tk implicitly passes the bound object reference (the Listbox) as the callback's first argument, which we assign to the variable `$lb`.

```
sub show_comic {

    my($lb) = @_;
```

Since we got here on a `<ButtonRelease-1>` event, we're guaranteed that the active Listbox entry is our target comic. We get it and index into the `%comics` hash to get the URL of the page containing the comic image URL. We return immediately if the transfer was interrupted.

```
my $comic = $lb->get('active');
my $comic_url = $comics{$comic};
my $comic_html = get_url
    $comic_url =~ /^http:/i ? $comic_url : "$comics_home$comic_url";
return if $eof == -1;
```

Now extract the image URL from the mass of HTML sitting in `$comic_html`. Unfortunately, web content changes over time, which is why we use multiple pattern matches. Once we actually find a URL, call `get_url` in list context to get both the response header and the binary comic image. If the transfer wasn't interrupted, we can assume all the returned data is correct. And given a valid data transfer, we can extract the image size (in bytes) from the response header's `Content-Length` attribute.

As an added touch, we'll adorn the comic's Listbox entry with this information, just to show we've already viewed the comic (see Figure 22-3).

```
my $image_url;

if ( ($image_url) = $comic_html =~ m\.*<IMG SRC="([^"]+)".*? ALT="(today|daily)\
is ) {
        print "1: $image_url!\n";
    } elsif ( ($image_url) = $comic_html =~ m\.*bgcolor="#FFFFCC" ALIGN="MIDDLE"
COLSPAN="3"><BR><IMG SRC="([^"]+)"\is ) {
        print "2: $image_url!\n";
    } else {
        status "Cannot find a comic image in $comic_url.";
        print STDERR $comic_html;
        return;
}

my ($response, $image) = get_url "$comics_home$image_url";
return if $eof == -1;
my($bytes) = $response =~ /Content-Length: (\d+)/is;
```

Perl/Tk images are generated from either an external file or embedded data. You may recall from Chapter 17 that because in Tcl "everything is a string,"* embedded image data must be in printable characters, which is why we first Base64 encode the image data. Now we do a little bookkeeping on the variable $photo; the second and subsequent invocations of this callback delete any previous image to stem a possible memory leak. Then we create an image of the appropriate format and configure the image Label to display it. Finally, we append the comic's size, in bytes, to its Listbox entry and update the status help message. The update method is carefully placed so Tk adjusts the application's geometry based on the new image's dimensions, ensuring that see positions the Listbox properly. selectionSet rehighlights the current comic name.

```
my $photo_data = encode_base64($image);
$photo->delete if UNIVERSAL::isa($photo => 'Tk::Photo');
my($ext) = $image_url =~ /\.(.*)?/;
$ext ||= 'gif';
status "Creating $bytes byte $ext Photo";
$photo = $mw->Photo(-data => $photo_data, -format => $ext{lc $ext});
$l->configure(-image => $photo);

my $index = $lb->index('active');
$comic .= " ($bytes)";
$lb->delete($index);
$lb->insert($index, $comic);
$lb->update;
$lb->see($index);
$lb->selectionSet($index);
```

---

* Well, more accurately, everything was a string; recent Tks can handle binary objects.

```
    status $help;

}  # end show_comic
```

Win32 Considerations

Under Win32, the code is sound and should work with Perl 5.6.0 and a recent Tk, such as Tk 800.022. But, alas, it doesn't. It hangs on the fileevent, which is never triggered. So, what can we do?

Threads are out, as Tk is not thread-safe. TCP/IP comes to mind and, since sockets are available on both Unix and Win32, this solution retains compatibility, if not simplicity. So let's rewrite get_url to fork a child that uses local Win32 sockets.

fork and local Win32 sockets

The parent begins by opening a listen socket on a well-known (but arbitrary) port on the localhost;* it then forks a second process to run *lwp-request*:

```
sub get_url {

    use IO::Socket;
    use POSIX;

    my $url = shift;
    my $port = 9917;
    my($pid, $handle);

    my $server = IO::Socket::INET->new(
        LocalHost => 'localhost',
        LocalPort => $port,
        Proto     => 'tcp',
        Listen    => SOMAXCONN,
        Reuse => 1,
    );
    die "Parent socket open failure: $!" unless defined $server;

    die "fork failure: $!" unless defined($pid = fork);
```

The Tk parent then waits on the accept call until it receives a connect, puts the socket in binary mode, unbuffers it, and then uses fileevent to read all the incoming HTML, just like in the pipe-open version of get_url.

```
    if ($pid) {          # parent
        $handle = $server->accept;
        binmode $handle;
        $handle->autoflush(1);

        $eof = 0;
        my $content;
```

---

* Similar to the *ipadm* daemon described in Chapter 19.

```
        $mw->fileevent($handle, 'readable' => sub {
            my($stat, $data);
            while ($stat = sysread $handle, $data, 4096) {
                $content .= $data;
            }
            die "sysread error: $!" unless defined $stat;
            $eof = 1 if $stat == 0;
        });
        $mw->waitVariable(\$eof);
        $mw->fileevent($handle, 'readable' => '');
        close $handle;
        $pid = undef;
        return $content;
```

Meanwhile, the child creates its unbuffered binary socket and outputs the HTML generated by a backticked *lwp-request*:

```
    } else {            # child
        $handle = IO::Socket::INET->new(
            PeerAddr => 'localhost',
            PeerPort => $port,
            Proto    => 'tcp',
        );
        die "Child socket open failure: $!" unless defined $handle;
        binmode $handle;
        $handle->autoflush(1);
        print $handle `lwp-request -m GET -t 20s -e $url`;
        close $handle;
        POSIX::_exit(0);

    } # ifend fork

} # end get_url
```

This code works perfectly well on Unix but, once again, hangs on the fileevent under Win32. Perhaps we're pushing Win32's new fork capability too far by using backticks within a forked process. Well, we can test that theory by replacing:

```
    print $handle `lwp-request -m GET -t 20s -e $url`;
```

with equivalent LWP code. The new code needs a 20-second timeout and must return the response headers in addition to the web content. Here's how we do it.

fork and LWP::UserAgent

We begin as before, by creating a new user agent and sending it a *timeout* message, building a request object, passing it to the user agent, and checking for errors. Now we return the response headers in the same format as *lwp-request*'s *–e* option, an empty line, and the web content:

```
    use LWP::UserAgent;
    my $ua = LWP::UserAgent->new;
    $ua->timeout(20);
    my $req_object = HTTP::Request->new('GET' => $url);
```

```
my $res_object = $ua->request($req_object);
die "request failed" if $res_object->is_error;
foreach my $response (keys %{$res_object->headers}) {
    print $handle "$response: ", $res_object->headers->{$response}, "\n";
}
print $handle "\n";
print $handle $res_object->content;
```

Once again, this code runs perfectly on Unix but fails on Win32, so we need to take a completely different tack. I suppose we could arrange for the child to write a file and signal the Tk parent by some means, perhaps a semaphore, but that lacks style. We can't use shared memory, since the Unix *shmctl/shmget/shmread/shmwrite* shared memory functions aren't available in Win32, right? True, but Win32 has its own shared memory capabilities, so let's investigate further.

Win32::Process and shared memory

A chance email with Grant Hopwell clued me in to his Tie::Win32MemMap module. With it, Grant would spin off Win32 children using Win32::Process::Create, and the two processes would talk using a shared Perl hash! This seemed an interesting possibility: create a shared hash with two keys, CONTENT and COMPLETE, and have the child run *lwp-request* and store web content in $shared_hash{CONTENT}, while the Perl/Tk parent watches (using waitVariable) for a change in $shared_hash{COMPLETE}, set by the child when ready.

Tie::Win32MemMap requires Storable, available from CPAN, and Win32::Mem-Map, written by Amine Moulay Ramdane, available at *http://www.generation.net/~aminer/Perl*.

As it happens, we can indeed write a drop-in replacement for the subroutine get_url, specifically for Win32, and keep the rest of *tkcomics* intact. Let's look at get_url for Win32 now.

```
sub get_url {

    my($url) = @_;

    status "Fetching $url";
```

Here we create and initialize a new chunk of shared memory and tie it to the hash %content. The shared memory is tagged with the name 'tkcomics', which any Win32 process can access if it uses the proper MapName.

```
use Win32::Process;
use Tie::Win32MemMap;

my %content;
tie %content, 'Tie::Win32MemMap', {
    Create  => MEM_NEW_SHARE,
    MapName => 'tkcomics',
};
```

```
    $content{'COMPLETE'} = 0;
    $content{'CONTENT'}  = '';
```

Now fire up the child process, another Perl program stored in the file *tkcwin32.kid*, whose job is to connect to the shared memory 'tkcomics', fill the CONTENT key with web data from the URL passed on the command line, and set the COMPLETE key when it's finished.

```
Win32::Process::Create(
    my $child,
    'c:\\perl\\bin\\perl.exe',
    "perl tkcwin32.kid $url",
    0,
    NORMAL_PRIORITY_CLASS,
    '.',
) or die Win32::FormatMessage(Win32::GetLastError);

$eof = 0;
$mw->update;
```

Here we wait for the signal from the child that it has completed. Normally we would use a waitVariable(\$content{'COMPLETE'}) statement, but there is competing magic between the Tie module and Tk, so we have to synthesize our own using this loop:

```
while ( $content{'COMPLETE'} != 1 ) {
    last if $eof == -1;
    $mw->after(10);
    $mw->update;
}
```

Once the child completes, we separate the response headers from the actual content and return the particular data required by our caller, just like the Unix version.

```
my $content = $content{'CONTENT'};
(my $response, $content) = $content =~ /(.*?)\n\n(.*)/is if $content;
return wantarray ? ($response, $content) : $content;

} # end get_url
```

For our purposes, the child, *tkcwin32.kid*, must reside in the current working directory, because we haven't qualified the pathname in the Win32::Process::Create call. It's certainly trivial to embed the child in *tkcomics* proper and create it during initialization; we'll do just that in short order. Until then, this is the Win32 child program.

Because we're not in the context of a subroutine, the naked shift statement uses as its argument @ARGV (the command line) rather that @_, thus providing the child the URL specified by the parent:

```
#!/usr/local/bin/perl -w
#
# Win32 tkcomics helper program that shovels web content to the Tk parent.

use Tie::Win32MemMap;

my $url = shift;
```

By this point in real time, the Tk parent has already created and tied the shared memory to its hash, so all the child need do is tie to the same MapName in "share" mode.

```
my %content;
tie %content, 'Tie::Win32MemMap', {
    Create  => MEM_VIEW_SHARE,
    MapName => 'tkcomics',
};
```

Once again, with Perl 5.6.0 and higher, the child is free to do a pipe open and run *lwp-request* in the same manner as the Unix code. Do not forget the binmode statement!

```
open(PIPE, "lwp-request -m GET -t 20s -e $url|") or die "open failure: $!";
binmode PIPE;
```

Once again, read 4K chunks of web content and build up the scalar $content{'CONTENT'}. When end-of-file is reached, close the pipe and set the complete marker, signaling the Tk parent to proceed.

```
my($stat, $data);
while ($stat = sysread PIPE, $data, 4096) {
    $content{'CONTENT'} .= $data;
}
die "sysread error:  $!" unless defined $stat;
close PIPE;

$content{'COMPLETE'} = 1;
exit(0);
```

If you don't believe all this actually works, gaze upon Figure 22-4 and witness *tkcomics* for Win32!

Figure 22-4. tkcomics works in Win32 too

Tidying an Ugly Mess

So now we have at least three distinct ways of fetching web content without blocking. If this has to be the state of the world, then so be it, but we can at least encapsulate the pipe-open, TCP/IP socket, and the Win32 memmap code directly into *tkcomics* and conditionally use the variant appropriate for the operating system at hand. We'll do this by testing $0 and eval-ing the correct code.

First, let's change get_url, effectively factoring out the essence of the subroutine, leaving _get_url (defined at compile time) to do the operating system–specific work.

```perl
sub get_url {

    my($url) = @_;

    status "Fetching $url";
    my $content = &_get_url($url);
    (my $response, $content) = $content =~ /(.*?)\n\n(.*)/is if $content;
    return wantarray ? ($response, $content) : $content;

}
```

Now, in a BEGIN block, store our three definitions for _get_url in three separate variables, then eval just the one desired for this invocation of *tkcomics*. Note that we can override the default selection from the command line and that we have to relax our coding strictness in order to eval the symbolic reference.

```perl
BEGIN {

    # Different mechanisms to get web content without blocking.

    use vars qw/
        $pipe_open_fileevent
        $tcp_socket_fileevent
        $win32_memmap_waitvariable
    /;

    $pipe_open_fileevent = <<'END';
    # Pipe/open/fileevent version of _get_url( ) here ...
END

    $tcp_socket_fileevent = <<'END';
    # TCP/IP socket/fileevent version of _get_url( ) here ...
END

    $win32_memmap_waitvariable = <<'END';
    # Win32 memmap/waitVariable version of _get_url( ) here ...
END

    my $get_url;
    if (defined $ARGV[0]) {
        $get_url = $ARGV[0];
    } else {
        if ($^O eq 'MSWin32') {
            $get_url = 'win32_memmap_waitvariable';
        } else {
            $get_url = 'pipe_open_fileevent';
        }
    }
```

```
    {
        no strict 'refs';
        print "Using $get_url method ...\n";
        eval $$get_url;
        die "_get_url eval error: $@" if $@;
    }

} # end BEGIN
```

Finally, here's *tkcomics* in its entirety. It fetches web content in a nonblocking mode so that Tk events flow and configures itself according to the operating system on which it's running. Enjoy.

```
#!/usr/local/bin/perl -w
#
# tkcomics - display comics courtesy of http://www.comics.com
#
# Because LWP::Simple and LWP::UserAgent can block, do the network
# I/O in another thread, or, child, and using fileevent() or
# waitVariable() to keep events flowing.
#
# Add a Stop/Cancel button that kills the pipe.
#
# Command line options:
#
#   pipe_open_fileevent
#   tcp_socket_fileevent
#   win32_memmap_waitvariable


use MIME::Base64;
use Tk;
use Tk::JPEG;
use Tk::PNG;
use subs qw/get_url show_comic status stop_get unix_pipe win32_memmap/;
use strict;

my $mw = MainWindow->new;
my $photo = '';
my $status = '';
my($eof, $pid);
my %ext = qw/
    gif gif
    jpg jpeg
    png png
    tif tiff
    xbm xbm
    ppm ppm
/;                      # file extension => Photo format map

my $s = $mw->Label(-textvariable => \$status, -width => 100);
my $lb = $mw->Scrolled(qw/Listbox -selectforeground blue/);
my $l = $mw->Label(
    -text       => 'tkcomics',
```

```
            -foreground => 'blue',
            -font       => [qw/-size 100 -slant italic/],
    );
    $s->pack(qw/-side bottom -fill x -expand 1/);
    $lb->pack(qw/side left -fill y -expand 1 -anchor w/);
    $l->pack(-side => 'right');

    # Fetch the main comics page, build a hash of comic URLs
    # indexed by comic name,  note the total comic count, and
    # populate a Listbox.  Listbox B1 fetches and displays a
    # comic. B2 anywhere cancels a transfer.

    my $comics_home = 'http://www.comics.com';
    my $comics = get_url $comics_home or die "Can't get $comics_home.";

    my(%comics, $comic_url, $comic);
    foreach (split /\n/, $comics) {
        next unless /OPTION\s+VALUE/i;
        if (($comic_url, $comic) = m\"([^"]+)">(.*)\) {
            $comic =~ s/\t//g;
            $comic =~ s/\r//g;
            $comics{$comic} = $comic_url;
        }
    }
    my $help = scalar(keys %comics) .
        ' comics, <Button-1> fetch comic, <Button-2> interrupt transfer';
    status $help;

    foreach (sort keys %comics) {
        $lb->insert('end', $_);
    }

    $lb->bind('<ButtonRelease-1>' => \&show_comic);
    $mw->bind('<ButtonRelease-2>' => \&stop_get);

    MainLoop;

    sub get_url {

        # Given a URL, return its contents. The exact nonblocking
        # mechanism is adjustable, and either defaults to the best
        # method for the operating system at hand, or is specified
        # on the command line.

        my($url) = @_;

        status "Fetching $url";
        my $content = &_get_url($url);
        (my $response, $content) = $content =~ /(.*?)\n\n(.*)/is if $content;
        return wantarray ? ($response, $content) : $content;

    } # end get_url

    sub show_comic {
```

```perl
    # Using the active listbox element, find the comic URL and fetch
    # its contents.  Within the content is another URL pointing to
    # the actual image, which we then fetch, convert to a Photo and
    # then display.  $eof is -1 if any transfer was aborted.

    my($lb) = @_;

    my $comic = $lb->get('active');
    $comic =~ s/\s\(\d+\)//;
    my $comic_url = $comics{$comic};
    my $comic_html = get_url
        $comic_url =~ /^http:/i ? $comic_url : "$comics_home$comic_url";
    return if $eof == -1;

    my($image_url);

    if ( ($image_url) = $comic_html =~ m\.*<IMG SRC="([^"]+)".*? ALT="(today|daily)\
is ) {
        print "1: $image_url!\n";
    } elsif ( ($image_url) = $comic_html =~ m\.*bgcolor="#FFFFCC" ALIGN="MIDDLE"
COLSPAN="3"><BR><IMG SRC="([^"]+)"\is ) {
        print "2: $image_url!\n";
    } else {
        status "Cannot find a comic image in $comic_url.";
        print STDERR $comic_html;
        return;
    }

    my ($response, $image) = get_url "$comics_home$image_url";
    return if $eof == -1;
    my($bytes) = $response =~ /Content-Length: (\d+)/is;

    my $photo_data = encode_base64($image);
    $photo->delete if UNIVERSAL::isa($photo => 'Tk::Photo');
    my($ext) = $image_url =~ /\.(.*)?/;
    $ext ||= 'gif';
    status "Creating $bytes byte $ext Photo";
    $photo = $mw->Photo(-data => $photo_data, -format => $ext{lc $ext});
    $l->configure(-image => $photo);

    my $index = $lb->index('active');
    $comic .= " ($bytes)";
    $lb->delete($index);
    $lb->insert($index, $comic);
    $lb->update;
    $lb->see($index);
    $lb->selectionSet($index);

    status $help;

} # end show_comic

sub status {
    $status = $_[0];
```

```
        $mw->idletasks;
}

sub stop_get {
    status "Stopping transfer ...";
    $mw->after(5000, sub {status $help});
    $eof = -1;
    kill 'TERM', $pid if defined $pid;;
}

BEGIN {

    # Different mechanisms to get web content without blocking.

    use vars qw/
        $pipe_open_fileevent
        $tcp_socket_fileevent
        $win32_memmap_waitvariable
    /;

    $pipe_open_fileevent = <<'END';

sub _get_url {

    my $url = shift;
    my $pid = open PIPE, "lwp-request -m GET -t 20s -e $url 2>&1 |" or
        die "Open error: $!";
    $eof = 0;

    my $content;
    $mw->fileevent(\*PIPE, 'readable' => sub {
        my($stat, $data);
        while ($stat = sysread PIPE, $data, 4096) {
            $content .= $data;
        }
        die "sysread error:  $!" unless defined $stat;
        $eof = 1 if $stat == 0;
    });
    $mw->waitVariable(\$eof);
    $mw->fileevent(\*PIPE, 'readable' => '');
    close PIPE;
    $pid = undef;
    return $content;

} # end pipe_open_fileevent

END

    $tcp_socket_fileevent = <<'END';

sub _get_url {

    # The parent opens a listen socket on a well known port on the
    # localhost, and then starts a second process to run lwp-request.
```

```perl
# When the parent receives a connect it reads all the HTML sent
# by the child.

use IO::Socket;
use POSIX;

my $url = shift;
my $port = 9917;
my($pid, $handle);

my $server = IO::Socket::INET->new(
    LocalHost => 'localhost',
    LocalPort => $port,
    Proto     => 'tcp',
    Listen    => SOMAXCONN,
    Reuse => 1,
);
die "Parent socket open failure: $!" unless defined $server;

die "fork failure: $!" unless defined($pid = fork);
if ($pid) {        # parent
    $handle = $server->accept;
    binmode $handle;
    $handle->autoflush(1);

    $eof = 0;
    my $content;
    $mw->fileevent($handle, 'readable' => sub {
        my($stat, $data);
        while ($stat = sysread $handle, $data, 4096) {
            $content .= $data;
        }
        die "sysread error:  $!" unless defined $stat;
        $eof = 1 if $stat == 0;
    });
    $mw->waitVariable(\$eof);
    $mw->fileevent($handle, 'readable' => '');
    close $handle;
    $pid = undef;
    return $content;

} else {        # child
    $handle = IO::Socket::INET->new(
        PeerAddr => 'localhost',
        PeerPort => $port,
        Proto    => 'tcp',
    );
    die "Child socket open failure: $!" unless defined $handle;
    binmode $handle;
    $handle->autoflush(1);

    use LWP::UserAgent;
    my $ua = LWP::UserAgent->new;
    $ua->timeout(20);
```

```perl
        my $req_object = HTTP::Request->new('GET' => $url);
        my $res_object = $ua->request($req_object);
        die "request failed" if $res_object->is_error;
        foreach my $response (keys %{$res_object->headers}) {
            print $handle "$response: ", $res_object->headers->{$response}, "\n";
        }
        print $handle "\n";
        print $handle $res_object->content;

        close $handle;
        POSIX::_exit(0);

    } # ifend fork

} # end tcp_socket_fileevent

END

    $win32_memmap_waitvariable = <<'END';

use vars qw/$kidfile/;
$kidfile = 'tkcwin32.kid';

sub _get_url {

    # The parent creates and initializes a new chunk of shared
    # memory, then starts a child process that shares the same
    # memory.  The parent waits for the child to run lwp-request
    # and save the web content by (essentially) doing a
    # waitvariable() on one particular hash element.

    use Win32::Process;
    use Tie::Win32MemMap;

    my $url = shift;

    my %content;
    tie %content, 'Tie::Win32MemMap', {
        Create  => MEM_NEW_SHARE,
        MapName => 'tkcomics',
    };
    $content{'COMPLETE'} = 0;
    $content{'CONTENT'}  = '';

    Win32::Process::Create(
        my $child,
        'c:\\perl\\bin\\perl.exe',
        "perl $kidfile $url",
        0,
        NORMAL_PRIORITY_CLASS,
        '.',
    ) or die Win32::FormatMessage(Win32::GetLastError);

    $eof = 0;
```

```perl
    $mw->update;

    while ( $content{'COMPLETE'} != 1 ) {
        last if $eof == -1;
        $mw->update;
    }
    return $content{'CONTENT'};

} # end win32_memmap

open(KID, ">$kidfile") or die "cannot open file $kidfile: $!";
print KID <<'END-OF-KID';
#!/usr/local/bin/perl -w
#
# Win32 tkcomics helper program that shovels web content to the Tk parent.

use Tie::Win32MemMap;

my $url = shift;

my %content;
tie %content, 'Tie::Win32MemMap', {
    Create  => MEM_VIEW_SHARE,
    MapName => 'tkcomics',
};

open(PIPE, "lwp-request -t 20s -e $url|") or die "open failure: $!";
binmode PIPE;

my($stat, $data);
while ($stat = sysread PIPE, $data, 4096) {
    $content{'CONTENT'} .= $data;
}
die "sysread error:  $!" unless defined $stat;
close PIPE;

$content{'COMPLETE'} = 1;
exit(0);
END-OF-KID
close KID;

END


    my $get_url;
    if (defined $ARGV[0]) {
        $get_url = $ARGV[0];
    } else {
        if ($^O eq 'MSWin32') {
            $get_url = 'win32_memmap_waitvariable';
        } else {
            $get_url = 'pipe_open_fileevent';
        }
    }
```

```
    {
        no strict 'refs';
        print "Using $get_url method ...\n";
        eval $$get_url;
        die "_get_url eval error: $@" if $@;
    }

} # end BEGIN
```

The PerlPlus Browser Plug-in

Now we'll briefly examine Frank Holtry's PerlPlus Plug-in, a loadable Netscape extension that executes Perl programs on a client computer. The Perl programs themselves can exist anywhere on the Net—the mere act of browsing a PerlPlus program (or any page with an HTML <EMBED> tag pointing to a PerlPlus program) may start it executing, subject to the result of an authentication procedure.

Netscape publishes an API for C language plug-ins that describes how to register a plug-in instance, read streaming data from a browsed URL, access system services, and so on. In 1996, Stan Melax used these specifications and developed the first plug-in for the Perl world so he could run Perl OpenGL programs in a browser. Basically, Stan's plug-in would read the browsed OpenGL program, wrap it in a Safe module, and feed the result to Perl. The Safe wrapper code provided security, and passed window information to the OpenGL code so it could properly embed itself within the browser.

In 1999, Frank rewrote the plug-in with an eye toward enhanced security. His idea was to use the *Opcode* module and restrict the opcodes available to the browsed Perl program. It's a multilevel scheme, from no security, in which all Perl opcodes are legal, to high security, where so many opcodes are forbidden that only the simplest Perl programs can run. Furthermore, a CGI program must first validate the browsed URL and return its opcode security level, a single digit from 0 through 5. The security CGI might be as crude as this simple table lookup:

```
#!/usr/local/bin/perl -w
#
# perlplus-secure.cgi - lookup a script's security level and inform the plugin.

use CGI qw/header param/;
use strict;

my $url_root = 'http://www.lehigh.edu/~solo/ptk/ppl';
my %urls = (
    "$url_root/clock-bezier.ppl" => 4,
    "$url_root/hw.ppl"           => 2,
    "$url_root/tkhanoi.ppl"      => 4,
);

my $url = lc param('URL');
my $sec_level = $urls{$url} || 0;

print header(-type => 'application/x-perlplus:.ppl:Perl'), "$sec_level\n";
```

Because the plug-in security model is under review, we won't examine this subject further.

As it happens, Perl/Tk programs generally have to run with most opcodes enabled, so browsing untrusted PerlPlus/Tk programs is a major security risk; imagine unleashing the full power of Perl inside your browser!* Nevertheless, it's easy to imagine a trusted environment where you know that the served PerlPlus programs are nonlethal.

Embedding Perl/Tk in Other Windows

Tk Toplevels, including the MainWindow, have an optional -use argument that indicates the window ID† within which the Toplevel should be embedded. (Normally a Toplevel appears inside the display's root window.) Any window you know the window ID of will work, even an *xclock*. Try it! Use *xwininfo* to determine an arbitrary window ID.

In our case, the PerlPlus plug-in makes Netscape's window ID available via a qualified Perl scalar, $Plugin::brinfo{xwindow_id}. Here's a bit of code that dumps the %brinfo hash key/value pairs and embeds a MainWindow within Netscape:

```
open PPLLOG, '>/tmp/ppl.log' or die $!;
foreach (sort keys %Plugin::brinfo) {
    print PPLLOG $_ . ' ' x (20 - length $_) . " : $Plugin::brinfo{$_}\n";
}
close PPLLOG;

my $mw = MainWindow->new(-use => $Plugin::brinfo{xwindow_id});
```

And here is what the file */tmp/ppl.log* shows us:

```
display            : 148717568
version            : 0.95.04
x_len              : 666
x_min              : 0
xwindow_id         : 88081995
y_len              : 272
y_min              : 0
```

The display hash key is the X display pointer, which you might find useful when performing low-level X11 functions, perhaps via X11::Protocol. x_min and y_min are the pixel coordinates of the top-left corner of the Netscape-provided window, and x_len and y_len are the width and height of the window, respectively.

---

* Think carefully, too, before you enable Java, or install your next plug-in and let boatloads of programs of unknown quality and origin execute on your machine.
† Use the window information command id to fetch the window ID of any Tk widget.

Embedded Versus Full-Screen Mode

Figure 22-5 depicts a full-screen Towers of Hanoi* simulation. A PerlPlus/Tk program runs in full-screen mode when its URL is browsed directly. In this case, your Tk program has an entire window all to itself. `$Plugin::brinfo{x_len}` and `$Plugin::brinfo{y_len}` define the window's width and height, and `$Plugin::brinfo{x_min}` and `Plugin::brinfo{y_min}` are both zero. If your MainWindow is larger than the Netscape window, it's clipped on the right and/or bottom.

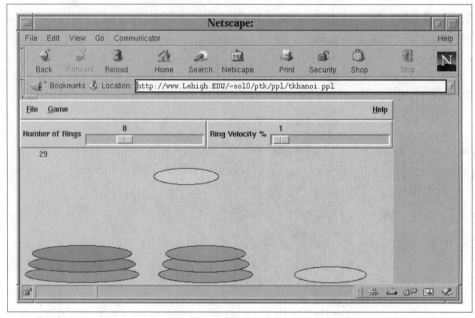

Figure 22-5. Full-screen Towers of Hanoi program

The other way to invoke a PerlPlus/Tk program is via an HTML `<EMBED>` tag:

```
<BODY>
    Countdown to 2038, <EMBED src="y2k.ppl" width=225 height=50> although
    there's not much hope I'll be around for the event!
</BODY>
```

This code produced Figure 22-6, a Perl/Tk program constrained to a 225 x 50 window.

For an embedded Perl/Tk window, `$Plugin::brinfo{x_min}` and `$Plugin::brinfo{y_min}` are the pixels offsets from the top-left corner of the Netscape window, not necessarily zero. If your code is flexible enough, it can use the following to resize itself to the area supplied by Netscape:

```
my $geom = $Plugin::brinfo{x_len} . 'x' . $Plugin::brinfo{y_len};
$mw->geometry($geom);
```

---

* See Appendix C for a complete *tkhanoi* program listing.

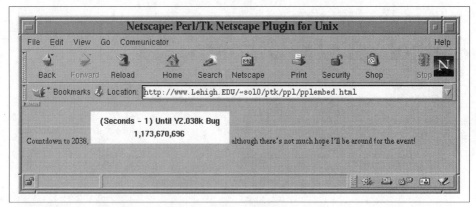

Figure 22-6. A constrained, embedded Perl/Tk window

How You Can Contribute to the PerlPlus Plug-in Project

The PerlPlus plug-in is available for public download and development at *http://sourceforge.net/projects/PerlPlusPlugin*. Head to Sourceforge; get yourself a username and password; ensure you have an environment that includes SSH, SSL, and CVS; and you're all set to web-over to the CVS repository to examine the source and get the entire source distribution or *diffs* of various versions, all from within your favorite browser.

If you want to work on the plug-in, contact Frank Holtry via the Sourceforge page, and he'll add you as a developer. Here's a sample CVS command to check out the source distribution:

```
export CVS_RSH=/path-to/ssh
cvs -z3 -dYOURNAME@cvs.PerlPlusPlugin.sourceforge.net:/cvsroot/PerlPlusPlugin co
PerlPlusPlugin
```

If you're behind a firewall, you'll need an SSH wrapper such as this, or else your CVS commands will appear to hang:

```
#!/bin/bash
exec /usr/local/bin/ssh -P $*
```

The -P option tells *ssh* to use a nonprivileged port. You'll end up with a directory named PerlPlusPlugin, a copy of the entire distribution.

## CHAPTER 23

Plethora of pTk Potpourri

In this chapter, we present a blast of miscellaneous widgets, methods, options, and cookbook ideas. There isn't a lot of depth in this chapter, just a jumble of material that didn't fit in the rest of the book, but that we know you'll need some day.

This chapter covers:

- Perl/Tk special variables and exporter symbols
- Cursor manipulation and customization
- Using dialogs for messages, errors, selecting colors, or opening and saving files
- The Adjuster widget, which allows users to resize frames in an application
- Calling up "help" windows via the Balloon widget
- The BrowseEntry widget, which is a composite of the Entry widget and a Listbox
- The LabFrame widget, which is a Frame with a label attached
- The NoteBook widget, which is a simple way to create multiple pages with tabs
- The Pane widget, essentially a scrollable Frame
- The ProgressBar widget, which can be used to display progress to a user during a time-consuming operation

pTk Special Variables and Exporter Symbols

Before we get to the interesting stuff, we need to list the special variables and symbols unique to Perl/Tk.

Global Variables

These global variables are available for your use:

$Tk::VERSION

> The Perl/Tk version, which incorporates the Tcl/Tk version it's based upon, plus the Perl/Tk subrelease number. '800.023' is the 23rd Perl/Tk release based on Tcl/Tk 8.0. '803.xxx' will be based on Tcl/Tk 8.3.

`$Tk::library`

The pathname where the Tk modules are installed; for example: `/usr/local/lib/perl5/site_perl/5.6.0/i686-linux/Tk`.

`$Tk::platform`

The platform, which is `'MSWin32'` for Win32 machines, otherwise `'unix'`.

`$Tk::version`

The base Tcl/Tk version, for example `'8.0'`.

`$Tk::patchLevel`

The Tcl/Tk patch level, for example `'8.0'`.

`$Tk::strictMotif`

A flag to force Tk to use pure Motif style windows.

Symbols Exported by Default

The use `Tk` statement exports these subroutines by default:

`DoOneEvent`

Handles Tk events. See Chapter 15.

`Ev`

Used in callback definitions to delay argument evaluation. See Chapter 15.

`exit`

Overrides Perl's `CORE::exit` to clean up Tk data structures.

`Exists($widget)`

Ensures that $widget is a valid Perl/Tk widget reference.

`MainLoop`

Starts the Tk event loop.

`tkinit(@args)`

Shorthand for `MainWindow->new(@args)`.

Optionally Exported Symbols

You can import these symbols if desired:

`catch`

Executes a block of code, trapping and ignoring any errors. The code should be enclosed in a Perl block: `catch {$widget->cget(-state)}`.

`*event`

A localized version of a callback's event structure. See Chapter 15.

`lsearch`

Searches a list for an exact string match. It returns the ordinal of the match, or –1 if no match. For example: `my $ord = lsearch(\@Selection,$i)`. The first argument is an array reference and the second the match string.

NoOp
> A No Operation subroutine, commonly used to disable a callback.

$XS_VERSION
> The XS version.

*widget
> A localized version of the widget that owns the callback. See Chapter 15.

DONT_WAIT, WINDOW_EVENTS, FILE_EVENTS, TIMER_EVENTS, IDLE_EVENTS, ALL_EVENTS
> DoOneEvent bit patterns. See Chapter 15.

NORMAL_BG, ACTIVE_BG, SELECT_BG, SELECT_FG, TROUGH, INDICATOR, DISABLED, BLACK, WHITE
> Common colors.

Exporter Tags

You can import several symbols at once using an Exporter tag (for example, to get all the DoOneEvent bit patterns, do use Tk ':eventtypes'):

- :eventtypes => qw/DONT_WAIT WINDOW_EVENTS FILE_EVENTS TIMER_EVENTS IDLE_ EVENTS ALL_EVENTS/

- :variables => qw/*widget *event/

- :colors => qw/NORMAL_BG ACTIVE_BG SELECT_BG SELECT_FG TROUGH INDICATOR DISABLED BLACK WHITE/

Manipulating the Cursor

Every Tk widget has a cursor shape associated with it. Most default to what's known as the left_ptr shape, shown in Figure 23-1.

Figure 23-1. The standard cursor for most widgets

The cursor shape can be changed on a widget-by-widget basis with the -cursor option:

```
$mw->Button(-text => 'Go ...', -cursor => cursor_name);
```

When the mouse is over the Button, the cursor changes to the one specified. The cursor change happens whether the Button is disabled or not. The set of available cursors is quite large. Figure 23-2 shows the cursor shapes available on most systems.

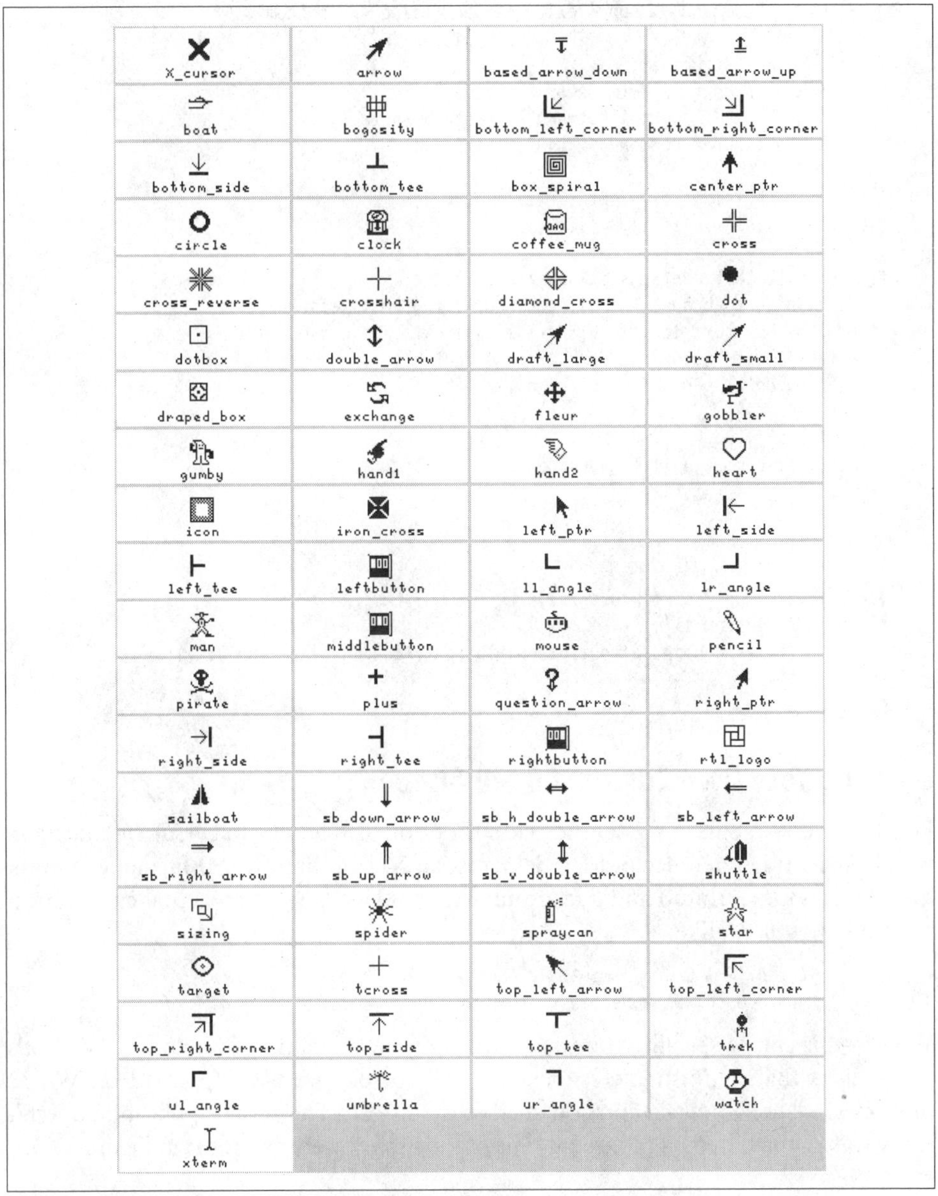

X_cursor	arrow	based_arrow_down	based_arrow_up
boat	bogosity	bottom_left_corner	bottom_right_corner
bottom_side	bottom_tee	box_spiral	center_ptr
circle	clock	coffee_mug	cross
cross_reverse	crosshair	diamond_cross	dot
dotbox	double_arrow	draft_large	draft_small
draped_box	exchange	fleur	gobbler
gumby	hand1	hand2	heart
icon	iron_cross	left_ptr	left_side
left_tee	leftbutton	ll_angle	lr_angle
man	middlebutton	mouse	pencil
pirate	plus	question_arrow	right_ptr
right_side	right_tee	rightbutton	rtl_logo
sailboat	sb_down_arrow	sb_h_double_arrow	sb_left_arrow
sb_right_arrow	sb_up_arrow	sb_v_double_arrow	shuttle
sizing	spider	spraycan	star
target	tcross	top_left_arrow	top_left_corner
top_right_corner	top_side	top_tee	trek
ul_angle	umbrella	ur_angle	watch
xterm			

Figure 23-2. Cursor shapes available on most systems

Here's a program to look at the different cursors interactively. It's really simple, just a Listbox full of cursor shape names and a button binding that changes the application's cursor. The hardest part is figuring out where the list of cursor names is hidden.

```
$mw = MainWindow->new;
$mw->Button(-text => "Exit",
```

```
                       -command => sub { exit })->pack(-side => "bottom",
                                          -fill => "x");
    $scroll = $mw->Scrollbar;
    $lb = $mw->Listbox(-selectmode => 'single',
                       -yscrollcommand => [set => $scroll]);
    $scroll->configure(-command => [yview => $lb]);

    $scroll->pack(-side => 'right', -fill => 'y');
    $lb->pack(-side => 'left', -fill => 'both');

    ## Open file that contains all available cursors
    ## Might have to change this if your cursorfont.h is elsewhere
    ## On Win32 systems look in C:\Perl\lib\site\Tk\X11\cursorfont.h
    open (FH, "/usr/X11R6/include/X11/cursorfont.h") ||
      die "Couldn't open cursor file.\n";

    while (<FH>) {
      push(@cursors, $1) if (/\#define XC_(\w+) /);
    }

    close(FH);

    $lb->insert('end', sort @cursors);
    $lb->bind('<Button-1>',
        sub { $mw->configure(-cursor => $lb->get($lb->curselection)); });

    MainLoop;
```

Creating Your Own Custom Cursor Shape

Besides a built-in cursor name, the -cursor option also accepts a *cursor specification*, which is an array reference of four elements: an X11 bitmap (XBM) filename, a mask filename, and foreground and background colors. Here's what an actual cursor specification might look like:

```
    my $cursor = $^O eq 'MSWin32' ? 'mouse' :
        [qw/@mouse.xbm mouse.mask brown white/];
```

We saw this cursor specification used in the *tkneko* program in Chapter 17. What it's telling us is that, unfortunately, home-brewed cursors are not supported on Win32 machines; we use a built-in cursor named mouse instead. The actual application doesn't really want a three-button mouse but one of the furry variety as shown in Figure 23-3.

Figure 23-3. The tkneko cursor

So, under Unix, Tk builds a custom cursor using the XBM files *mouse.xbm* and *mouse. mask* and colors the mouse brown and white. Note that *mouse.xbm* starts with an @ character, which signals to Tk that this is a custom cursor specification rather than a built-in cursor name. This is an artifact of Tcl's "everything is a string" heritage.

Dialog Boxes

There are several reasons you might want to create a dialog box in Perl/Tk. This section will show you what your choices are and how to configure dialog boxes.

The Dialog Widget

The most basic widget provided in Tk to create a dialog box is Dialog. It's perfect when you need a quick way to display information or get an answer from a user.

```
$answer = $mw->Dialog(-title => 'Please Reply',
   -text => 'Would you like to continue?',
   -default_button => 'yay', -buttons => [ 'yay', 'nay'],
   -bitmap => 'question' )->Show( );
if ($answer eq 'yay') {
  # ... do something ...
}
```

Figure 23-4 shows the output from our code snippet.

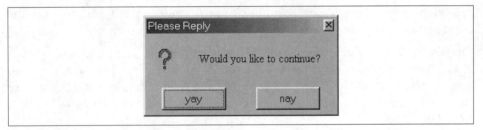

Figure 23-4. A typical dialog box

Instead of calling Show immediately, you can save a reference to the dialog and reuse it throughout your application. The options you can use with a Dialog are as follows:

-bitmap => *bitmap*
    Displays a bitmap to the left of the text in the Dialog. Optional.

-buttons => [*button list*]
    An anonymous list of buttons to display on the dialog. Buttons will be displayed in the same order they are listed.

-default_button => *button text*
    Whichever button matches this string will be highlighted as the default button for the Dialog. The string match is case senstive, and if the string doesn't match anything, there will be no default.

-text => *text*
    Text displayed above the buttons in the Dialog.

-title => *title*
    The title of the dialog box.

The messageBox Method

If you need only a one-shot dialog, you can use the messageBox method. The options are slightly different, but the result looks almost the same, shown in Figure 23-5. Keep in mind that every time you call messageBox, a new Dialog is created and there is no Show method.

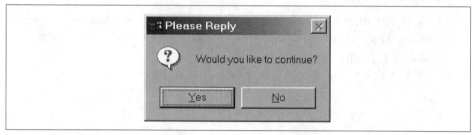

Figure 23-5. Dialog created using messageBox

Like a Dialog widget, messageBox returns the selected Button's string, but its case may vary depending on your operating system. Therefore, it's best to treat the response in a case-insensitive manner.

The messageBox Buttons are specified with the -type option, so, for example, a -type of AbortRetryIgnore produces three Buttons with the labels Abort, Retry, and Ignore. Any of these Button labels can be specified as the default Button. Once again, case issues are present; see -default. It's anticipated that these case issues will be taken care of in Tk 800.024.

```
$answer => $mw->messageBox(-title => 'Please Reply',
    -message => 'Would you like to continue?',
    -type => 'YesNo', -icon => 'question', -default => 'yes');
```

The options used with messageBox are as follows:

-default => *string*

> The string specified will be used as the default button. Depending on the version of messageBox you have, the default string needs to be all lowercase on a Win32 system, whereas on Unix the first letter should be capitalized. Either way, if the string doesn't match properly, you'll get an error.

-icon => *bitmap*

> The bitmap to display to the left of the message text. The bitmap displayed is operating system dependent.

-message => *message*

> The message to display above the buttons on the dialog.

-title => *title*

> The title for the dialog.

-type => *buttontypes*

    Specifies a predefined set of buttons to be displayed. The following values are possible: `'AbortRetryIgnore'`, `'OK'`, `'OKCancel'`, `'RetryCancel'`, `'YesNo'`, or `'YesNoCancel'`. An invalid type will result in an error.

The DialogBox Widget

The DialogBox widget is a more customizable version of Dialog. Instead of just a text message above the buttons, you can put anything you'd like in that area. There are only three options available with DialogBox:

-buttons => [*button list*]

    An anonymous list of buttons to display on the dialog. Buttons will be displayed in the same order they are listed.

-default_button => *button text*

    Whichever button matches this string will be highlighted as the default button for the Dialog. The string match is case-sensitive, and if the string doesn't match anything, there will be no default.

-title => *title*

    The title of the dialog box.

After creating the DialogBox, you can call the add method to insert items, and pack will display the widgets inside the dialog. Here's an example of creating a login DialogBox:

```
require Tk::LabEntry;
    ...
$db = $mw->DialogBox(-title => 'Login', -buttons => ['Ok', 'Cancel'],
                     -default_button => 'Ok');
$db->add('LabEntry', -textvariable => \$uname, -width => 20,
         -label => 'Username', -labelPack => [-side => 'left'])->pack;
$db->add('LabEntry', -textvariable => \$pw, -width => 20,
         -label => 'Password', -show => '*',
         -labelPack => [-side => 'left'])->pack;
$answer = $db->Show( );

if ($answer eq "Ok") {
  print "Username = $uname, Password = $pw\n";
}
```

Figure 23-6 shows the outcome.

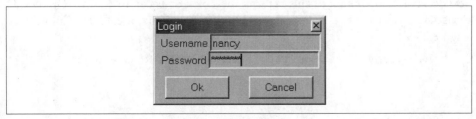

Figure 23-6. A login dialog created using DialogBox

Using ErrorDialog

When working with a graphical application, it makes sense to display errors to your user in a graphical manner. Normally if something goes wrong in your application, Tk::Error is called, and the error message(s) is printed on the console where the program was run from. This is a less-than user-friendly way to communicate to your users that something is wrong. By including use Tk::ErrorDialog in your application, you will start getting error messages in dialog boxes.

This magic happens because ErrorDialog overrides Tk::Error with a version of its own. If you're unsatisfied with either version of Tk::Error, write your own. It's called with three arguments:

```
my ($w, $error, @msgs) = @_;
```

$w is a widget reference, $error is the current error message, and @msgs is an array of traceback messages.

Figure 23-7 shows an example error dialog, when we used the wrong default button to create another dialog.

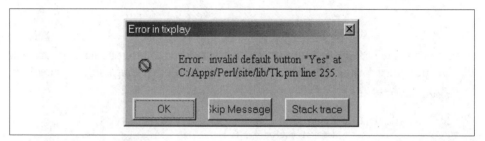

Figure 23-7. An error dialog

Execution of your application doesn't halt when an error shows up, but the user is required to click through any error messages that are displayed.

chooseColor Dialog

There are times you would like the user to select his own color, perhaps when customizing the look of the application windows or when drawing text in a Text or Canvas widget. Using chooseColor, you can pop up a dialog box to select a color name or hexadecimal color number. This returns the color or undef to $color. On Win32 chooseColor calls a native dialog (Figure 23-8), and on Unix, it calls Tk::ColorEditor (Figure 23-9).

```
$color = $widget->chooseColor(-title => 'string', -initialcolor => color);
```

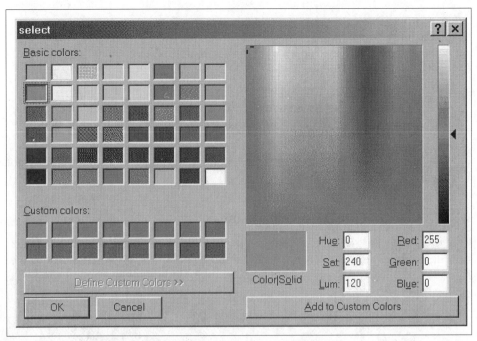

Figure 23-8. Version displayed when calling chooseColor on Win32

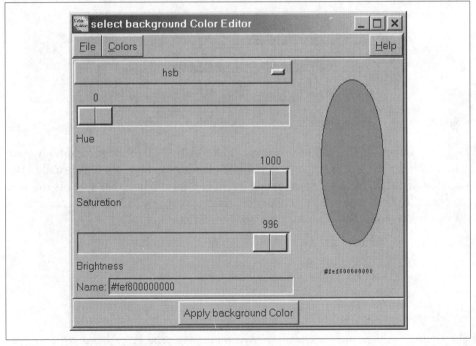

Figure 23-9. The Tk::ColorEditor dialog

Valid options are:

`-initialcolor => 'color'`

Specifies the color to display in the color dialog when it pops up. We talked about valid color values in Chapter 4.

`-parent => $widget`

Makes $widget the logical parent of the color dialog. The color dialog is displayed on top of its parent window. This option is not normally required.

`-title => 'title'`

Specifies a string to display as the title of the dialog box. If this option is not specified, a default title is displayed.

getOpenFile and getSaveFile Dialogs

Often you will want the user to locate an existing file or the location for a new file on her filesystem. The methods getOpenFile and getSaveFile let you do this easily. Figure 23-10 illustrates the getOpenFile dialog.

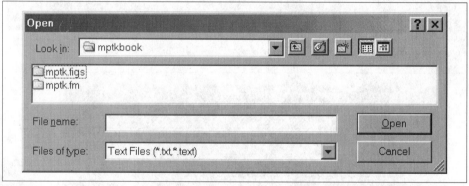

Figure 23-10. Version of getOpenFile (getSaveFile looks the same except for the title)

To give you a quick idea of how these are used, getOpenFile is most commonly associated with the "Open" command in the File menu, and getSaveFile is usually associated with the "Save as..." command in the File menu. In either case, if the user selects a file, both methods return the full pathname of this file. If the user cancels the operation, both methods return an undefined value.

The easiest way to invoke them both is:

```
my $file = $mw->getOpenFile( );
&do_something($file) if defined $file;

my $sfile = $mw->getSaveFile( );
&do_somethingelse($sfile) if defined $sfile;
```

The only real difference between the two methods is the error handling they perform. For instance, if you try to select a preexisting file from the Save dialog, you will be asked if you want to overwrite that file. Your program is still required to actually create or open the returned filename; these dialogs are just a consistent way of requesting the information from the user.

If you would like to customize your open or save dialog, use one or more of the following optional arguments:

-defaultextension => *string*
> Specifies a string that will be appended to the filename if the user enters a filename without an extension.

-filetypes => [*filePatternList*]
> You can specify some predefined file patterns for the user to choose from (if applicable on your platform). The *filePatternList* is a list itself, so you end up with a list of lists. Each inner list should contain a file type description, an extension (or list of extensions), and an optional type. Here's an example to clarify:

```
my $types = [
    ['Text Files',        ['.txt', '.text']],
    ['Java Source Files', '.java'          ],
    ['C Source Files',    '.c',      'TEXT'],
    ['GIF Files',         '.gif',          ],
    ['All Files',         '*',             ],
];

my $filename = $mw->getOpenFile(-filetypes => $types);
```

-initialdir => *directory*
> The starting directory for the user to browse from. If not specified, the files in the current working directory are displayed.

-initialfile => *filename*
> Default filename to start with. This option is ignored by the getOpenFile method.

-title => *string*
> A title to use for the dialog. A default title will be used if this isn't specified.

The Adjuster Widget

There are times you would like the user to have control over how large a frame is in part of the application. Let's say you're listing a large number of font styles along the left side of the application, and the right side of the application contains a Text widget. It would be nice if users could make the font styles list wider or smaller depending on their preferences. We can do this using the Adjuster widget.

Here's a simple example using two frames that contain a Listbox and a Text widget, respectively:

```
use Tk;
use Tk::Adjuster;
```

```
$mw = MainWindow->new(-title => "Adjuster example");

$leftf = $mw->Frame->pack(-side => 'left', -fill => 'y');
$adj = $mw->Adjuster(-widget => $leftf, -side => 'left')
  ->pack(-side => 'left', -fill => 'y');
$rightf = $mw->Frame->pack(-side => 'right', -fill => 'both', -expand => 1);

# Now put something into our frames.
$lb = $leftf->Scrolled('Listbox', -scrollbars => 'osoe')
  ->pack(-expand => 1, -fill => 'both');
$lb->insert('end', qw/normal bold italics code command email emphasis
                    emphasisBold Filename FirstTerm KeyCode KeySymbol/);
$rightf->Scrolled('Text', -scrollbars => 'osoe')
  ->pack(-expand => 1, -fill => 'both');

MainLoop;
```

You can see in Figure 23-11 that the thin line with the small box at the bottom is our adjuster. If you hover your mouse over the line, the cursor will change to a horizontal double-ended arrow, indicating you can click and drag. As you drag to the right, the Listbox becomes larger. As you drag to the left, the Listbox becomes smaller.

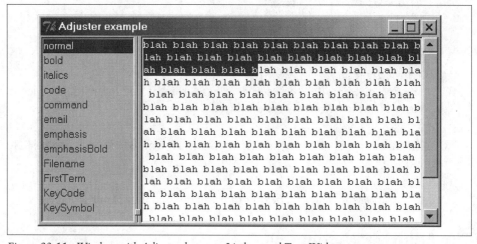

Figure 23-11. Window with Adjuster between Listbox and Text Widgets

Instead of calling pack on the Adjuster widget, you can call packAdjust, which shortens your argument list and eliminates having to use any pack-specific options:

```
$adj1->packAdjust($leftf, -side => 'left');
```

The options you can use to customize the Adjuster include:

-restore => 1 | 0

When the top level window changes size, setting -restore to 1 will make the Adjuster keep room for itself in the window.

```
-side => 'left' | 'right' | 'top' | 'bottom'
```
Indicates where the managed widget lies in relation to the Adjuster. Values of
'top' or 'bottom' will cause the Adjuster to be horizontal and manage height
instead of width.

```
-widget => widget
```
The widget to be managed by the adjuster.

The Balloon Widget

Using a Balloon widget, you can create help-text–like labels that appear as the mouse
hovers over a widget. You can also use it to create help text that appears in a status bar.
Let's look at a very simple example, then go over the relevant options and methods:

```
use Tk;
use Tk::Balloon;

$mw = MainWindow->new(-title => "Simple Balloon example");
$button = $mw->Button(-text => "Exit", -command => sub { exit })->pack;
$msgarea = $mw->Label(-borderwidth => 2, -relief => 'groove')
  ->pack(-side => 'bottom', fill => 'x');
$balloon = $mw->Balloon(-statusbar => $msgarea);
$balloon->attach($button, -balloonmsg => "Exit the App",
  -statusmsg => "Press the Button to exit the application");
$balloon->attach($msgarea, -msg => 'Displays the help text for a widget');
MainLoop;
```

Figure 23-12 illustrates this example.

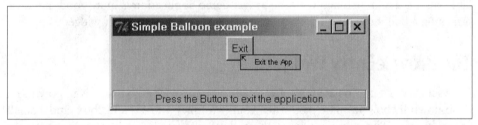

Figure 23-12. Using a Balloon as both help text and a status message

Using a status bar is optional. We've just included it here to show you how easy it is.
Here are the options you can use when creating your Balloon widget:[*]

```
-state => 'balloon' | 'status' | 'both' | 'none'
```
Determines if the Balloon widget will be displaying only balloons, only status
messages, both (the default), or nothing.

---

[*] Not all the options are detailed here, only those used 99% of the time. See the documentation included with
the widget for a complete listing.

`-statusbar => `*`widget`*

> Tells the Balloon what widget to use for displaying status messages. The widget specified must have a -text or -textvariable option.

`-balloonposition => 'widget' | 'mouse'`

> Determines the position in which the Balloon is displayed. Specify mouse to use the cursor position.

`-initwait => `*`time`*

> The amount of time in milliseconds to wait before showing the balloon message or status message. Default is 350 milliseconds.

Once the Balloon is created, you can both attach and detach widgets. Here's the attach method:

```
$balloon->attach($widget, option => value, ... );
```

This method takes a widget and a list of the following option/value pairs:

`-msg => `*`string`*

> The message to be displayed in both a balloon and the status bar

`-balloonmsg => `*`string`*

> The message to be displayed only as a balloon

`-statusmsg => `*`string`*

> The message to be displayed only in the status bar

You can override any of the -initwait, -state, -statusbar, or -balloonposition options with each individual call to attach.

The balloon demo included with the *widget* demo application is quite good; it shows attaching a Balloon to text widgets, canvas items, and various other widgets.

The BrowseEntry Widget

BrowseEntry is a composite widget created to be like a combo box (also known as a drop-down listbox on some platforms) using an Entry widget, a Listbox, and a small arrow button. The combination of these three widgets in the BrowseEntry is very powerful.

Before we list the options and methods for a BrowseEntry, let's look at an example:

```
use Tk;
use Tk::ROText;
use Tk::BrowseEntry;

$mw = MainWindow->new(-title => "Text search using BrowseEntry");

# Create Browse Entry to enter search text in, and save off
# already entered text that you've searched for.
$f = $mw->Frame(-relief => 'ridge', -borderwidth => 2)
  ->pack(-fill => 'x');
```

```perl
# Use ROText so user can't change speech
$t = $mw->Scrolled('ROText', -scrollbars => 'osoe')
  ->pack(-expand => 1, -fill => 'both');

$t->insert('end', <<'EOD'
"Give Me Liberty or Give Me Death"
March 23, 1775
By Patrick Henry
No man thinks more highly than I do of the patriotism, as well as abilities, of the
very worthy gentlemen who have just addressed the house. But different <snipped...> I
know not what course others may take; but as for me, give me liberty or give me
death!

EOD
);

# define a new tag to use on selected text
# (making it look just like normal selection)
# This way the Text widget doesn't need focus to show selection
$t->tagConfigure('curSel', -background => $t->cget(-selectbackground),
                 -borderwidth => $t->cget(-selectborderwidth),
                 -foreground => $t->cget(-selectforeground));

my $search_string = "";

# If user selects item from list manually, invoke do_search
$be = $f->BrowseEntry(-variable => \$search_string,
                      -browsecmd => \&do_search)->pack(-side => 'left');
# If user types in word and hits return, invoke do_search
$be->bind("<Return>", \&do_search);
$be->focus;  # Start w/focus on BrowseEntry

# Clicking the Search button will invoke do_search
$f->Button(-text => 'Search', -command => \&do_search)
    ->pack(-side => 'left');
$f->Button(-text => 'Exit', -command => \&do_exit)
    ->pack(-side => 'right');

sub do_search {
  # Add search string to list if it's not already there
  if (! exists $searches{$search_string}) {
    $be->insert('end', $search_string);
  }
  $searches{$search_string}++;

  # Calculate where to search from, and what to highlight next
  my $startindex = 'insert';
  if (defined $t->tagRanges('curSel')) {
    $startindex = 'curSel.first + 1 chars';
  }
  my $index = $t->search('-nocase', $search_string, $startindex);
  if ($index ne '') {
    $t->tagRemove('curSel', '1.0', 'end');
    my $endindex = "$index + " .  (length $search_string) . " chars";
```

```
      $t->tagAdd('curSel', $index, $endindex);
      $t->see($index);
    } else { $mw->bell; }

    $be->selectionRange(0, 'end'); # Select word we just typed/selected
}

# print stats on searching before we exit.
sub do_exit {
    print "CountWord\n";
    foreach (sort keys %searches) {
        print "$searches{$_}$_\n";
    }
    exit;
}

MainLoop;
```

Take a look at Figure 23-13 to see the screenshot of this application. The BrowseEntry is in the upper-left corner. We have shown it with the list part of the BrowseEntry down (after the down arrow button has been pressed).

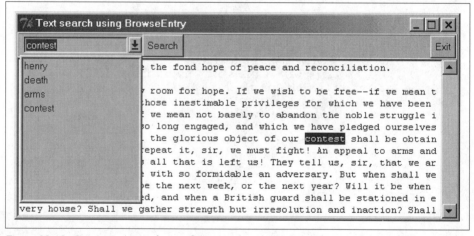

Figure 23-13. BrowseEntry used to perform searches in a Text widget

In this example, we are using the BrowseEntry with mostly default settings. We added a callback so that when the user selected an entry from the list manually, the search subroutine was invoked as well. The easiest way to know what the user has selected/typed is to use the -variable option. Most of the code for this example has to do with figuring out where the word is in the Text widget.

The BrowseEntry supports all the options a LabEntry does (see Chapter 5), except -textvariable. Additional BrowseEntry options are:

-arrowimage => *image*

　　This option changes the picture on the little button.

-browsecmd => *callback*

This callback will be invoked whenever the user selects something from the list. BrowseEntry already performs the work to display the new selection in the edit box.

-choices => *list*

You can put choices in the list using this option. Examples are: -choices => [qw/ one two three/] or -choices => @init_choices. You can also add items to the list using the insert method ($be->insert('end', 'newchoice');).

-listcmd => *callback*

Specify a callback to be invoked when the arrow button is pushed. This will be called before the list is displayed, so if you need to change the contents of the drop-down list, this is a great place to do so.

-listwidth => *amount*

The width of the popup listbox. The listbox will not automatically grow to fit your choices if you have long strings in it.

-variable => \$scalar

Place the user's selection in $scalar.

-state => 'normal' | 'readonly' | 'disabled'

A state of 'normal' that the user can type in new entries and select entries from the list. A 'readonly' state limits the user to only selecting items from the list. A state of 'disabled' will not allow any interaction with the user at all.

In addition to all the methods of Tk::Entry, the BrowseEntry widget supports its own insert and delete methods:

```
$be->insert('index', 'string');
$be->delete('index1', 'index2');
```

The insert method adds a new item into the list at the specified index. The delete method removes list entries that are between the two indexes.

The LabFrame Widget

A LabFrame widget has all the features of a Frame and additionally provides a text label on the 'top', 'bottom', 'left', or 'right' of the Frame. The special placement option 'acrosstop' creates a grooved Frame around the central Frame and puts the label near the northwest corner such that it overlays the groove.

```
use Tk;
use Tk::LabFrame;
use strict;

my $mw = MainWindow->new(-title => 'LabFrame example')
my $lf = $mw->LabFrame(-label => "This is the label of a LabFrame",
    -labelside => 'acrosstop')->pack;
$lf->Text(qw/-width 40 -height 5/)->pack;
MainLoop;
```

This code produces the widget shown in Figure 23-14.

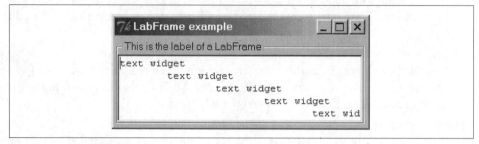

Figure 23-14. A LabFrame widget

LabFrame Options

LabFrame supports the same options as the Frame widget, plus:

-label => *text*
> The text of the label to be placed with the Frame

-labelside => 'left' | 'right' | 'top' | 'bottom' | 'acrosstop'
> Where to put the label on the frame

The NoteBook Widget

Displaying a lot of information in a small space is often the biggest challenge given to GUI programmers. The NoteBook widget is designed to help do just this. It allows us to have many pages of text, but lets only one be shown at a time. Each page in the NoteBook has a tab associated with it. The tab can display text or an image. Let's look at a simple example:

```
use Tk;
$mw = MainWindow->new();
# Create the notebook and fill the whole window
$nb = $mw->NoteBook()->pack(-expand => 1, -fill => 'both');
# Page 1 on the notebook, with button on that page
$p1 = $nb->add('page1', -label => 'Page 1');
$p1->Button(-text => 'Click me!')->pack();
# Empty page 2
$nb->add('page2', -label => 'Page 2');
MainLoop;
```

It creates a window with a NoteBook widget, shown in Figure 23-15. The notebook has two pages, named Page 1 and Page 2, respectively. Page 1 has a button on it, so the size of the NoteBook is determined by Page 1 (because it is the largest).

Figure 23-15. Simple NoteBook example

Creating Pages

When you create a page in a NoteBook, you assign it a name using the add method. From then on, when calling NoteBook methods, you refer to that page by that name. In our example, we used page1 and page2 as the internal page names. The displayed label can either be the same or something completely different. It is important that you use different internal names for every single page in the NoteBook, or you'll get an error. Here are some examples using the add method:

```
$p = $notebook->add('internalname', -label => 'Displayed Name');
$p2 = $notebook->add('internalname2', -bitmap => 'bitmapname');
```

The first argument passed to add is the internal storage name of the page. There are several options that will determine how the tab information is displayed:

-anchor => *anchordir*
    Anchors the text or image within the notebook tab. Values are: 'n', 'ne', 'e', 'se', 's', 'sw', 'w', 'nw', or 'center'.

-bitmap => *bitmap*
    A bitmap to use on the tab, instead of a label.

-image => *imageptr*
    An image to display instead of a label. Overrides both -bitmap and -label.

-label => *string*
    A string with which to label the tab.

-justify => 'left' | 'right' | 'center'
    Direction for the text to justify within the tab.

-createcmd => *callback*
    A callback that is invoked the first time the page is shown. This is useful if you have a lot of processing that can be delayed.

-raisecmd => *callback*
    Invoked every time the page is shown to the user.

-state => 'normal' | 'disabled'
    The state of the page.

`-underline => ` *index*

> Which character to underline in the tab. Starts at 0.

`-wraplength => ` *length*

> The maximum length of a line of text on the tab.

Once the page is created, you still need to put something on it. Use the reference returned by the `add` method and create widgets using that reference as the parent widget.

There are three ways to put something on a page:

- Using `MainLoop` when you create the page, before the window is displayed.
- Using the `-createcmd` option, which creates the page the first time the user clicks on that tab.
- Using the `-raisecmd`, which can change what is displayed on the page every time the user raises that page.

To delete a page, use the `delete` method and pass it the internal name of the page:

```
$notebook->delete("page1");
```

There are two methods used to get and set information associated with a page: `pagecget` and `pageconfigure`. Both methods will work only with the same options that can be used with the `add` method.

To get the value of an individual option, use `pagecget`:

```
$state = $notebook->pagecget("pagename", -state);
```

To change the value of one or more options, use `pageconfigure`:

```
$notebook->pageconfigure('pagename', -label => 'new label');
$notebook->pageconfigure('pagename', -label => 'new label', -underline => 3);
```

You can cause a page to be displayed (or raised) by using the `raise` method:

```
$notebook->raise("page4");
## OR check to see if that page is already showing:
$page = $notebook->raised();
if ($page ne "page4")
    $notebook->raise("page4");
```

WordCount Example Using a NoteBook

A NoteBook allows us to display data in an organized fashion. In this example, we are going to parse through some files (passed in as command-line parameters) and index out all the words contained within the files. The resulting window is shown in Figure 23-16; the code follows.

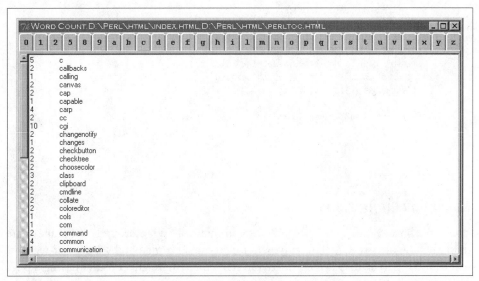

Figure 23-16. WordCount results displayed using a NoteBook

Half of the following code preps the list of words to display and the other half does the work of displaying it. To sort the words, we use a hash based on the first character in each word.

```
use Tk;
require Tk::NoteBook;

$mw = MainWindow->new( );
# Show the user the names of files we are parsing
# This might end up too long to see it all
$mw->title('Word Count:' . join (',', @ARGV));

# Use a courier font to display the tab text
$nb = $mw->NoteBook(-font => 'Courier 10 bold')->pack;

my %textWidgets;

%seen = ( );
while (<>) {
  while ( /(\w['\w-]*)/g) {
    $seen{lc $1}++;
  }
}

# go through the index in order and create the tabs and text widgets.
foreach my $word (sort (keys %seen)) {
  if ($word =~ /^(.)/) {
    $letter = $1;
```

```
    $t = $textWidgets{$letter};

    # Create the text widget if it doesn't already exist
    if (! defined $t) {
      my $p = $nb->add($letter, -label => $letter);
      $t = $p->Scrolled("Text")->pack(-expand => 1, -fill => 'both');
      $textWidgets{$letter} = $t;
    }
    $t->insert("end", $seen{$word} . "        " . $word . "\n");
  }
}

MainLoop;
```

NoteBook Limitations

You can't have the tabs for a NoteBook automatically wrap around and make more than one line of tabs. Consequently, you might make so many tabs that your window will be too big to be displayed properly. In that case, you might consider having a page contain another NoteBook widget, which will essentially give you two rows of tabs.

In order to disable a tab page, the recommended solution is to use an InputO widget, which covers everything on that tab page. However, InputO isn't supported on Win32 systems.

The Pane Widget

The Pane widget is essentially a Frame widget that may be scrolled. Within the Pane, you can pack whatever widgets however you like:

```
my $pane = $mw->Scrolled(qw/Pane -scrollbars osw/)->pack;

foreach (1 .. 20) {
    $pane->Label(-text => "Label $_")->pack;
}
```

The previous code produced Figure 23-17.

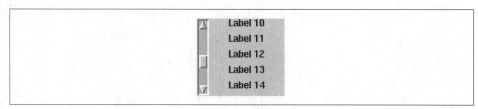

Figure 23-17. A Pane widget with a Scrollbar

Pane Options

The following options are available for Pane:

-gridded => 'x' | 'y' | 'xy'

Specifies if the top and left edges of the pane should snap to a grid column. This option is useful only if the widgets in the pane are managed by the grid geometry manager.

-sticky => *style*

If the Pane is larger than its requested dimensions, this option may be used to position (or stretch) the slave widgets within their cavity. *style* is a string that contains zero or more of the characters n, s, e, or w. Each letter refers to a side (north, south, east, or west) to which the slave sticks. If both n and s (or e and w) are specified, the slave is stretched to fill the entire height (or width) of its cavity.

There are also various methods to position the Pane's view. See the POD documentation for more information.

The ProgressBar Widget

Using a ProgressBar is a great way to show the user something is still happening when you are doing lots of processing. Without it, the user wonders, "Is the application still running? Why isn't it responding?" Figure 23-18 shows what a fairly typical progress bar looks like. This screenshot was generated with the following code:

```
use Tk;
use Tk::ProgressBar;

my $mw = MainWindow->new(-title => 'ProgressBar example');

$progress = $mw->ProgressBar(
        -width => 30,
        -from => 0,
        -to => 100,
        -blocks => 50,
        -colors => [0, 'green', 50, 'yellow' , 80, 'red'],
        -variable => \$percent_done
    )->pack(-fill => 'x');

$mw->Button(-text => 'Go!', -command=> sub {
    for ($i = 0; $i < 1000; $i++) {
      $percent_done = $i/10;
      print "$i\n";
      $mw->update;  # otherwise we don't see how far we are.
    }
  })->pack(-side => 'bottom');

MainLoop;
```

Figure 23-18. A ProgressBar

The callback that is part of the Go button is just a quick way of showing how to do something and update the ProgressBar as part of the process. You could be loading a file, doing some number crunching, or anything else that seems to cause your program to pause.

ProgressBar Options

Here is a list of options available for ProgressBar:

-anchor => 'n' | 's' | 'e' | 'w'
> Determines the starting point of the bar. For horizontal bars (such as our example), use 'e' or 'w'. Vertical bars use 's' or 'n'.

-blocks => *number*
> The number of blocks used in constructing the bar. The larger the number, the more blocks. The default is 10.

-colors => [*pos0, color0, pos1, color1, ...*]
> An anonymous list containing positions and colors. The position is where to start using that particular color in the bar. That color will be used until it finds another position/color or runs out of room in the bar.

-from => *number*
> The lower limit on the progress bar. Defaults to 0. Nothing is displayed if you try to use a value on the bar below this number.

-gap => *amount*
> Controls the amount of space left between blocks. Default is 1. Use 0 to get a solid bar.

-length => *amount*
> The long dimension of the progress bar as a valid screen distance. This is ignored if you use -fill with the pack command. If this is a vertical progess bar, this value will be used for the height.

-resolution => *amount*
> A real value specifying the resolution for the scale. If greater than zero, the scale's value will always be rounded to an even multiple of this value, as will tick marks and the endpoints of the scale. If the value is less than zero, no rounding occurs. Defaults to 1 (i.e., the value will be integral).

`-to => `*`number`*

    Sets the the upper limit of the progress bar. Defaults to 100. If you ask the progress bar to display a value higher than this limit, the bar will be completely filled.

`-variable => \$var`

    A scalar variable that holds the progress bar's current value. Use this instead of configuring the `-value` option all the time.

`-value => `*`amount`*

    The value currently displayed on the progress bar.

`-width => `*`amount`*

    The amount of screen distance allocated to the thin portion of the progress bar. For a horizontal bar, this is the height; for a vertical progress bar, this becomes the width.

Widgets Not in the Perl/Tk Distribution

There are many user-contributed widgets on CPAN and elsewhere on the Web. Most are registered on the Tk Modules page. Occasionally, this page finds a new home, so the following link, as far as is possible, is guaranteed to point to the proper page:

http://www.Lehigh.EDU/~sol0/ddumont/ptk_module_list.html

Other than telling you where these additional widgets are, we won't examine any of them, for various reasons. Mainly, there are too many widgets, some aren't documented at all, and there are questions of support. Use them with these thoughts in mind. Nevertheless, many of those widgets are quality code.

Installing Perl/Tk

Chapter 1 describes the litmus tests you can use to see if Perl and Tk are available and properly installed in your environment. We assume something is amiss, and that's why you're visiting this chapter. Here we detail the installation directions for both Perl and Tk under Unix and Win32.

For either operating system, installing Perl/Tk is ultimately simple. For Unix, we typically compile and build from source, but for Win32, we use a binary distribution from ActiveState.

Installing Perl/Tk for Unix

First, create a new subdirectory for the build process, change directory into it, and download the stable Perl source distribution from the Comprehensive Perl Archive Network (CPAN), at *http://www.cpan.org/src/stable.tar.gz*.

Now unzip and untar the distribution. Sometimes this is a one-step process since *tar* (or *gtar*) can unzip the file automatically. In this case, you'd use a command similar to this:

```
% gtar -zxvpf stable.tar.gz
```

This creates a directory named *perl-5.6.1* (or something similar). If *tar* cannot automatically unzip, you must unzip it manually before running *tar*:

```
% gunzip stable.tar.gz
% tar -xvpf stable.tar
```

Move into the new directory and type:

```
% sh Configure -des
% make
% make test
% make install
```

The previous commands configure *perl* with all the defaults suitable for your Unix environment, then build it, test it, and install it in the default location for your platform. You most likely have to have root privileges to do the install. Alternatively, you can install *perl* in your private space by changing `Configure`'s prefix variable:

```
sh Configure -des -Dprefix=/home/bug/perl
```

Then, perform the *make* as before.

Installing Tk is even easier. Ensure that your Unix path is set to include the *bin* directory from the *perl* install. In the previous example, that would be */home/bug/perl/bin*.

Now download the Tk source distribution from CPAN, at *http://www.cpan.org/authors/id/NI-S*.

Look for the latest file whose name is of the form *Tk800.0xx.tar.gz*, where *xx* represents the Tk version (currently 22). Fetch the file *Tk800.022.tar.gz*. When the new Perl/Tk based on Tcl/Tk 8.3 is available, look for filenames of the form *Tk803.0xx.tar.gz*.

Then unzip, untar, and install as follows:

```
% gtar -zxvpf Tk800.022.tar.gz
% perl Makefile.PL
% make
% make test
% make install
```

Test the configuration to ensure that all is well by running *widget* from the *bin* directory where *perl* is installed. The *widget* program demonstrates most of the Tk widget set.

Installing Perl/Tk for Win32

First, fetch the Perl binary distribution from *http://www.activestate.com*. Click on the ActivePerl Distribution link, which takes you to the downloads page.

Fetch ActivePerl for Windows MSI installer and save it somewhere on your computer, perhaps the desktop. As the *.MSI* file is downloading, you are taken to the Requirements page. For Windows 2000, you have everything you need; just click on the ActivePerl icon and follow the instructions.

For Windows 98, you must also fetch and install Microsoft Windows Installer and DCOM98 before installing ActivePerl. Install Microsoft Windows Installer first, followed by DCOM98. DCOM98 requires that you restart the computer to complete the installation.

Now double click the ActivePerl icon and follow the Setup Wizard's instructions. Then restart your computer a second time to update your path.

To install Tk, open a DOS window and type:

```
% ppm install Tk
```

Test the configuration to ensure that all is well by running *widget* from a DOS window. The program's pathname is typically *c:\perl\bin\widget*.

Options and Default Values for Each Widget

In Chapter 13 we discussed how to use the configure and cget methods on our widgets. This appendix shows the output from configure on each of the widgets we cover in this book. The program used to generate the data is as follows:

```perl
use Tk;
use strict;

my $mw = MainWindow->new;
while (my $w = <DATA>) {
    next if $w =~ /^#/;
    chomp $w;
    print "\n\n====== $w\n";
    my $o = $mw->$w;
    my(@o) = $o->configure;
    foreach my $opt (@o) {
    @$opt = map {defined($_) ? $_ : 'undef'} @$opt;
     printf "%s\t%s\t%s\t%s\t%s\n", @$opt;

     if ($$opt[4] =~ /^System/) {
      my ($r, $g, $b) = $mw->rgb($$opt[4]);
      print "$r $g $b\n";
     }
    }
}

__DATA__
Adjuster
Balloon
Bitmap
BrowseEntry
Button
## ... list shortened ...
Toplevel
Tree
```

Adjuster

Option name	Xdefault's name	Class name	Default value	Current value
-background	background	Background	undef	#d9d9d9
-bd	borderwidth	Borderwidth		
-bg	background			
-borderwidth	borderwidth	Borderwidth	0	0
-class	class	Class	Frame	Adjuster
-colormap	colormap	Colormap		undef
-container	container	Container	0	0
-cursor	cursor	Cursor		undef
-delay	delay	Delay	1	1
-fg	foreground	Foreground		
-foreground	foreground	Foreground	black	black
-height	height	Height	0	0
-highlightbackground	highlightBackground	HighlightBackground	#d9d9d9	#d9d9d9
-highlightcolor	highlightColor	HighlightColor	Black	Black
-highlightthickness	highlightThickness	HighlightThickness	0	0
-label	undef	undef	undef	undef
-labelPack	undef	undef	undef	
-labelVariable	undef	undef	undef	undef
-offset	offset	Offset	0 0	ARRAY(0x82d6abc)
-relief	relief	Relief	flat	flat
-restore	restore	Restore	1	1
-side	side	Side	top	top
-takefocus	takeFocus	TakeFocus	0	0
-tile	tile	Tile	undef	

Option name	Xdefault's name	Class name	Default value	Current value
-visual	visual	Visual		undef
-widget	widget	Widget	MainWindow=HASH(0x80f4d dc)	MainWindow=HASH(0x80f4d dc)
-width	width	Width	0	0

Balloon

Option name	Xdefault's name	Class name	Default value	Current value
-background	background	Background	#C0C080	#C0C080
-balloonmsg	balloonMsg	BalloonMsg		
-balloonposition	balloonPosition	BalloonPosition	widget	widget
-bd	borderWidth	BorderWidth		
-bg	background	Background		
-borderwidth	borderWidth	BorderWidth	1	1
-cancelcommand	cancelCommand	CancelCommand	undef	undef
-class	class	Class	Toplevel	Balloon
-colormap	colormap	Colormap		undef
-container	container	Container	0	0
-cursor	cursor	Cursor		undef
-fg	foreground	Foreground		
-font	font	Font	-*-helvetica-medium-r-normal--*-120-*-*-*-*-*	Tk::Font=SCALAR(0x8310e34)
-foreground	foreground	Foreground	Black	Black
-height	height	Height	0	0
-highlightbackground	highlightBackground	HighlightBackground	#d9d9d9	#d9d9d9

Option name	Xdefault's name	Class name	Default value	Current value
-highlightcolor	highlightColor	HighlightColor	Black	Black
-highlightthickness	highlightThickness	HighlightThickness	0	0
-initwait	initwait	InitWait	350	350
-installcolormap	installColormap	InstallColormap	0	0
-menu	menu	Menu		undef
-motioncommand	motionCommand	MotionCommand	undef	undef
-offset	offset	Offset	0 0	ARRAY(0x8310034)
-overanchor	undef	undef	undef	undef
-popanchor	undef	undef	undef	undef
-popover	undef	undef	undef	undef
-postcommand	postCommand	PostCommand	undef	undef
-relief	relief	Relief	flat	flat
-screen	screen	Screen		undef
-state	state	State	both	both
-statusbar	statusBar	StatusBar	undef	undef
-statusmsg	statusMsg	StatusMsg		
-takefocus	takeFocus	TakeFocus	0	0
-tile	tile	Tile	undef	
-title	undef	undef	Balloon	Balloon
-use	use	Use		undef
-visual	visual	Visual		undef
-width	width	Width	0	0

Bitmap

Option name	.Xdefault's name	Class name	Default value	Current value
-background	undef	undef	undef	undef
-data	undef	undef	undef	undef
-file	undef	undef	undef	undef
-foreground	undef	undef	#000000	#000000
-maskdata	undef	undef	undef	undef
-maskfile	undef	undef	undef	undef

BrowseEntry

Option name	.Xdefault's name	Class name	Default value	Current value
-arrowimage	arrowImage	ArrowImage	undef	undef
-background	background	Background	#d9d9d9	#d9d9d9
-bd	borderWidth			
-bg	background			
-borderwidth	borderWidth	BorderWidth	2	2
-browsecmd	browseCmd	BrowseCmd	undef	undef
-choices	choices	Choices	undef	
-colorstate	colorState	ColorState	undef	undef
-command	browseCmd			
-cursor	cursor	Cursor	xterm	xterm
-disabledtile	disabledTile	Tile	undef	undef
-exportselection	exportSelection	ExportSelection	1	1
-fg	foreground			
-fgtile	foregroundTile			

Option name	Xdefault's name	Class name	Default value	Current value
-font	font	Font	Helvetica -12	Tk:: Font=SCALAR(0x83af8ac)
-foreground	foreground	Foreground	Black	Black
-foregroundtile	foregroundTile	Tile	undef	undef
-highlightbackground	highlightBackground	HighlightBackground	#d9d9d9	#d9d9d9
-highlightcolor	highlightColor	HighlightColor	Black	Black
-highlightthickness	highlightThickness	HighlightThickness	1	1
-insertbackground	insertBackground	Foreground	Black	Black
-insertborderwidth	insertBorderWidth	BorderWidth	0	0
-insertofftime	insertOffTime	OffTime	300	300
-insertontime	insertOnTime	OnTime	600	600
-insertwidth	insertWidth	InsertWidth	2	2
-invalidcommand	invalidCommand	InvalidCommand	undef	undef
-invcmd	invalidCommand			
-justify	justify	Justify	left	left
-label	undef	undef	undef	undef
-labelActivetile	activeTile	Tile	undef	undef
-labelAnchor	anchor	Anchor	center	center
-labelBackground	background	Background	#d9d9d9	#d9d9d9
-labelBitmap	bitmap	Bitmap	undef	undef
-labelBorderwidth	borderwidth	BorderWidth	2	2
-labelCursor	cursor	Cursor	undef	undef
-labelDisabledtile	disabledTile	Tile	undef	
-labelFont	font	Font	Helvetica -12 bold	Tk:: Font=SCALAR(0x83649a0)
-labelForeground	foreground	Foreground	Black	Black
-labelHeight	height	Height	0	0

Option name	Xdefault's name	Class name	Default value	Current value
-labelHighlightbackground	highlightBackground	HighlightBackground	#d9d9d9	#d9d9d9
-labelHighlightcolor	highlightColor	HighlightColor	Black	Black
-labelHighlightthickness	highlightThickness	HighlightThickness	0	0
-labelImage	image	Image	undef	undef
-labelJustify	justify	Justify	center	center
-labelOffset	offset	Offset	0 0	0
-labelPack	undef	undef	undef	undef
-labelPadx	padx	Pad	1	1
-labelPady	pady	Pad	1	1
-labelRelief	relief	Relief	flat	flat
-labelTakefocus	takeFocus	TakeFocus	0	0
-labelText	text	Text		
-labelTextvariable	textVariable	Variable		SCALAR(0x80f5434)
-labelTile	tile	Tile	undef	
-labelUnderline	underline	Underline	-1	-1
-labelVariable	undef	undef	undef	undef
-labelWidth	width	Width	0	0
-labelWraplength	wrapLength	WrapLength	0	0
-listcmd	listCmd	ListCmd	undef	undef
-listwidth	listWidth	ListWidth	undef	undef
-offset	offset	Offset	0 0	ARRAY(0x83b0c80)
-options	choices			
-relief	relief	Relief	sunken	sunken
-selectbackground	selectBackground	Foreground	#c3c3c3	#c3c3c3
-selectborderwidth	selectBorderWidth	BorderWidth	1	1

Option name	.Xdefault's name	Class name	Default value	Current value
-selectforeground	selectForeground	Background	Black	Black
-show	show	Show	undef	undef
-state	state	State	normal	normal
-takefocus	takeFocus	TakeFocus	undef	undef
-textvariable	textVariable	Variable	undef	SCALAR(0x8310b28)
-tile	tile	Tile	undef	none
-validate	validate	Validate	undef	undef
-validatecommand	validateCommand	ValidateCommand	undef	undef
-variable	textVariable			
-vcmd	validateCommand			
-width	width	Width	20	20
-xscrollcommand	xScrollCommand	ScrollCommand	undef	undef

Button

Option name	.Xdefault's name	Class name	Default value	Current value
-activebackground	activeBackground	Foreground	#ececec	#ececec
-activeforeground	activeForeground	Background	Black	Black
-activetile	activeTile	Tile	undef	undef
-activeimage	activeImage	ActiveImage	undef	undef
-anchor	anchor	Anchor	center	center
-background	background	Background	#d9d9d9	#d9d9d9
-bd	borderWidth			
-bg	background			
-bitmap	bitmap	Bitmap		undef
-borderwidth	borderWidth	BorderWidth	2	2

Option name	Xdefault's name	Class name	Default value	Current value
-command	command	Command		undef
-cursor	cursor	Cursor		undef
-default	default	Default	disabled	disabled
-disabledforeground	disabledForeground	DisabledForeground	#a3a3a3	#a3a3a3
-disabledtile	disabledTile	Tile	undef	
-fg	foreground			
-font	font	Font	Helvetica -12 bold	Tk::Font=SCALAR(0x8364 a0)
-foreground	foreground	Foreground	Black	Black
-height	height	Height	0	0
-highlightbackground	highlightBackground	HighlightBackground	#d9d9d9	#d9d9d9
-highlightcolor	highlightColor	HighlightColor	Black	Black
-highlightthickness	highlightThickness	HighlightThickness	1	1
-image	image	Image	undef	undef
-justify	justify	Justify	center	center
-offset	offset	Offset	0 0	ARRAY(0x83b0bd8)
-padx	padX	Pad	3m	9
-pady	padY	Pad	1m	3
-relief	relief	Relief	raised	raised
-state	state	State	normal	normal
-takefocus	takeFocus	TakeFocus	undef	undef
-text	text	Text		
-textvariable	textVariable	Variable		undef
-tile	tile	Tile	undef	
-underline	underline	Underline	-1	-1
-width	width	Width	0	0

Option name	.Xdefault's name	Class name	Default value	Current value
-wraplength	wrapLength	WrapLength	0	0

Canvas

Option name	.Xdefault's name	Class name	Default value	Current value
-activegroup	activeGroup	ActiveGroup	0	undef
-background	background	Background	#d9d9d9	#d9d9d9
-bd	borderwidth			
-bg	background			
-borderwidth	borderWidth	BorderWidth	0	0
-closeenough	closeEnough	CloseEnough	1	1
-confine	confine	Confine	1	1
-cursor	cursor	Cursor	undef	undef
-disabledtile	disabledtile	Tile	undef	
-height	height	Height	7c	199
-highlightbackground	highlightBackground	HighlightBackground	#d9d9d9	#d9d9d9
-highlightcolor	highlightColor	HighlightColor	Black	Black
-highlightthickness	highlightThickness	HighlightThickness	1	1
-insertbackground	insertBackground	Foreground	Black	Black
-insertborderwidth	insertBorderWidth	BorderWidth	0	0
-insertofftime	insertOffTime	OffTime	300	300
-insertontime	insertOnTime	OnTime	600	600
-insertwidth	insertWidth	InsertWidth	2	2
-offset	offset	Offset	0 0	ARRAY(0x83c6fd4)
-relief	relief	Relief	flat	flat
-scrollregion	scrollRegion	ScrollRegion	undef	undef

Option name	Xdefault's name	Class name	Default value	Current value
-selectbackground	selectBackground	Foreground	#c3c3c3	#c3c3c3
-selectborderwidth	selectBorderWidth	BorderWidth	1	1
-selectforeground	selectForeground	Background	Black	Black
-state	state	State	normal	normal
-takefocus	takeFocus	TakeFocus	undef	undef
-tile	tile	Tile	undef	undef
-width	width	Width	10c	284
-xscrollcommand	xScrollCommand	ScrollCommand		undef
-xscrollincrement	xScrollIncrement	ScrollIncrement	0	0
-yscrollcommand	yScrollCommand	ScrollCommand		undef
-yscrollincrement	yScrollIncrement	ScrollIncrement	0	0

Checkbutton

Option name	Xdefault's name	Class name	Default value	Current value
-activebackground	activeBackground	Foreground	#ececec	#ececec
-activeforeground	activeForeground	Background	Black	Black
-activetile	activeTile	Tile	undef	
-anchor	anchor	Anchor	center	center
-background	background	Background	#d9d9d9	#d9d9d9
-bd	borderWidth			
-bg	background			
-bitmap	bitmap	Bitmap		undef
-borderwidth	borderWidth	BorderWidth	2	2
-command	command	Command		undef
-cursor	cursor	Cursor		undef

Option name	.Xdefault's name	Class name	Default value	Current value
-disabledforeground	disabledForeground	DisabledForeground	#a3a3a3	#a3a3a3
-disabledtile	disabledTile	Tile	undef	
-fg	foreground			
-font	font	Font	Helvetica -12 bold	Tk::Font=SCALAR(0x83649a0)
-foreground	foreground	Foreground	Black	Black
-height	height	Height	0	0
-highlightbackground	highlightBackground	HighlightBackground	#d9d9d9	#d9d9d9
-highlightcolor	highlightColor	HighlightColor	Black	Black
-highlightthickness	highlightThickness	HighlightThickness	1	1
-image	image	Image	undef	undef
-indicatoron	indicatorOn	IndicatorOn	1	1
-justify	justify	Justify	center	center
-offvalue	offValue	Value	0	0
-offset	offset	Offset	0 0	ARRAY(0x83cc32c)
-onvalue	onvalue	Value	1	1
-padx	padX	Pad	1	1
-pady	padY	Pad	1	1
-relief	relief	Relief	flat	flat
-selectcolor	selectColor	Background	#b03060	#b03060
-selectimage	selectImage	SelectImage	undef	undef
-state	state	State	normal	normal
-takefocus	takeFocus	TakeFocus	undef	undef
-text	text	Text		
-textvariable	textVariable	Variable		undef
-tile	tile	Tile	undef	undef

Option name	Xdefault's name	Class name	Default value	Current value
-underline	underline	Underline	-1	-1
-variable	variable	Variable		SCALAR(0x83c7130)
-width	width	Width	0	0
-wraplength	wrapLength	WrapLength	0	0

ColorEditor

Option name	Xdefault's name	Class name	Default value	Current value
-background	background	Background	#d9d9d9	#d9d9d9
-bd	borderWidth			
-bg	background			
-borderwidth	borderWidth	BorderWidth	0	2
-class	class	Class	Frame	ColorSelect
-color	background	Background	#d9d9d9	#d900d900d900
-color_space	undef	undef	hsb	hsb
-colormap	colormap	Colormap	undef	undef
-command	undef	undef	Tk::Callback=ARRAY(0x8297d5 4)	Tk::Callback=ARRAY(0x8297d5 4)
-container	container	Container	0	0
-cursor	cursor	Cursor	left_ptr	left_ptr
-display_status	undef	undef	0	0
-fg	foreground			
-foreground	foreground	Foreground	Black	Black
-height	height	Height	0	0
-highlight	undef	undef	background	background

Option name	.Xdefault's name	Class name	Default value	Current value
-highlightbackground	highlightBackground	HighlightBackground	#d9d9d9	#d9d9d9
-highlightcolor	highlightColor	HighlightColor	Black	Black
-highlightthickness	highlightThickness	HighlightThickness	0	0
-initialcolor	background	background		
-offset	offset	Offset	0 0	ARRAY(0x841b300)
-overanchor	undef	undef	undef	undef
-popanchor	undef	undef	undef	undef
-popover	undef	undef	undef	undef
-relief	relief	Relief	flat	raised
-takefocus	takeFocus	TakeFocus	0	0
-tile	tile	Tile	undef	0
-title	undef	undef		
-visual	visual	Visual		undef
-widgets	undef	undef	ARRAY(0x84d685c)	ARRAY(0x84d685c)
-width	width	Width	0	0

Dialog

Option name	.Xdefault's name	Class name	Default value	Current value
-activetile	activeTile	Tile	undef	
-anchor	anchor	Anchor	center	center
-background	background	Background	undef	#d9d9d9
-bd	borderWidth			
-bg	background			
-bitmap	undef	undef	undef	undef
-borderwidth	borderWidth	Borderwidth	2	2

Option name	Xdefault's name	Class name	Default value	Current value
-command	undef	undef	undef	undef
-cursor	cursor	Cursor		undef
-disabledtile	disabledTile	Tile	undef	
-fg	foreground			
-font	font	Font	-*-Times-Medium-R-Normal--*-180-*-*-*-*-*	Tk::Font=SCALAR(0x850f46c)
-foreground	foreground	Foreground	black	black
-height	height	Height	0	0
-highlightbackground	highlightBackground	HighlightBackground	#d9d9d9	#d9d9d9
-highlightcolor	highlightColor	HighlightColor	Black	Black
-highlightthickness	highlightThickness	HighlightThickness	0	0
-image	undef	undef	undef	undef
-justify	justify	Justify	center	left
-offset	offset	Offset	0 0	ARRAY(0x8510b4)
-overanchor	undef	undef	undef	undef
-padx	padX	Pad	1	1
-pady	padY	Pad	1	1
-popanchor	undef	undef	undef	undef
-popover	undef	undef	undef	undef
-relief	relief	Relief	flat	flat
-takefocus	takeFocus	TakeFocus	0	0
-text	text	Text		
-textvariable	textVariable	Variable		
-tile	tile	Tile	undef	undef
-title	undef	undef	Dialog	Dialog
-underline	underline	Underline	-1	-1

Option name	Xdefault's name	Class name	Default value	Current value
-width	width	Width	0	0
-wraplength	wrapLength	WrapLength	0	216

DirTree

Option name	Xdefault's name	Class name	Default value	Current value
-background	background	Background	#d9d9d9	#d9d9d9
-bd	borderWidth			
-bg	background			
-borderwidth	borderWidth	BorderWidth	2	2
-browsecmd	browseCmd	BrowseCmd		undef
-closecmd	closeCmd	CloseCmd	CloseCmd	CloseCmd
-columns	columns	Columns	1	1
-command	command	Command		undef
-cursor	cursor	Cursor		undef
-dircmd	dirCmd	DirCmd	DirCmd	DirCmd
-directory	directory	Directory	.	.
-dragcmd	dragCmd	DragCmd		undef
-drawbranch	drawBranch	DrawBranch	true	1
-dropcmd	dropCmd	DropCmd		undef
-exportselection	exportSelection	ExportSelection	0	0
-fg	foreground	Foreground		
-font	font	Font	-Adobe-Helvetica-Bold-R-Normal-*-120-*	Tk::Font=SCALAR(0x8581284)
-foreground	foreground	Foreground	Black	Black
-gap	gap	Gap	5	5

Option name	Xdefault's name	Class name	Default value	Current value
-header	header	Header	0	0
-height	height	Height	10	10
-highlightbackground	highlightBackground	HighlightBackground	#d9d9d9	#d9d9d9
-highlightcolor	highlightColor	HighlightColor	Black	Black
-highlightthickness	highlightThickness	HighlightThickness	2	2
-ignoreinvoke	ignoreInvoke	IgnoreInvoke	0	0
-image	image	Image	folder	folder
-indent	indent	Indent	20	20
-indicator	indicator	Indicator	1	1
-indicatorcmd	indicatorCmd	IndicatorCmd	IndicatorCmd	IndicatorCmd
-itemtype	itemtype	Itemtype	imagetext	imagetext
-opencmd	openCmd	OpenCmd	OpenCmd	OpenCmd
-padx	padx	Pad	2	2
-pady	pady	Pad	2	2
-relief	relief	Relief	sunken	sunken
-selectbackground	selectBackground	Foreground	#ececec	#ececec
-selectborderwidth	selectBorderWidth	BorderWidth	1	1
-selectforeground	selectForeground	Background	Black	Black
-selectmode	selectMode	SelectMode	browse	browse
-separator	separator	Separator	/	/
-showhidden	showHidden	ShowHidden	0	0
-sizecmd	sizeCmd	SizeCmd		undef
-takefocus	takeFocus	TakeFocus	1	1
-value	directory			
-wideselection	wideSelection	WideSelection	true	1
-width	width	Width	20	20

Option name	Xdefault's name	Class name	Default value	Current value
-xscrollcommand	xScrollCommand	ScrollCommand		undef
-yscrollcommand	yScrollCommand	ScrollCommand		undef

Entry

Option name	Xdefault's name	Class name	Default value	Current value
-background	background	Background	#d9d9d9	#d9d9d9
-bd	borderWidth			
-bg	background			
-borderwidth	borderWidth	BorderWidth	2	2
-cursor	cursor	Cursor	xterm	xterm
-disabledtile	disabledTile	Tile	undef	
-exportselection	exportSelection	ExportSelection	1	1
-fg	foreground			
-font	font	Font	Helvetica -12	Tk:: Font=SCALAR(0x83af8ac)
-foreground	foreground	Foreground	Black	Black
-fgtile	foregroundTile			
-foregroundtile	foregroundTile	Tile	undef	
-highlightbackground	highlightBackground	HighlightBackground	#d9d9d9	#d9d9d9
-highlightcolor	highlightColor	HighlightColor	Black	Black
-highlightthickness	highlightThickness	HighlightThickness	1	1
-insertbackground	insertBackground	Foreground	Black	Black
-insertborderwidth	insertBorderWidth	BorderWidth	0	0
-insertofftime	insertOffTime	OffTime	300	300
-insertontime	insertOnTime	OnTime	600	600

Option name	Xdefault's name	Class name	Default value	Current value
-insertwidth	insertWidth	InsertWidth	2	2
-invalidcommand	invalidCommand	InvalidCommand	undef	undef
-invcmd	invalidCommand			
-justify	justify	Justify	left	left
-offset	offset	Offset	0 0	ARRAY(0x8581494)
-relief	relief	Relief	sunken	sunken
-selectbackground	selectBackground	Foreground	#c3c3c3	#c3c3c3
-selectborderwidth	selectBorderwidth	Borderwidth	1	1
-selectforeground	selectForeground	Background	Black	Black
-show	show	Show	undef	undef
-state	state	State	normal	normal
-takefocus	takeFocus	TakeFocus	undef	undef
-textvariable	textVariable	Variable	undef	undef
-tile	tile	Tile	undef	undef
-validate	validate	Validate	undef	none
-validatecommand	validateCommand	ValidateCommand	undef	undef
-vcmd	validateCommand			
-width	width	Width	20	20
-xscrollcommand	xScrollCommand	ScrollCommand		undef

ErrorDialog

Option name	Xdefault's name	Class name	Default value	Current value
-appendtraceback	undef	undef	1	1
-background	background	Background	#d9d9d9	#d9d9d9
-bd	borderwidth			

Option name	.Xdefault's name	Class name	Default value	Current value
-bg	background			0
-borderwidth	borderwidth	BorderWidth	0	0
-class	class	Class	Toplevel	ErrorDialog
-cleanupcode	undef	undef	undef	undef
-colormap	colormap	Colormap		undef
-container	container	Container	0	0
-cursor	cursor	Cursor		undef
-fg	foreground			
-foreground	foreground	Foreground	Black	Black
-height	height	Height	0	0
-highlightbackground	highlightBackground	HighlightBackground	#d9d9d9	#d9d9d9
-highlightcolor	highlightColor	HighlightColor	Black	Black
-highlightthickness	highlightThickness	HighlightThickness	0	0
-menu	menu	Menu		undef
-offset	offset	Offset	0 0	ARRAY(0x8628a4c)
-relief	relief	Relief	flat	flat
-screen	screen	Screen		undef
-takefocus	takeFocus	TakeFocus	0	0
-tile	tile	Tile	undef	
-use	use	Use		undef
-visual	visual	Visual		undef
-width	width	Width	0	0

FileSelect

Option name	Xdefault's name	Class name	Default value	Current value
-accept	undef	undef	undef	undef
-acceptlabel	undef	undef	Accept	Accept
-background	background	Background	#d9d9d9	#d9d9d9
-bd	borderWidth			
-bg	background			
-borderwidth	borderWidth	BorderWidth	2	2
-cancellabel	undef	undef	Cancel	Cancel
-command	undef	undef	undef	undef
-create	undef	undef	0	0
-cursor	cursor	Cursor	undef	undef
-defaultextension	undef	undef	undef	undef
-directory	undef	undef	.	/home/bug/perl/atk
-dirlabel	undef	undef	Directory	Directory
-dirlistlabel	undef	undef	Directories	Directories
-exportselection	exportSelection	ExportSelection	1	1
-fg	foreground			
-filelabel	fileLabel	FileLabel	File	File
-filelistlabel	undef	undef	Files	Files
-filter	undef	undef	undef	*
-font	font	Font	Helvetica -12 bold	Tk::Font=SCALAR(0x8364 9a0)
-foreground	foreground	Foreground	Black	Black
-height	undef	undef	14	14
-highlightbackground	highlightBackground	HighlightBackground	#d9d9d9	#d9d9d9

Option name	Xdefault's name	Class name	Default value	Current value
-highlightcolor	highlightColor	HighlightColor	Black	Black
-highlightthickness	highlightThickness	HighlightThickness	1	1
-homelabel	undef	undef	Home	Home
-initialdir	undef	undef	undef	
-initialfile	undef	undef	undef	
-label	undef	undef	undef	Files
-labelActivetile	activeTile	Tile	undef	
-labelAnchor	anchor	Anchor	center	center
-labelBackground	background	Background	#d9d9d9	#d9d9d9
-labelBitmap	bitmap	Bitmap		undef
-labelBorderwidth	borderwidth	BorderWidth	2	2
-labelCursor	cursor	Cursor		undef
-labelDisabledtile	disabledTile	Tile	undef	
-labelFont	font	Font	Helvetica -12 bold	Tk:: Font=SCALAR(0x83649a0)
-labelForeground	foreground	Foreground	Black	Black
-labelHeight	height	Height	0	0
-labelHighlightbackground	highlightBackground	HighlightBackground	#d9d9d9	#d9d9d9
-labelHighlightcolor	highlightColor	HighlightColor	Black	Black
-labelHighlightthickness	highlightThickness	HighlightThickness	0	0
-labelImage	image	Image	undef	undef
-labelJustify	justify	Justify	center	center
-labelOffset	offset	Offset	0 0	0
-labelPack	undef	undef	undef	-in
-labelPadx	padX	Pad	1	1
-labelPady	padY	Pad	1	1

Option name	Xdefault's name	Class name	Default value	Current value
-labelRelief	relief	Relief	flat	flat
-labelTakefocus	takeFocus	TakeFocus	0	0
-labelText	text	Text		Files
-labelTextvariable	textVariable	Variable		SCALAR(0x8672490)
-labelTile	tile	Tile	undef	
-labelUnderline	underline	Underline	-1	-1
-labelVariable	undef	undef	undef	SCALAR(0x8672490)
-labelWidth	width	Width	0	0
-labelWraplength	wraplength	WrapLength	0	0
-offset	offset	Offset	undef	ARRAY(0x8692dd0)
-overanchor	undef	undef	undef	undef
-popanchor	undef	undef	undef	undef
-popover	undef	undef	undef	undef
-regexp	undef	undef	undef	undef
-relief	relief	Relief	sunken	sunken
-resetlabel	undef	undef	Reset	Reset
-scrollbars	scrollbars	Scrollbars	sw	se
-selectbackground	selectBackground	Foreground	#c3c3c3	#c3c3c3
-selectborderwidth	selectBorderWidth	BorderWidth	1	1
-selectforeground	selectForeground	Background	Black	Black
-selectmode	selectMode	SelectMode	browse	browse
-setgrid	setGrid	SetGrid	0	0
-takefocus	takeFocus	TakeFocus	undef	undef
-tile	tile	Tile	undef	
-title	undef	undef	FileSelect	FileSelect
-transient	undef	undef	1	1

Option name	Xdefault's name	Class name	Default value	Current value
-verify	undef	undef	ARRAY(0x868c9f4)	ARRAY(0x868c9f4)
-width	undef	undef	14	14
-xscrollcommand	xScrollCommand	ScrollCommand	undef	undef
-yscrollcommand	yScrollCommand	ScrollCommand	undef	undef

Frame

Option name	Xdefault's name	Class name	Default value	Current value
-background	background	Background	#d9d9d9	#d9d9d9
-bd	borderwidth			
-bg	background			
-borderwidth	borderwidth	BorderWidth	0	0
-class	class	Class	Frame	Frame
-colormap	colormap	Colormap	undef	undef
-container	container	Container	0	0
-cursor	cursor	Cursor	undef	undef
-fg	foreground			
-foreground	foreground	Foreground	Black	Black
-height	height	Height	0	0
-highlightbackground	highlightBackground	HighlightBackground	#d9d9d9	#d9d9d9
-highlightcolor	highlightColor	HighlightColor	Black	Black
-highlightthickness	highlightThickness	HighlightThickness	0	0
-label	undef	undef	undef	undef
-labelPack	undef	undef	undef	undef
-labelVariable	undef	undef	undef	undef
-offset	offset	Offset	0 0	ARRAY(0x8692d7c)

Option name	Xdefault's name	Class name	Default value	Current value
-relief	relief	Relief	flat	flat
-takefocus	takeFocus	TakeFocus	0	0
-tile	tile	Tile	undef	undef
-visual	visual	Visual		undef
-width	width	Width	0	0

HList

Option name	Xdefault's name	Class name	Default value	Current value
-background	background	Background	#d9d9d9	#d9d9d9
-bd	borderwidth			
-bg	background			
-borderwidth	borderwidth	BorderWidth	2	2
-browsecmd	browseCmd	BrowseCmd		undef
-columns	columns	Columns	1	1
-command	command	Command		undef
-cursor	cursor	Cursor		undef
-dragcmd	dragCmd	DragCmd		undef
-drawbranch	drawBranch	DrawBranch	true	1
-dropcmd	dropCmd	DropCmd		undef
-exportselection	exportSelection	ExportSelection	0	0
-fg	foreground			
-font	font	Font	-Adobe-Helvetica-Bold-R-Normal--*-120-*	Tk::Font=SCALAR(0x8581284)
-foreground	foreground	Foreground	Black	Black
-gap	gap	Gap	5	5

Option name	Xdefault's name	Class name	Default value	Current value
-header	header	Header	0	0
-height	height	Height	10	10
-highlightbackground	highlightBackground	HighlightBackground	#d9d9d9	#d9d9d9
-highlightcolor	highlightColor	HighlightColor	Black	Black
-highlightthickness	highlightThickness	HighlightThickness	2	2
-indent	indent	Indent	10	10
-indicator	indicator	Indicator	0	0
-indicatorcmd	indicatorCmd	IndicatorCmd		undef
-itemtype	itemType	ItemType	text	text
-padx	padX	Pad	2	2
-pady	padY	Pad	2	2
-relief	relief	Relief	sunken	sunken
-selectbackground	selectBackground	Foreground	#ececec	#ececec
-selectborderwidth	selectBorderWidth	BorderWidth	1	1
-selectforeground	selectForeground	Background	Black	Black
-selectmode	selectMode	SelectMode	browse	browse
-separator	separator	Separator	.	.
-sizecmd	sizeCmd	SizeCmd		undef
-takefocus	takeFocus	TakeFocus	1	1
-wideselection	wideSelection	WideSelection	true	1
-width	width	Width	20	20
-xscrollcommand	xScrollCommand	ScrollCommand		undef
-yscrollcommand	yScrollCommand	ScrollCommand		undef

Label

Option name	Xdefault's name	Class name	Default value	Current value
-activetile	activeTile	Tile	undef	center
-anchor	anchor	Anchor	center	#d9d9d9
-background	background	Background	#d9d9d9	
-bd	borderwidth			
-bg	background			undef
-bitmap	bitmap	Bitmap		2
-borderwidth	borderwidth	BorderWidth	2	undef
-cursor	cursor	Cursor		
-disabledtile	disabledTile	Tile	undef	
-fg	foreground			Tk::
-font	font	Font	Helvetica -12 bold	Font=SCALAR(0x83649a0)
-foreground	foreground	Foreground	Black	Black
-height	height	Height	0	0
-highlightbackground	highlightBackground	HighlightBackground	#d9d9d9	#d9d9d9
-highlightcolor	highlightColor	HighlightColor	Black	Black
-highlightthickness	highlightThickness	HighlightThickness	0	0
-image	image	Image	undef	undef
-justify	justify	Justify	center	center
-offset	offset	Offset	0 0	ARRAY(0x86948a4)
-padx	padX	Pad	1	1
-pady	padY	Pad	1	1
-relief	relief	Relief	flat	flat
-takefocus	takeFocus	TakeFocus	0	0

Option name	Xdefault's name	Class name	Default value	Current value
-text	text	Text		undef
-textvariable	textVariable	Variable	undef	
-tile	tile	Tile		-1
-underline	underline	Underline	-1	0
-width	width	Width	0	0
-wraplength	wrapLength	WrapLength	0	

LabEntry

Option name	Xdefault's name	Class name	Default value	Current value
-background	background	Background	#d9d9d9	#d9d9d9
-bd	borderWidth	BorderWidth		
-bg	background			
-borderwidth	borderWidth	BorderWidth	2	2
-cursor	cursor	Cursor	xterm	xterm
-disabledtile	disabledTile	Tile	undef	
-exportselection	exportSelection	ExportSelection	1	1
-fg	foreground			
-fgtile	foregroundTile			
-font	font	Font	Helvetica -12	Tk::Font=SCALAR(0x83af8ac)
-foreground	foreground	Foreground	Black	Black
-foregroundtile	foregroundTile	Tile	undef	
-highlightbackground	highlightBackground	HighlightBackground	#d9d9d9	#d9d9d9
-highlightcolor	highlightColor	HighlightColor	Black	Black
-highlightthickness	highlightThickness	HighlightThickness	1	1

Option name	Xdefault's name	Class name	Default value	Current value
-insertbackground	insertBackground	Foreground	Black	Black
-insertborderwidth	insertBorderwidth	BorderWidth	0	0
-insertofftime	insertOffTime	OffTime	300	300
-insertontime	insertOnTime	OnTime	600	600
-insertwidth	insertWidth	InsertWidth	2	2
-invalidcommand	invalidCommand	InvalidCommand	undef	undef
-invcmd	invalidCommand			
-justify	justify	Justify	left	left
-label	undef	undef	undef	undef
-labelPack	undef	undef	undef	undef
-labelVariable	undef	undef	undef	undef
-offset	offset	Offset	0 0	ARRAY(0x8697d8)
-relief	relief	Relief	sunken	sunken
-selectbackground	selectBackground	Foreground	#c3c3c3	#c3c3c3
-selectborderwidth	selectBorderwidth	BorderWidth	1	1
-selectforeground	selectForeground	Background	Black	Black
-show	show	Show	undef	undef
-state	state	State	normal	normal
-takefocus	takeFocus	TakeFocus	undef	undef
-textvariable	textVariable	Variable	undef	undef
-tile	tile	Tile	undef	none
-validate	validate	Validate	undef	undef
-validatecommand	validateCommand	ValidateCommand	undef	undef
-vcmd	validateCommand			
-width	width	Width	20	20
-xscrollcommand	xScrollCommand	ScrollCommand	undef	undef

LabFrame

Option name	Xdefault's name	Class name	Default value	Current value
-background	background	Background	#d9d9d9	#d9d9d9
-bd	borderwidth			
-bg	background			
-borderwidth	borderwidth	BorderWidth	0	2
-class	class	Class	Frame	Frame
-colormap	colormap	Colormap		undef
-container	container	Container	0	0
-cursor	cursor	Cursor		undef
-fg	foreground			
-foreground	foreground	Foreground	Black	Black
-height	height	Height	0	0
-highlightbackground	highlightBackground	HighlightBackground	#d9d9d9	#d9d9d9
-highlightcolor	highlightColor	HighlightColor	Black	Black
-highlightthickness	highlightThickness	HighlightThickness	0	0
-label	undef	undef	undef	undef
-labelPack	undef	undef	undef	-in
-labelVariable	undef	undef	undef	undef
-labelside	labelSide	LabelSide	acrosstop	acrosstop
-offset	offset	Offset	0 0	ARRAY(0x86a6310)
-relief	relief	Relief	flat	groove
-takefocus	takeFocus	TakeFocus	0	0
-tile	tile	Tile	undef	undef
-visual	visual	Visual		undef
-width	width	Width	0	0

Listbox

Option name	Xdefault's name	Class name	Default Value	Current value
-background	background	Background	#d9d9d9	#d9d9d9
-bd	borderWidth			
-bg	background	Background		
-borderwidth	borderWidth	BorderWidth	2	2
-cursor	cursor	Cursor	undef	undef
-exportselection	exportSelection	ExportSelection	1	1
-fg	foreground			
-font	font	Font	Helvetica -12 bold	Tk:: Font=SCALAR(0x83649a0)
-foreground	foreground	Foreground	Black	Black
-height	height	Height	10	10
-highlightbackground	highlightBackground	HighlightBackground	#d9d9d9	#d9d9d9
-highlightcolor	highlightColor	HighlightColor	Black	Black
-highlightthickness	highlightThickness	HighlightThickness	1	1
-offset	offset	Offset	undef	ARRAY(0x86a5ff8)
-relief	relief	Relief	sunken	sunken
-selectbackground	selectBackground	Foreground	#c3c3c3	#c3c3c3
-selectborderwidth	selectBorderWidth	BorderWidth	1	1
-selectforeground	selectForeground	Background	Black	Black
-selectmode	selectMode	SelectMode	browse	browse
-setgrid	setGrid	SetGrid	0	0
-takefocus	takeFocus	TakeFocus	undef	undef
-tile	tile	Tile	undef	
-width	width	Width	20	20

Option name	Xdefault's name	Class name	Default Value	Current value
-xscrollcommand	xScrollCommand	ScrollCommand		undef
-yscrollcommand	yScrollCommand	ScrollCommand		undef

MainWindow

Option name	Xdefault's name	Class name	Default value	Current value
-background	background	Background	#d9d9d9	#d9d9d9
-bd	borderWidth			
-bg	background			
-borderwidth	borderWidth	BorderWidth	0	0
-class	class	Class	Toplevel	Make-appB
-colormap	colormap	Colormap		undef
-container	container	Container	0	0
-cursor	cursor	Cursor		undef
-fg	foreground			
-foreground	foreground	Foreground	Black	Black
-height	height	Height	0	0
-highlightbackground	highlightBackground	HighlightBackground	#d9d9d9	#d9d9d9
-highlightcolor	highlightColor	HighlightColor	Black	Black
-highlightthickness	highlightThickness	HighlightThickness	0	0
-menu	menu	Menu		undef
-offset	offset	Offset	0 0	ARRAY(0x86a7b80)
-overanchor	undef	undef	undef	undef
-popanchor	undef	undef	undef	undef
-popover	undef	undef	undef	undef
-relief	relief	Relief	flat	flat

Option name	.Xdefault's name	Class name	Default value	Current value
-screen	screen	Screen		192.168.1.27:0.0
-takefocus	takefocus	TakeFocus	0	0
-tile	tile	Tile	undef	
-title	undef	undef	Make-appB	Make-appB
-use	use	Use		undef
-visual	visual	Visual		undef
-width	width	Width	0	0

Menu

Option name	.Xdefault's name	Class name	Default value	Current value
-activebackground	activeBackground	Foreground	#ececec	#ececec
-activeborderwidth	activeBorderWidth	Borderwidth	2	2
-activeforeground	activeForeground	Background	Black	Black
-activetile	activeTile	Tile	undef	
-background	background	Background	#d9d9d9	#d9d9d9
-bd	borderWidth			
-bg	background			
-borderwidth	borderWidth	BorderWidth	2	2
-cursor	cursor	Cursor	arrow	arrow
-disabledforeground	disabledForeground	DisabledForeground	#a3a3a3	#a3a3a3
-disabledtile	disabledtile	Tile	undef	
-fg	foreground			
-font	font	Font	Helvetica -12 bold	Tk:: Font=SCALAR(0x83649a0)
-foreground	foreground	Foreground	Black	Black

Option name	.Xdefault's name	Class name	Default value	Current value
-offset	offset	Offset	0 0	ARRAY(0x86a62d4)
-overanchor	undef	undef	undef	undef
-popanchor	undef	undef	undef	undef
-popover	undef	undef	undef	undef
-postcommand	postCommand	Command	undef	undef
-relief	relief	Relief	raised	raised
-selectcolor	selectColor	Background	#b03060	#b03060
-takefocus	takeFocus	TakeFocus	0	0
-tearoff	tearOff	TearOff	1	1
-tearoffcommand	tearOffCommand	TearOffCommand	undef	undef
-tile	tile	Tile	undef	undef
-title	title	Title	undef	undef
-type	type	Type	normal	normal

Menubutton

Option name	.Xdefault's name	Class name	Default value	Current value
-activebackground	activeBackground	Foreground	#ececec	#ececec
-activeforeground	activeForeground	Background	Black	Black
-activetile	activeTile	Tile	undef	
-anchor	anchor	Anchor	center	center
-background	background	Background	#d9d9d9	#d9d9d9
-bd	borderWidth			
-bg	background			
-bitmap	bitmap	Bitmap		undef
-borderwidth	borderWidth	BorderWidth	2	2

Option name	Xdefault's name	Class name	Default value	Current value
-cursor	cursor	Cursor		undef
-direction	direction	Direction	below	below
-disabledforeground	disabledforeground	DisabledForeground	#a3a3a3	#a3a3a3
-disabledtile	disabledtile	Tile	undef	undef
-fg	foreground			
-font	font	Font	Helvetica -12 bold	Tk:: Font=SCALAR(0x8364a0)
-foreground	foreground	Foreground	Black	Black
-height	height	Height	0	0
-highlightbackground	highlightBackground	HighlightBackground	#d9d9d9	#d9d9d9
-highlightcolor	highlightColor	HighlightColor	Black	Black
-highlightthickness	highlightThickness	HighlightThickness	0	0
-image	image	Image	undef	undef
-indicatoron	indicatorOn	IndicatorOn	0	0
-justify	justify	Justify	center	center
-menu	menu	Menu		undef
-padx	padX	Pad	4p	4
-pady	padY	Pad	3p	3
-offset	offset	Offset	0 0	ARRAY(0x86a7050)
-relief	relief	Relief	flat	flat
-state	state	State	normal	normal
-takefocus	takeFocus	TakeFocus	0	0
-text	text	Text		
-textvariable	textVariable	Variable		undef
-tile	tile	Tile	undef	undef
-underline	underline	Underline	-1	-1

Option name	Xdefault's name	Class name	Default value	Current value
-width	width	Width	0	0
-wraplength	wrapLength	WrapLength	0	0

Message

Option name	Xdefault's name	Class name	Default value	Current value
-anchor	anchor	Anchor	center	center
-aspect	aspect	Aspect	150	150
-background	background	Background	#d9d9d9	#d9d9d9
-bd	borderWidth			
-bg	background			
-borderwidth	borderWidth	BorderWidth	2	2
-cursor	cursor	Cursor		undef
-fg	foreground			
-font	font	Font	Helvetica -12 bold	Tk::Font=SCALAR(0x83649a0)
-foreground	foreground	Foreground	Black	Black
-highlightbackground	highlightBackground	HighlightBackground	#d9d9d9	#d9d9d9
-highlightcolor	highlightColor	HighlightColor	Black	Black
-highlightthickness	highlightThickness	HighlightThickness	0	0
-justify	justify	Justify	left	left
-padx	padX	Pad	-1	5
-pady	padY	Pad	-1	2
-relief	relief	Relief	flat	flat
-takefocus	takeFocus	TakeFocus	0	0
-text	text	Text		

Option name	.Xdefault's name	Class name	Default value	Current value
-textvariable	textVariable	Variable		undef
-tile	tile	Tile	undef	
-width	width	Width	0	0

NoteBook

Option name	.Xdefault's name	Class name	Default value	Current value
-background	background	Background	#d9d9d9	#d9d9d9
-backpagecolor	backPageColor	BackPageColor	#d9d9d9	#d9d9d9
-bd	borderWidth			
-bg	background			
-borderwidth	borderWidth	BorderWidth	2	2
-cursor	cursor	Cursor	undef	undef
-disabledforeground	disabledForeground	DisabledForeground	#a3a3a3	#a3a3a3
-dynamicgeometry	dynamicGeometry	DynamicGeometry	0	0
-fg	foreground			
-focuscolor	focusColor	FocusColor	Black	Black
-font	font	Font	-Adobe-Helvetica-Bold-R-Normal--*-120-*	Tk::Font=SCALAR(0x8581284)
-foreground	foreground	Foreground	Black	Black
-inactivebackground	inactiveBackground	Background	#c3c3c3	#c3c3c3
-ipadx	ipadX	Pad	0	0
-ipady	ipadY	Pad	0	0
-relief	relief	Relief	sunken	raised
-slave	slave	Slave	1	1
-tabpadx	tabPadX	Pad	6	6

Option name	.Xdefault's name	Class name	Default value	Current value
-tabpady	tabPadY	Pad	5	5
-takefocus	takeFocus	TakeFocus	0	1
-width	width	Width	10	10

Optionmenu

Option name	.Xdefault's name	Class name	Default value	Current value
-activebackground	activebackground	Foreground	#ececec	#ececec
-activeforeground	activeforeground	Background	Black	Black
-activetile	activeTile	Tile	undef	
-anchor	anchor	Anchor	center	center
-background	background	Background	#d9d9d9	#d9d9d9
-bd	borderWidth			
-bg	background			
-bitmap	bitmap	Bitmap		undef
-borderwidth	borderWidth	BorderWidth	2	2
-command	undef	undef	undef	undef
-cursor	cursor	Cursor	undef	undef
-direction	direction	Direction	below	below
-disabledforeground	disabledforeground	DisabledForeground	#a3a3a3	#a3a3a3
-disabledtile	disabledTile	Tile	undef	
-fg	foreground			
-font	undef	undef	undef	Tk::Font=SCALAR(0x83649a0)
-foreground	foreground	Foreground	Black	Black
-height	height	Height	0	0

Option name	Xdefault's name	Class name	Default value	Current value
-highlightbackground	highlightBackground	HighlightBackground	#d9d9d9	#d9d9d9
-highlightcolor	highlightColor	HighlightColor	Black	Black
-highlightthickness	highlightThickness	HighlightThickness	1	1
-image	image	Image	undef	undef
-indicatoron	indicatorOn	IndicatorOn	0	1
-justify	justify	Justify	center	center
-menu	menu	Menu		Tk::Menu=HASH(0x86d748c)
-offset	offset	Offset	0 0	ARRAY(0x86ddfe0)
-options	undef	undef	undef	undef
-padx	padx	Pad	4p	4
-pady	pady	Pad	3p	3
-relief	relief	Relief	raised	raised
-state	state	State	normal	normal
-takefocus	takefocus	Takefocus	1	1
-text	text	Text		
-textvariable	textVariable	Variable		SCALAR(0x82983a8)
-tile	tile	Tile	undef	
-underline	underline	Underline	-1	-1
-variable	undef	undef	undef	undef
-width	width	Width	0	0
-wraplength	wrapLength	WrapLength	0	0

Pane

Option name	Xdefault's name	Class name	Default value	Current value
-background	background	Background	#d9d9d9	#d9d9d9

Option name	Xdefault's name	Class name	Default value	Current value
-bd	borderWidth			
-bg	background			
-borderwidth	borderWidth	BorderWidth	0	0
-class	class	Class	Frame	Frame
-colormap	colormap	Colormap		undef
-container	container	Container	0	0
-cursor	cursor	Cursor		undef
-fg	foreground			
-foreground	foreground	Foreground	Black	Black
-gridded	undef	undef		undef
-height	height	Height	0	0
-highlightbackground	highlightBackground	HighlightBackground	#d9d9d9	#d9d9d9
-highlightcolor	highlightColor	HighlightColor	Black	Black
-highlightthickness	highlightThickness	HighlightThickness	0	0
-label	undef	undef	undef	undef
-labelPack	undef	undef	undef	
-labelVariable	undef	undef	undef	undef
-offset	offset	Offset	0 0	ARRAY(0x86ffb24)
-relief	relief	Relief	flat	flat
-sticky	undef	undef	undef	undef
-takefocus	takeFocus	TakeFocus	0	0
-tile	tile	Tile		
-visual	visual	Visual	undef	undef
-width	width	Width	0	0
-xscrollcommand	undef	undef	undef	undef
-yscrollcommand	undef	undef	undef	undef

Photo

Option name	.Xdefault's name	Class name	Default value	Current value
-data	undef	undef	undef	undef
-format	undef	undef	undef	undef
-file	undef	undef	undef	undef
-gamma	gamma	Gamma	1	1
-height	undef	undef	0	0
-palette	palette	Palette		
-width	undef	undef	0	0

ProgressBar

Option name	.Xdefault's name	Class name	Default value	Current value
-activegroup	activegroup	ActiveGroup	0	undef
-anchor	anchor	Anchor	w	w
-background	background	Background	#d9d9d9	#d9d9d9
-bd	borderwidth	BorderWidth		
-bg	background	Background		
-blocks	undef	undef	10	10
-borderwidth	borderwidth	BorderWidth	0	0
-closeenough	closeEnough	CloseEnough	1	1
-colors	undef	undef	undef	undef
-confine	confine	Confine	1	1
-cursor	cursor	Cursor		undef
-disabledtile	disabledtile	Tile	undef	undef
-fg	foreground			

Option name	Xdefault's name	Class name	Default value	Current value
-foreground	foreground	Foreground	Black	Black
-from	undef	undef	0	0
-gap	undef	undef	1	1
-height	height	Height	7c	199
-highlightbackground	highlightBackground	HighlightBackground	#d9d9d9	#d9d9d9
-highlightcolor	highlightColor	HighlightColor	Black	Black
-highlightthickness	highlightThickness	HighlightThickness	0	0
-insertbackground	insertBackground	Foreground	Black	Black
-insertborderwidth	insertBorderWidth	BorderWidth	0	0
-insertofftime	insertOffTime	OffTime	300	300
-insertontime	insertOnTime	OnTime	600	600
-insertwidth	insertWidth	InsertWidth	2	2
-length	undef	undef	0	0
-offset	offset	Offset	0 0	ARRAY(0x87244ac)
-padx	padX	Pad	0	0
-pady	padY	Pad	0	0
-relief	relief	Relief	sunken	sunken
-resolution	undef	undef	1	1
-scrollregion	scrollRegion	ScrollRegion		undef
-selectbackground	selectBackground	Foreground	#c3c3c3	#c3c3c3
-selectborderwidth	selectBorderWidth	BorderWidth	1	1
-selectforeground	selectForeground	Background	Black	Black
-state	state	State	normal	normal
-takefocus	takeFocus	TakeFocus	undef	undef
-tile	tile	Tile	undef	
-to	undef	undef	100	100

Option name	Xdefault's name	Class name	Default value	Current value
-troughcolor	troughColor	Background	grey55	grey55
-value	undef	undef	undef	0
-variable	undef	undef	undef	undef
-width	undef	undef	0	0
-xscrollcommand	xScrollCommand	ScrollCommand		undef
-xscrollincrement	xScrollIncrement	ScrollIncrement	0	0
-yscrollcommand	yScrollCommand	ScrollCommand		undef
-yscrollincrement	yScrollIncrement	ScrollIncrement	0	0

Radiobutton

Option name	Xdefault's name	Class name	Default value	Current value
-activebackground	activeBackground	Foreground	#ececec	#ececec
-activeforeground	activeForeground	Background	Black	Black
-activetile	activeTile	Tile	undef	undef
-anchor	anchor	Anchor	center	center
-background	background	Background	#d9d9d9	#d9d9d9
-bd	borderWidth			
-bg	background			
-bitmap	bitmap	Bitmap		undef
-borderwidth	borderWidth	BorderWidth	2	2
-command	command	Command	undef	undef
-cursor	cursor	Cursor	undef	undef
-disabledforeground	disabledForeground	DisabledForeground	#a3a3a3	#a3a3a3
-disabledtile	disabledTile	Tile	undef	undef
-fg	foreground	Foreground		

Option name	Xdefault's name	Class name	Default value	Current value
-font	font	Font	Helvetica -12 bold	Tk:: Font=SCALAR(0x83649a0)
-foreground	foreground	Foreground	Black	Black
-height	height	Height	0	0
-highlightbackground	highlightBackground	HighlightBackground	#d9d9d9	#d9d9d9
-highlightcolor	highlightColor	HighlightColor	Black	Black
-highlightthickness	highlightThickness	HighlightThickness	1	1
-image	image	Image	undef	undef
-indicatoron	indicatorOn	IndicatorOn	1	1
-justify	justify	Justify	center	center
-offset	offset	Offset	0 0	ARRAY(0x87244e8)
-padx	padX	Pad	1	1
-pady	padY	Pad	1	1
-relief	relief	Relief	flat	flat
-selectcolor	selectColor	Background	#b03060	#b03060
-selectimage	selectImage	SelectImage	undef	undef
-state	state	State	normal	normal
-takefocus	takeFocus	TakeFocus	undef	undef
-text	text	Text		
-textvariable	textVariable	Variable	undef	undef
-tile	tile	Tile	undef	
-underline	underline	Underline	-1	-1
-value	value	Value		
-variable	variable	Variable	selectedButton	SCALAR(0x8724494)
-width	width	Width	0	0
-wraplength	wrapLength	WrapLength	0	0

ROText

Option name	Xdefault's name	Class name	Default value	Current value
-background	background	Background	#d9d9d9	#d9d9d9
-bd	borderwidth			
-bg	background			
-borderwidth	borderwidth	BorderWidth	2	2
-cursor	cursor	Cursor	xterm	xterm
-disabledtile	disabledtile	Tile	undef	
-exportselection	exportSelection	ExportSelection	1	1
-fg	foreground			
-font	font	Font	Courier -12	Tk::Font=SCALAR(0x8731bf0)
-foreground	foreground	Foreground	Black	Black
-height	height	Height	24	24
-highlightbackground	highlightBackground	HighlightBackground	#d9d9d9	#d9d9d9
-highlightcolor	highlightColor	HighlightColor	Black	Black
-highlightthickness	highlightThickness	HighlightThickness	1	1
-insertbackground	insertBackground	Foreground	Black	Black
-insertborderwidth	insertBorderwidth	BorderWidth	0	0
-insertofftime	insertOffTime	OffTime	300	300
-insertontime	insertOnTime	OnTime	600	600
-insertwidth	insertWidth	InsertWidth	2	2
-offset	offset	Offset	0 0	ARRAY(0x8733838)
-padx	padX	Pad	1	1
-pady	padY	Pad	1	1
-relief	relief	Relief	sunken	sunken

Option name	Xdefault's name	Class name	Default value	Current value
-selectbackground	selectBackground	Foreground	#c3c3c3	#c3c3c3
-selectborderwidth	selectBorderWidth	BorderWidth	1	1
-selectforeground	selectForeground	Background	Black	Black
-setgrid	setGrid	SetGrid	0	0
-spacing1	spacing1	Spacing	0	0
-spacing2	spacing2	Spacing	0	0
-spacing3	spacing3	Spacing	0	0
-state	state	State	normal	normal
-tabs	tabs	Tabs	undef	undef
-takefocus	takeFocus	TakeFocus	undef	undef
-tile	tile	Tile	undef	undef
-width	width	Width	80	80
-wrap	wrap	Wrap	char	char
-xscrollcommand	xScrollCommand	ScrollCommand		undef
-yscrollcommand	yScrollCommand	ScrollCommand		undef

Scale

Option name	Xdefault's name	Class name	Default value	Current value
-activebackground	activeBackground	Foreground	#ececec	#ececec
-activetile	activeTile	Tile	undef	
-background	background	Background	#d9d9d9	#d9d9d9
-bigincrement	bigIncrement	BigIncrement	0	0
-bd	borderWidth			
-bg	background			
-borderwidth	borderWidth	BorderWidth	2	2

Option name	.Xdefault's name	Class name	Default value	Current value
-command	command	Command		undef
-cursor	cursor	Cursor		undef
-digits	digits	Digits	0	0
-fg	foreground			
-disabledtile	disabledTile	Tile	undef	
-font	font	Font	Helvetica -12 bold	Tk:: Font=SCALAR(0x83649a0)
-foreground	foreground	Foreground	Black	Black
-from	from	From	0	0
-highlightbackground	highlightBackground	HighlightBackground	#d9d9d9	#d9d9d9
-highlightcolor	highlightColor	HighlightColor	Black	Black
-highlightthickness	highlightThickness	HighlightThickness	1	1
-label	label	Label		undef
-length	length	Length	100	100
-offset	offset	Offset	0 0	ARRAY(0x8734204)
-orient	orient	Orient	vertical	vertical
-relief	relief	Relief	flat	flat
-repeatdelay	repeatDelay	RepeatDelay	300	300
-repeatinterval	repeatInterval	RepeatInterval	100	100
-resolution	resolution	Resolution	1	1
-showvalue	showValue	ShowValue	1	1
-sliderlength	sliderLength	SliderLength	10m	28
-sliderrelief	sliderRelief	SliderRelief	raised	raised
-state	state	State	normal	normal
-takefocus	takeFocus	TakeFocus	undef	undef
-tickinterval	tickInterval	TickInterval	0	0

Option name	Xdefault's name	Class name	Default value	Current value
-tile	tile	Tile	undef	
-to	to	To	100	100
-troughcolor	troughColor	Background	#c3c3c3	#c3c3c3
-troughtile	troughTile	Tile	undef	undef
-variable	variable	Variable		undef
-width	width	Width	5m	14

Scrollbar

Option name	Xdefault's name	Class name	Default value	Current value
-activebackground	activeBackground	Foreground	#ececec	#ececec
-activerelief	activeRelief	Relief	raised	raised
-activetile	activeTile	Tile	undef	
-background	background	Background	#d9d9d9	#d9d9d9
-bd	borderWidth	BorderWidth		
-bg	background	Background		
-borderwidth	borderWidth	BorderWidth	2	2
-command	command	Command		undef
-cursor	cursor	Cursor		undef
-elementborderwidth	elementBorderWidth	BorderWidth	-1	-1
-highlightbackground	highlightBackground	HighlightBackground	#d9d9d9	#d9d9d9
-highlightcolor	highlightColor	HighlightColor	Black	Black
-highlightthickness	highlightThickness	HighlightThickness	1	1
-jump	jump	Jump	0	0
-orient	orient	Orient	vertical	vertical
-relief	relief	Relief	sunken	sunken

Option name	.Xdefault's name	Class name	Default value	Current value
-repeatdelay	repeatDelay	RepeatDelay	300	300
-repeatinterval	repeatInterval	RepeatInterval	100	100
-takefocus	takeFocus	TakeFocus	undef	undef
-tile	tile	Tile	undef	
-offset	offset	Offset	0 0	ARRAY(0x8734204)
-troughcolor	troughColor	Background	#c3c3c3	#c3c3c3
-troughtile	troughTile	Tile	undef	
-width	width	Width	4m	11

Table

Option name	.Xdefault's name	Class name	Default value	Current value
-background	background	Background	#d9d9d9	#d9d9d9
-bd	borderWidth			
-bg	background			
-borderwidth	borderWidth	BorderWidth	0	0
-class	class	Class	Frame	Table
-colormap	colormap	Colormap		undef
-columns	columns	Columns	10	10
-container	container	Container	0	0
-cursor	cursor	Cursor		undef
-fg	foreground			
-fixedcolumns	fixedColumn	FixedColumns	0	0
-fixedrows	fixedRows	FixedRows	0	0
-foreground	foreground	Foreground	Black	Black
-height	height	Height	0	0

Option name	Xdefault's name	Class name	Default value	Current value
-highlightbackground	highlightBackground	HighlightBackground	#d9d9d9	#d9d9d9
-highlightcolor	highlightColor	HighlightColor	Black	Black
-highlightthickness	highlightThickness	HighlightThickness	2	2
-label		undef	undef	undef
-labelPack	undef	undef	undef	undef
-labelVariable	undef	undef	undef	undef
-offset	offset	Offset	0 0	ARRAY(0x875ae58)
-relief	relief	Relief	flat	flat
-rows	rows	Rows	10	10
-scrollbars	scrollbars	Scrollbars	nw	nw
-takefocus	takeFocus	TakeFocus	1	1
-tile	tile	Tile	undef	
-visual	visual	Visual		undef
-width	width	Width	0	0

Text

Option name	Xdefault's name	Class name	Default value	Current value
-background	background	Background	#d9d9d9	#d9d9d9
-bd	borderWidth			
-bg	background			
-borderwidth	borderWidth	BorderWidth	2	2
-cursor	cursor	Cursor	xterm	xterm
-disabledtile	disabledtile	Tile	undef	
-exportselection	exportSelection	ExportSelection	1	1
-fg	foreground			

Option name	Xdefault's name	Class name	Default value	Current value
-font	font	Font	Courier -12	Tk::Font=SCALAR(0x8731bf0)
-foreground	foreground	Foreground	Black	Black
-height	height	Height	24	24
-highlightbackground	highlightBackground	HighlightBackground	#d9d9d9	#d9d9d9
-highlightcolor	highlightColor	HighlightColor	Black	Black
-highlightthickness	highlightThickness	HighlightThickness	1	1
-insertbackground	insertBackground	Foreground	Black	Black
-insertborderwidth	insertBorderwidth	BorderWidth	0	0
-insertofftime	insertOffTime	OffTime	300	300
-insertontime	insertOnTime	OnTime	600	600
-insertwidth	insertwidth	InsertWidth	2	2
-offset	offset	Offset	0 0	ARRAY(0x875ae58)
-padx	padX	Pad	1	1
-pady	padY	Pad	1	1
-relief	relief	Relief	sunken	sunken
-selectbackground	selectBackground	Foreground	#c3c3c3	#c3c3c3
-selectborderwidth	selectBorderwidth	BorderWidth	1	1
-selectforeground	selectForeground	Background	Black	Black
-setgrid	setGrid	SetGrid	0	0
-spacing1	spacing1	Spacing	0	0
-spacing2	spacing2	Spacing	0	0
-spacing3	spacing3	Spacing	0	0
-state	state	State	normal	normal
-tabs	tabs	Tabs	undef	undef
-takefocus	takeFocus	TakeFocus	undef	undef

Option name	Xdefault's name	Class name	Default value	Current value
-tile	tile	Tile	undef	
-width	width	Width	80	80
-wrap	wrap	Wrap	char	char
-xscrollcommand	xScrollCommand	ScrollCommand		undef
-yscrollcommand	yScrollCommand	ScrollCommand		undef

TextUndo

Option name	Xdefault's name	Class name	Default value	Current value
-background	background	Background	#d9d9d9	#d9d9d9
-bd	borderWidth			
-bg	background			
-borderwidth	borderWidth	BorderWidth	2	2
-cursor	cursor	Cursor	xterm	xterm
-disabledtile	disabledtile	Tile	undef	
-exportselection	exportSelection	ExportSelection	1	1
-fg	foreground			
-font	font	Font	Courier -12	Tk:: Font=SCALAR(0x8731bf0)
-foreground	foreground	Foreground	Black	Black
-height	height	Height	24	24
-highlightbackground	highlightBackground	HighlightBackground	#d9d9d9	#d9d9d9
-highlightcolor	highlightColor	HighlightColor	Black	Black
-highlightthickness	highlightThickness	HighlightThickness	1	1
-insertbackground	insertBackground	Foreground	Black	Black
-insertborderwidth	insertBorderWidth	BorderWidth	0	0

Option name	Xdefault's name	Class name	Default value	Current value
-insertofftime	insertOffTime	OffTime	300	300
-insertontime	insertOnTime	OnTime	600	600
-insertwidth	insertWidth	InsertWidth	2	2
-offset	offset	Offset	0 0	ARRAY(0x87a13ac)
-padx	padX	Pad	1	1
-pady	padY	Pad	1	1
-relief	relief	Relief	sunken	sunken
-selectbackground	selectBackground	Foreground	#c3c3c3	#c3c3c3
-selectborderwidth	selectBorderWidth	BorderWidth	1	1
-selectforeground	selectForeground	Background	Black	Black
-setgrid	setGrid	SetGrid	0	0
-spacing1	spacing1	Spacing	0	0
-spacing2	spacing2	Spacing	0	0
-spacing3	spacing3	Spacing	0	0
-state	state	State	normal	normal
-tabs	tabs	Tabs	undef	undef
-takefocus	takeFocus	TakeFocus	undef	undef
-tile	tile	Tile	undef	undef
-width	width	Width	80	80
-wrap	wrap	Wrap	char	char
-xscrollcommand	xScrollCommand	ScrollCommand	undef	undef
-yscrollcommand	yScrollCommand	ScrollCommand	undef	undef

Tiler

Option name	Xdefault's name	Class name	Default value	Current value
-background	background	Background	#d9d9d9	#d9d9d9
-bd	borderwidth			
-bg	background			
-borderwidth	borderwidth	BorderWidth	0	0
-class	class	Class	Frame	Tiler
-colormap	colormap	Colormap		undef
-columns	columns	Columns	5	5
-container	container	Container	0	0
-cursor	cursor	Cursor		undef
-fg	foreground			
-foreground	foreground	Foreground	Black	Black
-height	height	Height	0	0
-highlightbackground	highlightBackground	HighlightBackground	#d9d9d9	#d9d9d9
-highlightcolor	highlightColor	HighlightColor	Black	Black
-highlightthickness	highlightThickness	HighlightThickness	2	2
-label	undef	undef	undef	undef
-labelPack	undef	undef	undef	
-labelVariable	undef	undef	undef	undef
-offset	offset	Offset	0 0	ARRAY(0x87b5870)
-relief	relief	Relief	flat	flat
-rows	rows	Rows	10	10
-takefocus	takeFocus	TakeFocus	1	1
-tile	tile	Tile	undef	
-visual	visual	Visual		undef

Option name	.Xdefault's name	Class name	Default value	Current value
-width	width	Width	0	0
-yscrollcommand	undef	undef	undef	undef

TList

Option name	.Xdefault's name	Class name	Default value	Current value
-background	background	Background	#d9d9d9	#d9d9d9
-bd	borderWidth			
-bg	background			
-highlightbackground	highlightBackground	HighlightBackground	#d9d9d9	#d9d9d9
-borderwidth	borderWidth	BorderWidth	2	2
-browsecmd	browseCmd	BrowseCmd		undef
-command	command	Command		undef
-cursor	cursor	Cursor		undef
-fg	foreground			
-font	font	Font	-Adobe-Helvetica-Bold-R-Normal-*-120-*	Tk::Font=SCALAR(0x8581284)
-foreground	foreground	Foreground	Black	Black
-height	height	Height	10	10
-highlightcolor	highlightColor	HighlightColor	Black	Black
-highlightthickness	highlightThickness	HighlightThickness	2	2
-itemtype	itemType	ItemType	text	text
-orient	orient	Orient	vertical	vertical
-padx	padX	Pad	2	2
-pady	padY	Pad	2	2
-relief	relief	Relief	sunken	sunken

Option name	Xdefault's name	Class name	Default value	Current value
-selectbackground	selectBackground	Foreground	#ececec	#ececec
-selectborderwidth	selectBorderWidth	BorderWidth	1	1
-selectforeground	selectForeground	Background	Black	Black
-selectmode	selectMode	SelectMode	browse	browse
-state	undef	undef	normal	normal
-sizecmd	sizecmd	SizeCmd		undef
-takefocus	takeFocus	TakeFocus	1	1
-width	width	Width	20	20
-xscrollcommand	xScrollCommand	ScrollCommand		undef
-yscrollcommand	yScrollCommand	ScrollCommand		undef

Toplevel

Option name	Xdefault's name	Class name	Default value	Current value
-background	background	Background	#d9d9d9	#d9d9d9
-bd	borderWidth			
-bg	background			
-borderwidth	borderWidth	BorderWidth	0	0
-class	class	Class	Toplevel	Toplevel
-colormap	colormap	Colormap		undef
-container	container	Container	0	0
-cursor	cursor	Cursor		undef
-fg	foreground			
-foreground	foreground	Foreground	Black	Black
-height	height	Height	0	0
-highlightbackground	highlightBackground	HighlightBackground	#d9d9d9	#d9d9d9

Option name	Xdefault's name	Class name	Default value	Current value
-highlightcolor	highlightColor	HighlightColor	Black	Black
-highlightthickness	highlightThickness	HighlightThickness	0	0
-menu	menu	Menu	undef	undef
-offset	offset	Offset	0 0	ARRAY(0x87d8b14)
-overanchor	undef	undef	undef	undef
-popanchor	undef	undef	undef	undef
-popover	undef	undef	undef	undef
-relief	relief	Relief	flat	flat
-screen	screen	Screen		undef
-takefocus	takeFocus	TakeFocus	0	0
-tile	tile	Tile	undef	
-title	undef	undef	Toplevel	Toplevel
-use	use	Use		undef
-visual	visual	Visual		undef
-width	width	Width	0	0

Tree

Option name	Xdefault's name	Class name	Default value	Current value
-background	background	Background	#d9d9d9	#d9d9d9
-bd	borderWidth			
-bg	background			
-borderwidth	borderWidth	BorderWidth	2	2
-browsecmd	browseCmd	BrowseCmd	undef	undef
-closecmd	closeCmd	CloseCmd	CloseCmd	CloseCmd
-columns	columns	Columns	1	1

Option name	Xdefault's name	Class name	Default value	Current value
-command	command	Command		undef
-cursor	cursor	Cursor		undef
-dragcmd	dragCmd	DragCmd		undef
-drawbranch	drawBranch	DrawBranch	true	1
-dropcmd	dropCmd	DropCmd		undef
-exportselection	exportSelection	ExportSelection	0	0
-fg	foreground	Foreground		
-font	font	Font	-Adobe-Helvetica-Bold-R-Normal--*-120-*	Tk::Font=SCALAR(0x8581284)
-foreground	foreground	Foreground	Black	Black
-gap	gap	Gap	5	5
-header	header	Header	0	0
-height	height	Height	10	10
-highlightbackground	highlightBackground	HighlightBackground	#d9d9d9	#d9d9d9
-highlightcolor	highlightColor	HighlightColor	Black	Black
-highlightthickness	highlightThickness	HighlightThickness	2	2
-ignoreinvoke	ignoreInvoke	IgnoreInvoke	0	0
-indent	indent	Indent	20	20
-indicator	indicator	Indicator	1	1
-indicatorcmd	indicatorCmd	IndicatorCmd	IndicatorCmd	IndicatorCmd
-itemtype	itemtype	Itemtype	imagetext	imagetext
-opencmd	openCmd	OpenCmd	OpenCmd	OpenCmd
-padx	padX	Pad	2	2
-pady	padY	Pad	2	2
-relief	relief	Relief	sunken	sunken
-selectbackground	selectBackground	Foreground	#ececec	#ececec

Option name	.Xdefault's name	Class name	Default value	Current value
-selectborderwidth	selectBorderWidth	BorderWidth	1	1
-selectforeground	selectForeground	Background	Black	Black
-selectmode	selectMode	SelectMode	browse	browse
-separator	separator	Separator	.	.
-sizecmd	sizeCmd	SizeCmd	undef	undef
-takefocus	takeFocus	TakeFocus	1	1
-wideselection	wideSelection	WideSelection	true	1
-width	width	Width	20	20
-xscrollcommand	xScrollCommand	ScrollCommand	undef	undef
-yscrollcommand	yScrollCommand	ScrollCommand	undef	undef

Complete Program Listings

This appendix contains program listings that, for one reason or another, did not appear in the book proper. This is mostly because only a small portion of the code was applicable to the chapter in which it appeared. Nonetheless, seeing the program in its entirety is useful, so here's a chapter full of code. Enjoy!

Tk::CollapsableFrame

Use a CollapsableFrame to hide information until the widget is opened. This widget is used by the MacCopy widget, described next. Both Tk::CollapsableFrame and Tk::MacCopy are more examples of composite mega-widgets, described in Chapter 14.

See Figure C-1 for a demonstration of a CollapsableFrame widget.

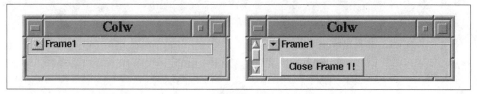

Figure C-1. A CollapsableFrame, shown both hidden and displayed

```
$Tk::CollapsableFrame::VERSION = '1.0';

package Tk::CollapsableFrame;

use Carp;
use Tk::widgets qw/Frame/;
use vars qw/$cf_height_bias $im_Close $im_Open/;
use strict;

use base qw/Tk::Frame/;
Construct Tk::Widget 'CollapsableFrame';

sub ClassInit {
```

```perl
# Define global variables and images for the class.

my($class, $mw) = @_;

$cf_height_bias = 22;

$im_Close = $mw->Photo(-data =>
  'R0lGODlhEAAQAKIAAP///9TQyICAgEBAQAAAAAAAAAAAAAAACwAAAAAEAAQAAADMxi63BMg
  yinFAyOHC3XjmLeA4ngpRKoSZoeuDLmo38mwtVvKu93rIo5gSCwWB8ikcolMAAA7');

$im_Open = $mw->Photo(-data =>
  'R0lGODlhEAAQAKIAAP///9TQyICAgEBAQAAAAAAAAAAAAAAACwAAAAAEAAQAAADNhi63BMg
  yinFAyOHC3Xj2EJoIEOM32WeaSeeqFK+say+2azUi+5ttx/QJeQIjshkcsBsOp/MBAA7');

$class->SUPER::ClassInit($mw);

} # end ClassInit

sub Populate {

# Create an instance of a CollapsableFrame.  Instance variables are:
#
# {frame} = the ridged frame, which contains the open/close
#           Label image, the id Label for the collapsable Frame,
#           and the container Frame within which the user manages
#           collapsable widgets.  It's ALMOST possible to forgo
#           this extra internal frame, were it not for the -pady
#           packer attribute we use to make the widget look pretty.
# {opcl}  = the open/close image Label.
# {ident} = the identifying Label.
# {colf}  = the user's container Frame, advertised as "colf".

my($self, $args) = @_;

my $height = $args->{-height};
croak "Tk::CollapsableFrame: -height must be >= $cf_height_bias" unless
    $height >= $cf_height_bias;
$self->SUPER::Populate($args);

$self->{frame} = $self->Frame(
    qw/-borderwidth 2 -height 16 -relief ridge/,
);
$self->{frame}->pack(
    qw/-anchor center -expand 1 -fill x -pady 7 -side left/,
);

$self->{opcl} = $self->Label(
    qw/-borderwidth 0 -relief raised/, -text => $height,
);
$self->{opcl}->bind('<Button-1>' => [sub {$_[1]->toggle}, $self]);
$self->{opcl}->place(
    qw/-x 5 -y -1 -width 21 -height 21 -anchor nw -bordermode ignore/,
);
```

```perl
    $self->{ident} = $self->Label(qw/-anchor w -borderwidth 1/);
    $self->{ident}->place(
        qw/-x 23 -y 3  -height 12 -anchor nw -bordermode ignore/,
    );

    $self->{colf} = $self->{frame}->Frame;
    $self->{colf}->place(qw/-x 20 -y 15/);
    $self->Advertise('colf' => $self->{colf});

    if (not defined $args->{-width}) {
     $args->{-width} = $self->parent->cget(-width);
     }

    $self->ConfigSpecs(
      -background  => [qw/SELF background Background/],
      -height      => [qw/METHOD height Height 47/],
      -image       => [$self->{opcl}, 'image', 'Image', $im_Open],
      -title       => '-text',
      -text        => [$self->{ident}, qw/text Text NoTitle/],
      -width       => [$self->{frame}, qw/width Width 250/],
    );

} # end Populate

sub bias {return $cf_height_bias}

# Instance methods.

sub toggle {
    my($self) = @_;
    my $i = $self->{opcl}->cget(-image);
    my $op = ($i == $im_Open) ? 'open' : 'close';
    $self->$op();
}

sub close {
    my($self) = @_;
    $self->{opcl}->configure(-image  => $im_Open);
    $self->{frame}->configure(-height => 16);
}

sub open  {
    my($self) = @_;
    $self->{opcl}->configure(-image  => $im_Close);
    $self->{frame}->configure(-height => $self->{opcl}->cget(-text));
}

sub height {
    my($self, $h) = @_;
    $self->{opcl}->configure(-text => $h);
}


1;

__END__
```

=head1 NAME

Tk::CollapsableFrame - a Frame that opens and closes via a mouse click.

=head1 SYNOPSIS

S<   >I<$cf> = I<$parent>-E<gt>B<CollapsableFrame>(I<-option> =E<gt> I<value>);

=head1 DESCRIPTION

This widget provides a switchable open or closed Frame
that provides for the vertical arrangement of widget
controls. This is an alternative to Notebook style
tabbed widgets.

The following option/value pairs are supported:

=over 4

=item B<-title>

Title of the CollapsableFrame widget.

=item B<-height>

The maximun open height of the CollapsableFrame.

=back

=head1 METHODS

=over 4

=item B<close>

Closes the CollapsableFrame.

=item B<open>

Opens the CollapsableFrame.

=item B<toggle>

Toggles the open/close state of the CollapsableFrame.

=back

=head1 ADVERTISED WIDGETS

Component subwidgets can be accessed via the B<Subwidget> method.
Valid subwidget names are listed below.

=over 4

```
=item Name:  colf, Class:  Frame

  Widget reference of the internal Frame widget within which user
  widgets are managed.

=back

=head1 EXAMPLE

 use Tk::widgets qw/CollapsableFrame Pane/;

 my $mw = MainWindow->new;

 my $pane = $mw->Scrolled(
     qw/Pane -width 250 -height 50 -scrollbars osow -sticky nw/,
 )->pack;

 my $cf = $pane->CollapsableFrame(-title => 'Frame1 ', -height => 50);
 $cf->pack(qw/-fill x -expand 1/);
 $cf->toggle;

 my $colf = $cf->Subwidget('colf');
 my $but = $colf->Button(-text => 'Close Frame 1!');
 $but->pack;
 $but->bind('<Button-1>' => [sub {$_[1]->close}, $cf]);

=head1 AUTHOR and COPYRIGHT

Stephen.O.Lidie@Lehigh.EDU, 2000/11/27.

Copyright (C) 2000 - 2001, Stephen O. Lidie.

This program is free software, you can redistribute it and/or modify
it under the same terms as Perl itself.

Based on the Tck/Tk CollapsableFrame widget by William J Giddings.

=head1 KEYWORDS

CollapsableFrame, Frame, Pane

=cut
```

Tk::MacCopy

This widget simulates a Macintosh file copy dialog. It uses a CollapsableFrame widget to hide copy details, and a MacProgressBar widget to indicate progress of the copy. See Figure C-2.

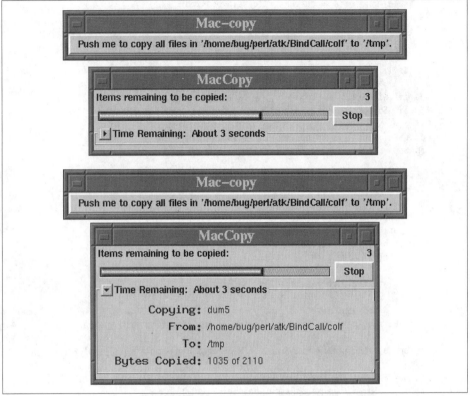

Figure C-2. Tk::MacCopy, shown with the CollapsableFrame both hidden and viewable

Here's the code:

```perl
$Tk::MacCopy::VERSION = '1.0';

package Tk::MacCopy;

use File::Copy;
use Tk::widgets qw/CollapsableFrame LabEntry MacProgressBar/;

use base qw/Tk::Toplevel/;
use strict;

Construct Tk::Widget 'MacCopy';

sub Populate {

    # Create an instance of a MacCopy widget.  Instance variables are:
    #
    # {bytes_msg}      = a string showing how many bytes copied,
    #                    as well as the total byte count.
```

```perl
# {file}             = current file being copied.
# {file_count}       = number of files left to copy.
# {from}             = source directory path.
# {to}               = destination directory path.

my($self, $args) = @_;

$self->withdraw;
$self->SUPER::Populate($args);

$args->{-width} = 300 unless exists $args->{-width};
my $pb = $self->MacProgressBar(%$args)->pack;

# Populate the top Frame of the MacProgessBar.

my $tf = $pb->Subwidget('tframe');
$tf->Label(-text => 'Items remaining to be copied:  ')->
    pack(qw/-side left -anchor w/);
$tf->Label(-textvariable => \$self->{file_count})->
    pack(qw/-side right -anchor e/);

# Populate the right Frame of the MacProgessBar.

my $rf = $pb->Subwidget('rframe');
$rf->Button(-text => 'Stop', -command => sub {$self->destroy})->pack;

# Populate the bottom Frame of the MacProgessBar with a CollapsableFrame.

my $bf = $pb->Subwidget('bframe');
my $cf = $bf->CollapsableFrame(-height => 110);
$cf->pack(qw/-fill x -expand 1/);
my $cf_frame = $cf->Subwidget('colf');

# Populate the CollapsableFrame with detail information.

foreach my $item (
    ['Copying', \$self->{file}],
    ['From', \$self->{from}],
    ['To', \$self->{to}],
    ['Bytes Copied', \$self->{bytes_msg}],
    ) {
my $l = $item->[0] . ':';
my $le = $cf_frame->LabEntry(
        -label       => ' ' x (13 - length $l) . $l,
        -labelPack   => [qw/-side left -anchor w/],
        -labelFont   => '9x15bold',
        -relief      => 'flat',
        -state       => 'disabled',
        -textvariable => $item->[1],
      -width         => 35,
    );
$le->pack(qw/ -fill x -expand 1/);
}
```

```
    $self->Advertise('collapsableframe' => $cf);
    $self->Advertise('progressbar'      => $pb);

} # end Populate

sub mcopy {

    # Perform the copy, updating copy information on-the-fly. Because
    # this is just a demo, we don't recursively copy subdirectories.

    my($self, $from, $to) = @_;

    $self->{from} = $from;
    $self->{to} = $to;
    $self->deiconify;

    opendir D, $from;
    my(@files) = grep(! -d $_, readdir D);
    closedir D;

    my $total_bytes = 0;
    foreach my $f (@files) {
        $total_bytes += -s $f;
    }

    $self->{file_count} = scalar @files;
    $self->update;

    my $filen = 0;
    my $bytes = 0;

    foreach my $f (@files) {
        $filen++;
        $self->{file} = $f;
        my $size = -s $f;
        my $stat = copy($f, "$to/$f");
        $self->messageBox(
                -title   => 'MacCopy Failure',
                -icon    => 'warning',
                -type    => 'OK',
                -message => "Copy of '$f' failed: $!",
            ) unless $stat;
        $bytes += $size;
        $self->{bytes_msg} = $bytes . " of $total_bytes";
        $self->{file_count}--;
        $self->Subwidget('collapsableframe')->configure(-text =>
                "Time Remaining:  About " . $self->{file_count} . " seconds");
            $self->Subwidget('progressbar')->set($filen / scalar(@files) * 100);
            $self->after(1000);
    }

    $self->destroy;

} # end mcopy
```

1;

__END__

=head1 NAME

Tk::MacCopy - simulate a Macintosh copy dialog.

=head1 SYNOPSIS

S<   >I<$cd> = I<$parent>-E<gt>B<MacCopy>(I<-option> =E<gt> I<value>);

=head1 DESCRIPTION

This widget simulates a Macintosh copy dialog using a MacProgressBar
and a CollapsableFrame. It does not truly emulate a real Macintosh
copy, since it doesn't:

 . check that the destination has enough room for the copy.
 . recursively copy subdirectories.
 . compute a time remaining figure.

=head1 METHODS

=over 4

=item B<mcopy($to, $from)>

Copies all files from $to directory to $from directory.

=back

=head1 ADVERTISED WIDGETS

Component subwidgets can be accessed via the B<Subwidget> method.
Valid subwidget names are listed below.

=over 4

=item Name: progressbar, Class: MacProgressBar

  MacProgressBar widget reference.

=item Name: collapsableframe, Class: CollapsableFrame

  CollapsableFrame widget reference.

=back

=head1 EXAMPLE

 use Cwd;
 use Tk;
 use Tk::MacCopy;

```
    my $mw = MainWindow->new;

    my $mc = $mw->MacCopy;
    my $cwd = cwd;

    $mw->Button(
        -text    => "Push me to copy all files in '$cwd' to '/tmp'.",
        -command => sub {$mc->mcopy($cwd, '/tmp'); exit},
    )->pack;

=head1 AUTHOR and COPYRIGHT

Stephen.O.Lidie@Lehigh.EDU

Copyright (C) 2000 - 2001, Stephen O.Lidie

This program is free software; you can redistribute it and/or
modify it under the same terms as Perl itself.

=head1 KEYWORDS

CollapsableFrame, MacCopy, MacProgressBar

=cut
```

Tk::ExecuteCommand

In Chapter 15, we discussed the Tk:ExecuteCommand program. Here it is in its entirety; see Figure 15-1 for a demonstration.

```
$Tk::ExecuteCommand::VERSION = '1.1';

package Tk::ExecuteCommand;

use IO::Handle;
use Proc::Killfam;
#use Tk::widgets qw/LabEntry ROText/;
use Tk::widgets qw/ROText/;
use base qw/Tk::Frame/;
use strict;

Construct Tk::Widget 'ExecuteCommand';

sub Populate {

    my($self, $args) = @_;

    $self->SUPER::Populate($args);

    my $f1 = $self->Frame->pack;
    $f1->LabEntry(
        -label => 'Command to Execute',
        -labelPack => [qw/-side left/],
```

```perl
            -textvariable => \$self->{-command},
        )->pack(qw/-side left/);

        my $doit = $f1->Button(-text => 'Do It!')->pack(qw/-side left/);
        $self->Advertise('doit' => $doit);
        $self->_reset_doit_button;

        $self->Frame->pack(qw/pady 10/);
        $self->Label(-text => 'Command\'s stdout and stderr')->pack;

        my $text = $self->Scrolled('ROText', -wrap => 'none');
        $text->pack(qw/-expand 1 -fill both/);
        $self->Advertise('text' => $text);
        $self->OnDestroy([$self => 'kill_command']);

        $self->{-finish} = 0;

        $self->ConfigSpecs(
            -command => [qw/METHOD command Command/, 'sleep 5; pwd'],
        );

} # end Populate

sub command {

    my($self, $command) = @_;
    $self->{-command} = $command;

} # end command

sub _flash_doit {

    # Flash "Do It" by alternating its background color.

    my($self, $option, $val1, $val2, $interval) = @_;

    if ($self->{-finish} == 0) {
        $self->Subwidget('doit')->configure($option => $val1);
        $self->idletasks;
        $self->after($interval, [\&_flash_doit, $self, $option, $val2,
                $val1, $interval]);
    }

} # end _flash_doit

sub _read_stdout {

    # Called when input is available for the output window.  Also checks
    # to see if the user has clicked Cancel.

    my($self) = @_;

    if ($self->{-finish}) {
        $self->kill_command;
```

```
        } else {
            my $h = $self->{-handle};
            if ( sysread $h, $_, 4096 ) {
                my $t = $self->Subwidget('text');
                $t->insert('end', $_);
                $t->yview('end');
            } else {
                $self->{-finish} = 1;
            }
        }
    }

} # end _read_stdout

sub _reset_doit_button {

    # Establish normal "Do It" button parameters.

    my($self) = @_;

    my $doit = $self->Subwidget('doit');
    my $doit_bg = ($doit->configure(-background))[3];
    $doit->configure(
        -text       => 'Do It',
        -relief     => 'raised',
        -background => $doit_bg,
        -state      => 'normal',
        -command    => [sub {
        my($self) = @_;
            $self->{-finish} = 0;
            $self->Subwidget('doit')->configure(
                -text   => 'Working ...',
                -relief => 'sunken',
                -state  => 'disabled'
            );
            $self->execute_command;
        }, $self],
    );

} # end _reset_doit_button

# Public methods.

sub execute_command {

    # Execute the command and capture stdout/stderr.

    my($self) = @_;

    my $h = IO::Handle->new;
    die "IO::Handle->new failed." unless defined $h;
    $self->{-handle} = $h;

    $self->{-pid} = open $h, $self->{-command} . ' 2>&1 |';
    if (not defined $self->{-pid}) {
```

```
            $self->Subwidget('text')->insert('end',
                    "'" . $self->{-command} . "' : $!\n");
            $self->kill_command;
            return;
        }
        $h->autoflush(1);
        $self->fileevent($h, 'readable' => [\&_read_stdout, $self]);

        my $doit = $self->Subwidget('doit');
        $doit->configure(
            -text    => 'Cancel',
            -relief  => 'raised',
            -state   => 'normal',
            -command => [\&kill_command, $self],
        );

        my $doit_bg = ($doit->configure(-background))[3];
        $self->_flash_doit(-background => $doit_bg, qw/cyan 500/);

    } # end execute_command

    sub kill_command {

        # A click on the blinking Cancel button resumes normal operations.

        my($self) = @_;

        $self->{-finish} = 1;
        my $h = $self->{-handle};
        return unless defined $h;
        $self->fileevent($h, 'readable' => ''); # clear handler
        killfam 'TERM', $self->{-pid} if defined $self->{-pid};
        close $h;
        $self->_reset_doit_button;

    } # end kill_command

    1;

    __END__

    =head1 NAME

    Tk::ExecuteCommand - execute a command asynchronously (non-blocking).

    =for pm Tk/ExecuteCommand.pm

    =for category Widgets

    =head1 SYNOPSIS

    S<    >I<$exec> = I<$parent>-E<gt>B<ExecuteCommand>;

    =head1 DESCRIPTION
```

Tk::ExecuteCommand runs a command yet still allows Tk events to flow. All
command output and errors are displayed in a window.

This ExecuteCommand mega widget is composed of an LabEntry widget for
command entry, a "Do It" Button that initiates command execution, and
a ROText widget that collects command execution output.

While the command is executing, the "Do It" Button changes to a "Cancel"
Button that can prematurely kill the executing command. The B<kill_command>
method does the same thing programmatically.

=over 4

=item B<-command>

The command to execute asynchronously.

=back

=head1 METHODS

=over 4

=item C<$exec-E<gt>B<execute_command>;>

Initiates command execution.

=item C<$exec-E<gt>B<kill_command>;>

Terminates the command. This subroutine is called automatically via an
OnDestroy handler when the ExecuteCommand widget goes away.

=back

=head1 EXAMPLE

I<$exec> = I<$mw>-E<gt>B<ExecuteCommand>;

=head1 KEYWORDS

exec, command, fork, asynchronous, non-blocking, widget

=head1 COPYRIGHT

Copyright (C) 1999 - 2001 Stephen O. Lidie. All rights reserved.

This program is free software; you can redistribute it and/or modify it under
the same terms as Perl itself.

=cut

Proc::Killfam

Also in Chapter 15, we used the killfam command. Here's the code we promised for that command:

```
$Proc::Killfam::VERSION = '1.0';

package Proc::Killfam;

use Exporter;
use base qw/Exporter/;
use subs qw/get_pids/;
use vars qw/@EXPORT @EXPORT_OK $ppt_OK/;
use strict;

@EXPORT = qw/killfam/;
@EXPORT_OK = qw/killfam/;

# We need Proc::ProcessTable to work properly.  If it's not available,
# then we act like Perl's builtin kill() command.

BEGIN {
    $ppt_OK = 1;
    eval "require Proc::ProcessTable";
    if ($@) {
        $ppt_OK = 0;
        warn "Proc::ProcessTable missing, can't kill sub-children.";
    }
}

sub killfam {

    my($signal, @pids) = @_;

    if ($ppt_OK) {
        my $pt = Proc::ProcessTable->new;
        my(@procs) =  @{$pt->table};
        my(@kids) = get_pids \@procs, @pids;
        @pids = (@pids, @kids);
    }

    kill $signal, @pids;

} # end killfam

sub get_pids {

    my($procs, @kids) = @_;

    my @pids;
    foreach my $kid (@kids) {
     foreach my $proc (@$procs) {
        if ($proc->ppid == $kid) {
```

```
            my $pid = $proc->pid;
            push @pids, $pid, get_pids $procs, $pid;
        }
    }
    }
    @pids;

} # end get_pids

1;

__END__

=head1 NAME

Proc::Killfam - kill a list of pids, and all their sub-children

=head1 SYNOPSIS

 use Proc::Kilfam;
 killfam $signal, @pids;

=head1 DESCRIPTION

B<killfam> accepts the same arguments as the Perl builtin B<kill> command,
but, additionally, recursively searches the process table for children and
kills them as well.

=head1 EXAMPLE

B<killfam 'TERM', ($pid1, $pid2, @more_pids)>;

=head1 KEYWORDS

kill, signal

=cut
```

tkmpg123

The *tkmpg123* program is an MPG player based on Apple's *itunes*. The explanation
and demonstration can be found in Chapter 15.

```
#!/usr/local/bin/perl -w
#
# tkmpg123 - keep mpg123 and Tk happily eventing w/o blocking.
#
# Stephen.O.Lidie@Lehigh.EDU, 2001/04/17.

use Audio::Play::MPG123;
use Tk;
use Tk::PNG;
use subs qw/build_player start_play  edit_menuitems file_menuitems
```

```perl
        help_menuitems init play/;
our ($c, , @info, $infov, $mw, $paus, $phand, $play, $player, $timev, $v);
use strict;


$v = '-0.97';

$player = Audio::Play::MPG123->new;
$phand = $player->IN;

$mw = MainWindow->new;
$mw->configure(-menu => my $menubar = $mw->Menu);
map {$menubar->cascade( -label => '~' . $_->[0], -menuitems => $_->[1] )}
    ['File', file_menuitems],
    ['Edit', edit_menuitems],
    ['Help', help_menuitems];


build_player;

MainLoop;

sub build_player {

    $c = $mw->Canvas(
        -width  => 1,
        -height => 1,
        -background => 'dark slate gray',
    )->pack;
    my $itunes = $c->Photo(-file => 'images/itunes.gif');
    $c->createImage(0, 0,
        -image => $itunes,
        -tag   => 'itunes',
        -anchor => 'nw',
    );
    $c->configure(-width => $itunes->width, -height => $itunes->height);

    $paus = $c->Photo(-file => 'images/paus.gif');
    $play = $c->Photo(-file => 'images/play.gif');

    $c->createImage(80, 40, -image => $play, -tag => 'play-image');
    $c->bind('play-image', '<1>' => \&pause);

    my $green = '#d5dac1';
    my $font = 'courier 12';

    my $f = $c->Frame(
        -width      => 250,
        -height     => 50,
        -background => $green,
        -relief     => 'sunken',
        -borderwidth => 3,
    );
    $f->packPropagate(0);
    $c->createWindow(170, 20, -anchor => 'nw', -window => $f);
```

```perl
    $infov = '';
    my $info = $f->Label(
        -textvariable => \$infov,
        -font         => $font,
        -background   => $green,
    );
    $info->pack(-side => 'top');

    $timev = 'Elapsed Time: 0:00';
    my $time = $f->Label(
        -textvariable => \$timev,
        -font         => $font,
        -background   => $green,
    );
    $time->pack(-side => 'top');

    my $f2 = $c->Frame(
        -width       => 570,
        -height      => 280,
        -background  => $green,
        -relief      => 'sunken',
        -borderwidth => 3,
    );
    $f2->packPropagate(0);
    $c->createWindow(15, 85, -anchor => 'nw', -window => $f2);

    my $mpgs = $f2->Scrolled('Listbox')->pack(-fill => 'y', -expand => 1);
    foreach my $mpg (<*.mpg>, <*.mp3>) {
        $mpgs->insert('end', $mpg);
    }
    $mpgs->bind('<1>' => sub {play $mpgs->get( $mpgs->nearest($Tk::event->y)  )});

} # end build_player

sub pause {
    $player->pause;
    $c->itemconfigure('play-image',
        -image => ($player->state == 1) ? $paus : $play
    );
}

sub edit_menuitems {
    [
      ['command', 'Preferences ...', -command => sub {$mw->bell}],
    ];
}

sub file_menuitems {

    [
      [
        qw/cascade ~Play -menuitems/ =>
        [
          [qw/command ~File... -command/ => \&play_file],
```

```
            [qw/command ~URL...  -command/ => \&play_url],
          ],
        ],
        [qw/command ~Quit  -command/ => \&exit],
    ];


}

sub help_menuitems {
    [
        ['command', 'Version', -command => sub {print "Version $v\n"}],
        '',
        ['command', 'About',   -command => sub {print "Playing songs\n"}],
    ];
}

sub play_file {
    play $mw->getOpenFile(-title => 'Pick A Song');
}

sub play_url {# for now
    my $song = 'http://www.lehigh.edu/solo/beat.mpg';;
    play $song;
}

sub play {
    my $song = shift;
    print "song=$song!\n";
    if (defined $song) {
        $player->load($song);
        @info = map {$player->$_} qw/title artist album/;
        start_play;
    }
}

sub ctm {
    my $s = shift;
    my $m = int($s / 60);
    sprintf("%02d:%02d", $m, $s - $m * 60);
}

sub start_play {

    my $info_tid = $mw->repeat(5000 => sub {
        $infov = $info[0];
        unshift @info, pop @info;
    });

    my $time_tid = $mw->repeat(1000 => sub {
    my(@toks) = split ' ', $player->stat;
        $timev = sprintf( "Elapsed Time: %s of %s\n",
            &ctm($toks[3]), &ctm($toks[3] + $toks[4]) );
    });
```

```
        my $in_hand = sub {
            $player->poll(0);
            $mw->update;
            if ($player->state == 0) {
                $player->stop;
                $mw->fileevent(\$phand, 'readable' => '');
                $mw->afterCancel($info_tid);
                $mw->afterCancel($time_tid);
            }
        };
        $mw->fileevent(\$phand, 'readable' => $in_hand);

    }
```

Tk::Trace

The Tk::Trace module can be used to trace Perl/Tk variables. See Chapter 15 for explanation and demonstration.

```
$Tk::Trace::VERSION = '1.0';

package Tk::Trace;

use Exporter;
use base qw/Exporter/;
@EXPORT = qw/traceVariable traceVdelete traceVinfo/;
use Tie::Watch;
use strict;

my %trace;                      # watchpoints indexed by stringified ref
my %op = (                      # map Tcl op to tie function
    'r' => ['-fetch',   \&fetch],
    'w' => ['-store',   \&store],
    'u' => ['-destroy', \&destroy],
);

sub fetch {

    # fetch() wraps the user's callback with necessary tie() bookkeeping
    # and invokes the callback with the proper arguments. It expects:
    #
    # $_[0] = Tie::Watch object
    # $_[1] = undef for a scalar, an index/key for an array/hash
    #
    # The user's callback is passed these arguments:
    #
    #    $_[0]        = undef for a scalar, index/key for array/hash
    #    $_[1]        = current value
    #    $_[2]        = operation (r, w, or u)
    #    $_[3 .. $#_] = optional user callback arguments
    #
    # The user callback returns the final value to assign the variable.
```

```
    my $self = shift;                               # Tie::Watch object
    my $val = $self->Fetch(@_);                      # get variable's current value
    my $aref = $self->Args(-fetch);                 # argument reference
    my $sub = shift @$aref;                          # user's callback
    unshift @_, undef if scalar @_ == 0;            # unshift "index" for a scalar
    my @args = @_;                                   # save for post-callback work
    $args[1] = &$sub(@_, $val, 'r', @$aref);        # invoke user callback
    shift @args unless defined $args[0];            # drop scalar "index"
    $self->Store(@args);                             # update variable's value

} # end fetch

sub store {

    # store() wraps the user's callback with necessary tie() bookkeeping
    # and invokes the callback with.the proper arguments. It expects:
    #
    # $_[0] = Tie::Watch object
    # $_[1] = new value for a scalar, index/key for an array/hash
    # $_[2] = undef for a scalar, new value for an array/hash
    #
    # The user's callback is passed these arguments:
    #
    #    $_[0]       = undef for a scalar, index/key for array/hash
    #    $_[1]       = new value
    #    $_[2]       = operation (r, w, or u)
    #    $_[3 .. $#_] = optional user callback arguments
    #
    # The user callback returns the final value to assign the variable.

    my $self = shift;                               # Tie::Watch object
    $self->Store(@_);                               # store variable's new value
    my $aref = $self->Args(-store);                 # argument reference
    my $sub = shift @$aref;                          # user's callback
    unshift @_, undef if scalar @_ == 1;            # undef "index" for a scalar
    my @args = @_;                                   # save for post-callback work
    $args[1] = &$sub(@_, 'w', @$aref);              # invoke user callback
    shift @args unless defined $args[0];            # drop scalar "index"
    $self->Store(@args);                             # update variable's value

} # end store

sub destroy {
    my $self = shift;
    my $aref = $self->Args(-destroy);               # argument reference
    my $sub = shift @$aref;                          # user's callback
    my $val = $self->Fetch(@_);                      # get final value
    &$sub(undef, $val, 'u', @$aref);                # invoke user callback
    $self->Destroy(@_);                              # destroy variable
}

sub traceVariable {
    my($parent, $vref, $op, $callback) = @_;
    die "Illegal parent." unless ref $parent;
    die "Illegal variable." unless ref $vref;
```

```perl
    die "Illegal trace operation '$op'." unless $op;
    die "Illegal trace operation '$op'." if $op =~ /[^rwu]/;
    die "Illegal callback." unless $callback;

    # Need to add our internal callback to user's callback arg list
    # so we can call it first, followed by the user's callback and
    # any user arguments.

    my($fetch, $store, $destroy);
    if (ref $callback eq 'CODE') {
        $fetch   = [\&fetch,   $callback];
        $store   = [\&store,   $callback];
        $destroy = [\&destroy, $callback];
    } else {                     # assume [] form
        $fetch   = [\&fetch,   @$callback];
        $store   = [\&store,   @$callback];
        $destroy = [\&destroy, @$callback];
    }

    my @wargs;
    push @wargs, (-fetch   => $fetch)   if $op =~ /r/;
    push @wargs, (-store   => $store)   if $op =~ /w/;
    push @wargs, (-destroy => $destroy) if $op =~ /u/;
    my $watch = Tie::Watch->new(
        -variable => $vref,
        @wargs,
    );

    $trace{$vref} = $watch;

} # end traceVariable

sub traceVdelete {
    my($parent, $vref, $op_not_honored, $callabck_not_honored) = @_;
    if (defined $trace{$vref}) {
        $trace{$vref}->Unwatch;
        delete $trace{$vref};
    }
}

sub traceVinfo {
    my($parent, $vref) = @_;
    return (defined $trace{$vref}) ? $trace{$vref}->Info : undef;
}

1;
__END__

=head1 NAME

Tk::Trace - emulate Tcl/Tk B<trace> functions.

=head1 SYNOPSIS

  use Tk::Trace;
```

```
$mw->traceVariable(\$v, 'wru' => [\&update_meter, $scale]);
%vinfo = $mw->traceVinfo(\$v);
print "Trace info  :\n  ", join("\n  ", @{$vinfo{-legible}}), "\n";
$mw->traceVdelete(\$v);
```

=head1 DESCRIPTION

This class module emulates the Tcl/Tk B<trace> family of commands by
binding subroutines of your devising to Perl variables using simple
B<Tie::Watch> features.

Callback format is patterned after the Perl/Tk scheme: supply either a
code reference, or, supply an array reference and pass the callback
code reference in the first element of the array, followed by callback
arguments.

User callbacks are passed these arguments:

```
 $_[0]       = undef for a scalar, index/key for array/hash
 $_[1]       = variable's current (read), new (write), final (undef) value
 $_[2]       = operation (r, w, or u)
 $_[3 .. $#_] = optional user callback arguments
```

As a Trace user, you have an important responsibility when writing your
callback, since you control the final value assigned to the variable.
A typical callback might look like:

```
 sub callback {
    my($index, $value, $op, @args) = @_;
    return if $op eq 'u';
    # .... code which uses $value ...
    return $value;      # variable's final value
 }
```

Note that the callback's return value becomes the variable's final value,
for either read or write traces.

For write operations, the variable is updated with its new value before
the callback is invoked.

Only one callback can be attached to a variable, but read, write and undef
operations can be traced simultaneously.

=head1 METHODS

=over 4

=item $mw->traceVariable(varRef, op => callback);

B<varRef> is a reference to the scalar, array or hash variable you
wish to trace. B<op> is the trace operation, and can be any combination
of B<r> for read, B<w> for write, and B<u> for undef. B<callback> is a
standard Perl/Tk callback, and is invoked, depending upon the value of
B<op>, whenever the variable is read, written, or destroyed.

=item %vinfo = $mw->traceVinfo(varRef);

Returns a hash detailing the internals of the Trace object, with these
keys:

```
 %vinfo = (
     -variable =>  varRef
     -debug    =>  '0'
     -shadow   =>  '1'
     -value    =>  'HELLO SCALAR'
     -destroy  =>  callback
     -fetch    =>  callback
     -store    =>  callback
     -legible  =>  above data formatted as a list of string, for printing
 );
```

For array and hash Trace objects, the B<-value> key is replaced with a
B<-ptr> key which is a reference to the parallel array or hash.
Additionally, for an array or hash, there are key/value pairs for
all the variable specific callbacks.

=item $mw->traceVdelete(\$v);

Stop tracing the variable.

=back

=head1 EXAMPLE

```
#!/usr/local/bin/perl -w
#
# Trace a Scale's variable and move a meter in unison.

package Tk;
    use Tk::Trace;

package main;

use Tk;
use constant PI => 3.1415926;
use strict;

my $mw = MainWindow->new;

my $c = $mw->Canvas(qw/-width 200 -height 110 -bd 2 -relief sunken/)->grid;
$c->createLine(qw/ 100 100 10 100   -tag meter -arrow last -width 5/);
my $s = $mw->Scale(qw/-orient h -from 0 -to 100 -variable/ => \my $v)->grid;
$mw->Label(-text => 'Slide Me for > 5 Seconds')->grid;

$mw->traceVariable(\$v, 'w' => [\&update_meter, $c, $s]);

$mw->after(5000 => sub {
    print "Untrace time ...\n";
    my %vinfo = $s->traceVinfo(\$v);
    print "Watch info  :\n  ", join("\n  ", @{$vinfo{-legible}}), "\n";
```

```
        $c->traceVdelete(\$v);
    });

    MainLoop;

    sub update_meter {
        my($index, $value, $op, @args) = @_;
        return if $op eq 'u';
        my($c, $s) = @args[0,1];# Canvas and Scale widgets
        my($min, $max) = ($s->cget(-from), $s->cget(-to));
        my $pos = $value / abs($max - $min);
        my $x = 100.0 - 90.0 * (cos( $pos * PI ));
        my $y = 100.0 - 90.0 * (sin( $pos * PI ));
        $c->coords(qw/meter 100 100/, $x, $y);
        return $value;
    }

    =head1 HISTORY

    Stephen.O.Lidie@Lehigh.EDU, Lehigh University Computing Center, 2000/08/01
    . Version 1.0, for Tk800.022.

    =head1 COPYRIGHT

    Copyright (C) 2000 - 2001 Stephen O. Lidie. All rights reserved.

    This program is free software; you can redistribute it and/or modify it under
    the same terms as Perl itself.

    =cut
```

tkhp16c

tkhp16c is an RPN calculator we used for a splash screen example in Chapter 15. See Figure 15-6.

```
    package Tk;

    use Tk::bindDump;

    # M A I N

    package main;

    use Tk;
    use Tk::MacProgressBar;
    use Tk::Splashscreen;
    use Tk::widgets qw/Compound ROText/;
    use subs qw/build_button_rows build_calculator build_help_window end splash/;
    use strict;

    my $mw = MainWindow->new;
    $mw->withdraw;
    $mw->title('Hewlett-Packard 16C Computer Scientist RPN Calculator');
```

```perl
$mw->iconname('HP 16C');
$mw->configure(-background => $GRAY_LIGHTEST);

my $splash = splash;# build Splashscreen
$splash->Splash;# show Splashscreen

build_help_window;
build_calculator;

$MAC_PB->set($MAC_PB_P = 100);
$splash->Destroy;# tear down Splashscreen

$mw->deiconify;# show calculator

MainLoop;

# Miscellaneous subroutines.

sub build_button_rows {

    my ($parent, $button_descriptions) = @_;

    foreach my $row (@$button_descriptions) {
        my $frame = $parent->Frame(-background => $GRAY_LIGHTEST);
        foreach my $buttons (@$row) {
            my ($p1, $p2, $p3, $color, $func) = @$buttons;

            $frame->Key(
            topl        => $p2,
                -butl       => $p1,
                -botl       => $p3,
                -background => $color,
                -command    => $func,
            );
        }
        $frame->pack(qw/-side top -expand 1 -fill both/);
        $MAC_PB->set($MAC_PB_P += 10);
    }

} # end build_button_rows

sub build_calculator {

    &on; &on; # on/off kluge to initialize HP stack

    # LED display, help button, and HP logo.

    my $tf = $mw->Frame(-background => $SILVER);
    $tf->pack(qw/-side top -fill both -expand 1/);

    $tf->Label(
        -relief      => 'sunken',
        -borderwidth => 10,
        -background  => 'honeydew4',
        -width       => 30,
```

```
    -foreground    => 'black',
    -font          => ['arial', 14, 'bold'],
    -textvariable => \$XV,
    -anchor        => 'w',
)->pack(qw/-side left -expand 1 -fill x -padx 70/);

my $hp = $tf->Button(-text => $MODEL, -relief => 'raised',
          -command => sub {$ONOFF = 1; &on; &exit});
$hp->pack(qw/-side right -expand 1 -fill both -padx 20 -pady 10/);
$hp->bind('<Enter>' => sub {$_[0]->configure(-text => "Quit\n--\n16C")});
$hp->bind('<Leave>' => sub {$_[0]->configure(-text => $MODEL)});

# Horizontal black and silver lines + vertical left/right silver lines.

$mw->Frame(qw/-background black -height 10/)->pack(qw/-fill x -expand 1/);
$mw->Frame(-bg => $SILVER, -height => 5)->pack(qw/-fill x -expand 1/);

my $frame0 = $mw->Frame(-background => $GRAY_LIGHTEST);
$frame0->pack(qw/-side top    -fill both -expand 1/);

$frame0->Frame(-width => 5, -bg => $SILVER)->
    pack(qw/-side left -expand 1 -fill y/);
$frame0->Frame(-width => 5, -bg => $SILVER)->
    pack(qw/-side right -expand 1 -fill y/);

# These frames hold all the calculator keys.

my $frame1 = $frame0->Frame->pack(qw/-side top    -fill both -expand 1/);
my $frame2 = $frame0->Frame->pack(qw/-side left   -fill both -expand 1/);
my $frame3 = $frame0->Frame->pack(qw/-side right -fill both -expand 1/);

# Bottom finishing detail.

$mw->Frame(
    -background => $SILVER,
    -width      => 20,
    -height     => 25,
)->pack(qw/-side left -expand 0/);
$mw->Label(
    -text       => 'H E W L E T T . P A C K A R D',
    -font       => ['courier', 14, 'bold'],
    -foreground => $SILVER,
    -background => $GRAY_LIGHTEST,
)->pack(qw/-side left -expand 0/);
$mw->Frame(
    -background => $SILVER,
    -height     => 25,
)->pack(qw/-side left -expand 1 -fill x/);
my $quest = $mw->Button(
    -text               => '?',
   -font                => '6x9',
    -relief             => 'flat',
   -highlightthickness  => 0,
   -background          => $SILVER,
    -borderwidth        => 0,
```

```perl
        -pady                 => 0,
        -command              =>
            sub {
          $HELP->deiconify;
            },
    )->pack(qw/-side left -expand 0 -fill y/);
    $quest->bind('<2>' => sub {
      my (@register) = ('(X)', '(Y)', '(Z)', '(T)');
      print "\n";
        for (my $i = $#STACK; $i >= 0; $i--) {
          print "stack+$i $register[$i] : '", $STACK[$i], "'\n";
      }
    });
    $mw->Frame(
        -background => $SILVER,
     -width       => 5,
        -height      => 25,
    )->pack(qw/-side left -expand 0/);

    # Create special Compound images for certain keys.

    my $rolu = $mw->Compound;
    my (@cargs) = (-foreground => $BLUE, -background => $GRAY);
    $rolu->Text(-text => 'R', -foreground => $BLUE);
    $rolu->Image(-image => $mw->Bitmap(-data => << 'END', @cargs));
#define up2_width 11
#define up2_height 12
static unsigned char up2_bits[] = {
  0x00, 0x00, 0x20, 0x00, 0x70, 0x00, 0xf8, 0x00, 0xfc, 0x01, 0xfe, 0x03,
  0x70, 0x00, 0x70, 0x00, 0x70, 0x00, 0x70, 0x00, 0x70, 0x00, 0x00, 0x00,
  };
END

    my $rold = $mw->Compound;
    @cargs = (-foreground => 'white', -background => $GRAY);
    $rold->Text(-text => 'R', -foreground => 'white');
    $rold->Image(-image => $mw->Bitmap(-data => << 'END', @cargs));
#define down2_width 11
#define down2_height 12
static unsigned char down2_bits[] = {
  0x00, 0x00, 0x70, 0x00, 0x70, 0x00, 0x70, 0x00, 0x70, 0x00, 0x70, 0x00,
  0xfe, 0x03, 0xfc, 0x01, 0xf8, 0x00, 0x70, 0x00, 0x20, 0x00, 0x00, 0x00,
  };
END

    my $swap = $mw->Compound;
    $swap->Text(-text => 'X', -foreground => 'white');
    $swap->Image(-image => $mw->Bitmap(-data => << 'END', @cargs));
#define swap_width 8
#define swap_height 15
static unsigned char swap_bits[] = {
  0x00, 0x00, 0x00, 0x06, 0x18, 0x60, 0x18, 0x06, 0x00, 0x60, 0x18, 0x06,
  0x18, 0x60, 0x00, };
END
```

```perl
$swap->Text(-text => 'Y', -foreground => 'white');

# Build the first 2 rows of the calculator, 10 calculator keys per row.

my $dv = sub {$_[1] / $_[0]}; # division
my $xr = sub {$_[1] ^ $_[0]}; # exclusive OR
my $dd = sub {$_[1] / $_[0]}; # double divide

my $sq = sub {sqrt $_[0]};   # square root
my $rp = sub {1 / $_[0]};    # reciprocal

my $ml = sub {$_[1] * $_[0]}; # multiplication
my $an = sub {$_[1] & $_[0]}; # AND
my $dm = sub {$_[1] * $_[0]}; # double multiply

build_button_rows $frame1, [
    [
        ['A',  'SL',    'LJ',   $GRAY,  \&err],
        ['B',  'SR',    'ASR',  $GRAY,  \&err],
        ['C',  'RL',    'RLC',  $GRAY,  \&err],
        ['D',  'RR',    'RRC',  $GRAY,  \&err],
        ['E',  'RLn',   'RLCn', $GRAY,  \&err],
        ['F',  'RRn',   'RRCn', $GRAY,  \&err],
        ['7',  'MASKL', '#B',   $GRAY,  [\&key, '7']],
        ['8',  'MASKR', 'ABS',  $GRAY,  [\&key, '8']],
        ['9',  'RMD',   'DBLR', $GRAY,  [\&key, '9']],
        ['/',  'XOR',   'DBL/', $GRAY,  [\&math3, $dv, $xr, $dd]],
    ],
    [
        ['GSB', 'x><(i)', 'RTN', $GRAY,  \&err],
        ['GTO', 'x><I',   'LBL', $GRAY,  \&err],
        ['HEX', 'Show',   'DSZ', $GRAY,  \&err],
        ['DEC', 'Show',   'ISZ', $GRAY,  \&err],
        ['OCT', 'Show',   'sqrt', $GRAY, [\&gmath, $sq]],
        ['BIN', 'Show',   '1/x', $GRAY,  [\&gmath, $rp]],
        ['4',   'SB',     'SF',  $GRAY,  [\&key, '4']],
        ['5',   'CB',     'CF',  $GRAY,  [\&key, '5']],
        ['6',   'B?',     'F?',  $GRAY,  [\&key, '6']],
        ['*',   'AND',    'DBLx', $GRAY, [\&math3, $ml, $an, $dm]],
    ],
];

# Build the leftmost 5 calculator keys of the last 2 rows.

build_button_rows $frame2, [
    [
        ['R/S', '(i)',      'p/r', $GRAY,  \&err],
        ['SST', 'I',        'BST', $GRAY,  \&err],
        [$rold, 'cPRGM',    $rolu, $GRAY,  \&roll_stack],
        [$swap, 'cREG',     'PSE', $GRAY,  \&swapxy],
        ['BSP', 'cPREFIX',  'CLx', $GRAY,  \&bspclrx],
    ],
    [
        ['ON',  '',         '',    $GRAY,  \&on],
```

```
          ['f',    '',       '',    $ORANGE,  \&f],
          ['g',    '',       '',    $BLUE,    \&g],
          ['STO',  'WSIZE',  '<',   $GRAY,    \&err],
          ['RCL',  'FLOAT',  '>',   $GRAY,    \&err],
    ],
];

# The 2 column high ENTER key divides the last 2 rows of calculator keys.

my $enter = $frame0->Key(
    -topl       => 'WINDOW',
    -butl       => "E\nN\nT\nE\nR",
    -botl       => 'LSTx',
    -background => $GRAY,
    -command    => \&enter,
    -height     => 6,
);
$enter->pack(qw/-side left -expand 1 -fill both/);

# Build the rightmost 4 calculator keys of the last two rows.

my $sb = sub {$_[1] - $_[0]}; # subtraction

my $ad = sub {$_[1] + $_[0]}; # addition
my $io = sub {$_[1] | $_[0]}; # inclusive OR

build_button_rows $frame3, [
    [
        ['1',    '1\'S',    'X<=y', $GRAY,    [\&key, '1']],
        ['2',    '2\'S',    'x<0',  $GRAY,    [\&key, '2']],
        ['3',    'UNSGN',   'x>y',  $GRAY,    [\&key, '3']],
        ['-',    'NOT',     'x>0',  $GRAY,    [\&math3, $sb, undef, undef]],
    ],
    [
        ['0',    'MEM',     'x!=y', $GRAY,    [\&key, '0']],
        ['.',    'STATUS',  'x!=0', $GRAY,    [\&key, '.']],
        ['CHS',  'EEX',     'x=y',  $GRAY,    \&chs],
        ['+',    'OR',      'x=0',  $GRAY,    [\&math3, $ad, $io, undef]],
    ],
];

# Now establish key bindings for the digits and common arithmetic
# operation, including keypad keys, delete, etcetera.

foreach my $key ( qw/0 1 2 3 4 5 6 7 8 9/ ) {
    $mw->bind( "<Key-$key>" => [\&key, $key] );
    $mw->bind( "<KP_$key>"  => [\&key, $key] );
}

foreach my $key ( qw/period KP_Decimal/ ) {
    $mw->bind( "<$key>"     => [\&key, '.'] );
}

foreach my $key ( qw/Return KP_Enter/ ) {
```

```
            $mw->bind( "<$key>"       => \&enter );
        }

        foreach my $key ( qw/plus KP_Add/ ) {
            $mw->bind( "<$key>"       => [\&math3, $ad, $io,   undef] );
        }

        foreach my $key ( qw/minus KP_Subtract/ ) {
            $mw->bind( "<$key>"       => [\&math3, $sb, undef, undef] );
        }

        foreach my $key ( qw/asterisk KP_Multiply/ ) {
            $mw->bind( "<$key>"       => [\&math3, $ml, $an,    $dm] );
        }

        foreach my $key ( qw/slash KP_Divide/ ) {
            $mw->bind( "<$key>"       => [\&math3, $dv, $xr,    $dd] );
        }

        $mw->bind( '<Delete>'         => \&bspclrx );

        $MAC_PB->set($MAC_PB_P = 90);

    } # end build_calculator

    sub build_help_window {

        $MAC_PB->set($MAC_PB_P = 10);

        $HELP = $mw->Toplevel(-tile => $mw->Photo(-file => 'hp16c-tile.gif'));
        $HELP->withdraw;
        $MAC_PB->set($MAC_PB_P = 15);
        $HELP->title('HP 16C Help');
        $HELP->protocol('WM_DELETE_WINDOW' => sub {});

        $MAC_PB->set($MAC_PB_P = 20);

        my $frame = $HELP->Frame->pack(qw/-padx 70 -pady 40/);
        $frame->Button(
            -text              => 'Close',
            -command           => sub {$HELP->withdraw},
            -background        => $BLUE_DARKER,
            -activebackground  => $BLUE,
        )->pack(qw/-expand 1 -fill both/);
        $frame->Label(
            -text => '? <B2> prints the stack.',
        )->pack(qw/-expand 1 -fill both/);

        $MAC_PB->set($MAC_PB_P = 25);

        $frame->Label(-image => $mw->Photo(-file => 'hp16c-help.gif'))->pack;

        $MAC_PB->set($MAC_PB_P = 30);
```

```perl
    $frame->Label(
        -text => ' ',
    )->pack(qw/-expand 1 -fill both/);

    $MAC_PB->set($MAC_PB_P = 35);

} # end build_help_window

sub splash {

    my $splash = $mw->Splashscreen(-milliseconds => 3000);
    $splash->Label(-text => 'Building your HP 16C ...', -bg => $BLUE)->
        pack(qw/-fill both -expand 1/);
    $MAC_PB = $splash->MacProgressBar(-width => 300);
    $MAC_PB->pack(qw/-fill both -expand 1/);
    $splash->Label(-image => $mw->Photo(-file => 'hp16c-splash.gif'))->pack;

    $splash->bindDump;

    return $splash;

} # end_splash

# Calculator key processors.

sub bspclrx {
    return unless $ONOFF;
    if ($F_PRESSED) {
        $mw->bell;
        end;
        return;
    }

    if ($G_PRESSED) {# clrX
        $STACK[0] = 0;
        $CLRX = 1;
        $PUSHX = 0;
    } else {
        if (length($STACK[0]) <= 2) { # BKSP
            $STACK[0] = 0;
            $CLRX = 1;
            $PUSHX = 0;
        } else {
            chop $STACK[0];
        }
    }
    end;
}

sub chs {      # change sign
    my $s = substr($STACK[0], 0, 1);
    substr($STACK[0], 0, 1) = ($s eq '-') ? ' ' : '-';
    end;
}
```

```perl
sub end {      # key cleanup
    $F_PRESSED = $G_PRESSED = 0;
    $XV = $STACK[0];
}

sub enter {   # enter key
    unshift @STACK, $STACK[0];
    $#STACK = $STACKM if $#STACK > $STACKM;
    $CLRX = 1;
    $PUSHX = 0;
    end;
}

sub err {$mw->bell if $ONOFF}# error

sub f {$F_PRESSED = 1};# F key

sub g {$G_PRESSED = 1};# G key

sub gmath {   # G key arithmetic operations

    # gmath( ) expects one code reference to an anonymous subroutine, which
    # expects one argument, X from the RPN stack.

    if (not $G_PRESSED) {
        $mw->bell;
        end;
        return;
    }

    $STACK[0] = &{$_[0]}($STACK[0]);
    $STACK[0] = " $STACK[0]" if substr($STACK[0], 0, 1) ne '-';
    $CLRX = $PUSHX = 1;
    end;
}

sub hpshift { # empty HP stack
    $#STACK = $STACKM if $#STACK > $STACKM;
    my $v = shift @STACK;
    $STACK[$STACKM] = $STACK[$STACKM - 1] if $#STACK == ($STACKM - 1);
    end;
    return $v;
}

sub key {      # process generic key clicks

    shift if ref $_[0];# toss bind( ) object
    my $key = $_[0];
    return unless $ONOFF;
    if ($F_PRESSED or $G_PRESSED) {
        $mw->bell;
        end;
        return;
    }
```

```
    &enter if $PUSHX;
    $STACK[0] = ' ' if $CLRX;

    $STACK[0] .= $key;
    $CLRX = $PUSHX = 0;
    end;
} # end key

sub math3 {   # tri-arithmetic keys

    # math3() expects three code references to anonymous subroutines, each
    # of which expects two arguments, X and Y from the RPN stack.
    #
    # $_[0] = normal button press
    # $_[1] = "f" qualified button press
    # $_[2] = "g" qualified button press

    shift if ref $_[0];# toss bind() object
    my $math = $_[0];
    $math = $_[1] if $F_PRESSED;
    $math = $_[2] if $G_PRESSED;
    if (not defined $math) {
        $mw->bell;
        end;
        return;
    }

    my $x = &hpshift;
    my $y = $STACK[0];
    $STACK[0] = &{$math}($x, $y);
    $STACK[0] = " $STACK[0]" if substr($STACK[0], 0, 1) ne '-';
    $CLRX = $PUSHX = 1;
    end;
}

sub on {      # power on/off
    if ($ONOFF) {
        $ONOFF = 0;
        if (open(RC, ">$RCFILE")) {
            foreach (reverse @STACK) {
            print RC "$_\n";
            }
            close RC;
        }
        end;
        $XV = '';
    } else {
        $ONOFF = 1;
        if (open(RC, $RCFILE)) {
            @STACK = () if -s $RCFILE;
            while ($_ = <RC>) {
            chomp;
            unshift @STACK, $_;
            }
```

```
            close RC;
        }
        $CLRX = $PUSHX = 1;
        end;
    }
} # end on

sub roll_stack {
    return unless $ONOFF;
    if ($F_PRESSED) {
        $mw->bell;
        end;
        return;
    }

    if ($G_PRESSED) {
        unshift @STACK, pop @STACK; # roll stack up
    } else {
        push @STACK, shift @STACK;  # roll stack down
    }
    end;
}

sub swapxy {
    return unless $ONOFF;
    if ($F_PRESSED or $G_PRESSED) {
        $mw->bell;
        end;
        return;
    }

    (@STACK[0, 1]) = (@STACK[1, 0]);
    end;
}
```

Tk::MacProgressBar

MacProgressBar is a widget designed to resemble a Macintosh progress bar. See
Figure 15-7 for a demonstration.

```
$Tk::MacProgressBar::VERSION = '1.0';

package Tk::MacProgressBar;

use base qw/Tk::Frame/;
use vars qw/$BASE $CAP $H $OTLW $W/;
use strict;

Construct Tk::Widget 'MacProgressBar';

$OTLW = 1 + 1;# inner black and outer grey outline width
$BASE = 2;    # left base segment width
$CAP = 6;     # right cap width
```

```perl
$H = 10;       # progress bar height

sub Populate {

    # Create an instance of a MacProgressBar.  Instance variable are:
    #
    # {photow} = Photo image width, including base and end cap.

    my($self, $args) = @_;

    $self->SUPER::Populate($args);

    my $w = $args->{-width};
    $w ||= 100;
    $self->{photow} = $w = $w + $BASE + $CAP;
    my $h = 2 * $OTLW + $H;

    # The MacProgressbar Label and its surrounding top/left/right/bottom
    # Frames, plus an empty Photo for the Label's image.  Pack things nicely.

    my $tf = $self->Frame;
    my $lf = $self->Frame;
    my $lb = $self->Label;
    my $rf = $self->Frame;
    my $bf = $self->Frame;

    my $i = $lb->Photo(-width => $w, -height => $h);
    $lb->configure(-image => $i);

    $tf->pack(qw/-fill both -expand 1 -side top/);
    $bf->pack(qw/-fill both -expand 1 -side bottom/);
    $lf->pack(qw/-fill both -expand 1 -side left/);
    $lb->pack(qw/-fill both -expand 1 -side left -ipadx 6/);
    $rf->pack(qw/-fill both -expand 1 -side left/);

    # Draw the outer and inner image outlines.

    my $left_top_outter = '#adadad';
    my $right_bottom_outter = '#ffffff';

    $i->put($left_top_outter,     -to =>        0,       0, $w - 0,        1);
    $i->put('#000000',            -to =>        1,       1, $w - 1,        2);
    $i->put($left_top_outter,     -to =>        0,       0,      1, $h - 0);
    $i->put('#000000',            -to =>        1,       1,      2, $h - 1);

    $i->put($right_bottom_outter, -to =>        0, $h - 0, $w - 0, $h - 1);
    $i->put('#000000',            -to =>        1, $h - 1, $w - 1, $h - 2);
    $i->put($right_bottom_outter, -to => $w - 1, $h - 0, $w - 0,        1);
    $i->put('#000000',            -to => $w - 2, $h - 1, $w - 1,        1);

    # Advertise important user subwidgets. All mega-widget configuration
    # requests default to the Label. Define a handler that will delete the
    # MacProgressBar image upon widget destruction.
```

```perl
    $self->Advertise('tframe' => $tf);
    $self->Advertise('lframe' => $lf);
    $self->Advertise('label'  => $lb);
    $self->Advertise('rframe' => $rf);
    $self->Advertise('bframe' => $bf);

    $self->ConfigSpecs(DEFAULT => [$lb]);

    $self->OnDestroy([$self => 'free_photo']);

} # end Populate

sub free_photo {

    # Free the MacProgressBar image.

    $_[0]->Subwidget('label')->cget(-image)->delete;

} # end free_photo

sub set {

    # This is the meat of the MacProgressBar mega-widget, where we
    # first "blank" the image by filling it with the background color,
    # then paint the base, a progress bar of the desired width, and
    # the end cap.

    my($self, $percent) = @_;

    warn "Tk::MacProgressBar: percent ($percent) > 100." if $percent > 100;
    my $l = $self->Subwidget('label');
    return unless defined $l;# Destroy in progress
    my $i = $l->cget(-image);
    my $w = ( $self->{photow} - ( $BASE + $CAP ) ) / 100 * $percent;
    if ($w >= $self->{photow} - $CAP) {
        $w = $self->{photow} - $CAP - 1;
    }
    my $h = 2 * $OTLW + $H;

    # Clear image with background color.

    $i->put('#bdbdbd',
        -to => $OTLW + 0, $OTLW + 0, $self->{photow} - $OTLW, $h - $OTLW);

    # Draw the two-pixel-wide progress bar base.

    $i->put('#6363ce', -to => $OTLW + 0, $OTLW + 0, $OTLW + 1, $h - $OTLW);
    $i->put([
        '#6363ce', '#9c9cff', '#ceceff',
        '#efefef', '#efefef', '#efefef',
        '#ceceff', '#9c9cff', '#6363ce', '#31319c',
    ], -to => $OTLW + 1, $OTLW + 0, $OTLW + 2, $h - $OTLW);

    # Draw an appropriately wide progress bar.
```

```
    $i->put([
        '#30319d', '#6563cd', '#9c9cff',
        '#ceceff', '#f0f0f0', '#ceceff',
        '#9c9cff', '#6563cd', '#30319d', '#020152',
    ], -to => $OTLW + $BASE, $OTLW, $OTLW + $BASE + $w, $h - $OTLW);

    # Draw the six-pixel-wide progress bar end cap.

    my $x = 0;
    foreach my $pixels (
            ['#31319c', '#6363ce', '#9c9cff', '#ceceff', '#ceceff',
             '#ceceff', '#9c9cff', '#6363ce', '#31319c', '#000082'],
            ['#31319c', '#6363ce', '#31319c', '#31319c', '#31319c',
             '#31319c', '#31319c', '#31319c', '#31319c', '#000052'],
            ['#31319c', '#000052', '#000052', '#000052', '#000052',
             '#000052', '#000052', '#000052', '#000052', '#000052'],
            ['#000000', '#000000', '#000000', '#000000', '#000000',
             '#000000', '#000000', '#000000', '#000000', '#000000'],
            ['#525252', '#525252', '#525252', '#525252', '#525252',
             '#525252', '#525252', '#525252', '#525252', '#525252'],
            ['#8c8c8c', '#8c8c8c', '#8c8c8c', '#8c8c8c', '#8c8c8c',
             '#8c8c8c', '#8c8c8c', '#8c8c8c', '#8c8c8c', '#8c8c8c'],
        ) {
    $i->put($pixels,
        -to => $OTLW + $BASE + $x + $w,          $OTLW,
            $OTLW + $BASE + $x + $w + 1, $h - $OTLW);
    $x++;
    }

    $self->update;

} # end set

1;

__END__

=head1 NAME

Tk::MacProgressBar - a blue, 3-D Macintosh progress bar.

=head1 SYNOPSIS

S<    >I<$pb> = I<$parent>-E<gt>B<MacProgressBar>(I<-option> =E<gt> I<value>);

=head1 DESCRIPTION
```

This widget provides a dynamic image that looks just like a Mac OS 9
progress bar. Packed around it are four Frames, north, south, east and
west, within which you can stuff additional widgets. For example, see
how MacCopy uses several Labels and a CollapsableFrame widget to create
a reasonable facsimile of a Macintosh copy dialog.

The following option/value pairs are supported:

=over 4

=item B<-width>

The maximun width of the MacProgressbar.

=back

=head1 METHODS

=over 4

=item B<set($percent)>

Sets the width of the progress bar, as a percentage of -width.

=back

=head1 ADVERTISED WIDGETS

Component subwidgets can be accessed via the B<Subwidget> method.
Valid subwidget names are listed below.

=over 4

=item Name: label, Class: Label

  Widget reference of the Label containing the MacProgressBar
  Photo image.

=item Name: tframe, Class: Frame

  Widget reference of the Frame north the MacProgressBar.

=item Name: bframe, Class: Frame

  Widget reference of the Frame south the MacProgressBar.

=item Name: lframe, Class: Frame

  Widget reference of the Frame west the MacProgressBar.

=item Name: rframe, Class: Frame

  Widget reference of the Frame east the MacProgressBar.

=back

=head1 EXAMPLE

 use Tk;
 use Tk::MacProgressBar;
 use strict;

```
my $mw = MainWindow->new;
my $pb = $mw->MacProgressBar(-width => 150, -bg => 'cyan')->pack;

while (1) {
    my $w = rand(100);
    $pb->set($w);
    $mw->update;
    $mw->after(250);
}

=head1 AUTHOR and COPYRIGHT

Stephen.O.Lidie@Lehigh.EDU

Copyright (C) 2000 - 2001, Stephen O.Lidie.

This program is free software; you can redistribute it and/or
modify it under the same terms as Perl itself.

=head1 KEYWORDS

MacProgressBar

=cut
```

TclRobots.pm

Chapter 20 discusses TclRobots in detail. *TclRobots.pm* allows you to write Robot Control Programs in Perl instead of Tcl.

```
$TclRobots::VERSION = '2.1';

package TclRobots;

# This module implements a thin API that interfaces Perl with tclrobots
# version 2, written by Tom Poindexter.  This means that you can write
# RCPs (Robot Control Programs) in your favorite language - Perl - and
# do battle with all the existing Tcl RCPs.
#
# This module is rather wierd - you're never supposed to use it!
# Instead, it's used when tclrobots runs an instance of perl, at which
# time this module is loaded and begins execution on behalf of your
# RCP.  It creates the main window of the required dimensions and at
# the proper location on the display, and adds all the widgets, text,
# and images
#
# When instructed by tclrobots, this module then loads your Perl RCP
# (via require, so be sure your code returns a TRUE value!), and the
# contest begins.  From that point on, incoming tclrobot messages are
# dispatched to Perl emulation handlers, and Perl RCP commands are
# converted to Tcl syntax and sent to tclrobots - the communication is
# via Tk::send() and Tk::Receive().
#
```

```
# Stephen.O.Lidie@Lehigh.EDU, 1999/05/07.
# Stephen.O.Lidie@Lehigh.EDU, 2000/04/13, for Perl 5.6.0.

use Exporter;
@ISA = qw/Exporter/;
@EXPORT = qw/after alert cannon damage dputs drive dsp heat loc_x loc_y
    scanner speed team_declare team_get team_send tick update/;

use File::Basename;
use Tk;
use Tk qw/after catch/;
use Tk::widgets qw/Dialog/;

use subs qw/_arrowshape_ _configure_widgets_ _customize_window_
    _disable_rcp_ _insult_rcp_ _destroy_rcp_ _load_rcp_
    _see_variable_ _set_variables_ _setup_window_ _start_rcp_/;
use vars qw/$_after_ $_alert_on_ $_debug $_dl_ $_fc_ $_fl_ $_fs_ $_mw_
    $_ping_proc_ $_rcp_filename_ $_resume_ $_robot_ $_start_ $_step_
    $_tclrobots_/;

use strict;

###########################################################################
#
# Note, we run tainted so that send() and receive() work.  Grab command line
# arguments:
#
# perl5 -Tw -I. -MTclRobots /dev/null RCP.ptr_2462 \
#     WidthxHeigh+X+Y rob2 tclrobots ./RCP.ptr
#
###########################################################################

return 1 if $ENV{TCLROBOTS_RCP_CHECK}; # if checking RCP syntax

$ENV{'HOME'} = '/tmp';
$_mw_ = MainWindow->new;
$_mw_->withdraw;

$ARGV[0] =~ /(.*)/;# robot's Tcl name
$_mw_->appname($1);
$_mw_->title($1);

$ARGV[1] =~ /(.*)/;# window geometry
$_mw_->geometry($1);

$ARGV[2] =~ /(.*)/;# robot's handle
$_robot_ = $1;

$ARGV[3] =~ /(.*)/;# tclrobot's name
$_tclrobots_ = $1;

$ARGV[4] =~ /(.*)/;# RCP filename
$_rcp_filename_ = $1;
```

```perl
$_mw_->deiconify;
MainLoop;

###############################################################################
#
# Robot Control Program commands available to your Perl controlware.  For
# the most part, they simply invoke Tcl subroutines in tclrobots.  We also
# handle single stepping in Debug mode.
#
###############################################################################

{
    local $^W = 0;
    eval 'sub after {$_mw_->after(@_)}';
}

sub alert {
    my($code_ref) = @_;
    $_ping_proc_ = $code_ref;
    if (defined $code_ref) {
        $_alert_on_ = 1;
    } else {
        $_alert_on_ = 0;
    }
}

sub cannon {
    my($deg, $range) = @_;
    $_mw_->after(100);
    $_mw_->update;
    my $val = Tk::catch {
        $_mw_->send($_tclrobots_, "do_cannon $_robot_ $deg $range");
    };
    $_mw_->waitVariable(\$_resume_) if $_debug and $_step_;
    &_ping_check_;
    $_mw_->update;
    return $val;
}

sub damage {
    $_mw_->after(100);
    $_mw_->update;
    my $val = Tk::catch {
        $_mw_->send($_tclrobots_, "do_damage $_robot_");
    };
    $_mw_->waitVariable(\$_resume_) if $_debug and $_step_;
    &_ping_check_;
    $_mw_->update;
    return $val;
}

sub dputs {
    my(@args) = @_;
    $_resume_ = 0;
```

```perl
    Tk::catch {
        $_dl_->insert('end', join(' ', @args));
        $_dl_->yview('end'); $_mw_->update;
    };
    $_mw_->waitVariable(\$_resume_) if $_debug and $_step_;
    $_mw_->update;
}

sub drive {
    my($deg, $speed) = @_;
    $_mw_->after(100);
    $_mw_->update;
    my $val = Tk::catch {
        $_mw_->send($_tclrobots_, "do_drive $_robot_ $deg $speed");
    };
    $_mw_->waitVariable(\$_resume_) if $_debug and $_step_;
    &_ping_check_;
    $_mw_->update;
    return $val;
}

sub dsp {
    $_mw_->after(100);
    $_mw_->update;
    my $val = Tk::catch {
        $_mw_->send($_tclrobots_, "do_dsp $_robot_");
    };
    $_mw_->waitVariable(\$_resume_) if $_debug and $_step_;
    &_ping_check_;
    $_mw_->update;
    my(@dsp) = split(' ', $val);
    return @dsp;
}

sub heat {
    $_mw_->after(100);
    $_mw_->update;
    my $val = Tk::catch {
        $_mw_->send($_tclrobots_, "do_heat $_robot_");
    };
    $_mw_->waitVariable(\$_resume_) if $_debug and $_step_;
    &_ping_check_;
    $_mw_->update;
    my(@heat) = split(' ', $val);
    return @heat;
}

sub loc_x {
    $_mw_->after(100);
    $_mw_->update;
    my $val = Tk::catch {
        $_mw_->send($_tclrobots_, "do_loc_x $_robot_");
    };
    $_mw_->waitVariable(\$_resume_) if $_debug and $_step_;
```

```perl
        &_ping_check_;
        $_mw_->update;
        return $val;
    }

    sub loc_y {
        $_mw_->after(100);
        $_mw_->update;
        my $val = Tk::catch {
            $_mw_->send($_tclrobots_, "do_loc_y $_robot_");
        };
        $_mw_->waitVariable(\$_resume_) if $_debug and $_step_;
        &_ping_check_;
        $_mw_->update;
        return $val;
    }

    sub scanner {
        my($deg, $res) = @_;
        $_mw_->after(100);
        $_mw_->after(100);
        $_mw_->update;
        my $val = Tk::catch {
            $_mw_->send($_tclrobots_, "do_scanner $_robot_ $deg $res");
        };
        $_mw_->waitVariable(\$_resume_) if $_debug and $_step_;
        &_ping_check_;
        $_mw_->update;
        return $val;
    }

    sub speed {
        $_mw_->after(100);
        $_mw_->update;
        my $val = Tk::catch {
            $_mw_->send($_tclrobots_, "do_speed $_robot_");
        };
        $_mw_->waitVariable(\$_resume_) if $_debug and $_step_;
        &_ping_check_;
        $_mw_->update;
        return $val;
    }

    sub team_declare {
        my($tname) = @_;
        $_mw_->update;
        my $val = Tk::catch {
            $_mw_->send($_tclrobots_, "do_team_declare $_robot_ $tname");
        };
        $_mw_->waitVariable(\$_resume_) if $_debug and $_step_;
        &_ping_check_;
        $_mw_->update;
        return $val;
    }
```

```
sub team_get {
    $_mw_->update;
    my $val = Tk::catch {
        $_mw_->send($_tclrobots_, "do_team_get $_robot_");
    };
    $_mw_->waitVariable(\$_resume_) if $_debug and $_step_;
    &_ping_check_;
    $_mw_->update;
    my @teams;
    foreach my $team (&SplitString($val)) {
        my($dsp, $data) = split ' ', $team;
        push @teams, [$dsp, $data];
    }
    return @teams;
}

sub team_send {
    my($args) = @_;
    $_mw_->update;
    my $val = Tk::catch {
        $_mw_->send($_tclrobots_, "do_team_send $_robot_ \"$args\"");
    };
    $_mw_->waitVariable(\$_resume_) if $_debug and $_step_;
    &_ping_check_;
    $_mw_->update;
    return $val;
}

sub tick {
    $_mw_->after(100);
    $_mw_->update;
    my $val = Tk::catch {
        $_mw_->send($_tclrobots_, "do_tick $_robot_");
    };
    $_mw_->waitVariable(\$_resume_) if $_debug and $_step_;
    &_ping_check_;
    $_mw_->update;
    return $val;
}

sub update {
    $_mw_->update;
}

#############################################################################
#
# Tcl -> Perl handlers.
#
#############################################################################

sub Tk::Receive {

    # Accept Tcl strings from tclrobots and invoke
    # Perl/Tk emulation code.
```

```perl
    my($mw) = shift;# main window
    $_ = shift;# Tcl command

    return 2 if /expr 1\+1/;
    return if /(Knuth|^rename)/m;

  CASE:
    {
        /setup window/m    and do {_setup_window_;          last CASE};
        /create|configure/ and do {_customize_window_ $_; last CASE};
        /set _start_ 0/    and do {_load_rcp_;            last CASE};
        /set _start_ 1/    and do {_start_rcp_;           last CASE};
        /^proc after/      and do {_disable_rcp_;         last CASE};
        /\.d\.1 insert/    and do {_insult_rcp_ $_;       last CASE};
        /^_a_\d+ 0 _e_\d+/ and do {_destroy_rcp_;         last CASE};
        /^set/             and do {_set_variables_ $_;    last CASE};
        /^format/          and do {return _see_variable_ $_;};
        print STDERR "UNHANDLED cmd=$_!\n";
    } # casend

} # end Tk::Receive

sub _arrowshape_ {
    my($cmd) = @_;
    my($cs, $ar) = $cmd =~ /\.f\.. create (.*) (-arrowshape.*)/;
    my(@cs) = split(' ', $cs);
    $ar =~ /"(\d+) (\d+) (\d+)/;
    my $as = [$1, $2, $3];
    $_fc_->create(@cs, -arrowshape => $as);
}

sub _configure_widgets_ {
    my($cmd) = @_;
    my($w) = $cmd =~ /\.f\.1/ ? $_fl_ : $_fs_;
    my($cs) = $cmd =~ /configure (.*)/;
    $cs =~ s/(;.*)//;
    my(@cs) = split(' ', $cs);
    $w->configure(@cs);
    $w->update;
}

sub _customize_window_ {
    $_ = $_[0];
    /configure/ and do {_configure_widgets_ $_; return};
    /create/    and do {_arrowshape_ $_;        return};
}

sub _destroy_rcp_ {
    $_mw_->after(1 => $_mw_->destroy);
}

sub _disable_rcp_ {
    {
        local $^W = 0;
```

```perl
        eval 'sub after {}';
        eval 'sub _ping_check_ {
            while (1) {
                $_mw_->update;
                $_mw_->after(100);
            }
        }';
    }
}

sub _insult_rcp_ {
    my($cmd) = @_;
    my($text) = $cmd =~ /insert end(.*)?;\.d\.1/;
    $_mw_->after(1 => sub {
        $text =~ s/\\//g;
        $_dl_->insert('end', $text);
        $_dl_->yview('end');
        $_mw_->update;
        $_mw_->waitWindow;
    });
}

sub _load_rcp_ {
    $_start_ = 0;
    $_mw_->after(100 => sub {
        $_mw_->waitVariable(\$_start_);
        eval "require \"$_rcp_filename_\"";
        if ($@) {
            my $bn = basename $_rcp_filename_;
            my $d = $_mw_->Dialog(
                -title => $_mw_->appname,
                -text  => "$@\nYour RCP failed to compile. To perform a
syntax " .
                    "check, do:\n\nTCLROBOTS_RCP_CHECK=1 perl -MTclRobots $bn",
                -font  => 'fixed');
            $d->Subwidget('message')->configure(-wraplength => '8i');
            $d->Show;
            $d->destroy;
        }
    });
}

sub _see_variable_ {
    my($expression) = @_;# including leading $
    $expression = substr $expression, 8;
    {
        no strict;
        # Perl bug: I want eval "$expression";
        # So for now, assume a scalar var name.
        $$expression;
    }
}

sub _setup_window_ {
```

```perl
    # Setup the RCP's debug and damage window.

    my $f = $_mw_->Frame;
    $f->pack(qw/-side top -fill x -ipady 5/);
    $_fc_ = $f->Canvas(qw/-width 20 -height 16/);
    $_fl_ = $f->Label(qw/-relief sunken -width 30  -text/ =>
                        "(loading robot code..)");
    $_fs_ = $f->Label(qw/-relief sunken -width 5   -text/ => "0%");
    $_fc_->pack(qw/-side left/);
    $_fs_->pack(qw/-side right/);
    $_fl_->pack(qw/-side left -expand 1 -fill both/);

    $_dl_ = $_mw_->Scrolled('Listbox', qw/-relief sunken -scrollbars se/);
    $_dl_->pack(qw/-side left  -expand 1 -fill both/);
    $_mw_->minsize(100, 70);
    $_mw_->update;

    $_resume_ = 0;
    $_step_ =  0;

}

sub _set_variables_ {
    my($cmd) = @_;
    foreach (split /;/, $cmd) {
        my($set, $var, $val) = /(set)\s+(\S+)\s+(.*)/;
        {no strict; eval {$$var = $val}}
    }
}

sub _start_rcp_ {
    $_mw_->after(100 => sub {$_start_ = 1});
}


############################################################################
#
# Auxiliary routines.
#
############################################################################

$_ping_proc_ = '';
$_alert_on_ = 0;
sub _ping_check_ {
    return unless $_alert_on_;
    my $val = Tk::catch {
        $_mw_->send($_tclrobots_, "do_ping $_robot_");
    };
    Tk::catch {&$_ping_proc_($val)} if $val != 0;
}

sub SplitString {

    # Swiped from Tk800.015 distribution - a weak attempt to
    # turn a Tcl LOL into a Perl LOL.
```

```perl
    local $_ = shift;
    my (@arr, $tmp);

    while (/\{(([^{}]*)\}|((?:[^\s\\]|\\.)+)/gs) {
        if (defined $1) {
            push @arr, $1;
        } else {
            $tmp = $2 ;
            $tmp =~ s/\\([\s\\])/$1/g;
            push @arr, $tmp;
        }
    }
    return @arr;
} # end SplitString

1;
```

Robot Control Program complex.ptr

This isn't really a Perl/Tk program, but we're including it anyway. It's a TclRobots Robot Control Program written in Perl.

```perl
map {
    dputs $_;
} split /\n/, <<'end-of-about';
-----
Robot Control Program complex.ptr

Even though I prefer simplicity, here's complexity, but it doesn't
always work very well, alas.  Basically, this RCP is completely state
driven and uses clock ticks to schedule internal events.  It moves in
a path described by an n-sided polygon that approximates a circle
(this was my idea, I didn't know one of Tom's RCP team samples also
used this technique!).  The direction of movement is randomly chosen
during preset, eliminating "wall" code (although the RCP may perform a
"crazy Ivan" if it cannot find an enemy).  The RCP also attempts to
move as fast as possible, thus tracks its cooling rate to coordinate
turns, eliminating "flee" code.  There is also some watchdog code that
periodically checks the RCP's health.  Finally, the robot list from
the first tournament is maintained, so it was simple to add a "friend"
field and thus implement team play.

Stephen.O.Lidie@Lehigh.EDU, 2000/09/24.
-----
end-of-about

# Syntax check: TCLROBOTS_RCP_CHECK=1 perl -MTclRobots -c complex.ptr

use Tk qw/lsearch/;

use vars qw/
    $ATTACK_LIST_ENTRY
    $CANNON_HEADING $CANNON_READY $CLIP_SIZE $COOLING @COST
```

```perl
    $DANGER_RANGE $DIRECTION $DRIVE_HEADING $DRIVE_SPEED
    $EMERGENCY_X $EMERGENCY_Y
    @HEAT $HOUSE_KEEP_COUNT $HOUSE_KEEP_TICK @HUNT_STATE_LIST
    @IWSL $IWSL_COUNT $IWSL_TICK
    $LAPS $LAP_INDEX $LAST_SEEN_TICK
    $MAX_CANNON_RANGE $MAX_X $MAX_Y $MID_X $MID_Y
    $MOVE_QUAD @MOVE_STATE_LIST $MY_STATE
    $NVERT
    %PATH $PATHI
    $REBOOST $RELOAD_CLIP $RELOAD_CLIP_TICK $RELOAD_ROUND
    $RELOAD_ROUND_TICK $ROUNDS_LEFT %ROB @ROBL $R2D
    $SCAN_HEADING @SINT $SPEED $SPEED_SLOW_TURN $SPEED_TROLL $SPEED_TURN
    $TEAM $TICK $TURN_ACTIVE
/;

use subs qw/
    bootstrap do_RCP emergency fifo house_keep initialize_RCP
    initialize_robot I_was_scanned  position_to_heading position_to_range
    process_IWSL scanner_to_position which_quad
/;
use subs qw/hunt hunt_aim hunt_atle hunt_cannon hunt_fire hunt_scan hunt_wait/;
use subs qw/move move_check move_goto move_wait/;

use strict;

initialize_RCP;
do_RCP;

sub bootstrap {

    # Initialize the RCP and start it circling.

    $TURN_ACTIVE = 1;
    my $q = which_quad;
    $PATHI = (( (($q+1)%4) * ($NVERT/4)) % $NVERT) + 1;
    $LAP_INDEX = $PATHI;
    $EMERGENCY_X = -2;
    $EMERGENCY_Y = -2;
    $HOUSE_KEEP_TICK = $TICK + $HOUSE_KEEP_COUNT;
    $IWSL_TICK = $TICK + $IWSL_COUNT;
    @HUNT_STATE_LIST = ();
    fifo 'hunt', 'in', ['SCAN', ''];
    @MOVE_STATE_LIST = ();
    fifo 'move', 'in', ['GOTO', 'DECELERATE'];
    $MY_STATE = 'move';        # initial state

} # end bootstrap

sub fifo {
    my($list, $action, $state) = @_;

    # Manipulate a (hunt|move) FIFO stack.

    dputs "Bad state list name $list" unless $list =~ /hunt|move/;
```

```perl
        my $list_ref = $list eq 'hunt' ? \@HUNT_STATE_LIST : \@MOVE_STATE_LIST;

    $_ = $action;
  CASE:
    {
        /^in/ and do {
            push @$list_ref, $state;
            last CASE;
        };
        /^out/  and do {
            if (@$list_ref == 0) {
                dputs "*** State Gag:  lst=$list, act=$action, state=$state";
                return -1;
            }
            return shift @$list_ref;
            last CASE;
        };
    } # casend

} # end fifo

sub do_RCP {

    bootstrap;

    while ( 1 ) {
        $TICK = tick;

        $_ = $MY_STATE;
      CASE:
        {
            /^hunt/ and do {hunt; last CASE};
            /^move/ and do {move; last CASE};
        }
        process_IWSL if $TICK >= $IWSL_TICK;
        house_keep   if $TICK >= $HOUSE_KEEP_TICK;
    }

} # end do_RCP

sub emergency {
    my($type) = @_;

    # Handle serious RCP anomalies.

    dputs "*** EMERGENCY=$type";
    if ($type =~ /^DRIVE/) {
        emergency 'DRIVE' unless drive $DRIVE_HEADING, $DRIVE_SPEED;
    } elsif ($type =~ /^RESTART/) {
        drive 0, 0;
        bootstrap;
    }

} # end emergency
```

```
sub house_keep {

    # Remove robots whom I haven't scanned recently from the robot list so
    # I don't have to worry about them (ignoring Me)!

    #for {set i [expr [llength $ROBL] - 1]} {$i > 0} {incr i -1} {
    #    set dsp [lindex $ROBL $i]
    #    if { $ms > [expr $ROB($dsp,'last_seen_tick') + $delta] } {
    #        set ROBL [lreplace $ROBL $i $i]
    #    }
    #}

    # "Crazy Ivan" if we haven't scanned a robot recently to ensure
    # an enemy RCP isn't stalking us.

    my $last_seen_tick = 0;
    foreach my $dsp (@ROBL) {
        $last_seen_tick = $ROB{$dsp,'last_seen_tick'} if
            $ROB{$dsp,'last_seen_tick'} > $last_seen_tick;
    }
    if ($last_seen_tick + $LAST_SEEN_TICK < $TICK) {
        $DIRECTION = 0 - $DIRECTION;
        foreach my $dsp (@ROBL) {
            $ROB{$dsp,'last_seen_tick'} = $TICK;
        }
        emergency 'RESTART';
    }

    # Restart the RCP if we seem to be stuck.

    emergency 'RESTART' if $EMERGENCY_X == $ROB{'Me','last_x'} and
        $EMERGENCY_Y == $ROB{'Me','last_y'};
    $EMERGENCY_X = $ROB{'Me','last_x'};
    $EMERGENCY_Y = $ROB{'Me','last_y'};
    $HOUSE_KEEP_TICK = $TICK + $HOUSE_KEEP_COUNT;

} # house_keep

sub hunt {

    # Hunt state processor.

    my $next_state = fifo 'hunt', 'out';
    if ($next_state == -1) {
        dputs "HUNT GAG!";
        fifo 'hunt', 'in', ['WAIT', ''];
        $MY_STATE = 'move';
        return;
    }

    $_      = $next_state->[0];
    my $arg = $next_state->[1];
  CASE:
    {
```

```perl
        /^ATLE/ and do {hunt_atle $arg;                     last CASE};
        /^FIRE/ and do {hunt_fire $arg;                     last CASE};
        /^SCAN/ and do {hunt_scan $arg;                     last CASE};
        /^WAIT/ and do {hunt_wait $arg; $MY_STATE = 'move'; last CASE};
    } # casend

} # end hunt

sub hunt_aim {
    my($rdir) = @_;

    my($ret, $min, $max);

    foreach my $t (qw/10 5 3 2 1 0/) {
        $min = ($$rdir - $t) % 360;
        $max = ($$rdir + $t) % 360;
        if      ( scanner( $max, $t ) > 0  ) {
            $$rdir = $max;
            $SCAN_HEADING = $$rdir - 40;
            $ret = scanner($$rdir, 1);
            return $ret if $ret > 0;
        } elsif ( scanner( $min, $t ) > 0  ) {
            $$rdir = $min;
            $SCAN_HEADING = $$rdir - 20;
            $ret = scanner($$rdir, 1);
            return $ret if $ret > 0;
        } else {
            return 0;
        }
    }
    return scanner($$rdir, 0);

} # end hunt_aim

sub hunt_atle {
    my($arg) = @_;

    # Make sure we have an attack list entry.  If not, generate a fresh attack
    # list and select the best entry.

    unless ($ATTACK_LIST_ENTRY) {
        my(@attack_list) = ( );
        foreach my $dsp (@ROBL) {
            next if $ROB{$dsp,'friend'};
            next if $ROB{$dsp,'last_x'} == -1;
            my $cr = position_to_range $ROB{$dsp,'last_x'}, $ROB{$dsp,'last_y'};
            if ($cr > $DANGER_RANGE and $cr <= $MAX_CANNON_RANGE) {
                push @attack_list, [$dsp, $cr];
            }
        }
        $ATTACK_LIST_ENTRY = shift @attack_list;
        if (@attack_list) {
            foreach my $f (@attack_list) {
                if ($f->[1] < $ATTACK_LIST_ENTRY->[1]) {
```

```
                    $ATTACK_LIST_ENTRY = $f;
                }
            }
        }
    }

    fifo 'hunt', 'in', ['WAIT', ''];
    if ($ATTACK_LIST_ENTRY) {
        fifo 'hunt', 'in', ['FIRE', ''];
    } else {
        fifo 'hunt', 'in', ['SCAN', ''];
    }

} # end hunt_atle

sub hunt_cannon {
    my($dir, $range) = @_;

    if ($range <= $MAX_CANNON_RANGE) {
        my $stat  = cannon $dir, $range;
        fifo 'hunt', 'in', ['WAIT', ''];
        $ROUNDS_LEFT--;
        $CANNON_READY = 0;
        if ($ROUNDS_LEFT <= 0) {
            $RELOAD_CLIP_TICK = $TICK + $RELOAD_CLIP;
        } else {
            $RELOAD_ROUND_TICK = $TICK + $RELOAD_ROUND;
        }
    }
    fifo 'hunt', 'in', ['WAIT', ''];
    fifo 'hunt', 'in', ['FIRE', ''];

} # end hunt_cannon

sub hunt_fire {
    my($arg) = @_;

    if ($CANNON_READY) {
        $ROB{'Me','last_x'} = loc_x;
        $ROB{'Me','last_y'} = loc_y;
        my $dsp =  $ATTACK_LIST_ENTRY->[0];
        my $cr  = $ATTACK_LIST_ENTRY->[1];
        $CANNON_HEADING = position_to_heading $ROB{$dsp,'last_x'},
            $ROB{$dsp,'last_y'};
        my $range = hunt_aim \$CANNON_HEADING;
        my(@dspl) = dsp;
        $dsp = $dspl[0];
        if ($dsp != 0) {
            if ($range > $DANGER_RANGE and not $ROB{$dsp,'friend'}) {
                hunt_cannon $CANNON_HEADING, $range;
            } else {
                $ATTACK_LIST_ENTRY = undef;
                fifo 'hunt', 'in', ['SCAN', ''];
            }
```

```
            } else {
                $ATTACK_LIST_ENTRY = undef;
                fifo 'hunt', 'in', ['SCAN', ''];
            }
        } else {
            fifo 'hunt', 'in', ['WAIT', ''];
            fifo 'hunt', 'in', ['SCAN', ''];
        } # ifend cannon ready

    } # end hunt_fire

    sub hunt_scan {
        my($arg) = @_;

        # Try to update information on all enemy robots.  Information is very
        # fuzzy, with range to target inaccurate up to 100 meters, and my
        # calculation of robot position inaccurate up to 200 meters!  We'll attack
        # later, narrowing the bad robot's position via a binary search.

        my $sd  = 9 * 20;            # hunks of 20 degrees
        my $sh;

        for (my $i = $SCAN_HEADING; $i <= $sd + $SCAN_HEADING; $i += 20) {
            $sh = $i % 360;
            my $sr = scanner $sh, 10;
            if ($sr > $DANGER_RANGE and $sr <= $MAX_CANNON_RANGE) {
                my($dsp, $damage) = dsp;
                initialize_robot($dsp) if lsearch(\@ROBL, $dsp) == -1;
                next if $ROB{$dsp,'friend'};
                $ROB{$dsp,'last_seen_tick'} = $TICK;
                $ROB{$dsp,'damage'} = $damage;
                scanner_to_position $dsp, $sr, $sh; # new enemy position
                last;
            }

        }

        $SCAN_HEADING = ($sh + 20) % 360;
        fifo 'hunt', 'in', ['ATLE', ''];

    } # end hunt_scan

    sub hunt_wait {
        my($arg) = @_;

        # Process auxiliary hunt tasks.

        if ($RELOAD_ROUND_TICK != -1 and $TICK >= $RELOAD_ROUND_TICK) {
            $CANNON_READY = 1;
            $RELOAD_ROUND_TICK = -1;
        }
        if ($RELOAD_CLIP_TICK  != -1 and $TICK >= $RELOAD_CLIP_TICK) {
            $CANNON_READY = 1;
            $ROUNDS_LEFT = $CLIP_SIZE;
```

```perl
        $RELOAD_CLIP_TICK = -1;
    }

} # end hunt_wait

sub initialize_robot {
    my($dsp) = @_;

    # Add an enemy or team robot to the robot list.

    push @ROBL, $dsp;
    $ROB{$dsp,'scanme_count'} = 0;          # times this robot has scanned me
    $ROB{$dsp,'last_scanme_count'} = 0;     # scanme_count last time around
    $ROB{$dsp,'last_seen_tick'} = $TICK;    # time last seen
    $ROB{$dsp,'damage'} = -1;               # robot's damage
    $ROB{$dsp,'last_x'} = -1;               # robot's last known X coordinate
    $ROB{$dsp,'last_y'} = -1;               # robot's last known Y coordinate
    $ROB{$dsp,'friend'} = 0;                # assume not a team member

    foreach my $response (team_get) {
        my $dsp2 = $response->[0];
        my $data = $response->[1];
        $ROB{$dsp2,'friend'} = 1 if $data eq $TEAM;
    }

} # end initialize_robot

sub I_was_scanned {
    my($dsp) = @_;

    # Note the fact that I was scanned by appending $dsp to IWSL.  It's up to
    # other code to shorten this list and update the scan_me count in the
    # robot table.

    push @IWSL, $dsp;

} # end I_was_scanned

sub move {

    # Move state processor.

    my $next_state = fifo 'move', 'out';
    if ($next_state == -1) {
        dputs "MOVE GAG!";
        fifo 'move', 'in', ['WAIT', ''];
        $MY_STATE = 'hunt';
        return;
    }

    $_       = $next_state->[0];
    my $arg  = $next_state->[1];
  CASE:
    {
```

```perl
            /^CHECK/ and do {move_check $arg;                         last CASE};
            /^GOTO/  and do {move_goto  $arg;                         last CASE};
            /^WAIT/  and do {move_wait  $arg; $MY_STATE = 'hunt'; last CASE};
        } # casend

} # end move

sub move_check {
    my($arg) = @_;

    # Change direction to next polygon vertex when proper.

    $ROB{'Me','last_x'} = loc_x;
    $ROB{'Me','last_y'} = loc_y;
    my $x0 = $ROB{'Me','last_x'};
    my $y0 = $ROB{'Me','last_y'};
    my $x  = $PATH{$PATHI,'x'};
    my $y  = $PATH{$PATHI,'y'};
    my $change_course = 0;

    $_ = $MOVE_QUAD;
    CASE:
    {
        /^1/ and do {$change_course++ if $x0 <= $x and $y0 >= $y; last CASE};
        /^2/ and do {$change_course++ if $x0 <= $x and $y0 <= $y; last CASE};
        /^3/ and do {$change_course++ if $x0 >= $x and $y0 <= $y; last CASE};
        /^4/ and do {$change_course++ if $x0 >= $x and $y0 >= $y; last CASE};
    }
    if ($change_course) {
        $PATHI = ($PATHI + $DIRECTION + $NVERT) % $NVERT;
        if ($PATHI == $LAP_INDEX) {
            $LAPS++;
            dputs "LAP COUNT=$LAPS, SPEED=" . speed . " *****";
        }
        fifo 'move', 'in', ['GOTO', 'DECELERATE'];
    } else {
        @HEAT = heat;
        my $h = $HEAT[0];
        if ($h and (not $COOLING)) {
            $COOLING = 1;
            $REBOOST = 1;
        }
        if ((not $h) and $REBOOST) {
            $COOLING = 0;
            $REBOOST = 0;
            fifo 'move', 'in', ['GOTO', 'REBOOST'];
        } else {
            fifo 'move', 'in', ['WAIT', ''];
            fifo 'move', 'in', ['CHECK', ''];
        }
    } # ifend change course

} # end move_check
```

```
sub move_goto {
    my($goto_state) = @_;

    # Goto next polygon vertex.  Slow to turn speed accounting for
    # turn delta and deceleration, make the turn and resume.

    $ROB{'Me','last_x'} = loc_x;
    $ROB{'Me','last_y'} = loc_y;
    my $x0 = $ROB{'Me','last_x'};
    my $y0 = $ROB{'Me','last_y'};
    my $x = $PATH{$PATHI,'x'};
    my $y = $PATH{$PATHI,'y'};
    my $new_heading = position_to_heading $x, $y;
    my $d1 = ($new_heading - $DRIVE_HEADING + 360) % 360;
    my $d2 = ($DRIVE_HEADING - $new_heading + 360) % 360;
    my $dheading = $d1 < $d2 ? $d1 : $d2;
    my $SPEED = speed;
    my $turn_speed = $dheading >= 75 ? $SPEED_SLOW_TURN : $SPEED_TURN;

    $_ = $goto_state;
    CASE:
    {
        /^DECELERATE/ and do {
            $TURN_ACTIVE = 1;
            my $dspeed = $SPEED - $turn_speed;
            my $decel = int($dspeed / 10.0 + 0.5);
            if ($decel <= 0) {
                fifo 'move', 'in', ['GOTO', 'TURN'];
            } else {
                my $stat = drive $DRIVE_HEADING, $turn_speed;
                emergency 'DRIVE' if $stat == 0;
                fifo 'move', 'in', ['GOTO', 'WAIT'];
            }
            last CASE;
        };
        /^WAIT/ and do {
            if ($SPEED <= $turn_speed) {
                fifo 'move', 'in', ['GOTO', 'TURN'];
            } else {
                fifo 'move', 'in', ['WAIT', ''];
                fifo 'move', 'in', ['GOTO', 'WAIT'];
            }
            last CASE;
        };
        /^TURN/ and do {
            $TURN_ACTIVE = 0;
            $DRIVE_HEADING = $new_heading;
            $DRIVE_SPEED = $SPEED_TROLL;
            my $stat = drive $DRIVE_HEADING, $DRIVE_SPEED;
            if ($stat == 0) {emergency 'DRIVE'}
            if ($x0 >= $x and $y0 <= $y) {
                $MOVE_QUAD = 1;
            } elsif ($x0 >= $x and $y0 >= $y) {
                $MOVE_QUAD = 2;
```

```
            } elsif ($xO <= $x and $yO >= $y) {
                $MOVE_QUAD = 3;
            } elsif ($xO <= $x and $yO <= $y) {
                $MOVE_QUAD = 4;
            } else {
                dputs "*** Turn error!";
            }
            fifo 'move', 'in', ['CHECK', ''];
            last CASE;
        };
        /^REBOOST/ and do {
            if (not $TURN_ACTIVE) {
                $xO = $ROB{'Me','last_x'};
                $yO = $ROB{'Me','last_y'};
                $x = $PATH{$PATHI,'x'};
                $y = $PATH{$PATHI,'y'};
                my $range = position_to_range $xO, $yO, $x, $y;
                $DRIVE_SPEED = 80 if $range < 100;
                my $stat = drive $DRIVE_HEADING, $DRIVE_SPEED;
                if ($stat == 0) {emergency 'DRIVE'}
            }
            fifo 'move', 'in', ['CHECK', ''];
            last CASE;
        };
    } # casend

} # end move_goto

sub move_wait {
    my($arg) = @_;

    # Process auxiliary move tasks.

} # end move_wait

sub position_to_heading {
    my($x, $y, $xO, $yO) = @_;

    # Given two absolute coordinate pairs, compute the heading (angle)
    # between them.  If only a single coordinate is given, use Me as the
    # second.  Typical usage is to determine the heading for this robot to
    # get somewhere else.
    #
    # The result is integer.

    if (not defined $xO) {
        $xO = $ROB{'Me','last_x'};
        $yO = $ROB{'Me','last_y'};
    }

    return int( $R2D * atan2( ($y - $yO), ($x - $xO) ) + 0.5) % 360;

} # end postion_to_heading
```

```perl
sub position_to_range {
    my($x, $y, $x0, $y0) = @_;

    # Given two absolute coordinate pairs, compute the range (relative
    # distance) between them.  If only a single coordinate is given, use Me
    # as the second.  Typical usage is to determine the range between this
    # robot and another.
    #
    # The result is floating point.


    if (not defined $x0) {
        $x0 = $ROB{'Me','last_x'};
        $y0 = $ROB{'Me','last_y'};
    }

    my $dx = $x - $x0;
    my $dy = $y - $y0;
    return sqrt( $dx*$dx + $dy*$dy );

} # end position_to_range

sub process_IWSL {

    # Empty the "I was scanned" list and update scanner counts.

    foreach my $dsp (@ROBL) {
        $ROB{$dsp,'last_scanme_count'} = $ROB{$dsp,'scanme_count'};
    }
    foreach my $dsp (@IWSL) {
        initialize_robot $dsp if lsearch(\@ROBL, $dsp) == -1;
        $ROB{$dsp,'scanme_count'}++;
    }
    @IWSL = ();

} # process_IWSL

sub scanner_to_position {
    my($dsp, $rng, $hdg) = @_;

    # Using the information from the scanner/dsp commands, compute the
    # absolute position of the scanned robot and save it.  $dsp is the
    # robot's digital signature, while $rng is the relative distance and
    # $hdg is the heading between Me and the robot.

    my $x = $rng * $COST[$hdg];
    my $y = $rng * $SINT[$hdg];
    $ROB{$dsp,'last_x'} = $ROB{'Me','last_x'} + $x;
    $ROB{$dsp,'last_y'} = $ROB{'Me','last_y'} + $y;

} # end scanner_to_position

sub which_quad {
    my($x, $y) = @_;
```

```perl
    # Determine a quandrant given an x/y coordinate pair (default is Me).

    if (not defined $x) {
        $x = $ROB{'Me','last_x'};
        $y = $ROB{'Me','last_y'};
    }
    my $q;
    if ( $x > $MID_X ) {
        $q =  $y > $MID_Y ? 1 : 4;
    } else {
        $q =  $y > $MID_Y ? 2 : 3;
    }

    return $q;

} # end which_quad

sub initialize_RCP {

    # Initialize the Robot Control Program.

    $TEAM = 'LUSOL2';              # kludge team capability
    team_declare $TEAM;
    team_send $TEAM;

    $TICK = -1;             # current RCP tick count
    my $clock = 500;           # tick resolution in milliseconds
    my $tps = 1000 / $clock;   # ticks/second

    my $pi = 3.141592654;    # pi
    $R2D = 180.0 / $pi;      # radians to degrees
    my $d2r = $pi / 180.0; # degrees to radians
    for (my $i = 0; $i < 360; $i++) {
        $SINT[$i] =  sin($d2r * $i); # sine table
        $COST[$i] =  cos($d2r * $i); # cosine table
    }

    $MAX_X = 999;             # battlefield X max
    $MAX_Y = 999;             # battlefield Y max
    $MID_X = $MAX_X / 2;      # X midpoint
    $MID_Y = $MAX_Y / 2;      # Y midpoint

    @ROBL = ();               # robot list
    initialize_robot 'Me';
    $ROB{'Me','last_x'} = loc_x; # last x coordinate
    $ROB{'Me','last_y'} = loc_y; # last y coordinate
    $ROB{'Me','friend'} = 1;    # of course

    @IWSL = ();               # "I was scanned" list
    $IWSL_COUNT = 4;          # tick interval
    $IWSL_TICK = -1;          # schedule at this tick value
    alert \&I_was_scanned;    # maintain a list of who scanned Me

    $ATTACK_LIST_ENTRY = undef; # no attack list entry
```

```perl
    srand $$;
    $SCAN_HEADING = rand 360;  # current scanner direction

    $CLIP_SIZE = 4;            # number of cannon rounds per clip
    $ROUNDS_LEFT = $CLIP_SIZE;

    $RELOAD_CLIP = 12 * $tps;  # ticks required before reload clip
    $RELOAD_CLIP_TICK = -1;

    $RELOAD_ROUND = 4  * $tps; # ticks required before reload round
    $RELOAD_ROUND_TICK = -1;

    $CANNON_HEADING = 0;       # cannon direction
    $CANNON_READY = 1;         # 1 IFF cannon is ready for firing
    $MAX_CANNON_RANGE = 700;   # I'm no robocop
    $DANGER_RANGE = 0;         # but there's always Heisenburg

    @HEAT = (0, 0);            # current heat results
    $COOLING = 0;              # 1 iff waiting for engine to cool
    $REBOOST = 0;              # 1 iff engine has just cooled

    $SPEED = 0;                # current speed
    $SPEED_TROLL = 100;        # normal speed to minimize heating
    $SPEED_SLOW_TURN = 20;     # slow turn speed
    $SPEED_TURN = 30;          # normal turn speed
    $TURN_ACTIVE = 0;          # 1 IFF we are turning
    $DRIVE_SPEED = $SPEED_TROLL;
    $DRIVE_HEADING = 0;

    # Compute vertices of an $NVERT sided polygon, the robot's continuous path.

    $NVERT = 8;                # polygon vertex count
    my $dangle = 360 / $NVERT;
    my $radius = 350;
    $MOVE_QUAD = 0;
    $PATHI = 0;
    for (my $angle = 0; $angle <= 359; $angle += $dangle) {
        my $i = $angle / $dangle;
        $PATH{$i,'x'} = int(($MID_X + $radius * $COST[$angle]) + 0.5);
        $PATH{$i,'y'} = int(($MID_Y + $radius * $SINT[$angle]) + 0.5);
    }
    $DIRECTION = int(rand(2)) ? 1 : -1; # +1 anti-clockwise, -1 clockwise

    $LAPS = 0;                 # lap count this battle
    $LAP_INDEX = 0;            # starting vertix index

    $HOUSE_KEEP_COUNT = 20;    # housekeep frequency in ticks
    $HOUSE_KEEP_TICK = 0;      # last housekeep tick
    $LAST_SEEN_TICK = int( rand(30) + 60 ); # reverse direction delta

    @MOVE_STATE_LIST = ( );
    @HUNT_STATE_LIST = ( );

} # end initialize_RCP
```

clock-bezier.ppl

In Chapter 22, we discussed the Netscape PerlPlus Plugin and used several PPL programs in our examples. We include two PPL programs in this appendix. The first is the *clock-bezier.ppl* program, shown in Figure C-3.

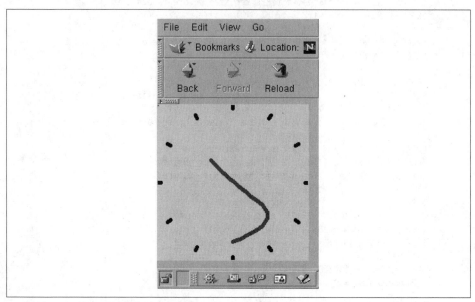

Figure C-3. clock-bezier.ppl

```perl
#!/usr/local/bin/perl -w
#
# This most entertaining program was written in Tcl/Tk by Scott Hess
# (shess@winternet.com).  It's a clock that uses a bezier curve anchored
# at four points -- the hour position, the minute position, the second
# position and the center of the clock -- to show the time.
#
# <Button-1> switches between display modes, and <Button-2> switches
# between line thicknesses.
#
# Perl/Tk version by Stephen.O.Lidie@Lehigh.EDU, 2000/02/05.

use POSIX qw/asin/;
use Tk;
use subs qw/buildclock hands setclock/;
use vars qw/$clock %hand $mw $pi180 $resize/;
use strict;

%hand = (
    hour    => 0.40,
    minute  => 0.75,
    second  => 0.85,
    0       => 0.00,
```

```
        intick  => 0.95,
        outtick => 1.00,
        width   => 0.05,
        scale   => 100,

        type    => 'bezier',
        types   => [qw/normal curve angle bezier/],
        tindx   => 3,
        normal  => [qw/minute 0 0 second 0 0 hour 0 0 minute/],
        curve   => [qw/minute 0 second 0 hour 0 minute/],
        angle   => [qw/minute second second hour/],
        bezier  => [qw/minute second 0 hour/],

        tick    => [qw/intick outtick/],
);
$pi180 = asin(1) / 90.0;
$resize = 0;

$mw = MainWindow->new;
$clock = $mw->Canvas(qw/-width 200 -height 200/);
$clock->pack(qw/-expand 1 -fill both/);
$mw->bind('<Configure>' => \&buildclock);
$mw->bind('<Button-1>'  => \&incrtype);
$mw->bind('<Button-2>'  => \&incrwidth);
buildclock;
$mw->repeat(1000 => sub {my(@t) = localtime; setclock @t[0 .. 2]});
MainLoop;

sub buildclock  {

    # Build the clock.  Puts tickmarks every 30 degrees, tagged
    # "ticks", and prefills the "hands" line.

    my $pi180 = asin(1)/90.0;

    Tk::catch {$clock->delete('marks')};
    $clock->update;
    my $w = $clock->width;
    $mw->geometry("${w}x${w}") if $resize; # ensure clock is square
    $resize++;
    $hand{scale} = $w / 2.0;

    # This is a horrid hack.  Use the hands() procedure to
    # calculate the tickmark positions by temporarily changing
    # the clock type.

    my $type = $hand{type};
    $hand{type} = 'tick';
    my %angles;
    for (my $ii = 0; $ii < 12; $ii++) {
        $angles{intick} = $angles{outtick} = $ii * 30 * $pi180;
        $clock->createLine(hands(\%angles), -tags => [qw/ticks marks/]);
    }
    $hand{type} =  $type;
```

```perl
    $clock->createLine(qw/0 0 0 0 -smooth 1 -tags/ => [qw/hands marks/]);
    $clock->itemconfigure(qw/marks -capstyle round -width/ =>
            $hand{width} * $hand{scale});
}

sub hands {

    # Calculate the set of points for the current hand type and
    # the angles in the passed array.

    my($aa) = @_;

    my $ss = $hand{scale};
    my @points;
    foreach my $desc ( @{ $hand{$hand{type}} } ) {
        push @points, sin($aa->{$desc}) * $hand{$desc} * $ss + $ss;
        push @points, $ss - cos($aa->{$desc}) * $hand{$desc} * $ss;
    }
    #print join(', ', @points), "\n";
    return @points;
}

sub incrtype {
    $hand{type} = $hand{types}->[ ++$hand{tindx} % @{$hand{types}} ];
}

sub incrwidth {
    my $w = $hand{width} + .05;
    $hand{width} = $w > .25 ? 0 : $w;
    $clock->itemconfigure('marks', -width => $hand{width} * $hand{scale});
}

sub setclock {

    # Calculate the angles for the second, minute, and hour hands,
    # and then update the clock hands to match.

    my($second, $minute, $hour) = @_;

    my %angles;
    $angles{0}       = 0;
    $angles{second} = $second *  6 * $pi180;
    $angles{minute} = $minute *  6 * $pi180;
    $angles{hour}   = $hour   * 30 * $pi180 + $angles{minute} / 12;

    my $sector  = int( $angles{second} + 0.5 );
    my(@colors) = qw/cyan green blue purple red yellow orange/;
    $clock->itemconfigure(qw/hands -fill/ => $colors[$sector]);

    $clock->coords('hands',  hands \%angles);
}
```

tkhanoi.ppl

This next PPL program is a classic Tower of Hanoi game.

```perl
#!/usr/local/bin/perl -w
#
# Towers of Hanoi, Perl/Tk style.  2000/06/14, solo@Lehigh.EDU

# Global package, subroutine and data declarations.

use Tk;
use Tk::Dialog;
use subs qw/do_hanoi fini hanoi init move_ring/;
use strict;

my $canvas;   # the Hanoi playing field
my @colors;   # 24 graduated ring colors
my $fly_y;    # canvas Y-coord along which rings fly
my $max_rings;# be nice and keep @colors count-consistent
my $num_moves;# total ring moves
my %pole;     # tracks pole X-coord and ring count
my %ring;     # tracks ring canvas ID, width and pole
my $ring_base;# canvas Y-coord of base of ring pile
my $ring_spacing;# pixels between adjacent rings
my $stopped;  # 1 IFF simulation is stopped
my $velocity; # pixel delta the rings move while flying
my $version = '1.0, 2000/06/14';

# Main.

my $mw = MainWindow->new(-use => $Plugin::brinfo{xwindow_id});
init;
MainLoop;

sub do_hanoi {

    # Initialize for a new simulation.

    my($n) = @_;# number of rings

    return unless $stopped;

    $stopped = 0;# start ...
    $num_moves = 0;# ... new simulation

    my $ring_height = 26;
    $ring_spacing = 0.67 * $ring_height;

    my $ring_width = 96 + $n * 12;

    my $canvas_width = 3 * $ring_width + 4 * 12;
    my $canvas_height = $ring_spacing * $n + $fly_y + 2 * $ring_height;

    $ring_base = $canvas_height - 32;
```

```
    # Remove all rings from the previous run and resize the canvas.

    for (my $i = 0; $i < $max_rings; $i++) {
        $canvas->delete($ring{$i, 'id'}) if defined $ring{$i, 'id'};
    }
    $canvas->configure(-width => $canvas_width, -height => $canvas_height);

    # Initialize the poles: no rings, updated X coordinate.

    for (my $i = 0; $i < 3; $i++) {
        $pole{$i, 'x'} = ($i * $canvas_width / 3) + ($ring_width / 2) + 8;
        $pole{$i, 'ring_count'} = 0;
    }

    # Initialize the rings: canvas ID, pole number, and width.

    for (my $i = 0; $i < $n; $i++) {
        my $color = '#' . $colors[$i % 24];
        my $w = $ring_width - ($i * 12);
        my $y = $ring_base - $i * $ring_spacing;
        my $x = $pole{0, 'x'} - $w / 2;
        my $r = $n - $i;
        $ring{$r, 'id'} = $canvas->createOval(
                $x, $y, $x + $w, $y + $ring_height,
                -fill => $color, -outline => 'black', -width => 1,
            );
        $ring{$r, 'width'} = $w;
        $ring{$r, 'pole'} = 0;
        $pole{0, 'ring_count'}++;
    }

    # Start the simulation.

    $mw->update;
    hanoi $n, 0, 2, 1;
    $stopped = 1;

} # end do_hanoi

sub hanoi {

    # Recursively move rings until complete or stopped by the user.

    my($n, $from, $to, $work) = @_;

    return if $n <=0 or $stopped;

    hanoi $n - 1, $from, $work, $to;
    move_ring $n, $to unless $stopped;
    hanoi $n - 1, $work, $to, $from;
}

sub init {
```

```perl
$fly_y = 32;# Y-coord rings use to fly between poles
$stopped = 1;
my $stop = sub {$stopped = 1};
my $about = $mw->Dialog(
    -title          => 'About tkhanoi',
    -bitmap         => 'info',
    -default_button => 'OK',
    -buttons        => ['OK'],
    -text           => "tkhanoi version $version\n\n" .
                       "r - run   simulation\n"       .
                       "s - stop simulation\n"        .
                       "q - quit program\n",
    -wraplength     => '6i',
);

# Menubar and menubuttons.

$mw->title("Towers of Hanoi");
$mw->configure(-menu => my $menubar = $mw->Menu);

my $file = $menubar->cascade(-label => 'File');
$file->command(-label => '~Quit', -command => \&fini,-accelerator => 'q');

my $game = $menubar->cascade(-label => 'Game');
$game->command(-label => '~Run',  -command => sub {}, -accelerator => 'r');
$game->command(-label => '~Stop', -command => $stop,  -accelerator => 's');

my $help = $menubar->cascade(-label => 'Help');
$help->command(-label => 'About', -command => sub {$about->Show});

my $info = $mw->Frame->pack;

# Number of rings scale.

my $rframe = $info->Frame(qw/-borderwidth 2 -relief raised/);
my $rlabel = $rframe->Label(-text => 'Number of Rings');
my $rscale = $rframe->Scale(
    qw/-orient horizontal -from 1 -to 24 -length 200/,
);
$rscale->set(4);
$game->cget(-menu)->entryconfigure('Run',
    -command => sub {do_hanoi $rscale->get},
);

$rframe->pack(qw/-side left/);
$rscale->pack(qw/-side right -expand 1 -fill x/);
$rlabel->pack(qw/-side left/);

# Ring velocity scale.

my $vframe = $info->Frame(qw/-borderwidth 2 -relief raised/);
my $vlabel = $vframe->Label(-text => 'Ring Velocity %');
my $vscale = $vframe->Scale(
```

```
        qw/-orient horizontal -from 0 -to 100 -length 200/,
        -command => sub {$velocity = shift},
    );
    $vscale->set(2);

    $vframe->pack(qw/-side left/);
    $vscale->pack(qw/-side right -expand 1 -fill x/);
    $vlabel->pack(qw/-side left/);

    # The simulation is played out on a canvas.

    $canvas = $mw->Canvas(qw/-relief sunken/);
    $canvas->pack(qw/-expand 1 -fill both/);
    $canvas->createWindow(40, 10, -window =>
        $canvas->Label(-textvariable => \$num_moves, -foreground => 'blue'),
    );

    # Each ring has a unique color, hopefully.

    @colors = (qw/
        ffff0000b000 ffff00006000 ffff40000000 ffff60000000
        ffff80000000 ffffa0000000 ffffc0000000 ffffe0000000
        ffffffff0000 d000ffff0000 b000ffff0000 9000ffff0000
        6000ffff3000 0000ffff6000 0000ffff9000 0000ffffc000
        0000ffffffff 0000e000ffff 0000c000ffff 0000a000ffff
        00008000ffff 00006000ffff 00004000ffff 00000000ffff
    /);

    $max_rings = 24;
    warn "Too few colors for $max_rings rings!" if $max_rings > $#colors + 1;

    # Global key bindings that emulate menu commands.

    $mw->bind('<KeyPress-r>' => sub {do_hanoi $rscale->get});
    $mw->bind('<KeyPress-q>' => \&fini);
    $mw->bind('<KeyPress-s>' => $stop);

} # end init

sub fini {
    $mw->destroy;
}

sub move_ring {

    # Move ring $n - its bounding box coordinates - to pole $to.

    my($n, $to) = @_;

    $num_moves++;
    my $r = $ring{$n, 'id'};
    my($x0, $y0, $x1, $y1) = map {int($_ + 0.5)} $canvas->coords($r);

    # Float the ring upwards to the flying Y-coordinate, and decrement
```

```
# this pole's count.

my $delta;
while ($y0 > $fly_y) {
    $delta = $y0 - $fly_y > $velocity ? $velocity : $y0 - $fly_y;
    $canvas->coords($r, $x0, $y0 -= $delta, $x1, $y1 -= $delta);
    $mw->update;
}
$pole{$ring{$n, 'pole'}, 'ring_count'}--;

# Determine the target X coordinate based on destination pole, and
# fly the ring over to the new pole. The first while moves rings
# left-to-right, the second while moves rings right-to-left.

my $x = $pole{$to, 'x'} - $ring{$n, 'width'} / 2;

while ($x0 < $x) {
    $delta = $x - $x0 > $velocity ? $velocity : $x - $x0;
    $canvas->coords($r, $x0 += $delta, $y0, $x1 += $delta, $y1);
    $mw->update;
}

while ($x0 > $x) {
    $delta = $x0 - $x > $velocity ? $velocity : $x0 - $x;
    $canvas->coords($r, $x0 -= $delta, $y0, $x1 -= $delta, $y1);
    $mw->update;
}

# Determine ring's target Y coordinate, based on the destination
# pole's ring count, and float the ring down.

my $y = $ring_base - $pole{$to, 'ring_count'} * $ring_spacing;

while ($y0 < $y) {
    $delta = $y - $y0 > $velocity ? $velocity : $y - $y0;
    $canvas->coords($r, $x0, $y0 += $delta, $x1, $y1 += $delta);
    $mw->update;
}

$pole{$to, 'ring_count'}++;
$ring{$n, 'pole'} = $to;

} # end move_ring
```

Index

We'd like to hear your suggestions for improving our indexes. Send email to *index@oreilly.com*.

O

O command (Perl), 16
Object-Oriented Perl (Conway), 309
-offset option, 172, 445
-offvalue option, 84, 92, 260
OnDestroy method, 305
-onvalue option
    Button widgets and, 84
    Checkbuttons and, 92, 260
open method, 469
-opencmd option, 469
openfold image, 471
OpenGL, glpOpenWindow command, 402
openLine method, 184
operating systems
    colormap complications and, 237
    differences for Listbox modes, 153
    identifer, 266
operators used with tags, 214
option database, 410–416
option menus, 275–278
-option option, 327
optionAdd method, 410, 415
optionClear method, 414
optionGet method, 415
Optionmenu widget, 275
optionReadfile method, 410, 415
-options option, 275, 311
options, order of precedence, 407
option/value pairs
    alignment suggestions, 14
    as resource, 406
    packInfo method and, 35
    qw operator and, 10
    syntax for, 9
-orient option
    Scale widgets and, 226, 227
    Scrollbars and, 139, 140
    TList widgets and, 458
Ousterhout, John K., 4
-outline option
    Canvas widgets and, 199
    createArc method and, 202
    createOval method and, 206
    createPolygon method and, 200
    createRectangle method and, 207
-outlinestipple option, 199, 202
-outlinetile option, 199
ovals, 206
-overanchor option, 273
overanchor point, 272
overridedirect method, 234, 272

-overstrike option, 73, 172
OverstrikeMode method, 184
owner method, 490

P

pack geometry manager
    advantages, 70
    features, 20–41
    overview, 10
    stacking with, 19
pack method
    demo programs, 37–41
    options available with, 22
    syntax, 10, 20
    Text widgets and, 165
__PACKAGE__ construct, 369
packaging
    for CPAN, 351–355
    for PPM, 355
packForget method, 34
packInfo method, 23
packing
    Scrollbars and, 138
    widgets and, 20, 31
packPropagate method, 23, 117, 232
packSlaves method, 35
-pad option, 23, 49
-padbottom option, 62
padding
    -padx option and, 23
    -pady option and, 23
    widget size, 32
    widgets, 23, 48, 62
-padx option
    Button widgets and, 84
    form method syntax, 62
    grid method and, 23, 48
    increasing Button size with, 102
    Label widgets and, 113
    Menubutton widgets, 269
    padding and, 23
    Text widgets and, 164
    Tix widgets and, 455
    windowCreate method and, 184
-pady option
    Button widgets and, 84
    form method syntax, 62
    grid method and, 45, 48
    increasing Button size with, 102
    Label widgets and, 113
    Menubutton widgets, 269
    padding and, 23

About the Authors

Steve Lidie has spent decades consulting, programming, and administering systems from Apple, CDC, DEC, HP, IBM, Microsoft, and SGI. Author of the *Perl/Tk Pocket Reference* (O'Reilly) and a graduate of Lehigh University, he currently manages Lehigh University's large-scale scientific computing complex and occasionally writes Tk articles for *The Perl Journal* and *PerlMonth*.

Nancy Walsh has been involved with Perl (and Perl/Tk) since 1996. Well before that, she honed her emerging technical skills playing Pong, Atari 5200 games, and working with hideously underpowered "computers." She received a computer science degree from the University of Arizona in 1993. Currently, Nancy works as a Principal Consultant for XOR, Inc. (*http://www.xor.com*), doing J2EE and Java work on various projects. Nancy has taught several Perl/Tk tutorials at the O'Reilly Open Source Conference and is also the author of *Learning Perl/Tk* (O'Reilly).

Colophon

Our look is the result of reader comments, our own experimentation, and feedback from distribution channels. Distinctive covers complement our distinctive approach to technical topics, breathing personality and life into potentially dry subjects.

The bird on the cover of *Mastering Perl/Tk* is an emu (*Dromaius novaehollandiae*). This large, flightless bird is found throughout the Australian bush steppes. The emu is one of the largest birds in existence, second only to its cousin, the ostrich. Adult emus stand about 5 feet high and weigh up to 120 pounds. The grayish-brown emu's small wings contain only six or seven feathers. They are hidden by the long, hairlike rump plumage. Emus have extremely long legs, which they use as defensive and offensive weapons when fighting. A human limb can be broken by a kick from an emu. Their powerful legs make emus strong swimmers and fast runners; they can reach speeds of up to 50 kilometers per hour.

Male emus, which are slightly smaller than females, tend to the incubation of eggs and the raising of the young. An emu nest contains as much as fifteen to twenty-five deep green eggs, laid by several hens. Incubation of the eggs takes from twenty-five to sixty days. The large discrepancy in incubation time occurs because the male needs to leave the nest periodically to find food and drink. The length of time he is away affects the time for incubation. Newly hatched emus weigh about 15 ounces. They are fully grown at two to three years.

The relationship between emus and Australian farmers has always been adversarial; three coastal subspecies of emu have been exterminated. Because emus can jump over high fences, it is difficult to keep them out of fields, where they eat and trample crops. In the arid Australian bush, emus also compete with cattle and sheep for grass and water. On the other hand, emus eat many insects that would otherwise eat crops. In 1932, Australian farmers declared war on the emus, making an all-out effort to eradicate them. Fortunately, the effort failed. The battle between emus and farmers continues to this day.

Linley Dolby was the production editor and copyeditor for *Mastering Perl/Tk*. Sada Preisch was the proofreader. Jeffrey Holcomb and Claire Cloutier provided quality control. Lucie Haskins wrote the index. Phil Dangler, Derek Di Matteo, Edie Shapiro, and Sarah Sherman provided production support.

Pam Spremulli designed the cover of this book, based on a series design by Edie Freedman. The cover image is a 19th-century engraving from *Johnson's Natural History II*. Emma Colby produced the cover layout with QuarkXPress 4.1, using Adobe's ITC Garamond font.

Melanie Wang designed the interior layout, based on a series design by David Futato. Neil Walls implemented the design in FrameMaker 5.5.6, using tools created by Mike Sierra. The text font is Linotype Birka; the heading font is Adobe Myriad Condensed; and the code font is LucasFont's TheSans Mono Condensed. The illustrations that appear in the book were produced by Robert Romano and Jessamyn Read, using Macromedia FreeHand 9 and Adobe Photoshop 6. This colophon was written by Clairemarie Fisher O'Leary.

Whenever possible, our books use a durable and flexible lay-flat binding.